FIFTH EDITION

Technical Communication

FIFTH EDITION

Technical Communication

Rebecca E. Burnett
Iowa State University

Harcourt College Publishers

Fort Worth • Philadelphia • San Diego • New York • Orlando • Austin • San Antonio
Toronto • Montreal • London • Sydney • Tokyo

Publisher	Earl McPeek
Acquisitions Editor	Julie McBurney
Market Strategist	John Meyers
Developmental Editor	Joseph W. Loftin III
Project Manager	Andrea Archer

Cover credit: Leonardo da Vinci, Design for Machinery. Art Resource, NY. Ferris wheel: Digital Imagery © copyright 2000 PhotoDisc, Inc.

ISBN: 0-15-506448-7
Library of Congress Catalog Card Number: 00-106794

Address for Domestic Orders
Harcourt College Publishers, 6277 Sea Harbor Drive, Orlando, FL 32887-6777
800-782-4479

Address for International Orders
International Customer Service
Harcourt College Publishers, 6277 Sea Harbor Drive, Orlando, FL 32887-6777
407-345-3800
(fax) 407-345-4060
(e-mail) hbintl@harcourtbrace.com

Address for Editorial Correspondence
Harcourt College Publishers, 301 Commerce Street, Suite 3700, Fort Worth, TX 76102

Web Site Address
http://www.harcourtcollege.com

Harcourt College Publishers will provide complimentary supplements or supplement packages to those adopters qualified under our adoption policy. Please contact your sales representative to learn how you qualify. If as an adopter or potential user you receive supplements you do not need, please return them to your sales representative or send them to:
Attn: Returns Department, Troy Warehouse, 465 South Lincoln Drive, Troy, MO 63379.

Printed in the United States of America

0 1 2 3 4 5 6 7 8 9   039   9 8 7 6 5 4 3 2 1

Harcourt College Publishers

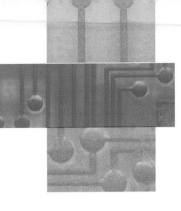

Contents in Brief

PART I Understanding the Communicator's Work 1
- **1** *Considering Communication 3*
- **2** *Writing: Processes and Production 31*
- **3** *Writing for Readers 61*
- **4** *Reading Technical Documents 99*
- **5** *Collaboration in Workplace Communication 131*

PART II Developing the Communicator's Tools 161
- **6** *Locating and Recording Information 163*
- **7** *Organization of Information 207*
- **8** *Information Design 245*
- **9** *Using Visual Forms 273*

PART III Understanding the Communicator's Strategies 325
- **10** *Creating Definitions 327*
- **11** *Creating Technical Descriptions 365*
- **12** *Creating Process Explanations 397*
- **13** *Ensuring Usability: Testing, Revising, and Editing 425*

PART IV Completing Documents 485
- **14** *Correspondence 487*
- **15** *Instructions 527*
- **16** *Proposals 571*
- **17** *Reports 603*

PART V Creating a Professional Image 657
- **18** *Oral Presentations 659*
- **19** *Addressing Career Concerns 693*

  Usage Handbook UH1

v

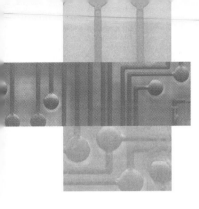

Contents in Detail

PART I Understanding the Communicator's Work 1

1 Considering Communication 3
Importance of Effective Communication 5
Defining Technical Communication 6
Contexts for Constructing Meaning 8
Texts That Communicate 11
Communicators 13
  Technical Communicators and Technical Experts 18
  Constraints That Communicators Face 18
End-of-Chapter Recommendations for Technical Communicators 21
Individual and Collaborative Assignments 23
INTERTEXT: Technical Writers Are in Demand: Do You Have
  the Right Stuff? 27

2 Writing: Processes and Production 31
Inventing and Exploring 34
Planning and Organizing 36
  Project Planning 36
  Document Planning 37
Drafting 40
Revising 42
  Using Data from Authorities 43
  Presenting Facts Without Drawing Inferences 43
  Drawing Inferences 44
  Establishing Causal Relationships 45
Editing 47
Differences Between Writing Processes 48
End-of-Chapter Recommendations for Technical Communicators 50
Individual and Collaborative Assignments 52
INTERTEXT: Care and Feeding of the Organizational Grapevine 54

3   Writing for Readers   61

Identifying Purposes   63
Identifying Readers   64
Analyzing Readers   66
    Context   68
    Attitudes and Motivations   70
    Education   71
    Professional Experience   71
    Reading Level   71
    Organizational Role   75
Adjusting to Readers   76
    Differences in Expertise   76
    Differences in Roles and Stances   78
    Readers Adjusting   80
End-of-Chapter Recommendations for Technical Communicators   83
PRACTICUM: Iowa Public Television (IPTV)   84
Individual and Collaborative Assignments   91
INTERTEXT: Baby Blues   97

4   Reading Technical Documents   99

Identifying Purposes   101
Reading–Writing Relationships   102
Strategies for Effective Reading   103
    Identify Structure   105
    Distinguish Main Points   110
    Draw Inferences   110
    Generate Questions   113
    Monitor and Adapt Reading Strategies   115
End-of-Chapter Recommendations for Technical Communicators   124
Individual and Collaborative Assignments   125
INTERTEXT: Sold on the Simplicity of Web Sites:
    Companies Are Getting Back to Basics with Web Designs
    That Enable Users to Find What They Need   128

5   Collaboration in Workplace Communication   131

Reasons for Collaboration   133
    Subject   134
    Process   134
    Product   135
    Interpersonal Benefits   135

Types of Collaboration   135
       Co-Authoring   136
       Consulting with Colleagues   137
       Contributing to Team Projects   137
Being a Good Collaborator   138
       Be Engaged and Cooperative   138
       Listen   139
       Conform to Conversation Conventions   139
       Ask Questions   140
       Share   141
       Use Technology Effectively   142
       Reflect   142
Negotiating Conflicts   144
       Affective Conflicts   144
       Procedural Conflicts   145
       Substantive Conflicts   146
       Cultural Differences and Expectations   150
End-of-Chapter Recommendations for Technical Communicators   151
Individual and Collaborative Assignments   153
INTERTEXT: The Rage for Global Teams   158

PART II   Developing the Communicator's Tools   161

6   Locating and Recording Information   163

Locating Primary and Secondary Sources   166
Personal Observations and Close Reading   168
       Personal Observations   169
       Close Reading   170
Calculations   170
Samples and Specimens   171
Empirical Investigations   171
Internal Records   172
Interviews and Letters of Inquiry   172
       Developing Questions   173
       Asking Questions   173
Surveys and Polls   176
Library Resources   180
       Research Librarians and Their References   180
       Reference Resources   182

Online Catalog 183
Indexes 183
Electronic Resources 186
Computerized Databases 186
Web Research 187
Government Documents and Offices 190
Recording Data 191
Field Journals 191
Lab Notebooks 192
Note Cards 192
Outlines 193
Tracings, Photographs, Drawings, Maps, Videotapes, Films 193
Audiorecordings 194
End-of-Chapter Recommendations for Technical Communicators 194
Individual and Collaborative Assignments 196
INTERTEXT: Internet Power Searching:
Finding Pearls in a Zillion Grains of Sand 198

7   Organization of Information 207
Outlining 209
Organizing Information 213
Parts/Whole Organization 215
Chronological Order 216
Spatial Order 217
Ascending/Descending Order 218
Comparison/Contrast 220
Cause and Effect 222
Using Organization 225
End-of-Chapter Recommendations for Technical Communicators 227
PRACTICUM: Engineering Associates at Work 228
Individual and Collaborative Assignments 234
INTERTEXT: How an Author Can Avoid the Pitfalls
of Practical Ethics 237

8   Information Design 245
Chunking and Labeling Information 248
White Space to Chunk Information 250
Headings to Label Chunked Information 252
Arranging Related Chunks of Verbal and Visual Information 253
Using Design Conventions 253
Avoiding Problems in Arranging Information 254

Emphasizing Information   257
    Typefaces   257
    Typographic Devices   262
Designing for the Web   263
    Why Using Grids Works   264
    Why Dumping Text on the Web Doesn't Work   264
End-of-Chapter Recommendations for Technical Communicators   265
Individual and Collaborative Assignments   267
INTERTEXT: Collaboration Revolutionizes Design Process   270

9   Using Visual Forms   273
Incorporating Visuals   276
    Visual/Verbal Combinations   276
    Adapting Visuals to Audiences   279
    Conventions in Referencing and Placing Visuals   280
Conventions in Use of Color   282
    Cautions Against Misuse of Color   282
    Suggestions for Appropriate Use of Color   283
    Color in Designing Online Documents   290
Visual Functions   291
    Function 1: Organize Numeric or Verbal Data   292
    Function 2: Show Relationships   294
    Function 3: Define Concepts, Objects, and Processes   300
    Function 4: Present Action or Process   303
    Function 5: Illustrate Appearance, Structure, or Function   306
    Function 6: Identify Facilities or Locations   310
End-of-Chapter Recommendations for Technical Communicators   314
Individual and Collaborative Assignments   316
INTERTEXT: Avoiding Distortion and Misuse of Visuals   319

PART III   Understanding the Communicator's Strategies   325

10   Creating Definitions   327
The Need for Definitions   330
    Multiple Meanings   330
    Complexity of Meaning   331
    Technical Jargon   331
    Symbols   334

Construction of Definitions   334
    Formal Definitions   335
    Informal Definitions   336
    Operational Definitions   339
    Expanded Definitions   340
Placement of Definitions   343
    Glossary   343
    Information Notes and Sidebars   343
    Incorporated Information   346
    Appendixes   346
    Online Help   347
End-of-Chapter Recommendations for Technical Communicators   347
PRACTICUM: Big Creek Forestry: Challenges in Becoming
   a SmartWood Certified Resource Manager   349
Individual and Collaborative Assignments   354
INTERTEXT: Sexual Harassment Training:
   Trust and Consequences   359

11   **Creating Technical Descriptions   365**
Defining Technical Description   368
Using Technical Description   369
    Observation Notes   369
    Reference and Training Materials and Manuals   370
    Proposals and Reports   371
    Marketing and Promotional Pieces   373
    Public Information and Education   373
Preparing a Technical Description   373
    Audience's Task   373
    Components   374
    Diction   374
    Visuals   378
    Organization   379
End-of-Chapter Recommendations for Technical Communicators   382
PRACTICUM: The Boeing Company   383
Individual and Collaborative Assignments   388
INTERTEXT: Cross-Cultural Communication:
   Is It Greek to You?   392

12   Creating Process Explanations   397

Defining Processes   399

Using Process Explanations   400

Manuals   400

Orientation and Training Materials   400

Marketing and Promotional Materials   402

Public Information and Education   404

Preparing Processes   405

Audience and Purpose   406

Identification of Steps   406

Visuals   407

Diction   407

Organization and Format   407

Examining a Sample Process Explanation:
    Developing Low-Cost Roofing Materials   409

End-of-Chapter Recommendations for Technical Communicators   412

PRACTICUM: Lockheed Martin   413

Individual and Collaborative Assignments   418

INTERTEXT: The Changing Face of Sexual Harassment   421

**13   Ensuring Usability:
    Testing, Revising, and Editing   425**

Document Testing   427

Procedures for Document Testing   427

Test-Based Testing   428

Expert-Based Testing   429

User-Based Testing   430

General Observations About Testing   431

Revising   431

Redesigning Documents   431

Revising for Plain Language   435

Editing   443

Use Concrete Details   446

Use Direct Language   446

Use Positive Phrasing   447

Eliminate Wordiness   448

Revise Noun Strings   449

Examining Revision and Editing Decisions   451

End-of-Chapter Recommendations for Technical Communicators   469

PRACTICUM: Using Style Guides to Ensure Usability   470

Individual and Collaborative Assignments   475

INTERTEXT: Readability   479

PART IV   Completing Documents   485

14   Correspondence   487

Characteristics of Correspondence   489
   Distinctive Features of Correspondence   489
   Written Correspondence or Telephone Calls   490
   Modes of Delivery   490
Domino Effect of Correspondence   493
Composing Letters, Memos, and Electronic Mail Messages   507
   Attitude and Tone   508
   Audience   509
   Organization of Information   510
Format   512
Visual Displays   514
End-of-Chapter Recommendations for Technical Communicators   516
PRACTICUM: Weisner Associates Inc.   518
Individual and Collaborative Assignments   522
INTERTEXT: Handling Customer Service on the Web:
   The Robots Are Here   525

15   Instructions   527

Defining and Designing Instructional Texts   529
   Task Analysis   529
   Analyzing and Adapting to Audiences   531
   Considering International Audiences   533
   Adapting Task to Audience   536
   Organizing Instructions   537
   Locating Information in Manuals   538
Constructing Instructional Texts   539
   Content Elements   540
   Visual and Design Elements   547
Document Testing   554
Examining Sample Instructions   555
End-of-Chapter Recommendations for Technical Communicators   556
PRACTICUM: Vidiom: The Case of the Multiple Versions   558
Individual and Collaborative Assignments   564
INTERTEXT: Design Learner-Friendly Training Manuals   567

16   Proposals   571

Characterizing Proposals   574
  Types of Proposals   574
  Sources of RFPs   575
Using Persuasion in Proposals   577
  Readers' Needs   577
  Persuaders' Credibility   578
  Logic of Message   578
Preparing Proposals   580
  Managing   581
  Planning   581
  Drafting   582
  Evaluating   583
  Revising   583
Organizing Proposals   584
Examining a Sample Proposal   589
End-of-Chapter Recommendations for Technical Communicators   589
Individual and Collaborative Assignments   596
INTERTEXT: Goof-Proofing Your RFPs   597

17   Reports   603

Differentiating Informal and Formal Reports   605
Purposes and Characteristics of Reports   606
Planning a Report   607
  Identify Audiences   608
  State Purpose   608
Organizing Informal Reports   609
  Task Reports   610
  Periodic Activity Reports   611
  Progress Reports   614
  Meeting Minutes   616
  Trip and Conference Reports   616
  "To File" Reports   620
Formats of Reports   620
  Prepared Forms   621
  Memos and Letters   621
Organizing Formal Reports   621
  Front Matter of a Report   623
  Body of a Report   625
  End Matter of a Report   627
  Format Elements   628

Examining a Sample Report   629
End-of-Chapter Recommendations for Technical Communicators   644
PRACTICUM: Responding to Change   645
Individual and Collaborative Assignments   648
INTERTEXT: Clearing the Air:
    Some Thoughts on Gender-Neutral Writing   651

PART V   Creating a Professional Image   657

18   **Oral Presentations   659**

Types of Presentations   661
    Informal Presentations   661
    Formal Presentations   662
    Class Presentations   663
Preparing a Professional Presentation   663
    Audience   664
    Purposes of Presentations   665
Organizing a Professional Presentation   666
    Engaging the Listeners   666
    Organizing for the Listeners   667
    Using Note Cards or Outlines   668
Preparing Materials for a Professional Presentation   670
    Visuals   671
    Handouts   676
    Poster Displays   678
Presenting Yourself   679
    Professional Appearance   679
    Vocal Characteristics   681
    Handling Questions   681
Evaluating Presentations   684
    Active Listening   684
    Assessing Presentation Skills   684
End-of-Chapter Recommendations for Technical Communicators   685
Individual and Collaborative Assignments   688
INTERTEXT: Using Copyrighted Works for Meetings, Seminars,
    and Conferences   690

19   Addressing Career Concerns   693

Learning About Jobs   695

Preparing Application Letters   698

Designing a Résumé   701

  Essential Elements   703

  Optional Elements   709

  Unnecessary Elements   709

  Design Elements   709

  Sample Résumés   712

  Your Résumé and Your Development   712

Preparing a Portfolio   716

  Portfolio Content   716

  Paper or Electronic?   717

  A Usable Portfolio   718

Interviewing   720

End-of-Chapter Recommendations for Technical Communicators   726

Individual and Collaborative Assignments   728

INTERTEXT: How Technology Is Changing Privacy Issues
in the Workplace   732

Usage Handbook   UH1

Words   UH2

  Acronyms   UH2

  Abstract Nouns Changed to Active Verbs   UH3

  Substitutes for Inflated Words   UH4

  Redundant Pairs, Modifiers, and Categories   UH5

Sentences   UH6

  Sentence Structure   UH6

  Sentence Fragments   UH9

  Comma Splices   UH11

  Run-On Sentences   UH13

  Subject–Verb Agreement   UH14

  Pronoun–Antecedent Agreement   UH16

  Pronoun Reference   UH18

  Dangling Modifiers   UH20

  Misplaced Modifiers   UH23

  Parallel Structure   UH25

  Sentence Combining   UH28

Punctuation   UH34

  Apostrophe   UH34

  Brackets   UH35

  Colon   UH35

Comma   UH35

Dash   UH37

Ellipsis   UH37

Exclamation Point   UH37

Hyphen   UH37

Italics   UH38

Parentheses   UH40

Period   UH40

Question Mark   UH40

Quotation Marks   UH41

Semicolon   UH41

Slash   UH42

Capitalization   UH42

Personal Names   UH42

Academic Degrees, Honors, and Awards   UH43

Groups of People   UH43

Place Names   UH43

Words Derived from Proper Nouns   UH44

Organizations   UH44

Historical and Cultural Terms   UH44

Calendar and Time Designations   UH45

Scientific Terms   UH45

Registered Trademarks   UH47

Titles of Works   UH47

Numbers—Figures or Words?   UH47

Ordinal vs. Cardinal   UH48

Beginnings of Sentences   UH48

Very Large Numbers   UH48

Physical Quantities   UH48

Percentages and Decimals   UH49

Age   UH49

Documenting Sources   UH49

Sources Cited   UH49

Source Notes   UH50

Formats for Documentation   UH51

Endnotes and Credits   C1

Index   I1

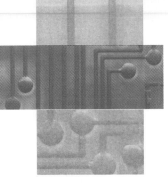

Preface

To Each Student

Technical Communication has a clear goal: to help you learn to communicate technical information—whether oral, visual, or written—to an audience. As you read this book and create technical documents and presentations, you'll learn to make decisions about elements that affect the effectiveness of your communication: context, purpose, audience, organization, and design.

What You Can Expect.   In using this textbook, you will find several of its features particularly helpful:

- Every chapter begins with a Chapter in Brief that introduces the key concepts you'll read about and concludes with End-of-Chapter Recommendations for Technical Communicators that summarize actions you can take.

- The examples—many created by workplace professionals, others created by students in technical communication classes—illustrate points in the discussion and provide you with models of effective technical communication.

- Marginal questions throughout each chapter help you focus on issues and problems that you'll have to deal with in the workplace.

- Each chapter includes an Ethics Sidebar that focuses on some complex issue that provokes controversy, an issue that you are likely to need to consider in the workplace.

- Annotated drafts and the resulting revisions offer examples of the process of drafting and revising technical documents.

- The numerous figures provide you with helpful explanations and guidelines to use when completing your own documents.

- Several of the chapters include a Practicum, each written by a workplace professional. The Practicums provide you with windows into workplace scenarios and invite you to solve complex problems.

- The Individual and Collaborative Assignments at the end of each chapter give you a chance to practice what you've learned by engaging in problem solving and writing, sometimes by yourself, but often in a group.

- Intertexts—special sections between chapters—deal with a range of important topics in technical communication, such as researching topics on the Web, considering ethics, avoiding sexism, and understanding cross-cultural communication.

- The Usage Handbook at the end of the textbook is especially useful if you need to settle a question about some point of grammar, confirm the conventional use of punctuation or capitalization, decide on effective sentence structure, or make decisions about ways to document information. The sentence and paragraph exercises in the Usage Handbook come from actual technical documents.

- Web and technology examples show the importance of electronic communication in the workplace. You will benefit from developing skills in both print and electronic formats.

What You'll Learn.   While accuracy is arguably the most critical aspect of any technical document, visual, or presentation, technical accuracy alone is not enough. Here are some of the things you can expect to learn from using this book:

- How to approach communication problems found in complex workplace environments.

- How to use strategies that help you become a more effective reader of technical documents.

- How to prepare more effective presentations, visuals, and documents by understanding the context in which communication occurs as well as knowing your purpose, the constraints of the situation, the needs of your readers, and strategies for organizing and presenting information.

- How to size up your audiences and develop strategies for adjusting material to different audiences to help you plan and prepare more effective presentations, visuals, and documents.

- How to design print and electronic visuals and documents for a powerful impact on your audience, including how to use color effectively.

- How to be an effective collaborator in the workplace.

- How to take advantage of the power of computer tools.

- How to test different kinds of documents and then use the results of testing as you revise and edit these documents.

Why Leonardo da Vinci?   As you skim through this book, you'll notice that the cover and the part dividers feature Leonardo da Vinci's mechanical drawings.

I use them because they are precise, detailed, functional, and focused. I hope your oral, visual, and written technical communication is equally accurate and engaging.

How You Can Help.   I have made changes in each edition of this book based on recommendations from students. I also have incorporated new student examples. If you have suggestions about changes I should consider, please let me know. If you have created exemplary documents and visuals I might use in the next edition, please send me copies.

Rebecca E. Burnett, Ph.D.
c/o Harcourt College Publishers
301 Commerce Street, Suite 3700
Fort Worth, TX 76102

To Colleagues Teaching Technical Communication

In writing *Technical Communication*, I have tried to bring together the best of workplace practice, current theory and research, and classroom pedagogy.

What's Distinctive in This Text?   In this fifth edition, I have continued the emphasis on a rhetorical, problem-solving approach to technical communication. Students learn to make decisions about rhetorical elements such as context, purpose, audience, organization, and design as they engage in the complex process of communicating technical information—whether in oral, visual, or written form.

I hope that students who use this text learn that effective technical communication contains elements of both creativity and craft, a point I make by the continued use of Leonardo da Vinci's drawings throughout *Technical Communication*. In the earlier editions I have noted that, like Leonardo da Vinci's mechanical drawings, technical communication should be precise, detailed, functional, and focused. That's not all it should be; it's the least it should be.

What's the Same?   You'll find that this fifth edition of *Technical Communication* maintains the strengths of the previous editions while incorporating important new developments in technical communication.

The traditional concerns of technical communication—techniques such as definitions, descriptions, and processes; and forms such as correspondence, instructions, reports, and proposals—are always related to rhetorical elements as well as to strategies for testing, revising, and editing documents. Beyond these concerns, however, the text continues to include detailed information about collaboration as well as design and visuals.

The Intertexts—those special sections between chapters—continue to give students opportunities to learn about a range of important topics in technical communication such as researching topics on the Web, considering ethics, avoiding sexism, and understanding cross-cultural communication.

Two sections in each chapter—Chapter in Brief, which introduces the key concepts, and End-of-Chapter Recommendations for Technical Communicators, which summarize actions students can take—provide strong pedagogical support for students as they preview and review critical information.

What's New in This Edition?   The improvements in this edition range from an entirely new chapter (created by conflating two chapters from the previous edition) to new Intertexts, from increased discussion throughout the text about both computers and intercultural communication to the addition of extensive information and examples of the use of color in technical documents.

- Increased information about computers is included throughout the text such as workplace applications of multimedia and Web research.

- Appropriate and inappropriate uses of color are discussed in relation to paper documents, oral presentations, and online documents. This edition also includes a full-color chapter that discusses carefully selected full-color technical visuals that use color effectively.

- Differences between print and online reading are discussed.

- Because the Intertexts are designed to encourage (and even provoke) students to think about issues associated with current critical topics in technical communication, this edition includes a number of new Inter-texts—ones about Web searches, intellectual property, RFPs, and corporate gossip.

- New annotated examples from a variety of disciplines and professions reflect the complex nature of technical communication.

- Each chapter includes new marginal questions designed to stimulate higher-level thinking skills in students and to encourage them to connect material in the text to their own experiences.

- Each chapter includes a new ethics sidebar that focuses on some complex issue that provokes controversy, an issue that professionals are likely to need to consider in the workplace.

- Half of the chapters include a new feature—Practicums. The Practicums, all written by workplace professionals, provide students with windows into workplace scenarios and invite them to solve complex communication problems.

- Finally, the expanded Usage Handbook includes detailed information about documenting electronic sources.

How Are Students Addressed?   This even more readable, teachable edition talks directly to students, offering them clear, practical advice based on current theory and practice. The elegant, usable design of this edition enables students to use the text's pages as models. The discussions and the classroom-tested exercises and assignments—both individual and collaborative—help students become better communicators, ones who can recognize the rhetorical, situational nature of communication and can manage processes and strategies to solve communication problems. The text stresses the integrated, recursive nature of producing effective print and electronic documents, encouraging writers to think of invention and revision as ongoing processes, to think of visuals as ways to present information, to think of language as having the power to shape and influence the readers' perceptions.

What Critical Concerns Are Addressed?   The text is effective with traditional and nontraditional students as well as with professionals in a variety of settings. I have tried to strike a balance between theory and pedagogy and between classroom and workplace needs. This balance is demonstrated in ten critical concerns:

Rhetorical base. The text uses rhetorical factors—for example, constraints of the situation, needs of the readers, purposes of writers, conventions of genre, complexity and organization of the subject—to guide writers through the process of producing documents. This analysis of factors such as context, audience, writers, and subject establishes a context for presenting information verbally and visually.

Writing for readers. Technical Communication provides in-depth coverage of audience analysis. The text moves from a theoretical to a practical level by providing suggestions for adjusting material to different audiences. The concern with audience analysis and the adjustment of material to different audiences continues throughout the text.

Visuals and document design. Technical Communication is unique in that it identifies and illustrates the rhetorical base of visual material and establishes parallels between visual and verbal presentations. The text also explores the role of color in technical documents and emphasizes the impact of document design on audience reactions.

Collaboration. The text not only presents a chapter that focuses on collaboration, but the end of each chapter includes collaborative activities and exercises. Throughout the text, students are reminded that the workplace is a collaborative environment and that documents are not produced or used in isolation.

Testing, revising, and editing. Creating an effective document should include document testing (e.g., text-based, expert-based, and user-based). The results of document testing can be used as the basis for revising and editing a document.

Process and product. Technical Communication shows how technical communicators are involved in a complex process to create a product. The text discusses ways to approach a writing problem, explains options available to writers, offers suggestions about logical organization, and illustrates appropriate language use.

Emphasis on technology. Because technical communication takes place in a rapidly changing electronic environment, this text discusses the impact of technology both on the writing process and on the resulting document. Students will find extensive discussion of technology in the chapters as well as the Intertexts.

Examples. Early in the text, students are introduced to examples of exemplary documents. Then, throughout *Technical Communication*, annotated examples by students and workplace professionals illustrate the key points and serve as models—from professions as varied as agriculture, astronomy, electronics, forestry, manufacturing, metallurgy, music, pediatrics, and robotics to name a few.

Style. Technical Communication is a reader-based text; it directly addresses students and workplace professionals in a straightforward style that is appealing and accessible.

Apparatus and computer support. The addition of marginal questions offers students ample opportunities to discuss ideas and apply the practices advocated in *Technical Communication.* The *Practicums* give students the opportunity to complete actual workplace tasks. The *Individual and Collaborative Assignments* encourage problem solving and writing that students will need for classroom as well as professional success. In addition, the sentence and paragraph exercises in the Usage Handbook provide practice with materials from actual technical documents.

What Support Materials Are Available?   Teachers have a range of support materials accompanying this edition of *Technical Communication.*

Anyone who teaches in a computer lab—from a few classes to the entire term—will appreciate the more than 25 supplementary activities, exercises, and assignments developed by David Clark and Mark Zachry and now available on the text's Web site. These activities will enrich any class, whether in a conventional class or a computer lab. You can access the Web site through the Harcourt Web site at www.harcourtcollege.com.

Teachers will find *Case Studies in Technical Communication,* developed by Andrea Breemer Frantz, an especially important addition to the support materials for *Technical Communication.* This book was developed to work as a supplement or as a stand-alone volume. The carefully researched and engaging cases give students the opportunity to negotiate complex workplace contexts as they prepare documents and presentations.

The *Instructor's Resource Manual* (IRM) includes a series of essays written especially to accompany this text—useful for new instructors as well as experienced ones—that discuss various issues central to teaching technical communication. In addition, the IRM includes practical, classroom-tested suggestions, quizzes, supplemental materials, and a series of masters for handouts and transparencies. The IRM is available free to all adopters of this new edition of *Technical Communication.* (To request the IRM, call 1-800-237-2665.)

I have made changes in each edition based on the recommendations of colleagues from colleges and universities around the country. If you have suggestions about changes I should consider, please let me know. If you have exemplary documents and visuals that would help readers of the next edition, please send me copies. I value your feedback.

Rebecca E. Burnett, Ph.D.
c/o Harcourt College Publishers
301 Commerce Street, Suite 3700
Fort Worth, TX 76102

Acknowledgments

Technical Communication would not exist without the personal and professional support of family, friends, and colleagues.

In preparing this edition, I have been thankful every single day for the skillful and thorough researchers who assisted me in preparing this revision: Irene Faass recommended ways to strengthen the Individual and Collaborative Assignments and suggested many of the new marginal questions; Matt Turner researched and drafted the very engaging ethics sidebars; Peggy Pollock provided computer examples and overall insights about technology as well as updated print documentation; Julie Zeleznik recommended relevant new Intertexts, provided information about posters and portfolios, and helped revise the Instructor's Resource Manual. Their assistance has been critical to this revision.

William Jeffries continues in his unwavering support and serves as an invaluable critical reviewer and voice of reason. I also appreciate the fruitful suggestions and contributions provided by friends, colleagues, students, and workplace professionals: David Clark, Patty Harms, Ken Jolls, Clay Spinuzzi, Don Stanford, and Judith Stanford. Their experiences and observations have shaped many places in this revision. Muriel McGrann keeps an eye out for good examples. As always, my family provides the confidence and support to make the revision possible.

I especially appreciate the workplace professionals who created Practicums for this revised edition: Arricka Brouwer from TelDocInc; Christopher Burnett from Big Creek Forestry; Elizabeth Herman from Wellmark; Kari Krumpel from Lockheed-Martin; Walden Miller from Vidiom; Kate Molitor from Weisner Associates; Janet Renze from Boeing; Daryl Seay from Engineering Associates; and Melissa Waltman from Iowa Public Television.

I also want to thank friends and colleagues at Iowa State University who see the wisdom in balancing theory, research, workplace practice, and pedagogy. Their curiosity, dedication, and insight are a constant inspiration to me. My undergraduate and graduate students at Iowa State University and technical professionals in workplace seminars have also been important to this edition; many seminar participants offered specific and helpful suggestions that have strengthened this edition. Doug Schaapveld, Jill Bigley, and Larry Chan have been especially helpful in recommending computer documentation.

The contributions by the following people to the fourth edition have been substantially retained: Susan Booker, Kaelin Chappelle, David Clark, Andrea Breemer Frantz, Woody Hart, William Jeffries, Lee-Ann Kastman, Elenor Long, Muriel McGrann, Ron Myers, Tom Myers, Mike Peery, Clay Spinuzzi, Don Stanford, Judith Stanford, Gary Tarcy, Lee Tesdell, Christianna White, Dorothy Winchester, Mark Zachry, and Stephanie Zeluck as well as friends, colleagues, and students at Iowa State University.

The contributions by the following people to the third edition have been substantially retained: Reva Daniel, Michael Hassett, William Jeffries, Muriel McGrann, Cindy Myers, and Christianna White as well as colleagues and students at Iowa State University.

The contributions by the following people to the second edition have been substantially retained: Philippa Benson, William Jeffries, and Barbara Sitko as well as my friends, colleagues, and students at Carnegie Mellon University.

The contributions by the following people to the first edition have been substantially retained: Geraldine Branca, Christopher Burnett, Bernard DiNatale, Arline Dupras, Elizabeth Foster, Nancy Irish, Elizabeth Carros Keroack, Marcia Greenman Lebeau, Muriel McGrann, Stephen Meidell, Leon Sommers, and Judith Dupras Stanford as well as students at Northern Essex Community College, Merrimack College, and the University of Massachusetts at Lowell.

Reviewers' detailed and practical suggestions were, of course, instrumental in revisions for this edition. I appreciate the helpful suggestions of many, many colleagues from colleges and universities around the country who reviewed the text for this revision.

Elena Dolhberg at Wadsworth Publishing Company was instrumental and supportive in the beginning stages of this revision, started when the text was still published by Wadsworth.

The team members for *Technical Communication* at my new publisher, Harcourt, have been extraordinary in their commitment: Julie McBurney provided excellent editorial direction; Joe Loftin aided in the complex process for this revision with intelligence, patience, expertise, and humor—for which I am immensely grateful; Martha Beyerlein and Andrea Archer have managed the production process with remarkable efficiency; and Cheri Throop has handled the complex task of permissions with thoroughness. Elm Street Publishing Services provided copyediting that saved me from embarrassing errors, further refined an already sophisticated, appealing, and usable design, and used the art of da Vinci to create a cover and part dividers that reflect the spirit of the text. For all, I am immensely thankful.

Rebecca E. Burnett
Iowa State University
Ames, IA

Understanding the Communicator's Work

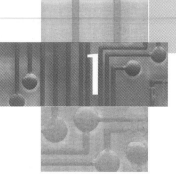

Considering Communication

Technical communication is a broad field that touches nearly every subject and profession through a vast array of oral interaction as well as print and electronic documents; it defines, describes, and directs activities in business and industry, government and research institutions, hospitals and farms.

Importance of Effective Communication

Technical professionals who communicate effectively—regardless of their area of expertise—usually achieve more career success and have greater job satisfaction than do those who have only technical expertise.

Defining Technical Communication

Technical communication can be defined through a cluster of characteristics dealing with factors such as content, context, purpose, audience, organization, visuals, and design.

Contexts for Constructing Meaning

Creating *reader-based documents*—ones that consider readers' needs and reactions and organize information for readers' understanding—requires awareness of the situation in which documents are generated and used. Readers construct meaning from the documents, influenced by the words as well as by ethics, attitudes, values, education, and experiences.

Texts That Communicate

Both internal and external audiences read many types of documents: correspondence; sales, marketing, and promotional materials; instructions and instructional manuals; proposals, and reports.

In preparing technical documents, you need to meet minimum standards:

- Identify the *context*, and assure the accuracy and completeness of the *content*.
- Identify the *purpose*, anticipate *audience* needs, and adapt content to meet those needs.
- Create an effective *organization* of key points, and establish connections between those points.
- Select appropriate *visuals* and an accessible, appealing *design* of the document.
- Confirm the *usability* of the document.
- Reflect professional *conventions* and standards.

Communicators

Workplace professionals who prepare documents generally work in one or more of these situations: as independent communicators responsible for their own work, as members of cooperative teams, or as contributors to projects. Workplace professionals have to manage a variety of constraints that influence their communication: time; subject and format; audience; collaboration; data collection; technology; and "noise."

**W**hat do astrophysicists, obstetricians, electrical engineers, ecologists, farmers, musicians, and veterinarians have in common? All read and write technical documents. What do the moons of Jupiter, in vitro fertilization, silicon chips, wetlands conservation, soybean crops, flutes, and foals have in common? All are technical subjects that professionals read and write about. Technical communication is a broad field that touches nearly every subject and profession because it connects ideas, people, and practices. Technical communication defines, describes, and directs activities in business and industry, government and research institutions, hospitals and farms.

Although certain professions such as engineering have traditionally been associated with technical communication, nearly every discipline and profession have technical documents, visuals, and oral presentations. For example, detailed information about sound formation is important for both speech pathologists and computer engineers designing a voice synthesizer. Knowledge about muscle conditioning is equally relevant to physical therapists, ballet dancers, and veterinarians. Data about weather changes are crucial to both meteorologists and commercial fishers.

Importance of Effective Communication

Technical professionals who communicate effectively usually achieve more career success and have greater job satisfaction than those without the skills to communicate their technical knowledge. Technical experts who cannot communicate effectively are not an asset to their organization. Successful professionals see reading and writing as integral parts of their job, not as something extra that they have to fit in. They assume responsibility for their own writing—from organizing ideas to final proofreading of documents.

How much do you anticipate communicating when you're in the workplace? Examine your profession's journals, trade magazines, and Web sites to see if you can determine the role of reading, writing, and speaking in your field.

People's reputations may be built largely on their communication. Although good communication skills are essential for all technical professionals, the higher a person is promoted, the more writing and public speaking are required. The following survey results show the importance placed by technical professionals on effective communication skills:

- Almost all (97 percent) of the respondents rated speaking skills either "very important" or "important" to their jobs.

- An overwhelming 91 percent stated that their writing was either "important" or "very important" to their jobs.

- About 80 percent said that the ability to communicate helped in their advancement.

- Approximately 73 percent responded that they spent more time writing (as their responsibilities increased).

- Approximately 42 percent spent between 20 percent and 40 percent of their time writing. More than 28 percent of the respondents spent between 40 percent and 100 percent of their time writing.[1]

As this survey shows, you gain tremendous professional advantages if you write and speak effectively. Your communication needs to be technically complete and accurate, logically organized for the audience, visually appealing, and interesting; it also needs to be mechanically and grammatically conventional, and it must say something worthwhile.

Defining Technical Communication

Although technical communication has existed as long as people have recorded information, technical communication as a profession evolved tremendously during the second half of the twentieth century. More recent definitions of technical communication focus on the collective characteristics of technical discourse as illustrated in Figure 1.1. With minor adjustments, these characteristics apply to all modes of technical communication—whether oral presentations, paper or electronic texts, or visuals. Figure 1.1 summarizes the characteristics that define technical communication. The following scenario about Jon Baliene, a manufacturing supervisor, illustrates these characteristics in a workplace situation. Jon's situation is typical of many technical professionals.

Can you find an example of a technical document that fulfills most of the characteristics in Figure 1.1?

Division manager Sandy Schaeffer asks her manufacturing supervisor, Jon Baliene, to prepare a report that recommends solutions to some production problems in his department. Although Jon presents verifiable information about the factors contributing to the problem, he also wants to prepare a reader-based report that persuades Sandy to accept his analysis. Because Sandy's background is in business, Jon adjusts the technical material by adding explanations of the highly specialized information. In addition, Jon includes an appendix with calculations and specifications appropriate for secondary readers who have more technical experience than his manager.

Beyond identifying and analyzing the problems, Jon includes recommendations, which, he stresses, are based on current projections and costs; in six months, he would have to write a different report. He hopes the background information along

PURPOSE informs and persuades

AUDIENCE identifies multiple needs of readers; adapts material to readers

ORGANIZATION uses conventional sequence of information; supports argument well

CONTENT presents accurate technical content adjusted to intended audiences

CONTEXT responds to specific situation; intends to fulfill identified needs

MORE ON CONTEXT provides current information that is easily dated

Part I: Understanding the Communicator's Work

FIGURE 1.1 ■ Characteristics of Technical Communication

Characteristic	Explanation
Content	◆ Conveys technical aspects of any field
	◆ Presents accurate, appropriate information adjusted to the audience
Context	◆ Responds to specific situations
	◆ Fulfills specific, identified needs
	◆ Often becomes easily dated
Purpose	◆ Informs *and* persuades
Audience	◆ Addresses identified readers, listeners, or viewers who often have multiple needs and constraints
	◆ Recognizes that multiple interpretations of text, oral presentation, or graphic will occur
Organization	◆ Presents information so that it is logical, accessible, and retrievable, so that it's easy to comprehend and recall
Visuals	◆ Often conveys content through various kinds of visuals and graphics (rather than text) that aid understanding and decision making
Document design	◆ Designs documents to contribute to the accuracy and speed of comprehension and recall of information
	◆ Uses standard paper and electronic formats to take advantage of audience expectations
Usability	◆ Assures that a document is functional, usable; that it enables users to easily and accurately complete the task or activity for which the document is intended
Language conventions	◆ Attempts to be straightforward; differentiates opinions from verifiable information
	◆ Uses clear and direct language without unnecessary complexity; often uses short- to medium-length sentences, subject-verb-object word order; stylistically varied but simple

with his carefully selected support and persuasive arguments convince Sandy to accept his recommendations. However, even though Jon has worked hard to prepare an effective report, he can't guarantee the way that Sandy Schaeffer will interpret the information and his argument. Jon checks the text as well as the visuals to make sure nothing seems ambiguous or confusing.

MORE ON AUDIENCE recognizes the report is open to interpretation

VISUALS conveys content in a table and graph; integrates visuals with text

Because he knows that information might be ignored if presented only in a narrative—without adhering to the conventions readers expect—Jon uses the report format recommended in his company's style guide. He uses his software to organize a great deal of numerical data into a table and to create a graph

DOCUMENT DESIGN uses standard report format

that shows the trends he has identified from the data. He places these visuals in the text immediately following his references to them.

USABILITY
ensures that readers will be able to locate information needed for decision making

Despite Jon's enthusiasm for his recommendations and his recognition that he has a definite bias, he clearly and directly explains the problems and proposes his recommended solution. He realizes that although his primary reader (Sandy Schaeffer) and secondary readers (others in management and manufacturing) are intelligent, well educated, and well informed, they have little time to read an unnecessarily complex report, so he checks his sentences for length and clarity and uses his computer's style option to set headings and subheadings that signal divisions in the report.

MORE ON
DOCUMENT DESIGN provides headings and subheadings to signal main sections and ease reading

LANGUAGE CONVENTIONS
uses clear, direct, and accessible style

Contexts for Constructing Meaning

As Jon planned his report, he identified two goals: one was to submit a report by the deadline in which he recommended solutions to the production problems in his department; the other goal was to persuade Sandy to accept his analysis of the situation and, thus, his recommendations. In preparing his report, Jon considered the situation that stimulated Sandy's request. In other words, he considered the overall context—the social and political situation in the organization as well as the professional expectations and constraints of the organization—that could influence what he would say and how Sandy might interpret it. He selected his information and organized it based on her needs. Thus Jon could not use a boilerplate report format and simply fill in the blanks; the dynamic nature of the situation required that he adjust the form and content to meet specific needs and expectations.

As this situation with Jon shows, technical documents do not occur in isolation; rather, they are part of a larger situation; the documents *and* the situation they are a part of are considered the *genre*. Both the documents and the situations have recurring, evolving patterns. Researchers Carol Berkenkotter and Thomas Huckin explain that rather than being fixed and immutable, the genre (documents and situations) tend to be *dynamic*—that is, they change over time in response to particular circumstances. They are also *situated* because they are part of a particular workplace task or activity. They also have *form and content* that are "appropriate to a particular purpose in a particular situation at a particular point in time." Professionals not only recognize the form of various genre, they also contribute to their creation and *reproduction*—that is, they regularly prepare them and modify them. And finally, professionals, because they are members of a discourse community, see workplace genre as part of their *community's activities*. This book as a whole is about genres in technical communication—that is, the ways documents and presentations are created and used for particular purposes in particular situations at particular points in time.[2]

Like Jon, your goal should be to create *reader-based documents* that consider the readers' needs and reactions and that organize information for readers' understanding. Creating reader-based documents requires awareness of the situation in which documents are generated and used. Readers are, of course, influenced by the actual words on the page, but these words carry slightly different meanings for each reader. And words themselves, whether spoken or written, are only part of what contribute to the understanding. Readers' comprehension of and response to a document are influenced by a range of factors including their attitudes, values, education, job security, political position, personality, and experiences.

What other factors can you think of that could affect the way readers respond to documents? What might affect readers' comprehension? What might affect their recall of information?

Because meaning is constructed by readers, as a writer you need to be especially careful to select words and visuals and then organize information so that readers are more likely to construct a meaning that is similar to the one you intend. No document completely conveys the meaning the writer intends, nor does any reader ever understand everything the writer wants to convey. As a writer, you both add and omit things that were part of the original situation. As a reader, your interpretation is affected by what linguists call *exuberance* (that is, your interpretation always adds something the writer didn't intend) and *deficiency* (that is, your interpretation always ignores things that the writer wanted you to notice).

Meaning is also constructed by the technology you use. What is broadly called *computer-mediated communication* (CMC) is a process of human communication via computers. CMC provides a way for people to communicate, interact, and retrieve information in a variety of contexts and to shape communication for a variety of purposes. The technology you use influences what you say and how you say it, specifically affecting privacy and immediacy.

- *Privacy.* Virtually all electronic communication in the workplace can be monitored; it is simply not private. Knowing that someone other than the intended audience might read your e-mail should promote some caution in what you choose to write and send. For example, e-mail messages and online chats are not necessarily protected by privacy laws. Some legal experts argue that "the writer of an e-mail message is implicitly consenting to its recording."[3]

- *Immediacy.* You can decide when to communicate by participating in synchronous or asynchronous communication. *Synchronous communication* is concurrent or simultaneous (real time) digital communication—for example, computer conferencing, chat rooms, or white board environments. Such environments often promote comments that are not carefully thought through. *Asynchronous communication* is digital communication that takes place independently in time—communication exchanges can be delayed by minutes, hours, or days such as voice mail, e-mail, or online newsgroups. While asynchronous communication allows more time for reflection, the informal nature often promotes casual, hurried responses.

What factors besides privacy and immediacy are influenced by computer-mediated communication?

Whether you're preparing an electronic or print document, writing grammatically conventional sentences and organizing information in coherent paragraphs

Public vs. Private: Ethics and the Technical Professional

Imagine the following workplace situation:

You are working on your first major report, a technical description of the company's latest product. You know your technical description should highlight the product's state-of-the-art features. Those features are a key selling point. However, some field tests indicate those features are unreliable under adverse weather conditions—conditions common in the intended market for this product. Other tests, though, are planned. You are faced with a decision: Do you include the current test results in your technical description? You know what your company would prefer, but you feel an obligation to let customers know about the possibility of problems. The description is due by the end of the day. What do you do?

Writing situations like this one require technical professionals to make ethical decisions. Ethics determine what we are willing to communicate and how we are willing to communicate. Ethics come from many different perspectives: personal beliefs, professional guidelines, organizational practices, cultural expectations, and legal or judicial requirements.

Communication researcher Cezar Ornatowski[4] believes ethical dilemmas for technical professionals occur because they have two "incompatible" goals: serving the interests of employers while attempting to write technical documents that are "objective, plain, factual." Placed under these conflicting pressures, technical professionals are at increased risk for ethical violations—either the technical professional produces a document that does not meet the employer's goals, or the technical professional produces a document that may not be verifiable. (For a discussion of ethical violations in written communication, see Herbert Michaelson's article at the end of Chapter 7.)

How can you decide what information to include in a document and what information to exclude?

Dealing with these ethical dilemmas is not always easy—sometimes, technical professionals must make difficult decisions. However, many ethical dilemmas can be addressed by knowing that these dilemmas exist and understanding various ways to resolve them. Even if you don't find ethical violations that challenge your personal beliefs, you should be aware of ways they might affect your standing among your colleagues and your profession. Ethical violations affect a document's credibility that, in turn, affects how you will be professionally perceived.

Re-read the scenario at the beginning of this sidebar. Upon consideration, how would you deal with this conflict? Would you include the questionable test results? Would excluding them be an ethical violation?

are not enough. To meet readers' needs, you must initially decide about your purposes to inform and persuade. Beyond this, you must respond to the context, define and focus the content, analyze the task and audience, organize the information, and design the specific document. But you still need more.

To be an effective communicator, you must also consider factors that influence you and your audience as you and they construct meaning. What's one of the most important factors that influences everyone involved in writing, reading, and responding to technical documents? Ethics. In this textbook, ethics are considered in every chapter—most prominently, in the sidebars where you'll read about a number of ethics issues. The first such sidebar is above.

Texts That Communicate

If you identified every type of technical document, the list would extend for pages, both because so many types exist and because the terminology is not standardized. One easy way to differentiate technical documents is by audience and function. The audience (readers who expect documents to respond to their particular needs) can be within your organization or outside your organization. The following types of documents are familiar to workplace audiences:

What are the most common types of technical documents in your career area? When are they used? What are their purposes? Who are their audiences? How much does it matter that you be able to read and write these types of documents?

- *Correspondence* includes paper notes, memos, and letters as well as electronic correspondence such as e-mail. Notes and memos are typically intended for internal readers, whereas letters are generally for external readers. Electronic mail can be for either internal or external readers, often replacing traditional print correspondence. Correspondence is discussed in Chapter 14.

- *Sales, marketing, and promotional materials* as well as specifications and product information sheets are intended for external readers (the customers) or for sales representatives who work with customers. Techniques to use in creating these paper and online documents are presented in Chapters 11, 12, and 13.

- *Instructions and manuals*, prepared for both internal and external readers, standardize everything from the operation of manufacturing equipment to procedures for personnel practices. Every product, whether for the commercial or consumer market, should be accompanied by paper or online manuals to direct assembly, guide operation, recommend maintenance, and troubleshoot common problems. Chapter 15 discusses instructions and manuals.

- *Proposals* written for internal audiences are often brief and informal, providing recommendations for anything from equipment purchase to staff reorganization. Lengthy, formal proposals are most frequently for external audiences, asking for approval or acceptance of a variety of services and products; sometimes proposals are even submitted electronically. Chapter 16 introduces guidelines for preparing proposals.

- *Reports*, for both internal and external audiences, may be brief and informal or extend to lengthy, formal documents. Reports fall into several broad categories: research, periodic activity, finance, personnel, decision making, and so on. General guidelines for short reports and formats for formal reports are discussed in Chapter 17.

To be effective, all these technical documents, regardless of function, must meet certain standards. Where a document falls on the range of standards—from minimal to most rigorous—depends on the situation. For example, you probably have lower standards for informal, internal, short-lived notes than for formal,

FIGURE 1.2 ■ Guidelines and Questions for Analyzing and Assessing Technical Documents

Photocopy and use this figure to help you analyze and assess documents.

Guidelines	Questions to Help Analyze and Assess Technical Documents
Understand the impact of context.	◆ What's the situation in which the document will be used? How does the situation affect the document's purpose? Audience? Organization?
Identify the multiple purposes.	◆ What is the document's stated purpose?
	◆ What is the writer's purpose? Is it different from the reader's purpose?
Select the content.	◆ What do you need to include for this situation? Purpose? Audience?
	◆ Which information is accurate? Misleading? Inaccurate?
Anticipate needs of multiple audiences.	◆ How is the audience identified? How is the document adapted to that audience?
	◆ What do various members of the audience already know? Need to know? Want to know? What might various readers misinterpret?
	◆ How can *analogies* and *metaphors* be used to help readers connect new information to what they already know?
	◆ Are unfamiliar terms defined? Are complex concepts explained?
Select the most appropriate, effective organization.	◆ How is the organization signaled so readers know what to anticipate?
	◆ What textual devices are used to establish *unity*—that is, logically relating the information to a central point? To establish *coherence*—that is, clearly relating the ideas to each other?
	◆ Can readers easily understand the *position* being taken in the document? What kind of *support* is used for this position?
Create or choose appropriate visuals.	◆ How does the document effectively integrate verbal and visual information?
	◆ What visuals increase readers' comprehension of the information?
	◆ How do these visuals both illustrate and clarify concepts?
	◆ How does the document use color?
Design the document so it is accessible and appealing.	◆ How does the design of the document aid readers' comprehension?
	◆ Do headings help readers keep track of where they are in the document?
	◆ What elements—such as table of contents, preview and review sections, glossary, references, and index—help readers locate information and navigate through the document?
	◆ What design and format conventions do readers expect in this document?
Assure that the document is usable.	◆ Can readers easily and accurately complete the task or activity for which the document is intended? How easily can key points be located?
	◆ What are readers' expectations? Does the document take advantage of them?
	◆ Can readers easily differentiate opinions from verifiable information?
Use professional standards for language conventions.	◆ How does the document meet mechanical and grammatical conventions?
	◆ How appealing and appropriate is the style of writing?
	◆ How well documented is information from other sources?

external proposals. In general, the factors in Figure 1.2 should be part of your assessment of any document. Figure 1.2 also suggests questions you can ask yourself to help analyze and assess technical documents—whether your own, those you're writing with a collaborator, or those you're reviewing for a colleague.

Now you're going to have an opportunity to look at two examples of technical documents (Figures 1.3 and 1.4) that have been annotated to highlight the characteristics that make them effective. The first example, an excerpt from an in-house technical report, provides a summary of information gathered in a site visit. The second example, from a section of a booklet for patients suffering from respiratory problems, defines and discusses occupational asthma.

At the beginning of this chapter, you read a list of guidelines to consider when you are planning and evaluating documents. As a result of seeing brief analyses of two examples, you now have some specifics to tag on to these general guidelines. Even though the examples in this chapter are intended for very different audiences (committee members involved in decision making about the battery supplier and nonexpert readers wanting to learn more about allergies), both have some common characteristics:

- Definitions of terms in the introductory section

- Foregrounding (previewing) of what's to come

- Selection of details appropriate for the readers' level of technical understanding

- An effective design (for example, headings and white space) that contributes to ease of reading

- Use of typographic devices (for example, bullets) and elements (for example, italics and boldfacing) to call attention to information

- Use of visuals (for example, a table) to reinforce the text

More important than simply recognizing these common characteristics, though, you can see that these examples use textual, organizational, and design features that are appropriate for the situation and meet the needs of the readers. If you were to select other pieces to analyze, you could use the guidelines to help you frame general questions. The specific points could be different, but they should reflect the general characteristics discussed in this chapter.

What additional guidelines do you think would be useful to you in planning or analyzing documents?

What are the advantages, if any, of being able to analyze the effectiveness of the documents that other people write?

Communicators

As customer satisfaction with products and services becomes more important, companies increase the attention they give to paper and electronic documents, which are now seen as essential parts of the products. Since operations increasingly depend on rapid, accurate communication, companies expect all employees to be good communicators. In fact, a poll by the National Association

FIGURE 1.3 ■ **Example of an Excerpt from a Technical Report**

PASTE PRODUCTION[5]

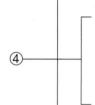

Paste production involves mixing lead oxide with water, sulfuric acid, organic fibers, and red lead to produce a dough-like substance called *paste*. In this section, I discuss Dalton's general paste formula and control parameters but not the exact formula. No comparison with other vendors can be made because these formulas are closely guarded secrets. However, I do provide a comparison of Dalton's control parameters both to industry standards and to optimum conditions for known parameters.

Formulations for the positive and negative paste differ primarily because red lead is added to the positive paste and not to the negative, while expander is added to the negative paste and not to the positive. In the battery industry, red lead is usually 10–30% of the total lead oxide: the higher the percentage of red lead the better. Dalton uses only 10% red lead. The expander, a mixture of lignin, carbon black, and barium sulfate, is usually added at about the 1% level. The best expander is Anzon-Kx. Instead, Dalton uses HL-120, from Harrington Lead Company. Harrington has the reputation for occasionally producing erratic quality expanders. Dalton's paste formulation—rounded off to 1%—is given in the table below.

	Positive Formula	Negative Formula
Oxide	72%	82%
Red Lead	8%	None
Water	11%	10%
Acid	9%	7%
Expander	None	2%

The quality of the paste is determined by three parameters: peak temperature, dump temperature, and cube weight. The temperatures are monitored continuously but are controlled by the rate of reaction between the lead oxide and sulfuric acid. The other two parameters are manually measured with each batch of paste prior to dumping into the pasting machine. Usually only one measurement is taken per batch.

Peak temperature is probably the most important of the control parameters because it sets the amount of nuclei of tetrabasic lead sulfate, the phase necessary for long life in the battery. The hotter the peak temperature the better. The industry standard for this critical parameter is 160°F; in contrast, Dalton's control point is 140°F +/− 10°F. (Note: I would prefer to see peak temperatures of 190°F.)

Unlike peak temperatures, *dump temperatures* should be kept as low as possible to prevent premature curing of the paste. The industry standard is 110–115°F, which is considerably cooler than Dalton's 125°F. Perhaps Dalton Battery is partially compensating for the low peak temperatures with high dump temperatures to increase their tetrabasic lead sulfate nucleation count.

Cube weights, which measure the density of the paste, are best if kept between 72–75 g/in^3 for the positive in order to achieve long battery life. The negative is less critical but traditionally has cube weights of 68–78 g/in^3. In comparison, Dalton uses cube weights of 66–68 g/in^3 and 72–74 g/in^3 for the positive and negative, respectively.

FIGURE 1.3 ■ Annotations for Figure 1.3

The example in Figure 1.3 is an excerpt from a long internal company report assessing the capabilities of one of several battery manufacturers being considered as a supplier for the company. The readers are company employees—engineers, industrial buyers, managers—who are members of a committee to review the capabilities of ten major battery manufacturers. (The names of all the companies referred to have been changed.) This committee will recommend which manufacturers the company should select as their primary and secondary suppliers. A major portion of the committee's decision rests on the capability of the battery manufacturer and the quality of the batteries. And that quality depends on the production processes. So, based on information obtained from site visits to each manufacturing facility, one of the engineers on the committee produced a separate, detailed, and lengthy report for each manufacturer being considered.

The engineer/writer decided that each of the ten reports—completed over a six-month period coinciding with the site visits—would include the same eight sections so that comparisons among the various manufacturers could be made easily (even though the process of collecting and evaluating the information took place over a lengthy period). Seeing the outline used for each report's table of contents gives a sense of the overall organization of each report:

1. Introduction
2. Metallurgical processes: alloy production and grid production
3. Chemical processes: lead oxide production and paste production
4. Plate production: pasting and curing
5. Cell production: assembly and case-to-cover sealing
6. Battery production: formation, packing, high-current testing
7. Product completion: finishing and shipping
8. Summary and evaluation table

The excerpt in Figure 1.3, from the report about the site visit to Dalton Battery, is the paste production subsection of the third main division of the report, chemical processes. The report is *unified* (all information in this section relates to paste production) and *coherent* (the points flow logically from one to the next).

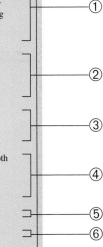

◆ Definitions and explanations enable the less technical members of the committee to follow the discussion but will not annoy the technical readers who don't need as much explanation.
  ◇ The writer includes critical definitions and explanations (for example, an overview of the process of paste production) because some members of the committee do not have an engineering background.
  ◇ The writer provides technical details that are important to the engineers on the committee. ①

◆ The writer effectively organizes the information and signals that organization for readers.
  ◇ The two kinds of paste are clearly distinguished in the second paragraph.
  ◇ Foregrounding of critical parameters in the third paragraph prepares readers for next three paragraphs. ②

◆ Readers are guided in their interpretation.
  ◇ Words such as "only" and "instead" help readers understand how the writer interprets the information. ③

◆ Details are organized into a table that identifies the percentages of components in the formulas for both positive and negative paste.
  ◇ The information in the table reinforces and illustrates the text.
  ◇ Readers are given help in interpreting the data. ④

◆ Each parameter is discussed in a separate paragraph so that it is easy to distinguish. ⑤

◆ Effective use of standard comparisons helps readers assess the information. ⑥

FIGURE 1.4 ■ Example of an Extended Definition from a Medical Booklet

OCCUPATIONAL ASTHMA[6]

① WHAT IS OCCUPATIONAL ASTHMA?

② *Occupational asthma* is generally defined as a respiratory disorder directly related to inhaling fumes, gases, or dust while on the job. Symptoms include wheezing, chest tightness, coughing, and may also include runny nose, nasal congestion, and eye irritation. The cause may be allergic or nonallergic in nature. The disease may persist for lengthy periods in some workers even if they are no longer exposed. Many workers with symptoms have been incorrectly diagnosed as having bronchitis.

It's important to remember that persons living in residential areas near factories are also exposed to fumes and may suffer symptoms as well.

④ In many cases, a previous family history of allergy will make a person more likely to suffer from occupational asthma. Yet many individuals who have no such history still develop this disease. Studies show that the length of exposure varies and can range from 4 to 36 months before symptoms occur.

① HOW PREVALENT IS OCCUPATIONAL ASTHMA?

② The exact prevalence of occupational asthma is not known. Researchers have found, however, that at least 15% of all male cases of asthma in Japan result from exposure to industrial vapors, dust, gases, or fumes. In the U.S., 5–10% of all cases of asthma are thought to have job-related origins.

① WHAT ARE THE CAUSES OF OCCUPATIONAL ASTHMA?
④ Occupational asthma may be caused by one of three mechanisms: irritants, allergic, or environmental factors:

③ • Examples of *irritants* that provoke cases of occupational asthma include exposure to hydrochloric acid, sulfur dioxide, or ammonia found in the petroleum or chemical industries. People who may already have asthma or some other respiratory disorder are particularly affected when exposure occurs. In instances where irritants are re-
④ sponsible for causing the asthma, allergic mechanisms are not actively involved. (An allergic mechanism refers to the body's immune system responding adversely to an offending substance.)

• *Allergic factors* do play a role, however, in the following instances: exposures to the enzymes of *Bacillus subtilis* in the washing powder industry, exposure to castor and green coffee beans, and contact with papain in the food processing industry. Other
② examples include complex salts of platinum in metal refining and other agents such as ethylene diamine, phthalic anhydride, toluene diisocyanate (TDI), and trimellitic anhydride (TMA) in the plastics, rubber, and resin industries.

• *Environmental factors* include the inhalation of dust or liquid extracts of dust from cotton, flax, or hemp. In these cases, tissue cells in the lung directly release chemi-cals, such as histamine, which can cause bronchial smooth muscle to contract and,
④ thus, block airways. Yet this reaction can occur in subjects who are not allergic to any of these substances. The exact role that these factors play in producing this drug-like effect is not yet completely known.

FIGURE 1.4 ■ Annotations for Figure 1.4

The example about occupational asthma in Figure 1.4 is an excerpt from *Allergy Relief Guide,* a booklet for people suffering from respiratory problems. The introduction to the booklet explains that it has been prepared by the American Academy of Allergy and Immunology, a group of physicians "who specialize in the diagnosis and management of asthma and allergy disorders of adults and children." The introduction explains that information in the booklet helps readers know more about their own health and, thus, take better care of themselves and their families.

The chapter this excerpt is from begins with a simple definition of asthma (an allergy that occurs in the lungs) and its triggers: allergens (such as pollen, mold), viral infections, irritants (such as tobacco smoke, air pollutants), distance running, sensitivity to drugs, and emotional anxiety. Thus, the information in the excerpt is presented after readers have some general background.

- ◆ Questions readers might ask a doctor are used to organize the information:
    - ◇ Questions as headings provide easy access to key points.
    - ◇ The series of topically related questions provides some coherence, but the text doesn't have the smooth flow of a well-written report—nor should it.
    - ◇ The questions act as simple foregrounding for the chunks of information that follow.
    - ◇ The question-and-answer format makes information in the booklet very accessible, in part because each question is capitalized and presented on a separate line from the beginning of the answer.

- ◆ Details are appropriate for readers:
    - ◇ Each cause is discussed in a separate paragraph.
    - ◇ Limited use of technical information is appropriate for this nonexpert audience.
    - ◇ Specific details are provided to help readers understand a point.

- ◆ Document design elements help readers:
    - ◇ Italics draw attention to key points.
    - ◇ Bulleted items draw attention and make reading easier.
    - ◇ Key causes are signaled in the heading and foregrounded in the text.

- ◆ Cause-effect explanations help readers understand symptoms.

After the basic information reproduced in the excerpt, the booklet includes a two-column list—material and industry—of specific "industrial materials known to cause occupational asthma." For example, flour can cause occupational asthma for bakers as well as for farmers and grain handlers. Similarly, phenylglycine acid chloride and sulphone chloramides can cause occupational asthma for workers in the pharmaceutical industry.

of Manufacturers stated that 37 percent of entry-level applicants aren't hired because of poor reading or writing skills; 25 percent aren't hired because of poor oral skills.

Technical Communicators and Technical Experts

Two broad categories of professionals are responsible for virtually all the technical documents and presentations in any organization: technical communicators and technical experts. Technical communicators have evolved as highly trained specialists whose primary responsibility is to design, develop, and produce a wide range of documents and visuals. As essential members of project teams, technical communicators support the products and services of an organization. Equally important are technical experts who communicate as a regular part of their job. These scientists, engineers, technicians, and managers regularly plan and prepare a wide range of technical documents and presentations. These individuals, whether technical communicators or technical experts, perform one or more of these roles:

- *Independent communicators.* In some organizations, you may be the single individual who is totally responsible for a writing project, from collection of data through publication of the document. If you are totally responsible for a project, you must be able to work with the support personnel who fulfill the responsibilities of editing, graphic design, word processing, and publication. In a very small company, you may also take on many of these support functions.

In what kinds of situations have you worked? In what kinds of situations are you most comfortable? Most productive?

- *Members of project teams.* In some organizations, you may be one member of a team of experts, all of whom collaborate on one or more long-term projects. If you're on a team, you must regularly coordinate your work with other members of the team. Sometimes a project or communication group manager assumes primary responsibility for working with editors, designers, word processing (wp) operators, and printers.

- *Contributors to projects.* In some organizations, you may be assigned to complete a section of a project—perhaps several chapters in a manual or one book in a series—with a managing or supervising editor overseeing the project. Here you may have little responsibility beyond completing your own assignment and sometimes working with editors. Group supervisors and managers coordinate work with designers, wp operators, and printers.

Constraints That Communicators Face

What kinds of constraints have you already faced in the workplace? How did you manage these constraints so they did not cause major problems?

Regardless of your organizational role, you'll not only need an aptitude for understanding and explaining technical information, but also an ability to manage the constraints that come with your role. These constraints affect the entire process of creating a document.

Time Constraints.   You'll often work within time limits that seem unreasonable; maybe the schedule has been set by someone unaware of the demands of the writing or the technical aspects of the project. Time considerations and deadlines limit every stage of preparing a document or presentation. Technical communicators realize that varying levels of professionally acceptable work exist, and you'll recognize the value of developing priorities to decide which projects deserve the most time. You will find, for example, that some projects require extensive exploring and planning or time-consuming revising and editing, whereas others need no more than cursory revisions, incorporated as the drafting proceeds.

Subject and Format Constraints.   The subject for a technical document or presentation is usually predetermined. However, you'll face the challenge of focusing on details appropriate for the intended audience and presenting what may be uninspiring information in an interesting, or at least useful, manner. You will seldom be given a specific approach for a document. Rather, you'll need to be able to narrow your subject, select and organize content, and then determine the limitations of the document. To do this, you'll need to assess the audience's needs and identify its purpose for reading the document.

Audience Constraints.   Sometimes you'll prepare a technical document or presentation for an audience in which everyone has similar education, experience, and expectations. Frequently, however, the members of the audience have varied backgrounds as well as different reasons for reading the document or listening to a presentation. For example, a business manager might have an advanced degree in management but little expertise in the technical field of the company. As a result, you'll need to make decisions about the level of technical complexity, organization, diction, and design to respond to the needs of a variety of readers or listeners. (See Chapter 3 for a more detailed discussion of audience.)

Collaboration as a Constraint.   Sometimes you'll work independently; sometimes collaboratively. Think of two extremes. In one, you'll work independently, assuming responsibility for exploring, planning, drafting, and perhaps even editing and publishing a document. In the other, you'll be a member of a group, a collaborator who shares the responsibility for one or more stages of the process. Realistically, your actual role in preparing any given document or presentation will probably fall somewhere between the isolation of working independently and the pressure of working collaboratively. (See Chapter 5 for a more detailed discussion of collaboration.)

Constraints in Data Collection.   The information you need won't always be easily or quickly accessible. To collect information, you must approach new equipment and unfamiliar processes with confidence. As you learn to operate the equipment or complete the process, you'll discover what your readers will need to know. Don't be surprised, however, when you are hampered by limited access to the necessary equipment or when the available information seems skimpy. Sometimes the deadlines will be too tight to learn everything you need to know. In these situations, you must depend on others for the information to prepare a document or presentation. Develop persuasive skills so that people who have packed schedules will agree to make time to talk with you. Once you've located the people who have the information and have made an appointment, you need strong interviewing skills to collect the data. (Chapters 6 and 19 provide guidelines for conducting successful interviews.)

Constraints in Technology.   Technology is becoming more and more a part of communication in every workplace from agribusiness to astrophysics laboratories, from endangered species breeding programs in zoos to software engineering departments. You face several potential constraints: You need access to appropriate technology as well as the capability and training to use it. You are at a tremendous disadvantage if you aren't familiar with and have the training to use a wide range of appropriate electronic tools. Other constraints you might encounter include limited access to electronic tools, lack of technical support for the hardware and software, and readers' unfamiliarity with the technology if they need to read electronic documents.

Constraints Caused by Noise.   Interference, or what is sometimes called *noise*, can come from any of the elements in the communication process, from the context or environment, from any of the communicators, or from the document itself. This interference influences the way that readers, listeners, or viewers interpret the messages of writers, speakers, or designers.

What constraints do you anticipate you might have in the future when preparing a technical document or presentation? How do you plan to deal with these constraints?

- *Noise from the context or environment.* One kind of environmental interference occurs because the physical reception of the information is garbled or masked. Physical interference may be as simple as a noisy air conditioner in a meeting room or static on a phone line. Another kind of environmental interference occurs because the social or political environment influences the way in which people interpret information. Social or political interference may be caused by organizational policies and practices. For example, if safety updates are typically given only cursory attention in a particular company, a writer has a more difficult time than if these updates are carefully read and implemented. No environment is neutral; some form of interference always exists.

- *Noise from any of the communicators.* Writers, speakers, and designers as well as readers, listeners, and viewers can generate noise. The experiences and attitudes of the writers, speakers, or designers (factors such as vested interests, emotional biases, perceptions) affect their selection and slant of information. This interference may also come from problems that writers, speakers, or designers have in formulating the information (for example, ambiguity or failure to consider audience needs). The experiences and attitudes of readers, listeners, and viewers (factors such as boredom, doubt, disagreement, anger, or indifference) affect their interpretation of information. No communicator is neutral; interference of some type is always part of those who generate the information as well as those who interpret it.

- *Noise embedded in the information and in the delivery of documents, presentations, and visuals.* Information can be incomplete, inaccurate, illogical, unsupported, or inflammatory, thus causing interference in understanding. Beyond that, documents, presentations, and visuals can embed noise in various ways. Interference can occur in documents or visuals because of factors such as confusing document design or low-quality reproduction. Interference can occur in oral presentations because of factors such as inadequate amplification or inappropriate visuals for the room size. No document, presentation, or visual is neutral; some form of interference always affects the information and the delivery.

Being aware of the constraints that communicators face—time, subject and format, audience, collaboration, data collection, technology, and noise—should help you anticipate and manage some of the problems that these constraints generate.

End-of-Chapter
Recommendations for Technical Communicators

1. Consider that speaking and writing skills are either "very important" or "important" to the success of many workplace professionals.

2. Define technical discourse by a cluster of characteristics dealing with factors such as purpose, subject matter, approach, and audience.

3. Consider the overall context—that is, social, political, and ethical factors in the organization, as well as the professional expectations and constraints of the organization—that could influence how you shape your communication and how listeners, readers, or viewers might construct your meaning as they interpret it.

4. Create reader-based documents that consider the readers' needs and reactions and that organize information so that readers can understand it.

5. Be familiar with the range of documents that both internal and external readers use:
   - Correspondence
   - Sales, marketing, and promotional materials
   - Instructions and instructional manuals
   - Proposals
   - Reports

6. Use these guidelines to help assess any document:
   - Understand the impact of context.
   - Select the content.
   - Identify the multiple purposes.
   - Anticipate needs of multiple audiences.
   - Select the most appropriate, effective organization.
   - Create or choose appropriate visuals.
   - Design the document so it is accessible and appealing.
   - Assure that the document is usable.
   - Use professional standards for language conventions.

7. Be prepared to work as an independent communicator, as a member of a project team, or as a contributor to projects.

8. Learn to manage these constraints: time, subject and format, audience, collaboration, data collection, technology, and noise.

Individual and Collaborative Assignments

1. **Define technical communication.** According to the Institute of Scientific and Technical Communicators, technical communication is defined as

   . . . all processes by which humans convey meaning about the development and use of technology. In essence, scientific and technical communication involves the gathering, analyzing, and distributing of scientific and technical information efficiently and accurately for specific audiences.[7]

   This ISTC definition focuses on conveying information but does not mention interpreting information—either by the writer or the reader/listener. How would you revise the ISTC definition to incorporate the idea of interpretation?

2. **Identify general audiences.** Read the following list of subjects. Identify at least two realistic technical audiences for documents, visuals, or presentations for any five of these subjects. Explain what technical information each audience might need to learn or use.

   Example: Renaissance paint might be of interest to any of these technical professionals: a museum curator—to authenticate a painting; an art historian—to characterize materials in a particular period; a chemist—to conduct a spectrographic analysis.

arrows	ethanol	magnifying glass	running shoes
ballet	fax machine	modem	soybeans
butter	frisbees	motor oil	steroids
CDs	furniture stripper	mouse	styrofoam
cellular phone	golf balls	peanut	synthesizer
coffee	hot dogs	perfume	tires
condors	jogging	plastic film	tricycles
daisies	kitty litter	poetry	trout
dreams	legumes	pup tents	wire cable
eggs	light bulbs	rainbows	ZIP drive

3. **Identify particular audiences.** Visit any five of the following Web sites, which represent a range of national and multinational corporations as well as not-for-profit organizations. Identify three intended audiences for each one, and briefly explain what information or features on the site would appeal to that audience.

<www.admworld.com>	<www.cokecc.com>	<www.monsanto.com>
<www.bayerus.com>	<www.foodsafety.org>	<www.oracle.com>
<www.birdseye.com>	<www.lucent.com>	<www.ups.com>
<www.cocacola.com>	<www.merck.com>	<www.whymilk.com>

4. **Assess a short memo.** The following memo was submitted as a weekly progress report about project activities. It is typical in several ways—amount of information, tone, length, and attention to detail—of the memos and reports produced by William Jackson, an associate engineer. Because Mr. Jackson has always been extremely careful to double-check his content for accuracy, he is surprised that his semiannual review identifies his writing as a block to rapid advancement. Examine the memo and use the factors for assessing documents presented in this chapter to help explain whether you agree with the assessment by Mr. Jackson's supervisor. What advice would you give Mr. Jackson to help him become a more effective communicator?

MEMO

September 26, 20—

To   Mark Hager
From   William Jackson *wj*
Subject   Project Update

We're on schedule except for setting up the grinding wheels because they haven't been recieved yet and calibrating the tools 'cause new master blocks haven't been uncrated and Joe Simons has been out all week with the flu.

Everything should be done next week.

The electrician is scheduled Tuesday to install new lines and wire equipment.

---

5. **Assess a technical explanation.** Read the following text, "Understanding and Avoiding the Leading Cause of Death Among Pilots," that was written for beginning student pilots. In the rubric on page 26, create criteria for *excellent* for each feature listed (e.g., content, context, purpose, audience, etc.): What makes content excellent? What makes response to context excellent? What makes presentation of purpose excellent? What makes adaptation to audience excellent? Then apply your criteria to this document for student pilots, deciding which features of this document you think are *unacceptable, weak, acceptable,* or *excellent.* Based on your completed rubric, explain whether the writer has created an effective technical document.

UNDERSTANDING AND AVOIDING THE
LEADING CAUSE OF DEATH AMONG PILOTS[8]

More pilots are killed in **stall-spin accidents** than in any other type of incident. The next cause of fatalities is inadvertent flight into bad weather by pilots not trained in instrument flight, which usually leads to a stall-spin scenario. At the end of this discussion, you should be able to answer these questions:

• What holds the airplane up?
• What is a stall?
• What is a spin?
• How can you recover from a stall?

The engine doesn't hold the airplane up in the air, the wing doesn't hold it up in the air, and (although we're reluctant to admit it) the pilot's skill doesn't hold it up in the air. Airplanes are held aloft by a physical force called lift. **Lift** is an upward force generated by the smooth flow of air over the wing's surfaces.

The illustration below uses tiny balloons to represent paired air molecules passing above and below a wing. In 1738, a Swiss physicist named Daniel Bernoulli suggested that the airmass remains undisturbed by the wing and that each pair of balloons would join again at the back of the wing. Wings have a certain shape: the top is convex; the bottom is flat. Slats at the leading edge of the wing and flaps at the trailing edge of the wing exaggerate the difference. As the illustration shows, the curved line traveled by the balloons above the wing is a greater distance than the straight line traveled by balloons below the wing.

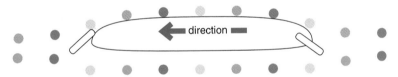
direction

In order for the balloons to rejoin, the speed and spacing of the upper balloons must be greater than the speed and spacing of the lower balloons; the difference in speed and distance causes a relatively lower **air pressure** along the top of the wing. This relative suction translates into a force called lift. Lift increases as the flow of air increases over the wings. When the speed of the airflow over the wings generates a lifting force stronger than gravity, the plane flies. The engine does not thrust the plane into the sky; the engine moves the plane forward at a speed permitting the wings to generate sufficient lift.

What happens when this goes wrong? When the airflow is disturbed, the subtle relative suction disappears, and gravity re-asserts itself over the mass of the aircraft. The airflow can be disturbed by ice or by an extremely nose-high attitude. The loss of lift is called a **stall,** a phrase that has nothing to do with the way a jalopy quits on the highway. One warning: Never attempt to takeoff with ice or frost on the wings. Keep the wings clean of dirt and bugs. Lift requires clean wings.

When one wing stalls before the other, the aircraft becomes asymmetrical, resulting in a disorienting rotation dive called a **spin.** Low-time pilots can be overwhelmed by the physical forces of a sustained spin and may be unable to regain controlled flight.

Recovery from the stall is straightforward: Level the wings to avoid a spin, drop the nose to increase airflow over the wings and restore lift, increase to full engine power to climb to safety, and reflect on the audacity of flight.

Your experienced flight instructor will show you how to intentionally stall and spin your aircraft to practice recovering from these situations. When you start these maneuvers at a safe altitude and with your instructor's guidance, you will learn how to avoid, recognize, and resolve the situations that put novice pilots at risk. Remember: Level the wings, drop the nose, and apply full power.

Document Features	1 Unacceptable	2 Weak	3 Acceptable	4 Excellent
Content				
Context				
Purpose				
Audience				
Organization				
Visuals				
Information Design				
Usability				
Language Conventions				

Note: Throughout this text, you will be asked to create and use rubrics as tools to help you assess documents, visuals, presentations, and Web sites. To fill in this rubric, you can draw from Figures 1.1, 1.2, 1.3, and 1.4 in this chapter. As you learn more, you'll develop additional criteria for assessing technical documents. See the Handbook at the end of the textbook for a more detailed description of rubrics and some suggested criteria for evaluation.

6. **Determine guidelines and criteria to add to the above rubric.** What additional document features do you think would be useful to you as you plan or analyze print documents? If possible, work with classmates in your discipline or career area and build on the suggestions in this chapter to add features that may be specifically useful in your discipline or career area. How might these criteria be changed if you were assessing or analyzing Web-based documents?

Intertext

Technical Writers Are in Demand: Do You Have the Right Stuff?[9]

- Do you think that you can write a user's manual that is better than the manual for the last computer you learned to use?

- Have you received compliments on the design and content of the Web site you created?

- Do you want to be part of the thriving information technology industry?

The U.S. Department of Commerce announced . . . that the information technology industry is responsible for more than one quarter of the country's real economic growth in the last five years. If you answered *yes* to any of the above questions, a technical writing career may be in your future.

What Do Technical Writers Do?

Technical writers explain things. They translate complex information and ideas into content that can be easily understood by a particular audience, from the general public to technically trained people. Technical writers create environmental impact statements, Web sites, magazine articles, proposals, instructions for taking medicine, training manuals for pilots, repair manuals for blood analyzers, instructions for using VCRs, online help for computer software, assembly instructions, newsletters, on-screen instructions for using your bank's ATM machine, specifications, user's guides for telephone answering machines, instructions for making microwaved popcorn, computer manuals, and many other types of documentation. Technical writers work in every industry, from automobiles to computers to finance to health care.

At one time, technical writers were primarily wordsmiths. Austin Brown began his technical writing career in Alaska in 1961, before the computer and the photocopier were commonplace. "Writers used a pencil or an ink pen and wrote words on paper," he recalls. "The paper was handed to a typist who used a typewriter to type the words. Documents were printed using a method called offset lithography. The word processing and desktop publishing software applications that we use today weren't introduced until the early 1980s."

[A decade ago] Brown retired from his position as head of the Technical Publications Branch of the Naval Surface Weapons Center in Virginia. Brown is now semi-retired and a communications consultant in Hawaii. Today he and his colleagues use not only words, but also illustrations, photographs, video, and computer-based multimedia. Now more than ever, technical writing is a craft that combines science, technology, and the humanities. Today's technical writers are also called information architects, analysts, technologists, developers, designers, and engineers; Web masters; technical communicators and editors; procedure writers; and documentation specialists. Whatever they are called, their objective is the same as always: to convey scientific and technical information concisely, accurately, and clearly.

Why Are Technical Writers in Demand?

Demand for technical writers is expected to continue to increase as technology continues to become more and more a part of our lives. Popular consumer magazines identified technical writing as a hot career as early as 1983 (*Ebony*) and as recently as 1996 (*Working Woman* and *Black Enterprise*). According to the . . . *Occupational Outlook Handbook,* published by the U.S. Department of Labor's Bureau of Labor Statistics, employment of writers and editors is expected to increase faster than the average for all occupations (that is, increase 21 to 35 percent) through the year 2006. The handbook also says that through the year 2006, opportunities will be good for technical writers because of the more limited number of writers who can handle technical material. The handbook says that online publications and services, which are relatively new, will continue to grow and require an increased number of writers and editors.

The number and variety of technical communication opportunities have enabled Angela Taylor, now a technical writer for IBM in Research Triangle Park in North Carolina, to thrive as a technical communications writing contractor for the last 16 years. "A contractor is an employee that a technical service agency hires to work for various companies for a specified period of time," Taylor explains. "The agency matches the contractor's skills with the position that the company needs to fill. It's analogous to an actor being hired to portray a particular character on a television show for just a few months." Taylor has worked under contract for periods as short as six months. Her current contract was supposed to last for only three months, but she has earned multiple extensions that have spanned more than five years and two states.

What Salaries Do Technical Writers Earn?

The Society for Technical Communication (STC) is an individual membership organization that is dedicated to advancing the arts and sciences of technical communication. With 22,000 members worldwide, STC is the largest organization of its type.

[A recent] STC Technical Communicator Salary Survey reported that the average annual salary of entry-level U.S. STC members was $36,100. The average annual salary of all U.S. STC members (all levels) was $48,250. Ten percent of U.S. STC members with 11 years or more of experience in technical communication earned more than $71,640 annually. See the STC Web site for more salary information (http://www.stc-va.org).

The handbook mentioned earlier reported that the average annual salary for technical writers and editors in the federal government in non-supervisory, supervisory, and managerial positions was about $47,440 in 1996; other writers and editors averaged about $46,590. . . .

Peter Kent's book . . . , *Making Money in Technical Writing,* has this tagline on its cover: "Turn Your Writing Skills Into $100,000 a Year." Kent believes that it is fairly easy for a freelance technical writer to make $70,000 a year, and he says that he has met technical writers earning $150,000 and up. See the Web site for his book at http://www.mcp.com/mgr/arco/techwr.

Taylor says she gets frequent calls from recruiters at technical service agencies. "If you have the skills that an agency is looking for," Taylor says, "the principles of supply and demand apply. You can almost name your own price. Rates will vary depending on where the job is located and the level of skill and experience needed." The living-on-the-edge aspects of contracting appeal to Taylor, as does the opportunity to travel and experience the various lifestyles of different parts of the country. "Contracting is good for those who like something different and a challenge and don't want to be locked in," Taylor says. "Also, it's a way to get an inside look at how a company operates before you take a permanent position there."

What Should Prospective Technical Writers Study?

Since the 1950s, when the first technical communication degree programs were offered, the number of colleges and universities offering courses as well as two-year, four-year, and graduate degrees in technical communication has been increasing. Today, you can even enroll in Internet-based distance learning programs for technical communication. The increases in the number of opportunities for education in technical communication are reflected in the following statistics. In 1974, 24% of STC members had studied English in school, 10% had studied journalism, 2.9% had studied technical communication, and 38% had studied science or engineering. In 1995, 42% of STC members had studied English in school, 10% had studied journalism, 23% had studied technical communication, and 19% had studied science or engineering. . . .

Technical Writing? If you are pursuing a degree in graphic design, communication, journalism, language arts, or English—and if you are interested in lifelong learning about science and technology—a career in technical writing might be ideal. Take elective courses in computer science, natural sciences, math, statistics, management business administration, human–computer interaction, or engineering. In some cases, if you have good writing skills, you can obtain specialized knowledge on the job. That's what the author of this article did after receiving a BS in Communication with a specialization in technical writing from Rensselaer Polytechnic Institute in Troy, N.Y. When I joined a company that made blood analyzers and other equipment used in medical laboratories, I was sent to numerous in-house training courses.

Science and Technology? Another option is that you can major in a scientific or technical subject area of your choice while taking elective courses in communication, technical writing, English, composition, illustration, journalism, graphic design, management, business administration, or human-computer interaction. . . . Some future technical writers transfer from jobs as technicians, scientists, or engineers. Others begin as research assistants, editorial assistants, or trainees in a technical information department, and then develop technical communication skills, and then assume writing duties. . . .

If you want to combine an interest in science and technology with writing and people skills, the dynamic world of technical communication needs you. Abundant opportunities, satisfaction, and rewards await.

Deborah M. Grimstead is a technical writer for Sun Microsystems, Inc., in Southeast Florida. In 1998, she was the first African-American woman elected a fellow of the Society for Technical Communication, the highest rank that the society can confer upon a member.

2

Writing: Processes and Production

The writing process, which is highly recursive, has several identifiable and overlapping stages:

Inventing and Exploring

During this stage, writers assess their knowledge, read and review available background references, ask questions and discuss ideas, conduct experiments, take notes, and make decisions about how they'll represent their task. Four problem-solving strategies used during this exploration include (1) brainstorming, (2) 5 Ws plus H, (3) cause-and-effect analysis, and (4) synectics, which encourages analogical thinking.

Planning and Organizing

Writers need to do two types of planning: First, they should use informal or formal time- and project-management tools. Second, they need to make decisions about a variety of elements: content, purpose, task, audience, constraints, organization, and design.

Drafting

This stage involves writing the text and preparing the visuals. Because writers also replan as they see a draft evolving in a different direction from their original plan, drafting overlaps with the next stage, revising.

Revising

Writers read and reread their drafts to examine and improve choices in content, structure, organization, logic, and design. Writers can use informal or formal document testing to gather feedback to help in revision. Potential problems in logic generally fall into four categories:

- Using data from authorities
- Presenting facts without drawing inferences
- Drawing inferences
- Establishing causal relationships

Editing

Writers identify and correct inconsistencies and errors in a draft. They can focus on content correctness, design accuracy and consistency, proofreading, and administrative tasks.

Differences Between Writing Processes

Experienced and inexperienced writers usually have different writing behaviors, particularly in their attention or inattention to elements such as planning, audience, and revision.

hat do writers do when they write? The writing process used to be described as consisting of three linear stages: prewriting, drafting, and revising. However, as researchers have charted writers' actions and ideas through the writing process, the notion that the process is linear has been dispelled. Writers say things like this: "Lots of times while I'm in the middle of writing, I'll get a terrific idea—something I've never thought of before, something that's not part of my outline." Or, "I'll write one word and immediately know it's not quite right, so I'll scratch it out and write a new one." These people are saying that the stages in their writing process do not necessarily happen consecutively; rather, they recur and overlap.

Producing a technical document or presentation isn't a linear process—and it isn't a solitary process, either. You'll work with other people for many different reasons: to get the necessary information, to verify your approach, to confirm technical accuracy, and to check readers' reactions. Figure 2.1 identifies some of the major categories you need to consider and some of the questions you need to ask. You can begin learning good questions to ask by starting at any category in Figure 2.1.

Many people begin by asking about the *context*, the *subject*, and the *document* itself. But you can also start with yourself, depending on whether your role is as a *writer*, *reader*, or *reviewer*. Take time to carefully read the questions in Figure 2.1—and get accustomed to asking them every time you plan a document or presentation. When you're working on a document or presentation for a specific organization, you'll add questions to those suggested here, ones that are based on the people and politics of that organization.

Let's look at the details of a process that you might use to create a document or presentation. Although you will change the specific elements to suit your individual approach and the requirements of a particular project, experienced writers of technical texts typically use these elements in their process:

- Inventing and exploring

- Planning and organizing

- Drafting

- Revising

- Editing

The writing process or creating technical documents and presentations is typically recursive and collaborative—that is, stages happen more than once (and

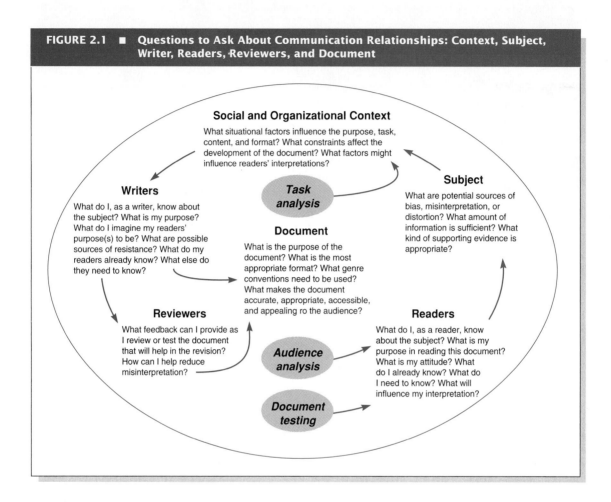

Social and Organizational Context

What situational factors influence the purpose, task, content, and format? What constraints affect the development of the document? What factors might influence readers' interpretations?

Task analysis

Writers

What do I, as a writer, know about the subject? What is my purpose? What do I imagine my readers' purpose(s) to be? What are possible sources of resistance? What do my readers already know? What else do they need to know?

Document

What is the purpose of the document? What is the most appropriate format? What genre conventions need to be used? What makes the document accurate, appropriate, accessible, and appealing ro the audience?

Subject

What are potential sources of bias, misinterpretation, or distortion? What amount of information is sufficient? What kind of supporting evidence is appropriate?

Reviewers

What feedback can I provide as I review or test the document that will help in the revision? How can I help reduce misinterpretation?

Audience analysis

Readers

What do I, as a reader, know about the subject? What is my purpose in reading this document? What is my attitude? What do I already know? What do I need to know? What will influence my interpretation?

Document testing

with more than one person), and more than one stage can happen at the same time. This chapter focuses on what happens in each stage.

Inventing and Exploring

Writers really do talk to themselves—inventing an idea and listening to how it sounds. During your inventing and exploring, you may assess your knowledge, read and review available background references, ask questions and discuss ideas, make observations, conduct experiments, and take notes. You may make tentative decisions about your task. Thinking about your options and your approach is part of this stage, one that you will return to many times while preparing a document, presentation, or visual.

This stage is a good place to explore writing problems related to a particular document; as you consider possible solutions, effective problem-solving strategies can make your work easier. For example, you may have problems coming up with what you think are good ideas or determining the focus. One way you can discover alternatives is to go through a problem-solving process (which, like writing, is recursive, so it has overlapping stages):[1]

- Recognize and define the problem (which may be defined differently by different people).

- Consider the broad situation of which the problem is a part (the politics, the policies, the parameters for solutions).

- Formulate several possible solutions (hypotheses) that may differ from traditional or conventional approaches; defer judgment.

- Gather information and ask questions to support possible solutions.

- Test and evaluate these solutions.

- Select and implement the most appropriate, efficient solution with consideration for technical as well as organizational and interpersonal factors.

Once you have recognized and defined a problem, you need ways to formulate possible solutions so that you can evaluate and then test them. This section identifies four commonly used and successful problem-solving strategies.

Which of the following problem-solving strategies have you used? How useful have they been? Which ones do you think you'll try in the future?

You're probably already familiar with the first one, *brainstorming*, a problem-solving technique that encourages you to suggest as many ideas as possible about a given problem or situation without making any judgments until after a number of ideas have been suggested. Remarkably simple, brainstorming is a problem-solving strategy that often works.

Two other strategies are commonly used by quality control circles.* One of these strategies is also a formula frequently associated with journalism: *5 Ws plus H*. These questions are effective for approaching any problem you are examining:

WHO	Who is involved? Who should be involved?
WHAT	What is involved? What should be changed? What should remain the same?
WHEN	When should it be done? When is the most appropriate or convenient time?
WHERE	Where should it be done?
WHY	Why should it be done?
HOW	How should it be done?

*Quality control circles is a group problem-solving process used in many companies. Small groups of people doing similar work go through a training period and then meet regularly to identify, analyze, and solve problems connected to the work they do. Many companies have established quality control circles, using work pioneered in Japan, to improve productivity as well as employee involvement.

Another strategy recommended by quality control circles is *cause-and-effect analysis*, which focuses on the causes of a particular problem. The initial causes are separated into four categories: *machine, employee, material,* and *method*. Any of these possible causes can be expanded with additional headings.

A final problem-solving strategy is *synectics*, often used collaboratively to stimulate creative thinking. *Synectics* is a coined word, "from the Greek *syn* (meaning 'to bring together') and *ectos* (for 'diversity'), which together suggest 'the bringing together of diversity.'"[2] This "bringing together" encourages workplace professionals to, for example, combine two unrelated ideas as a means of analyzing a particular problem. The goal is to develop new perspectives and solutions. Using a variety of techniques—including metaphors, analogies, role playing, and simulations—synectics asks participants to first define a particularly difficult problem. Then participants put themselves *into* the problem by creating a metaphor or an analogy or by acting out a component of the problem. Synectics encourages participants to engage in a variety of strategies: search for ideal solutions, imagine that they *are* the subject, compare the subject to something concrete, and compare the subject to something abstract. You can, of course, use similar problem-solving strategies at any time during the writing process.

Planning and Organizing

When you're planning a document, you need to determine the schedule for the project by arranging the sequence of activities. You also need to recognize the specific elements to consider in planning an individual document or presentation.

Project Planning

Early in the process of planning a document, writers often help themselves manage their time by sketching out what needs to be done and when it needs to be done. Your informal plan may be nothing more than a Post-it note stuck on a bulletin board or on the edge of your computer screen. Or you may prefer notes jotted on a calendar or Palm Pilot. Maybe your style is to make a list of tasks that you paper clip to the front of a manila folder containing notes for the project. Whatever the form you choose, though, it serves an important time-management function by encouraging you to make a preliminary assessment of the tasks that need to be done, their order, and their deadlines.

For larger projects, writers often turn to more formal time- and project-management tools. Two common tools are PERT (Program Evaluation Review Technique) charts and Gantt charts, both of which keep track of the various tasks in projects. PERT charts not only track various project activities, but they also show how these activities depend on each other. Gantt charts track project activities on a time line. Both of these project management tools enable you to plan projects and determine what should be accomplished at each stage.

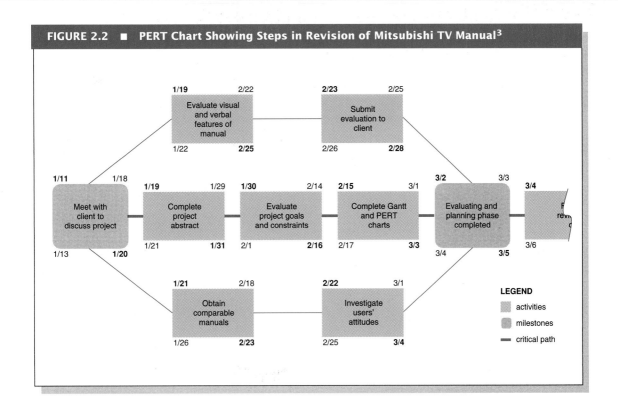

FIGURE 2.2 ■ PERT Chart Showing Steps in Revision of Mitsubishi TV Manual[3]

Figure 2.2 (PERT) and Figure 2.3 (Gantt) illustrate the same project so that you can easily compare the two tools.

Computer software is available that helps you construct both kinds of time-management charts. Project planning software can make creating PERT and Gantt charts very easy; managers can print up-to-date charts, status reports, and graphs of the project's progress. More sophisticated packages allow users to link the charts for various projects so that managers can see conflicts in deadlines and balance workloads. Project planning software used on a computer network helps managers automatically update the schedule and inform project members. For example, when a manager changes the project schedule, all project members are notified, and then they receive e-mail reminding them of changes in upcoming deadlines.

Document Planning

Planning often occurs simultaneously with inventing and exploring. When you plan, you need to make decisions about a variety of rhetorical elements (already presented in Chapter 1). Figure 2.4 lists these rhetorical elements again, this time as areas that skillful writers consider as they plan their documents. The critical

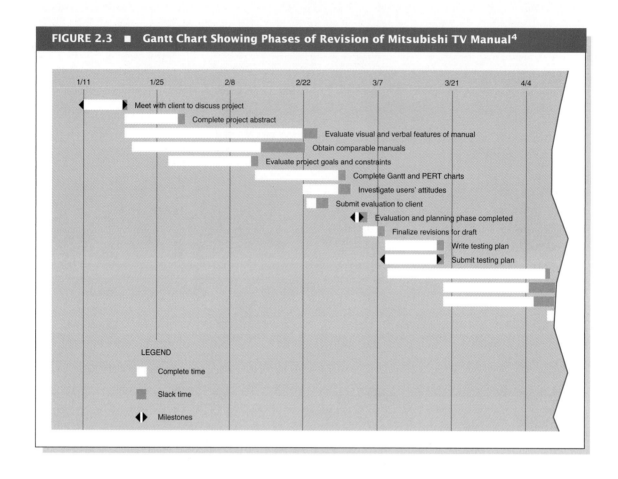

FIGURE 2.3 ■ Gantt Chart Showing Phases of Revision of Mitsubishi TV Manual[4]

Meet with client to discuss project
Complete project abstract
Evaluate visual and verbal features of manual
Obtain comparable manuals
Evaluate project goals and constraints
Complete Gantt and PERT charts
Investigate users' attitudes
Submit evaluation to client
Evaluation and planning phase completed
Finalize revisions for draft
Write testing plan
Submit testing plan

LEGEND

Complete time

Slack time

Milestones

What planning questions do you believe will be useful for the kinds of writing you expect to do in your career?

questions in Figure 2.4 provide suggestions you can use as you make decisions about how to approach a document or presentation. As you use these questions, you should jot down additional ones that also help.

What you read at the beginning of this chapter about the overall process of writing being recursive also applies to the process of planning; each element affects the others. The sequence in which you consider these elements has no best order. As your work on a document progresses, you can change your plans, but you need to begin with a sense of what you're doing and where you're going, in part because changes in one element influence the other elements. Although writers plan often and re-plan as their work progresses, careful planning can minimize the number of major changes that are needed later. Simply put, you'll find changing a plan easier than changing a fully drafted document.

Planning may be more productive if it is collaborative, even if you are going to draft the document independently. Working with someone else often generates ideas and approaches that you might not come up with alone. Unfortunately, you will almost always be under a deadline, so make time for planning—whether it be a few minutes alone as you develop ideas for a short letter or a few weeks with

FIGURE 2.4 ■ Critical Questions to Ask During Document Planning	

Photocopy and use this figure to help you during document planning.

Rhetorical Elements	Critical Questions
Content	◆ What do you already know? What do you need to learn to write this document?
	◆ What information do you want to include and exclude?
	◆ What examples and explanations will help achieve the purpose?
Context	◆ What is the situation necessitating the document? How does this situation influence the rest of your planning?
	◆ What are the constraints—for example, time, subject and format, audience, collaboration, data collection, technology, and noise—that you face in planning?
	◆ How should you deal with these constraints?
Purpose	◆ Do you want to inform? Persuade? Instruct? Train?
	◆ What argument are you making?
	◆ What is the best way to accomplish your purpose?
Audience	◆ Who are the readers of your document?
	◆ What are their characteristics? What do they expect? What do they need?
	◆ How will the reader use the document?
Organization	◆ What is the most effective way to organize the information?
	◆ How will you ensure that key points are easy to locate?
	◆ What have you done to ensure that readers can follow the argument? That the points are coherent?
Visuals	◆ Which information should be presented verbally, and which should be presented visually?
	◆ What visual conventions need to be followed?
Document design	◆ How can the design reinforce the purpose of the document?
	◆ What design features will appeal to the audience?
	◆ What document design conventions need to be followed?
Usability	◆ How will you determine that the information is accurate?
	◆ How will you determine that the information in the document is usable for all of the intended users?
Language conventions	◆ What professional standards are you using?
	◆ What will readers expect?

others as you collaborate on a complex proposal. Despite temptations to jump right into the actual drafting, you should not skimp on exploring and planning.

One of the most important things you should pay attention to during planning is the ethics of the situation. The ethics sidebar on the next page specifically

"Is the communication honest?": Ethics and the Writing Process

Technical professionals face ethical decisions throughout the writing process. From initial brainstorming, through the creation of the document, to post-production distribution, technical professionals must continually be aware of the ethical aspects of their communication. Researcher Brenda Sims provides a useful list of questions to ask yourself as you plan, draft, and revise documents and presentations:[5]

- Is the communication honest and truthful?
- Am I acting in the organization's best interest? In the public's? In my own?
- What if everybody acted or communicated in this way?
- Does the action or communication violate the rights of any of the people involved?
- Am I treating similar situations similarly?
- Am I willing to take responsibility for the action or communication publicly and privately?

Asking yourself these questions helps you look at your communication from personal and public perspectives. Ethical problems can occur when we don't look at how communication is perceived privately and publicly.

If you are willing to take responsibility for a communication privately, but not publicly, then your behavior may be viewed as unethical by your colleagues or the general public. For example, if you send a private memo to a colleague objecting to company hiring practices, but you are unwilling to voice the same concerns publicly, you may be perceived by some colleagues as acting unethically because you will not take a public position.

How can you revise documents so that they are acceptable privately and publicly?

If, on the other hand, you take a public position but it conflicts with your private view, then your personal ethics may also be in question. For example, if you tell sales representatives that an owner's manual covers all possible problems that owners will encounter, but you neglect to mention that you personally believe that some explanations are very difficult to understand, some people may question your ethics.

Ethical problems like these affect your professional standing and credibility. In most companies, organizations, and agencies, you will be held responsible for what you communicate. Using checklists like the one provided by Sims helps you avoid potential ethical problems that could negatively affect your writing and career.

What issues in your discipline might cause you to consider inconsistencies between your private and public positions?

addresses ethical questions you need to answer early in your planning. The bottom line is that having accurate content or an appealing design doesn't much matter if you're perceived as unethical. The sidebar focuses on achieving a balance between your personal (or private) positions and your public positions.

Drafting

The drafting stage involves writing the text and preparing the visuals—both for print and electronic documents. Writers have many different ways of approaching this stage of the process:

- You may be the kind of writer who creates bits and pieces of the draft during the planning stage, recording key sentences you don't want to forget. When your planning seems to be done, you take these ideas, develop them, and fill in the spaces.

- You may be the kind of writer who sits down and composes the draft from beginning to end without interruption.

- You may be a writer who prepares an outline and notes, then sets them aside and starts to write, checking your planning materials only when you get stuck.

- You may be the kind of writer who generates an online outline as the framework of your draft and then sticks to this outline.

- You may be a writer who works slowly, pondering and polishing every phrase and sentence and paragraph as you go along.

What kinds of drafting are typical of your writing?

If you are drafting a document that will be read on a computer—for example, a document for an electronic journal or a section on a Web site—you have additional constraints that affect your work. You not only need to think about your own process, but you need to be conscious of how your document will be read on a computer screen. Author Steve Outing, writing in the online publication, *Editor & Publisher Interactive* <http://www.mediainfo.com/>, summarizes some of the advice given by Crawford Kilian in his recent book, *Writing for the Web*. Of course, this advice also works equally well for drafting print documents.[6]

- *Be concise.* The low resolution of computer screens makes reading from a monitor more difficult than reading on paper. Monitor reading can be 25 percent slower than paper reading.

- *Keep chunks of text short.* Readers of electronic documents need minimal text. Write chunks of text between 150 and 200 words, then edit so you get each chunk to about 60 words. Kilian advises that writers "pack the maximum meaning into the minimum text, so your readers will get the message in the shortest possible time."

- *Use bulleted lists.* Long paragraphs don't work well on computer screens. Instead, use bulleted lists so the text can be easily scanned.

- *Use active voice.* Active voice identifies the do-er of the action and, thus, is usually clearer and more engaging for readers. And sometimes active voice even uses fewer words. Say "You need to review the draft" or "The committee needs to review the draft" rather than "The draft needs to be reviewed."

- *Consider international readers.* The whole world may read your message—with your name on it. Your text may be read in Australia, Germany, Israel, Japan, Saudi Arabia, South Africa, and Venezuela; therefore, avoid culture-specific idioms and metaphors.

What features make your Web reading easier? What features are annoying or distracting?

The key to drafting—whether for print or electronic documents—is to try several approaches in order to find out which ways work best for you. (Refer to Chapter 7 for a detailed discussion of outlining for planning and drafting.) Drafting is not an isolated stage. Because writers also re-plan as they see a draft evolving in a different direction from their original plan, drafting overlaps with the next stage, revising.

Revising

During the revision stage, you'll read and reread your draft critically to examine choices in content, structure, organization, logic, and design. You can add, delete, and rearrange material in order to produce a document that is more accurate and effective for the audience. You may be the kind of writer who begins revising almost as soon as you start planning, or you may defer most of your revising until you have written a chunk of text.

Ideally, you'll have time to compose the draft and then set it aside for a while before thoroughly revising it. All documents are improved when you check them to verify the accuracy and logic of the content, note needed changes in the examples or organization, and keep an eye open for violations of mechanical and grammatical conventions. In other words, you need to maintain the minimum specifications for good writing identified in Chapter 1. (Refer to the revision checklist on the inside back cover of this book for a review of critical points you need to consider during revision.)

Most of the time, though, checking the document isn't enough. For important documents—for example, instructions, politically sensitive memos and letters, major reports, proposals—you need to enlist reviewers who can assess the accuracy and appropriateness.

However, these reviewers aren't enough either because a key part of the situation is missing: the reader. Writers need to know how readers will react to and interpret the information. And you need to know how readers will actually view the document. So, when you write a document that will be read on a computer, try to view it on at least a couple different monitors to see how it shows up. Sometimes you'll be surprised that the document that looked professional on your monitor is not nearly so appealing when viewed on another system.

Typically, document testing is separated into three broad categories: text-focused testing, expert-judgment testing, and reader-focused testing. Testing throughout the development of a document is important so that writers can make necessary revisions based on accurate and timely feedback. (Refer to Chapter 10 for a detailed discussion of document testing.)

One of the most difficult parts of revising is checking the document for logic. You must first recognize potential problems in logic and then know how to correct them. Problems in logic generally fall into four categories:

- Using data from authorities

- Presenting facts without drawing inferences

- Drawing inferences

- Establishing causal relationships

Once you recognize these pitfalls, you are likely to judge your evidence more critically. The following discussion defines these four categories of logic problems, analyzes examples, and suggests possible ways to eliminate the problems.

Using Data from Authorities

Your readers will often respond positively to evidence from a recognized authority in the field. However, the evidence loses its effectiveness if the expert's qualifications are suspect or if the expert has a vested interest. If people or organizations have a vested interest (that is, a proprietary concern in supporting a particular position), their views might be more self-serving than objective. For example, imagine that the New England Soy Dairy prints a flier that states, "People everywhere are excited about the prospect of adding tofu to their diets." The business of the New England Soy Dairy is to market soy products, so it is in their interest to promote positive attitudes about soy products. Before accepting their word about the widespread excitement regarding soy products, you should verify the information with less vested sources.

What problem(s) have you observed that involved using data from authorities?

Presenting Facts Without Drawing Inferences

Writers often present facts in the form of statistics, quotations, or visuals intended to support points in a document. If these supporting facts are incomplete, out of context, oversimplified, or distorted, readers will be misled.

Omitted or Incomplete Data. Omitted or incomplete data, whether done purposefully or accidentally, affects the accuracy and credibility of a document. Imagine a novice computer user trying to follow instructions that omit a critical piece of information, such as "Press Enter after completing each step"—information that is second nature to anyone who has some computer experience. Omitted or incomplete data sometimes result from failure to check and recheck facts, but the problem also occurs when a researcher hopes to influence a reader by omitting discrepant or conflicting data, as the following example shows:

What problem(s) have you observed that involved at least one of the following kinds of presenting facts without drawing inferences?

Statement Soy-based infant formula is generally the best food for infants with milk allergies.

Comment The statement fails to mention that breast milk is the best food for infants and greatly reduces the likelihood that an infant will develop milk allergies.

| Revision | When breast-feeding is impossible or is not the feeding method of choice, soy-based infant formula is generally the best alternative for infants with milk allergies. |

Out-of-Context Data.   Out-of-context information may be accurate in itself, but relevant background or related information is omitted, thus giving readers a distorted view. Out of context, even indisputable information can be misleading, as seen in this example:

Statement	American farmers often prefer planting corn to soybeans.
Comment	Although the statement is true, taking it out of context ignores both the important reasons that influence farmers' decisions and the relationship between soybeans and other major crops.
Revision	Soybean crops compete with other major crops in the principal production areas, so the amount of land planted with soybeans depends on a complex interaction of factors that affect both soybeans and the competing crops. Most significant appears to be the price relationship between corn and soybeans in the major Midwest area, and between cotton and soybeans in the Mississippi Delta. This relationship, in turn, depends on world market factors, which most recently have tended to favor corn over soybeans and soybeans over cotton.[7]

Oversimplified or Distorted Data.   Oversimplification reduces a complex situation or concept to a few simple ideas, ignores relevant details, and gives readers a distorted view, as the following example illustrates:

Statement	Adding soy protein to a person's diet improves the quality of the diet.
Comment	Many factors determine the quality of a diet; the interrelationships of all dietary components must be considered. Adding soy protein to some diets may result in an excess protein intake, limit the intake of other necessary nutrients, and so on.
Revision	The inclusion of soy protein in a person's diet may have economic, nutritional, and sensory benefits.

Drawing Inferences

What problem(s) have you observed that involved at least one of the following kinds of drawing inferences?

In general, documents present data, and then the writer draws inferences based on that data. These inferences will be faulty if a writer makes hasty generalizations, assumes irrelevant functions, or falls prey to fallacies of composition and division. A writer should make sure the data represent the general condition or situation.

Hasty Generalizations.   A hasty generalization occurs when a particular case or situation is mistakenly assumed to be typical or representative of a group. This error usually takes place when the writer has not examined enough cases to warrant a generalization, as seen in the following example:

Statement   In a survey of food cooperative members, 90 percent stated they would like to increase the amount of soy in their diets. Therefore, Americans are willing to eat more soy foods.

Comment   Food cooperative members may not be representative of the greater population.

Revision   The willingness of co-op members surveyed to increase soy food intake suggests a potential for increased soy food consumption in at least some segments of the American population.

Irrelevant Functions.   When writers criticize something for not having a characteristic it was never intended to have, they are guilty of assuming an irrelevant function:

Statement   Tofu and tempeh (a traditional Indonesian cultured soybean food) do not taste like meat.

Comment   Tofu and tempeh, traditional foods in several cultures, should be appreciated for their own characteristics. They are not intended to taste like meat.

Revision   Tofu and tempeh are alternative sources of protein for people who choose to eat less meat in their diet.

Fallacies of Composition and Division.   The fallacy of composition assumes that the characteristics of the individual components can be attributed to the whole. The reverse occurs in the fallacy of division, in which the characteristics of the whole are attributed to each of the individual components composing the whole. The following example illustrates the fallacy of division:

Statement   Peanut butter on wheat bread is a protein dish of high biological value (it is a "complete protein"); therefore, peanut butter alone or wheat bread alone has a high biological value (is a "complete protein").

Comment   In this example of the fallacy of division, the basic assumption is faulty. In fact, peanuts (peanut butter) and grain (bread) proteins complement each other to provide protein of high biological value.

Revision   Peanut butter combined with wheat bread is a protein dish of high biological value.

Establishing Causal Relationships

One of the most frequent relationships employed in technical documents establishes causes and resulting effects. Readers can be misled by poorly drawn

What problem(s) have you observed that involved at least one of the following kinds of establishing causal relationships?

causal relationships in several ways, including a condition not being sufficient cause, variables not being correlated, and the fallacy of *post hoc, ergo propter hoc*.

Condition Not a Sufficient Cause.

An effect that results from multiple causes must have sufficient causes, and it may also have contributing causes. A *sufficient cause* is one that by itself can produce the effect. A *contributing cause* may help bring about the effect, but if all other causes are eliminated, any one contributing cause by itself cannot produce the effect. The following example demonstrates how poorly established cause–effect relationships can mislead readers:

Statement	The patient's heart attack was caused because his diet contained too much cholesterol.
Comment	Heart disease is caused by a number of contributing factors, such as diet, obesity, smoking, heredity, hypertension, amount of exercise. Evidence has not yet shown that cholesterol alone is a sufficient cause, but it is usually a contributing cause.
Revision	The high cholesterol may have contributed to the patient's heart disease.

Variables Not Correlated.

This principle is based on the concept that even though a number of factors frequently occur in sequence, a cause–effect relationship does not necessarily exist:

Statement	In the 1970s, the U.S. production of soybeans rose, and soon after, Americans began eating more soybeans.
Comment	The increase in soy production was primarily to help the balance of trade. Most of the soy was exported and used as animal feed. Americans' increase in soy consumption has resulted from a number of factors such as increased awareness, marketing, and availability.
Revision	In the 1970s, the U.S. production of soybeans rose to help the balance of trade. At the same time, Americans began eating more soybeans in response to a combination of factors, such as increased awareness, marketing, and availability.

Fallacy of Post Hoc, ergo Propter Hoc.

This line of reasoning (usually simply called *post hoc*) claims that because one event follows another, the first event must cause the second. The Latin translates as "after this, therefore because of this." The following example demonstrates how such fallacious logic can undermine a document's credibility:

Statement	Japanese women eat a high proportion of soy protein in their diets. Japanese women also have a low incidence of breast cancer; therefore, eating soy lowers the likelihood of breast cancer.

FIGURE 2.5 ■ Questions to Ask Yourself During Revision About the Logic of a Document	
Photocopy and use this figure to help you assess the logic of a document. **If you answer *I agree* to each of these statements, you can be fairly sure the logic in your document or presentation will withstand scrutiny.**	I agree
◆ All the evidence and data are accurate.	❏
◆ No information has been purposely or accidentally omitted, oversimplified, or distorted.	❏
◆ No sources have special vested interests.	❏
◆ Examples and cases are representative of the general condition(s) or situation(s).	❏
◆ Data are presented with appropriate background information or discussion so that they are meaningful to readers.	❏
◆ Sources have expertise in the area being discussed.	❏
◆ Visuals are presented without distortion of any kind.	❏
◆ Nothing is criticized for something that is not part of its nature or function.	❏
◆ Causes and effects are clearly differentiated and not mistakenly assumed because of a sequence of events.	❏

Comment   Even though eating soy precedes the low incidence of breast cancer, the chronology does not necessarily indicate a causal relationship. Japanese women also have a high intake of fish. Does eating fish also lower the risk of breast cancer?

Revision   Japanese women eat a high proportion of soy protein in their diets. Japanese women also have a low incidence of breast cancer. Emphasizing low-fat foods in the diet (such as soy and some types of fish) may be a contributing factor in lowering the risk of breast cancer.

When you're finished revising a document or presentation, checking the statements in Figure 2.5 will help you evaluate whether the information will withstand scrutiny.

Editing

Editing generally refers to identifying and correcting inconsistencies and errors in a draft—whether a paper or electronic document. When you're working on your own documents, editing and revising have many similarities. When you are preparing a document that will be read primarily or exclusively on a computer screen, most professional writers and editors recommend that you print everything out on paper for final editing and proofreading; otherwise, you'll miss things that need revision. You'll also find that reading aloud helps catch problems—omissions, awkward phrasings, grammatical errors—that you might miss when proofreading silently, especially proofreading on a computer screen.

However, editing is a broader function than revising and is frequently done by someone other than the writer. Many organizations employ full-time editors who perform various levels of editing. Sometimes, in small organizations, these editorial functions are lumped together in the single role of "editor" and sometimes even melded with other parts of the writing process. Editorial functions can be separated into four broad categories. (Refer to Chapter 13 for a detailed discussion of these categories.)

What are your strengths in editing?

- Content correctness

- Design consistency

- Proofreading

- Administrative tasks

In very large organizations, tasks in these categories can be performed by different people according to their respective levels of experience and expertise.

Editors are not necessarily responsible for the technical accuracy of a document. In fact, accuracy is almost always the responsibility of the writer. In situations in which the editor does make changes in content, final approval for the changes usually remains with the writer (unless the changes involve institutional policies and practices more familiar to the editor). (Refer to the list of editing and proofreading marks on the inside front cover.)

People who work on a networked computer system often use the network's capabilities to help with *document cycling*—the part of the process that takes a document through several rounds of reviewing, revising, and editing. They can electronically send their document to several reviewers simultaneously and receive the reviewers' comments the same way. Using the network can potentially speed document cycling, which in many organizations is a required part of preparing important documents, especially ones for external readers.

Differences Between Writing Processes

Although the writing process divides into broad general stages of inventing and exploring, planning and organizing, drafting, revising, editing (which includes proofreading), and finally publishing, individual writers differ in the time they spend in various stages, in the sequence of the stages, and in their thought processes. When you find a writing process that works for you, examine it, use it, develop it. Once you're confident of an approach, branch out and try another one. If it works, integrate it with your writing practices. You may find it useful to review some of the habits, concerns, and working procedures that are used by experienced workplace writers, as summarized in Figure 2.6.

FIGURE 2.6 ■ Composing Processes of Experienced Writers

Stage	Experienced Workplace Writers
Inventing and exploring	◆ Spend time inventing and exploring. Experienced writers see value in activities such as cause-and-effect analysis.
	◆ Spend time considering and contemplating the implications of various alternatives.
Planning and organizing	◆ Plan before drafting. Experienced writers plan and organize ideas in their heads, in conversations with other people, on their computers, and on paper.
	◆ Consider a lot more than content. They ask themselves questions about their purpose, audience, and organization.
	◆ Create notes and sketches so that they have a record to go back to.
	◆ Reconsider their plans as they write and revise their plans whenever necessary. They don't stop planning when they start writing.
Drafting	◆ Respond to readers' needs.
	◆ Frequently stop to rescan, reread, reflect.
	◆ Respond to all aspects of the writing situation: content, context, audience, purpose, organization, design.
	◆ Show concern with a document's accuracy, appropriateness, accessibility, and appeal.
Revising and editing	◆ Revise globally first for organization and logic, then locally for sentence- and word-level conventions.
	◆ See revising as ongoing throughout the process of preparing a document.
	◆ Proofread with care.

Writing research has shown that experienced writers recognize the importance of exploring and planning, using this time to investigate the subject and organize the information. For experienced writers, revising is recursive, occurring both during the drafting and after the draft is complete. They are concerned with accuracy of the material as well as appropriateness, accessibility, and appeal of the presentation for the intended audience.

Experienced writers usually match their planning process to the writing task. They seem to shift among three types of planning—*schema-driven planning*, *knowledge-driven planning*, and *constructive planning*—depending on the situation. Knowing about these types of planning can help you select the most appropriate kind for a particular task.

If you create a document according to an existing format or template for a text, you'll follow what is called a *schema*. A schema is your knowledge, your mental image of what is expected or appropriate in a given situation. You already have schema for many texts like memos and business letters. If you use *schema-driven planning*, you can often complete a document without much thought about format or the kind of information to include. For example, if you have a memo schema, you can quickly produce a memo announcing a meeting. If you have a business letter schema, you can quickly produce a letter requesting product specifications. Writers who use schema-driven planning can usually produce successful documents if their schema is appropriate for the situation.

In another situation, you might not have a schema, but you might have a great deal of knowledge about the subject. In this case, planning a document becomes a matter of your telling what you know about the subject. For *knowledge-driven planning* to work, your information must be well organized and appropriate for the task. For example, a chemist who has a great deal of experience with gas chromatography has the procedural knowledge to make it fairly easy to write instructions for technicians to operate the equipment.

In contrast, if you have a difficult writing problem, you probably can't depend on existing schema or knowledge. Instead, you'll have to do *constructive planning*, which requires careful analysis of the purpose, audience, task, and a variety of constraints. Although constructive planning usually requires more time and effort than other kinds of planning, it helps you set goals and criteria as well as establish procedures for composing your document.

What planning strategies discussed in this section have you personally found useful in your writing?

Often you may use a combination of schema-driven planning, knowledge-driven planning, and constructive planning. For example, writers preparing a proposal for municipal recycling of refuse need to be familiar with the format and language of proposals and also need to have extensive knowledge about the subject. But the specific problem of preparing a proposal for recycling in a particular community requires constructive planning so that writers can solve the problems of the task and establish procedures for completing it.[8]

End-of-Chapter
Recommendations for Technical Communicators

1. Remember that the stages in your writing process do not happen consecutively; rather, they recur and overlap.

2. Use your inventing and exploring to assess and add to your knowledge about the subject. Make tentative decisions about how you're representing your writing task. Think about your options and your approach.

3. Use effective problem-solving strategies to make your work easier:

   - Recognize and define the problem.
   - Formulate possible solutions (hypotheses) that may differ from traditional or conventional approaches; defer judgment.
   - Gather information, and ask questions to support possible solutions.
   - Test and evaluate these solutions.
   - Select and implement the most appropriate, efficient solution with consideration for technical as well as interpersonal factors.

4. Use quality control circles strategies for problem solving: the 5 Ws plus H, cause-and-effect analysis, and synectics.

5. Determine the schedule for a project by arranging the sequence of activities. For big projects, use project-management tools such as PERT (Program Evaluation Review Technique) charts and Gantt charts.

6. Make decisions about a variety of elements: scope and content, purpose, task, audience, constraints, organization, and design. Understand that your document planning often occurs simultaneously with inventing and exploring.

7. Adapt your process and the sequence activities to the particular project. Remember that there's no best way, just a workable plan for each project.

8. Consider drafting as an ongoing process, not an isolated stage. Plan and re-plan as you see a draft evolving.

9. Revise to critically examine your choices in content, structure, organization, and design. Seek outside readers, reviewers, and users to help sharpen the textual and technical accuracy. Carefully examine the logic of your evidence:
   - Use data from authorities.
   - Present facts without drawing inferences.
   - Draw inferences.
   - Establish causal relationships.

10. Edit to identify and correct inconsistencies and errors in your draft dealing with content, design accuracy and consistency, proofreading, and a variety of administrative tasks.

11. Remember that experienced writers tend to do more exploring, planning, and revising than inexperienced writers.

Individual and Collaborative Assignments

1. **Track your writing process.** One way to learn about your writing process is to track your own process as you prepare a document. You will need to maintain careful records. Use one of the following methods to track your own process as you prepare a document.

   (a) Tape record your planning, drafting, or revising. (Note: Trying to track the entire process of preparing the document takes too much time; pick just one part of the process.) Afterward, you can listen to the tape to identify interesting patterns in what you observe.

   (b) Keep a log (in a notebook or on your computer) in which you record every time you work on the document (even thinking about it counts). Record the date and time you start and stop. Describe what happens during the time—what gets accomplished, what goes wrong, what you expected to get done but didn't (and why), and so on. Record the facts, but also jot down your attitudes and feelings. Try to be as accurate and complete as possible.

2. **Analyze your writing process.**

   (a) Use the data you have collected in Assignment 1 to write a one- to two-page discussion about one aspect of your writing process. Focus on some specific aspect—for example, the way you defined the task, the way you considered your audience, the way you decided to organize or design the document. Use quotations from the tape or log to support your decision.

   (b) Review this discussion and determine what problem-solving strategies you found useful in your writing. Will this help as you write more documents?

   (c) Assume the time from the beginning to the end of the writing project in Assignment 1 is 100 percent. Design a chart to show the typical proportion of time you spend on each stage of your writing process. Explain in what stage(s) you're most effective. And in which you're the weakest. What might you do to improve your process?

3. **Create a rubric.** The only way to make sure that your writing is effective is to analyze it (as in Assignment 2) to determine what areas you need to improve. Use the rubric from Chapter 1 (and modify it to fit your document) to analyze a document that you created so that you can assess your own skills as a technical communicator. Each time you create a new document, use the rubric to establish where you have made improvements.

4. **Interview a professional.**

   (a) Arrange to interview a professional technical writer or a technical professional in your field who writes frequently. During the interview, inquire about the person's approach to writing, including his or her approach to problem solving. Consider asking some of the following questions:

- Where/how do you get the information you use?
- Do you ever have problems getting the information?
- How are these problems handled?
- Who are the readers of the documents you prepare?
- What kind of noise needs to be filtered out for these readers?
- What's your background? Technical communication? Science? Engineering?
- How does this background affect your writing?

(b) Organize the information you find into a brief oral or written report.

5. **Look at the process of translation.** Because your audience is not always made up of native English speakers, you need to consider how to translate your documents into the language that your audience uses. Translation of technical documents is not as easy as it may sound. In order to test your translation, you should have a native speaker of that language read your document and the translation of your document to look for errors or miscommunications caused by direct translation. This is called back-translation. In this assignment, you will be asked to look at the process of translation and back-translation. Visit the following Web site:

(a) Type in a short paragraph from a document that you have written in English.

(b) Ask the "translator" to translate your paragraph to another language.

(c) Find a native speaker of that language on your campus and ask her or him to read the translation and the original (English).

(d) Write a short memo to your classmates about the process of translation. Consider the effectiveness of the Web site translation program and the value of the native speaker.

Intertext

Care and Feeding of the Organizational Grapevine[9]

The term *grapevine* can be traced back to the United States Civil War. Because the battle fronts moved frequently, army intelligence telegraph wires were loosely strung from tree to tree across battlefields, much like grapevines. Due to the reckless way the lines were hung, the messages sent over them were often garbled and confusing, leading to inaccurate communication. Soon, any rumor or unofficial command was said to have been heard "via the grapevine." During this time the correlation between the grapevine and inaccuracy began. The grapevine has been an identifiable aspect of American culture ever since.

The organizational grapevine is part of the modern business world and has long been considered a necessary evil of conducting business. Managers typically have done their best to suppress this method of communication. However, some are beginning to consider it an asset rather than a liability. The grapevine will remain a part of any assembled work force, so why not harness its potential to ease communication within the organization instead of trying in vain to smother it? The grapevine is a valuable means of communication within an organization; attempts to phase it out are unwarranted and unproductive. The grapevine does not always deliver information in an ideal manner and is sometimes difficult to manage, but its advantages outweigh its disadvantages. Therefore, it should be nurtured, not pruned—and management must cultivate it carefully to reap the greatest benefits for the organization.

The grapevine in business

Webster's dictionary defines grapevine as "an informal person-to-person means of circulating information or gossip." Psychologists G. A. Fine and R. C. Rosnow define gossip as "small talk with a purpose," and gossip columnist Liz Smith has added, "Gossip is usually the news running ahead of itself in a red satin dress—it is rumor about to become fact." No matter how the grapevine is defined, one thing is certain: The grapevine is the informal and unsanctioned communication network found within every organization.

Organizational members require information to perform their jobs. When information is not transmitted through a formal system in a timely fashion, the grapevine is called upon to communicate the essential facts throughout the organization. In fact, most organizational communication consists of person-to-person informal contacts. These contacts are necessary for the smooth functioning of the organization, and they contribute to improved job performance. Some research has found that communicatively isolated workers in a large organization have lower job satisfaction, organizational commitment, and job performance than their counterparts who are engaged actively in a communication network.

The grapevine has a discernible structure . . . [described by] Keith Davis: . . . four primary chains of communication in an organization's grapevine:

- *The single-strand chain.* A tells B, who tells C, who tells D, and so on. The longer this chain continues, the greater the potential for alterations to the original message. Consequently, this chain tends to produce the least accurate messages.

- *The gossip chain.* A tells everyone he or she comes into contact with. This chain often transmits messages slowly, as there is only one active disseminator of information.

- *The probability chain.* A conveys information randomly to C and E. They, in turn, randomly tell others. In this chain, some in the organization will, by chance, get this information and some will not.

- *The cluster chain.* A tells those he or she frequently contacts, C and D. They continue the chain by revealing the message to those they have close contact with. Selectivity determines the pattern in this chain. As a result, some will not hear the information.

Elements of the grapevine
Three roles have to be filled for grapevine activity to take place:

- *Bridgers or "hey" communicators.* These individuals gather information and pass it on to others. These people

are most responsible for the health of the grapevine.

- *Baggers or dead-enders.* These individuals hear rumors but either do not pass them along or repeat them to other dead-enders.

- *Beaners or isolates.* These organizational members are outside the grapevine and thus not privy to its messages. Therefore, they neither hear nor pass along correspondence.

Messages transmitted through the grapevine are normally referred to as "rumors." However, to label a message a rumor is a simplification. There are actually at least four types of messages:

- *Pipe dreams or wish fulfillment.* These rumors identify the wishes and hopes of employees. It naturally follows, then, that these rumors are positive in constitution, yet they still reflect employee anxieties.

- *Bogie rumors.* These rumors originate from employees' fears and concerns and result in a general restlessness within the organization. Often, these rumors are damaging.

- *Wedge-drivers.* These rumors are marked by aggression and animosity. As a result, they are characteristically negative and serve to cleave groups and dissolve allegiances.

- *Home-stretchers.* These rumors are initiated in anticipation of final decisions or announcements. They tend to fill in the gap during times of ambiguity.

Benefits of the grapevine
The contemporary grapevine has kept its reputation for disseminating unreliable

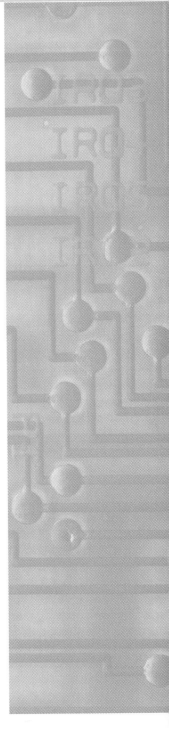

information. However, research shows that grapevine information is highly reliable and accurate, making this means of communication an asset to the organization. Studies done by Keith Davis have demonstrated accuracy ratings of nearly 80 percent for many grapevine transmissions, with a range of accuracy between 75 percent and 95 percent. The grapevine's precision is not surprising when one considers the origins of its messages. Research has shown that rumors passing through the grapevine begin as testimonies of an actual event. Thus, someone or some group has witnessed an event and feels it is worthy of passing on to others in the organization.

Still, people are wary of embracing information gleaned through the grapevine. This is partly due to the grapevine's poor reputation. Grapevine information is also considered inaccurate because its errors are often dramatic. Therefore, the mistakes are more memorable than the grapevine's normal daily accuracy. This skepticism is healthy and contributes to the benefits of the grapevine.

Many people think of the grapevine as an uncensored, "the rest of the story" source of information. As Jack Levin, Ph.D., professor of sociology at Northeastern University, put it, "If you want to know about the kind of insurance coverage your employer offers, look in the company handbook. But if you want to know who to avoid, who the boss loathes or loves, who to go to when you need help, what it really takes to get a promotion or raise, and how much you can safely slack off, you're better off paying attention to the company grapevine."

Probably the best feature of the grapevine is the timeliness of the message it carries. Its speed of transfer is far faster than messages coming through formal channels, partly because formal communication has traditionally been written in the form of memos, reports, and newsletters.

Since formal communication channels tend to transmit information slowly, gaps between the time information is needed and when it arrives are common. As a result, formal networks tend to be inadequate for handling unplanned communication requirements, for competently transmitting complicated or detailed information, or for sharing personal information.

The grapevine, on the other hand, thrives on quicker word-of-mouth conversations. And although electronic communications have made the formal methods of interaction faster, they have made informal means of conveying information even swifter. Because the grapevine is fast, it can serve as an early warning system for members of an organization.

Knowing this, management sometimes purposely sends messages through the grapevine to test the waters, allowing individuals to plan for and ponder formal statements to come. This may give employees the opportunity to provide input to senior management before final decisions are made. Thus grapevine timeliness often gives employees a chance to become more participatory, which is known to enhance an organization. These advantages are particularly beneficial when bad news will be coming through formal communication channels.

Another advantage of the grapevine is that it can transmit messages in a multi-directional manner. Unlike the formal communication network, which follows a highly rigid, linear path from supervisors to subordinates, the grapevine can leap from department to department and jump between various management levels. It moves up, down, horizontally, vertically, and diagonally in an organization at an incredible pace.

Furthermore, the grapevine can serve as an outlet for stress release. Subordinates frequently need an opportunity to let off steam but are unable to do so through formal communication lines, fearing embarrassment or repercussions. The grapevine provides them a way to share their personal opinions and feelings.

Another important aspect of grapevine messages is their personal nature. Instead of impersonal, faceless transmissions via the formal communication networks, the grapevine frequently facilitates enjoyable face-to-face interactions between co-workers. Research suggests that subordinates prefer to get their information in this manner. While this is not always possible, a healthy grapevine makes it more likely.

One other positive aspect of the grapevine is its immunity to time constraints. While the formal communication network typically starts up at 9 a.m. and shuts down at 5 p.m., the grapevine is in effect nearly 24 hours a day. It begins in the morning in car pools on the way to work and may last late into the night through company softball teams, golf games, or bowling leagues.

Finally, the grapevine serves as an index of organizational health, morale, trends, and productivity. The grapevine can spotlight issues and problems important to an organization. Effects of policies and procedures often can be measured with informal communication. Also, it seems that organizations with strong formalized structures that inhibit communication outside these structures may benefit from an active grapevine that supplements formal channels of communication. Indeed, this informal communication network seems to blossom when certain common denominators exist in organizations. If formal channels are rigid and narrow, if vital intelligence is kept from employees, if an overabundance of free time is allowed to subordinates, or if employees feel the pressures of job insecurity, be assured that the grapevine will be very active.

Potential pitfalls

As mentioned earlier, grapevine information tends to be accurate 80 percent of the time. This means there is at least a 20 percent inaccuracy factor. Nearly all the information passed along the grapevine is undocumented, and thus is in a prime position to be altered and misinterpreted as it flows. The central theme is usually resistant to severe alterations, but critical details are eliminated constantly in a process known as "leveling." The most dramatic details are "sharpened"—hyped up—each time the message is recycled. And details are sometimes adjusted to correspond with the prior attitudes and experiences of the participants in a process called "assimilation." Together, leveling, sharpening, and assimilation have the potential to alter the facts significantly. Nevertheless, the correspondence is still grounded in the truth and remains an important vehicle for communication.

Electronic communication such as "cybergossip" (gossip through the computer) has made the grapevine an even faster means of communication. Though a potential advantage, cybergossip is often misinterpreted because it is flat: no voice inflection, no room for subtleties of language. It may be more difficult to tell whether someone is making a joke, being sarcastic, or passing on the gospel.

Like cybergossip, another modern-day phenomenon has changed the nature of the grapevine: The new generation of workers seems to disdain it. Historically, most baby boomers (those born between 1946 and 1964), as much as they deny it, believe in playing office politics and do their utmost to become proficient in this area. Conversely, the younger generation of employees takes offense to those proficient at politics and feels sorry for those who seek mastery in it. This present attitude could be a major blow to the informal communication network as it now stands. In fact, these "baby busters" or "generation Xers" (those born between 1965 and 1977) seem to prefer that crucial messages be presented one-on-one by supervisors—if not in person, then by voice mail or e-mail. Thus, they are ultimately unwilling to tap into the grapevine for information.

Another potential problem with the grapevine is the threat of legal action arising from inaccurate rumors traveling this network. Many organizations have been defendants in legal suits arising from false information circulating in the workplace. Lawsuits based on defamation, fraud, invasion of privacy, harassment, emotional distress, and disability discrimination have all taken place because of grapevine inaccuracies (Zachary, 1996).

Implications for leaders

As the previous section indicates, the grapevine is not all pinot noir. It is no wonder many managers feel they must attempt to silence the grapevine in order to avoid the problems just mentioned. But the potential for using the grapevine advantageously is well documented. To ensure that the grapevine remains primarily an asset and minimally a liability, there are some ground rules that management must follow in order to foster an effective, healthy environment for the grapevine to operate.

- Accept that the grapevine exists and has the potential to add value to the organization. Management must not try to eliminate it—they did not hire it and they cannot fire it.

- Acknowledge the fact that the grapevine must, for the most part, remain unrestrained. If management tries to take control of it, they do not allow it to operate effectively and it ceases to provide its potential benefits.

- Do not underestimate the grapevine's power or value to the organization. Ignoring the grapevine can do more harm than good, and managers cannot afford to attempt to escape putting the necessary effort into managing it.

- Become part of the grapevine rather than remaining a passive observer. If the main concern about the grapevine is false information, being privy to grapevine messages will allow management to monitor them most effectively. If management chooses to ignore the grapevine, they fail to use its potential. In fact, the grapevine can serve as a vital mechanism in the "management by wandering around" approach. This philosophy suggests that when managers wander around the workplace without any particular objective, they are likely to pick up highly relevant information. This is information that may never have become available if the manager stayed in his or her office all day or communicated only in the normally structured manner.

- Maintain activity within formal communication channels. The grapevine is not a substitute for formal communication, but it can be an effective supplementary tool when fostered properly.
- Encourage organizational members to question and assess grapevine exchanges prior to responding to them. This will help keep the grapevine from becoming a facilitator of false rumor.

The grapevine is alive and well. In the past, such a statement would have made management cringe, since the grapevine was often perceived as an impediment to organizational well-being. However, research, in addition to verifying the existence of a vibrant grapevine, supports the idea that an active grapevine correlates positively with a well-functioning organization. Organizations need a constant, consistent flow of information in order to operate in today's dynamic environment. Formal channels of communication are often unable to keep up with this informational demand. The informal communication network, the grapevine, picks up the slack and keeps organizations moving forward rather than stagnating.

No medium of communication is perfect, and the grapevine is no exception. It must be managed correctly to yield positive results. However, the cost of this management is well worth the effort when one considers what the grapevine can provide an organization: the fast, timely, and relevant flow of information from those who have it to those who need it.

Sources Cited

Keith Davis, "Grapevine Communication Among Lower and Middle Managers," *Personnel Journal* (April 1969).

M. Zachary, "The Office Grapevine: A Legal Noose?" *Getting Results* (August 1996).

Patricia Karathanos, Ph.D., is chair of the department of administrative services at Southeast Missouri State University, Cape Girardeau, Missouri. She teaches management communication and leadership in the M.B.A. program and has written extensively for both academics and practitioners.

Anthony Auriemmo earned his bachelor's degree in business administration in 1993. At the time this article was written, he was a graduate student at Southeast Missouri State University seeking a master's degree in business administration. He works as a strength and conditioning coach at the U.S. Olympic Education Center in Marquette, Michigan.

3

Writing for Readers

Identifying Purposes

Writers of technical documents usually have two broad purposes: to convey verifiable information and to persuade readers to attend to this information.

Identifying Readers

You need to identify your *initial reader, primary reader, secondary readers,* and *external readers.* You also need to determine whether these readers are *experts, professional nonexperts, technicians, equipment operators, students, general readers,* or *children.*

Analyzing Readers

You can plan more effectively once you learn more about several aspects of your audience—the context in which they work, their attitudes and motivations, education, professional experiences, reading level, and organizational role—by talking with the readers themselves and the people who work with them. Several factors work together to affect the ease or difficulty of text.

Adjusting to Readers

Writers can adjust material for different audiences in three broad ways: (1) address readers with *different levels of expertise* by adjusting the complexity of the material; (2) address readers with *different organizational roles* by shifting the focus of the discussion and the choice of details, including an acknowledgement of readers' ethical stance or point of view; and (3) address readers by designing Web sites that enable readers to *construct unique sequences of information* to meet their own needs and interests.

Nearly anything can be the subject of a technical document, but the treatment of that subject changes for different readers. For example, the same polymer resin used to make baby bottles is also used for media storage disks. Many kinds of readers could be interested in the same subject—but with different purposes: Parents and pediatricians might want to know about material safety; media librarians and managers might focus on material stability; chemists might be interested in ways to modify material composition; production supervisors might want to know how to best extrude the resin.

The way you define and visualize your readers influences your choices as you prepare documents and presentations. This chapter discusses the importance of identifying your purpose and then categorizes readers and analyzes factors that influence them.

Identifying Purposes

Writers of technical documents usually have two broad purposes: to convey verifiable information in a straightforward manner and to persuade readers to attend to this information. Figure 3.1 shows questions you need to ask yourself about your readers during planning.

FIGURE 3.1 ■ Questions Stimulated by Purpose	
Writer's Purpose	**Writer's Questions**
To convey information	What information do I (the writer) want readers to learn? Why do I want them to learn this information?
	What decisions do readers need to make? What information do readers need in order to make a decision?
	What background information do I need to provide? What questions do I want to answer?
To persuade	What ideas or actions of the readers do I want to influence?
	What information and approaches will persuade the readers?
	What constraints will affect the persuasiveness of my argument?

How could you convince a colleague who thinks that technical documents are only to convey information that they also have a persuasive function?

People may have both primary and secondary purposes for reading. Typical reasons for reading technical documents include reading *to assess*, *to learn*, *to learn to do*, or *to do*. These purposes appear separately and in combination. For example, a reader's primary task might be to *do:* to make a decision that approves or rejects a proposal. A secondary task might be to *learn:* to gather information about important areas for future research. (See Chapter 4 for further discussion of readers' purposes.)

Identifying Readers

Before you analyze an audience, you must identify it. Every technical document has an *intended audience*—a specific individual (Elizabeth Jones, research and development [R&D] director) or a category of users (operators of Macintosh computers)—each with identifiable needs. Readers of technical documents often want information about specific rather than general issues, so they usually can be more precisely described than readers of most other types of writing.

Complicating matters, the same document is often read by a number of different readers. For example, a proposal for new product development could be read by people on various levels in several areas in a company—finance, marketing, engineering, manufacturing. As a result, you often are expected to create material that simultaneously meets the needs of several categories of readers. You can accomplish this most easily by directing different readers to particular sections of a report. For example, managers or executives would usually be most interested in the summary and the major recommendations, whereas engineers would usually be most interested in the application of these recommendations.

You can help yourself by distinguishing the various reader roles:

- The *initial reader* is often the person to whom you submit a document, though not necessarily the decision maker. This initial reader directs your material to the appropriate primary reader(s).

What might be the ramifications of misjudging who is actually the primary reader of a document?

- The *primary reader* is the person for whom your document is actually intended, the one who will actually use the information, the decision maker.

- *Secondary readers* have an indirect interest because they are affected by the information or by decisions based on it.

- Many documents also have *external readers* who are outside the immediate organization.

For example, a general contractor could be the initial reader of a request for a quotation on wiring a condominium's new community center. The primary reader could be the electrical contractor. The secondary readers might include the condominium's board of directors. An external reader might be a local building inspector.

Readers form a continuum of knowledge about the subject, from those with expertise and interest to those with little knowledge and some interest. Readers typically fit on more than one place on a continuum, especially if they have multiple interests and responsibilities.

- *Experts* have a theoretical as well as practical background that enables them to understand the most technical information in their own field. For example, engineers, ecologists, and economists typically read a range of print and electronic material, from specifications to professional journals.

- *Professional nonexperts*, including managers, supervisors, and executives, are interested in and required to read print and electronic material that is outside their own professional specialty. For example, a department manager in a computer firm may have a degree in business but little specialized knowledge of computers. A manager of an engineering department may have earned an engineering degree twenty years ago or have a degree in industrial management, not engineering.

- *Technicians* frequently work in highly specialized fields and read complex print and electronic material as part of their jobs. Although their work is most often practical (for example, calibrating equipment or completing processes), many technicians have a theoretical understanding as well. In one company, chemical technicians helping develop new applications for carbon fibers were able to contribute to the project because of their theoretical background in polymer chemistry.

- *Equipment operators* are concerned primarily with having clear directions to follow. If operators understand how their role in the operation fits into the larger process, they'll often do a better job. For example, word processing operators will probably do a better job if they know the workflow process. In some fields, equipment operators may have limited literacy skills, which must be considered when preparing documents with information they're expected to use.

- *Students*, from those in advanced high school courses to those majoring in technical subjects in college, read print and electronic documents as part of their academic preparation, including work-study and internship programs. They are interested in learning disciplinary knowledge and forming opinions to gain a broad background and eventually to become professionals in a specialized field.

- *General readers* want to read about science and technology, but their interests usually have little or nothing to do with their job. General readers are interested in how and why things happen, so they read the science and technology articles in their daily newspaper, on Web sites, in the bulletins sent from the local medical center, and in weekly and monthly magazines.

Which audience(s) do you think you will write to most frequently in your professional work?

What are specific examples that justify including children as readers of technical documents?

- *Children* are increasingly reading technical documents adapted to their level. Many of them enthusiastically read science books, have their own subscriptions to children's science magazines, and regularly surf Web sites. They also read the technical documents that come with their computers, models, and video games.

This continuum of readers is not absolute; an individual reader often fits into more than one category. For example, a polymer technician who is comfortable reading reports about composite materials may be a general reader or a professional nonexpert when reading about learning disabilities, astronomy, or kidney failure. A company vice president is an expert in business matters, but may be a student reader in a flying class and a general reader regarding agronomy or microwaves. Figure 3.2 identifies the familiarity these readers typically have with various kinds of subject matter, the kinds of expectations they often hold, and the education many of them have. Such generalizations, of course, don't fit the profile of every reader, but may help you make preliminary decisions about ways to approach a particular audience.

Analyzing Readers

Once you have identified the purposes for a document and the general category of readers (expert, technician, and so on), you need to learn more about this audience. Several strategies exist for analyzing audiences. While no approach is foolproof, one of the most frequently used involves considering a number of demographic characteristics as you plan to meet readers' needs and expectations:

1. Context in which a document is interpreted and used

2. Attitudes and motivations of the readers

3. Education of the readers

4. Professional experience(s) of the readers

5. Reading level of the readers

6. Organizational role of the readers

The best way to assess your intended readers is to talk with them and the people who work with them. Imagine that you are responsible for writing the user manual for a new computer system. Whether the manual is usable for the intended audience is critical. So, you need to find out about the actual users— what they're likely to have trouble with, what they'll probably find helpful, what they're likely to know and not know. To gain a sense of what should and shouldn't be included in the new manual, you could talk with people in these areas:

- Design and development—to learn what features the system will have and what kind of background a user would need

Readers	Familiarity	Expectations	Education
Experts	Most know theories as well as practical applications, abbreviations, jargon, and complex abstractions in their own field	Most prefer straightforward presentations; want to know purpose; do not want explanations of what they already know; use information to assess, learn, learn to do, and do	Usually have undergraduate or graduate degrees or equivalent experience in specialized fields
Professional nonexperts	Most know general concepts of the field in which they're working	Most prefer definitions and explanations of concepts and procedures; prefer information that lets them focus on learning what they need for decision making	Usually have undergraduate or graduate degrees or equivalent experience, often in areas peripheral to the technical areas for which they are responsible
Technicians	Most know specialized area in which they're working; sometimes have general understanding of the broader field	Most prefer straightforward definitions and explanations; prefer information that focuses on learning to do and doing	Usually have a degree from a two-year or four-year college or on-the-job training
Equipment operators	Most know tasks they're assigned to do; will do a better job if they understand the way their job relates to broader processes	Most seem to prefer explanations that let them focus on doing	Usually have on-the-job training (often oral rather than written) instead of formal education related to the job
Students	Often know generalizations in a field; typically need information that provides technical details as well as implications	Most prefer information that helps them assess, learn, learn to do, and do; interested in theory as well as practice	May have specialized training from summer or part-time jobs, internships, or co-op programs
General readers	Often know generalizations in a field; want information that explains how and why things happen	Most prefer information that helps them assess, learn, learn to do, and do; widely varied interests	May be highly educated but not in what they're reading about; may have specialized knowledge from hobbies
Children	Often want information that explains how and why things happen; need consideration for limited concepts and vocabulary	Most prefer information that helps them with learning, learning to do, and doing; widely varied interests	Usually have completed elementary, middle, or junior high school; may have specialized knowledge from hobbies and activities

- Marketing—to learn how the target market has been characterized

- Sales—to learn how customers have reacted to similar manuals

- Customer service (those who answer hot-line calls)—to find out what causes the most difficulties for users of similar products

Even more useful would be talking with representative users—the actual people who will use the computer system and the manual you plan to write. You can interview them about their needs, their expectations, and the problems they've had with other systems and documentation. You also should arrange for some users to test the manual at various stages during your drafting.

To help you collect information about the users of a document you're preparing, refer to the questions on the audience analysis worksheet in Figure 3.3. This worksheet helps you focus your audience analysis by asking you specific questions. Initially, you will find it helpful to actually photocopy and then fill in the worksheet. The more frequently you use it, however, the more familiar you will become with the questions. Eventually, you will automatically ask yourself the questions whenever you plan a document or presentation.

Context

An often ignored but vital consideration for technical communicators is the physical and political context and the general working conditions in which readers will interpret and use a document.

Regardless of a person's reading ability or knowledge of the subject, if the physical context is distracting or noisy, reading difficult material may be nearly impossible. A writer might adjust elements such as paragraph division, headings, page design, type and size of illustrations, and binding to make the document easier to use. For example, a repair manual used by technicians while they are troubleshooting equipment needs a sturdy cover, pages that lie flat, a detailed and easy-to-read table of contents and index, and headings and visuals that can be scanned easily. A report read by a busy executive needs an accurate abstract, clear headings, an initial statement of conclusions and recommendations, and brief explanations and justifications.

Just as the physical context is important, so too is the political context. For example, the attitude people in an organization have toward particular documents affects how these documents are read. Is a new employee told, "The manager's memos are a waste of time; just put them directly in the circular file" or told, in contrast, "The manager's memos are important; make sure to keep them for reference"?

The general working conditions of an organization—including how information is presented to readers—affects not only the way the documents are read but whether they're read at all. For example, if important memos are simply posted on hallway or lunchroom bulletin boards, many readers will skip them; most will think the memos are unimportant. If important internal documents are sent as attachments to e-mail, but some employees cannot access attachments,

FIGURE 3.3 ■ Audience Analysis Worksheet

Photocopy and use this figure to help your audience analysis.

Context: Where will the readers use the material? What distractions will they face in the physical and political context? What are the readers' working conditions (e.g., access to e-mail, available time)? _____

_____

_____

Audience: Who are the intended readers? What are their purposes? Do you need to consider differences among the initial, primary, secondary, and external readers?

_____

_____

Attitudes and motivations: What are the attitudes of the readers? What factors might contribute to their resistance or receptivity? How might these factors influence the way they read a document? How can you decrease resistance and increase receptivity? _____

_____

_____

Education: What level of education do you anticipate that the readers have? Theoretical or practical focus? How does this affect your plans for the document?

_____

_____

Professional experience: How much on-the-job experience do the readers have? How does this affect your plans? _____

_____

_____

Reading level: What is your best estimate about the level of material the readers can handle without difficulty? How can you make the document more accessible to readers? How have you used visuals and document design to aid reading? _____

_____

_____

Organizational role: What are the readers' positions in the organization? What professional experiences and organizational roles do the readers have? Job title? Areas of responsibility? Years of experience? Familiarity with the subject? How do these factors affect what they need to read? What constraints are at work? _____

_____

_____

these readers may presume that they are unimportant, that the documents are unimportant, or both.

Another aspect of working conditions is the available time the audience has to read the material. Because time is valuable, documents should be designed so that readers can understand and use the information as quickly and easily as possible. Technical communicators use organizational or graphic devices that ease the readers' task. The following strategies are particularly helpful:

- Initial abstracts or summaries

- Headings and subheadings

- Use of descending order so that the most important information comes first

- Definition of terms if necessary

- Transitions that show how sections of the document relate to each other

- Visuals that make information easily accessible

- Page layout that is not crowded or cluttered

Attitudes and Motivations

Analyzing readers' attitudes and motivations is relatively easy if you know the intended audience—individual or group—personally; however, most of the time, you don't personally know the audience. The task that readers do influences their motivation to read a particular document. For example, a computer technician might be motivated to read an operation manual, whereas a manager might be motivated to read theory about design or system architecture. A patient might be motivated to read instructions and side effects printed on a sheet packaged with medication but probably would not care much about the constituents used to synthesize the medication, which might be of great interest to a pharmacist.

Knowing readers' attitudes and motivation helps you adjust the organization of a document so that you increase receptivity and decrease resistance.

Explain whether you think professional colleagues might ignore verifiable information in a report because they didn't agree with the overall position of the writer.

- *Receptive readers:* You can present recommendations initially and then support them in subsequent sections of the document.

- *Resistant readers:* You can present the problem, discuss the alternatives, and then lead to the most appropriate and feasible solution, hoping readers are persuaded by your interpretation. You try to prevent or eliminate approaches that might interfere with readers' interpretation of information.

Attitude and motivation are abstract qualities and, thus, hard to quantify. So, how do you make this assessment? Imagine an actual reader in your intended audience. How will this reader feel about the document—pleased, neutral, or negative? For example, a repair technician may be highly motivated in referring to the repair manual when equipment breaks down, but feel neutral or negative about checking repair procedures if there's no problem. A manager may feel neutral about the proposal he has to read and be completely unmotivated to begin.

Education

If you can estimate readers' level of knowledge, which may be largely the result of formal education or experience, you will be able to determine the appropriate vocabulary and content. The level of education suggests readers' orientation:

- *Vocational-technical training* generally focuses on providing a practical or applied knowledge.

- *Professional or academic training* generally focuses on providing a theoretical understanding as well as a practical experience.

A physician or nurse practitioner might consult the *Physician's Desk Reference* to review the side effects of a new medication. A patient would read the much less technical insert accompanying the medication. A child might just see the Mr. Yuk poison symbol on the bottle and know enough to leave it alone.

Professional Experience

Readers' professional experience may influence their reactions to a document. Experienced professionals are more likely to be aware of corporate policies and to understand the influence of different personalities in support of or opposition to a document's recommendations. A more important part of professional experience, however, involves readers' expertise in the subject. This includes the readers' level of responsibility, years of professional experience, and familiarity with the field, including new developments.

Although estimating professional experience—and thus the readers' ability to understand the information and its practical application—is difficult, you can generalize about the amount needed to hold a job. The primary benefit of such information is the confidence writers derive from selecting appropriate vocabulary, technical complexity, and format.

Why is equating people's ability or intelligence with their amount of formal education a risky thing to do?

Reading Level

Reading level refers to the degree of difficulty of material readers are able to comprehend. Writing for the audience's level is important; if readers cannot understand and act on the written information, it is useless. Technical accuracy, completeness, logical organization—all are irrelevant if the intended audience cannot comprehend the material.

Knowing an audience's reading ability helps you adjust content and approach. Writers should not automatically assume, however, that the smarter the readers, the more difficult the material should be. A very intelligent person may not have a high reading level; another person may be able to read complex material in one specialized area but not in another. Someone capable of reading nearly any material might be constrained by lack of time or interest and thus prefer short, easy-to-read information. Your writing should be as easy as possible to read without oversimplifying or distorting the content.

This section discusses both readability formulas and limited literacy—two critical issues that affect workplace communication.

Readability Formulas.   Your computer's word processing program very likely comes with a function that supposedly calculates the *readability* of any text you write. The problem is that readability calculations simply use one of several formulas to determine a ratio between word length and sentence length. A readability formula—despite its name—doesn't really tell you how easy or difficult a text is for readers.

Readability formulas operate on the premise that shorter words and sentences are always easier to read. This is simply not so. The three-syllable word *elephant* is easier for virtually everyone to understand than the three-letter word *erg*. Such an oversimplified view of reading ignores many factors.

Calculation of readability for the paragraphs in this section of the text about Reading Level using the Flesch-Kincaid grade level says this section is appropriate for grade 11.9. However, with only a few changes to the text, the formulas can be manipulated to show a higher or lower level of difficulty. For example, making the text into many more short, simple sentences reduces the grade level. And other changes (such as making the entire section one long, dense, undifferentiated paragraph) result in no change at all to the readability results. Trusting readability formulas to assess the appropriateness of your documents for readers is risky at best.

Although word and sentence length certainly do influence the accessibility of information and ideas in a document, readability formulas, unfortunately, do not take into account many of the factors that affect reading. Figure 3.4 identifies some factors that affect the ease or difficulty of a text—factors that simply are not considered by readability formulas. Of course, all the factors in Figure 3.4 have to be considered comparatively and in context. For example, for a food scientist, understanding how beans grow is probably as easy as understanding why beans cause flatulence; to a botany student, understanding how beans grow is probably much easier; and to a first-grade student, both topics are probably beyond reach.

If readability formulas don't really measure how easy or difficult a text is to read, why are they so widely used?

Despite the value of understanding the factors in Figure 3.4, by themselves they do not make a text easy or difficult to read. In fact, how easy a document is to read depends largely on the interaction between the reader and the document, on the meaning that the reader creates during reading. As a writer, you can try to make a document accurate, accessible, appropriate, and appealing, but the ultimate readability test is what the reader gets out of the document.

Limited Literacy.   When people talk about "limited literacy" they can mean two different things: (1) people who are skillful readers in some circumstances

FIGURE 3.4 ■ Factors that Affect the Ease or Difficulty of a Text		
Photocopy and use this figure to help you assess your documents. The more "yes" responses, the easier a document will be to read.		
Factor	**Questions about Text Ease or Difficulty**	**✓ Yes**
Content	◆ Is the content concrete?	❏
	◆ Are abstractions supported with explanations and/or examples?	❏
	◆ Do readers have the necessary prior knowledge to understand the content?	❏
Context	◆ Does the document acknowledge and explain the context?	❏
	◆ Is the type of document familiar to the readers?	❏
Purpose	◆ Is the purpose clearly stated?	❏
	◆ Are readers likely to agree with the document's purpose?	❏
Audience	◆ Is the document adapted to the audience's level of understanding, needs and expectations, and organizational role?	❏
Organization	◆ Is the content logically organized? Are readers given cues about the organization?	❏
	◆ Is the document coherent (for example, using topic sentences and transitions)?	❏
	◆ Is the argument clearly presented and well supported?	❏
Visuals	◆ Is the verbal and visual information appropriately integrated?	❏
	◆ Are the kinds of visuals appropriate and appealing?	❏
	◆ Does the document conform to conventions for visuals?	❏
Document Design	◆ Is information appropriately chunked and labeled? Is the hierarchy clear?	❏
	◆ Are the choices for font, type style, type size, white space, and line length appropriate for the documents and the readers?	❏
	◆ Is the overall design of the document accessible and appealing?	❏
Usability	◆ Is the document usable for the intended context, purpose, and audience?	❏
Language Conventions	◆ Does the document conform to conventions of language—both grammar and mechanics?	❏

(for example, reading engineering reports) but not necessarily skillful in other circumstances (for example, reading legal briefs); or (2) people who don't get much information from any written documents. This section discusses this second kind of literacy problem.

Limited-literacy workers may see documents as difficult, intimidating, confusing, or even incomprehensible; thus, they may ignore the documents entirely. These workers can often read single words and short phrases, but they have great difficulty reading sentences, paragraphs, and entire documents. Limited-literacy workers also may not understand document conventions, which may result in literacy problems such as these:

- May not know how to use a table of contents or an index

- May not use headings to preview upcoming text

- May not treat boxed, shaded, boldfaced, or italicized text as more important than plain text

- May skip parts of the text they don't understand

- May misread parts of the text but believe they do understand it

- May expect that all relevant information will be in the visuals

The problem of limited literacy is widespread in the workplace. The recent National Adult Literacy Survey reports the results of interviews with more than 26,000 randomly selected adults in the United States. Between 47 and 51 percent of the adult population (the equivalent of 90 to 94 million adults) could not complete very simple literacy tasks. These simple tasks included locating a single piece of information in a short article, entering a signature on a form, and locating information about eligibility for employee benefits in a table.

Surprisingly, the majority of people who performed at this level described themselves as being able to read and write English "well" or "very well," so their limited skills may "allow them to meet some or most of their personal and occupational literacy needs." In the same National Adult Literacy Survey, only 18 to 21 percent of the adult population (the equivalent of 34 to 40 million adults) performed at the highest literacy levels. More complex literacy tasks included interpreting information from an article, identifying patterns from information in a table, and summarizing information in a table.[1]

What compensatory skills might a person develop in order to make up for limited reading skills?

As a person responsible for creating technical documents, you need to be especially careful if your audience has limited literacy skills. If time and budget allow, consider alternative forms of presentation such as one-on-one conferences, face-to-face small group meetings, buddy training programs, videocassettes, videodisks, or multimedia computer programs.

If these options are out of the question, create documents that are largely visual. However, keep in mind that sequences of information on a page and ways of interpreting color are not universal; U.S. conventions are not worldwide conventions. Consider that moving through a document from left to right and from top to bottom is a convention for reading English; if a person doesn't read, this may not be a familiar convention; thus, arrows as well as numbers are useful. Consider that design elements such as color and icons to signal information can work well; thus, high risks can be marked in yellow (caution) or red (stop). But check that your readers are from a culture (like North America or Europe) where these colors have these meanings.

Organizational Role

Organizations are generally categorized as hierarchical or nonhierarchical. In practice, most organizations incorporate both hierarchical and nonhierarchical characteristics:

- *A hierarchical organization* has bosses at the top, managers in the middle, and workers at the bottom. Hierarchical organizations generally assume that people work best when directed.

- *A nonhierarchical organization* has everyone contributing equally to the productivity of the organization. Nonhierarchical organizations regard people as most productive when they participate in decision making.

Explain where you would prefer to work— a hierarchical organization or a nonhierarchical organization. Why?

A hierarchical organization can be analyzed by examining where a person fits into the organizational structure of the company—who reports to whom, who is a decision maker, who holds ultimate responsibility for a process or a project. Curiously, e-mail is flattening hierarchies in some organizations because all employees are easily accessible simply by sending an e-mail message. But the ease of sending such a message doesn't mean it's necessarily appropriate. An assessment of hierarchy in an organization requires sensitivity to and awareness of any subtle differences between the formal structure and the actual working structure.

So far, the discussion has focused on internal readers—those within the writer's organization. Frequently, however, readers are external, belonging to another organization. Such readers might be customers or a funding agency. They would not know many of the things that are apparent to internal readers, so the writer needs to provide more background information than may be customary for an internal reader. This background might include elements such as definitions, a brief history, and the relation of the subject to the overall operation.

The tone used for external readers is often more formal than the tone used for internal readers. However, *formal* does not mean pompous; rather, the document just does not include casual language common in internal memos. For example, an internal memo might say, "I'll get back to you by Monday about the revised schedule," whereas a document for an external reader would be more likely to say, "I will send you information about the revised schedule by Monday, October 22" or "Information about the revised schedule will reach you by Monday, October 22."

Adjusting to Readers

After you have identified and analyzed your readers, you can prepare documents that respond to their reasons for reading as well as to factors such as contexts, levels of expertise, organizational roles, stances on issues, attitudes, and prior knowledge. This section focuses on adjusting content complexity for different audiences in three broad ways:

- Address readers with *different levels of expertise* by adjusting the complexity of the material.

- Address readers with *different organizational roles* by shifting the focus of the discussion and the choice of details.

- Address readers by designing Web sites that enable readers to *construct unique sequences of information* to meet their own needs and interests.

Differences in Expertise

Readers vary in their level of technical knowledge. When you adjust material for readers with various levels of technical competence, you need to change the complexity of the concepts, language, details, and examples. The following examples show how workplace professionals can adapt information to meet the needs of different audiences. The director of medical technology for an urban hospital produced three paragraphs about coagulation, each intended for a different audience.[2]

The first paragraph (Figure 3.5) is for high school biology students learning new concepts. These students need to learn the vocabulary as well as the process of coagulation. The writer uses the run-in heading to pose a question to focus the students' attention and let them know what to anticipate. The writer then reviews common knowledge about clots before presenting and defining new terms. The writer organizes details using a familiar cause-and-effect organization.

The second paragraph (Figure 3.6) is for college students majoring in a four-year medical technology degree program. These students can handle technical vocabulary and already understand the basic causal relationships. What they need to learn, though, are concepts that explain coagulation. The writer signals this focus with the run-in heading. The paragraph itself explains the process of coagulation, which includes introducing and defining new terms (such as procoagulants and fibrinogen) and providing specific details (for instance, procoagulants are activated by damaged tissue, phospholipids, and calcium ions).

The third paragraph (Figure 3.7) is for professional medical technologists who are enrolled in a review course given in their hospital. These medical professionals understand the basic process of coagulation, but they need a review. After using a run-in heading to signal the topic, the writer uses a topic sentence to preview the content and the organization of the paragraph (intrinsic, extrinsic, and common pathways). Italicizing each main term provides a typographic cue that helps readers keep track of where they are in relation to the whole.

FIGURE 3.5 ■ Paragraph for High School Students

What is coagulation? If a blood vessel ruptures, the blood thickens and forms a gel called a clot, which slows the flow of blood from the wound. This process is called *coagulation,* a mechanism to prevent blood loss when a blood vessel is ruptured. This process is initiated both by the damaged blood vessel tissue and by substances released from the damaged tissue. The substances activate proteins in the blood called *procoagulants.* The activated procoagulants act as enzymes in a series of chemical reactions that culminate in the conversion of a molecule of fibrinogen to a smaller molecule, fibrin. The fibrin molecules link together into strands. These strands form a tight mesh that is known as a *fibrin clot.*

AUDIENCE: high school students

VOCABULARY: simple; terms defined; new terms italicized

APPROACH: reviews common knowledge before presenting causal relationship

FIGURE 3.6 ■ Paragraph for Medical Technology Majors in College

The Process of Coagulation. A major function of the hemostatic mechanism of the cardiovascular system is the coagulation of blood. Coagulation plays a vital role in preventing blood loss in episodes of vessel injury, allowing the body to maintain blood volume and retain blood products. The process of coagulation is achieved through the chain of chemical reactions of procoagulants (a group of plasma proteins) and tissue cell constituents. The procoagulants circulate through the bloodstream as inert enzymes, activated by damaged tissue, phospholipid from cell membranes, and calcium ions. After a series of enzymatic reactions, the procoagulants cleave a protein peptide from fibrinogen, a glycoprotein, to form a fibrin monomer. The fibrin monomers polymerize into strands that form an insoluble mesh known as a fibrin clot.

AUDIENCE: college students

VOCABULARY: technical; terms defined

APPROACH: offers a causal explanation of the process, which includes new vocabulary

FIGURE 3.7 ■ Paragraph for Professional Medical Technologists in a Hospital Review Course

Pathways in coagulation. Three pathways are involved in the coagulation of the hemostatic mechanism: intrinsic, extrinsic, and common pathways. Each pathway consists of a cascade of proteolytic enzyme reactions in which procoagulants, a series of inert circulating proteolytic enzymes called coagulation factors, activate one another. The *intrinsic pathway* is activated by the presence of damaged endothelium tissue and a high molecular weight activator, kallikren. The extrinsic pathway is activated by tissue factor, a phospholipid of endothelium, and calcium ions. The *common pathway* is activated by the resultant coagulation factors of the intrinsic and extrinsic pathways. The result of the common pathway is the conversion of fibrinogen to fibrin monomers, which polymerize into strands. The strands mesh through covalent bonding to form an insoluble fibrin clot.

AUDIENCE: medical technologists

VOCABULARY: technical

APPROACH: uses a parts/whole approach (types of pathways) and causal explanation of each type of pathway

Differences in Roles and Stances

The technical complexity of documents usually remains the same for readers with similar organizational positions or political stances; instead, you adjust to the audience by emphasizing different aspects of the subject. Writers can appeal to readers by focusing on factors directly relevant to their organization role. Writers can also appeal to readers by acknowledging their particular point of view.

The following three memos—all written by the vice president of plant operations—are about the same subject: the purchase of a mill that is intended to increase product uniformity, reduce waste, and increase product availability. Each memo is directed to a separate manager, each of whom has specialized interests and responsibilities. These three memos have approximately the same level of content difficulty, yet the focus shifts in each one to emphasize the content that is relevant to each reader.

In the first memo, which appears in Figure 3.8, the writer addresses the production supervisor of the Mill Department. Because the recipient of this memo is interested primarily in production, the writer identifies a critical problem that will be eliminated with the new machine and identifies a series of benefits—including product uniformity and a reduction in rejections and downtime—which should increase productivity.

The second memo, which appears in Figure 3.9, is written to the controller, the person responsible for the company's financial operations. A controller is primarily concerned about money matters, so he would be interested in cost savings that come about because of waste reduction and increased equipment efficiency. The controller would also be interested in the payback period. The

FIGURE 3.8 ■	Memo from the VP of Plant Operations to the Production Supervisor

The writer focuses on the reader's interest—product availability. This topic is signaled in the subject line of the memo and is the primary topic of the paragraph.

The memo provides a critical date and identifies anticipated production benefits.

INTEROFFICE MEMO

To	Peter Smith, Prod. Supervisor, Mill Dept.
From	Thomas White, VP Plant Operations tw
Date	8 September 200–
Subject	Expected increase in product availability

The recently purchased mill is scheduled to be on line by October 15. This machine will solve the problems of the thermal stabilization times you have been plagued with, while increasing product uniformity. When the department has less product rejection and machine downtime, I look forward to seeing increased rates per shift. You will be notified of the new rate production schedule on October 15.

FIGURE 3.9 ■ Memo from the VP of Plant Operations to the Controller

INTEROFFICE MEMO

To	Edward Daily, Controller
From	Thomas White, VP Plant Operations *tw*
Date	8 September 200–
Subject	New Wolverine Cereal Flaking Mill

The addition of the new mill to our production line is an effective solution to the production waste problems we have been experiencing. With the minimal waste expected combined with the machine's operating efficiency, the payback period should be within the next fiscal year. Early signs indicate that purchasing the mill has been a smart investment.

In writing to the controller, the writer focuses on financial matters.

Because the controller does not regularly work with production line equipment, he needs to be reminded (tactfully, in the subject line) about the specific machine.

The memo identifies ways the mill will save money and reviews the length of the payback period.

difficulty of the content, sentences, and vocabulary in this memo is much the same as that in Figure 3.8.

In the third memo to the director of marketing and sales (Figure 3.10), the writer concentrates on product availability—the amount, the date, the implications. There is no mention of production details or costs, which are only peripherally relevant to someone in marketing and sales. The emphasis is on the need to develop a new short-term marketing plan.

INTEROFFICE MEMO

To	David Parker, Director of Mkting & Sales
From	Thomas White, VP Plant Operations *tw*
Date	8 September 200–
Subject	Expected increase in product availability

Due to the addition of capital equipment in the production department, product availability will increase by approximately 50%. A short-term plan in marketing strategy should be initiated to increase sales and expand to new territories. Product stockpiling begins October 15.

The writer wants the director of marketing and sales to concentrate on a marketing plan.

Mentioning the increase in availability and the product stockpiling should reinforce the need for new territories.

What are the advantages and disadvantages of a writer preparing separate documents for the variety of audiences who need the same information?

Should you write three separate memos? Yes, if you have the time and believe that the special attention increases reader comprehension and support. However, you may not have the time to write separate memos, and sometimes political realities dictate that all readers receive an identical memo. In these circumstances, you need to write one memo for multiple readers who differ in their interests, familiarity with the project, and levels of expertise. To make this one memo as effective as possible, consider these suggestions:

- *Identify and write for the primary readers:* Organize the information for the people who need the information for decision making, putting first what is most important to them.

- *Identify and consider the secondary readers:* Include information of interest to secondary readers based on its value to the primary readers and the influence these secondary readers have on the primary readers.

- *Use design elements to make information accessible:* Use headings, typographic elements (such as boldface and italic), and typographic devices (such as bullets and boxes) to signal important topics.

Explain which is easier for you to do—write for audiences with different levels of expertise or for audiences with different organizational roles.

So far, you've read about adjusting communication to meet needs established largely by readers' organizational roles and responsibilities. Sometimes, however, concentrating solely on the verifiable information relevant to particular roles is not sufficient. For example, communication that ignores readers' stance—points of view, attitudes, values, and beliefs—is likely to be ineffective. In fact, readers may dismiss documents and presentations that ignore affective concerns, feeling that such documents or presentations simply do not adequately consider them or the situation—despite being filled with verifiable information. The sidebar on the next page addresses this important issue.

Readers Adjusting

The previous discussion focuses on ways you can adjust for readers with different levels of expertise or different organizational roles or stances. This section illustrates how readers can take responsibility for constructing their own unique document, one that is tailored to their individual needs and interests.

What defines information as critical? Who should determine what is critical—Web writers/designers or Web users?

When an effective Web site is constructed, writers and designers take special care to see that a range of intended users will find the site usable; thus, links to critical information need to be easy to find. On the Web, readers can choose links that may create a unique document. At a minimum, the sequence of links they select leads to an individual interpretation of the information. For example, Figure 3.11 shows a screen from a food safety Web site. Depending on a user's prior knowledge, needs, and interests, this site could be "read" in a number of different ways. Visitors to this food safety Web site can select their own sequence of information. This page on the site gives readers choices about links to the Food and Drug Administration (FDA), the Centers for Disease Control (CDC), safe food practices, ongoing research, and definitions of common pathogens.

"Their approaches are culturally insensitive": Ethics and Public Policies

Effective technical documents typically present clear, precise, verifiable information. Focusing on such details reflects the belief that the more readers know, the better decisions they will make. However, technical professionals who rely too much on precise information sometimes ignore other equally important aspects of a document. Focusing on precision can sometimes lead a writer to provide too much information or to present information in confusing or unfamiliar terms. Often, the result is a document that contains all the relevant information but does not sufficiently consider the ethics of the context, content, or purpose as they affect the audience.

Researchers Patricia Hynds and Wanda Martin, reviewing the public outcry over a city water project, outline how an unethical approach can derail a much-needed project.[3] Hynds and Martin describe a debate that arose when the City of Albuquerque, New Mexico, began the process of drilling a well in one of the city's suburbs, the South Valley. Albuquerque relies heavily on wells to provide water for its communities; city planners assumed that South Valley's residents would readily recognize the value of the new well. When South Valley residents voiced concerns about the effects of drilling the new well, Albuquerque's mayor asked the public works department to meet with South Valley residents to work out a new location (although resident approval for a new well's location was not legally necessary). Three community meetings later, communication between the city and residents had degenerated, and lawsuits were filed. The well has yet to be drilled.

Why did such a necessary project reach this impasse? Hynds and Martin believe the problem occurred because the city's representatives failed to adequately recognize the cultural and social viewpoints of the residents. The residents voiced concerns about the negative impact of the well; they did not want their small community to become too industrial or overcrowded with new construction. The city's representatives, however, viewed these concerns as simply a lack of understanding by the residents. In each meeting, the city's representatives continually emphasized the technical aspects of the well to support their position: they believed "that when the technical facts are clearly communicated, all reasonable hearers will arrive at similar conclusions." The residents, however, felt the technical explanations were patronizing and did not feel that their concerns were respected. For the residents, the issue was about more than facts; it was about respecting the traditions and heritage of the area. Eventually, the animosity the residents felt towards the city reached a point where the residents boycotted the last meeting and filed lawsuits to stop the drilling.

Hynds and Martin believe that despite the city's good intentions, the city planners failed to treat the audience ethically. Instead of talking to the residents about their concerns, they continually tried to make the residents see the situation from the city's point of view. They relied too much on precise facts and too little on the concerns of their audience. The unfortunate result was a breakdown in communication. If the city planners used an ethical approach to communication, they would have considered more than their verifiable information about water needs and well locations.

How would you convince the city planners that listening to their audience matters? What would you do if your audience rejected carefully presented and verifiable information in favor of emotional and unverifiable opinions?

How can you determine when your audience has concerns beyond the technical data?

After quickly scanning these links, users could choose to go in a number of different and equally productive directions—depending on their needs. For

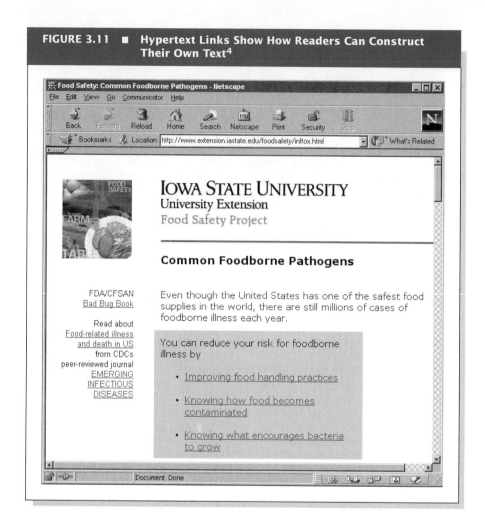

FIGURE 3.11 ■ **Hypertext Links Show How Readers Can Construct Their Own Text[4]**

example, by following different links, users could do any of these things in whatever order they chose. And, of course, each link they go to might have additional links that enable them to explore the idea in greater depth.

Access this Web site: <http://www.extension.iastate.edu/foodsafety/inftox.html> Keep track of the links you follow and compare your sequence with others in the class.

- View an online video presentation about kitchen safety
- Learn how food can become hazardous
- Conduct research at the Centers for Disease Control
- Discover the characteristics of a specific bacteria

When hypertext documents are reader-centered, readers can easily construct their own paths through online text by choosing their own sequence of links. Researcher Paul Levinson calls this "empowerment of the author through the empowerment of readers."[5] Simply put, hypertext documents allow writers and readers to link related concepts and restructure knowledge. A document that is read interactively is rarely experienced the same way twice; different readers can arrive at the same point in a document but have discovered different things along the way because they activated different links. Hypertext documents that offer readers this empowerment respect audience needs.

End-of-Chapter
Recommendations for Technical Communicators

1. Identify your purpose in preparing a document or presentation: to convey information and to persuade readers to attend to that information.

2. Identify the readers' task(s): to assess, to learn, to learn to do, to do.

3. Distinguish the various reader roles: initial reader, primary reader, secondary readers, and external readers.

4. Determine the readers' level of expertise and organizational role: expert, professional nonexpert, technician, equipment operator, student, general reader, child.

5. Analyze your readers to assess the context in which they'll use the documents as well as their attitudes and motivations, education, professional experience, reading level, and organizational role.

6. Adjust to your readers' level of expertise by changing such things as the complexity of the concepts and the difficulty of the language you use.

7. Adjust to your readers' organizational role by changing such things as the focus of your document and the kinds and amount of details you include.

8. Acknowledge your readers' ethical stance about issues.

9. Design reader-centered Web sites that empower people to construct their own unique document, one that is tailored to their individual needs and interests.

Practicum

Iowa Public Television (IPTV)

Iowa Public Television (IPTV), a statewide network located in Johnston, Iowa, employs slightly over 150 people. Its primary mission is to provide viewers with high-quality programs with a special emphasis on educational programming. One IPTV department, EdTel (Educational Telecommunications), zeros in on educational products, including the project I work on—the Mississippi River Heritage Project, which includes live interactive broadcasts, Internet resources, virtual fieldtrips using distance learning, and multimedia CD-ROMs.

In 1997, EdTel received a Star Schools Grant from the U.S. Department of Education. This federal grant encourages "improved instruction" using telecommunications in all subject matter for under-served audiences. EdTel has taken a significant portion of its Star Schools Grant and established InteractiveMedia, a team that creates multimedia educational products for middle-school students. InteractiveMedia is a collaborative team of six IPTV professionals—instructional designers, producers, graphic designers/computer modelers, and writers—all chosen for our specific communication and technical skills. We also work with 3-D modelers, sound engineers, programmers, curriculum designers, and content writers.

I function as a technical writer, editor, and instructional designer. But this team has had lots of turnover, so of the 13 original people who started the project, only six remain. Why? The project entails complex technology tasks and subject matter expertise coupled with pay lower than that provided by for-profit industry. Finding the right professionals for the project is challenging because the work requires collaboration, a willingness to learn instructional design methodology, an interest in educational content, and work with cutting-edge digital technology.

Scenario

The Mississippi River Heritage project involves the development and production of a CD-ROM with accompanying classroom materials for middle school students in the state of Iowa, with possible national distribution.

When I first joined the project, the previous editor had been gone for several months. Because of imminent deadlines, I was allowed a very short learning curve. Two of the other team members had arrived only months before I did.

Unfortunately, even though the project had been going on for over two years, previous team members had maintained only minimal print files about the subject for the CD. Most of the information was rudimentary and required more research to make it useful. When I was hired, a pilot version of the CD had to be out within two months, including the documentation (user guides for the CD-ROM program, classroom activities for teachers, copies of assignments, and evaluation materials such as surveys and observation checklists).

In spite of the mayhem, I was excited about the challenge. The hardest part was using the document specifications, established early in the project, to create meaningful text (see pages 88–89 for examples). In essence, I needed to complete these steps:

1. Meet with the team and determine eight content themes for the Mississippi River—one of them: *river formation*—as they would fit into science, math, language arts, social studies curricula.

2. Determine what students need to know about the theme. (Students should understand the following river formation concepts: geology, glacial impact, hydrology/limnology, and delta formation.)

3. Brainstorm ways to present information in a multimedia environment. (We decided to create a "river formation room" where students could dynamically interact with 3-D models that demonstrate concepts like "discharge," "velocity," "turbidity," and "sediment load.")

4. Research the topics and write according to specifications.

5. Pass off all documentation to the graphic designer or producer for production.

Examples

All of our technical documents for the CD-ROM are written for middle school students. Preliminary user testing of the CD in middle schools allows us to adapt our process to students' needs and desires. Two of the common forms for presenting information are "books" and infocards.

Book script. During testing, I found that most students did not read the original electronic "books" that we placed on the CD-ROM. Students told me that these "books" were too long (even though they didn't exceed 10 pages) and didn't have enough pictures. This feedback has allowed us to rethink the way we produce reading materials.

The following example presents part of a revised "book" script that takes into account the students' preferences.

Infocard. Another way we present content is through an electronic *infocard*, which presents a detail that students can click on within the program to read textual information. The infocard, designed to look like a typical index card, provides information about a graphic (for example, a picture, a statue, an artifact) that students may need to know in order to complete an assignment.

Excerpt from a "Book" Script: How Did the USS Cairo Float?

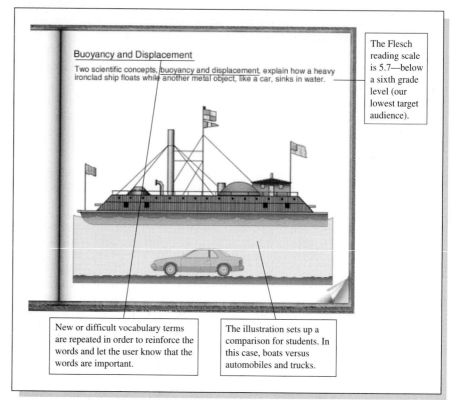

Buoyancy and Displacement

Two scientific concepts, buoyancy and displacement, explain how a heavy ironclad ship floats while another metal object, like a car, sinks in water.

The Flesch reading scale is 5.7—below a sixth grade level (our lowest target audience).

New or difficult vocabulary terms are repeated in order to reinforce the words and let the user know that the words are important.

The illustration sets up a comparison for students. In this case, boats versus automobiles and trucks.

Infocards can contain a title that is no more than 60 characters and text that is no more than 340 characters, as illustrated in the example on page 87. Because of these specifications, infocards are very difficult to write.

Assignment

Imagine that you have been hired as a freelance writer for the IPTV multimedia team. According to your 700-hour contract, you need to submit one topic—of the nine topics listed below—every two weeks:

- flyways on the Mississippi River
- northern pine forests (like those found near Lake Itasca in Minnesota)
- historical business along the Mississippi River
- recreation along the Mississippi River
- an important Civil War battle that took place along the Mississippi River
- jazz music's relationship with the Mississippi River
- how the levee system on the Mississippi River works

Example of Infocard

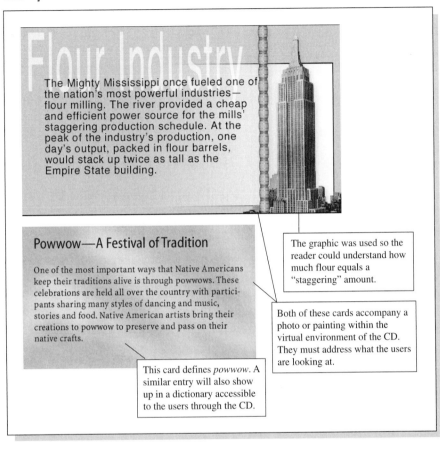

- African-Americans' relationship to the Mississippi River
- steamboats on the Mississippi River

For this class, your assignment is to complete only one of the topics for the IPTV team. You need to do the following tasks:

1. **Prepare.** Research your selected topic (from the list above) using print and Web resources. Keep a complete list of your references to include.

2. **Plan.** Outline the topic into the constituent parts you choose to present (an example about flyways follows) and write short (300–1200 characters) paragraphs for each part of the main topic. (You define what is important; you're the content expert.) As you plan and write, you may discover that you need more information.

1. Define a flyway.

2. Define the four major U.S. flyways (map the boundaries, establish overall importance, and identify typical birds in each):

   a. Pacific

   b. Central

   c. Atlantic

   d. Mississippi Flyway

3. Identify regions within Mississippi Flyway.

   a. Identify specific *habitats* within those regions (e.g., marsh, swamp etc.).

   b. Identify *uses* typical of those regions and habitats (e.g., wintering in Midwest, breeding in Delta).

      i. Identify specific species that exemplify those uses (e.g., neo-tropical songbirds breed in the barrier islands).

      ii. Map the migration cycle of some dominant species.

4. Identify threats to the regions.

Notes

* If you find useful graphics, cite them and include copies.

* If you find information that we haven't identified as a need but you feel is important to the concept of a flyway, include it.

3. **Design and Draft.** List several ways you could present the content information for the Mississippi River Heritage project's CD-ROM. Then select two of these forms to actually complete, according to the specifications that follow.

Specifications for Project Forms

Infocard—3 card maximum (1 preferred)		*Body*	12-pt Myriad Bold
Title	14-pt Minion Web Regular		10 lines maximum
	2 lines maximum		34 characters per line
	30 characters per line		340 characters maximum
	60 characters maximum		left justified
	left justified		
		Book (see magazine) (10-page maximum)	

Museum Placard (1 per topic)

Title	30-pt Myriad Web Bold
	20 characters maximum
	2 lines maximum
	10 characters per line maximum
	200w x 50 h pixel width
Body	14-pt Minion Web Regular
	1450 characters maximum
	21 lines maximum
	70 characters per line maximum
	390w x 320h pixel width

Magazine Article (4-page maximum)

Title	specified by graphic designer
Body	12-pt Myriad Bold
	1400 characters maximum
	(includes space for graphics)

Brochure 420w x 350h; limited to 1 page

Title	20 characters maximum
	2 lines maximum
	10 characters per line
Body	800-character maximum
	heavy use of visuals

Script (2-minute maximum)

- Used as a voice over (recorded audio track)

Movie (2-minute maximum)

- Produced with audio and video

Miscellaneous graphics

- Includes maps, charts, timelines, posters, mural, etc.
- User can select details within the image to zoom in on.
- Pixel dimensions no larger than 640w x 350h

4. Consider Critical Factors.

- *Audience.* The audience is middle school students (grades 6-8). Don't throw around 25 cent words when a nickel word will do. There is *always* an easier way to get your message across. Rewrite. Revise. And revise again. Remember, a picture really is worth a thousand words.

- *Resources.* Technical books and scientific journals are good places to start, but don't forget about recreational magazines, environmental newspapers/journals, interviews with researchers in the field, and the Web. Stay away from personal Web pages because they are often poorly documented and unreliable. Instead, use government-sponsored Web sites: U.S. Park Service, U.S. Geological Service, and the Army Corps of Engineers, a site with great technical reports.

- *Sensory appeal.* Kids learn better if multiple channels are stimulated; thus, try to develop visual, oral, auditory, tactile, and kinesthetic activities to explain technical concepts and practices.

- **Visuals.** Select informative visuals, especially if they can be inter-active. For example, we are producing a map display from which users can click on *button 1* to show barge networks on the Missis-sippi River; *button 2* for train routes along the river; and, *button 3* for major highways along the river. The whole display allows users to see how the Mississippi River is still an integral part of transportation. And there are fewer than 150 words used on the whole display.

Melissa Waltman is an editor and technical writer for Iowa Public Television. She received her B.A. in English from Iowa State University and is completing her M.A. there in rhetoric, composition, and professional communication.

She is interested in languages of all kinds and works to make written communication accessible to multiple audi-ences. She says, "The Mississippi River Heritage Project gives me an opportunity to explore and research ways in which writers can improve scientific, technical, and educa-tional texts, especially for young readers." She can be reached at <melissa@iptv.org>, or you can check the IPTV Web site <www.interactive.iptv.org>.

Individual and Collaborative Assignments

1. **Determine the audiences.** Read the following sets of sentences intended for different audiences. Determine the audience for each sentence and then answer the following questions:

   - How has the writer adjusted for the different audiences? Which set is adjusted for differences in audience expertise? Which set is adjusted for differences in organizational role?
   - What information did the writer need to make these adjustments?
   - Why are the changes necessary if the statements in each set convey essentially the same information?

   Set 1   The sun damages many human-made materials.

   The sun causes degeneration and weakening of any synthetic fibers.

   Ultraviolet radiation causes polymer degeneration by attacking links in the polymer chain and reducing the molecular weight of the material.

   Set 2   The shipment was delayed because of manufacturing equipment malfunction and misjudgment about the resulting delays.

   Because your shipment has again been unavoidably delayed, we will credit your rental fee for fourteen days—the anticipated length of this second delay.

   Occasional brief delays in shipping have a minimal impact on attaining projected third-quarter goals.

2. **Determine the audiences.** Visit the following Web sites and ask the questions about different audiences for whom the Web sites are intended:

   - Who are the various audiences for the Web site?
   - How have the writer and designer adjusted for the different audiences? How have the writer and designer acknowledged and responded to the needs and interests of specific segments of the audience—for example, people of color and international readers?
   - What information did the writer and designer need to make these adjustments?

   <www.dairynetwork.com>   <www.campbellsoup.com>
   <www.discovery.com>   <www.ibm.com>
   <www.nsf.com>   <www.sch-plough.com>

3. **Differentiate the audiences.** For each of these three paragraphs about the Cessna T-37B (an aircraft used for pilot training), identify a likely intended audience, and explain your choice by using specific textual examples as support.[6]

   (a) The Cessna T-37B is a low-wing aircraft. It is a dual-control trainer with side-by-side seating, which simply means that the plane has two sets of controls, one for the instructor and one for the student, who sit next to each other as opposed to one in front of the other. The aircraft is powered by two Continental jet engines and is equipped with a bird-resistant windshield. Designed for utility, ruggedness, and safety, the T-37B provides a channel for student transition to the next aircraft trainer, the T-38.

   (b) The Cessna T-37B is a low-wing, dual-control trainer with side-by-side seating. It is powered by two turbojet engines and is equipped with a two-position speed brake that is located on the bottom of the fuselage and is activated to decelerate the aircraft during approaches and landings. The aircraft is also equipped with spoilers for artificial stall warnings because the actual stall warning does not function due to the change in airflow. The spoilers, when extended, create a turbulent airflow that causes the aircraft to buffet. Some other features include full instrumentation and lighting for both day and night flying, oxygen equipment, an air-conditioning and defrost system, and bird-resistant windshields. Designed for utility, ruggedness, and safety, this aircraft provides a channel for student transition to the next trainer, the T-38.

   (c) The Cessna T-37B is a low-wing, dual-control trainer with side-by-side seating and powered by two Continental turbojet engines. The aircraft is equipped with a two-position speed brake, spoilers for artificial stall warning, thrust attenuators, a jettisonable canopy, and ejection seats. Other noteworthy features include full instrumentation and lighting for day and night flying, oxygen equipment, and an air-conditioning and defrost system. The aircraft is also equipped with bird-resistant windshields. Designed for utility, ruggedness, and safety, the T-37B provides a channel for pilot transition to heavier and faster jet aircraft.

4. **Rewrite a paragraph.** Read the following paragraph and rewrite it to lower the difficulty.

   A new concept that greatly improves the economics of outdoor storage of grain and other free-flowing bulk materials includes a self-erecting cover and new methods of aeration. The cover is laced together from triangular sections of vinyl-coated nylon fabric and raised to the top of a central filling tower before the filling operation is begun. During filling, it is lifted and spread by the growing grain pile and provides a form-fitting cover that completely encases the pile during all stages of fill. This form-fitting cover is highly resistant to lifting effects of high winds and protects the pile against rainfall. This protection allows the filling operation to be continued during the heaviest downpours. It also completely contains dust particles that would otherwise be carried into the atmosphere to settle on the surrounding countryside. When full, the covering, tightly fitted to the finished pile, is held in place without need of the usual tires or cable tie-downs and provides long-term protection against crusting and other surface spoilage effects caused by the weather. This protection is obtained at a very low cost, as the cost of the cover can be completely paid off by the spoilage eliminated by a single year of the cover's use.

5. **Analyze audiences for different paragraphs.**

   (a) Read and analyze the audiences and some of the related factors for the following two paragraphs about the same subject—why stars twinkle.

   Paragraph A. The stars twinkle because the earth's air scatters the light that comes from them. So during windy weather, stars appear to twinkle more than when the weather is calm. Also, stars near the horizon twinkle more than stars higher in the sky because the light has a thicker layer of air to go through. Observed from the moon, stars do not appear to twinkle at all because the moon does not have any air. Planets do not appear to twinkle as much as most stars because planets usually appear much brighter than most stars, making it harder for their light to be scattered.

   Paragraph B. Stars twinkle because of atmospheric diffraction, the scattering of light caused by the earth's atmosphere. Stars appear to twinkle much more when the atmosphere is extremely turbulent, as it is just before a weather front passes through. Stars near the horizon appear to twinkle much more than those near the zenith because light has to pass through a thicker layer of atmosphere and has more of a chance to be diffracted. The moon's lack of an atmosphere causes a very small amount of diffraction. The light from planets is not diffracted as much as that from stars because planetary disks subtend a much larger area than do stellar disks (40 arc seconds as compared to 0.001 arc second). This larger area causes the light to be more intense and results in less diffraction.

   (b) Complete a matrix based on your analysis of the paragraphs. Describe, explain, and illustrate each factor. (Create a larger version of the matrix below to actually fill in the cells of the matrix.)

	Paragraph A	*Paragraph B*
Audience		
Context		
Content		
Purpose		
Vocabulary		

6. Contrast articles written for different audiences.

(a) Select an article from *Science Digest*, *Science News*, the *New York Times* science section (published on Thursdays), or a local newspaper's science section, and then locate the original article from which it was abridged or on which it was based. Identify and comment on the changes.

(b) Create a table to present your analysis—one column to identify the features you examined and the other two columns (one for each publication) to present examples of the differences. Provide complete citation information for each article.

(c) Find a Web site that deals with the same information. Identify and comment on differences in the presentation of the information on the Web site. Revise your table (additional column and rows) to present the information from your Web site analysis.

7. Write memos for two audiences.

(a) Read the following two memos written by a production supervisor about the purchase of hand cutters for assembly workers on a production line.

■ **Memo from Production Supervisor to Engineer in Manufacturing Engineering**

Marlborough Science, Inc.

October 11, 20—

TO: Charles Faria
                  PCB Manufacturing Engineering
FROM: Marty Holmann *mh*
SUBJECT: EREM Hand Cutters

From September 23, 200-, to October 10, 200-, the SPS assembly personnel evaluated three styles of EREM ergonomic hand cutters. The assemblers preferred cutter style 711E-BH to cutter styles 511E-BH or 512E-BH.

Nine line assemblers as well as six post solder operators had the opportunity to use the three styles of cutters. They all agreed that the 711E-BH cutter was the most comfortable, durable, and versatile. The padded handles and quick-action internal spring reduce the fatigue factor experienced by the assemblers with their current cutters. The cutters were used to cut leads varying from 0.019 inch to 0.050 inch and showed little sign of wear, even after being used to cut soldered leads.

In summary, the assemblers strongly preferred the EREM hand cutters to the Lindstrom or Utica cutters. They are still willing to evaluate any new cutters that you may consider equivalent or applicable to their needs.

Note the places that make each memo appropriate for the intended audience.

- The first memo is to an engineer in manufacturing whose projects are affected by the quality of the work the assembly workers do. He wasn't involved in the testing, so he needs a summary of test information. He is particularly interested in the function and capability of the cutters.

- The second memo is to a finance representative. Her primary concern is cost—initially, total expenditure, then cost comparison. Least important to her is the reason for the choice.

(b) After reading the two memos, write two additional memos about the same subject. Direct one of the memos to the assembly workers themselves. Direct the other memo to the manager of the manufacturing division, who is the immediate supervisor of the production supervisor who is writing the memos.

■ Memo from Production Supervisor to Finance Department Representative

Marlborough Science, Inc.

October 11, 20—

TO: Diane Martin
            Finance Representative
FROM: Marty Holmann *mh*
SUBJECT: EREM Hand Cutters

PCB Manufacturing Engineering and PCB Management are requesting approval from the Finance Department to purchase 400 EREM hand cutters for the assembly-line workers for a one-time total purchase price of $9,200.

From September 23, 200-, to October 10, 200-, three styles of EREM hand cutters were evaluated by the assembly-line workers and the manufacturing engineer of the department. The three styles are similar in size and shape and contrast only in material and price.

Style #	Unit Price	Discount Price (over 100)
711E-BH	**$30.00**	**$23.00**
511E-BH	$31.00	$25.00
512E-BH	$32.00	$25.00

The assemblers on the line preferred cutter style 711E-BH for its comfort, versatility, and durability. They also found that the cutter reduced their operator fatigue, which is a factor in our processes.

(c) In a small group, choose people to role-play the responses of the recipients to the memos. Discuss your decisions as a group.

8. **Write for three audiences.** Write three separate paragraphs about the same subject for three different audiences.

Example: If you are writing about treating runners' knee injuries, you could write for any of these audiences. Each reader would be interested in some aspect of treating knee injuries, but the focus, as well as the amount and kind of detail would differ.

EMT (emergency medical technician)	sports physician
coach	physical therapist
athlete	therapy equipment manufacturer
athletic trainer	running shoe designer

Be sure to make appropriate adjustments in content focus and complexity, clarity, diction, sentence structure, and organization. Label each paragraph to indicate the intended audience. Consider one of the following suggested topics, or select your own:

architecture for Web site	hybrid seed development
artificial insemination	laser optics
cable TV operation	manufacture of plastic film
capability of computer software	new treatment for cavities
conformation of show animal	operation of microwave oven
construction of road bed	propagation of house plants
development of photographic film	safety standards in paint shop
effects of aerobic exercise	setting a fractured bone
effects of cigarette smoking	shifting sand barriers
fetal alcohol syndrome	treatment for hangovers
gene splicing	weather tracking

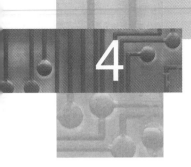

4

Reading Technical Documents

Identifying Purposes

Workplace professionals read for a variety of purposes, which usually fall into one or more of these categories:

1. To assess

2. To learn

3. To learn to do

4. To do

Reading–Writing Relationships

Thinking about how your documents will be read helps you both as a writer and as a reader.

Strategies for Effective Reading

Four factors affect online reading: screen and page size, legibility, responsiveness, and tangibility. These factors influence formatting, proofreading, reorganizing, and sense of place in the text.

Experienced readers adapt the following strategies in their reading.

1. Identify structure: visual cues, previews, and reviews.

2. Distinguish main points.

3. Draw inferences: tacit assumptions, implications, ethics, and impact of implications.

4. Generate questions about knowledge, comprehension, application, analysis, synthesis, and evaluation.

5. Monitor and adapt strategies before, during, and after reading.

**W**hat is reading? Some people think of reading as simply looking at words and decoding them—that is, figuring out their pronunciation and definitions. However, experts in reading consider reading a complex activity and believe that making meaning involves interpreting ideas rather than decoding words. Meaning comes from more than the words on a page because interpretation is strongly influenced by that individual's prior experiences and knowledge as well as by the context in which the document is written and read. As a result, the same document can be interpreted in different ways by different readers.

Throughout your professional life, you'll read and respond to a variety of documents. Some of these documents will require very little effort or attention; others will be exceedingly difficult to understand. This chapter suggests ways to make all of your reading easier and more productive. Your workplace literacy— that is, your ability to read and create paper and electronic documents—will influence your professional success.

The chapter begins by summarizing reasons that workplace professionals might have for reading and then discusses the strong relationship between reading and writing, both on paper and computers. Most of the chapter is devoted to discussing strategies used by effective readers.

Identifying Purposes

As a workplace professional, you'll read for a variety of purposes. Virtually all of these workplace purposes can be categorized into one of four often overlapping categories—reading to assess, reading to learn, reading to learn to do, and reading to do—as shown in Figure 4.1.[1]

Regardless of their purpose for reading, workplace professionals expect information in documents to be accurate and accessible. Information is usually more accessible if a document has a clear purpose, well-organized and appropriately developed points, and an effective balance of verbal and visual information.

A document—say, a technical report—will probably be read for a number of purposes, depending on the reader's needs in a particular context. For example, an engineer might read an interim project report for any of the four purposes described in Figure 4.1. She might skim to *assess* whether she should read the report thoroughly later; she might read to *learn* how well a modification she designed for the production line was working; she might read to *learn to do* the

What purposes for reading are you likely to have in your professional work? How will strategies differ for each purpose?

FIGURE 4.1 ■ Purposes for Reading

Purpose	Examples
Reading to assess. This reading—often skimming—enables you to decide whether a document will be useful for you or someone else, usually at a later time.	A forester might skim summaries of legislation about support for reforestation that he or someone else in his Department of Natural Resources office might need to study.
Reading to learn. This reading enables you to learn information for problem solving, decision making, and background knowledge.	A small-animal veterinarian might read an article in a professional journal to learn about new medication for feline colitis.
Reading to learn to do. This reading enables you to learn how to complete tasks.	A dental assistant might read a continuing education booklet about ways to minimize pain and anxiety for pediatric patients.
Reading to do. This reading—which serves largely as an external prompt—enables you to complete tasks.	A furniture refinisher might read the product label and information sheet to determine safety requirements for using a new paint remover.

calibration of the new furnace controls; she might read to *do* a procedure for mechanical inspection that is outlined in the report.

Reading–Writing Relationships

Your reading and writing are closely related, whether you're working on a document that you read and write on paper or on a computer monitor. Consider these typical examples:

- A shipping manager writes instructions for sending products overseas; she rereads these instructions as she revises them following user testing. Later, her revised instructions are read by shipping clerks preparing an order.

- A greenhouse worker reads the package insert that came with a pesticide, specifically studying the section about application. Later he records changes in greenhouse plants treated with this pesticide.

What kinds of documents are you likely to read electronically? What complicating factors of reading electronically are likely to be the most problematic for readers?

- A heating contractor reads the troubleshooting section of the manual for a new computer-controlled thermostat that is not working properly. Later she completes a form to return the defective computer-controlled thermostat to the manufacturer.

- A hospice nurse makes notes about a patient's weekly medication; he rereads these notes as he writes a recommendation for modifying the patient's care. Later, the patient's doctor reads the recommendation in order to make a decision about patient care.

FIGURE 4.2 ■ Predict Readers' Questions[2]

Since 1986, all irradiated products must carry the international symbol called a radura, which resembles a stylized flower.

What is a radura?

What are the legal requirements of using a radura?

What is the history of using the radura?

What protection does the use of the radura provide consumers?

As a writer, imagine yourself as a member of your intended audience and then try to read the document you're preparing from one of the reader's perspectives. For example, if you are working on a food safety Web site that is discussing food irradiation, you should try to anticipate reader questions. One of the symbols that would appear on this site is the radura, an international symbol identifying foods that have been irradiated. You realize that some readers will not recognize the radura; thus, it needs to be defined. Other readers will recognize the symbol, but they do not necessarily know its purpose. The marginal questions next to Figure 4.2 show some of those questions readers might have about the radura.

As a reader, you need to be conscious of a text's features. On a Web site, this means recognizing the links that you can follow to obtain necessary information. As an active reader, you ask yourself questions—ones that you hope the text answers. Of course, the questions you have are not necessarily the ones that other readers will have. Readers using a Web site, like the excerpt in Figure 4.2, will construct different meanings, depending on which links they choose to follow; thus, the same Web site—or print document—can be interpreted in different ways by different readers.

Strategies for Effective Reading

How do people read technical documents on the job? You may think of reading as simply looking at a page with words, decoding what they mean, and stringing them together so they mean the same thing the writer intended. But the process of reading is not so simple. Reading researchers know that reading is remarkably complex and has less to do with decoding the meanings of words than with the way readers interpret those meanings in particular situations. How well people read has a great deal to do both with their *prior knowledge* and with their *reading strategies.*

Experienced readers tend to see technical documents and the situation they're part of as a whole—that is, the documents cannot be separated from the situations in which they're created and used. Both the documents and the situations have recurring, evolving patterns that are familiar to experienced readers. These familiar patterns help experienced readers select and adapt appropriate strategies to read documents—both print and electronic. This chapter is largely about these strategies. Figure 4.3 identifies five of the strategies used by experienced readers for increased comprehension and then explains how you can also use your knowledge of these strategies to improve your writing.

What are your strongest strategies as a reader?

Reading on the Web is different from reading on paper because it involves an interface—that is, reading on the Web is not simply an electronic display of information; instead, it is interactive and brings with it a number of complications. Researcher Christina Haas at Kent State University[4] and Karen McGrane Chauss at Rensselaer Polytechnic Institute[5] have identified factors that are particularly important in online reading:

Which features of electronic text do you find most influential in reducing your comprehension and/or speed in reading?

- **Screen and page size.** How much text can a reader see at one time? Larger screens (and larger windows on those screens) enable readers to see more. But even with large screens, readers sometimes have difficulty because reading on a computer monitor reduces their awareness of where they are in relation to the whole document.

- **Legibility.** How easy is it to read what's on the screen? Factors such as screen flicker, spacing, and background and text color affect legibility. Readers also sometimes have difficulty because visual cues such as boldface and italics may not show on the screen (as in some e-mail systems), and spacing is sometimes difficult to judge; thus, proofreading is often more difficult to do on a monitor.

- **Responsiveness.** How quickly does the system respond to readers' actions? Human factors research involving mainframe users at IBM has shown that users are most productive when the time between hitting a function key and getting the requested screen is less than a second. So far, that's not possible on the Web; ten seconds is the current standard for Web sites; longer than that and people lose attention and wander to other tasks.

- **Navigation.** How easily can readers navigate the Web site—that is, how easily can readers move through and locate places in the text? Web readers/users are influenced by images and icons that affect their ability to navigate on the Web, by color, by links and backgrounds, and, of course, by typography and layout. But even with navigational aids, it's easier to get lost in an electronic document than in a paper document.

- **Equipment and service.** How much are readers constrained by physical realities? Recent research at Georgia Tech suggests that even though fast modems and higher bandwidths are available, the modems and lines used by most people are too slow for decent Web response times.

FIGURE 4.3 ■ Reader Strategies and Text Characteristics[3]

Strategies Used by Effective Readers to Increase Comprehension and Recall	Strategies Used by Writers to Create More Effective Documents
Identify the document's structure. Readers who discern the form and structure of a document usually recognize the document's purpose and can remember more information than readers who don't discern the structure.	◆ Use the document's structure to help readers identify the purpose and anticipate how to use a document. ◆ Add headings, subheadings, and other visual cues to help readers distinguish and recall the hierarchy of ideas. ◆ Include previewing segments and summaries to reinforce a document's structure or organization.
Distinguish main points. Readers who distinguish main ideas from subordinate and supporting ideas usually have greater recall of important information. Skillful readers often make mental gists and summaries based on their interpretation of a document's verbal and visual cues and then they synthesize those ideas.	◆ Select sentence structures, coherence devices, and other textual cues to help readers distinguish main ideas from subordinate and supporting ideas.
Draw inferences. Readers who draw inferences based on a combination of prior knowledge and the information in a document usually have increased understanding and recall of information. Skillful readers often extend ideas in the document by imagining situations in which these ideas might be used.	◆ Present necessary and expected information so readers have a basis for decision making. Anticipate what readers might want to know that's *not* in the document.
Generate questions. Readers who ask themselves questions about their reading generally have a better comprehension of the information. Skillful readers often interrogate the text by thinking of examples and counterexamples that support or contradict what's in a document and what they know from their own experience.	◆ Encourage readers to ask questions to increase their comprehension and recall of information and then to apply, analyze, synthesize, and evaluate that information.
Monitor and adapt your own reading strategies. Readers who monitor their own reading process use their self-reflective feedback to adjust their strategies to get the most out of a document. They're aware of their own comprehension and adjust their strategies when comprehension is low.	◆ Use *visuals cues* (such as boldfacing, italics, and marginal annotations), *text support* (such as glossaries and checklists), and *reader appeals* (such as narratives, examples, and details) to increase reader comprehension and engagement.

Identify Structure

Many technical documents have a clear and identifiable structure that includes using conventional document features, using headings and other visual cues, and previewing what's upcoming in the document.

Document Features.   The standard features of a document can help readers know what to anticipate. For example, the features of abstracts—often described as the most important part of a technical report—are influenced by the purpose: to provide an overview of a report.

Well-written abstracts maintain the tone and focus of the original document, presenting key points. The *Journal of the American Medical Association* (*JAMA*) recommends that articles about a clinical investigation be accompanied by an abstract with these features:

> . . . *the objective(s) or purpose, the design (e.g., randomized, double-blind, placebo-controlled, multicenter trial), the setting (e.g., university clinic, hospital), the patients or participants, the intervention(s), the measurements and main results, . . . the conclusion . . . ; [and] important outcome measures or endpoints.*

JAMA recommends that review articles intended to "identify, assess, and synthesize" information be accompanied by an abstract that contains these features:

> . . . *purpose, data identification (a summary of data sources), study selection (how many studies were chosen and how they were selected), data extraction (guidelines for abstracting articles), results of data synthesis, and conclusions (which should include potential applications and research needs).*[6]

You are likely to read abstracts more quickly and with greater comprehension if you anticipate their features (this is also true of other kinds of documents you read). The example in Figure 4.4 provides a useful approach to help you anticipate and locate four kinds of information that often appears in abstracts:

- purpose or rationale of study

- methodology

- results

- conclusions

The example in Figure 4.4 is an abstract from *Science*, a professional journal for experts interested in a wide range of scientific research, including work in both natural and physical sciences. The abstract accompanied an article written by researchers in environmental studies who were interested in finding ways to monitor pollution. In the style of *Science*, the original abstract was set in italics to distinguish it from the main text of the article. Most readers would have an easy time identifying the features of the abstract.

Whenever you are reading, you can make good use of your time by knowing the features of that particular type of document. Just as abstracts have predictable features, so do the other documents you'll read. Recognizing and then anticipating the features and their organization will help you read efficiently.

FIGURE 4.4 ■ Abstract from *Science* with Features that Readers Should Anticipate[7]

1. *Purpose of study:* Determine if honey bees are effective biological monitors of environmental contaminants.

2. *Methodology:* Collect pollen and bees for chemical analysis.

POLLUTION MONITORING OF PUGET SOUND WITH HONEY BEES

Abstract. To show that honey bees are effective biological monitors of environmental contaminants over large geographic areas, beekeepers of Puget Sound, Washington, collected pollen and bees for chemical analysis. From these data, kriging maps of arsenic, cadmium, and fluoride were generated. Results, based on actual concentrations of contaminants in bee tissues, show that the greatest concentrations of contaminants occur close to Commencement Bay and that honey bees are effective as large-scale monitors.

3. *Results:* Kriging maps show concentrations of arsenic, cadmium, and fluoride based on concentrations of contaminants in bee tissue.

4. *Conclusions:* (a) Greatest concentrations of contaminants occur close to Commencement Bay; (b) honey bees are effective as large-scale monitors.

Visual Cues.   Various kind of visual cues help readers distinguish the hierarchy of ideas in a document. Typically, readers have an easier time with documents that have the following features:

- Information is *chunked* so that relationships are clear. How can you chunk information?
  - ◇ Add headings and subheadings to signal and separate topics.
  - ◇ Adjust leading (spacing) between lines and sections to group related information.
  - ◇ Indent to indicate subordinate ideas.

- Information is *arranged* so that the sequence is clear. How can you arrange information?
  - ◇ For ideas in a paragraph, make sure the logic is clear and then use transitions that indicate the relationship of the points you're making.
  - ◇ For items in a list, use numbers, letters, or bullets to signal the sequence.

- Information is *emphasized* so that important elements are signaled. How can you emphasize information?
  - ◇ Vary typeface and size to differentiate headings and text.
  - ◇ Use type-style variations—for example, SMALL CAPS, **bold,** or *italics*—to draw readers' attention to important terms or ideas.
  - ◇ Use icons to signal important categories.

Readers use visual cues to help them decide what's important in a document, but careful writers use such cues judiciously—that is, they don't overdo their use because when too many cues are used, they lose their effectiveness.

FIGURE 4.5 ■ Table of Contents Showing Structure[8]

TECH BRIEFS

March 2000 • Vol. 24 No. 3

ENGINEERING SOLUTIONS FOR DESIGN & MANUFACTURING

FEATURES

24 InReview
28 Application Briefs
32 Mass 3D: From Design, to Manufacturing, to Supply Chain

BRIEFS

42

80

84

34 **Special Coverage: CAD/CAE/CAM**
34 Computer Code Generates Two-Dimensional Unstructured Grids
36 Designing Composite Repairs and Retrofits for Infrastructure
38 A Method for Designing Low-Pass FIR Digital Filters
41 Software for Predicting Life of Metal-Matrix Composites

44 **Electronic Components and Systems**
44 Security System Based on Bragg Gratings in an Optical Fiber
46 Higher-Resolution Optoelectronic Shaft-Angle Encoder
48 High-Power Laser Illuminator
49 Communication Controller Board for a Wind-Tunnel Model

52 **Software**
52 Software for Simulating Progressive Fracture in Braided PMCs

54 **Materials**
54 Molecular-Sieve Type 3Å
56 Composite Graphite Anodes Containing Cyclic Ether Additives
57 Polypyrrole and Polyaniline Doped With Lignosulfonic Acid

58 **Mechanics**
58 Leak-Free Pressurizing Valve
60 Afterbody Cushions for Instrumented Penetrator Projectiles
62 Ultrasonic Measurement of Bending of Bolts

64 **Manufacturing/Fabrication**
64 Improvements in Rapid Prototyping

66 **Physical Sciences**
66 Efficient Ionizer for an Array of Mass Spectrometers
67 Analyzing Rocket Exhaust by Atomic-Absorption Spectroscopy
68 Adjustable Optics for Spectral Analysis of Rocket Exhaust
69 Thickness-Independent Ultrasonic Characterization of Tubes
71 Detecting Metal Ions by Voltammetry Using Diamond Electrodes

DEPARTMENTS

14 **Commercial Technology Team**
16 **UpFront**
20 **Reader Forum**
22 **This Month in RPD Online**
26 **Who's Who at NASA**
30 **Commercialization Opportunities**
42 **Special Coverage Products: CAD/CAE/CAM**
80 **Special Coverage Products: Industrial Automation**
84 **New on the Market**
86 **New on Disk**
87 **New Literature**
87 **Editorial Index**
88 **Advertisers Index**

SPECIAL SUPPLEMENT

1a - 32a
Photonics Tech Briefs

Follows page 16 in selected editions only.

6   www.nasatech.com   NASA Tech Briefs, March 2000

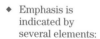

♦ Chunking *is signaled by increased spacing between sections of related information.*

♦ Arrangement is clear because of page numbers.

♦ Emphasis is indicated by several elements:
   ◇ Font size and style—*large, boldface font for the major sections; small, plain font for the individual articles*
   ◇ Icons—*familiar to the audience and in a contrasting color to signal important categories*

A well-designed table of contents demonstrates how these visual cues can be used. (See Chapter 8 for additional discussion about visual cues to help design information.) The table of contents in Figure 4.5, from *NASA Tech Briefs*, gives readers multiple visual cues about chunking, arrangement, and emphasis. The annotations identify cues you might use in documents that you design.

Previews and Reviews.   Preview and reviewing reinforce the structure or organization of a document. Helping readers identify the structure of a document increases the likelihood that they will understand and recall the information. Visual and verbal cues—numbered or bulleted lists, parallel terms, design and typography—signal readers as to the relative relationship among the terms. To reduce the chance of misinterpretation, the language in the preview should match the language used later in the document.

Figure 4.6 is the first half of a page from a manual for farmers, *How to Grow Shiitake Mushrooms Outdoors on Natural Logs*. In this preview, readers are signaled about the purpose of the section: "Let's quickly preview the factors to

FIGURE 4.6 ■ Previewed Information[9]

Readers are clearly signaled about the purpose of this section.

The five critical factors are previewed.

Visual cues help readers:
- *numbered list with hanging indents*
- *boldface terms*
- *factors set off by colon from comment about each factor*

The language of the first item in the preview anticipates the language of the first heading.

PART 2. BEDLOGS: SELECTING, CUTTING, & GROWING

If you want to grow a few shiitake *noncommercially,* all you really need to know about choosing bedlogs is to get fresh, healthy logs, of the proper size and species, that were cut in late winter. However, if you have a *commercial* interest, there's a lot more worth learning about bedlog selection. Let's quickly preview the factors to consider. Then, we'll take a close look at each of them.

BEDLOG CONSIDERATIONS
1. **Tree Selection:** You must decide which tree species to use and how to select the best individual trees to fell.
2. **Bedlog Selection:** You must know how to cut suitable logs from the trees felled.
3. **Season of Felling:** The trees must be felled at the right time of year.
4. **Bedlog Handling:** Harvested bedlogs must be carefully handled and properly stored until they are inoculated.
5. **Bedlog Silviculture:** If you plan to have an ongoing operation, you probably need to carry out some woodland management practices to ensure a future supply of bedlogs. Or, if you plan to buy logs, you have to find a logger who is willing to meet your specifications.

What Tree Species Should be Selected?

. . .

consider. Then we'll take a close look at each of them." Readers are introduced to the five critical factors that are distinguished by a series of visual cues:

- ALL CAP section heading (acceptable for these very short phrases)

- numbered list with hanging indents

- boldface terms

- a colon separating each factor from the comment

The language of the first item in the preview (Tree Selection) anticipates the language of the first subheading (What Tree Species Should be Selected?). Similar repetition is used throughout the section so that the language of the preview matches the language in the subheadings and the text itself. Knowing what to anticipate helps readers call on their relevant prior knowledge and begin to organize what they'll be reading.

Distinguish Main Points

Distinguishing between the main points and the subordinate points helps readers understand the relationships among ideas in a document. Sometimes the main points are easy to distinguish because the writer uses typographic cues. For example if you look again at Figure 4.6, you'll see that in the first paragraph the writer has italicized the terms *noncommercial* and *commercial,* so readers immediately know that this distinction matters.

Sometimes, though, the main points are more difficult to identify, and you must be able to generate a series of questions to help you identify them. The example in Figure 4.7 is an informative abstract for a technical report about a component failure in a computer system. People who need an informative abstract want a clear, straightforward presentation that answers their questions about the subject.

Experienced readers of this kind of document might begin by asking—and expecting their reading to answer—questions such as these:

- What is the issue or problem?

- Who and what are involved in the issue or problem?

- What is the approach to the solution to the problem?

- How will the approach be addressed or the solution be implemented?

Answers to these questions help you identify the main points of virtually any abstract or technical report.

Draw Inferences

Not everything that readers learn from a text is explicitly stated. Sometimes readers draw inferences: They make connections and draw conclusions beyond

Abstract

The XC-2000 display has a serious problem—a 20 percent field failure rate since July—that has resulted in a shipping delay. The failure is caused when the display's 4305 driver components short internally, producing smoke that concerned customers.

Failure evaluations of both the 4305 driver and the 4503 receiver have been conducted by Design Component Engineering. The evaluations included pin-to-pin electrical testing, external and internal visual inspection, and failure-mode duplication testing in and out of the application. The cause of failure is a 10,000-volt transient on the 12-volt supply (pin 8) of the 4305, and a similar transient on the input (pin 5) of the 4503 receiver.

Investigation confirms that the damage occurs in transit, between final system test and delivery to the customer site. Because of the difficulty encountered in locating the exact cause of the transient damage, efforts have been channeled toward protecting the parts rather than removing the cause.

XC-2000 display driver/receiver boards were tested with several bypass protection techniques. The most effective and economical protection is the placement of two 1N7211 zener diodes across selected pins on the J1 and J4 connectors. Three hundred reworked units have been shipped through normal methods and have arrived in working order at the customer sites. Therefore, a corrective action has been identified and should be used on all future production of the XC-2000.

What is the issue or problem?
The main point is signaled by the language ("a serious problem") as well as the punctuation (an explanation offset by dashes). The cause of the problem is clearly indicated.

Who and what are involved in the issue or problem?
The who and what are clearly identified.

What is the approach to the solution to the problem?
The rationale for the solution is placed in a subordinate clause: "Because of the difficulty . . ."; the solution itself is presented in the main clause.

How will the approach be addressed or solution be implemented?
Critical information is signaled by the word choice: "The most effective and economical protection . . . ."

The corrective action is encouraged.

the words and visuals that are presented. For example, if you look again at Figure 4.7, you can draw some inferences. Although the second sentence of this abstract is not at all alarmist, you can infer that smoke coming from a new computer drive might have "concerned customers" a great deal—perhaps, in fact, enough to speed up the failure evaluations. Because the damage occurred during the transportation of the system (paragraph 3), you might also infer that a great deal of discussion occurred with the shipping department, the shipping company, and the insurance company dealing with locating the cause of the damage and with terms of financial liability.

You can draw inferences from virtually any document that you read. Most experienced readers draw inferences as they read, forming and reforming their

What problems in understanding a document might occur if the writer and reader have different tacit assumptions about the subject?

opinions as they move through a document. Three specific strategies help you draw inferences:

- *Identify the tacit assumptions* on which you believe the document is based—that is, what's presumed but not articulated.

- *Extend the ideas* to pose reasonable but unstated implications—what's implied but not articulated.

- *Speculate on the impact of the implications*—what's possible but not articulated.

Drawing inferences involves identifying tacit assumptions, extending ideas, and speculating on the possible impact of what you've read—in relation to what you already know. Figure 4.8 provides an example of a reader drawing inferences while reading. The boxed section presents an excerpt from the first part of an online article about the Xanadu system, a concept for a worldwide electronic repository of documents. The comments are the questions and inferences drawn by David Clark, a cautious—perhaps even skeptical—reader who brings expertise and prior experience in a variety of fields to his reading: computer science, World Wide Web page design, literature, teaching, editing, and technical communication. As you read the figure, you can consider how David identified tacit assumptions, extended the article's ideas, and speculated on the possible impact of the ideas in the article.

Figure 4.8 shows one way readers can be engaged with a text by articulating their own reactions as they read. Readers' reactions are shaped, in part, by prior experiences and knowledge as well as by the context in which the document is written and read. The ethics sidebar on the next page explains the critical importance of context, showing how it affects interpretation and decision making.

Generate Questions

Readers can ask themselves questions that will help them understand a document. Sometimes readers benefit from using a traditional taxonomy (a formal method of classification) that increases their chances of understanding important information. One particularly well-known taxonomy uses six levels of questions:[13]

- ***Knowledge questions*** emphasize the recall of specifics amid abstractions. Such questions require recall of specialized terminology and symbols, quantifiable facts, conventions of organizing information, awareness of trends, knowledge of classification systems, evaluation criteria, methodology, principles, and theories.

- ***Comprehension questions*** require responses that incorporate knowledge as well as understanding. Responses to comprehension questions can involve translation, interpretation, or extrapolation.

- ***Application questions*** require specific applications of principles or theories.

FIGURE 4.8 ■ Drawing Inferences While Reading[11]

THE XANADU IDEAL

Theodor Holm Nelson

WHAT IS XANADU PUBLISHING?

The term *universal electronic library* has been suggested. Perhaps *universal bookstore* is more like it. World Publishing Repository™ is perhaps the most appropriate term.

The Xanadu system has been designed from the literary point of view, the computer point of view, the business point of view and the legal point of view.

The Xanadu publishing system will be a licensed method of online electronic publication provided by vendors throughout the world. "Publication" consists of placing a digital document somewhere in the repository network. A document may include text, pictures, audio, movies and any other form of digital information. Readers, or users, are of course at screens. Any user in the world may send for any document, or any part of a document. The publisher pays only for the storage; the user pays for delivery, including a royalty to the publisher. **Clark's Comment:** Nelson assumes that users can afford these costs and will want to pay for documents. Isn't this exclusionary, making it possible only for people with money to have access to this "World Publishing Repository™"? Even if the charge is only a few cents per document, it's still more expensive than local libraries.

The user obtains a digital copy of everything he or she sends for—to keep or discard. The user may point and click to travel among documents, obtaining only the small part needed to keep going. **Clark's Comment:** Nelson's assumption is that pointing and clicking are better, or more efficient, than shelf browsing at the library. How will users know which documents they want? Will they be paying for documents, whether they "keep or discard" them? If so, every click would be an investment, and this doesn't seem like an improvement over shelf browsing.

Staying within the Xanadu online world, anyone may publish a connection to a document—a comment, illustration, disagreement, or link of any other type; and anyone may quote from a published Xanadu document, since the quotation is bought from the original publisher at the time of delivery. The publisher agrees to be legally responsible for the contents and agrees to interconnection by anyone. **Clark's Comment:** Again, we see "anyone"; do "anyone's" documents cost the same as famous authors' documents? This would be an interesting democratic move, but how would readers find credible and useful information if they must slog through piles of information by people they've never heard of, whose work may well not be useful or interesting?

- *Analysis questions* emphasize the separation of objects, mechanisms, systems, organisms, operations, or ideas into constituent parts, clearly establishing the relationship between these parts.

- *Synthesis questions* expect the reader to focus on organizing or structuring the parts to form a unique whole. The response may either serve as an overall plan or explain a particular phenomenon.

"It's only a report": Ethics and Context

The following is an excerpt from a technical report:

> The van's normal load is usually nine [pieces] per square yard. In Saurer vehicles, which are very spacious, maximum use of space is impossible, not because of any possible overload, but because loading to full capacity would affect the vehicle's stability. So, reduction of the load space seems necessary. It must absolutely be reduced by a yard, instead of trying to solve the problem, as hitherto, by reducing the number of pieces loaded.[12]

Researcher Steven Katz points out that this report meets many of the formal criteria necessary for an effective document. The report addresses a concern shared by both the readers and the writer and provides answers relevant to their concerns. However, Katz also points out that we must look at this document in the context in which it was written.

This report comes from Nazi Germany in 1942. The "pieces loaded" are Jews, Poles, gypsies, and other humans who are being transported to their deaths in concentration camps.

Katz examines this report to suggest that not only the content of a document can make it unethical. How readers interpret it and use it also matters. Technical professionals must recognize the purposes behind technical documents and the effects those documents might have. Many involved in indirectly supporting the Holocaust argued that they should not be held responsible for their actions. They were "only doing their jobs." Most scholars believe that we cannot accept this argument. When individuals are not held accountable for the contexts in which they perform their jobs, when they are not held responsible for interpreting and implementing ideas, then atrocities like the Holocaust continue.

How can you make sure you don't lose sight of the context for a document you are writing?

The context in which technical professionals work is not as horrific as the Holocaust of World War II. Even so, technical documents affect readers. We must be aware of those effects and be willing to examine their ethical consequences. As you write, ask yourself: Do I know who is affected by this document? Am I willing to be responsible for those effects? Perhaps, if the writer of the 1942 report had asked himself this question, such documents would not exist.

- **Evaluation questions** require readers to judge something's qualitative and quantitative value. Such questions examine internal elements for logic and consistency as well as external comparisons to establish the relationship of the subject with accepted principles, theories, and works of recognized excellence.

Figure 4.9 presents "Slowing the Progress of Aortic Regurgitation," reprinted from the *Harvard Heart Letter*, a monthly newsletter written to interpret complex medical information for general readers interested in heart-related medical issues. In addition, Figure 4.9 presents questions—based on the taxonomy—that a reader asked when reading this article. You can see how the reader used the taxonomy to develop questions that could help check comprehension.

Whenever you read, you should ask yourself questions about the text and the accompanying visuals. You can jot these questions in the margins of the document you're reading (if it belongs to you), or you can keep a separate pad for taking notes and recording questions.

Monitor and Adapt Reading Strategies

Effective readers are aware of what they're doing. They're actively engaged in their reading; they're aware of their comprehension of concepts and terms. When their comprehension or speed decreases, they can adjust their strategies to meet the needs of the situation.

Your goal is to develop effective reading strategies for yourself. Effective readers usually consider certain questions before, during, and after reading.

Before Reading
- What prereading strategies are helpful?
- What's your purpose(s) for reading a particular document?
- What's likely to be difficult about the document?

During Reading
- How will you reduce (or prevent) distractions or interruptions during reading?
- How will you annotate your reading?
- How will you ask and record your questions about the reading?
- How will you make meaning from your reading?

After Reading
- What is the most productive way to respond to the document?

Figure 4.10 gives you practical approaches for addressing each of these questions as you try to understand the visual and verbal information in technical documents. Although the list of questions seems long, after you use it for a while, asking these questions and handling the reading this way will become second nature. Like other effective readers, you'll learn what you need to do so that your reading is productive.

Monitoring your reading process may feel uncomfortable at first, but like reflecting on your writing processes as you plan, draft, and revise documents, this monitoring will soon become second nature to you. As with writing, one of the things that distinguishes experienced readers is their ability to adjust strategies to match the situation they're in.

To demonstrate the differences that may occur with readers of the same text, you'll have a chance to "listen in" on two different professionals as they read the opening three paragraphs from an article in *Scientific American*, "Smart Rooms." The article is about the potential benefits of a project at MIT to create computer systems that recognize human faces, expressions, and gestures. Two expert

FIGURE 4.9 ■ **Applying Taxonomy of Questions to Reading**

SLOWING THE PROGRESS OF AORTIC REGURGITATION[14]

A leaky aortic valve allows blood that has just been pumped out of the heart and into the aorta—the large blood vessel that distributes blood to the body—to flow backwards, or regurgitate, into the left ventricle. This problem, which is also known as aortic regurgitation or aortic insufficiency, forces the left ventricle to do extra work, since this blood must be pumped out a second time. Only by doing this additional work can the heart sustain a normal flow of blood to the body.

Over time, this added burden can take a toll on the heart. The left ventricle enlarges to accommodate the blood flowing back into it from the aorta and works less efficiently when its architecture becomes distorted. Eventually, some people with aortic regurgitation develop congestive heart failure, which may not be reversible even if the valve is replaced surgically. In heart failure, the heart is unable to pump enough blood to maintain normal circulation; the result is a buildup of fluid in the body.

Until recently, aortic-valve surgery was the only way to stop this process. Although the surgery is usually successful, the patient must live thereafter with the problems associated with an artificial valve. However, scientists have been searching for a medication that might decrease the damage from aortic regurgitation and thereby delay or eliminate the need for surgery. A recent randomized trial reports the first long-term positive results of such drug therapy.

A NEW ROLE FOR NIFEDIPINE

The drug used in this study was nifedipine—a medication that is used most commonly to treat high blood pressure and angina (the chest pain or discomfort that occurs when the heart muscle is not getting enough blood from the coronary arteries). Nifedipine (Procardia, Adalat) is a calcium-channel-blocking agent, which causes muscle cells to relax by blocking the movement of calcium across cell membranes. This medication is believed to help people with coronary artery disease, in part by dilating the coronary arteries and preventing spasm of these blood vessels. It also lowers blood pressure by dilating arteries in the rest of the body.

These "vasodilator" effects of nifedipine are believed to be the beneficial mechanism for patients with aortic regurgitation. The dilated arteries and the lowered blood pressure decrease the force that "pushes" blood back through the leaky aortic valve. Since less blood flows the wrong way, the strain on the left ventricle decreases.

Two relatively short-term studies previously showed that nifedipine and another vasodilator, hydralazine, might have a beneficial effect on the heart's function, but whether these drugs could actually prevent the need for surgery remained uncertain. Therefore, a team of researchers from Padua, Italy, designed a long-term study to test this idea (*New England Journal of Medicine*, 494, pp. 689–694).

BEFORE SYMPTOMS BEGIN

All 143 people who were enrolled in this study had severe aortic regurgitation, which was documented by echocardiography, an examination that uses sound waves to produce a video of the beating heart (see August 493 *Harvard Heart Letter*). None of the patients started with symptoms or evidence of damage to the left ventricle. About half were assigned to receive daily digoxin (0.25 mg) to increase the strength of the heart's contractions; the rest took nifedipine (20 mg) twice a day.

Comprehension question: How does the extra work the heart must do because of aortic regurgitation lead to an irreversible problem?

Knowledge question: What side effects might be caused by taking nifedipine?

Application question: How does a vasodilator such as nifedipine delay the need for surgery?

Analysis question: How does nifedipine treat the symptoms of high blood pressure and angina?

FIGURE 4.9 ■ Applying Taxonomy of Questions to Reading (continued)

Over the next six years, the patients who received nifedipine were about half as likely to need an aortic-valve replacement as those who took digoxin. During the first two years, there were no valve replacements in the nifedipine group versus about 10% of those who took digoxin. At the end of six years, 34% of the patients who took digoxin had undergone valve replacement compared with only 15% of those assigned to nifedipine. The decision to perform surgery was made according to specific criteria, so it is unlikely that knowledge of which drug the patient was taking influenced the rate of valve replacements.

Nifedipine's benefits were not without a price. At least one new mild symptom was reported during the first three months by 42% of the patients who took nifedipine versus 12% of those who used digoxin. The most common side effects were a sensation of a rapid heart beat and headache among those who used nifedipine, and fatigue among those who used digoxin. At six years of follow-up, some side effects were still reported by 5% of those who used nifedipine, but no patient in this study discontinued medication because of complications.

Synthesis question: How does the use of a drug such as nifedipine contribute to the treatment of cardiac patients?

ENCOURAGING DATA

This encouraging study suggests that the course of aortic regurgitation can be altered and that nifedipine can delay the need for surgery if given early enough in the course of this disease. Whether other vasodilators can reduce the need for surgery is unknown; in theory, other drugs could be as effective, but none have been studied as comprehensively as nifedipine.

Vasodilator therapy is not a replacement for surgery. If medical therapy with a vasodilator is unsuccessful, patients and their physicians should not continue to rely on that treatment. If the left ventricle is substantially dilated or damaged, patients should have surgery before the problem becomes so severe that even replacing the valve cannot restore normal function. Nevertheless, this study represents wonderful news to many of those with aortic regurgitation. People who have this condition should consult with their physician to determine whether the findings from this investigation are relevant to them.

Evaluation question: In what ways does research into the use of vaso-dilators appear to be promising?

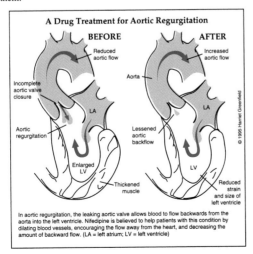

A Drug Treatment for Aortic Regurgitation

In aortic regurgitation, the leaking aortic valve allows blood to flow backwards from the aorta into the left ventricle. Nifedipine is believed to help patients with this condition by dilating blood vessels, encouraging the flow away from the heart, and decreasing the amount of backward flow. (LA = left atrium; LV = left ventricle)

FIGURE 4.10 ■ Practical Approaches for Reading Technical Documents

Before Reading

What prereading strategies are helpful?

- Skim and preview the title, abstract, headings, and summary.

- Mentally review what you already know about the subject.

- Note and check meanings of unfamiliar terms that catch your eye.

- Check the works cited or bibliography of the document to review the sources the writer used.

- Decide what's potentially relevant about the document.

What's your purpose(s) for reading a particular document?

- Determine your purpose for reading a particular document: reading to assess? reading to learn? reading to learn to do? reading to do?

What's likely to be difficult about a particular document?

- Anticipate possible problems: an unfamiliar genre? a new topic? limited time to read? difficult concepts? no supporting examples? limited or inadequate visuals? poor document design?

During Reading

How will you reduce (or prevent) distractions or interruptions during your reading?

- Given the difficulty and importance of the document, estimate the amount of time you'll need and set other work aside for that time.

- Work in an isolated area, wear headphones, or post a DO NOT DISTURB sign.

How will you annotate your reading?

- Determine the approach you'll use for annotating important information: take marginal notes? highlight important phrases? make an outline? create diagrams or charts?

How will you ask and record your questions about the reading?

- Determine the kinds of questions you should ask: knowledge, comprehension, application, analysis, synthesis, and/or evaluation questions.

- Decide how you'll record these questions: on a note pad? in the margins? in a computer file?

How will you make meaning from your reading?

- Determine the possible meanings of what you've read.

- Identify possible alternative interpretations.

After Reading

What is the most productive way to respond to the document?

- Decide what information belongs chunked together. Consider relationships among ideas.

- Identify the writer's key point(s). Identify the support for these points. Decide whether you agree with the writer.

- Consider how information adds to your knowledge or influences your position about the topic.

- Decide the most effective way to increase your recall of the information in the document: summarize the key ideas? reorder the information? write reactions and responses?

readers were asked to read these paragraphs and to "interrogate" the article—
to record the questions and comments they had while reading.

- Figure 4.11 presents the introductory paragraphs that embed the questions and comments made by Clay, who has a computer science degree. Clay read the article as preliminary background for work he was doing about the computer–human interface.

- Figure 4.12 presents the introductory paragraphs that embed the questions and comments made by Susan, who has a degree in journalism. Susan read the article to learn more about the interaction that takes place in smart rooms for a feature article she was writing for a local newspaper.

Can identical paragraphs mean different things to different readers? The questions posed by Clay and Susan show that from the very beginning they had different reactions. While their general purpose was the same (to learn), their specific purposes were quite different. Clay was interested in the technical interface and Susan in the human interaction and application. The meaning of a document is shaped by the reading process and interpretation brought to the document by the readers. As you'll see in Figures 4.11 and 4.12, the opening paragraphs of this *Scientific American* article sometimes provoked similar comments and questions from Clay and Susan.[15] At other times, though, their interpretations were startlingly different. The following list highlights some of their similarities and differences:

- Both remark that the term *smart room* sounds familiar. Both make connections to their prior knowledge, Clay mentioning a journal he reads and Susan drawing on her prior knowledge.

- Both are curious about who wrote the article. Susan immediately searches through the article until she finds the author's bio at the end. The information in this bio shapes Susan's reading, since she wonders whether the listed sponsors might influence the nature of the article.

- Clay and Susan both start eagerly, but they read the article in different sequences. Clay starts at the beginning and reads straight through the first three paragraphs, referring to photographs as he needs them. Susan reads the title, teaser, and author's name; then she searches for biographical information. Before moving back to the beginning of the article, she reads one of the article's sidebars, looks at a couple of the color photos in the article, and reads their captions.

- Clay and Susan both draw frequently on their prior knowledge, which shapes their reading. But their prior knowledge is remarkably different. Clay talks about UNIX-based systems, Silicon Graphic terminals, and limitations of VR goggles. Susan talks about the value of imperative mood, balanced examples, and personal anecdotes as well as ways to make information relevant to general readers.

SMART ROOMS

Smart rooms. I heard about these in a *Communications of the ACM* a few years ago. The picture looks interesting. [Clay reads the caption.] Okay, it's a giant screen and the user appears on it, sort of like a shadow projected on the wall, only more colorful. It's not 3D. How is it better?

[article's teaser] In creating computer systems that can identify people and interpret their actions, researchers have come one step closer to building helpful home and work environments.

Not sure if I buy this. What do they mean by "interpret actions"? Physical actions, maybe—that's what the picture looks like. It reminds me of the haunted house ride in Disneyland; there's one point at which you pass a mirror and see ghosts sitting beside you in the reflection. You turn around and they're not there. Same with this screen.

by Alex P. Pentland

Who is this guy? Guess I'll find out.

Imagine a house that always knows where your kids are and tells you if they are getting into trouble. Doesn't look like it'll be purely you facing the screen, then. I wonder how they're managing that? Cameras? How are they rendering the people they monitor— C++ objects? Shades of Big Brother here. Or an office that sees when you are having an important meeting and shields you from interruptions.

Artificial intelligence—this isn't strictly graphical interface. Or a car that senses when you are tired and warns you to pull over. How? Scientists have long tried to design computer systems that could accomplish such feats. Examples? What research was this built from? Despite their efforts, modern machines are still no match for babysitters or secretaries. But they could be.

The problem, in my opinion, is that our current computers are both deaf and blind; they experience the world only by way of a keyboard and a mouse. And that's the way some of us like them. Even multimedia machines, those that handle audiovisual signals as well as text, simply transport strings of data. So this probably won't be referring to a UNIX-based system, since UNIX relies on data strings. Probably an object-oriented operating system. I see that the diagram has what looks like a Macintosh in it. Is this technology Mac-based? No, the next page shows someone rendering his face on a Silicon Graphics terminal, thank God. [Clay skims the article looking for a mention of

■ Clay and Susan form different views of the author. When Clay reads about software developed by the author and another programmer, he talks about the author's credibility going up: "This isn't a journalist trying to interpret hardware or software.] Here's a piece of software called Pfinder—apparently the writer and another programmer developed it. Well, the writer's credibility just went up: this isn't a journalist trying to interpret an expert's words, but someone who knows what he's talking about! But he doesn't want to tell us what OS he's using. Perhaps Pfinder IS the OS.

They do not understand the meanings behind the characters, sounds, and pictures they convey. I believe computers must be able to see and hear what we do before they can prove truly helpful. So is he talking about artificial intelligence? The experts say that true AI is a long ways away. Or is he speaking metaphorically?

What's more, they must be able to recognize who we are and, as much as another person or even a dog would, make sense of what we are thinking. Yep, that's AI all right, or an impoverished imitation of it.

To that end, my group at the Media Laboratory at the Massachusetts Institute of Technology has recently developed a family of computer systems for recognizing faces, expressions, and gestures. That might be interesting. But maybe irritating. I mean, voice-activated technology at present involves having the user train herself to speak the way the computer wants her to—voice-pilots tend to sound pretty stilted when talking to the computer. Are we going to have to exaggerate our expressions to operate the software now? I don't like the idea of taking mime lessons just to get to my files. And different cultures use different expressions to express their emotions; would we have to have a library of expressions for each culture? The technology has enabled us to build environments that behave somewhat like the house, office, and car described above. These areas, which we call smart rooms, are furnished with cameras and microphones that relay their recordings to a nearby network of computers. Sounds expensive. High-end users, office security, etc. Could lessen need for security guards. Military installations? Corporate headquarters? The computers assess what people in the smart room are saying and doing. Thanks to this connection, visitors can use their actions, voices, and expressions—instead of keyboards, sensors, or goggles—to control computer programs, browse multimedia information, or venture into realms of virtual reality. . . . Arrgh. VR. Well, I have heard that VR goggles are too limiting for real work and collaboration—where was that, *Wired?* Makes sense. Maybe this would be useful, but I'd like to see more examples. This sounds too specialized and too expensive for the sort of tasks desktop users would perform—writing code, word processing, etc.

. . .

an expert's words. . . ." Susan talks about the author's credibility having "taken a large dive" when she anticipates that he may be promoting his own work.

FIGURE 4.12 ■ **Journalist "Interrogating" a Text (Reader Comments in Green)**

SMART ROOMS

OK, this is a term I have heard before, maybe in relation to missiles and other military applications. Hmmm. Wonder what smart rooms are like. Is this a virtual reality thing? I bet the subheads will help clarify.

[article's teaser] In creating computer systems that can identify people and interpret their actions, researchers have come one step closer to building helpful home and work environments.

Oh, my. This sounds incredible. So, how will the writer "sell" this to readers? Assume that they are sympathetic, excited about this technology? Approach the subject with soft sell? Do these work environments and home environments interact? Are they separate smart rooms?

by Alex P. Pentland

Who wrote this article? [Susan searches through the article to find a bio of the author.] It's not at the bottom of the first page, which would have been more convenient; instead, it's at the end of the article next to the references. Geez. He has a Ph.D. from MIT—so, he's a technical person who writes rather than a reporter who's covering a technology beat. Awards, awards, awards. Honors, honors, honors. Oh, and he's a researcher on smart rooms. The sponsors of his research are listed; I'll be reading the article with an eye toward whether he mentions these sponsors explicitly. If so, I have to wonder about the piece.

[Susan doesn't immediately go back to the beginning of the article. Instead, she looks at the PERSON FINDER sidebar and glances from it to the four-color photo to its right.]

So, now I know how this person finder application works. Why would I want to track this? A general reader of a feature article would be asking for this kind of answer, too.

[Susan's attention is attracted to the SURPRISED caption.] The information is intriguing, but why? This looks a lot like the artists' renditions of suspects in crimes. Sort of the computerized drawings (a la Unabomber!) but these images are a comparison of "smart-room users" and the visual images of animated models. And, again, who are these smart room users?

Imagine a house that always knows where your kids are and tells you if they are getting into trouble. All right! The connection to the general reader of my feature! It's imperative mood. That's good. Those blasted question leads are deadly. Or an office that sees when you are having an important meeting and shields you from interruptions. Or a car that senses when you are tired and warns you to pull over. The three examples—

Explain why it's inaccurate to say that if a document is written clearly enough, each reader will gain the same meaning from it.

Regardless of the differences in the details of their reading, Clay and Susan both interrogate the article at about the same level of detail and for about the same amount of time, inserting occasional wry comments and regularly that nice, odd number—offering general readers different, but recognizable examples. Scientists have long tried to design computer systems that could accomplish such feats. "Feats" makes me think that this technology is a good thing. Despite their efforts, modern machines are still no match for babysitters or secretaries. Pentland is reaching for the connection with the general reader with "babysitters and secretaries." But they could be.

The problem, in my opinion, is that our current computers are both deaf and blind; they experience the world only by way of a keyboard and a mouse. This is the same sentiment of the guy who wrote *Being Digital*—that computers are great, but they can be so much greater. So much more interactive. Even multimedia machines, those that handle audiovisual signals as well as text, Good. I needed a simple definition of what "multimedia machines" are. simply transport strings of data. They do not understand the meanings behind the characters, sounds, and pictures they convey. I believe computers must be able to see and hear what we do before they can prove truly helpful. Here's the opinion, an odd addition for the reporter to put himself into the story—even for a magazine. I guess I would have expected a first-person approach to be made explicitly from the start. Beginning with a personal anecdote. What is more, they must be able to recognize who we are and, as much as another person or even a dog would, make sense of what we are thinking. But why?

To that end, my group at the Media Laboratory at the Massachusetts Institute of Technology Uh, huh, here it comes. The ad for this guy's own work. His credibility has just taken a large dive. has recently developed a family of computer systems for recognizing faces, expressions, and gestures. The technology has enabled us to build environments that behave somewhat like the house, office, and car described above. These areas, which we call smart rooms, At last, a definition of smart room. I wonder if this wouldn't have been more effectively introduced earlier. I wonder if other readers remember the smart bomb rhetoric from the Gulf War and might have more easily connected with that. Probably endangers the negative rather than the positive for this guy's research. are furnished with cameras and microphones that relay their recordings to a nearby network of computers. Nearby, where? The computers assess what people in the smart room are saying and doing. Thanks to this connection, visitors can use their actions, voices and expressions—instead of keyboards, sensors or goggles—to control computer programs, browse multimedia information or venture into realms of virtual reality. The why? is missing . . . or at least not made explicit and real and desirable for general readers. Why do we want smart rooms?

. . .

reminding themselves about their own purpose for reading. They both read critically; the meaning they create is shaped by their prior knowledge and their use of various reading strategies.

1. Consider your purposes for reading:
   - To assess
   - To learn
   - To learn to do
   - To do

2. Recognize that you regularly move back and forth between writing and reading.

3. Develop your strategies for making gists, noting important points, comparing authorities, thinking of examples, imagining applications, and synthesizing ideas.

4. Be aware of factors that influence your online reading: screen and page size, legibility, responsiveness, and tangibility.

5. Consciously practice strategies often used by effective readers:
   a. Identify structure.
       Know the structure of the genre.
       Look for visual cues.
       Use previews and reviews.
   b. Distinguish main points.
   c. Draw inferences.
       Tacit assumptions
       Implications
       Impact of implications
   d. Generate questions.
       Knowledge questions
       Comprehension questions
       Application questions
       Analysis questions
       Synthesis questions
       Evaluation questions
   e. Monitor and adapt strategies before, during, and after reading.

Individual and Collaborative Assignments

1. **Identify the purpose, methodology, result(s), and conclusion.** The example that follows is an abstract from *Medicine and Science in Sports and Exercise.* This abstract accompanied an article written by researchers from the University of California, San Diego, who are interested in the effects of late-night exercise on sleep patterns. Carefully read the abstract and identify the purpose, methodology, result(s), and conclusion.

   Is sleep disturbed by vigorous late-night exercise? This experiment examined the influence of prolonged, vigorous late-night exercise on sleep. Sixteen highly fit male cyclists completed each of two 60-h laboratory treatments involving a base-line night, an experimental treatment night, and a recovery night. In the counter-balanced order, subjects (1) cycled for 3 h at 65-75% of heart rate reserve combined with bright light exposure (3000 lux), and (2) were exposed to a 3 h pulse of bright light (3000 lux) alone. On the baseline and recovery nights, subjects maintained their usual sleep-wake schedules. On the treatment night, exercise + bright light or bright light alone were centered at 6 h before their usual wake times, followed by bedtimes 30 min after the treatments. Illumination was 3000 lux during the experimental treatments, 0 lux during the sleep periods, and 50 lux at other times. Sleep was assessed with an Actillume (Ambulatory Monitor-ing, Inc., Ardsley, NY) wrist monitor to define sleep onset latency (SOL), wakeful-ness after sleep onset (WASO), and total sleep time. Subjective assessments of SOL, WASO, and insomnia were also gathered each morning. No significant differ-ences in objective or subjective sleep variables were found between treatments. These data are inconsistent with the general opinion that vigorous exercise shortly before bedtime disturbs sleep.[16]

2. **Determine kinds of reading.** Read the following brief scenarios and determine the primary kind(s) of reading each workplace professional is doing—reading to assess, reading to learn, reading to learn to do, or reading to do:

   - Engineer reading a company newsletter to learn about what other research projects in the division have been funded
   - Agronomy technician reading product label and instruction sheet to select proportions for mixing an herbicide to apply on an experimental plot
   - Division manager reading a report about market trends in order to propose a new product line
   - Chemical technician reading product abstract to see if the report will be useful for herself and the rest of her research group to read
   - Engineer reading an operator's manual to learn to calibrate a piece of equipment

- Mechanical engineer reading product descriptions to decide which spectrometer to order for the lab
- Hospital dietician reading product labels to see if any of the goods in the supply room meet the restricted needs of a new patient
- Office supervisor reading in an operator's manual about ways to change the toner cartridge in the photocopying machine
- Lab technician reading an article from published conference proceedings to learn general background information about a process that a competing firm is using
- Equipment supervisor reading product safety sheets to learn to do the most appropriate first-aid treatment in the case of an emergency
- Maintenance team leader reading the online manual that identifies step-by-step troubleshooting procedures in order to repair a piece of equipment
- Microbiologist skimming specifications sheets to decide which air filtration systems to consider closely for a new clean room

3. **Compare differences in reading purposes.** (a) Work with a small group to obtain additional readings/interrogations of the following excerpt—three paragraphs exactly as they appeared in the *Scientific American* article (or use another text of similar interest and length). Locate two people who would be interested in reading the document but have different purposes for reading it and who would bring different backgrounds to their reading. Ask the two to read and interrogate the text. If you can, give them an online version for their interrogation. They can write their comments directly into the online text, as Clay and Susan did. If they are reading a paper version, they can record their comments on a cassette tape recorder or jot them in the margins. (b) With your group, compare the differences and speculate about the possible reasons for the differences. (c) Write a memo to the class in which you report what your group identifies as the key similarities and differences between the two readers' interpretations.

4. **Interrogate a document.** Use the World Wide Web to locate a document that addresses some controversial aspect of a subject in your professional discipline. As David Clark did with the online document in Figure 4.8, interrogate the document:
   - Identify the *tacit assumptions* on which you believe the document is based—what's presumed but not articulated?
   - *Extend the ideas* to pose reasonable but unstated implications—what's implied but not articulated?
   - Speculate on the *impact of the implication*—what's possible but not articulated?

SMART ROOMS[17]

*In creating computer systems that can identify people and interpret
their actions, researchers have come one step closer to building
helpful home and work environments.*
by Alex P. Pentland

Imagine a house that always knows where your kids are and tells you if they are getting into trouble. Or an office that sees when you are having an important meeting and shields you from interruptions. Or a car that senses when you are tired and warns you to pull over. Scientists have long tried to design computer systems that could accomplish such feats. Despite their efforts, modern machines are still no match for babysitters or secretaries. But they could be.

The problem, in my opinion, is that our current computers are both deaf and blind; they experience the world only by way of a keyboard and a mouse. Even multimedia machines, those that handle audiovisual signals as well as text, simply transport strings of data. They do not understand the meanings behind the characters, sounds, and pictures they convey. I believe computers must be able to see and hear what we do before they can prove truly helpful. What is more, they must be able to recognize who we are and, as much as another person or even a dog would, make sense of what we are thinking.

To that end, my group at the Media Laboratory at the Massachusetts Institute of Technology has recently developed a family of computer systems for recognizing faces, expressions, and gestures. The technology has enabled us to build environments that behave somewhat like the house, office, and car described above. These areas, which we call smart rooms, are furnished with cameras and microphones that relay their recordings to a nearby network of computers. The computers assess what people in the smart room are saying and doing. Thanks to this connection, visitors can use their actions, voices and expressions—instead of keyboards, sensors, or goggles—to control computer programs, browse multimedia information or venture into realms of virtual reality. . . .

Intertext

**Sold on the Simplicity of Web Sites:
Companies Are Getting Back to
Basics with Web Designs That Enable
Users to Find What They Need**[18]

Officials at T. Rowe Price Associates Inc. know that, on the Internet, their competition is just a click away. That's why as T. Rowe Price's Web site content grew to the point where it was difficult for customers to find what they were looking for, the Baltimore-based financial services company took a fresh look at its Web design with an eye toward making the site easier to navigate.

Last September, the company launched a redesigned site—www.troweprice.com—that makes it possible for customers to find information about any of the company's 76 mutual funds in two clicks.

Like T. Rowe Price, many companies are learning that Web site clutter can kill the customer experience. As sites grow in complexity, with more content and functions, too much information can take away from rather than add to the user's time online by causing navigation problems. Ultimately, a bad user experience can sabotage a company's Web effort, whether it's an intranet, a business-to-consumer, or a business-to-business electronic commerce site. The answer is, as IT officials at T. Rowe Price found out: Get back to basics.

The first step on the road back to a basic Web design, experts say, is to make sure the site is set up based on how users access it, not according to a company's own organizational structure. Second, provide information quickly while avoiding marketing and business jargon. And last, design the site to work with the lowest common platform, which means avoiding graphics-intensive introductory pages that can hijack customers' browsing time or, worse, alienate them from the site because their browsers are not compatible with the Web page.

These are the guidelines T. Rowe Price followed, and now finding information on its latest home page is easier than ever. When the site launched in January 1996, it used a graphical site map, where links were embedded in graphics, for navigation. As content on the site expanded, however, that became too clunky, often leaving information such as investor reports buried five or six clicks deep, said Emmett Higdon, T. Rowe Price's assistant vice president of Internet marketing.

"While it looked fairly attractive, it wasn't user-friendly," Higdon said. He quickly learned that having a visually appealing site is not as powerful as a less glamorous yet functional design. As a result, Higdon and his team developed a Web framework where users would not need to click more than twice to find what they want.

Analysts agree that cutting down on clicks is a courtesy more companies need to offer their customers. A Forrester Research Inc. survey of 25 corporate sites found that users could find information by the third page on only half the sites they visited. Moreover, the Cambridge, Massachusetts, market researcher found that unnecessary clicks not only turn off customers but can also hurt business. The study estimated that each additional layer of menus could cut sales by as much as half because potential buyers get confused or lose interest.

Ultimately, experts say, a well-designed site comes down to understanding the user. For companies, that means knowing their customers and testing designs on them. Such testing must go beyond a few focus groups and include watching how customers navigate a site and react to its design, said Marc Rettig, an analyst at Cambridge Technology Partners Inc., in Cambridge, Massachusetts.

"The cost of doing usability testing is so cheap compared to redoing it later," Rettig said.

In fact, Forrester estimates that usability labs charge between $25,000 and $50,000 for thorough testing. Compare that with the cost of a site tear-down and overhaul: $780,000 to $1.56 million. While most will take a less dramatic path, even tinkering with design problems can cost as much as $90,000, Forrester found.

Don't push, pull

As T. Rowe Price mapped out its strategy to minimize clicks, it became obvious that achieving the "two-click" goal would mean adding more links from the home page. But how could it do so without causing clutter? The answer: Present a variety of ways to get at the information. In its case, the solution came in the form of pull-down menus.

Those that lose their way in the site can click on a menu in the upper right corner of the page that provides one-click access to the site's main sections and home page.

Other companies have moved in a similar direction, pumping up their home pages as a way of minimizing user maneuvers. Take Eastman Kodak Co. The company's first redesign, in 1995, created a vertical home page with seven basic links. But as the content grew and grew— from 500 to 30,000 Web pages—users wanted quicker routes to information.

After a series of usability tests and another redesign in December 1997, kodak.com moved toward a fuller home page with 30 links. By moving more content to the home page, Kodak provided direct access to popular content, said Kodak officials in Rochester, N.Y.

The new focus seems to be reaping benefits for Kodak and its customers. In online surveys of the latest site version, about 80 percent of the respondents rated it "better" or "much better" than the earlier site design, said Lee Corkran, the site's design manager. More visits to the site also have followed, Corkran said. Kodak.com estimates that about 60,000 unique visitors browse the Web pages each day, which is double the traffic of 18 months ago when the new design went live.

Not all companies agree, however, that this is the right approach to Web design, especially if you're trying to sell a product. For instance, Sears, Roebuck and Co. went the opposite route with its Web site. The retailer got rid of the 50 different links that packed its site's home page and replaced them with a picture of a washer and dryer to represent the online appliance store it launched this year. There are only a few links to other sections, such as company information, lining the top of the page.

"If you try to give everything equal weight on the home page, it really confuses the customer," said Mike Jacob, director of Sears Online, in Hoffman Estates, Illinois. So in Sears' case, designers concentrated on the most important people to their business—consumers. And to consumers, Sears reasoned, a picture is worth a thousand words.

Still, analysts say, even retailers like Sears can't go overboard with bandwidth-intensive graphics. The full-screen bouncing graphic that works well for a designer connected to a T-1 line and using a 21-inch monitor falls apart for a dial-up user viewing pages on a standard 15-inch monitor.

Easy does it

Worse yet, a site created for the latest Web browsers can block customers running older versions. As a result, companies need to design sites "for the lowest common denominator," said Shelley Taylor, president and founder of management consultancy Shelley Taylor & Associates, in Palo Alto, California. "Stop thinking of the latest technology, and get back to the basics."

That can hold true even when designing a site for more sophisticated users. For instance, T. Rowe Price fought the urge to add many of the latest Web design technologies. When a design company suggested it use dynamic HTML in its site navigation, the company declined because officials realized that only about 20 percent of its users had upgraded to a required 4.x version browser, T. Rowe Price's Higdon said.

And the effort to cut out technologies whose drawbacks outweigh their benefits has continued at the company. For instance, the original Web site redesign incorporated a Java script that highlighted a navigation button when the mouse crossed it. The feature looked nice but added time to downloading the home page—so much so that users complained. T. Rowe Price ditched the script and is planning to remove it from other pages on the site.

Matching technology with users isn't easy. Higdon estimates that 20 percent to 30 percent of development time for the new site was spent on testing different versions of browsers from Netscape Communications Corp., Microsoft Corp. and America Online Inc. And the company continues to study user logs as often as once a month to track the browsers being used.

While T. Rowe Price, Kodak and Sears took different approaches to Web design, they all had a common goal: to create a home page with clear navigation.

Ultimately, it all comes down to good ol' WYSIWYG, industry experts say. Providing a clean view for the user will likely keep them coming back.

5

Collaboration in Workplace Communication

As much as 75 to 85 percent of the writing you will do in the workplace may involve collaboration.

Reasons for Collaboration

You'll generally collaborate for one or more of these reasons:

- *The subject of the project.* Some subjects require the expertise of more than one person.
- *The process that results.* The collaborative process encourages multiple perspectives and offers feedback.
- *The product that collaborators create.* Some products such as manuals and newsletters are better done collaboratively.
- *Interpersonal benefits.* For many professionals, collaborative projects are more enjoyable than individual ones.

Types of Collaboration

You'll probably participate in three different types of collaboration: co-authoring, consulting with colleagues, and contributing to team projects.

Being a Good Collaborator

Individuals are influenced by a range of affective factors in their task environment: interpersonal relationships and social groups, organizational expectations and policies, and a variety of technological and ergonomic factors.

Individuals who are engaged and cooperative, who listen, ask questions, share, and reflect will be more effective. Groupware—which is changing the way collaborators plan, share documents, give and receive feedback, and make decisions—helps this interaction, whether it is synchronous or asynchronous or is in the same or distance locations.

Effective collaborators consider content, purpose and key point(s), audience, organization and support, and document design elements.

Negotiating Conflicts

Collaborators should discourage *affective* (interpersonal) conflicts; negotiate potential *procedural* conflicts that could interfere with a group's operation; and encourage *substantive* conflicts, which promote alternatives and disagreements about critical aspects of the document. Conflicts are sometimes the result of differences in cultural attitudes, beliefs, and practices.

"I look for a team player. . . . I want someone who understands that people are human and doesn't pick at the behavior of others until it becomes disruptive. I want someone who is not afraid to throw a bad idea out, in the hopes that it may spark a good idea." So says Sharon Burton-Hardin, the Chief Operations Officer at Anthrobytes Consulting in Riverside, California, and President of the Inland Empire chapter of the Society for Technical Communication (www.iestc.org). Burton-Hardin posted her comment on TECHWR-L, a listserve for professional technical communicators. "Too many times all the employees are doing what they want, regardless of what they have been told the joint effort is. Bickering, deception, destruction."[1] Her opinions give some indication of things that can go wrong with collaboration: disruption, bickering, deception, destruction. And she hints at another problem—the reluctance to be wrong.

Because 75 to 85 percent of the writing you will do in the workplace may involve collaborating with another person, knowing how to be effective is critical.[2] What do you need to know to be an effective collaborator? What pitfalls do you need to be aware of in collaboration? In what ways can collaboration be more productive or effective than writing individually? This chapter should help you answer these questions. You'll learn about the reasons professionals give for collaboration, various types of collaboration, techniques for effective collaboration, and ways to deal with conflicts and resolve problems in collaboration.[3]

Reasons for Collaboration

Collaborative relationships generally have some common elements: two or more people cooperatively completing some agreed-on task and a specific goal or product to be accomplished over time. Physical proximity is not a necessity; in fact, computer-mediated communication makes long-distance collaboration commonplace.

Professionals enter collaborative relationships by individual choice, by circumstance, and even by management directive. Your reasons will generally fall into one or more of these four categories:

- The subject of the project

- The process that results

- The product that collaborators create

- Interpersonal benefits

Subject

The *subject* of some projects makes collaboration essential. Some tasks require expertise from more than one person. For example, a research project in biomedical engineering to help paraplegics walk might require professionals with backgrounds in biomedical engineering, electronics, neurophysiology, and physical therapy. A paper resulting from such a collaboration could include input from all the individuals involved; thus, each could be acknowledged as a co-author. Some research is conducted by teams so large—for example, in high-energy physics—that the papers appear under the names of institutions rather than the individual authors. Examining articles in professional journals for various branches of science shows that many are co-authored; for example, in chemistry, 83 percent of journal articles are co-authored.[4]

What subjects in your professional area are well suited to collaborative efforts?

Closer to what you'll probably be doing is an example from Kaufer Computing, Inc. The general manager heads a team that is preparing a proposal to install a new CAD/CAM (computer-aided design/computer-aided manufacturing) system in a lab for a local technical college. His team includes professionals with experience in drafting and design, education, electronics, computer systems and software, and, of course, technical communication—expertise unlikely to be found in a single individual. When you're working on a project that requires experience and expertise beyond your own, you should feel comfortable in forming or being a member of a team that works collaboratively to reach a common goal.

Process

Collaboration sometimes enriches the *process* of preparing a document in ways that are impossible for an individual working alone. One major advantage of collaboration is the consideration of a variety of alternative viewpoints. Imagine that an industrial engineer is exploring ways to improve the production capability for Northern Pacific Cabinet Company, Inc., an OEM (original equipment manufacturer) that provides handcrafted wood cabinets for high-quality electronic entertainment systems. The engineer realizes that this investigation will be much more productive if it involves buyers, cabinetmakers, schedulers, and shippers, all of whom can offer unique perspectives about ways to increase production.

How do you react when a collaborator poses an alternative that counters what you've already suggested?

Another way that collaboration can help you prepare documents is by providing feedback seldom available if you're working independently. Collaborators often provoke reflection about the content and product as well as about the process—simply because you are faced with other perspectives. For example, the industrial engineer for Northern Pacific Cabinet Company not only will receive a variety of alternatives for improving production, but also will receive feedback about all the proposed suggestions, her own as well as everyone else's. This feedback enriches any work by providing you with reactions that you're not likely to think of alone. The ideas and reactions of your collaborators usually stimulate your ideas and reactions, which not only makes the process more enjoyable but also improves the document.

Product

Sometimes the type of *product* signals the need for collaboration, simply because some products—such as newsletters, user manuals, and proposals—are usually better if they're created collaboratively. Imagine that your task is creating a newsletter for families dealing with a relative who has cystic fibrosis. The newsletter might be more valuable and appealing if it contained articles from a variety of health care professionals (physicians, nurse practitioners, nurses, home health care workers); from patients themselves and their relatives; and from medical researchers. A newsletter written by you alone is not likely to have the range of perspectives necessary to sustain the interest of such a variety of readers.

Similarly, long documents such as user manuals or major proposals demand a collaborative effort because of the complexity of the content. For example, Ecological Recycling Associates wants to submit a proposal to the town of Sheffield for dealing with recyclable trash. One of the company's environmental engineers is responsible for coordinating a five-member team to prepare the proposal. The team meets to plan the proposal, but various sections are prepared individually by different members of the team. The comprehensive nature of the proposal and the amount of technical detail require expertise impossible to be found in one person, especially given the deadlines for submission. Having a project coordinator contributes to the collaborative proposal's consistency in style, tone, and format.

When you're working on a team in which each person is responsible for a separate section, how could you ensure overall consistency in style, tone, and format?

Interpersonal Benefits

Many professionals advocate collaborative writing because of the *interpersonal benefits*. They say the collaborative process is often more enjoyable than working independently. They have a chance to work with colleagues with whom they might not otherwise have a chance to interact. In fact, some professionals admit that they sometimes establish collaborative projects, rather than individual ones, just for the opportunity to work with particular people.

Working collaboratively also has social and organizational benefits. Many people like being part of a team. As a member of a team, you will have a group identity that provides support when the workload and schedule are especially difficult. Beyond the fact that companies like having employees who are satisfied with their work environment, a smoothly running team can be more productive than the same number of individuals working separately.

How can you increase the interpersonal benefits of belonging to a team?

Types of Collaboration

In the workplace, collaboration often takes many different forms. As long as the collaborators agree on their interpersonal roles and their tasks, numerous collaborative relationships are possible. For example, collaborators might work together during only one phase of a project—such as during planning—but then one person could draft and revise the entire document. Or after the initial collaborative planning, each person could complete a different portion of a major document. Another example occurs when collaborators work together on only one portion of a project. An engineer might collaborate with a colleague in finance when preparing the budget section for a proposal and with another colleague in quality control when preparing the testing and evaluation section of the same proposal. Regardless of the nature of the collaboration, when collaborators assume unequal responsibility for different aspects of a project, they should expect to receive unequal recognition and compensation.

One useful way to examine collaboration is to analyze the role of the individual in relation to the other collaborators. For example, consider the work of Paula Thompson, a manager at Dover Systems, a company that designs hardware and software for commercial architects and contractors. Three of Paula's current projects involve different types of collaboration: co-authoring, consulting with colleagues, and contributing to team projects.

What types of collaboration are you likely to do as an entry-level professional? As a more senior professional?

Co-Authoring

To many people, collaboration means that the contributions of the collaborators are equivalent and the exchange of information is reciprocal. In a co-equal collaboration, each collaborator contributes ideas but is willing to abandon or modify them. Co-equal collaborators analyze both the strengths and weaknesses of their own ideas and also evaluate the ideas of the other collaborator(s). Any arguments that arise are explored in light of mutually agreed-on purposes, tasks, and products. Because each collaborator assumes responsibility for creating and criticizing, the team is able to build new ideas by taking the best from each collaborator. Each collaborator takes equal responsibility and receives equal credit as co-author.

One project Paula Thompson is responsible for involves working with a colleague, Chris McCaffrey, to prepare an article for publication in the company's technical report series. As co-authors, Paula and Chris share responsibilities for planning, drafting, and revising their technical report.

Paula and Chris have agreed to an initial meeting to discuss content, purpose, audience, organization, and evidence as well as to plan their schedule. They agree to rough-out ideas separately and then meet again. Although they each take responsibility for writing separate sections of the report, they read each other's drafts and make suggestions that influence the other's work. Because they both write on a networked computer system, they can share each other's drafts and exchange e-mail about the drafts. Even though they communicate regularly by e-mail, they also have face-to-face meetings to resolve problems. Once the draft of their co-authored report is completed, Paula and Chris establish another series of collaborative relationships as the document moves through the review and editing cycles.

Consulting with Colleagues

Another of Paula's projects is preparing a packet of information sheets for a new product line. Initially, Paula sketches notes for information sheets that should accomplish these five goals: draw attention to a new product or product line that solves a problem, unify the product conceptually with the design of the information sheet, create a sense of corporate competence, arouse customers' interest enough for them to seek additional information, and summarize the marketable features of the product.

Paula also knows that information sheets should not become merely a list of technical features, so she works with colleagues in a number of departments to complete her project:

- Engineering—to get accurate product specifications

- Marketing—to get information about the target market

- Graphic design—to work with the artist to design the information sheets and pocket folder they'll go in

- Communication—to work with an editor assigned to the project

- Publication—to get corporate publishing specifications and printing costs

- Quality control—to arrange for technical review and user testing

Although Paula is responsible for the development of the information sheet packet, she consults with a variety of colleagues who have expertise that she needs.

This type of collaboration—consulting with colleagues—is common and expected. You should willingly seek information from colleagues and be prepared to reciprocate when they need information from you. Naturally, Paula lets her colleagues (and their managers) know how helpful they have been.

Contributing to Team Projects

A third project Paula is responsible for is coordinating the efforts of a team of hardware engineers, software designers, systems analysts, information designers, and budget planners. She must organize their individual efforts into a proposal for a state-of-the-art laboratory that will be submitted to one of the country's leading architectural schools. The team has had numerous planning meetings, but each person is responsible for an individual section of the document. Part of Paula's job is to facilitate the planning meetings and to coordinate the separate sections that people prepare into a coherent, cohesive, persuasive proposal.

However, even on a team, collaboration does not necessarily mean co-equal contributions. When one person assumes a greater responsibility, that person might initially identify the purpose of the collaboration, define the task, and perhaps even specify the product. Individual contributions do not have to be equivalent. However, if the collaboration is to be successful, all the individuals involved need to have some say in what responsibilities each person should assume and suggest the collaborative approach that should be used.

Being a Good Collaborator

Allan Ackerson, lead technical writer working for the Colorado Springs division of Logicon Applied Technology, Inc., recently commented on TECHWR-L that collaborators—especially if they're team leaders—should follow three guidelines:

1. Treat people like you'd like to be treated.

2. Identify strengths and weaknesses of team members and use them accordingly.

3. Insist on excellence.[5]

Ackerson's advice is valuable because it reminds people that being an effective collaborator and team leader requires common sense and courtesy. Following Ackerson's advice is a good start. Whether you are preparing a document as a co-author, as a consultant with colleagues, or as a member of a project team, you can do several things that will help you be more effective:

- Be engaged and cooperative

What are your strengths as a collaborator? What areas would you like to strengthen?

- Listen

- Conform to conversation conventions

- Ask questions

- Share

- Use technology effectively

- Reflect

Be Engaged and Cooperative

Several things increase the likelihood that your collaborations can be enjoyable and productive. You can begin by coming to the collaborative session with an open mind. Leave at the door any prejudices or negative preconceptions about the people you're working with or the project you're working on. Be receptive to the likelihood that the collaboration improves whatever ideas you already have. Once you have an open mind and a receptive attitude, you will find the following general guidelines useful:

- Always *come prepared* for any collaborative meeting, which means gathering necessary information and having something to contribute to the collaboration.

- Be able to *articulate the purpose* of your collaborative work. What's the goal? What's the task? Do others on the team have the same ideas? What's the process you'll use to complete the project? How can you get all the collaborators in your group to represent or interpret the goals, task, and process in the same way?

- *Be articulate* in expressing your views. Don't assume body language or silence will sufficiently (or accurately) convey your views.

- *Be cooperative* and *supportive* rather than competitive and antagonistic.

- Be direct in stating your own opinions, but *don't trample* on the ideas of other collaborators.

Listen

You can learn a great deal if you are an *active listener* instead of a passive listener. An active listener is engaged—attentive, involved, interested. Being an active listener means paying attention to what your collaborators say—and what they don't say. Be aware, too, of their manner of speaking. Tone of voice, pacing, and inflection all reflect attitudes about the content. Sometimes knowing those attitudes is as important as knowing the content.

Being involved and interested while listening to your collaborators means asking questions when you're confused and periodically summarizing what you hear the speakers saying. Getting immediate clarification lessens the chance that you'll misinterpret what you hear. Paraphrasing what speakers say is a good way to verify that your understanding matches their intent.

An additional benefit is that if you listen actively to your collaborators, they're more likely to listen to you. As a result, you'll all have a better understanding of one another's views, and the project will have an increased chance of being successful.

Conform to Conversation Conventions

Collaboration requires conversation—face to face or at a distance. Certainly having something to say matters, but, beyond that, following a few conventions makes the face-to-face, telephone, and computer conversations move more smoothly and productively.

All conversations
- Select an appropriate location (minimal background distractions).

- Look, sound, and act interested.

- State your points clearly.

- Provide explanations and examples as needed.

- Share the turn taking.

- Respond to the other person's ideas.

Face-to-face conversations

- Make direct eye contact (be aware of gaze, part of a person's cultural comfort zone).

- Respect personal space (be aware of proxemics, a person's spatial comfort zone).

Telephone conversations

- Don't eat, drink, or chew gum while you're on the phone.

- Don't put people on hold for more than a few seconds.

Computer conversations *(See Chapter 14 for netiquette about e-mail.)*

What are your best habits—and your worst—in each kind of conversation?

- Keep in mind that all electronic messages can be forwarded, printed, or permanently stored by any recipient, so be sensible—perhaps even cautious—about what you send electronically.

- Copy only enough of the message you're responding to in order to provide a context or a reminder; do not copy the entire message.

Ask Questions

To be an effective collaborator, you need to ask questions to get the necessary information. These questions can be powerful tools for helping you to assess what you already know and what you need to know to prepare an effective document. These two guidelines are particularly useful:

- Ask questions that require comments or discussions rather than questions that ask for *yes* or *no* responses.

- Ask questions that focus attention on a range of elements important to the project: content, purpose, key points, audience, conventions of organization and support, and conventions of document design.

When you have primary responsibility for preparing a document, you can get a great deal of help from a supporter who asks you questions such as those in Figure 5.1. A good supporter encourages you to extend your ideas, questions you about points that seem inconsistent or contradictory, and offers suggestions about ways to improve the document. Of course, you can work with a supporter at any stage in planning, drafting, and revising a document. This kind of collaboration can help you focus your ideas, consider alternatives that may not have occurred to you if working alone, and give you feedback for improving the document. You can also reciprocate by acting as a supporter for colleagues.

The questions in Figure 5.1 are designed to help collaborators, whether they are acting as supporters for another writer, working as co-authors, or participating as members of a team. Although these questions are listed in separate categories, many concerns are relevant to more than one area. For example, the following question integrates several concerns: "How will the *organization* and

FIGURE 5.1 ■ **Questions to Help Collaborators Deal with Content and Other Concerns[6]**	
Photocopy and use this figure during your collaborative planning sessions.	
Content	◆ What critical information needs to be included in this document?
	◆ What additional information might you/we include?
	◆ Have you considered including _____?
	◆ What content can be omitted?
Purpose and key point(s)	◆ What do you see as your/our main purpose?
	◆ What main point(s) do you/we want to make?
	◆ How will the audience react to the purpose and points?
	◆ I see a conflict between _____ and _____. How can you/we resolve it?
Audience	◆ Who is your/our intended audience?
	◆ What do the readers expect to learn?
	◆ How do you think the readers will react to _____?
	◆ What problems, conflicts, inconsistencies, or gaps might readers see?
Organization and support	◆ How can you/we organize the content to achieve the purpose?
	◆ What evidence can you/we use to support the purpose and appeal to the audience?
	◆ What examples (anecdotal, statistical, visual, and so on) should you/we use?
	◆ How are you/we going to connect _____ and _____?
Document design elements	◆ How can design features be used to convey the main point(s)?
	◆ What design features will the audience expect? What will they respond to?
	◆ How can verbal and visual information be balanced?
	◆ How can the design be used to reflect the organization of the content?

What questions would you like to add to Figure 5.1? Why are these useful questions to add?

design convey our *purpose* to the *audience*?" Periodically, you may want to consolidate two or more concerns into one question.

Share

Not only do you need to get information from your colleagues by listening and asking questions, but you also must be willing to provide them with detailed and accurate information. Unless prior agreements among all parties restrict sharing information (usually for proprietary reasons), you should make every effort to keep your collaborators informed about the work you're doing. You should also provide feedback to your collaborators about their work. This exchange of information should be done regularly.

The most effective way to ensure that information is exchanged regularly is to establish a schedule and a method when the project begins. For example, you can all agree to provide weekly update memos. Or you can provide read-only privileges for selected computer files. Or you can have weekly meetings to discuss the status of the project. Or you can circulate updated drafts of the document—on paper or electronically. The method is not nearly as important as the fact that regular communication occurs among collaborators.

Use Technology Effectively

Technology can help with sharing, especially if you use *groupware*, software designed to facilitate group interaction. Groupware—which usually changes the way collaborators plan, share documents, give and receive feedback, and make decisions—considers two important factors:

1. *Time:* Are you and your collaborators working together at the same time (synchronous) or at different times (asynchronous)?

2. *Location:* Are you and your collaborators working in the same place (co-located; face-to-face) or in different places (non-co-located; distance)?

Groupware enables the formation of groups for special projects. Whether you need synchronous or asynchronous communication, whether you and your collaborators are in the same room or separated by thousands of miles, group-ware can bring together multiple perspectives and expertise. Groupware also enables structured interactions so that aggressive people are less likely to dominate conversations.[7]

One of the most convenient groupware tools is a group calendar, which helps schedule meetings, reserve rooms and equipment, manage projects, and coordinate activities among people. Despite the convenience of a group calendar, some people worry about *privacy* (for example, some users may feel that their activities can be scrutinized) and *accuracy* (other users may not want to take time to enter their schedule). Figure 5.2 identifies additional types of groupware that aid collaboration and teamwork.

Reflect

Take time to reflect. Mull over the ideas you've heard. A good collaborator carefully considers ideas and opinions from other people. Planning a specific time for reflection is difficult when time is scarce—when deadlines slip, when your day is filled with back-to-back responsibilities, when you barely have time to eat lunch—but it is nonetheless an important part of the collaborative process. You

FIGURE 5.2 ■ Common Types of Groupware[8]

		Time	
		synchronous interaction (same time)	*asynchronous interaction (different time)*
Location	*co-located interaction (same location)*	◆ **Presentation support systems** aid speakers in formal or informal presentations with computer slides, often accompanied by audio and animation. ◆ **Decision support systems** (DSS) facilitate group decision-making by helping collaborators with brainstorming, critiquing, weighing probabilities and alternatives, and voting. DSS may facilitate meetings by encouraging equal participation through anonymity or enforcing turn taking.	◆ **Shared computers** with word processing software enable collaborators to track changes and annotate each other's work.
	distance interaction (different locations)	◆ **Shared whiteboards** permit two or more people to view and draw on a shared drawing from different locations. Color-coded telepointers identify each person. ◆ **Video communications systems** allow two-way or multi-ways calling with live video. Video is advantageous when visual information is being discussed. ◆ **Chat systems** permit multiple people in real-time to write messages in a shared space. Many chat rooms control access or permit moderators for discussions. Issues in real-time groupware include anonymity, following the stream of conversation, scalability with number of users, and abusive users. ◆ Also **DSS** (see above)	◆ **E-mail** can forward messages to individuals or groups, send messages to groups, sort and file messages, and attach files to messages. ◆ **Workflow systems** help documents move through organizations electronically. For example, employees can submit an expense report by routing it to a manager who electronically approves it for payment. Simultaneously, the report is debited to the group's account and then forwarded to the accounting department for payment.
		◆ **Collaborative writing systems** provide both synchronous and asynchronous support. Collaborators may be given tools to help plan and coordinate as well as link separately authored documents. Synchronous support usually provides an additional communication channel to the authors as they work, such as videophones or chat. Asynchronous support usually uses shared computers (see above).	

need to sift through the information you've collected and assess its value, decide what information to use and what to discard, and pinpoint areas of confusion that should be clarified and areas of disagreement that should be resolved. Your reflection may also show that you need to go back to your colleagues or team for additional information or clarification; more decisions may be needed. In short, without reflection, you won't be able to effectively use the information you gain through collaboration.

Negotiating Conflicts

As you learn to be a more effective collaborator by being engaged and cooperative, listening, adhering to conventions, asking questions, sharing, using technology effectively, and reflecting, you'll also need to manage problems and negotiate the various kinds of conflicts—affective, procedural, and substantive—that arise.

Affective Conflicts

Affect involves your attitudes and biases, your personality and values. These factors shape your interpersonal communication and influence the way you approach collaboration. With effective interpersonal communication, your collaborations are more likely to be successful.

Interpersonal relationships are as important to collaboration as the task itself. A project is more likely to succeed if you respect your collaborators and get along with them, if you're comfortable working with them and feel free to share ideas and voice concerns. You and your collaborators need to trust one another; you can help build and maintain this trust by frequent contact and sharing information.

Affective conflict, defined simply as interpersonal disagreement, can seriously impede any collaborative interaction, perhaps even signaling the end of the collaborative relationship. Affective conflicts might arise because of strongly held beliefs about religion; politics; business ethics; or gender, racial, or ethnic prejudices. For example, a collaborator who says, "I'll never work with a ____" (fill in the blank with some personal bias) has let affective conflict interfere with a working relationship. One way you can avoid affective conflict is to acknowledge your biases and prejudices and then make a special effort to not be negatively influenced by them during your collaboration.

What affective problems have you had in collaboration? What might you have done to decrease or eliminate these problems?

Another way you can avoid affective conflict is by paying attention to differences and changes in footing during collaboration. *Footing* is a term used by cultural anthropologists to describe the underlying assumptions people make about a particular situation; those assumptions govern the way people act. Of course, your assumptions change as you learn new information about the people you're working with—their knowledge, their attitudes, their behavior—and the task you're working on. Even though you have established a relationship with your collaborators, you should recognize that changes are inevitable. In fact, as you react to new information and recognize subtle shifts in footing, your views about your collaborators and the task will gradually change. Being aware of this evolution will make it easier to handle.

Procedural Conflicts

For a collaborative group to function smoothly, you and your collaborators need to discuss how the group sessions will run—that is, the procedures that govern the group's operation. Many experienced collaborators find it efficient and productive to begin their work together by agreeing on several concerns:

Deciding about meeting details
- Settle details of meetings: time, place, duration.

- Agree on what preparation should be done for meetings.

- Discuss the collaborative approach the group will use.

Deciding about team roles and responsibilities
- Identify the responsibilities each individual will assume.

- Determine how to monitor the group's progress.

- Decide on order of authorship based on some mutually acceptable criteria.

Discussing ways to manage conflict productively
- Agree on ways to minimize affective and procedural conflict.

- Agree on ways to encourage substantive conflict.

- Decide how to negotiate among alternatives and resolve disagreements.

Deciding such concerns up front can reduce your chances of having a group derailed by procedural conflict. Discussions about procedures can strengthen the group cohesiveness—both the feeling of group identity and the group's commitment to the task.

Anticipating procedural conflict can be critical to a group's success. Don't wait until your third meeting at 4:30 in the afternoon to discover that one member always has to leave early because of child-care responsibilities or a second job. Don't wait until people are shouting at each other to agree that you should withhold criticism until all the options have been presented. Don't wait until someone fails to meet a deadline to discover that he or she doesn't have the time or skills to do that part of the project effectively. Don't wait until the first progress report is due to discover that no one is keeping track of what's already completed, what is being done, and what needs to be done. Sometimes just asking questions about procedural concerns makes people aware of potential problems that can be easily managed by some preliminary discussions and agreements.

A group of workplace professionals in a course to study collaboration compiled a list of surefire ways to sabotage any collaborative effort. If you want to ensure failure, follow the suggestions in Figure 5.3.

Other procedural concerns have to do with the costs and materials of a project—procedures regarding the allocation of resources. Because collaborative projects often take a long time to complete, they can be expensive. And because the projects are often complex, they require purchase of or access to a variety of equipment, tools, supplies, and services, which also can be costly.

What would you add
to this list of ways to
sabotage collaboration?

FIGURE 5.3 ■ Ways to Sabotage Excellence in Collaboration[9]

Miss meetings.	Expect that many hands make quick work.
Show up late.	
Don't bother to talk about what the group goal is.	Keep meetings going for more than two hours.
Don't ever allow discussion of anything not on the agenda.	Compete for individual recognition.
Don't establish an agenda.	Elevate personal success above group success.
Ignore established agendas and procedures.	Don't bother to keep track of what is discussed.
Disagree with everything just because you don't want to be there.	Don't establish ways of communicating outside of scheduled meetings.
Agree with everything just because you don't want to be there.	Rely solely on guesses to make decisions.
Keep quiet, even when you have another idea.	Don't establish any way to assess individual progress.
Hoard your information.	Attempt to include everything anyone ever said.
Give up on your idea without even explaining it.	Expect the worst from your group members.
Make yourself responsible for everything.	Don't let the group get to know you.
Don't take responsibility for anything.	Strive for quick consensus on every issue.
Plan to get everything done in one big work session.	Believe that everything runs smoothly in good collaboration.
	Never laugh.

A limited budget can affect the nature of a collaborative project, restricting employee time and access to necessary resources. However, realistic long-range planning often allows an organization to budget for collaborative projects.

The extraordinary problems created by inattention to or short circuiting of procedural concerns are discussed in the ethics sidebar on the next page. Initial discussions—rather than assumptions—about who would receive credit for important work would have reduced the chances that people would have been passed over. And as the situation discussed in the sidebar illustrates, procedural conflicts quite predictably spilled over into affective conflicts as well.

Substantive Conflicts

Substantive concerns deal with the substance of a document or presentation—decisions about things such as content, purpose, audience, conventions of organization and support, and conventions of design. Just as you may make preliminary agreements about procedural concerns, you should also adopt the

"They were all there to grasp all the credit for themselves": Ethics and the Culture of Credit

Picture the story of Susan Berget. Berget was a postdoctoral student researching human genes in a lab at the Massachusetts Institute of Technology (MIT). Berget's research revealed a puzzling connection between different strands of human chromosomes. Berget, working with Phillip Sharp, who headed the lab, later uncovered the concept of gene splicing. The discovery of gene splicing was a major development in the field of molecular biology. The concept was so important that the 1993 Nobel Prize for medicine was awarded to its discovers: Phillip Sharp of MIT and Richard Roberts of New York's Cold Spring Harbor Laboratory (CSHL), a lab that had discovered gene splicing at about the same time. Notably missing from the list of prize winners was Susan Berget's name. Berget says that she and Sharp have settled their differences about the lack of acknowledgment for her role in the discovery, but "she acknowledges that the distribution of credit was not a perfectly smooth process" (Cohen and Taubes, page 1707).[10]

Reporters Jon Cohen and Gary Taubes investigated gene splice research and found that Berget was not the only researcher left out. As results from separate steps in the research were publicly released, contributions from many researchers went unacknowledged. John Hassell, a member of the CSHL group, believes that "Ninety percent of the people at Cold Spring Harbor didn't get the credit they deserved." Cohen and Taubes attribute the winnowing of contributors to the "drive for individual credit—stoked by prize committees and the media." Focusing on individual credit "overshadows the collaborative nature of the scientific process, distorting the record and leaving researchers feeling bruised" (Cohen and Taubes, page 1706).[11]

How can technical professionals avoid these conflicts in giving credit? Researchers Mark Haskins, Jeanne Liedtka, and John Rosenblum believe a possible solution is to develop an ethic of collaboration that is based on relationships and not tasks. They identify four important elements in a collaboration that focuses on relationships:

- a caring attitude about the well-being of colleagues and about the work
- a recognition of the importance of the work for themselves and others
- a personal passion for the work
- a creative energy that fuels risk and innovation[12]

Focusing on relationships, Haskins and his colleagues believe, induces an ethic of collaboration that helps members see the advantages of group accomplishments over individual credit. If an ethic of collaboration had existed in Susan Berget's case, all the different researchers who played a role in the discovery would have been acknowledged for their role in the group's achievements.

How would you keep the need for individual recognition from damaging a collaborative project?

Do you approach teamwork with an ethic of collaboration? Would you be willing to forgo individual credit for the sake of the group's success? Think of Susan Berget's story. How would you feel if your contributions to a project were not acknowledged?

practice of experienced collaborators who often address substantive concerns early in their discussions:

- Agree on the purpose of the collaboration.
- Agree on project objectives and outcomes.

Collaborators who do not agree about these substantive concerns run the risk of producing unfocused, poorly designed documents that don't respond to the needs or interests of any particular audience. Making decisions about these concerns doesn't lock you in, it gives you a direction—and re-planning is always possible. You always have the flexibility to change any of your initial decisions, realizing that each one influences the others. For example, changing the purpose influences the organization and design of a document. Changing the design can change the impact on the audience.

Collaborators need to reach consensus, but not too quickly. One effective and productive way of deferring consensus is to engage purposely in substantive conflict. Unlike affective conflict (which deals with interpersonal tensions) or procedural conflict (which deals with disagreements about things such as meeting times), substantive conflict focuses on the issues and ideas of your collaborative work. Substantive conflict includes two specific types of interaction:

- *Voicing explicit disagreements:* For example, when one collaborator suggests, "Let's do Z," the other collaborator might respond, "No," or "I disagree," or "I think that's wrong."

- *Considering alternatives:* For example, when one collaborator suggests, "Let's do X," the other collaborator might respond, "Yes, X is a possibility, but let's consider Y as another way to solve the problem."

Deferring consensus can give you more time to identify and consider opposing points, more time to generate and critically examine issues and ideas. Resolution of substantive conflict can lead to your increased commitment to your team effort and to a potentially higher-quality product. Because engaging in substantive conflict should be cooperative rather than competitive (after all, you're all going after the same goal: high-quality decisions and high-quality products), the resolution can be described as win–win.[13]

Here are some suggestions for engaging in substantive conflict during a cooperative collaborative session:

Ask provocative questions
- Ask questions that focus on potential problems between various elements: "How can we use the design to help show our purpose?" "How can we explain these examples so the readers will be able to understand them?"

- Ask your collaborators for elaborations, clarifications, and explanations of statements, and be prepared to offer clarifications and explanations of your own statements.

- Ask for reasons to support arguments and work on developing and supporting well-formed arguments of your own.

Take a productive and critical perspective
- Try never to settle on one solution or decision without first having considered a couple of alternatives.

- Assume the role of devil's advocate.

- When you disagree with something, say so; support your disagreement with a reason and, if possible, an alternative that will work.

- If other collaborators don't generate substantive conflict by raising alternatives and voicing disagreements about your ideas, bring up alternatives and possible objections yourself.

Separate ideas and personality

- Don't mistake an objection to your ideas as an attack on your character, personality, or intellect.

Substantive conflict should be viewed as a way to strengthen a project rather than weaken it. Such conflict enables collaborators to rethink their own positions, delineate the perimeters of their views, and make decisions about key issues. Collaborators who establish interpersonal relationships know that disagreements aren't personal attacks; instead, they're ways of reexamining issues critical to the project.

Of course, as the Dilbert cartoon shows, successful collaboration depends on an ability to think and communicate clearly, but it also depends on everyone involved being willing to interact and being receptive to the ideas they hear—even when they don't necessarily agree. Summarily dismissing collaborators when they disagree is not productive.

Where can agreement begin? Collaborators should agree about the content of their project, the conceptual core that reflects their ideas and ideals. Collaborators should be able to define their concepts and explain why they're important.

14

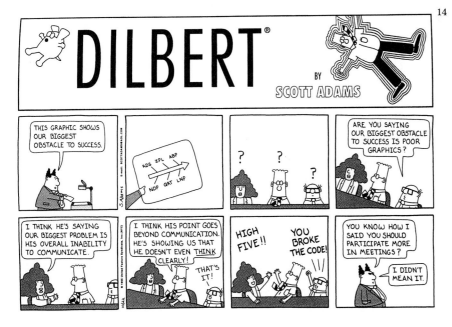

Explain whether you believe the attitudes and behaviors in the Dilbert cartoon accurately reflect the workplace.

Some documents are confusing because they seem to present inconsistent and sometimes even conflicting views.

During planning, collaborators need to explore the concepts from a variety of angles: accuracy, logic, underlying theory, related issues, and implicit values. If the ideas aren't clear to the collaborators, they certainly won't be clear to the readers. Such investigating helps collaborators examine alternative views, bolster arguments against attack, refine explanations, delete weak positions, and clarify vague or misleading statements. Considering these alternatives makes the eventual agreement much stronger.

Cultural Differences and Expectations

When a conflict arises, you need to ask yourself not only if it is affective, procedural, or substantive, but also if it is generated by cultural differences. Collaboration is a complex process of decision making and compromise that is influenced by cultural beliefs and practices. You can't assume that people from different cultural groups, backgrounds, or geographic regions will react the same way. Although all individuals have unique attitudes and behaviors that influence their collaborative style, within cultural groups you can often find common patterns of behavior.

Collaborators may inadvertently misjudge the behaviors of their colleagues, not realizing that these behaviors are perfectly normal in another culture. For example, a colleague may agree with the clearly conflicting positions of two collaborators to avoid having to reject the ideas of either one. This behavior, regarded by some as indecisive or even wimpy, may simply be a reflection of the person's cultural practice not to insult another by publicly rejecting his or her ideas.

What cultural differences, other than country of birth, might cause problems?

In some cultures colleagues seldom directly express objections to problematic plans that are on the table for discussion. This reluctance to voice explicit disagreements may stem from a cultural practice that avoids criticizing others (which could embarrass them) and perceives disagreements as criticism or from a cultural perspective that values group harmony above potential benefits that substantive conflict might generate.[15] All sorts of behaviors—a reluctance to engage in substantive conflict, a hesitancy to spell out the procedural expectations, or an unwillingness to volunteer—may be the result of cultural practices different from yours.

You can help guard against inadvertent cultural bias by encouraging people you work with to exchange information about their patterns and practices dealing with collaboration—their individual preferences as well as their cultural behaviors. When you are establishing the procedures the group will follow, collaborators can ask each other questions in categories such as these:

Moving the collaboration forward
- Are you willing to suggest an idea or plan that differs from the one accepted by the majority of the group?

- When you don't understand something, do you ask for explanations and clarifications?

Reacting to disagreement

- When you don't agree with something, are you willing to express objections? Criticisms? How do you express your disagreement?

- How do you think disagreements should be resolved?

Reacting to personal comments

- How do you react to being put on the spot?

- How do you respond to criticism?

- How do you respond to praise?

Considering team roles

- Do you think the group should have a leader? What are the responsibilities of the leader?

- What are the responsibilities of the other collaborators?

Talking about these aspects of individual behavior may help collaborators understand that people respond in different ways. Understanding—and perhaps even anticipating—behaviors different from your own will help you be a more responsive and effective collaborator.

End-of-Chapter Recommendations for Technical Communicators

1. Remember that collaboration is important; 75 to 85 percent of the writing you will do in the workplace may involve collaboration.

2. Decide whether collaboration is appropriate for any given project based on the subject of the project, the process that should be used, the product that you'll create, or the interpersonal benefits you might gain.

3. Learn to be skillful in three different types of collaboration: co-authoring, consulting with colleagues, and contributing to team projects.

4. Develop your skills as a collaborator:

    - Be engaged and cooperative.

    - Listen actively by paying attention to both verbal and nonverbal cues.

    - Conform to conversation conventions.

    - Ask rigorous questions—especially during planning—about your project's content, purpose, audience, organization, support, and document design.

    - Share information regularly with your classmates or colleagues.

    - Understand that groupware—which can be categorized in two ways: time (synchronous and asynchronous) and location (face to face and distance)—helps collaborators plan, share documents, give and receive feedback, and make decisions.

- Reflect about the collaborative process so that you learn more about your own interaction and can pinpoint areas for improvement.

5. Discourage affective conflict because it nearly always short-circuits a collaborative relationship.

6. Eliminate potential procedural conflict by identifying and negotiating the procedures that enable a group to function efficiently and productively.

7. Encourage substantive conflict—posing alternatives and voicing disagreements—as a way to explore issues related to your project's content, purpose, audience, organization, support, and document design.

8. Be sensitive to ways in which cultural differences can influence collaborative attitudes and behaviors.

Individual and Collaborative Assignments

1. **Address a complex problem.** Before coming to class or meeting with your collaborator, carefully read the case situation for Sundance Systems, Inc., and the Sundance Information Sheet. Before you meet with your collaborator, prepare notes about a way to approach the technical memo and the information sheet redesign.

   (a) **Write a memo.** Work with a collaborator to prepare a technical memo in response to the Sundance Systems case situation. The memo needs to include an analysis of the problems and propose a plan to address them. Take into account the task, the content, and concerns such as purpose, audience, organization and support, document design, and consolidation of these concerns. As part of your planning, discuss your approach to the issues and your collaborator's approach before you both decide how to prepare the memo.

   ### Case Situation: Sundance Systems, Inc.

   Examine the accompanying information sheet. In response to mail-in and telephone inquiries from potential customers (small businesses and homeowners), Sundance Systems, Inc., has sent out approximately 5,500 information sheets during the past 12 months. During this same period, the company has sold and installed 470 systems, at costs ranging from $5,000 to $25,000.

   Unfortunately, a recent survey of customers indicates that although 47 percent of customers who purchased a Sundance System said they had read the information sheet, only 17 percent of customers who read it said it positively influenced their decision. In contrast, 22 percent of those who read it said it was confusing, and the remaining 61 percent said it didn't affect them one way or the other.

   The information sheet was prepared by Lou Battle, founder of the company, who is considered an industry leader. Lou likes the idea of responding to inquiries with factual information. The current information sheet has been used for the past two years. In last week's staff meeting, Lou mentioned that he's heard some people want to update it, but he thinks it's pretty good as it is—it's short and accurate.

   You've just been hired as an information designer in Sundance Systems' expanding corporate communication group. This group has consolidated the management of all published company documents, documents that until recently were handled by individual departments as needed. You were the top choice of Judith Dupras, the company's general manager. Part of your job is to work with another information designer to decide what to do about the survey results. What's the problem? What should be done? Present your collaborative assessment. (*Note:* You can create appropriate information to complete the assessment as long as it doesn't conflict with the minimal information provided.)

(b) **Revise the information sheet.** Continue working with the same collaborator. Your task now is to revise the Sundance Information Sheet. Take into account the content as well as purpose, audience, organization and support, visuals, and document design. Discuss your approach to the

---

SUNDANCE INFORMATION SHEET

Although most active solar systems are fairly simple in design and operation, the air-cooled system is the simplest. Unlike a liquid system, an air system needs needs no considerations for freeze protection, expansion, air bleeding, or vacuum relief. Since air-cooled systems run at lower operating temperatures than liquid-cooled systems, heat loss throughout the system is kept at a minimum while efficiency is kept at a maximum. The simplicity of the air-cooled solar system, its high efficiency, and its low cost should convince you to install a SUNDANCE SYSTEM in your home or business.

The heart of the air-cooled system is the solar collectors. The SUNDANCE solar collectors collect and convert the solar energy into usefull heat energy. The SUNDANCE collector is basically an air-tight insulated box. The inside of this box contains a black aluminum absorber plate, and the box is covered with a special transparent cover that allows light to pass through, but doesn't allow heat to escape. Light from the sun enters the box through the transparent cover, strikes the black aluminum absorber plate, and is converted to heat. Cool air enters the bottom of the solar collector, passes over the absorber plate, and exits from the top of the collector as heated air. Typically, this cool air entering the SUNDANCE collector is about 60F, and the heated air leaving the collector is about 140F. This heated air is brought via the ductwork into the building for water or space heating.

The ductwork is used to convey the cool air from the building (the return line) to the SUNDANCE collectors, and the heated air from the SUNDANCE colectors (the supply line) to the building. Ductwork is also used to connect the individual SUNDANCE collectors together to form an array and to vent this array during a period of nonuse such as a vacation. It is imperative that the ductwork system be thoroughly sealed from leakage. Leakage adversely affects the efficiency of the SUNDANCE SYSTEM by drawing cold outside air into the return line or by leaking heated air from the supply line. All ductwork done by SUNDANCE SYSTEMS is heavily insulated to keep heat loss at a minimum. Dampers are used to direct air into the house for space heating in the winter or to divert this heated air through a special water heater for summer operation.

A one-third horsepower two-speed blower provides air movement through the SUNDANCE SYSTEM. The fast speed is more suitable for winter operation since the system maintains a maximum output temperature of about 140F at this speed. This 140F air is usefull for space heating since it is about 70F warmer than the air already in the house. The difference between the temperature of the air leaving the house and the temperature of the air returning to the house is called the temperature differential. During summer operation however the lower operation speed is used since a higher operating temperature is necessary. The lower operating speed provides a collector output temperature of about 180F. This higher operating temperature is necessary for heating water since as the water becomes increasingly hotter the temperature differential and therefor the efficiency of the system are decrease. Therefore the SUNDANCE SYSTEM has a two-speed blower to maximize output year-round.

---

issues and your collaborator's approach as you decide how to revise the information sheet. Create a completely revised document.

(c) **Write an analysis of the revised information sheet.** With your collaborator, prepare a memo to accompany the revised information

The SUNDANCE water heater is a three-shell design. The stainless steel inner shell contains the pressurized water. The middle shell provides the space for the heated air to circulate around the inner water tank. The outer shell contains the fiberglass insulation that is wrapped around the middle shell. Heated air enters the top of the water heater and circulates around the inner water tank, giving up its heat to the tank. Cooler air leaves the bottom of the water heater and is returned to the SUNDANCE collectors for reheating and the cycle continues. The heated water from the SUNDANCE solar water tank is piped into the existing electric hot water heater. By providing preheated water to the electric water heater, the amount of time this water water would be required to run is substantially reduced. This arrangement results in a continuous flow of hot water and an uncomplicated system

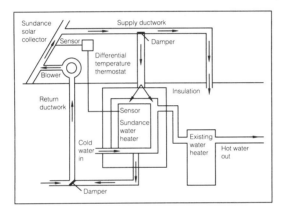

The differential temperature thermostat provides control over the entire SUNDANCE SYSTEM by controling the operation of the blower. In the winter operational mode, the unit turns the blower on when the collectors reach a preset temperature and off when they reach a preset minimum temperature. There is also a thermostat that will override the differential temperature thermostat and turn the system off if the building becomes too hot. In the summer mode, the operation of the temperature differential thermostat is a little more complex. The thermostat has two sensors connected to it. One from the SUNDANCE collector, and the other from the SUNDANCE hot water tank. The thermostat continuously monitors the temperatures at these two locations. The thermostat turns on the SUNDANCE SYSTEM when the temperature differential between the water tank and the collectors is greater than 40F, and off when the temperature differential is less than 20F. By maintaining a proper temperature difference between the collectors and the water tank and the collectors and the building, the SUNDANCE SYSTEM maintains maximum output and effeciency.

sheet. This memo should identify the major changes you made and provide a rationale for them. Including "before" and "after" examples could be used to illustrate your points. The memo should specifically address how the purpose, audience, organization and support, visuals, and document design affected your decisions.

2. **Evaluate your collaboration.** While conducting assignment #1, tape record a planning session with your collaborator. After the assignment is completed, arrange a time when both you and your collaborator can listen to the tape together and then discuss the following questions. What interesting behaviors and patterns did you notice? Did anything surprise either of you when you listened to your collaboration? What does the tape reveal about the following issues:

   - Who was in charge? Was authority shared between the collaborators?
   - Was the time productively used?
   - Where did the ideas come from?
   - What did each person contribute to the collaborative effort?
   - What kinds of problems occurred? How were the problems resolved?

3. **Examine collaboration in your discipline.**
   (a) Survey a key professional journal in a specific discipline (your own field or another one that interests you). Select three years—say, 1950, 1970, and 1990, or 1960, 1980, and 2000—to determine changes in the percentage of co-authored articles. Present your findings in a table or a graph, and prepare a brief oral explanation of the results.
   (b) Interview a professional in your discipline (or one that interests you) to learn about the kinds of collaboration in which you'll be expected to participate. Prepare a series of questions based on the information presented in this chapter. Ask for specific examples of collaboration. Discuss the information you learn in a paper for your classmates. Be prepared to give an oral summary of your findings.

4. **Evaluate computer software.**
   (a) Establish criteria for the effectiveness of a software program that enables some form of collaboration.
   (b) Use your criteria to determine whether the software is effective.
   (c) Write a short review suitable for trade publication.

5. **Track your own collaborative behavior.** One way to learn more about your collaborative processes is to track yourself as you prepare a technical document. The tracking process has three basic steps.
   (a) Keep a log (in a notebook or online) in which you record every time you work on the document (even just thinking about it counts). Indicate whether you are working individually or collaboratively. Record the date

and the time you start and stop. Describe what happens during the time—what gets accomplished, what goes wrong, what you expected to get done but didn't (and why), and so on. Focus particularly on the interaction. Record the facts, but also jot down your attitudes and feelings.

(b) Review and analyze the log, looking for interesting incidents and patterns of behavior that you believe characterize your collaboration.

(c) Use your analysis to describe the nature of your own collaborative behavior. Prepare a detailed memo that focuses on no more than four specific aspects of your own collaborative behavior—for example, the way you approach tasks, the way you handle disagreements, and the way you approach leadership. Include some discussion about the way the collaboration affected the document you prepared.

Intertext

The Rage for Global Teams[16]

In technology, teams are tops. And for the most innovative companies, U.S.-only teams are old hat. Global teams are the rage. Consider the following:

- In Penang, Intel taps the talents of top Malaysian engineers, not only by hiring them as employees but also by helping them launch their own businesses—and then hiring the new firms as contractors who at times work alongside Intel's own employees.

- Engineers from Colorado, Australia, Germany, India and Japan converge on a hotel in trendy Los Gatos, Calif. This isn't a vacation but a rare face-off between members of a Hewlett-Packard software team.

- In Gemenos, France, a half-dozen French engineers at Gemplus, a leading supplier of smart cards, are managed by an American who speaks only enough French to converse with a waiter. His counterpart at Gemplus' research lab in Redwood City, Calif., is a Frenchman who manages a group of Americans.

The spread of global teams is probably inevitable, given the ease and low cost of communication. It also helps that engineers and scientists around the world share the same basic education. Many multinationals, meanwhile, run worldwide training programs that further the trend toward a shared mentality among the world's technical elite.

To be sure, there are plenty of barriers to global teamwork. Look at the life of Radha Basu, who manages Hewlett-Packard software teams that stretch across six countries and 15 time zones. Just communicating is a challenge. She tries to visit each piece of every team four times a year, flying more than 100,000 miles. She's on the road so much that she frequently sends a single five-minute-long voice mail to hundreds of people.

Though all her business is conducted in English, this common language can obscure cultural differences. When talking to an engineer in Brazil about deadlines, she must realize that a due date of Monday may mean that code will arrive any time that week. "By contrast, when one of my engineers in Germany commits to a day," she says, "he usually gives me a time of the day he'll deliver."

Jealousies across cultures can also undermine teamwork. In developing countries, engineers at some multinationals may resent their much-better-paid teammates in the United States and Europe. At one big disk-drive company, engineers in Thailand and Malaysia provide crucial process innovations that make mass production of new drives possible. Yet they fume privately that their American teammates consider them less creative and resist giving them more demanding assignments.

Not surprisingly, some companies eschew global teams altogether. Microsoft, for instance, keeps all its teams within its sprawling campus in Redmond, Wash. It only recently announced plans to open its first non-U.S. facility—and this will be a laboratory in "exotic" Cambridge, England.

Despite the inherent risks and difficulties of global teams, they are increasingly popular. The reason is simple: With demand red-hot for skilled engineers, companies have more incentive than ever to build their ranks abroad. After all, there are only so many code writers and hardware jocks that can be brought legally into the United States. Besides, it's expensive to import foreign talent, and engineers in their native lands are usually a bargain (the exceptions: those in Western Europe and Japan). From Seoul to Singapore, engineers earn roughly one-third to one-half of their American counterparts. Indian or Russian engineers, meanwhile, are happy with a paycheck that is one-tenth of what a Yank gets.

"Discount" foreign engineers often are assigned to banal tasks such as teasing another model out of an aging hardware line or writing ancient COBOL code for so-called "legacy" software. But companies are increasingly making foreign engineers, even those from developing countries, equal members of far-flung technical teams.

While multinational companies say they can't offer equal pay to top team members in the developing world, they can shower them with perks. In another unit of Hewlett-Packard, for instance, a star Malaysian engineer in Penang lives as if he were in Silicon Valley. He has a posh pad, a new car and trendy holidays such as a weekend of rock climbing. He also gets bonuses, stock options, special equipment at work and a high-powered ISDN line and a computer at home. The company even periodically flies him to see teammates in California. All this effort is expended simply to keep him happy on his own turf.

When global teams work, the results are impressive. Product cycles are cut in half; Ms. Basu says her teams either write code or test it an average of 22 hours a day. Different parts of the world, meanwhile, specialize in different techniques. They can also cater to the needs of customers in the region.

Such global teamwork isn't going to win Ms. Basu a Nobel Peace Prize, but it is good business. Despite the inevitable headaches, bringing diverse people together is the future of innovation.

Developing the Communicator's Tools

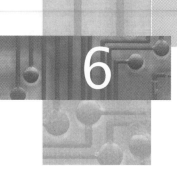

6

Locating and Recording Information

CHAPTER 6 IN BRIEF

Locating Primary and Secondary Sources

Primary source information is first-hand information, reported by people directly involved with an action or event. Secondary source information is, instead, passed to a second or third person, who reports it. You can collect information from any of ten different categories of sources.

Personal Observations and Close Reading

Your own observations can be an important source of primary information, especially if you're a trained observer.

Calculations

If you calculate information for a specific situation, the results constitute primary source information.

Samples and Specimens

Actual objects or specimens can be primary sources. Descriptions of these samples can appear in a paper.

Empirical Investigations

You conduct an empirical investigation to test a hypothesis or supposition or to observe an identifiable pattern.

Internal Records

Internal company records might provide details about finances, personnel, manufacturing, marketing, or shipping.

Interviews and Letters of Inquiry

Interview questions can be convergent (having one correct answer) or divergent (being open ended).

Surveys and Polls

Questions include dual alternatives, multiple choice, rank ordering, Likert scales, completions, and essays or open-ended questions.

Library Resources

Conventional library resources include reference resources, online catalogs, and indexes.

Electronic Resources

Computer databases and the World Wide Web provide access to an additional array of resources.

Government Documents and Offices

A search can begin with the Government Printing Office and the Congressional Research Service of the Library of Congress.

Recording Data

Various methods of recording data include field journals; lab notebooks; note cards; outlines; visual forms such as tracings, photographs, drawings, maps, videotapes, films; and audiorecordings.

T he quality of your communication depends on your care and thoroughness in collecting evidence. The credibility and completeness of your evidence affect readers' acceptance of the points you're making. The following examples are typical of situations in which you might collect evidence for a document or presentation:

- Holly Craig has spent several hours searching a computerized database to locate information about new techniques to strengthen carbon fibers.

- Ayami Ogura is calculating the expected heat loss in a new office complex using passive solar energy.

- Herb Kane has just designed a survey to use for market research about industrial degreasers.

- Philip Benson has spent three weeks trying to find out from his product design engineer about the status of a new product, which he is responsible for documenting.

- Gina Salmone is collecting water samples from a local brook that runs through an industrial park.

- Richard Minkoff has spent an hour reading abstracts in indexes such as *Pollution Abstracts* and *Water Resources Abstracts* to locate relevant research on contamination of ground water.

For major projects, you'll need to collect information in the workplace as well as in the library. For example, Nancy Irish, a nutritionist who has worked for government agencies as well as private groups, is investigating the ecological and nutritional benefits of soy protein and its potential for greater use in the diets of Americans. Her preliminary work involves academic research, using library resources to review available literature about soy proteins and tofu. Then she conducts interviews and surveys to determine people's attitudes toward tofu and obtains tofu samples from local stores and food cooperatives to determine availability and quality. Some of her research techniques are included as examples in this chapter.

Locating Primary and Secondary Sources

You can collect information from any of these ten categories of sources:

- Personal observations and close reading
- Calculations
- Samples and specimens
- Empirical investigations
- Internal records
- Interviews and letters of inquiry
- Surveys and polls
- Library resources, including reference resources, the online catalog, and indexes
- Electronic resources, including computerized databases, the Internet, and the World Wide Web
- Government documents and offices

Your choice of sources depends on your document's purpose and audience. For example, if you are providing general background information for professional nonexperts, you can confidently employ summaries of calculations, experiments, or expert opinions. However, if you are writing for experts who will implement the solutions, you need precise details rather than summaries. (Refer to Chapter 3 to review the process of audience analysis.)

In preparing technical documents, you need to decide whether to use quantitative or qualitative data—or both—as evidence to support your positions. *Quantitative data* describe measurable elements (quantities) in mathematical or statistical terms. *Qualitative data* describe observed or reported information (qualities). However, after qualitative data are recorded, the information can sometimes be treated quantitatively. For example, an anthropologist would record observations of a native population over a period of months (qualitative data). The number of observations of a particular phenomenon could then be counted (quantitative data).

The methods used to collect and record information—whether quantitative or qualitative data—often get people into hot water. Some methods, quite simply, are considered unacceptable. The ethics sidebar on the next page addresses a number of situations that many workplace professionals consider unethical.

Even before selecting specific evidence, though, you need to consider the relative advantages of primary and secondary sources. Then, whether you decide on primary or secondary sources, check the credentials of the source, the sponsoring agency, and the date the information was obtained.

Primary source information is first-hand information, reported by people directly involved with an action or event. Because primary source information

Explain whether you believe that primary information is or is not more reliable than secondary information.

On-the-Job Pressures: Ethics and Technology in the Workplace

Consider the following on-the-job actions:

- Sabotaging the systems or data of a current or former coworker or employer
- Accessing private computer files without permission
- Listening to a private cellular phone conversation
- Accessing pornographic Web sites using office equipment
- Using office equipment to search for another job
- Copying the company's software for home use
- Wrongly blaming an error on a technological glitch
- Making multiple copies of software for office use
- Using office equipment to shop on the Internet for personal needs

Which of these actions would you find unethical? All of them are unethical, according to the Ethics Officer Association (EOA), the professional association for managers of corporate ethics and compliance programs. In 1998, the EOA, along with the American Society of Chartered Life Underwriters and Chartered Financial Consultants, conducted a nationwide survey of American workers "to measure whether or not the presence of new technologies in the workplace increases the risk of unethical and illegal business practices."[1] Nearly half (45%) of the respondents to the survey indicated they had engaged in at least one unethical act.

The survey found that business and technical professionals feel pressured by new workplace technologies. The pressures caused by workplace technologies include increased productivity expectations; the continual need to change or update the technology; increased frustration with coworkers who are not up to date on the technology; less tolerance for errors; inadequate manuals and/or training; and the fear of losing data. Female respondents felt more pressure than male respondents, largely due to a "lack of understanding terminology or lingo" (70% women vs. 51% men). "New technologies have changed the way we do our jobs and the way we work with one another," said EOA Executive Director Ed Petry when the survey results were announced. "We're expected to do more, to do it faster, and we're also working more independently."

What are some solutions to these ethical problems? Survey respondents offered several, including creating guidelines for the personal use of company technology resources, installing Internet blocking software, and encouraging employees to police themselves. For technical professionals, perhaps the best individual advice is to be aware of how these actions can cause unnecessary workplace conflicts. Avoiding these conflicts will help make workplace technology more of an asset and less of a liability. (See discussion of unproductive conflicts in Chapter 5.)

What constitutes unethical use of your office computer? How could you keep yourself from using your office computer unethically?

Have you engaged in any of the unethical actions listed above? Did you consider them unethical at the time? What would be the most effective deterrent to keep you from engaging in them in the future?

has not been interpreted through a second or third person, it is often considered reliable. However, primary sources can be slanted or biased. For example, two firefighters who worked to put out a chemical fire in a warehouse could give

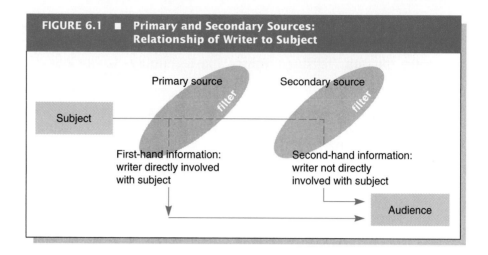

FIGURE 6.1 ■ Primary and Secondary Sources: Relationship of Writer to Subject

first-hand reports about fighting chemical fires. But if one of the firefighters had been injured during the chemical fire, that firefighter might give a different account of the specific fire and have a different opinion about safety in firefighting.

Another problem with first-hand information is that a particular situation might be an exception. Unless you are concentrating on exceptions to the rule, evidence you cite should be representative. For example, Nancy Irish would not assume that the experiences of one farmer or one supermarket manager are necessarily representative of all farmers or supermarket managers.

Secondary source information does not come directly from people involved in the action or event. Instead, the information is interpreted by a second or third person, who reports it. If an engineer conducts an experiment and then reports her findings, the document is a primary source. However, if that same engineer is interviewed about her research by a technical writer who writes the report, that document is a secondary source.

Secondary sources are sometimes considered less desirable than primary sources because some people believe that secondary sources have a greater chance of being distorted, incomplete, or misrepresented. This view does not consider the possible bias of the primary source. Figure 6.1 illustrates one way to depict the relationship of a writer to the subject in primary and secondary sources.

Ten types of sources are all accessible as both primary and secondary sources. In this chapter, they are arranged in order from those you can do most easily yourself, thus producing primary source materials, to those that are most difficult to produce as primary sources.

Personal Observations and Close Reading

Personal observations are legitimate primary sources if the observer is trained in the area of investigation. For example, botanists can identify a bog by observing and classifying the vegetation in a geographic area. Physicians can diagnose many illnesses by observing the symptoms of a patient. Opticians can make remarkably accurate judgments about the flatness of a mirror surface by observing light refraction. Veterinarians can determine when a mare is ready to foal by observing physical changes. Psychologists can observe changes in behavior that signal a patient's progress or decline.

Your own involvement—even if you're not a specialist—in completing a procedure is an important source of primary information. If you are a technical communicator who operates a computer system, you are better equipped to explain its operation than a colleague who merely hears about it. Similarly, if you are a supervisor who can actually run the equipment in a machine shop, you are better qualified to train new employees than a colleague who knows the theory but not the actual operation. A nutritionist experienced in dietary analysis is better equipped to teach such analysis than is an inexperienced nutritionist. Do not underestimate the value of your hands-on experience.

Personal Observations

If you choose to use your own or others' personal observations and experiences as evidence in a document, consider several guidelines to increase the likelihood that the data will be accepted as credible:

- Select observations that are representative, not outliers.

- Support generalizations with specific details and examples.

- Quantify observations whenever possible.

- Use standard terminology and notation.

- Identify the situation, the context. Identify clearly biased observations.

- Indicate the expertise of the observer.

Before the days of sophisticated test and measuring equipment, technical knowledge depended on recording the personal observations and experiences of trained experts. For instance, in 1628, William Harvey wrote *De Motu Cordis (On the Motion of the Heart)*, part of which is quoted here, based entirely on his personal observations and activities. Modern medicine, in fact, has derived in part from this method based on Harvey's observations made more than 300 years ago.

■ EXAMPLE

In the motion, and interval in which this is accomplished, three principal circumstances are to be noted:

1. That the heart is erected, and rises upward to a point, so that at this time it strikes against the breast and the pulse is felt externally.

2. That it is everywhere contracted, but more especially toward the sides, so that it looks narrower, relatively longer, more drawn together. The heart of an eel taken

out of the body of the animal and placed upon the table or the hand shows these particulars; but the same things are manifest in the hearts of small fishes and of those colder animals where the organ is more conical or elongated.

3. The heart, being grasped in the hand, is felt to become harder during its action. Now this hardness proceeds from tension, precisely as when the forearm is grasped, its tendons are perceived to become tense and resilient when the fingers are moved.

4. It may further be observed in fishes, and the colder-blooded animals, such as frogs, serpents, et cetera, that the heart when it moves becomes of a paler color; when quiescent, of a deeper blood-red color.

From these particulars it appeared evident to me that the motion of the heart consists in a certain universal tension—both contraction in the line of its fibers and constriction in every sense. It becomes erect, hard, and of diminished size during its action; the motion is plainly of the same nature as that of the muscles when they contract in the line of their sinews and fibers; for the muscles, when in action, acquire vigor and tenseness, and from soft become hard, prominent, and thickened: in the same manner the heart.[2]

Close Reading

You can often identify valuable resources by close reading of the footnotes, endnotes, and references in articles and reports. Close reading is a kind of personal observation (of a text rather than an actual situation) that many people overlook. For example, in reading *Protein Resources and Technology: Status and Research Needs*, an anthology edited by three Massachusetts Institute of Technology professors, Nancy Irish found a reference to a mimeographed report, National Soybean Research Needs, that had not been mentioned in the periodical and abstract indexes or in her computerized database search. The reason was obvious: It was an unpublished committee report from the University of Missouri. This resource would never have been part of her research base if she hadn't taken the time to read the references listed at the end of relevant articles.

Calculations

If you calculate information for a specific situation, the results constitute primary source information. Standard formulas exist for determining such things as heat in a house, strain on the foundation of a building, and quality of protein.

By using well-known, widely accepted formulas, you are more likely to produce unquestioned calculations. In the body of a document, the results of calculations are most important, but the actual formulas and calculations should also be included in a footnote or an appendix. For example, a nutritionist can apply a formula to calculate the biological value of protein, based on the amount of nitrogen absorbed.

■ EXAMPLE

$$BV = \frac{\text{Dietary } N - (\text{Urinary } N + \text{Fecal } N)}{\text{Dietary } N - \text{Fecal } N} \times 100$$

BV = biological value
N = nitrogen

A nutritionist doing case study research to determine the biological value of consumed protein in a group of patients suffering from gallbladder problems could use this formula. The resulting biological values might be presented in a table, with the formula itself placed in an information note. If the writer wanted to include the formula and the individual calculations, they could all be placed in an appendix.

Samples and Specimens

Actual objects or specimens can be primary sources. Geologists often take core samples of earth, ecologists take water samples, physicians take biopsies (tissue samples), and dairy farmers take milk samples. In her investigation of tofu in retail food stores, Nancy Irish collected samples—randomly selected packages of tofu—to determine type, quality, and freshness.

Obviously, samples themselves are not included in a document, but a description focusing on the significant characteristics of the sample should appear. For example, Nancy Irish assembled a trained tasting panel to rate samples of dishes made from the selected packages of tofu. One of the dishes, tofu cheesecake, was given an average rating of 7.5 on a 10-point scale; this figure would be cited in her report.

Empirical Investigations

You conduct an empirical investigation to test a hypothesis or supposition or to observe an identifiable pattern. One kind of empirical investigation is an experiment designed to establish whether the hypothesis is accepted. Such a study may have a control group and a test group, which have the same characteristics; results are measured by applying experimental treatments only to the test group, not to the control group. Other kinds of empirical investigations don't start with a hypothesis; instead, investigators carefully observe a subject group in order to identify patterns, and then they use these patterns to develop a hypothesis.

When you report the results of a study, check that they are both valid and reliable. *Validity* represents the extent to which the study produces the intended results—its capability to prove or disprove the hypothesis. *Reliability* represents the extent to which the study consistently produces similar results. If a study is valid, it is also reliable; that is, if it substantiates what you want to prove or disprove, it does so consistently. However, a study can be reliable without being valid; it can produce consistent results that do not prove or disprove the hypothesis. When you use information from studies, make sure to check both the validity and reliability. If the methodology is not rigorous enough, you cannot be confident in using the results.

Internal Records

Internal records—the data a company keeps about its own transactions in business—often serve as supporting material in a document. Such records might provide facts and details about finances, personnel, manufacturing, marketing, or shipping. For example, in submitting a memo proposing the addition of three employees to his sheet metal department, a departmental manager used a variety of data, including personnel information about salaries and benefits, monthly productivity sheets, backlogged orders, and projected sales figures. His proposal wouldn't have any impact if he merely said his department needed three additional workers. All the evidence he needed to support his proposal was available in the files and internal documents of his own company.

Internal records must be analyzed before you can use them. For instance, a report with an appendix of 100 pages of raw computer printout—perhaps detailing manufacturing quotas and actual production figures—isn't helpful for most readers. Instead, the writer needs to analyze the data in the printout by comparing the quotas with actual production. Once the figures are accessible, the writer can evaluate, draw conclusions, and finally make recommendations.

Can you justify the use of proprietary or confidential material in a report or presentation if someone ultimately benefits from the release of the information?

Internal records are not always an appropriate source of information, even if the conclusions and recommendations are accurate. You must consider the legal and ethical implications of using internal records, particularly in a document intended for external readers. Many companies require key employees to sign statements (usually considered legally binding) to restrict the dissemination of proprietary information.

Interviews and Letters of Inquiry

Interviewing is one of the most important professional skills. Often the information you need is not written in any book or article, but is in the mind or indecipherable notes of another person. You have to ask the right questions in order to elicit this information. Be prepared and persistent.

Preparing effective questions for an interview requires some homework. You need to prepare in two ways:

- *Gather necessary information about the subject:* What do you already know? What do you need to know? What do you expect this particular person to be able to tell you?

- *Approach the person you want to interview:* How should you contact the person? What's the best place for the interview? What's the most convenient time? Be aware when you select the site that time and place can affect the quality of the interview. How should you refer to the person?

The answers to these questions provide a focus for the interview. An essential courtesy is learning to pronounce the name of the person you're interviewing. You should also be familiar with the terminology you'll use during the interview.

Developing Questions

Questions can be divided into two broad categories: convergent questions, which have only one correct answer, and divergent questions, which are open ended and therefore more useful in problem solving. The following general suggestions should make your interviewing more successful:

- Identify in advance key topics for questions.

- Ask direct, unambiguous questions, using simple language.

- Allow sufficient time for answers; give people time to think.

- Build on a respondent's answers by asking follow-up questions.

Identify the categories of questions you want to ask, and plan the specific topics that you want to explore. Listing topics rather than specific questions gives you more flexibility. The guidelines in Figure 6.2 are illustrated by some of the questions that Nancy Irish used in her interviews.

Asking Questions

What you ask is important. How you ask it is also important. Figure 6.3 identifies actions and attitudes that will make your interviews more efficient and effective. Far more than the content of the questions is important. You also need to consider your behavior and body language, respect conventions of interviewing, and decide how to manage mechanical considerations.

If time is limited or distance a problem, you may be able to convince a person to be interviewed by telephone or e-mail. Although this is a good alternative to an in-person interview, you should consider certain problems that result from not

In a report about equipment for a company's new daycare facility for employees' children, what information about the equipment should you verify beyond that provided by manufacturers? Why?

FIGURE 6.2 ■ Guidelines for Asking Effective Interview Questions

Guidelines	Negative and Positive Examples	
◆ Design questions whose answers require a definition or an explanation rather than a simple yes or no.	*Weak:*	Are people's diets improved by using soy protein?
	Effective:	In what ways are people's diets improved by using soy protein?
◆ If you must ask a yes or no question to establish a position, follow it with a question requiring some explanation. Generally, you should know the answers to basic questions. Don't waste interview time asking questions when you already know the answers. Instead, use this basic information to develop more fruitful questions.	*Weak:*	Has there been an increase in the past five years in soy protein used in processed food for human consumption?
	Effective:	Has there been an increase in the past five years in soy protein used in processed food for human consumption? What has contributed to this increase (or decrease)?
	Better:	What has contributed to the increase (or decrease) in the past five years in soy protein used in processing food for human consumption?
◆ Ask questions that require a focused response, not a broad, rambling discussion.	*Weak:*	What do you think of the public attitudes about soy use?
	Effective:	What specific strategies work to persuade the public to incorporate soy into regular meals?
◆ Ask a single question at a time, not combined (complex) questions that require multiple answers.	*Weak:*	Describe the progress that has been made in identifying those components responsible for undesirable flavors and colors and in developing processing technology to eliminate these from food products.
	Effective:	Describe the progress in identifying components responsible for undesirable flavors and colors in soy products.
	Follow up:	What processing technology has been developed to eliminate these from food products?

Should you send questions for an interview in advance to the person you're interviewing? Should you agree to submit material written from the interview for clarification? For approval?

being able to see the person. Questions need to be particularly clear and focused because you cannot reword or clarify them based on the quizzical expression on the person's face. Further, determining a person's attitude is more difficult because you cannot see his or her body language and facial expressions. Pauses, an inevitable part of interviews while a person is thinking, are more disconcerting on the telephone.

When a person is simply not available in person, on the telephone, or by e-mail, a letter of inquiry is an appropriate vehicle for collecting information. In some situations, a person may even agree to record answers on a tape that

FIGURE 6.2 ■ Guidelines for Asking Effective Interview Questions *(continued)*

Guidelines	Negative and Positive Examples	
◆ Use terminology that narrows the area of response.	*Weak:*	In what ways have soybeans been improved?
	Effective:	In what ways has the nutritive value of soybeans been improved, specifically the amino acid profile and the digestibility?
◆ Prepare questions to tactfully redirect a respondent who has begun to ramble.	*Weak:*	Getting back to the subject, I'd like to ask you again to describe the ways in which soybeans have been improved.
	Effective:	I'd be interested to hear more of the ways in which the nutritive value of soybeans has been improved.
◆ Research other interviews in the field to avoid asking what have become cliché questions; instead, find a new angle so that the respondent will be interested in what you ask and will know you have done your homework.	*Weak:*	What are the ecological benefits of soy foods?
	Effective:	How do you think the ecological benefits of soy foods could be used in marketing to increase the American public's interest in them?
◆ Refer specifically to the respondent's published work.	*Weak:*	I liked your recent article on soybeans for human consumption.
	Effective:	Your article in last month's *Soy Research Journal* effectively supports the importance of increasing human consumption of soybeans.
◆ Prepare questions the respondent might perceive as hostile so that the respondent is not offended but, instead, answers.	*Weak:*	How can you carry out objective research on soy foods when your research is funded by the National Soy Growers of America?
	Effective:	I understand that your research is funded by the National Soy Growers of America. Does that make it difficult for you to conduct your research objectively?

you provide so that he or she is spared writing detailed responses. Figure 6.4 displays a letter of inquiry that Nancy Irish wrote to Chris Morgan.

Whether you obtain your information through a personal interview, telephone interview, e-mail interview, written questionnaire with taped response, or written response to a letter of inquiry, take the time to write a thank-you letter, acknowledging your appreciation for the time and effort the person took to assist you.

You can give the letter a personal tone by mentioning one or two things that were particularly helpful. If the person is someone you regularly see in your company, you can write an informal note or send an e-mail message; even a person

FIGURE 6.3 ■ Actions and Attitudes for Effective Interviewing

Category	Actions and Attitudes
Interpersonal behavior	◆ Be attentive and courteous.
	◆ Know how to pronounce the person's name.
	◆ Generally address the person formally ("Dr. Greenough" rather than "Pat") unless you know him or her personally.
Body language	◆ Convey interest through your tone of voice, facial expressions, and body language.
	◆ Make direct eye contact with the person you're interviewing.
	◆ Note the person's body language as a signal to how well the interview is going.
Interviewing conventions	◆ Confirm arrangements beforehand regarding the time, place, and duration of the interview.
	◆ Arrive or call on time, and do not exceed the agreed-on length. If you want to record the interview, ask for permission; it's usually granted.
	◆ Prepare questions in advance. You can modify or extend them if you need to, but don't go into the interview unprepared.
	◆ Give the person time to respond to your questions.
	◆ Don't interrupt unless the person strays off track or becomes too long-winded.
Mechanical considerations	◆ Be prepared to take notes, paraphrasing the person's comments, in case there are mechanical problems with the recorder or the person prefers that you don't use it.
	◆ Consider asking the person to prepare responses to statistical questions prior to or after the interview itself.

you see every day appreciates a brief thank you. If the person is someone you do not see every day, make the thank you more formal.

Surveys and Polls

Surveys and polls can be misleading if care has not been taken in constructing the questions, selecting the test group, and compiling the results. If you are conducting your own survey, you need to be attentive to each of these areas. If you are using the data from surveys by others, you need to investigate how carefully the surveys were constructed and conducted.

Survey design is important. The questions should be both valid (the questions really ask what the survey takers intend to ask) and reliable (the questions are likely to be interpreted in a similar way by people completing the survey). In order to determine the validity and reliability of questions, you need to test them with representative members of the survey group. If changes are necessary, you can make them before officially administering the survey.

Part II: Developing the Communicator's Tools

FIGURE 6.4 ■ Letter of Inquiry

112 North Riverside Drive
Ames, IA 50010-5971
October 30, 20—

Make sure to include your return address so the person can contact you.

Chris Morgan, Research Director
National Soybean Institute
731 Jefferson Street
Dubuque, IA 52086

If you don't know the gender of the person (because of a name such as Robin, Pat, or Chris), use the full name.

Dear Chris Morgan:

Identify your role and goal.

As part of my work designing educational programs for members of food co-ops, I am investigating the role of soybeans in an ecologically and nutritionally sound food system. I am particularly interested in the increased use of soybeans in the American diet.

State specifically what you want.

Could you please provide information on the following topics?

1. Percentage of annual U.S. soybean crop consumed by humans vs. livestock; domestic vs. foreign markets
2. Percentage of U.S. arable land (acreage) planted in soybeans
3. Nutrient composition of traditional Asian soy foods
4. Resource efficiency of soybean products vs. grain-fed livestock production
5. Current research to develop new soy products for human consumption

I appreciate your assistance. If you wish, I will be glad to send you a copy of my final report outlining program options.

Thank the person for assisting you.

Sincerely,

Nancy Irish

Nancy Irish
515-555-1234 (office)
515-555-6779 (fax)
nirish@iastate.edu (internet)

Provide a telephone number and, if available, a fax number and e-mail address to give the person alternative and perhaps more convenient ways of contacting you.

Surveys can be designed using any of six different types of questions; each type has advantages and disadvantages you should consider when designing a questionnaire for a survey or poll:

- *Dual alternatives*, the simplest questions to tabulate, offer only two choices: yes/no, positive/negative, true/false, and so on. Such questions adequately address simple issues, but they often unrealistically limit the range of responses needed to portray complex situations. If you want to use this type of question, assure yourself that there really are only two possible answers so that the respondent does not feel as if the choices are inadequate.

- *Multiple choice questions* give respondents alternatives, sometimes limiting them to a single answer, at other times permitting them to check all applicable answers. Because the survey designer provides all the choices, multiple choice questions may not offer an answer with which respondents agree, thus distorting the results. A well-designed multiple choice question does not have two or three choices that are obviously wrong, nor does it have choices in which the distinctions are so slight that the respondent must guess the correct answer.

- *Rank ordering* provides respondents with a series of items and asks them to order the items according to preference, frequency of use, or some other criterion. Tabulating rank ordering is easy, but distortion may occur if the mean (arithmetic average) differs significantly from the mode (most frequently occurring number). If the items in a particular grouping are similar, respondents will have a difficult time ranking them and may assign an arbitrary value rather than an actual preference.

- *Likert scales* provide a method for respondents to express their opinion by rating items either numerically or verbally on a continuum. As with rank ordering, tabulation is easy but may give distorted results if the mean and mode are significantly different. Scales are most effective if they have an even number of choices (usually four or six). If a scale has a middle choice (as occurs when the scale has an odd number of choices), respondents choose it a disproportionately large percentage of the time.

- *Completions* expect respondents to fill in information to complete an item. The answers are simple to tabulate if the responses are quantitative, such as age, frequency, or amount. But even short, open-ended opinion questions present problems in tabulation if respondents give a variety of answers; the evaluator must decide which terms respondents use are synonymous.

- *Essays or open-ended questions* give respondents the opportunity to fully express themselves, presenting both facts and opinions, but the responses are difficult to tabulate. Essays are much more effective if they ask respondents to focus on specifics rather than requesting general opinions or reactions.

FIGURE 6.5 ■ Variations of Questions that Could Produce the Same Response

Dual Alternative	Would you include tofu in your meals if you knew good recipes? ❑ Yes *(23 percent)* ❑ No
Single Multiple Choice	Tofu is a traditional Asian soybean food high in protein and other nutrients and low in calories and fat. Considering the high nutrient value of tofu, check the one item you most agree with. ❑ Willing to try tofu if I had a good recipe *(14 percent)* ❑ Use tofu regularly *(9 percent)* ❑ Tried tofu and didn't like it ❑ Not interested in trying tofu ❑ Never heard of tofu
Rank Order	Rank order the following soy items in order of preference as additions to your current diet. __ Soy sauce __ Tofu *(23 percent ranked tofu second)* __ Miso __ Natto __ Tempeh

Continuum (Likert)	Mark your preference for each food item on the scale.
	Tofu: Would not Might Would if Use
	        ever use consider knew how now
	
	           |_____|_____|_____|
	                                        (23 percent)

Completion	Which soy product are you most willing to include in your meal planning? _____ *("tofu"–23 percent)*

Do the types of questions really make a difference? Imagine that Nancy Irish read a claim that 23 percent of people questioned agreed they would include tofu in their diets. The statistic doesn't mean much unless she knows the question. The same answer may be a response to several variations of the question. Dual alternatives, for example, could elicit far more positive responses than completion questions. Figure 6.5 illustrates some of the possible questions that could have elicited such a response.

Designing an effective series of questions is only the first step in preparing a survey. After you have designed and tested your questions, you need to administer the survey to a representative random sample of the target population. Compiling and reporting the results should not be difficult if your questions have been carefully designed. Even when the questions are valid and reliable, the population sample random and representative, and the data compiled accurately, the results may be disappointing, particularly with mail-in surveys, which have a very low return rate.

Library Resources

Knowing how to locate information in a library is invaluable. Academic, public, and corporate libraries are no longer defined by their walls or the print materials on their shelves. Several major resources will be useful in your professional work:

- Research librarians who can ferret out information where those less well trained fail

- Online catalogs that give you access to the complete holdings of your library and other libraries

- Periodical indexes and abstract indexes (available in print, microforms, and CD-ROM)

The amount of library resources available is astounding. For example, the Library of Congress has holdings of more than 16 million books, more than 13 million other volumes, and nearly 80 million other items, including everything from newspapers to maps to movies, in its other collections. This number increases every year because thousands of new books are published every year—more than 47,000 in the United States in a single year, nearly 3,000 of those about science and another 2,100 about technology. In addition to books, there are more than 141,000 different periodicals in *The Serials Directory: An International Reference Book*, which lists both print and electronic serials (that is, periodical publications).

The largest university libraries hold millions of volumes of books (more than 12 million at Harvard, 8 million at the University of Illinois at Urbana, nearly 4 million at the University of Pennsylvania). With these vast resources, you obviously must develop techniques to sort and select the information.

Research Librarians and Their References

The best resources in any library—academic, public, or corporate—are the research librarians and staff members who know alternative search strategies and can locate information often inaccessible to average library users. One of the reasons librarians are so effective is their familiarity with a variety of bibliographic references, that is, reference books for locating other books.

- *Cumulative Book Index* (CBI), published monthly, with a bound cumulative volume published annually, provides the bibliographic details for any book published in English.

- *Books in Print* (BIP), an annual publication, lists every book published in the United States (if the publisher supplies the information), beginning in its year of publication and continuing until it goes out of print. BIP lists books two ways: in an author index (with title, publisher, and price) and in a subject index (the Library of Congress subject headings).

- *Library of Congress Subject Headings* is helpful as a reference tool because it offers alternative headings for a subject.

- Specialized resources of books in science and technology include *Scientific and Technical Books in Print* and *Technical Book Review Index*.

- Both *Winchell's Guide to Reference Books* with Sheehy's supplements and Walford's *Guide to Reference Material* are valuable. These volumes do overlap in their coverage of various fields in science and technology; however, Walford has more than twice as many entries dealing with science and technology. A third resource, *American Reference Books Annual* (ARBA), covers a broad range of science subjects. The ARBA evaluates all reference books published in the United States in brief reviews (up to 300 words).

The services offered by large corporate libraries, often called information services, give a clear picture of the importance of librarians to your own professional work. Unlike public and college libraries, where people usually locate their own information, the librarians in a corporate information service often locate the information for their internal clients, which has important benefits. The Information Services division of 3M Corporation, headquartered in St. Paul, Minnesota, is a good illustration. 3M employees who request in-depth information surveys from Information Services estimate that, on the average, receiving this information saves them some 28 hours per project. Barbara Peterson, Director of Information Services for 3M, explained in a recent interview how the 75 professionals in Information Services help meet her division's four distinct responsibilities:[3]

1. Information Services responds to three kinds of questions:
    - Answering fact-based questions that range from locating potential consultants for a project to identifying regulatory requirements that may affect project development
    - Identifying publications related to a particular topic requested by 3M professionals, from state-of-the-art sources to newspaper articles
    - Monitoring ongoing developments with selective dissemination of information (SDI) so that searches can be tailored to an individual's information needs

2. Information Services provides 3M professionals with easy access to library materials, ranging from journals to the Internet.

3. Information Services organizes and maintains systems that track two kinds of 3M's R&D information:
    - Internal research and development documents—research proposals, laboratory notebooks, research reports

- An online database of skills of 3M scientists and engineers—so that project teams have a good chance of locating a needed expert from among 3M's 8,000 technical employees

4. Information Services provides ongoing education to help 3M employees use, manage, and share information effectively.

Although corporate libraries in other companies may provide a different range of services, you can depend on a good corporate library to be a tremendous help to you in identifying and collecting information useful for your projects.

Reference Resources

What are the implications of taking a "not-for-circulation" periodical or reference book that is critical to your current work from any library— public, academic, or corporate?

The reference section of a library provides easy access to a large collection of volumes containing a vast array of data. These resources include handbooks, specialized dictionaries, specialized encyclopedias, and business and industrial guides.

Handbooks are compact and carefully organized one-volume reference works, usually presenting information in tables, charts, diagrams, graphs, and glossaries. Handbooks are available in astronomy, biological science, biomedical science, chemistry, computer science, engineering, environmental science, geoscience, mathematics, physics, and virtually every other major field of technical and scientific inquiry.

Specialized dictionaries concentrate on providing precise, current meanings of technical terms. Having one or more specialized dictionaries—for example, the *Chambers Dictionary of Science and Technology* or the *Dictionary of Technical Terms*—on your personal reference shelf makes your professional work easier. In addition, several other types of technical dictionaries are commonly used. For example, translators and technical professionals who work with international vendors and clients use a variety of specialized bilingual and foreign-language dictionaries. In other situations, dictionaries of acronyms are necessary. Many companies create so many acronyms that they publish an acronym glossary of company-related terms for their own employees and customers.

Specialized encyclopedias and a variety of *business and industry guides* are invaluable for an initial inquiry because the entries provide an overview, summarizing and discussing essential facts and theories about a subject. Beyond the discussion, the entries often present statistical data in various graphic forms, provide historical background, and list bibliographic references.

Other valuable references that are often overlooked include *annotated bibliographies and bibliographic essays*, available in every scientific and technical field. Annotated bibliographies not only identify authoritative sources but also provide a descriptive abstract of the material. Bibliographic essays go further; they categorize and discuss the relative merits of significant sources.

Online Catalog

The online catalog has information about all the books, bound periodicals (a year's issues of a particular journal bound into a single volume), and audiovisual (av) holdings (films, records, audio- and videotapes) in a particular library. You can use the online catalog to determine if the library has books, bound periodicals, or av materials relevant to your subject.

Each book or other item is assigned an individual number, based on one of two classification systems: the Dewey decimal system or the Library of Congress system. Public libraries generally use the Dewey decimal system, whereas college and university libraries use the Library of Congress system. The Dewey decimal system divides books into ten categories, each identified by a range of numbers. The Library of Congress system divides books into twenty categories, each identified by a letter followed by specific numbers. The broad letter categories represent major subject areas.

In both the Dewey decimal and the Library of Congress systems, the broad categories are further subdivided until each book has an individual number—the *call number*—which helps you locate specific volumes in library stacks. Being familiar with call numbers enables you to go into the stacks and browse though the books in your specific field of interest. Browsing does not constitute efficient use of time, but you often find volumes of interest that you might have ignored had you only read the online information about a book.

Nancy Irish began her search using the online catalog at Iowa State University in order to locate current resources about nutritional benefits of soy protein. Folowing the on-screen directions, she had several choices: She could search for information by *author, title, subject,* or *keyword.* The keyword option is the one Nancy decided to use. Figure 6.6 shows three of the screens that appeared when Nancy was conducting her search.

The *Library of Congress Guide to Subject Headings* is also valuable to use here. After one or two attempts at identifying the term(s) under which a subject is cataloged, check this guide for alternative labels and related areas of study. Figure 6.7 reproduces a section of the guide used by Nancy Irish during her research.

Indexes

Indexes can give you access to information that would otherwise be very difficult to locate. Virtually all the commonly used indexes for periodicals, newspapers, and abstracts have an introductory section that explains how to use that index. Although some of these indexes are available only in printed versions, many have electronic versions (online or CD-ROM) that are easy to use. You'll

FIGURE 6.6 ■ Online Catalog Screen

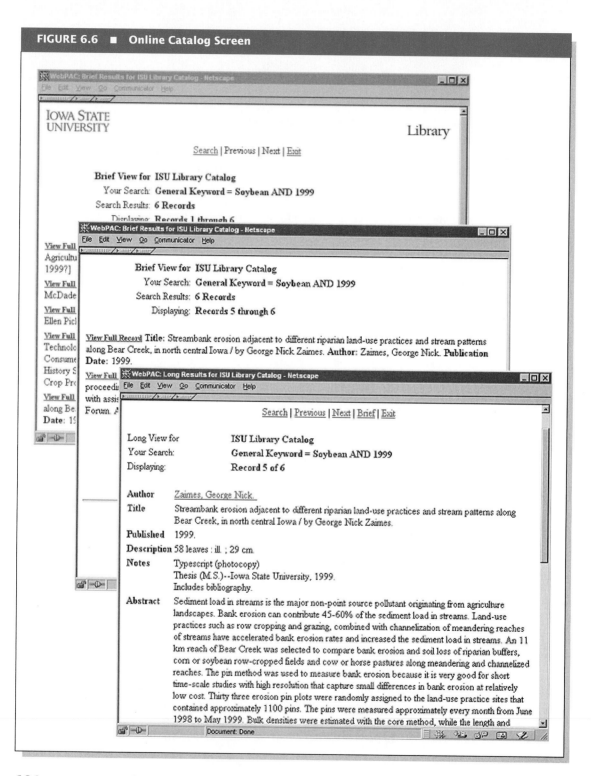

IOWA STATE
UNIVERSITY

Library

Search | Previous | Next | Exit

Brief View for ISU Library Catalog

Your Search: **General Keyword = Soybean AND 1999**

Search Results: **6 Records**

Displaying: **Records 1 through 6**

View Full
Agricultu
1999?]

View Full
McDade

View Full
Ellen Picl

View Full
Technolo
Consume
History S
Crop Pro

View Full
along Be
Date: 19

Brief View for ISU Library Catalog

Your Search: **General Keyword = Soybean AND 1999**

Search Results: **6 Records**

Displaying: **Records 5 through 6**

View Full Record Title: Streambank erosion adjacent to different riparian land-use practices and stream patterns along Bear Creek, in north central Iowa / by George Nick Zaimes. Author: Zaimes, George Nick. Publication Date: 1999.

View Full
proceedi
with assi
Forum. A

Search | Previous | Next | Brief | Exit

Long View for ISU Library Catalog

Your Search: General Keyword = Soybean AND 1999

Displaying: Record 5 of 6

Author Zaimes, George Nick.

Title Streambank erosion adjacent to different riparian land-use practices and stream patterns along Bear Creek, in north central Iowa / by George Nick Zaimes.

Published 1999.

Description 58 leaves : ill. ; 29 cm.

Notes Typescript (photocopy)
Thesis (M.S.)--Iowa State University, 1999.
Includes bibliography.

Abstract Sediment load in streams is the major non-point source pollutant originating from agriculture landscapes. Bank erosion can contribute 45-60% of the sediment load in streams. Land-use practices such as row cropping and grazing, combined with channelization of meandering reaches of streams have accelerated bank erosion rates and increased the sediment load in streams. An 11 km reach of Bear Creek was selected to compare bank erosion and soil loss of riparian buffers, corn or soybean row-cropped fields and cow or horse pastures along meandering and channelized reaches. The pin method was used to measure bank erosion because it is very good for short time-scale studies with high resolution that capture small differences in bank erosion at relatively low cost. Thirty three erosion pin plots were randomly assigned to the land-use practice sites that contained approximately 1100 pins. The pins were measured approximately every month from June 1998 to May 1999. Bulk densities were estimated with the core method, while the length and

Document: Done

Soy	UF Soybean oil industry	Soybean curd
USE Soy sauce	[Former heading]	USE Tofu
Soy-bean	BT Oil industries	**Soybean cyst nematode** *(May Subd*
USE Soybean	Soybean industry	*Geog)*
Soy-bean as feed	**Soy proteins** *(may Subd Geog)*	[QL391.N4 *(Zoology)*]
USE Soybean as feed	UF Proteins, Soy	[SB9098.S68 *(Pest)*]
Soy-bean as food	BT Plant proteins	UF Heterodera glycines
USE Soyfoods	Soybean products	[Former Heading]
Soy-bean flour	NT Textured soy proteins	Soybean nematode
USE Soybean as flour	Soy pulp	BT Heterodera
Soy-bean meal	USE Okara	Soybean flour
USE Soybean meal	**Soy sauce** *(may Subd Geog)*	USE Soy flour
Soy-bean meal as feed	[TP438.56 *(Manufacture)*]	**Soybean glue**
USE Soybean meal as feed	[TX407.569 *(Nutrition)*]	BT Glue
Soy-bean milk	UF Sauce, Soy	Soybean products
USE Soymilk	Soy	Soybean hulls
Soy-bean mosaic virus	Soya sauce	USE Soy bran
USE Soybean mosaic virus	BT Fermented soyfoods	**Soybean industry** *(May Subd Geog)*
Soy-bean oil	RT Cookery (Soy sauce)	[HD9235.S6-HD9235.S62]
USE Soy oil	**Soy sauce industry** *(may Subd*	BT Vegetable trade
Soy~~ oil mills~~	*Geog)*	NT Soy oil industry

need to ask your librarian which indexes are available in online or CD-ROM versions in your library.

Periodical Indexes.

Most subject areas have periodical indexes, many of which you can access on CD-ROM in the reference or periodical section of your library. There are many more indexes than those listed here.

Accountants' Index
Bibliography and Index of Geology
Biological and Agricultural Index
Business Periodicals Index
Cumulative Index to Nursing Literature

Engineering Index
Index Medicus
Index of Economic Journals
Index to Legal Periodicals
Natural History Index-Guide

Each index includes an introductory section that clearly explains how to use that particular volume. These indexes are generally organized much like the commonly used *Readers Guide to Periodical Literature*.

An interesting and useful resource is the *Science Citation Index*, which indexes authors or sources cited in footnotes and bibliographies of periodical articles, government documents, and published reports. This resource is valuable in identifying significant and frequently cited documents that influence the direction of work in science.

Newspaper Indexes.

Newspaper indexes are helpful, particularly in pinpointing dates of specific events and announcements. *New York Times Index* and *Wall Street Journal Index* are the most widely used newspaper indexes.

Abstract Indexes.   Abstract indexes not only give author, subject, and title references, but they also provide an abstract—a summary of each article. Abstract indexes can save a researcher a great deal of time. Imagine that you have identified the titles of 20 articles that appear to be relevant to your research. If the articles average 10 pages each, you have 200 pages of technical material to read. If you had initially read 20 abstracts, you could have selected the relevant articles without having to read the others.

Bibliographic resources identify the abstracts and indexes that are published. Check with your librarian to determine which ones your library carries. In some cases, several different abstracting indexes are available for a single discipline. For example, computer science abstracts are cataloged in three different indexes: *Computer and Control Abstracts*, *Computer and Information Systems*, and *Computer Reviews*. In other cases, specialized abstract indexes that concentrate on relatively narrow subfields include material that is also available in a broader index. For example, the information in *Rheology Abstracts* and *Acoustics Abstracts* is also contained in *Physics Abstracts*.

Electronic Resources

Less than a decade ago, electronic resources were available only for a fee and with the assistance of a specially trained librarian. Now, however, electronic resources are widely available—not only in public, college, and corporate libraries, but also through the Internet, which you can access with your personal computer. In this section, you'll read about two categories of electronic resources: computerized databases and the World Wide Web.

Computerized Databases

Your university or company library as well as your link to the Internet give you access to a vast array of computerized databases. Because available information is increasing at a rate faster than anyone can manage to read, professionals in most fields learn to use computerized databases that give them an overview of current information and research. Database searches can be helpful to you in several different ways:

- To prepare a literature review

- To stay abreast of current information and research

- To locate answers to specific questions

- To locate resources

Two kinds of databases are generally available. *Reference databases* include bibliographic databases that provide citations to published works, as well as referral databases that refer users to another source for more information. *Source databases* include original information, ranging from the results of survey data to the results of experimental studies to the full text of documents.

Librarians are trained to help you use databases. Most CD-ROM databases have helpful search suggestions that can save you a great deal of time. Whether you're doing a search yourself or working with a librarian, the following general guidelines will help:

- *Specify the time frame of your search.* Do you want information from the past ten years? Five years? Only the current year?

- *Specify the types of materials.* Do you want only books? Articles? Audio-visual materials? Presentations?

- *Specify the language(s).* Do you want materials only in English? Also in German? French? Russian? Spanish? Chinese?

- *Specify the print format.* Do you want to print from the online screen (expensive but available immediately), or do you want an off-line printout (usually less expensive but takes longer). Do you want only the titles? The full citation? The complete record with the abstract if it's available?

Developing a search strategy helps you focus your ideas so that you get information that is useful, but a search strategy also saves you time (and money). Some libraries ask you to complete a questionnaire that helps you conduct a more efficient and effective database search. In general, you need to know the following information:

- *What are your key terms?* What are synonyms for these terms? What alternative terms are used to refer to the topic? For example, if your topic is breast-feeding, you'll need to check breast-feeding, lactation, and infant feeding.

- *What indexing source does the database use* (for example, the Library of Congress subject headings)? Knowing the indexing source will help you identify relevant terms (much like knowing that in the Yellow Pages you need to look under "physician" rather than "doctor").

- *How do you want to combine the terms?* For example, do you want to search for *chocolate and candy* or *chocolate or candy*? The first combination would give you all citations that contain both the words *chocolate* and *candy*. The second combination would give you all the citations with only *chocolate*, only *candy*, and both *chocolate and candy*.

Web Research

The World Wide Web (WWW or Web), a global computer network, makes possible quick, cheap access to documents from around the world. WWW use has expanded enormously since it was introduced in the early 1990s. Many millions of documents are available from millions of Web sites, or pages. Web sites are sets of hypertext pages created by individuals or organizations that are generally located at a single Internet address. Web pages at a single site often have a common appearance and purpose. You can browse through Web sites created by private companies, libraries, government agencies, research institutes, universities, and individuals. Many hundreds come online every day.

Locating Information on the Web.   The Web is essentially an enormous set of documents stored in computers around the world. Users gain access to these documents by typing a URL (Uniform Resource Locator) address into their Web browser (a special program used for locating information on the Web) that tells the program where the document is stored. The browser then accesses the document and displays it on the user's screen, where it can be read and printed. Most documents also provide links that can connect users to other documents.

The Web makes it possible for anyone with access to a Web server (a computer that connects a group of users to one another and to the Web) to publish documents on the Web. Because of the Web, very little time is needed to make new information available around the world, with minimal printing or delivery costs. For instance, photographs from the Hubble telescope were made available by NASA on the Web minutes after they were taken. In contrast, most of a day is needed for photographs to be published in newspapers, months to be published in professional journals, and sometimes years to be published in scholarly books.

You locate information on the Web by using a *search engine*, a navigational tool that lets you search the Web by topic or key word. Search engines have three major components: the spider, the index, and software. *Spiders*, or crawlers, visit Web pages, read them, and follow links to other pages within a site. They are programmed to return regularly to look for changes. Whatever the spider finds goes into an *index*. This index, or catalog, contains a copy of every Web page the spider finds. When a Web page changes, the "book" is updated with the new information. This may take a while, so a Web page may have been "spidered" but not yet "indexed." Until information is indexed, it is not available to those using the search engine. Search engine *software* filters through millions of pages recorded in the index to find matches to a search request. The software ranks potential matches in the order it perceives to be most relevant.

Search engines have specific characteristics, so some are better than others for particular jobs:

- *Indexed engines* catalog computer-generated databases that contain information on Web pages or Usenet newsgroup articles. AltaVista and HotBot are typical index search engines.

- *Hierarchical (directory) engines* are list categories of subjects. Web directories may help you narrow your search by offering related ideas associated with the topic. Yahoo is a typical hierarchical search engine.

- *Combined types* such as Excite, Infoseek, Lycos, and WebCrawler combine features of both indexes and hierarchical directories. Some search engines,

FIGURE 6.8 ■ List of Popular Search Engines

Indexed Engines

AltaVista	<http://www.altavista.com/>
Google	<http://www.google.com/>
HotBot	<http://www.hotbot.lycos.com/>

Hierarchical (Directory) Engines

Yahoo	<http://www.yahoo.com>

Combined Types

Ask Jeeves	<http://www.askjeeves.com/>
Excite	<http://www.excite.com/>
InfoSeek	<http://infoseek.go.com/>
MetaCrawler	<http://www.metacrawler.com/>
Northern Light	<http://www.northernlight.com/search.html>

such as Northern Light, group results into meaningful categories contained in subfolders on the left side of your screen.

The most popular search engines are listed in Figure 6.8.

Beyond search engines, which are the most likely source of Web information, both newsgroups and lists are also potential sources for gathering information. *Newsgroups* and mailing *lists* are similar in spirit to e-mail systems except that they are intended for messages among large groups of people instead of one-to-one communication. In practice the main difference between newsgroups and mailing lists is that newsgroups only show messages to a user when they are explicitly requested (an "on-demand" service), while mailing lists deliver messages as they become available (an "interrupt-driven" interface).[5] Keep in mind that all electronic messages can be forwarded, printed, or permanently stored by any recipient, so be sensible—perhaps even cautious—about what you send electronically. (See Chapter 14 for netiquette about e-mail.)

Newsgroups allow users to correspond by "posting" and "replying to" messages from other users. *Lists* (e.g., LISTSERV and Majordomo) are automatic mailing list servers that transmit e-mail only to individuals who have subscribed to the list. Newsgroups are separated into many different subjects (more than 25,000) with titles that usually begin with a prefix followed by a "." and then a suffix such as alt, soc, comp, misc, rec, or sci.[6] Lists are often associated with professional organizations or particular professions. (See Chapter 14 for netiquette for newsgroups and lists.)

Chapter 6: Locating and Recording Information

When are information sources on the Web more useful than more traditional library sources? Are they always? Why or why not?

In what ways might information sources on the Web be more or less reliable or credible than traditional library sources?

Credibility. A search engine is unlikely to find every document about your subject, so finding useful documents on the Web often requires patience and resourcefulness. Not only can documents be difficult to locate, you may have difficulty knowing how credible they are. Readers of articles in professional journals usually assume that the articles have been through a thorough peer review and editing processes. But the Web makes possible the publication of documents with no editing or review; thus, you may have difficulty judging the expertise or credibility of the authors of a document. You need to consider possible biases and inaccuracies in information obtained from the Web; users should think critically about the origin of a document. For example, documents published by companies may be biased in favor of their products; documents published by individuals may be partially or entirely inaccurate.

Government Documents and Offices

Which repository of government documents is closest to you? What reference guides can you use to locate government documents that are useful to you?

A final way to locate potentially useful government information is to access the World Wide Web, as you have just read in the previous section. Virtually all agencies of the U.S. government have Web sites, making their information easily and cheaply accessible. For example, the U.S. Census Bureau has the most recent census online <http://www.census.gov>, the FBI posts its Most Wanted list < http://www.fbi. gov/toplist.html>, and the Federal Aviation Administration publishes many of its regulations <http://web.fie.com/web/fed/faa>.

The government agencies can provide updates whenever they have more current information (as opposed to waiting for next year's edition of a printed report), and users can access the documents whenever they like from wherever there is a connection. Several government sites are particularly interesting and useful:

- Federal Deposit Insurance Comm (FDIC)—<http://www.fdic.gov>
- Fish and Wildlife Service—<http://www.fws.gov>
- Library of Congress—<http://www.loc.gov>
- Patent and Trademark Office—<http://www.uspto.gov>
- Securities and Exchange Commission (SEC)—<http://www.sec.gov>
- Smithsonian Institution—<http://www.si.edu>

A recent addition to the available government Web resources includes Pub-SCIENCE <http://www.osti.gov/pubsci>, which enables users to search across a large collection of peer reviewed journal literature with a focus on physical sciences and technology. Similarly, the EnergyFiles <http://www.osti.gov/EnergyFiles/> of the Virtual Library of Energy Science and Technology provide information, tools, and technologies to facilitate the use of scientific resources and capabilities in planning and conducting energy-related research. EnergyFiles has more than 56,000 full-text R&D literature reports (approximately 3.8 million pages), representing a major portion of the Department of Energy and global R&D output since 1996.

Recording Data

No single method for recording the information you collect from various sources is best. Thus, you need to develop several techniques for recording data in different situations. In most cases, your choice of technique depends on the source of the original material as well as personal preferences in organizing a draft. Before you choose the method of collecting data and design the way to record it, think about how you're going to use the information so that it will be easy to retrieve. Also think about how you might need to select sections of the data for different audiences. The completeness and accuracy of the information you use influence your reputation. Beyond this, the sources you select reflect your expertise, but they also reflect your biases.

Careful record keeping is also important because it allows you to track changes that you (or others) make to documents as they are developed and later revised. For example, as a maintenance manual is developed, a writer needs to keep track of all the ECOs (engineering change orders). The easiest way to record such changes is to maintain a computer file so that the changes can be categorized and retrieved as they are needed. A writer might want to track the categories of changes, the chronology of changes, or the levels of importance of changes.

You should be familiar with various methods of recording data: field journals; lab notebooks; note cards; outlines; such visual forms as tracings, photographs, drawings, maps, videotapes, and films; and audiorecordings.

Field Journals

Field journals are maintained by professionals who work literally in the *field:* wildlife biologists recording feeding habits of deer; civil engineers noting rechanneling of a river where a new highway is planned; ecologists studying the impact of noise on the reproductive cycles of marsh animals.

- Record activities and observations in chronological order—what, when, where, and how.

- Place name of the investigator and the year at the top of the consecutively numbered pages.

- Note the exact location of each observation—country, state, and county— as well as date, time, mileage, and direction relative to a permanent map feature.

- Use waterproof ink that is resistant to alcohol, formalin preservatives, grease, animal fluids, and ammonia.

- Use durable paper that is resistant to water damage and age deterioration. Specially treated all-weather paper is available for field use, and loose-leaf binders enable you to remove field notes and keep them in a safe place.

Because of environmental hazards, professionals using field journals are selective in their materials for recording data. A particularly useful type of field journal is a parallel notebook. One version places factual notes on one page and comments on the facing page, which allows you to clearly distinguish between facts and opinions; another has notes on one side and drawings on the facing page. More recent tools are PDAs—that is, electronic personal digital assistants used for recording data.

Commenting on data when you collect them is very important because if you wait until all of your data have been accumulated, you may well forget some of your insights.

Lab Notebooks

Experimental data and primary observations in laboratory situations are recorded in lab notebooks, which are intended as documentation of activities. Occasionally, such notebooks are used to establish proprietary rights in cases of patent infringement.

- Use a bound notebook with consecutively numbered pages so that pages cannot easily be torn out without the gap being obvious.

- Number, date, and sign each page after the information is recorded.

- Place name of the investigator and the year at the top of the consecutively numbered pages.

- When recording calculations in tables or graphs, provide essential identifying information: name, date, method or formula, and labels on the columns or axes.

- Write a few sentences about the importance of the calculated data.

Note Cards

Information from other sources that will later need to be reorganized can be recorded on note cards—whether paper cards or electronic cards in a hypertext program. For example, cards are an effective technique for recording information from periodicals for a literature search to discover state-of-the-art developments for a new research and development project in a company. Cards work equally well for collecting and organizing information for traditional academic research. Cards are convenient because you can rearrange the cards (and thus, the information) in a variety of ways after collecting the data.

- Record the source and topic at the top of each card.

- Mark direct quotations clearly.

- Label or differentiate your comments and opinions about the source or information.

- Limit each card to one subtopic of information.

- Record biographical data about authors' expertise.

- Make a bibliography or source card for each source.

Outlines

Outlines—whether on paper or online—list major and subordinate points and summarize ideas from either documents or speeches. Outlines are less useful than notebooks or note cards for recording data simply because written and oral material may not be sufficiently organized to permit a note taker to make an effective outline. However, if you can easily and logically outline material, you can generally assume that it is well organized.

Tracings, Photographs, Drawings, Maps, Videotapes, Films

In many situations, data that cannot be fully recorded in writing, whether in notebooks, on note cards, or in outlines, are more accurately and efficiently recorded visually, by tracings, photographs, drawings, maps, videotapes, or films. For example, tracings are used to record information in a variety of fields—medical tests such as electroencephalograms, geologic data such as seismographs, stress/strain tests for engineering materials, and chemical assays using chromatography. These tracings can be directly interpreted by experts and then explained to nonexperts.

- Use photographs, drawings, and maps to provide accurate visual depictions of objects, processes, and locations.

- Use photographs when overall physical characteristics are important.

- Use drawings to focus on important components, especially if photographs may contain distracting details.

- Use maps to depict geographic and topographic features more effectively than photographs or drawings of the same area.

- Use videotapes and films when recording action is crucial.

Sometimes, a combination of photographs, drawings, and maps is particularly valuable. For example, a field biologist photographs the interior of a cave containing bats and then draws a map identifying the locations of various bat colonies. The photograph of a finished metal optic for a satellite becomes even more impressive when accompanied by a mylar overlay of a blueprint that specifies that dimensions on the actual part vary by no more than 0.0001 inch.

Audiorecordings

Audiorecordings are particularly effective for data where sound is essential. An environmental engineer uses audiotapes to record the highway noise that spills into adjacent residential areas. A speech pathologist records a client's progress. Without audiotape, the information could not be recorded as accurately or quickly.

- Use audiotapes in situations where the actual sound is essential (for example, bird calls).

- Use audiotapes in situations where exact wording is critical (for example, interviews and depositions).

- Use audiotapes if you don't have the time to record observation notes or write the draft of a document.

End-of-Chapter
Recommendations for Technical Communicators

1. Use evidence to substantiate your general points. The credibility of your work will depend, in part, on the credibility of your evidence.

2. Know when to use *quantitative data* (which describe measurable elements—quantities—in mathematical or statistical terms) and *qualitative data* (which describe observed or reported information—qualities).

3. Understand the difference between *primary sources*, which are first-hand, and *secondary sources*, which do not come directly from people involved in the action or event.

4. Seek out information from a variety of sources. Know how to collect information from any of ten different categories of sources:
    - Personal observations and close reading
    - Calculations
    - Samples and specimens
    - Empirical investigations
    - Internal records
    - Interviews and letters of inquiry
    - Surveys and polls
    - Library resources

- Electronic resources
- Government documents and offices

5. Select appropriate methods for recording data:
   - Field journals
   - Lab notebooks
   - Note cards
   - Outlines
   - Tracings, photographs, drawings, maps, videotapes, films
   - Audiorecordings

Individual and Collaborative Assignments

1. **Learn about your academic library and design a hands-on orientation for others.** Some academic libraries have cooperative arrangements with local businesses so that academic library facilities are available for practicing professionals. Work in small groups with others who share your academic major (or a closely related one).

   (a) Design questions for a librarian about services and resources available to local businesses and industries.

   (b) Select a representative to arrange and conduct an interview with a college librarian.

   (c) Design a hands-on library orientation for local business professionals to develop skills in using library references and resources. Go beyond the usual orientation by including information about the services of reference librarians, database searches, periodical and abstract indexes, technical reference materials, government documents, microfilm and microfiche files, and audiovisual materials. Present the information in a guidebook that also serves as a convenient reference for professionals after the orientation.

2. **Learn about a corporate library and design a hands-on orientation for others.** Learning about corporate library resources is important for technical professionals and for technical writers. Work in small groups with others who share your academic major (or a closely related one).

   (a) Design questions for a corporate librarian about the differences between a university and a corporate library, frequency of use, and the types of professionals who use them.

   (b) Select a representative to arrange and conduct an interview with corporate librarians at different local businesses and industries.

   (c) Design a hands-on library orientation to introduce new professional employees to the references and resources in a corporate library. Include information about services of professional librarians, available books and periodicals, loan privileges, database searches, periodical and abstract indexes, technical reference materials, government documents, microfilm and microfiche files, and audiovisual materials. Present the information in a guidebook that also serves as a convenient reference for employees.

3. **Recommend resources.** Corita Muir is investigating the cost-effectiveness of her company, GeoTech, Inc., instituting a longer lunch hour and flex-time with the goal of having a variety of company-sponsored fitness programs available to all employees from 6:00 to 8:00 A.M., 11:00 A.M. to 1:00 P.M., and 4:00 to 7:00 P.M. She plans to use the following resources to prepare her proposal:

   - Company records providing the number of sick days employees used in the past twenty-four months

- Recent articles in the local newspaper describing the benefits of regular exercise

What additional resources would you recommend?

4. **Identify alternative labels and terms.** You are trying to locate information about one of the following topics. Before looking in the *Library of Congress Guide to Subject Headings*, brainstorm possible alternative labels and terms for the topics.

- Midwives
- Medical applications of lasers
- New coal-mining techniques
- Proper use of farming equipment
- Wellness programs

5. **Compare sources in your field.**
    (a) Do a search for information on a particular topic in your field using both Internet sources and library sources. Determine what you believe are advantages and disadvantages of each type of information source.
    (b) Compile and then annotate a list of reference books and Internet sources that are particularly helpful to a person in your career field.

6. **Compare Internet sources.** Visit the following Web site: <http://www.nist.gov/weblinks.htm>

Choose three different government Web sites to visit and analyze. Determine what you believe are purposes, audience, and advantages or disadvantages of each Web site. In a memo to the class, report your analysis of the government Internet sites.

Intertext

Internet Power Searching: Finding Pearls in a Zillion Grains of Sand[7]

During the past two years, Web content has expanded enormously. Global access to hundreds of government resources and agencies worldwide, more than 1,400 Internet-based online public access catalogs (OPACs) from libraries on every continent [1], professional and trade associations, and experts in millions of subjects are just a few examples of categories of information not readily found online in the past. As the Internet erupted, search engines, metasearch engines, and intelligent agents with value-added features came on the scene and gradually began to refine their offerings, turning information retrieval into a more organized process than ever before.

Traditional vendors used by professional searchers also became accessible on the Web. For example, The Dialog Corporation, Dow Jones Interactive, LEXIS-NEXIS, OCLC FirstSearch, Ovid, silver Platter, and STN all now provide Web-based database searching [2]. In addition, a 1997 survey of database producers on the Web found remarkable progress [3]. Of 54 leading databases from 38 database producers, 35 searchable databases were either on the Web or had been announced. Added to these, new entrepreneurial publishers, also called niche market research boutiques, entered the market. This incredible growth has made the Internet the major research tool of the late twentieth century—although not without some serious shortcomings.

Unfortunately, much time can be spent—and wasted—when searching without knowing the tricks of the trade. Furthermore, the search engines are constantly changing, growing, and improving in their quality and capabilities for locating needed information. . . .

Search Engine Size

An April 1998 article in *Science* measured the size of the Internet and reported 320 million pages at that time [4]. This figure has grown to more than 380 million, plus hundreds of databases, in recent months. Nevertheless, one of the search engines, HotBot, has estimated that only 200 million pages are searchable within their system. These numbers, along with other information about search engine coverage, indicate that a large proportion of the Web is not reachable at all through search engines. According to Danny Sullivan (http://searchenginewatch.com), there are both technical and physical reasons that search engine coverage is incomplete:

- Information retrieval technology may not necessarily require exact matches and returns pages with related words. Documents that don't exist anymore are returned.

- Documents are changed after an index picks it up.

- Most search engines cannot index frames or image maps.

198

- Search engines do not index sites that deliver information from complex databases, for example, such sites as Amazon.com (http://www.amazon.com), an online bookstore, or Mediafinder.com (http://www.mediafinder.com), a database of magazines, newsletters, journals, and mail order catalogs.

- Sites that require passwords are not returned.

- Sites that use a robots.txt file to keep files and/or directories off limits prevent search engine results. Since so many Web sites can not be reached, it is important for researchers to amass knowledge about a range of resources useful for uncovering information not found by search engines, as well as to learn how to use search engines for a range of requests.

Focus on Big

The new Internet economy has brought about the development of competing search engine companies, each with its own proprietary software. Sites are collected and updated differently. After a search is conducted, one search engine provides exactly what's required within the first ten hits whereas another is useless. Frequently, there is tremendous overlap, although no two search engines are exactly alike. Since the outcome varies from search engine to search engine, researchers often find it necessary to use several search engines for the same question for either the best or more comprehensive results.

The larger the index compiled by a search engine, the more likely the chance of finding obscure material. Spiders or crawlers constantly visit sites to create catalogs or indexes of Web pages that are searchable. Results are sorted or ranked by relevancy based on individual proprietary algorithms. Although dozens of search engines now exist, the focus here is on those that are big.

One of the major search engines is AltaVista (http://www.altavista.com). It began operation in 1995 and is one of the largest. It remained unchallenged until September 1997 when HotBot (http://www.hotbot.com) began to compete and surpassed it in terms of number of pages indexed at that time. Other search engines of note are Excite (http://www.excite.com) and Northern Light (http://www.northernlight.com). In fact, Greg R. Notess (http://www.notess.com/search) suggested that Northern Light now ranks first, followed by AltaVista and HotBot. Another very well known and useful site is Yahoo, (http://www.yahoo.com), the oldest Web directory with some 750,000 sites. It is based on user submissions and staff selections.

All of the search engines mentioned here, plus Yahoo, have expanded and improved whereas others have tapered off in size or completely disappeared. Some key features of the largest search engines follow.

AltaVista (http://www.altavista.com)

- One of the most powerful and popular search engines.

- Good for specific searches.

- Offers an advanced query feature with more search options.

- Allows for a natural language query.

- Provides a translator between English and five languages that is useful but has been criticized as not "too good."
- Offers Boolean and proximity searching.
- Includes field searching.
- Flaws in the retrieval algorithm have been found in the past.
- AltaVista is not as user-friendly as Hotbot, but once mastered is the favorite for many.

Excite (http://www.excite.com)
- Good for searches on broad, general topics.
- Fast access to a small number of relevant sites.
- Adds interesting extras like a simultaneous search of the Web, news headlines, sports scores, and company information and groups the relevant results on a single page.
- If you find a site that is on target, you can click on search for more documents like this one and the search engine finds more of the same, although it doesn't work well for all types of queries.
- Includes a service called NewsTracker for selecting subjects of interest and receiving daily alerts from 300 news sources.
- Provides a user-friendly travel site for booking airline reservations.
- A power search capability broadens the scope of a search.
- Boolean searching is available by default on the home page.

HotBot (http://www.hotbot.com)
- Provides a very user-friendly interface with pull-down menus.
- Search results appear quickly.
- Recent changes integrate material generated by human editors into the service.
- Users can review one hundred results at a time, important for quick scanning when there are a large number of hits that are worth reviewing.
- Boolean searching is an option.
- Searching by continents can prove useful for some research.
- Hotbot was the most current search engine at one time, providing a new index every two weeks in the past, although more recently it has been criticized for lack of freshness. This is supposed to be corrected.
- Field searching can narrow research.
- Stemming is now provided.

Northern Light (http://www.northernlight.com)
- Provides content that encompasses both the Web and Northern Light's Special Collections, which are articles that can be purchased from more than 5,000 publications on a pay-as-you-go basis for $1.00 to $4.00 each. Some of these publications are not available from other major commercial vendors.
- Advanced, power, and industry searches narrow results by document type such as press release or product type.

- Automatically refines every search by creating Custom Search Folders with similar sites by subject, source, or type.
- Enterprise accounts for corporations and organizations are available.

Yahoo (http://www.yahoo.com)
- A directory or catalog of Web sites, valuable for searching broad general topics.
- Contains 750,000 sites
- World Yahoos, i.e., country versions.
- Drill down through categories or with a click, the query originally sent to Yahoo is "piped" or forwarded to a major search engine. This is especially useful since Yahoo is selective rather than as all encompassing as the other search engines mentioned here.
- Inclusion/exclusion, phrases, wildcards, title, and URL limiters.

DejaNews (http://www.dejanews.com) and Reference.com (http://www.reference.com)
Both DejaNews and Reference.com are search engines for newsgroups or mailing lists and can be used to identify experts who participate in various discussion groups, review major trends, or discover what's being said about a company, product, or topic.

Where to Start
Where and how to search depends on research goals and needs. Indeed, whether to use the Internet or a traditional database is often the first decision, and whether to use a narrow or broad strategy is another consideration. Fundamentally, it's necessary to become familiar with several major search engines and select the right one for the job.

Much Internet research is trial and error and serendipity, too. Nonetheless, self-education is necessary. Preparing for Internet research involves visiting major search engine sites to review how each works. The more that is known about a particular search engine, the better prepared the searcher will be to decide which is appropriate for each request. Each search engine provides detailed instructions about basic or simple searches and how to use more advanced or powerful searching techniques.

Before searching, it's important to plan the search by considering unique words, phrases, and synonyms that describe the topic. Once a search is conducted, a review of results can lead to reformulating the search when what you are looking for is not found. If you find yourself spending too much time at one site, move on to the next search engine. Search results often improve when taking a search elsewhere.

Search Engine Basic Hints & Tips
- Some search engines permit Boolean searching with *and, or,* or *not.*
- Many search engines require the use of quotations around phrases.
- Some search engines allow you to truncate a word and pick up variations, but others do not.
- Search engines typically do not look for articles such as *the, a,* etc., conjunctions such as *and, with,* or heavily used adjectives.

201

- Some search engines will not search on common words. Hotbot, for example, ignores the search terms *Internet* and *Web*.

Search Engine Advanced Hints & Tips

One of the best ways to refine searches is with power features such as field searching. Ran Hock explains that, "fortunately, some Web search engines do provide at least a rudimentary field search capability, but because of the immature nature of the engines, the options are neither very numerous nor particularly sophisticated." AltaVista allows date, title, URL, and language searching, plus a half-dozen other fields, all related to the types of features included on the page, such as image and sound files. HotBot, similarly, provides date, title, and URL searching. In addition, it lets a user search for records that contain a sound or video file, search by page depth, by what words are included in hypertext links, and for the presence of a variety of scripting languages and plug-ins. For a detailed discussion on this subject, see Hock's article "How to Do Field Searching in Web Search Engines: A Field Trip"[5].

Metasearch Engines

Metasearch engines are Web sites that send a search to several search engines all at once. Often, only a selected number of sites from each search engine is identified and then incorporated into what are blended results from many search engines into one page. Some well-known metasearch engines are described below.

Dogpile (http://www.dogpile.com). Dogpile integrates many search engines as well as other types of sources and sorts the results by search engine. Included in the search are (1) Search engines: Yahoo!, Lycos' A2Z, Excite Guide, GoTo.com, Planetsearch, Thunderstone, What U Seek, Magellan, Lycos, WebCrawler, InfoSeek, Excite and AltaVista; (2) Usenet: Reference.com, Dejanews, AltaVista and Dejanews' old database; (3) more than two dozen online news services or other types of sources. Dogpile includes an advanced search and allows Boolean operators. Dogpile is a good way to check to see which search engine works best for a particular question.

Internet Sleuth (http://www.isleuth.com). Internet Sleuth is a 3,000-strong collection of specialized online databases, which can also simultaneously search up to six other search sites for Web pages, news, and other types of information. It's excellent for highly specialized searches of any subjects in its detailed directory.

- Links popular Net search engines and allows you to specify categories like business, computers, education, sports, etc. MetaCrawler (http://www.metacrawler.com).

- Searches several popular search engines and sorts the results. It is excellent for getting a quick hit of what's out there. But if you don't see what you want in the results, its limited search options make it tough to issue really precise queries.

ProFusion (http://www.profusion.com). Lets you select what search engines to search including AltaVista, InfoSeek, Lycos, Excite, WebCrawler, and others. Filters results to remove duplicates and broken links.

SavvySearch (http://www.savysearch.com). Searches multiple Internet search engines, Web directories such as Yahoo or Magellan, Usenet, and other sources via just one query and then returns the linked results.

Intelligent Agents

Metasearch engines can be advantageous for getting a quick overview, but because every search engine differs in how it functions and because metasearch engines provide limited results per each search engine, the outcome is incomplete. In addition, some metasearch engines are rather slow and create another problem, that of duplicates. A better solution is to consider using *intelligent agents,* software programs that search many search engines at once, similarly to metasearch engines, but which add other features such as automatically finding, analyzing, filtering, and presenting information rapidly.

BullsEye, one of the most recent entrants to the marketplace, offers a trial version for download (http://www.intelliseek.com). One valuable feature is that the user can specify the number of total hits and the number desired from each search engine. As a result, a much larger list of hits is created than when using metasearch engines on the Web. A unique and automated feature of Bulls-Eye is that it can track and update searches based on the time frame selected by the user—either hourly, daily, weekly—and then e-mail updates to you.

Hard-to-Find Information

Two categories of hard-to-find information are industry statistics and market data. Often, this information is developed and provided by two distinct types of organizations—government agencies or professional and trade associations. Consider what agency or association would typically generate the required information and search for that first. For example, when looking for U.S. population statistics, consult the U.S. Bureau of the Census at http://www.census.gov since it is the governmental agency responsible for compiling these statistics. If you need market data about restaurants, try the National Restaurant Association at http://www.restaurant.org. A reference book for additional help with hard-to-find information is *Finding Statistics Online* by Paula Berinstein, Information Today, Inc., 1998 (http://www.infotoday.com). Here are some additional Web sites that are useful for finding information not readily available or indexed by search engines.

Price's List of Lists (http://gwis2.circ.gwu.edu/~gprice/listof.htm). The Internet contains many lists of information in the form of rankings of different people, organizations, companies, etc. This site contains a collection that is designed to be a clearinghouse for these types of resources.

Direct Search (http://gwis.circ.gwu.edu/~gprice/direct.htm). This site contains links to resources not easily searchable by search engines such as archives & library catalogs, books, news sources, and ready reference.

Internet Publishers & Databases

Although there is an astounding amount of free information, professional researchers have also seen the commercialization

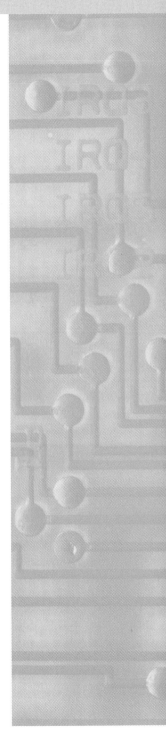

of the Web during the past year. As mentioned previously, many traditional commercial database vendors who were available only through dial-up telecommunications have launched Web products, and new publishers have entered the market with unique products. Here are examples of some of the new producers or products that have come onto the scene:

- Hoover's Inc. (http://www.hoovers.com) provides company snapshots.

- Research Bank Web (http://www.investext.com) includes three major database collections—investment research, market research, and trade association research.

- Vista Information Solutions (http://www.vistainfo.com) provides information on environmental, property, and business-risk information on any property, business, or address in the United States.

- XLS (http://www.xls.com) contains financial databases with information that can be downloaded as preformatted spreadsheets.

- Integra (http://www.integrainfo.com) provides financial ratios based on 3.5 million private companies in 900 industries in the form of industry profiles as a way to benchmark against financial information of a specific company that the user already knows about. Also offers a new product called Prospect Profiler that includes a range of important information for sales prospecting.

- VentureOne (http://www.ventureone.com) provides a database of venture capital companies, transactions, and funds.

Web Tools & Specialty Search Engines

A very interesting Web navigation service is Alexa (http://www.alexa.com). It works in conjunction with a Web browser and resides as a tool bar at the bottom of the browser. Alexa provides useful information about the sites you are visiting and suggests related sites with links to click on. This can immediately add relevant sites to the search process as one way to save time on a search. An example of a specialty search engine is Liszt (http://www.liszt.com). Liszt provides brief descriptions of some 90,000 electronic mailing lists and discussion groups. These are especially valuable for keeping up with current trends in your own profession or those related to your areas of subject expertise and interest. A search can be initiated by key word, or there are broad categories from which to choose such as Business, Computer, Education, Politics, or Science. Another specialty search engine for finding companies from all over the world is Corporate Information (http://www.corporateinformation.com). Its new search engine and A-Z list of countries with links to sites make this a unique source for global company information.

Keeping Up

Keeping up with changes in search engines and the latest information necessary for professional information workers is quite a challenge. Here are some selected sources:

- Cyberskeptic Guide to Internet Research (http://www.bibliodata.com) is a newsletter with articles about useful sites for searchers.

- Free Pint (http://www.freepint.co.uk) is a British-based free e-mail newsletter that includes information on quality and reliable information on the Web. It contains tips, tricks, and articles written by information professionals in the United Kingdom and is currently sent to more than 12,000 information professionals every two weeks.

- On the Net (http://www.onlineinc.com), a column by Greg Notess covers the information side of the Internet and is published in Online and Database.

- The Search Engine Update (http://searchenginewatch.com) is a free site with a subscription-based e-mail newsletter e-mailed twice monthly with access to "in progress" projects and detailed information only available to subscribers.

- Web Wise Ways (http://www.infotoday.com), a column by Amelia Kassel, began in October 1998 and is published in *Searcher* magazine. This column provides in-depth reviews of new Web-based research products and compares them to traditional commercial database products when applicable.

What's Next for Internet Power Searchers?

Just when searchers have conquered methods and idiosyncrasies of a search engine, it changes. My very first personal favorite, Open Text, has disappeared. I then discovered that Hotbot was easy to use and most satisfactory for the majority of my research requests. Of late, Northern Light, the most significant entry to the playing field during the past year and half, continues to add new content and features while others have remained either fairly static or in some cases deteriorated.

In recent months, there has been a hush in new search engine development. Nothing much new! Nevertheless, Reva Basch points out that, with regard to search engines, "the only constant is change" [6]. This insightful comment implies, to me, that information professionals will want to continue their experimentation with search engines, and acclimate themselves to changes or new features. For the moment, we can hone our skills using existing products while waiting to see what the next generation will bring.

For now, searchers will need to continue to identify, collect, evaluate, and organize useful Web sites and learn new tools that come onto the scene since so much on the Web is not accessible via search engines. Many of the same skills that we learned in graduate schools of library and information science are applicable to this new searching environment that we have had to meet head on.

References

1. Nelson, Bonnie R. (1998) OPAC Directory 1998: A Guide to Internet-Accessible Online Public Access Catalogs, Information Today, *Inc.* Medford, NJ.

2. Kassel, Amelia. (1998) Dialog Alternatives: A Power Searcher's Checklist. SEARCHER, *The Magazine for Database Professionals,* September, 1998, pp. 31-56 (http://www.infotoday.com/searcher/sep/kassel.htm).

3. Kassel, Amelia. (1997) Here They Come! Database Producers on the Web, SEARCHER, *The Magazine for*

Database Professionals, July/August 1997, pp. 26-29+.

4. Lawrence, Steve and C. Lee Giles. (1998) Searching the World Wide Web, *Science,* April 3, 1998, Vol. 280 (5360) pp. 98-100.

5. Hock, Ran. (1998) How to Do Field Searching in Web Search Engines: A Field Trip Online, May/Jun 1998 Vol. 22(3). pp. 18-22. (http://www.onlineinc.com/onlinemag/OL1998/hock5.html)

6. Basch, Reva. *Researching Online for Dummies,* IDG Books Worldwide, Inc., 1998.

Amelia Kassel is president and owner of MarketingBASE, a successful information brokerage specializing in market research, competitive intelligence, and worldwide business information since 1984. Kassel holds a Masters Degree in library science (1971, UCLA) and combines an in-depth knowledge of information sources with an emphasis on the use of databases and a knowledge of business and marketing strategies.

7

Organization of Information

Your intent should be to create reader-based documents, ones that consider the needs and reactions of your readers and organize information so that they can understand the issues.

Outlining

Any working outline you develop should be flexible and easy to change as you arrange and rearrange ideas, add new information, and delete unnecessary material. Outlines are tools to help you manage the material for a document. Think of them as document blueprints that show overall structure and primary features.

Organizing Information

The organization of a document affects the meaning your readers' construct. Changing the organization of information can change your readers' understanding.

Some common ways to organize information—either verbally or visually— are parts/whole organization, chronological order, spatial order, ascending/ descending order, comparison/contrast, and cause and effect.

Effective topic sentences can identify both the content and organization of a paragraph so that your readers begin with definite expectations.

Transitions are one important technique you can use to achieve coherence.

T he purpose of a document is to communicate information to readers; thus, making your document understandable is critical. As you initially explore a topic, you may outline and then draft a *writer-based document*, one that helps you examine and organize the information. A writer-based document may be helpful in your preliminary investigations because it uses your point of view, focus, and organization. However, it doesn't consider whether they'll be effective for your readers. Your end goal should be to create a *reader-based document*, one that considers the needs and reactions of your readers and organizes information so that they can understand the issues.

Outlining

You may decide to outline your information simply because (as you read in Chapter 6) changing an outline is usually easier than changing the draft of a text. Any outline you develop should be flexible and easy to change as you arrange and rearrange ideas, add new information, and delete unnecessary material. Outlines are not intended to restrict you; rather, they are tools to help you manage the material for a document. Think of them as document blueprints that show overall structure and primary features. As with buildings that exist only on paper, changes in documents are easier to make before drafting.

Outlines can help you arrange and examine collected information. They do not have to be formal, complete-sentence outlines. Initially, you can just jot down information and then rethink, rearrange, and reorganize it in an outline. For example, the following list is simply a series of unorganized points for a paper reporting a Harvard ethnobotanist's attempts to explain the zombies of traditional Haitian voodoo:[1]

- Natives believe in zombies (walking dead); fertile ground for mind control

- Natives believe in power of a bocor, malevolent voodoo priest

- Zombies created by a bocor, sophisticated knowledge of pharmacology and psychology

- Poisons from puffer fish contain powerful neurotoxin, tetrodotoxin

- Initially produces hypothermia, nausea, respiratory difficulties, hypertension, hypotension, paralysis

- Long-term control maintained with hallucinogenic plant containing daturas; causes disorientation, amnesia
- Bocor have variety of poisons, all with same main ingredient
- Tetrodotoxin reduces metabolic functions to deathlike state

Figure 7.1 shows a computer screen of an outline that was developed from this preliminary list. Outlining is an option with most word processing software. An online outline offers you a different *view* of your document rather than creating a separate document. The online changes you make in the outline auto-

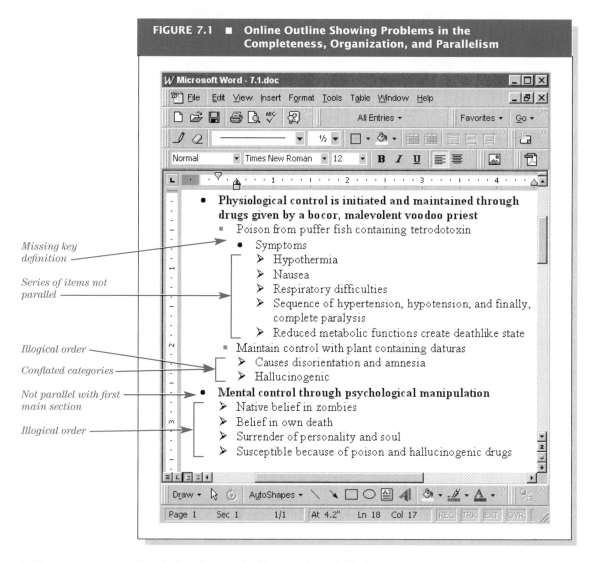

FIGURE 7.1 ■ **Online Outline Showing Problems in the Completeness, Organization, and Parallelism**

matically become part of the document, and vice versa. You can easily switch back and forth between an *outline view* of your document and a full *text view*.

The writer could examine the online outline in Figure 7.1 to determine whether the information is complete and parallel—equivalent in importance, sequence, and wording. In this case, the outline has incomplete information, needs reordering, and isn't parallel. But without the outline (whether online or on paper), the writer might not see these inadequacies.

Figure 7.2 shows a revised online outline in which the writer has corrected the problems. The changes are more than cosmetic. First, expressing ideas

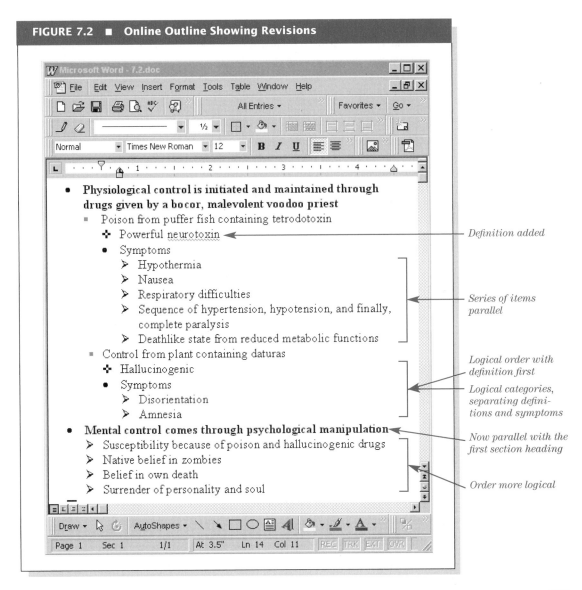

FIGURE 7.2 ■ Online Outline Showing Revisions

in parallel structure demonstrates that the writer intends to treat them equally, as shown in the revision of the sections. Next, the sequence of entries must be logical, as shown in the revision in the order of entries. Here, indicating native susceptibility logically comes first; instances of their beliefs resulting from this susceptibility follow. Finally, essential information must not be inadvertently omitted, as shown by the omission of the type of poison in the first section. In each case, changing the outline is easier than changing the draft of the paper.

The original and revised outlines about zombies (Figures 7.1 and 7.2) show how helpful outlines can be to organize and reorganize information before starting to draft a document. These outlines identified gaps in data, inconsistencies in the relative importance of various segments, and problems in sequencing information. If you use outlines as tools for planning and revision, you may save yourself a great deal of frustration and time.

As you plan your material, you can ask yourself the questions in Figure 7.3 to check whether your outline is likely to result in a successful document. If you can answer yes to all the questions in Figure 7.3, your outline will probably be useful in planning, organizing, and drafting your document.

Outlines have additional uses besides help in planning and revising. In a long document, an outline's main headings can provide ready-made headings for the document itself. Outlines can also be modified for use as a table of contents. And sometimes outlines actually form the body of a document, as in the excerpt in Figure 7.4 from "External and Internal Parasites—Causes, Symptoms, Treatment, and Control," which appeared in a professional journal for farmers.[2] Using an outline for the body of a document can make it easy for readers to skim the document to locate main points.

FIGURE 7.3 ■ Questions to Ask About Your Outline

Content and context

- ◆ Is all important information included and all unnecessary information omitted?
- ◆ Are contextual factors that will influence the document's interpretation acknowledged?

Audience

- ◆ Do the headings give readers an accurate overview of the document?
- ◆ Is the level of detail appropriate for the purpose and audience?

Purpose and key points

- ◆ Are the main headings and subheadings logically arranged?
- ◆ Is the organization in the outline appropriate to the content, purpose, audience, and genre?

Organization

- ◆ Is all information in the outline in the appropriate places—both in the main sections and the subsections?
- ◆ Do the details in each subsection reflect the emphasis for that heading?

Professional standards

- ◆ Are main headings in the outline written in parallel grammatical form (so that you can use them as headings in the document)?

Part II: Developing the Communicator's Tools

Organizing Information

The way the information in a document is organized affects the meaning that readers construct. Once you've decided how to organize your information, you

FIGURE 7.4 ■ Outline Forming the Body of a Document

INTRODUCTION

Dairy goats, like other animals, wild or domestic, have their share of parasites (both external and internal) and effective parasitic treatment, prevention and control play an integral part in milk and meat production . . .

There are two main types of parasites in most domestic animals including the dairy goat. In this article, basic information will be presented on the common signs and symptoms of the most prevalent external and internal parasites along with their treatment, prevention and control.

1. EXTERNAL PARASITES

A. Lice

Lice are the most common external parasites of dairy goats. The two primary types of lice which affect goats are:
   1. Biting louse—Bovicola caprae
   2. Sucking louse—Linognathus stenopsis

The biting louse, red in color, feeds on the skin and burrows into the hair follicles causing severe itching. The blood-sucking louse, blue in color, is larger and more visible. It pierces the skin to feed and is prevalent on the sides of the neck, underline and around the udder.

Symptoms
   a. Excessive scratching against the sides of the barn, fence post and wire
   b. Weight loss
   c. Decreased milk production
   d. The appearance of dry, crusty or scabby areas on the back, side of the face, and underside of the neck

Treatment and Control

The best time to control and treat lice is in the fall. Dipping or spraying using "Coral" (coumaphos) is the drug of choice even in lactating animals. Good control is obtained if spraying is repeated once or twice at least 10-14 days apart to kill all the lice that hatch from eggs. Lice must live on their host to survive; thus, neither barns nor bedding need be treated.

B. Mange

Two types of mange are common in dairy goats:
   1. Sarcoptes scabei, var. caprae
   2. Demodectic spp

Sarcoptic mange, Sarcoptes scabei var. caprae is seen mostly around the neck, the underline, and face, while demodex is generalized but can be commonly found in the flank and udder areas. Demodex, the more prevalent of the two, is caused by Demodex caprae. The mites that burrow into the hair follicles leave blebs (or small raised welts) that are mainly detected by shaving the hair close or passing the hand over the areas involved.

Symptoms
   a. In addition to excessive scratching, sarcoptic mange exhibits a relative thickening of the (epidermal) layer of skin in the areas of irritation.
   b. With demodex, when the hair is shaved, the blebs or subcutaneous swellings laden with mites are seen. These swellings or nodules, ranging in size from pin head to hazel-nut, contain thick grayish material of waxy consistency, which can be easily expressed. Numerous demodectic mites are found in this material.

Treatment

Frequent dips with an insecticide are necessary, and "Coral" (coumaphos) does an effective job even with lactating animals.

C. Ear Mites

Ear mite infestation in the dairy goat is a common problem and is easy to misdiagnose. The infestation is caused by a mite of the genus Psoroptes spp. . . .

can help readers by using signals that identify that organization. Two tools are helpful for signaling: topic sentences and transitions.

- A *topic sentence* identifies both the content and organization of a paragraph so that readers have definite signals about what a paragraph is about and how the information is organized.

- *Transitions* are words and phrases that act as the glue connecting ideas and sentences within a single paragraph, linking one paragraph to another and relating one section of a document to the next section.

For a reader who is an expert in the subject, why are transitions necessary? Won't an expert understand the relationships among the ideas?

Technical communicators organize information to make it clear and accessible to readers. Some common ways to organize information are presenting parts/whole organization, chronological order, spatial order, ascending/descending order, comparison/contrast, and cause and effect.

No communicator settles down to write and says, "I'm about to begin a document using chronological order." Instead, the communicator may ask questions like these: "What's the situation or problem this document is responding to?" "What's my purpose?" "Who's the audience, and what are their expectations?" "How can I help my readers understand this information?" "What's the appropriate genre?" And then the communicator may ask, "What's the most appropriate way to organize the information—given the situation, purpose, audience, and genre?" In organizing the information, technical communicators use topic sentences and transitions to help make the information more accessible and appealing to readers.

In what ways do topic sentences make technical information easier to read?

Does every paragraph in a document have a topic sentence? Not necessarily. Some paragraphs are transitional, connecting one main paragraph or section to the next. Occasionally, an excessively long paragraph is separated into two or more to make the paragraph easier to read and give readers a chance to breathe. Usually, however, most of the paragraphs in a well-constructed document have clear topic sentences, which can be separated from the document and listed together as a summary. If the message from this topic sentence summary is clear and logical, then the document is probably well constructed.

So far, the focus of this chapter has been on organizing information that is usually presented in print documents. However, organizing information for Web sites is also very important. Jakob Nielsen, an expert of Web usability, reports on some of the problems that result from poorly organized Web sites:[3]

- In one recent study of 15 large commercial sites, users were taken to the correct home page before they started the test tasks; even with that help, they found information only 42 percent of the time.

- In another study of online shoppers, 62 percent of them gave up looking for the item they wanted to buy because they couldn't find it.

- A third study analyzed 20 major sites to determine whether these sites followed simple Web usability principles: Is the site organized by user goals? Does a search list retrievals in order of relevance? Only slightly more than half of the sites—51 percent—complied with basic principles of organization.

What's the impact of such poorly organized Web sites?

- Sites lose approximately 50 percent of potential sales because people can't find what they want.

- Sites lose repeat visits from up to 40 percent of users who do not return to a site after an initial negative experience.

What's the most effective solution? Jakob Nielsen recommends usability testing of all Web sites (see Chapter 13). If a site is well organized, users should be able to find what they want. The strategies in this chapter can be part of your repertoire for organizing print and Web documents.

Parts/Whole Organization

A document that uses parts/whole organization presents readers with a relationship between the *whole* (whether an idea, object, or entire system) and *parts* of that whole (whether on a micro level or a macro level). Sometimes this parts/whole organization involves separating a single item into individual components. At other times, it involves identifying related types of an item. It may also involve identifying the broad category to which something belongs.

A parts/whole organization to present the categories of integrated circuits is shown in Figure 7.5. The paragraph shows the relationship between the whole (the category of devices called integrated circuits) and the parts of that whole (three types of circuits: programmable devices, memory devices, and linear

---

FIGURE 7.5 ■ Parts/Whole Organization of Information

Integrated circuits are divided into three categories, depending on their function and capability in the final product. (See the diagram below.) The first type is a programmable integrated circuit, a multifunctional component designed to be programmed by the supplier or by in-house technicians. The second type of integrated circuit is the memory device, used to store memory in an end product. The third type is a linear device designed to do many specific predetermined functions and used in conjunction with other components to operate computers.

Whole: *integrated circuits*

Parts:
first type
second type
third type

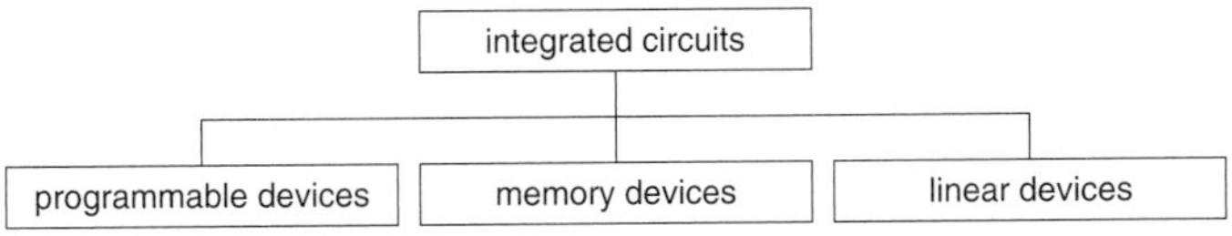

devices). This example (and those that follow related to integrated circuits) were written by the supervisor of a testing line in an inspection group of a plant that manufactured and assembled integrated circuits. This supervisor was required to train the unskilled entry-level workers assigned to her area. She decided to provide these workers with short, easy-to-read explanations about the inspection process. She believed that helping them understand how their specific job fit into the larger process would increase the quality of their work.

Chronological Order

Researcher Lance Stewart is preparing a report about the results of his work during the past six months. He wants his readers to follow the progress of his experiments step by step, not knowing the results until they read the conclusion and recommendations at the end of the report. He says he worked hard to get the results; he wants the readers to appreciate all of his work. What do you think of his decision? What would you say to persuade him to reconsider his plan?

Chronological order presents readers with material arranged by sequence or order of occurrence. When the purpose is to give instructions, describe processes, or trace the development of objects or ideas, chronology is appropriate. For example, chronologically organized information about computer disks might include a description identifying each step of the manufacturing process or an explanation of the historical development of electronic storage media, from paper tape to mylar disks. Information can be presented chronologically in visual forms, as shown in Figure 7.6, which also lists an example of each form.

A topic sentence conveying chronology includes words or phrases that indicate a process or a sequence of actions, as illustrated in the following sentences:

■ EXAMPLES

Seven operations are necessary to fabricate sheet metal. . . .

Most poultry farms are vertically integrated, from breeding to egg to packaged product. . . .

FIGURE 7.6 ■ Visual Forms for Chronological Order	
Form	**Example**
Flow chart	Sequence of manufacturing process
Time line	Development of synthetics for medical use
Genealogy chart	History of family with Huntington's disease
Sequential photos	Embryo development
Sequential drawings	Steps in resuscitation of drowning victim
Story board	Public service ad urging water conservation
Time-lapse photos	Emergence of butterfly from cocoon
Line graph	Increase in restlessness during REM sleep
Calendar	Production schedule for new product
Chart	Stratification of rock layers according to geologic periods

Readers can justifiably expect the paragraph that follows the first topic sentence to identify and explain the seven steps of sheet-metal fabrication. The paragraph that follows the second topic sentence should identify each stage in the process of poultry production.

Transitions in chronological paragraphs can indicate the sequence of events or the passage of time. Figure 7.7 presents an example that explains the *chronology* of incoming inspection that integrated circuits go through. The reader easily follows the process because the chronological transitions highlight each step of the five-step process.

Spatial Order

Spatial order—arrangement by relative physical location—describes for readers the physical parts of nearly anything, from cellular structures to the orbital path

---

FIGURE 7.7 ■ Information Organized Using Chronological Order

Integrated circuits received at incoming inspection go through a five-step process. As the flowchart shows, the first stage of inspection ensures that the parts have been purchased from a predetermined qualified vendor list. The parts are then prioritized according to daily back-order quantities and/or line shortages assigned by the production floor. Next the parts are moved into the test area, where a determination is made as to which lots will be tested at 100 percent and which will be sample tested. After this, the parts are electrically tested for specific continuity and direct current parameters using MCT handlers. The final step of incoming inspection is distributing the parts according to need on the production floor.

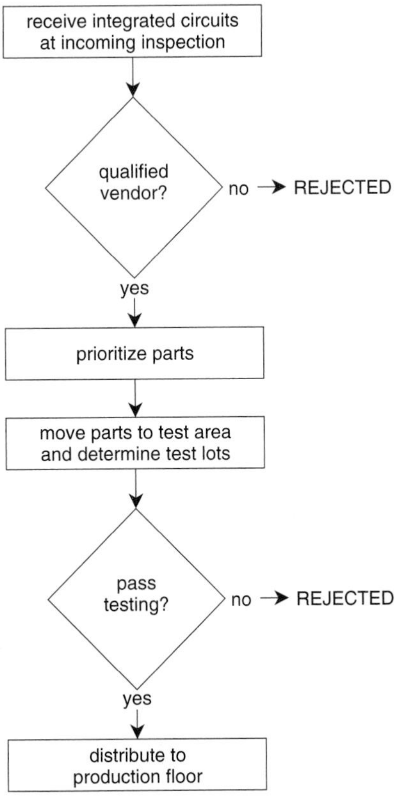

receive integrated circuits at incoming inspection

qualified vendor? no → REJECTED

yes

prioritize parts

move parts to test area and determine test lots

pass testing? no → REJECTED

yes

distribute to production floor

Chronological transitions:

the first stage

then

Next

After this

The final step

FIGURE 7.8 ■ Visual Forms for Spatial Order

Form	Example
Map	Identification of migration stopovers
Blueprint	Specification of dimensions for machined part
Navigational chart	Location of sand bars and buoys
Celestial chart	Sequence of moons around Jupiter
Exploded view	Assembly of disk brake
Cutaway view	Interior components of pool filter
Wiring diagram	Wiring of alarm system
Floor plan	Workflow in busy area
Set design	Arrangement of furniture/props for *Hamlet*
Architectural drawing	Appearance of building with solar modifications

of a satellite. Spatial organization could explain parts of a computer disk or the location of the disk drives in relation to the other parts of the computer. Figure 7.8 presents examples of several visual forms. You may find visual presentations are particularly effective for spatially arranged material because they help your readers see the actual physical relationships.

Because spatial arrangement deals with the relative physical location of objects, the topic sentence suggests their placement, as seen in these examples.

■ EXAMPLES

Unnecessary or damaged inventory that is scheduled to be scrapped is placed on skids in one of six bin locations in the Defective Stockroom. . . .

Sound is a ripple of molecules and atoms in the air that travels from its source to our ears. . . .

Readers of the first sentence anticipate the identification of each bin's location according to type of scrap material. The second topic sentence indicates to readers that the paragraph will track the sound as it moves through the air from source to listener.

Transitions in spatial paragraphs suggest the relative physical location of components or objects. Figure 7.9 presents an example that uses *spatial order* to describe the incoming inspection of an integrated circuit.

Ascending/Descending Order

Ascending and descending orders present readers with information according to quantifiable criteria.

FIGURE 7.9 ■ Information Organized Using Spatial Order

The movement of the IC (integrated circuit) chip through the test area is very efficient. The chips arrive from the supplier, already set—24 at a time—into a removable channel within a clear tube. The chips are aligned in the same direction within the tube. This tube is inserted by the operator into the MCT handler so that pin 1 of the first chip, marked by a small dot, is in the upper left. The tube slides through a slot, into the testing compartment, where each chip is tested individually. Automatically, the good chips are placed in one channel, the rejects in another. The channels are moved so the operator can slip on the protective tubes. The good chips are sent to the manufacturing area; the rejects are sent to another engineering station for further testing.

Spatial transitions:
through the test area
from the supplier
into a removable
*   channel within a*
*   clear tube*
in the same direction
into the MCT handler
in the upper left
*   through a slot*
to the manufacturing
*   area*
to another engi-
*   neering station*

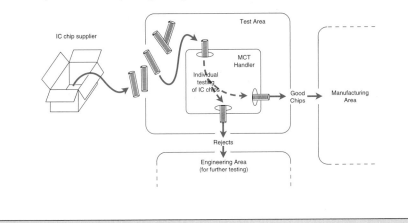

appeal	durability
authority	ease of manufacture, operation, repair
benefit	frequency
cost	importance
delivery	size

Descending order uses a most-to-least-important order; ascending order, a least-to-most. Descending order is found in workplace writing more frequently than ascending order because most readers want to know the most important points first. In business and industry, readers generally form opinions and make decisions based on what they read initially; they expect descending order in nearly all technical documents. Descending or ascending order would be appropriate for organizing the relative convenience of various forms of electronic data storage or for identifying the disk specifications in various price ranges. If you wanted to arrange information visually, one of the forms illustrated in Figure 7.10 would work.

Unlike topic sentences for paragraphs organized in other ways, those beginning descending or ascending paragraphs do not give an immediate clue about

FIGURE 7.10 ■ Visual Forms for Ascending/Descending Order

Form	Example
Numbered list	Priority of options for treating breast cancer
Bull's-eye chart	Population affected by nuclear explosion
Percent graph	Percent of different economic groups receiving balanced nutrition
Pareto diagram	Productivity using different methods (bar graph arranged in descending order)
Line graph	Increasing success for breeding endangered species in captivity over twenty-year period

the subsequent organization. The reader understands that the paragraph will present a series of related ideas, but the specific relationship is not clear until the second sentence. The topic sentence in the next example begins a paragraph about the master satellite station in Beijing, presenting the characteristics of the Beijing antenna in descending order of importance.

■ **EXAMPLE**

The largest earth station in China is a 15-to-18-meter-diameter dish antenna in Beijing for domestic satellite communications.

A paragraph using a descending organization to identify the various sized antennas in China begins with a general statement before going on to identify each type of station.

■ **EXAMPLE**

Three types of earth stations are planned for domestic satellite communication in China. The largest is a 15-to-18-meter-diameter dish antenna of the master station in Beijing. . . . Regional stations are equipped with a 10-to-13-meter-diameter antenna. . . .[4]

Readers would expect the remainder of the paragraph to identify a series of satellite dish antennas, arranged by size, from largest to smallest.

Transitions in ascending/descending paragraphs indicate the relative priority of points in the paragraph or document. Figure 7.11 uses *descending order* to identify the priorities for testing circuits.

Comparison/Contrast

Comparison and contrast tell readers about similarities and differences. Comparison identifies the similarities of various ideas, objects, or situations; contrast,

FIGURE 7.11 ■ Information Organized Using Descending Order

Integrated circuits received at incoming inspection are processed according to priorities. As the following figure shows, the most important integrated circuits are those that fill line shortages on the production floor. These parts take first priority at incoming inspection and are handled according to frequency of use and critical demand. These priority parts are further separated according to how fast they can be accurately tested and sent to the production floor. All other integrated circuits are then prioritized by back-order demand and the availability of open test equipment.

INSPECTION PRIORITIES

1   Fill line shortages

    2   Determine speed of testing

        3   Determine back-order demand
            and equipment availability

the differences. A comparison or contrast organization could present the advantages and disadvantages of certified versus uncertified computer disks or the ease or difficulty of various methods of storing electronic data. Any of the techniques in Figure 7.12 could visually present information that you want to compare and contrast.

Readers expect comparison and contrast topic sentences to present ideas dealing with similarities and differences, or both, as illustrated by the following two sentences:

■ **EXAMPLES**

The Honey Bee Lens, with three telescopic lenses for each eye, is patterned after the compound eye of a bee. . . .

Computers can now analyze measurable differences between the cries of healthy newborns and high-risk infants. . . .

The first sentence introduces a paragraph that compares new lenses to the compound eyes of bees. The second sentence leads readers to expect the paragraph to deal with characteristics that differentiate cries of healthy and high-risk infants.

Transitions in comparison and contrast paragraphs identify various similarities and differences. Figures 7.13 and 7.14 use *comparison and contrast* to differentiate the responsibilities of incoming inspection and in-process inspection of integrated circuits. Figure 7.13 shifts back and forth between incoming

Chapter 7: Organization of Information

FIGURE 7.12 ■ Visual Forms for Comparison and Contrast

Form	Example
Paired photos or drawings	Before/after of patient treated for scoliosis
Multiple or paired bar graphs	Expenditures for utilities for each quarter of the fiscal year
Multiple or paired percent graphs	Utilization of nutrients with and without coconut oil to increase absorption
Line graph	Changes in toxicity of emissions since installation of scrubbers
Multiple or paired gauges	Illustration of danger/no-danger in training manual for pilots
Table	Data collected on species size of bats according to age, sex, and location
Dichotomous key	Distinction of edible wild plants
Pareto diagram	Distinction between major and minor causes of shipping delays
Histogram	Women, grouped by age, affected by lung cancer
Columned chart	Physical symptoms of substance abuse

inspection and in-process inspection, explaining how each deals with specific responsibilities.

Figure 7.14 takes the same paragraph and rearranges it to present all the information about incoming inspection first and then discusses the in-process inspection.

Cause and Effect

The cause-and-effect organization of information focuses on precipitating factors and results. You can move from cause to effect or from effect to cause. For example, you could carry the disk through an electronic surveillance scanner and then trace the effects—the various disk errors that appear. Or beginning with the effect—a damaged disk—you could investigate the causes of the damage. Figure 7.15 identifies and illustrates various visuals that are effective for presenting cause-and-effect relationships.

One type of cause and effect—*inductive reasoning*—moves from specific instances to broad generalizations, forming the basis for the *scientific method* used in much research and experimentation. You begin by collecting data in support of an unproved hypothesis. After you have organized and examined a sufficient body of data, you draw a conclusion. When your conclusion proves consistently to be valid, it is considered a generalization. Most scientific principles and theories are based on this method of inquiry.

FIGURE 7.13 ■ Information Organized Using Comparison and Contrast

Integrated circuits are inspected and/or tested by two separate quality control departments: incoming quality control and in-process quality control. Incoming quality control is responsible for ensuring that all integrated circuits sent to the production floor meet all electrical standards set by the Component Engineering Department. In-process quality control is only responsible for ensuring that the parts are properly mounted on the printed circuit board. Incoming quality control also has to verify the markings on the integrated circuits in order to do proper testing and make certain that the company has purchased a qualified product. In contrast, in-process quality control only has to do random inspections of the circuit markings to ensure that qualified parts are being used in the manufacturing process. Although incoming and in-process inspection are two different areas, they do share the same goal of building a quality product. The following lists summarize each department's responsibilities.

Organization of
information:
incoming inspection

in-process inspection
incoming inspection

in-process inspection

mutual goal

Component Engineering Department responsible for *in-coming inspection*	Quality Control Department responsible for *in-process inspection*
• verify parts meet standards • verify IC markings • confirm qualified vendors	• ensure proper mounting • do random inspections

FIGURE 7.14 ■ Information Organized Using Comparison and Contrast

Integrated circuits are inspected and/or tested by two separate quality control departments: incoming quality control and in-process quality control, as shown in the lists below. Incoming quality control is responsible for ensuring that all integrated circuits sent to the production floor meet all electrical standards set by the Component Engineering Department. Incoming quality control also has to verify the markings on the integrated circuits in order to do proper testing and make certain that the company has purchased a qualified product. In-process quality control is only responsible for ensuring that the parts are properly mounted on the printed circuit board. In-process quality control only has to do random inspections of the circuit markings to ensure that qualified parts are being used in the manufacturing process. Although incoming and in-process inspection are two different areas, they do share the same goal of building a quality product.

Organization of
information:
incoming inspection

incoming inspection

in-process inspection
in-process inspection

mutual goal

Component Engineering Department responsible for *in-coming inspection*	Quality Control Department responsible for *in-process inspection*
• verify parts meet standards • verify IC markings • confirm qualified vendors	• ensure proper mounting • do random inspections

FIGURE 7.15 ■ Visual Forms for Cause and Effect	
Form	**Example**
Paired photos or drawings	Effects of two different treatments for removing facial birth marks
Weather map	Impact of cold front on majority of Midwest
Bar graph	Efficiency of various methods for harvesting cranberries
Line graph	Destruction of American chestnut by blight during this century
Cause-and-effect diagram	Identification of multiple contributing factors to contamination of drinking water
Pareto diagram	Identification of major causes in low birth weight

Because there is no way to test every instance, induction has a certain risk, and researchers must be careful to avoid basing their reasoning on invalid assumptions. They must not assume chronology is the same as causality, and they must examine a large sample before drawing a conclusion.

The first of these problems, equating chronology with causality, represents an error in reasoning. Just because B follows A does not mean that A causes B. Because inductive reasoning moves from specifics to a generalization, an investigator should not assume that sequence of events alone causes the effect. (Such an error in reasoning is called *post hoc, ergo propter hoc,* Latin for "after this, therefore because of this.") For example, a donor may become ill the day after donating blood to the Red Cross, but he cannot logically conclude that donating blood caused him to become ill. Guard against fallacious reasoning by examining all possible causes.

You also need to examine a large number of instances before drawing a conclusion. For example, before a new drug is allowed on the market, the Food and Drug Administration requires extensive tests with a broad segment of the target population. As a result of testing, a powerful painkiller such as propoxyphene, when taken according to directions and under a physician's care, is certified as safe even though all propoxyphene tablets and capsules have not been individually tested. Unfortunately, errors occur, although rarely, causing some people to suspect all inductive reasoning. So make sure your methodology is sound, your sample large, and your analysis free from bias or distortion.

When a generalization is widely accepted, you can use it as a base from which to predict the likelihood of specific instances occurring. This process is called *deductive reasoning*—moving from general premises to specific causes. A patient taking propoxyphene trusts that the pills are safe even though those particular ones have not been tested.

In paragraphs that show cause and effect, both should be identified in the topic sentence, as seen in the next examples.

One hypothesis about the formation of mineral-rich marine nodules suggests that marine bacteria break down organic material into free-floating minerals that eventually collect to form nodules. . . .

The Zephinie Escape Chute (ZEC) can rapidly evacuate people from 10-story burning buildings because of its unique construction. . . .

Readers of the first sentence expect the information in the paragraph to explain how minerals form marine nodules. The second sentence develops a paragraph that explains how the ZEC's unique construction aids rapid evacuation.

Transitions in cause-and-effect paragraphs signal the relationship between an action and its result. The example in Figure 7.16 uses *cause and effect* to organize information about IC testing. In this example, the cause-and-effect transitions indicate the descending order of the reasons an IC chip can be rejected.

Using Organization

These ways of organizing information are frequently used in technical documents—as short, self-contained segments (like the examples about integrated circuits) and also combined in longer pieces of writing.

FIGURE 7.16 ■ Information Organized Using Cause and Effect

Reasons for rejection of IC chips during incoming inspection fall into three categories (see figure). Most often, rejections occur because of some flaw in the chip itself. For example, a chip may have a short in the circuitry or fail to perform at the specified voltage or current. A second reason for rejection occurs when the supplier sends the wrong parts or a mixed batch of parts; therefore, assembly is delayed and production schedules slip. The final reason, which happens infrequently, occurs when the automatic test equipment has the wrong program or a program with a bug, so the contacts for the electrical testing are misplaced.

Causal transitions:
because

therefore

so

```
                    ┌─────────────────────┐
                    │  Causes of rejection │
                    └─────────────────────┘
          ┌───────────────┼───────────────┐
  most frequent      occasional       infrequent
  ┌──────────┐    ┌──────────────┐  ┌──────────────┐
  │ flaw in  │    │ wrong parts  │  │   wrong      │
  │ the chip │    │  or mixed    │  │ program or   │
  │          │    │   batch      │  │   bug in     │
  └──────────┘    └──────────────┘  │  program     │
                                    └──────────────┘
```

You can make a paragraph or document more understandable, as well as overcome some of the noise that interferes with readers' acceptance or comprehension of information, by organizing information so that it meets the needs of the content, purpose, and audience. For example, processes, procedures, and directions are best organized chronologically for all audiences. Descriptions of physical objects, mechanisms, organisms, and locations frequently make the most sense to readers if the information is organized spatially. Reasons and explanations are usually presented in descending order so that the audience reads the most important information first. Explanations of problems and their

ETHICS SIDEBAR

"Is This Ethical?": Ethics and Document Design

Consider the following scenarios:

Scenario 1: "You have been asked to evaluate a subordinate for possible promotion. In order to emphasize the employee's qualifications, you display these in a bulleted list. In order to de-emphasize the employee's deficiencies, you display these in a paragraph. Is this ethical?"

Scenario 2: "You are designing materials for your company's newest product. Included is a detailed explanation of the product's limited warranty. In order to emphasize that the product carries a warranty, you display the word "Warranty" in a large size of type, in upper and lower case letters, making the word as visible and readable as possible. In order to de-emphasize the details of the warranty, you display this information in smaller type and in all capital letters, making it more difficult to read and thus more likely to be skipped. Is this ethical?"[5]

Are these ethical or unethical document design choices? If you are uncertain, then you are not alone. Technical professionals and teachers, responding to these same scenarios (and others) in a survey, revealed differing opinions about the ethics involved. A majority of respondents (54.6%) considered the design choices of the evaluation ethical although a significant number were uncertain (26.7%) or found the evaluation unethical (18.7%). The warranty document divided opinions even more: a statistically similar number found the document ethical (33.3%), unethical (44.1%), or were uncertain (22.6%).

Researcher Sam Dragga, who coordinated the survey, believes the survey indicates the thin line separating rhetorically savvy design from deceptive design. He did find, however, that the survey revealed a general guideline most technical professionals follow for producing ethical document design: "The greater the likelihood of deception and the greater the injury to the reader as a consequence of that deception, the more unethical is the design of the document."[6] Determining the degree of deception and injury requires a technical communicator to weigh different items, "including typical communication practices, professional responsibilities, explicit specifications and regulations, as well as rhetorical intentions and ideals."[7] Dragga recognizes that workplace pressures can sometimes lead us to choose convenience over ethics. To avoid making unethical document design choices, Dragga advises "periodic self-examination" for technical professionals to help them create ethical communications.

| *What can help you decide whether a document's design is misleading?* | Follow Dragga's advice for self-examination by reviewing the scenarios. Is the reader deceived by the different formats in the evaluation? Does the difference in font size in the text of the warranty increase the likelihood of injury for the reader? |

solutions often make the most sense to readers if the information is organized using comparison/contrast and cause and effect.

You can also use organization of information to adapt your material to readers' attitudes. Specifically, you can take advantage of what you know about induction (specific to general) and deduction (general to specific). If you think readers might be reluctant to accept your conclusions or recommendations, you can organize the material inductively, moving from various specifics to your conclusion. Thus, readers can follow your line of reasoning and, perhaps, be persuaded by your analysis. If you think readers will agree with your conclusions, you can organize the information deductively, presenting the conclusion initially and then following it with the specifics that led to it. Deductive organization is more common in technical documents.

Sometimes decisions about organizing information aren't obvious or easy. The ethics sidebar on the previous page focuses attention on unethical design choices, ones that distort information and, thus, mislead readers because of the way information is organized. Decision making might be easier if workplace professionals agreed about what was unethical, but as you'll read in the sidebar, opinions are divided.

End-of-Chapter
Recommendations for Technical Communicators

1. Prepare *reader-based documents* that consider the needs and reactions of your readers.

2. Use a working outline to help you arrange and rearrange ideas, add new information, and delete unnecessary material.

3. Decide whether information is better presented verbally or visually, given your purpose and audience.

4. Organize your document so that the information is clear to your readers and helps you accomplish your purpose. Consider these standard ways to organize information verbally or visually:
   - Parts/whole organization
   - Chronological order
   - Spatial order
   - Ascending/descending order
   - Comparison/contrast
   - Cause and effect

5. Use topic sentences to identify both the content and organization of a paragraph.

6. Use transitions as one way to achieve coherence in a document.

Practicum

Engineering Associates (EA) is an established telecommunications consulting firm located in Atlanta, Georgia. We have been in business for more than 45 years, employing over 100 employees and providing a wide range of professional analysis and design services. Our present portfolio provides leading-edge design services for all of the most current technologies affecting fiber optics, microwave, digital switching, and CATV as well as wired and wireless voice/data networking.

Our clients are geographically dispersed throughout the nation and the world. They include but are not limited to Southern Bell, Cox Communications, ALLTEL, U.S. Navy, NASA/Kennedy Space Center, GTE, major universities, Fortune 500 corporations, the Republic of Hungary, and various divisions of the United Nations. Of particular value to our clients is our delivery of well-designed design documents and recommendations. EA's service to any given client may range from handling all of the particulars involved in conducting a simple data traffic study, requiring only a few weeks, to a large voice/data network design requiring several years.

Because each project is unique in its requirements, the delivery is often challenged by the difficulties associated with the development of an effective communication process. That is to say, we always expect to work very closely with each client in establishing a specific communication strategy that will best serve the needs of the project. This strategy may be as simple as e-mailing all communication to several key people on a weekly basis. On other projects we may have to establish a communication process that includes e-mails, faxes, letters, conference calls, and electronic drawings, all of which must contain accurate, relevant, and timely information.

The difficulties in these cases are linked primarily with identifying essential correspondents, their exact physical and virtual location(s), the expected communication format, content, and version where applicable. We must also carefully plan for when we originate and reply to each communication, considering both the overall project deadlines and the uncertainty of each recipient's work schedule.

Scenario: Designing Telecommunications Systems

I work in the Systems Engineering department. This department, as the name suggests, is primarily involved in the analysis and design of telecommunications systems. These systems may be a subset of a larger system or may be the entire system. Our target market consists of telephone companies, universities, and government installations. All of our work is project oriented with objectives that vary depending on the present needs of each client. Typically, the projects may involve upgrading or creating new designs for telephone central office transmission equipment, CATV systems, LAN (Local Area Network) integration, inside-plant and outside-plant cabling, and PBX/Centrex voice services.

For each project we provide any desired mix of professional services including feasibility studies, product evaluations, budget estimates, detailed designs, and project management. All of our clients have a general feel for what their telecommunication needs are, but they may or may not know how best to satisfy those needs. Even clients who know exactly how to define their needs and how to correct them usually do not wish to dedicate their own resources to implementing these changes. This is where we enter. The nature/extent of our involvement is determined primarily by the client's wishes and our professional recommendations at the onset of the project

My oral, visual, and written communication is cyclical. Specifically, similar tasks tend to recur within each project and from project to project. Further, most communication tasks within a project are recursive. (That is, the development is not linear; I move back and forth among thinking, drafting and revising.)

The form, objective, and target of my communication depends on where I am in the project. For a typical project, I invariably produce dozens upon dozens of e-mails, construction drawings, spreadsheets, and letters both to internal readers and to the client to satisfy the project requirements. My client contacts are primarily the budget gatekeepers and the supervisory persons responsible for the maintenance and operation of the finished product provided by EA. My secondary and tertiary contacts are any possible combination of end users, installation contractors, technical staffers, material suppliers, and departmental administrative assistants. My communication is generally technical: designed to request information, summarize meetings, provide clarification, train the client's end users, report test results, and state study conclusions.

Example: Coordinating a Corporate Move

Engineering Associates' work with DialTone America is an example of our work. This project involved relocating thousands of DialTone America employees from many different locations throughout Atlanta into one central headquarters building. A series of moves were scheduled sequentially over a period of months to maintain continuity in the operation of the company. The moves involved abandoning old PBX's at each building and assuming essentially the same telephone service functionality at the new headquarters. (Phone service would then be provided by the telephone company's Centrex service.)

Engineering Associates was contracted to coordinate the identification and activation of all desktop telephone, fax, and modem lines in the new building. Provision also had to be made for training the relocated employees on the use of their new phone sets and voice-mail system. In addition, we were responsible for receiving, configuring, transporting, placing, and testing all the various types of desktop telephone sets at each new work location. The documents that I produced had to be explicit enough to capture and represent the data needed to program the remote Centrex telephone switch.

Gathering, organizing and presenting this information from and to the client at times was a real challenge, largely because no established policies existed for gathering the volumes of necessary information. Also, the documents had to be updated regularly to reflect omitted, incorrect, or changed information. I also had to deal with the complexity of communicating with a large and diverse end-user group concurrently and in real time.

I had a number of important questions to answer as I worked on this project. How could I best create communication designed for mass distribution that would be understood by all recipients? How would I get the client/users to respond promptly and accurately? How could I track the communication process and ensure that all affected parties were adequately informed of the status and impact of these communications? In short, how would I keep track of all the information necessary to produce documents that accurately reflected the new telecommunications needs at the new building and ensure that all employees were properly trained?

One way to track the information was to create the following checklist. This checklist was distributed to each department's move coordinator before each move. Each coordinator was responsible for seeing that all employees within their group were accounted for and that their specific telecommunications requirements were identified. I could make no presumptions in regard to the coordinator's experience with providing such information. So, this checklist was intended to serve as a guide for them as they filled in the accompanying spread-sheet for the benefit of their departmental employees. A kick off meeting was held between myself and all move coordinators prior to each move to explain the documents personally and to answer any move-related questions.

Assignment

Consider the preceding scenario and create two documents, which together should result in the collection and organization of all needed telecommunication requirements for each moved employee. Both documents are intended for the move coordinator.

Document 1. Design a cover letter for the checklist. This letter should be brief (1 page maximum) and contain the following information:

- Time, place and length of kick-off meeting

- Purpose of kick-off meeting

- Purpose of checklist and spreadsheet

- Coordinator's role in the data-gathering process

- Coordinator's contact information (i.e., name, address, phone number, etc.)

**DIALTONE AMERICA—
MAIN HEADQUARTERS
MOVE COORDINATOR INPUT
CHECKLIST**

Please use the following checklist to identify your group's telecommunication requirements on the attached spreadsheet. Your spreadsheet is due by **Tuesday, August 17.**

1. *Personnel.* Who's involved?
   - Who are the people in your group, their location (i.e., cube or room number), telephone extension and pager number?
   - What's the group manager's name?
   - On what date will each person move?
   - Who is your administrative assistant? Do you or does anyone in your group need an appearance on the administrative assistant's set?
   - Who will telecommute?

2. *Lines.* What's needed?
   - Where are fax lines needed?
   - Who needs modem/data lines?
   - Who requires second lines?

3. *Set.* Set type—Who gets what set?
   - 5316 digital business set (management & admin. assistants)
   - 9316 analog set (all others)

4. *Hunt Groups.* Do you require incoming calls to ring in sequence starting at the main number and rolling over to other phones until the call is answered?

5. *ACD Groups.* For your call center environments, do you require incoming calls to ring in sequence starting at the main number and rolling over to the least idle agent until the call is answered?

6. *Connections.* Who requires LAN/WAN connection(s)?

7. *Other requirements.* Who requires international dialing? What special needs or features are unique to your operation (800 numbers that need to be moved, lines for servers, auto attendant systems in use, etc.)? Comments explaining requirements for the department or for any given specific employee not already addressed elsewhere.

Thank you for your assistance.

- Specified form of kick-off meeting attendance confirmation (i.e., e-mail, phone, fax, etc.)

- How questions will be handled by you before, during, and after the kick-off meeting

- Deadlines for completing and returning the spreadsheet

- Your contact information

- The attached check list

- An attached specimen spreadsheet (to be used as a basis for discussion during the kick-off meeting)

Document 2. Design an electronic spreadsheet. In general, construct the spreadsheet so that for any given cell in the spreadsheet, the coordinator will input either a name, number, None, N/A or yes/no. You will tell them in the kick-off meeting to choose the input that provides the most information. While spreadsheet cells will accept any number and arrangement of alpha-numeric characters (as do word processing programs), be careful to segregate your input fields so as to make the document sortable by the most variables possible.

Build the document to accommodate, for every employee, the answers to all applicable questions presented in the checklist. Conserve valuable space on your spreadsheet by thoughtfully presenting information only as often as necessary (e.g., if you produce your spreadsheet by department, you will not have to represent the department manager's name along with each employee entry). Headers and footers are also an efficient way to use space.

This spreadsheet should be designed to fit on legal paper (printed landscape), and each page should additionally contain the following information:

- Spreadsheet title

- Client's name (the company)

- Department

- Sufficient space to handle information for a minimum of 175 employees

- Easily readable font sizes

- Your company's name

- Spreadsheet filename

- Automatic page numbering

- Date

Think smart. Have fun!

Daryl Seay, a Registered Communications Distribution Designer (RCDD), is a Senior Project Engineer at Engineering Associates in Atlanta, Georgia. He received a B.S. in Electrical Engineering from the University of Tennessee. He is also a Licensed Low-Voltage Contractor. He has a successful track record with over 15 years of engineering, marketing, and

testing. His background includes project management, electrical design, scheduling, inspections, field operations, home office engineering, and product development. At Engineering Associates, Daryl Seay contributes to all aspects of premise wiring and outside-plant design affecting voice, data, and video projects. He also provides client-based internal telecommunications support.

In commenting about this practicum, Daryl Seay said, "Professionals are often required to render services that rely heavily on the collection, organization, and representation of lots of information from third parties—with no precedents to aid them. The ability to think critically and to use clear and orderly communication techniques are of inestimable value."

For a comprehensive look at Engineering Associates, please visit the company Web site at www.engineeringassociates.com.

Individual and Collaborative Assignments

1. **Identify expectations based on topic sentences.** Read the following topic sentences and identify expectations that readers might have if they read them. What content would readers expect in each paragraph? One example is provided.

   Example The use of a sulfur-asphalt mixture for repaving the highway will result in several specific benefits.

   Analysis The sentence presents a cause-and-effect relationship between using a sulfur-asphalt mixture and specific benefits. The paragraph will identify these benefits.

   a. The CAT scan creates an image resembling a "slice" that clearly visualizes anatomical structures within the body.
   b. The fetus is in the birth position by the ninth month of a normal pregnancy.
   c. The routine use of drugs in labor and delivery sometimes has adverse effects on otherwise healthy, normal infants.
   d. The stages of normal labor and delivery begin at term when the fetus reaches maturity and end with the expulsion of the placenta.
   e. Two major forms of leukemia—chronic myelocytic and acute myelocytic— have distinct differences.
   f. Improper downstroke and follow-through can cause the golf ball to either hook and fade to the left or slice and fade to the right.
   g. Three main types of parachutes are used for sky diving. The most widely used parachute has a round, domelike canopy. . . .
   h. A square parachute provides more maneuverability and a better overall ride than does a conventional round parachute.
   i. Two methods of disinfecting treated wastewater are chlorination and ozonation.
   j. The chlorinator room contains the evaporators, chlorinators, and injectors, three of each. The evaporators are used only when liquid chlorine is being drawn from the containers. . . .

2. **Revise a memo by improving organization.** Read the memo on the next page. Revise it so that the subject line in the heading, the topic sentences, and the paragraphs are unified and coherent. The intended readers are interested in information that will help decrease rejects during manufacturing. They are not particularly concerned with personnel or cost.

3. **Revise paragraphs by adding topic sentences.** Read the two paragraphs on the next page and write topic sentences that anticipate the organizational structure presented.

Stanford Engineering, Inc.

February 14, 20—

To: Quality Control Supervision
From: T. R. Hood, Engineer   TRH
Subject: Increased scrap and customer rejects

The Engineering Department is recommending the purchase of an International glue
line inspection system to strengthen standard visual inspection. Machine operators
will not be slowed down by the addition of this new glue line inspection system. The
system will detect breaks in the glue line and eject a carton from the run before it
reaches shipping. If the system detects more than five consecutive rejects, it will automatically stop the machine.

   Purchasing this International system is a better solution than purchasing a new glue
pot for $6,500. The savings in purchasing the $4,000 International system will allow us
to rebuild the existing glue pot.

Paragraph 1

Buss bars, the smallest of the parts the Sheet Metal Fabrication Shop
produces, are made of grade-A copper and are tin-plated before being used
for internal grounding. Paper deflectors, used in printers, are made of stainless steel and do not require any plating or painting. Deflectors guide the
paper through the printer and usually measure 4" in width and 15" in length,
depending on the size of the printer. A larger box-like structure, made of
aluminum and requiring plating in the enclosure chassis, is designed to hold
a variety of electronic devices within an even larger computer main frame.
A steel door panel requiring cosmetic plating and painting is the largest of the
parts produced by the Sheet Metal Fabrication Shop.

Paragraph 2

The fetal causes for abortion are infectious agents: protozoa bacteria, viruses,
particularly rubella virus. Drugs such as thalidomide cause fetal abnormali-
ties. When radiation is given in therapeutic doses to the mother in the first
few months of pregnancy, malformation or death of the fetus may result.

4. **Characterize and evaluate the organization of a Web site.** Work with
   a small group of people in your major or a closely related field of study.
   (a) Visit several Web sites that are related to your field of study. How
       would you characterize the organizational strategies used (parts/whole,

chronological, spatial, ascending/descending, comparison/contrast, or cause and effect)?

(b) Establish criteria for evaluating the effectiveness of Web site organization based on your responses to Assignment 4(a).

(c) Create a rubric for these criteria, and choose one Web site from the list you've identified to evaluate.

(d) Share your rubric and evaluation with your classmates.

5. **Tour and evaluate a Web site.** Visit the following Web site: <www. illustructions.com>. Follow the links to learn as much as you can about the Web site and its purpose. Write a review for your instructor of the Web site and the integration of visual and verbal information.

Intertext

How an Author Can Avoid the Pitfalls of Practical Ethics[8]

Abstract—An author's violations of ethics can be either intentional or unintentional. Sometimes the sins of the pen (or keyboard) creep unawares into a manuscript, only to emerge after publication as awkward ethical problems for the writer. Examples show how such indiscretions can damage the author's professional reputation.*

Why are ethical questions important in engineering writing, which is inherently factual and straightforward communication? The answer lies in the rather subtle conflict between an author's self-interest and the obligation to provide adequate information for readers. Because of this conflict, an author could violate accepted standards of practical ethics in any of several ways; for example, one might run afoul of the following:

- *Moral ethics,* by misrepresenting facts;
- *Professional ethics,* by omitting credit to peers' contributions; or
- *Legal ethics,* by violating copyright laws [1].

Such definitions of practical ethics, however, are fraught with contradictions. For example, legal positions are not necessarily moral, and moral positions are often not legal [2]. Standards, both legal and moral, may also vary geographically. The seriousness of an author's offense can vary in a wide range from little white

*This Intertext is based on a chapter in a book by H. B. Michaelson, *How to Write and Publish Engineering Papers and Reports*, Oryx Press, Phoenix, AZ, 3rd ed.

lies and exaggerations to brazen plagiarism and stolen information. The sins of the pen (or keyboard) may seem trivial, such as a little fudging of the engineering data to make results look better. But can a writer be only a little dishonest—and can an expectant mother be only a little pregnant? Hardly.

Besides, the minor infraction that seems innocuous to an author may be quite unacceptable to readers. Although there are no hard and fast, enforceable rules for ethical writing, the substandard practices described below are generally recognized as being unethical.

Engineers will seldom fake data or make fraudulent claims, but the subtler forms of ethical irregularities—either deliberate or unintentional—are not unusual in engineering writing. Indeed, *unintentional* violations of ethics are rather common. These are usually due either to lapses in memory or just plain thoughtlessness. But to the reader a statement may be unethical, even though the author didn't phrase it that way deliberately.

Suppose, for example, you read a journal paper by Jones describing a novel idea for the design of a widget. Later you seize upon this idea, forgetting the source, and consider it your own. Your paper on the subject then claims that you originated the design methodology. Readers who know Jones's work will brand your lapse of memory as deliberate dishonesty.

The *intentional* slip in ethical behavior is something else. As a writer of product literature you may decide to omit hazard warnings to help the marketing effort; as a proposal writer you may exaggerate claims of the competence and experience of the personnel for the project; or as the ambitious author of an engineering research paper you may gild your lily by wrongly claiming credit for a colleague's concept.

In another kind of situation imagine that you are developing a new type of electronic camera and face pressures from your manager to publish research results before the competition can announce a similar development. You are anxious to promote your technical ideas and also to establish your professional reputation. In your haste to get published, you could be tempted to force the issue by omitting significant limitations of your design or by polluting the facts with speculation.

Such violations of practical ethics can defeat your purposes. The attempts to bolster your professional reputation will fall flat—instead they disturb the integrity of the manuscript and will eventually expose you to criticism. But you can avoid being trapped by these pitfalls of practical ethics by weeding out from your first draft those subtle indiscretions that may have crept in and by searching for the kinds of ethical problems discussed below. Because you can easily overlook them in your own writing, ask a colleague to help seek out the improprieties. An independent review of the initial draft could also show where important information was omitted.

Sins of Omission

Readers can be misled, not only by your ambiguities and exaggerations, but also by what you deliberately leave out. Here are typical reasons for omitting technical information:

To hide defects and limitations of engineering designs or procedures: No engineering design is perfect. Even the Brooklyn Bridge, a designer's triumph, will rust and decay eventually. When you describe a novel engineering object or a new process, be fair to the reader—explain what it can do and what it can't—and also what it is and what it isn't.

To avoid giving credit to prior accomplishments of others: In reporting R&D work it is wrong not to include short statements of who did what in previous developments, especially in published papers.

To withhold contradictory information: Omitting certain data that would detract from an honest description of your engineering design isn't cricket. One example is the omission of outlier points from a graph because they wouldn't look good, as illustrated in Fig. 1. Another is neglecting to mention significant failures that occurred during the course of the design effort. Burying mistakes doesn't help you or the reader! Remember Santayana's famous remark, "Those who cannot remember the past are condemned to repeat it," and if your record of the past is incomplete or misleading, you risk condemnation by your readers.

To omit data that would lead to legal entanglements: Burying information on defects can be legally right but morally wrong. For example, withholding of pub-

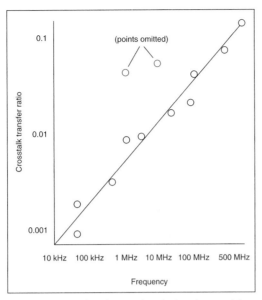

Fig. 1. *Example of sins of omission in graphics.*

lic reports on mechanical failures to protect the defendant from accusations of neglect in an accident insurance litigation is legally correct but ethically wrong [3].

To avoid commitments to accuracy or reliability: In an engineer's description of a device, the user is entitled to know how accurately it performs and how reliably it operates. The lack of such information in a formal description hints strongly that the author is not willing to discuss these properties and implies an unethical decision to omit information.

If you rely on such devious reasons for omitting data when writing an R & D paper or an engineering report, you may well be cheating the reader out of useful information.

To the observant reader, certain kinds of omissions from a technical manuscript will be considered a breach of ethics. To others the missing information will pass unnoticed. Regardless, omitting certain types of items from a formal paper or report can be downright troublesome.

Limits of performance: The objective of engineering design is to provide usability and function, to prevent operational failures, and to avoid potential hazards. An engineering description of a system or device should indicate the upper limits of operation and its expected lifetime and should identify safety concerns. For example, a detailed report on a microwave unit should point out that it may affect the operation of nearby pacemakers. And if pesticides are banned in the U.S., any technical descriptions for use in other countries (however legal) should include appropriate caveats for the buyer. In recent years product safety [4] and product liability have attracted much attention.

Limitations of reported tests: Engineering tests should be explained in clear detail to show their validity: the test parameters, the number of samples tested, the nature of the test population, and so on. A mere listing of tabulated numbers isn't always the adequate and honest way to present results.

Significant details of research or development work: Details can be *legitimately* omitted for reasons of national security, patent rights, or a company's trade secrets and proprietary data [6]. However, an author is unethical if these reasons are used as a false excuse for withholding details. An engineer author, for example, who borrowed and adopted some unclassified ideas but claimed to be the inventor, could refuse to divulge certain data because the details were "classified." Hiding self-interest behind a nonexistent curtain of security is certainly unethical.

Credit to coworkers: Today's engineering achievements are usually the result of teamwork. Any important coworker who is not a coauthor of the final report or paper deserves mention. To ignore those contributors, even if an oversight, is questionable behavior.

Proper qualifications: Without adequate qualifiers, claims of superiority can get out of hand, to the discredit of the author. An engineer's presentation about a new manufacturing process, for example, would be unethical if the claims of lower production costs omitted any mention of the lower product integrity due to fewer quality control procedures.

Unfair Bias

Inserting biased information into your manuscript can be just as unfair to readers as omitting important data. But not always! A distorted presentation is legitimate if it emphasizes and expands upon the significant aspects of your engineering work, while deemphasizing the routine and well-known portions. On the other hand, slanting your manuscript to gain an unfair advantage is, of course, unethical. Some distortions of this kind will be obvious to the careful readers; others, which are described here, are more subtle.

One of the less obvious kinds of biased reporting occurs in the author's *selection* of literature references:

> *The detailed analysis and conclusions of the present investigation are similar to those of Carter [16] and Wright [17].*

The citation of the two prior papers will seem convincing support of the author's analysis unless the reader knows about a paper published by Jones and Abernathy (deliberately unmentioned by the writer in the above example), which disproved the claims of Carter and Wright.

There is another way an author's bias can shape a manuscript to gain an unfair advantage. In our example a senior investigator, planning to report on a controversial piece of engineering research, can choose co-authors selectively because there are no real conventions for co-authorship. In some cases coworkers on the engineering team share the writing load. In other cases a professional writer becomes a coauthor or the department manager does some of the writing. In this particular case the senior author has an axe to grind and decides to slant the text in the desired direction by selecting colleagues who happen to agree with the chosen point of view.

Another type of bias occurs in the cropping of photographs. It is quite acceptable to delete those portions of a picture that are not discussed in the text. It is unethical, however, to hide the parts of a photograph that the reader is entitled to know about. For example, if the photomicrograph of a metallic specimen is cropped to show only one type of strong grain structure, any hint in the text that these grains are representative of the entire sample could be due to the author's bias and would be downright misleading.

The biased treatment of graphics can also hide defects in an engineer's development work. Large charts or diagrams of routine data tend to attract the reader's eye and draw attention away from technical weaknesses in the text. Such a ploy has been labeled "The Houdini Syndrome" [7]. The great magician frequently focused the attention of his audience on a remote item, drawing the eye away from his method of escaping.

Another way of hiding weak links in the information chain is to use a language strategy. The following is an example of selectively "overstating the positive":

> *The vibration test data for the beam supports, tabulated in Table 6, are convincing evidence of the ruggedness of our new structural design.*

Here the facts are misrepresented because the favorable results listed in Table 6 showed vibration tests in only one of three possible planes. Indeed, the table is unethical as much as the explanation. Any explanation of tabular data should be complete and unambiguous.

Ambiguity and Speculation

The ambiguity that lurks everywhere in written language may either innocently cause misunderstandings or deliberately invite misinterpretation. The latter kind of vague statement, *unethical ambiguity* [8], is rare, but it is one of the many ways communication can be thrown out of focus in engineering writing. The example below attempts to stress the advantages of modern technologies:

> *This method of bridge design has employed sophisticated computer techniques of structural analysis, using the Bensonhurst algorithm to achieve strong supporting members.*

This statement is misleading because it implies that the use of "sophisticated techniques" resulted in a bridge design of great strength. The fact is, however, that computer analytic methods are generally used to plan economical construction with the least expensive materials. These methods can produce a structural design of minimum acceptable strength [3].

The illusions derived from language manipulation take many forms. The double meanings, for example, that pop up everywhere can be a potent tool for distorting engineering information. Again, the confusion could be due either to the author's accidental choice of the wrong words or to a studied attempt at obfuscation. Here is one way the unsuspecting reader can be misled:

> *For many years no satisfactory method was known for sealing together these two alloys for use in a vacuum system, but seals have now been made successfully.*

In this case the passive verb in the last clause suggests that the author himself had developed the sealing method. Actually he did not deserve credit for the method because it had "now been made successfully" in a previous unrelated project.

In any kind of engineering work either evading or misstating the accuracy or precision of data is unprofessional. Misleading statements of precision are frequently seen in feature stories in the public press, but they should never appear in formal engineering writing. When, for example, the increase in ductility of a metal after heat treatment is cited as a 12.07 percent average improvement, those four significant digits express a false degree of precision if ductility can actually be measured only within ±2 percent.

One obfuscation that is particularly frustrating and unfair to the reader is the citing of technical details that are buried in an obscure source or—worse still—in a nonexistent reference. This is the "hand-waving reference":

The details of controlling this diffusion process[18] demand close control of time, temperature, and pressure.

The reader is now saddled with the job of finding a foreign language book without the benefit of the full name of the author, the name of the publisher, the date of publication, and the page numbers of the cited critical information on the close control of the process.

A more flagrant violation of the ethics of the literature reference is the citation

---
[18]J. Schmidt, *Warmpressversuche an hochdispersen Metallpulvern.*

of an internal report that is not available to external readers on request. Even if such a citation were an unintentional and thoughtless mistake of the writer, readers will be offended by what seems a deliberate attempt to shield their eyes from privileged information.

To the reader who needs specific technical information, thinly veiled speculation is just as bad as ambiguity. One popular way of speculating in a seemingly legitimate way is to extrapolate the existing data to a future time, to a better reliability, to an improved performance, and so on. With the aid of modern automated computation, extrapolation is a guessing game in which the thread of logic and the assumption of technical conditions can be conveniently obscured by the author's favorite computational method. An example:

These accelerated life tests of the water pump over a period of two weeks indicate an average time-to-failure of ten years.

Unless some explanation of the extrapolation method is added to the above statement, the audience may question the validity of the reliability data.

Plagiarism

One of your responsibilities as an engineer author is to respect the intellectual property of others. Any attempt to pass off another's published work as your own or to assume credit for another's ideas is a gross violation of practical ethics. When you plan to include in your report a substantial portion of published material, cite the source. If the material was copyrighted, you must also request approval of the holder of the copyright. If you do not take these standard precautions, you run the risk of, at least, unpleasant accusations. In more flagrant cases you risk the loss of your professional reputation and possible legal action against you. Of course plagiarism sometimes goes unnoticed. If so it reposes like a time bomb in your document. When you are eventually exposed in the theft of someone else's technical ideas and text your career may be destroyed. Even if you have been merely thoughtless and neglected to cite your sources, you run the same risks as the intentional plagiarist. This kind of forgetfulness is what Garfield called "citation amnesia," [9] which readers may confuse with intellectual thievery.

Self-plagiarism is a different kind of transgression. If you rework some of your old, published data and represent it as a new finding, it can be exposed as a fraud, as unethical as any other form of plagiarism. It is legitimate, of course, to prepare a second paper based on your first one if you add significantly new data and modify the conclusions. But simply regurgitating your old results in new contexts without proper citation is wholly unethical. . . .

Indiscriminate Publication

Although getting published and becoming known for your engineering accomplishments should be one of your professional goals, you must avoid the unethical aspects of publishing. One of these is indiscriminate publication, fueled by your desire to rush into print or to pad your personal bibliography.

One way of building up your list of published papers, self-plagiarism, has already been mentioned. Unfortunately the literature is full of redundant articles which not only contribute to the soaring expenses of journal publishers, but also add to the burdens of literature searching. The indexing and abstracting systems become clogged with material that is repeated many times, published mainly for the benefit of the authors. And what of the readers? An unscrupulous author who offers his or her old stuff under the guise of a "new" manuscript may claim it is for a "different audience" or that it has a "different message." This may be true. But when it is only a thin excuse for getting republished it becomes wasteful—and unethical.

Another example of indiscriminate publication is the premature paper. But there is nothing inherently wrong with publishing an R & D article or report before the work is fully completed. However, when such a premature publication makes claims or draws conclusions that are not supported in the article, the pie-in-the-sky presentation violates ethical principles. Even in professional journals papers of this kind sometimes survive the referee procedures and find their way into print.

One more questionable practice is the submission of an article to several journal editors at once. An author may commit this sort of offense out of ignorance, not realizing that magazine editors dislike investing time and effort in appraising an article, only to find that the writer has suddenly found acceptance elsewhere. Other authors brazenly commit the sin of multiple submissions, fully understanding the imposition on editors and reviewers. This inconsiderate behavior is foolish because it breeds poor relations with journal editors and burdens the system. Some journals, however, may accept multiple submission papers. Read a journal's "advice to authors." If you are unsure,

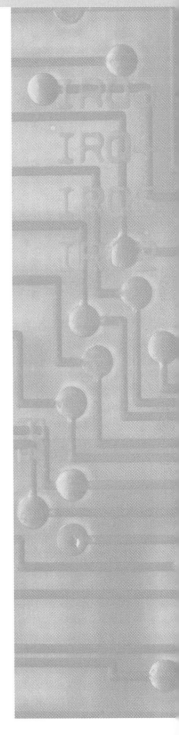

query the editors involved before submitting the same paper to several journals.

Conclusion

You can be trapped by accusations of unethical statements unless you conscientiously review the rough draft of your manuscript with the help of a colleague or a competent technical editor. The ethical aspects to look for are adequate data, acceptable standards of good taste, credibility of the exposition—all of which contribute to the integrity of your manuscript. Rooting out ethical improprieties is not easy. Some may have been buried deep in the writing in the same way they may have been hidden deep within your personal motivation. Others may have been conscious and deliberate on your part even in the face of the consequences discussed here. But readers are not always fooled by distortions of meaning. Remember that even when your readers discover a trivial bit of fakery in your writing, its credibility is destroyed. And your standing among peers will suffer. Discretion has to be your keynote when your professional reputation is at stake.

References

[1] F. Radez, "STC and the professional ethic," *Tech. Commun.*, vol. 27, no. 3, 1980, pp. 5–7.

[2] H. L. Shimberg, "Technical communicators and moral ethics," *Tech. Commun.*, vol. 27, no. 3, 1980, pp. 10–12.

[3] H. Petroski, *To Engineer Is Human*. New York: St. Martin's Press, pp. 199, 211, 1985.

[4] K. Kipnis, "Engineers who kill: Professional ethics and the paramountcy of public safety," *Bus. Prof. Ethics Journal*, vol. 1, no. 6, 1981, pp. 253–256.

[5] D. E. Zimmerman and D. G. Clark, *Guide to Technical and Scientific Communication*. New York: Random House, p. 380, 1987.

[6] J. G. Bronson, "Unfriendly eyes," *IEEE Trans. Prof. Commun. PC 30*, 1987, p. 173.

[7] C. Reimold, "Games of deception," *IPCC Conf. Record*, 1989, IEEE Professional Communication Society, p. 99.

[8] M. A. Zeidner, "Constructive ambiguity: The new road to prestige in science and engineering," *Tech. Commun.*, vol. 28, no. 3, 1981, pp. 25–26.

[9] E. Garfield, "More on the ethics of scientific publication," *Current Contents*, July 26, 1982, no. 30, pp. 5–10.

Additional References

Technical Communication and Ethics, R. John Brockmann and Fern Rook, eds. Anthology Series, Washington: Society of Technical Communication, 1989.

A. L. Caplan, "Ethical engineers need not apply: The state of applied ethics today," *Science, Tech., and Human Values*, vol. 6, no. 6, Fall 1980, pp. 9–23.

P. M. Rubens, "Reinventing the wheel? Ethics for technical communicators," *Journal Tech. Writing and Commun.*, vol. 11, no. 4, 1981, p. 205.

Herbert B. Michaelson (M'49–LS'87) is a consultant in technical communication in Jackson Heights, NY.

8

Information Design

CHAPTER 8 IN BRIEF

A document's appearance affects readers' attitudes as well as their ease and speed in reading.

Chunking and Labeling Information

Chunks are topically related groupings of information that are influenced by context, purpose, and audience. White space differentiates chunks of information in documents and makes information more accessible.

- The four margins on a page are usually different widths.
- A justified right-hand margin gives a document a neat, clean appearance; fully justified text is not as easy to read as text with a ragged-right margin.
- Changes in leading and adjustments in justification and line length can have a great impact on ease of reading.

Headings and subheadings label chunks of information and signal their relative importance in a document.

Arranging Related Chunks of Verbal and Visual Information

The easiest and most efficient way to approach the design is to see a page as a *grid*—columns and rows that help you organize the space on a page. In most situations, you will use one-column, two-column, or three-column grids.

Many engineers and scientists prefer visuals integrated in the text rather than placed in an appendix. Design errors resulting from *chartjunk, tombstoning,* heading placement, and widows and orphans should be avoided.

Emphasizing Information

Typeface (also called type font) affects readers' attitudes and reactions, as well as their ability to read the text easily and quickly, so you should know some basic characteristics about typefaces:

- Serif or sans serif
- Typeface variations
- Type size
- Style choices

Effective visual devices include numbered lists, bulleted lists, underlining, boxes, shading or tints, and colors. Overuse diminishes their impact.

Designing for the Web

Using grids helps you create effective, consistent pages. Dumping text on the Web doesn't work, in part because it doesn't account for differences in the way print and electronic documents are read.

Everyone knows the sinking feeling of turning to a page filled with tiny print and virtually nonexistent margins. Unquestionably, a document's appearance affects readers' attitudes as well as their ease and speed in reading. Whereas Chapter 7 discusses selection and organization of information, this chapter deals with the visual design of information, focusing on how that design affects the accessibility, appropriateness, and appeal of a document or a Web site.

Regardless of your technical specialty—from aviation and biology to computers, from mechanical engineering and nursing to oceanography, from writing and xerography to zymurgy—part of your job will involve the design of information—in print documents and on Web sites. Your knowledge of ways to effectively combine visual and verbal forms to communicate to readers may distinguish you from others. And if you are lucky enough to have designers and graphic artists to work with, you need to be able to communicate your vision of the document.

Information design is a field concerned with the ways in which you can organize and present information to affect readers' comprehension. Document design, a term you're probably more familiar with, is part of information design. As you design the information in your documents, you manage three categories of elements:[1]

- **Textual elements:** letters, numbers, and symbols (for example, the characters that form the words in a document as well as headings, labels, and page numbers)

- **Spatial elements:** spaces between textual elements (for example, the spacing between paragraphs, the margins, and the page breaks) as well as the size and location of textual and graphic elements

- **Graphic elements:** punctuation marks, typographic devices (for example, bullets and icons), geometric forms (for example, diamond-shaped decision boxes on flowcharts), and visuals themselves (for example, diagrams and drawings)

These three elements are important whether you're designing print documents or Web pages. Regardless of how carefully you design a document, though, you need to know that reading online is about 25 percent slower than reading from paper. Furthermore, many people simply do not like to read extended chunks of text on a computer monitor. And, finally, they don't like to scroll, so short pages are likely to get more careful attention. To compensate for these reading preferences, when you're writing an electronic document, you should "write 50 percent less text and not just 25 percent less since it's not only a matter of reading speed but also a matter of feeling good."[2]

This chapter discusses strategies of information design for managing these textual, spatial, and graphic elements for both print documents and Web pages:

- Chunking and labeling information by effective use of white space and headings

- Arranging information by appropriate integration of visual and verbal chunks

- Emphasizing information by effective use of typographic devices and typefaces

Chunking and Labeling Information

You can approach the design of information in your print document or Web site by grouping, or chunking, topically related information and then labeling it for readers. In simple terms, chunking makes the information in undifferentiated text accessible to readers. Decisions about chunking information involve two factors:

- Logical topical relationships

- Audience needs for the information

Figure 8.1a–c shows the sequence of chunking and labeling information. Figure 8.1a includes information about several topics related to hornbills, an exotic bird found in Africa and Asia.[3] Unfortunately, the information is in no particular order and is without any design of the information to aid readers. Figure 8.1b groups all the information about the various subtopics and then visually separates these topical chunks into paragraphs. Figure 8.1c labels the subtopics and uses a bulleted list to make reading easier.

Decisions about the most appropriate way to chunk and label information are not necessarily as simple as grouping topically related information, as in Figure 8.1a–c. For example, if you are preparing a fact sheet about the rivets your company sells, you could chunk the information by characteristics such as types of materials, strength of materials, applications, dimensions, resistance to corrosion, distinctions from competitors, price, and so on. Information from all these categories could appear on the fact sheet, but you could make a decision about how to chunk the information based on the needs of your audience. At the top of page 250, the list on the left chunks information about materials for rivets according to type; the list on the right according to strength.

(a) Twenty-three species of hornbills inhabit the savannas and forests of Africa, and twenty-seven more species are found in Asia, mostly in tropical rain forests. The Tangkoko red knobs are a species bothered by few dangerous predators; their unusual nesting behavior seems a holdover from earlier times. The nesting behavior of the Tangkoko red knobs is thought to have evolved from one or more of these reasons: protection from predators; defense against intruding hornbills; ensurance of mate fidelity (female can't escape to the nest of another; or, variously, male is too exhausted feeding one female and chick to seek an additional mate). Tangkoko red knobs weigh more than five pounds and produce a variety of honks, croaks, squawks, and barks some of which can be heard more than 300 yards away. The female Tangkoko red knob nests in a tree cavity or rock crevice and then seals the nest entrance—with mud delivered by the male and her own fecal matter—leaving only a narrow slit for receiving food from the male. One of the Borneo species of hornbills, the Tangkoko red knobs, is large and loud. Only four species are found to the east of the biogeographical boundary between Borneo and Sulawesi.

The information about hornbills is raw, run-together text—undifferentiated, except for capital letters and periods to mark the beginnings and ends of sentences. The information is unordered and is in a sans serif font without any spatial or graphic elements to aid readers.

(b) Twenty-three species of hornbills inhabit the savannas and forests of Africa, and twenty-seven more species are found in Asia; mostly in tropical rain forests. Only four species are found to the east of the biogeographical boundary between Borneo and Sulawesi.

One of the Borneo species of hornbills, the Tangkoko red knobs, is large and loud. They weigh more than five pounds and produce a variety of honks, croaks, squawks, and barks some of which can be heard more than 300 yards away.

The female nests in a tree cavity or rock crevice and then seals the nest entrance—with mud delivered by the male and her own fecal matter—leaving only a narrow slit for receiving food from the male. This behavior is thought to have evolved from one or more of these reasons: protection from predators; defense against intruding hornbills; ensurance of mate fidelity (female can't escape to the nest of another; or, variously, male is too exhausted feeding one female and chick to seek an additional mate). However, the Tangkoko red knobs are bothered by few dangerous predators, so their unusual nesting behavior seems a holdover from earlier times.

All the information about the three subtopics, now in a serif font, is topically chunked and then visually separated into paragraphs with a ragged-right margin.

(c) **Hornbill Territory.** Twenty-three species of hornbills inhabit the savannas and forests of Africa, and twenty-seven more species are found in Asia, mostly in tropical rain forests. Only four species are found to the east of the biogeographical boundary between Borneo and Sulawesi.

Tangkoko Red Knobs. One of the Borneo species of hornbills, the Tangkoko red knobs, is large and loud. These birds weigh more than five pounds and produce a variety of honks, croaks, squawks, and barks some of which can be heard more than 300 yards away.

Unusual Nesting Behavior. The female nests in a tree cavity or rock crevice and then seals the nest entrance—with mud delivered by the male and her own fecal matter—leaving only a narrow slit for receiving food from the male. This behavior is thought to have evolved from one or more of these reasons:
- protection from predators
- defense against intruding hornbills
- ensurance of mate fidelity (female can't escape to the nest of another; or, variously, male is too exhausted feeding one female and chick to seek an additional mate)

However, the Tangkoko red knobs are bothered by few dangerous predators, so their unusual nesting behavior seems a holdover from earlier times.

The subtopics in each paragraph are labeled with run-in, boldfaced headings. A bulleted list makes reading easier.

What information could you chunk in two different ways, similar to these lists categorizing rivets?

■ **EXAMPLE**

This chunking would be useful for readers interested in marine applications where anticorrosion is a critical factor.

This chunking would be useful for readers interested in bridge construction where strength is a critical factor.

Types of Rivet Materials
- Steel
- Aluminum
- Brass
- Plastic

Strength of Rivet Materials
- Tensile strength
- Compressive
- Flexure
- Torsion
- Shear

White Space to Chunk Information

Once you have determined the chunks of information, you can signal these chunks by using white space and then you can label them with headings.

White space is the part of any page that is blank—no print or visuals. Not only does white space signal chunks of information, it also makes documents more appealing. Although no hard and fast rules exist concerning the use of white space, several conventions suggest that white space be used for margins, between lines within a paragraph (called leading), between paragraphs and sections of a document, and around visuals. The amount of white space is also affected by the justification and length of the lines of text. The impact of white space is illustrated by the two segments in Figure 8.2a and b—the first with crowded printing and skimpy margins; the second with wider margins and more space between lines.

Margins. The four margins, which usually have different widths, are also used to chunk information. The top (head) margin is the narrowest. The inner margins (gutters) are wider to ensure that no words are lost in the binding; the outer margin is wider still. Type that runs nearly to the edge of the paper not only is unattractive but also leads readers' eyes off the page. Sometimes, outside margins are even wider to provide space for note taking or a running gloss, marginal notes that emphasize particular points. The widest margin is usually at

FIGURE 8.2a ■ Skimpy White Space	FIGURE 8.2b ■ Appropriate White Space
This paragraph is more difficult to read because little attention is given to physical features of the presentation. Narrow leading and full justification create greater eye strain. The small margins give an impression of crowding. The proportion of text is too great for the amount of space.	This paragraph is easier to read because the physical features consider the reader. The material has sufficient space between the lines and is surrounded by margins. The white space and text are balanced.

FIGURE 8.3 ■ Changes in Margins

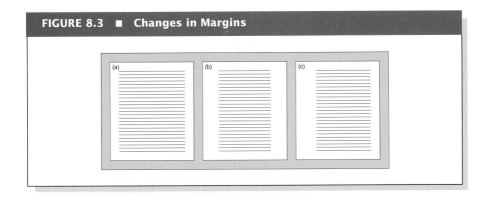

the bottom of the page. The thumbnail sketches in Figure 8.3 show the flexibility you have in adjusting margins: the typical 1-inch margins in version a; the wide equal margins in version b; the extra-wide left margin in version c.

Justification.   Another element that affects chunking is justification. If all the lines of type on a page are exactly the same length, the lines have been justified—adjusted to equal length by proportional spacing between words on each individual line. A justified right-hand margin gives a document a neat, clean appearance, as Figure 8.4a illustrates. If the lines all begin at the same left-hand margin, and the right margin is ragged, the right margin is unjustified, as Figure 8.4b shows.

Although some editors prefer that both left and right margins be justified—both because of tradition and because more words can be fit on a page—fully justified text is not as easy to read as text with a ragged right margin. Because all the lines in a fully justified text are the same length, it's easy for readers to lose their place. An additional benefit of ragged-right margins is that the text lines are less difficult to revise in typing or typesetting and less expensive to typeset.[4] In addition, a recent survey in the journal *Technical Communication* indicated that a clear majority of both managers and nonmanagers preferred documents with ragged-right margins.[5]

FIGURE 8.4 ■ Justification

Fully justified text has a formal, neat look, but reading many pages of justified text is difficult, especially if the print is small and the lines are long.

Most ragged-right text (justified only on the left) is easier to read than fully justified text.

Explain which you think is more important: a neat, clean appearance or an easy-to-read document.

Generally, readers find texts with shorter line lengths and ragged-right margins easier to read; however, these generalizations need to be applied with an awareness of the type of document you're producing. For example, a formal corporate annual report might have one column with justified left and right margins, whereas a monthly newsletter for the same company might use a two-column format with ragged-right margins.

Leading and Line Length. The spacing between lines of type (leading) is another way of chunking information that improves legibility and thus increases ease and speed of reading. Generally, text that is easiest to read has line spacing that is one-and-one-half times the letter height. (See Chapter 4 for discussion about reading online.)

Lines that are too short are annoying for readers; lines that are too long are difficult to read. But "short" and "long" are relative, related to font type and size rather than to absolute line length. In general, font size larger than 12 points has a "primer" look and reminds people of their elementary school reading. (Exceptions to this, of course, are materials for visually impaired readers.) And a font size smaller than 7 points is usually too tiny to read easily. However, changes in leading and adjustments in justification and line length can have a great impact on ease of reading, as the following two examples show:

8-point Geneva, 8-point leading, full justification, and long lines

. . . The whole world ocean extends over about three-fourths of the surface of the globe. If we subtract the shallow areas of the continental shelves and the scattered banks and shoals, where at least the pale ghost of sunlight moves over the underlying bottom, there still remains about half the earth that is covered by miles-deep, lightless water, that has been dark since the world began. (Rachel Carson, from "The Sunless Sea" in The Sea Around Us)

8-point Geneva, 12-point leading, ragged-right margin, and shorter lines

. . . The whole world ocean extends over about three-fourths of the surface of the globe. If we subtract the shallow areas of the continental shelves and the scattered banks and shoals, where at least the pale ghost of sunlight moves over the underlying bottom, there still remains about half the earth that is covered by miles-deep, lightless water, that has been dark since the world began. (Rachel Carson, from "The Sunless Sea" in The Sea Around Us)

Headings to Label Chunked Information

Headings and subheadings can label chunked information and identify the relative importance of these chunks in a document. Headings not only establish the subject of a section, but they also give readers a chance to take both a literal and a mental breath while previewing the upcoming content. Some writers try to use a heading or subheading every three to five paragraphs to avoid visual

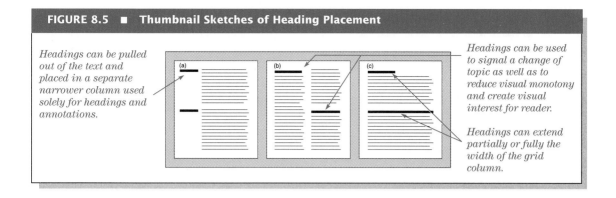

FIGURE 8.5 ■ Thumbnail Sketches of Heading Placement

Headings can be pulled out of the text and placed in a separate narrower column used solely for headings and annotations.

Headings can be used to signal a change of topic as well as to reduce visual monotony and create visual interest for reader.

Headings can extend partially or fully the width of the grid column.

monotony and keep the reader focused. Although you may find such breaking too frequent, the concept is important. As noted in Chapter 7, a well-designed outline can serve as the structure for the table of contents and also provide headings and subheadings that make a document easier to read.

The thumbnail sketches in Figure 8.5 show various ways you can incorporate headings into your documents. Relative importance is signaled by capitalization, type size, and typeface. When you test the draft of a document with readers, check that they are helped, not confused, by your titles, headings, and subheadings.

Arranging Related Chunks of Verbal and Visual Information

In arranging verbal and visual information, you can draw on design conventions as well as avoid design problems.

Using Design Conventions

Two practices used by professional designers will help you produce more effective documents:

- Selection of appropriate grids
- Placement of visuals near related text

The easiest and most efficient way to design a page (or an entire document) is to see the page as a *grid*—columns and rows that help you organize the verbal and visual chunks. In most situations, you will use one-column, two-column, or three-column grids, illustrated in thumbnail sketches in Figure 8.6. When you are using more detailed grids, you'll probably be working with a designer or graphic artist. When you are working independently, you'll be able to use your word processing or desktop publishing software to create a grid and then place the text and visuals within it.

Why should subject matter experts spend time learning about the design of documents?

FIGURE 8.6 ■ **Columns for Grids**

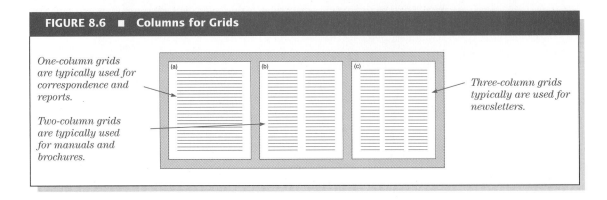

One-column grids are typically used for correspondence and reports.

Two-column grids are typically used for manuals and brochures.

Three-column grids typically are used for newsletters.

Different grids are appropriate for different purposes and audiences. Imagine, for example, that the one-column grid in Figure 8.6a could be for an in-house technical report about reconfiguring computer workstations. The two-column grid in part (b) could be for an operator's manual for office workers using desktop publishing. The three-column grid in part (c) could be for a corporate newsletter.

Readers appreciate not having to constantly turn back and forth between the page they're reading and visuals placed in an appendix. A recent survey of management and nonmanagement engineers and scientists concerning the format of NASA technical reports indicated that 80 percent preferred visuals integrated into the text rather than placed in an appendix. The only exceptions noted were if several consecutive pages of visuals interrupted the flow of the text and thus distracted the reader.[6] Figure 8.7 shows several acceptable possibilities for incorporating visuals into your text.

Avoiding Problems in Arranging Information

Before you design a document, you need to be aware of four potential problems:

- Chartjunk
- Tombstoning

FIGURE 8.7 ■ **Placement of Visuals**

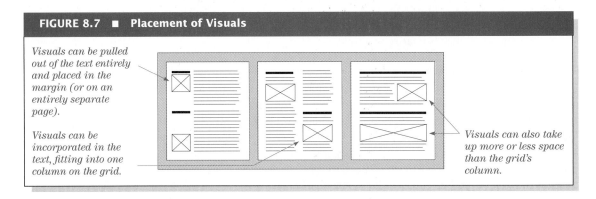

Visuals can be pulled out of the text entirely and placed in the margin (or on an entirely separate page).

Visuals can be incorporated in the text, fitting into one column on the grid.

Visuals can also take up more or less space than the grid's column.

- Heading placement
- Widows and orphans

One problem involves the temptation to clutter visuals with unnecessary *chartjunk*. This temptation is multiplied when you are using computer software that entices you to add fancy features to visuals. Figure 8.8 contrasts a graph with unnecessary and distracting chartjunk and one with less chartjunk and more white space. Whatever is included on visuals should contribute to the meaning and make the information more accessible and appealing.

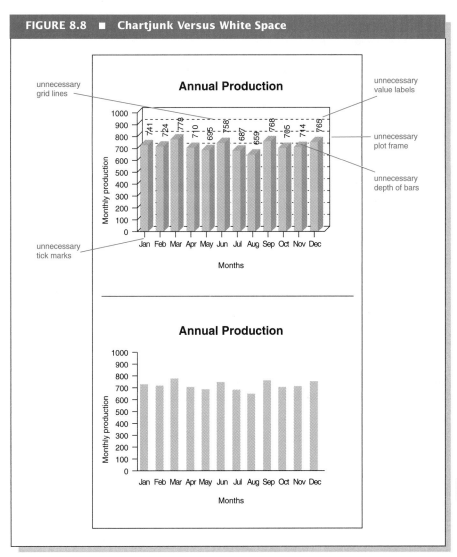

FIGURE 8.8 ■ Chartjunk Versus White Space

This version has too much chartjunk and too little white space, so the data are obscured.

This version, without the chartjunk, has more white space, so the changes in monthly production are easier to see.

What arguments can you think of for and against using chartjunk?

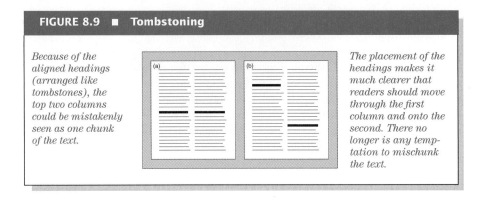

FIGURE 8.9 ■ Tombstoning

Because of the aligned headings (arranged like tombstones), the top two columns could be mistakenly seen as one chunk of the text.

The placement of the headings makes it much clearer that readers should move through the first column and onto the second. There no longer is any temptation to mischunk the text.

Another problem called *tombstoning* involves aligning headings so that readers mistakenly chunk the text when they look at the page. In Figure 8.9a, readers could easily believe that the top half of the page was one section and the bottom half was another. Figure 8.9b shows that you can rearrange the headings to avoid this potential "tombstoning" confusion.

A third problem comes from leaving too few lines after a heading or subheading at the top or bottom of a column or page. Figure 8.10a shows the problem of not leaving at least three lines in a column or on a page before beginning a new heading or having at least three lines following a new heading at the bottom of a column. Figure 8.10b shows the adjustment to include a few more lines.

A final problem deals with widows and orphans. *Widows* are leftover words—one or two words hanging on awkwardly as the last line of a paragraph. You can avoid them by revising the sentences in the paragraph to add or delete a few words so that one or two are not left on a line alone. *Orphans* occur when a column or page break occurs in a paragraph after the first line of the paragraph (see Figure 8.11). Try to arrange paragraph breaks after a few lines rather than at the very beginning or end.

Sometimes problems in arranging information are more serious than simply inconveniencing readers whose time may be wasted or understanding restricted because of careless or inadequate attention to design of information. The ethics

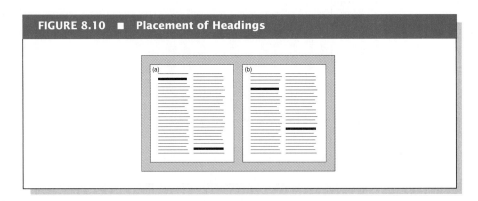

FIGURE 8.10 ■ Placement of Headings

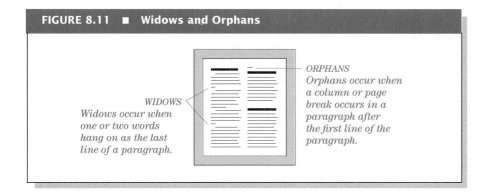

FIGURE 8.11 ■ Widows and Orphans

WIDOWS
Widows occur when one or two words hang on as the last line of a paragraph.

ORPHANS
Orphans occur when a column or page break occurs in a paragraph after the first line of the paragraph.

sidebar on the next page discusses the document design of a government document and the ways that type size, white space, and bolded type potentially biased readers.

Emphasizing Information

Once information is chunked, labeled, and arranged, you may still need to emphasize selected portions of the text to make the information more accessible, appropriate, and appealing.

On print pages, your decisions about chunking, labeling, and arranging are fixed for the readers. However, readers can alter the way they view Web pages by changing browser preferences. For example, readers can choose to "view pictures and text," "pictures only," or "text only" (because they turn graphics off to speed up the download time). They can choose for their browser to use fonts on their machine as a default and turn off the fonts specified in the document, disable dynamic fonts, and so on. Readers can also specify link and background colors.

Explain whether knowing a great deal about making documents appealing to readers increases the likelihood that carelessly done work—perhaps flawed in accuracy or inaccurately supported—could be presented in an effective "package" that might disguise its inadequacies.

Despite a designer's careful and considered choices, some readers may choose to override the designer's decisions. Most readers, though, use the design on the Web page; thus, typeface and typographic devices remain important for creating emphasis for both print and Web pages.

Typefaces

Typeface (also called type font) affects readers' attitudes and reactions to a document, as well as their ability to read the text easily and quickly. The desktop publishing revolution makes it imperative that you know some basic characteristics about typefaces:

- Serif or sans serif
- Typeface variations

"A Wound to the Hand": Ethics and Document Design

Can technical professionals provide verifiable facts in a technical document but still be at fault for presenting an unethical document? Yes, they can—if those facts are found in a document that is designed to deceive and mislead the audience. So found researcher TyAnna Herrington in her review of research on the relationship between ethics and document design.[7] Herrington's research indicates the way facts are presented in a document is as important as the facts themselves. Design elements like headings, titles, spacing, and font size guide readers in determining the inherent value of the information and the relative importance of that information when compared to other information inside (and outside) of the document. These design elements can, intentionally or unintentionally, lead readers to interpretations and conclusions that may not be supported by the facts or that hide more credible or relevant explanations.

Herrington believes an example of unethical document design can be found in a government report about the ATF siege at the Branch Davidian compound in Waco, Texas, in 1998. The Branch Davidians, a small religious group, and the U.S. Department of Alcohol, Tobacco, and Firearms (ATF) clashed in February of that year when the ATF attempted to confiscate weapons they believed the Branch Davidians had obtained illegally. The violent confrontation between the ATF agents and the Branch Davidians at the Davidian's housing compound led to multiple deaths on both sides.

Herrington reviewed the tables in the government report and found that type size, white space, and bolded type emphasized the ATF injuries and de-emphasized the Branch Davidian injuries, even though more Davidians than agents died during the attack. For example, the titles for the ATF tables are in bold and are a larger type size (14-point vs. 12-point) than the Branch Davidian titles, which are not in bold. She also found additional white space around the titles in the ATF tables that helped these tables stand out more in the overall document. These visual differences, Herrington believes, help accentuate the ATF casualties.

The descriptions in tables listing ATF and Davidian injuries also accentuate the ATF casualties. In the ATF table, the wording of the descriptions is more understandable to the untrained reader than the descriptions in the Davidian tables. For example, the ATF table lists a "gunshot wound to the hand" while the Davidian table lists a "craniocerebral trauma-gunshot wound." Herrington believes these differences are unethical because they may lead to unsupported and misleading interpretations of the events in Waco.

What are some techniques you could use to avoid using font sizes deceptively?

Emphasizing information is an important part of document design in technical communication, but technical professionals must be aware of the ethical line between emphasis and deception. Where is this line for you? How much does document design, in elements like type size or spacing, affect how a document is interpreted?

- Type size

- Style choices

You have the same choices when you're selecting typefaces for a print document or for a Web page, but the constraints are considerably different. For a Web page, follow these general guidelines:

- Select conventional fonts that you can be fairly sure users will have installed on their computer.

- Remember that in print the relationship between typographical elements is fixed on a page. However, on a Web site, users scroll and link in different (and sometimes unanticipated) ways so reaction to typographical elements is never to a fixed page.[8]

- Web sites can use technology to build in interaction—for example, overlays or pop-ups—to engage users.[9]

Serif or Sans Serif. Typefaces can be serif or sans serif. Serifs are the tiny fine lines, usually at the top or bottom of letters. These are examples of lowercase and uppercase versions of the letter r in serif and sans serif typefaces:

serif: r R (10-point Times Roman)   sans serif: r R (9-point Helvetica)

Sans serif typefaces have a neat, appealing appearance and are often used for short documents. Because sans serif typefaces are simpler, the letters don't have as many distinguishing features, making them slightly more difficult for some people to read. Thus, long documents often use a serif typeface so that readers won't tire so quickly.

Typeface Variations. Your selection of typeface should be influenced both by the kind of document and your sense of how the readers will react. Readers are discouraged if typefaces are inappropriate for the document or situation or are difficult to read.

This typeface is called Zapf Chancery and is usually used only for social announcements.

This typeface is called Helvetica and is often used for standard business letters.

This typeface is called ITC Century Book and is usually used for typesetting lengthy reports and books, including this one, because it is easy to read.

Figure 8.12 illustrates ways in which typographical conventions—including typeface—are used in a Dell user's manual as visual cues to help readers. Each typeface has a specific meaning. For example, all items on the manual's menu screens are presented in Helvetica; all commands lines are presented in Courier. Associating meaning with various fonts and other typographic cues helps readers because they have the verbal content as well as the visual cues to help them construct meaning.

Type Size. You can also affect readers by the size of the type. You can discourage, insult, or alienate readers by using an inappropriate type size. For example, although tiny type reduces the number of pages in a user manual, it also makes the manual difficult for readers to use. Unnecessarily large type can make a document seem elementary because many people associate large type with children's books. You generally use 10- or 12-point type for the text of business documents. Headings may use larger type. The type used for

FIGURE 8.12 ■ Typographical Conventions Used in a Dell User's Manual[10]

The following list defines (where appropriate) and illustrates typographical conventions used as visual cues for specific elements of text throughout this document:

- *Keycaps,* the labeling that appears on the keys on a keyboard, are presented in uppercase and enclosed in angle brackets.

  Example: <ENTER>

- *Key combinations* are series of keys to be pressed simultaneously (unless otherwise indicated) to perform a single function.

  Example: <CTRL><ALT><ENTER>

- All items on a menu screen are presented in the **HELVETICA** font and in uppercase bold.

  Example: **SETUP PASSWORD** category

- *Commands* presented in lowercase bold are for reference purposes only and are not intended to be typed at that particular point in the discussion.

  Example: "Use the **format** command to . . ." In contrast, commands presented in the `Courier` font are intended to be typed as part of an instruction.

  Example: "Type `format a:` to format the diskette in drive A."

- *Filenames* and *directory names* are presented in lowercase bold.

  Example: **autoexec.bat** and **c:\windows**

- *Syntax lines* consist of a command and all its possible parameters. Commands are displayed in lowercase bold; variable parameters (those for which you substitute a value) are displayed in lowercase italics; constant parameters are displayed in lowercase bold. The brackets indicate items that are optional.

  Example: **chkdsk** [*drive:*] [[*path*] *filename*] [**/f**] [**/v**]

- *Command lines* consist of a command and may include one or more of the command's possible parameters. Command lines are presented in the `Courier` font.

  Example: `chkdsk a:/f`

- *Screen text* is text that appears on the screen of your monitor or display. It can be a system message, for example, or it can be text that you are instructed to type as part of a command (referred to as a *command line*). Screen text is presented in the `Courier` font.

  Example: "Type `md c:\dos`, and then press <ENTER>."

  Example: The following message appears on your screen:

  `No boot device available`

- *Variables* are symbols for which you substitute a value. They are presented in italics.

  Example: SIMM*n* (where *n* represents the SIMM number)

PowerPoint presentations or transparencies (vu-graphs) should be larger (18-point, 24-point, or 36-point type works well for making visuals to accompany oral presentations) so that the information can easily be read from the back of the room.

Variation in type size can also be used to capture your readers' attention. This warning, printed in 18-point Berkeley Old Style, is intended to grab readers.

WARNING! Ingestion of this chemical could be fatal!

However, the warning would not be nearly as effective if it were printed in 8-point type. Reducing the type size reduces the impact.

WARNING! Ingestion of this chemical could be fatal!

Typeface itself influences the size; all 10-point type does not look like it's the same size. Small type enables you to fit more into a space; however, if the type size is too small, the material looks crowded and may be difficult to read. Slightly larger type can make material more accessible and appealing; however, type that is too large may create an elementary rather than a professional image. Combinations of type size and typeface provide visual appeal and variety. For example, the body of this book is set in 9.5-point Century Book with 13-point Lucida Sans Bold main headings; 9.5-point Officina Sans Book is used for the examples.

If particular material must fit into a prescribed and limited amount of space, you can use type size to make minor adjustments. For example, information for a résumé could fit attractively on a single 8-1/2-by-11-inch sheet using a 10-point font, whereas the information might take up one and a quarter sheets using a 12-point font.

Flexibility in type size depends on the equipment being used. Some printers may restrict your choices of typeface and type size. However, most inkjet and laser printers offer tremendous flexibility. Many inkjet printers offer the option of color cartridges so that you can print in color for a relatively low cost. Many word-processing packages let you select from 9-point to 72-point type in a great variety of typefaces (fonts).

And what about fonts for Web sites? Fonts—even the same fonts—are displayed differently on Macintosh and Windows operating systems. In general, fonts on Windows Web browsers look two to three points larger than the equivalent fonts on Macintosh browsers. The difference in the way fonts are displayed can have a major impact on your page design.[11]

What federal mandates exist for making information accessible to visually impaired readers? What AARP guidelines exist to help design documents for elderly readers?

Style Choices.   The style of the type you select can also influence readers. Depending on the equipment you're using, you have the capability of using CAPITALIZATION, SMALL CAPS, **boldface,** and *italics,* as well as fancier variations such as shadow or outline.

Using ALL CAPS for occasional emphasis can be effective; however, your use of ALL CAPS should be limited to headings and single words or short phrases in the text. WHEN YOU USE ALL CAPS FOR ENTIRE SECTIONS OF TEXT, THE READER IS NOT ABLE TO RAPIDLY DIFFERENTIATE THE WORDS BECAUSE ALL THE LETTERS ARE THE SAME HEIGHT. THUS, READING IS SLOWED. YOUR INTENT TO EMPHASIZE A POINT IS LOST IN THE VISUAL MONOTONY OF CONSISTENT CAPITALIZATION.

Visual emphasis can be created by using **boldface** or **BOLD SMALL CAPS** or **BOLD ALL CAP.** These techniques are usually reserved for signaling warnings, cautions, and dangers and for calling attention to important points and terms. Use all these type variations with restraint. Try to work within a general guideline of using no more than four variations of typeface, type size, or style on a single page.

Typographic Devices

Sometimes you need to emphasize information by separating it or visually distinguishing it from the text. Effective devices include numbered lists, bulleted lists, underlining, boxes, shading or tints, and colors. As with any devices, their impact diminishes with overuse. Too many visual devices make a page look so cluttered that the reader cannot concentrate on content.

Numbered lists are particularly common elements in sets of instructions, but they also appear frequently in reports and proposals. Numbered lists suggest one of three things to the reader:

- Sequence or chronology of items is important.

- Priority of items is important.

- Total count of items is important.

When all items in the list are equivalent, a bulleted list is preferable, as illustrated in the preceding lines. The bullets draw attention to each item in the list but infer no priority to the sequence. You can make bullets with most word processing software by using one of the option keys or menu items.

<u>Underlined words or phrases</u> are converted to italics when the material is typeset. A useful summary of these conventions appears in the Usage Handbook at the end of this text. Beyond these conventions, *italics* are sometimes used as a typographic variation to identify a subsection.

Boxed and shaded information is emphasized. Information that is boxed should be surrounded by white space so that the text does not run into the box. Sometimes the boxed material relates directly to the text; other times it is supplemental. Too much shading diminishes its impact. Note particularly the use of shading for boxed figures in this text.

Boxes are often effective in the following situations:	Shading highlights and emphasizes material. Sometimes shaded areas are used in conjunction with boxes. Readers are drawn to shaded material because it is differentiated from the rest of the text.
- Identify major headings - Highlight key terms - Emphasize formulas or equations - Separate anecdotal material	

Color is an especially appealing visual device, often contributing significantly to the effectiveness and clarity of a document. Some technical materials require color. For example, as you'll see in Chapter 9, anatomical diagrams need shading and color. Color-coded electronic components should be accompanied by color-

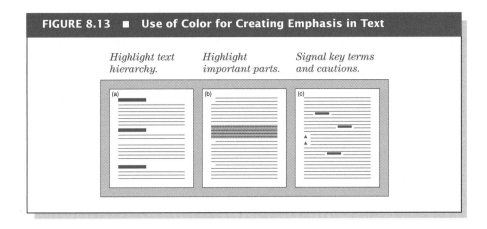

FIGURE 8.13 ■ Use of Color for Creating Emphasis in Text

Highlight text hierarchy.　　Highlight important parts.　　Signal key terms and cautions.

coded troubleshooting diagrams. In documents with difficult material, color can create visual interest, highlight section headings, identify examples, and emphasize important points. In this text, color is used to highlight important textual elements as well as to help distinguish parts of visuals.

Color has a number of specific benefits, as illustrated in the thumbnail sketches in Figure 8.13.[12]

- *Identify text hierarchy.* Color can help readers locate the main sections in a text. For example, Figure 8.13a shows how color can be used to highlight headings, but color can also be used for section dividers.

- *Chunk information.* Color can effectively chunk related information for readers. For example, Figure 8.13b shows how color can be used to highlight an important part of a paragraph.

- *Emphasize key points.* Figure 8.13c shows how color can be used to highlight terms, which helps readers recall and remember that information. Similarly, color can be used to emphasize critical parts of the text—for example, to signal cautions and warnings.

Despite its value, the use of color is often restricted by cost. A separate printing run is needed for each color added to a page. Often, a well-designed document employing a variety of visual devices other than color will be as effective.

Designing for the Web

Being able to design effective Web pages is as important as being able to design effective print pages. You can get a good start on a Web page by using a consistent grid and choosing not to dump (that is, simply scan) print documents onto a Web site.

Why Using Grids Works

When you're designing a Web page, use a grid—just as you do for a print page. Figure 8.14 shows a typical diagram for a Web grid, 535 pixels wide, a width preferred by designers who are trying to be sensitive to all the modes in which a Web page may be viewed or used. For example, this size, while not typically used for intranet pages or Internet pages, is safe for WebTV. The left-hand column in a grid (like the one in Figure 8.5a) can list the topics—much like the table of contents in a print document—but each topic is actually a link to that section of the Web page.

Why Dumping Text on the Web Doesn't Work

The more popular and widespread the Web becomes, the more companies talk about putting their internal and external documents on their internal intranet

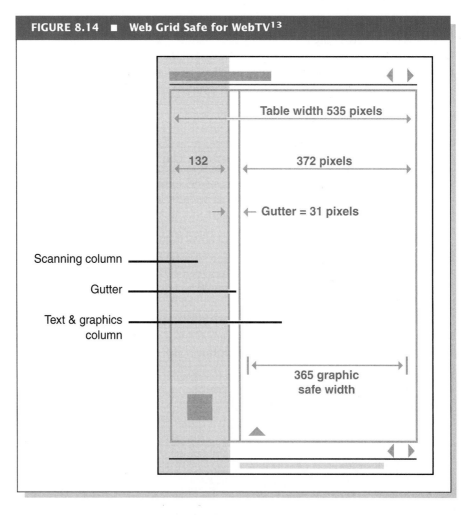

FIGURE 8.14 ■ Web Grid Safe for WebTV[13]

Table width 535 pixels

132

372 pixels

Gutter = 31 pixels

Scanning column

Gutter

Text & graphics column

365 graphic safe width

site or on their external Web site. However, simply taking paper documents—even well-designed ones—and scanning them onto a Web site is not likely to be effective.

Because paper and online documents exist in different mediums, they have different features that readers respond to and use. Paper documents are linear, static, physical forms of communication (for example, brochures, news releases, instruction manuals, textbooks) that come with their own established text features, so that readers already have expectations when they pick up a paper document.

In contrast, online documents are nonlinear, changing, virtual forms of communication that must create their context visually. Because readers can arrive at any Web page from anywhere else on the Web, the context must be immediately obvious. Online documents have these elements:[14]

- **Site architecture** is the framework that structures content. The structure should meet the goals and expectations of the user. The site structure can be *sequential* (each page links to the next in a linear style), *hierarchical* (outline format), or *nonlinear* (unstructured, random links).

- **Navigational cues** should answer these questions: Where am I? Where have I been? Where can I go? Consistent navigational elements (for example, toolbars, buttons, and site map) let the users know where they are in relation to the rest of the site.

- **Usability** is increased by incorporating these elements:
  - *Easy-to-locate identifier* on each page so readers are less likely to lose their place
  - *Clear transitions* from one page to the next, which may include simple links, pop-up windows, zooming
  - *Short downloading time . . .* the longer it takes, the less happy users will be
  - *User testing on different browsers*
  - *Opportunity to disable graphics*

- **Design**—that is, the look and feel of a site—is another mechanism to help users understand location and context.

End-of-Chapter
Recommendations for Technical Communicators

1. Use grids—columns and rows that help you organize the space on a page so that you can balance text, visuals, and white space.

2. Choose ragged-right margins as your default. Use full justification only when you have a specific reason.

3. Improve legibility and increase ease and speed of reading by using leading one-and-one-half the letter height.

4. Use headings and subheadings to identify the relative importance of these sections in your document.

5. Consider what readers will learn from the placement of visuals on a page. When possible, integrate visuals into the text rather than placing them in an appendix.

6. Anticipate problems:
    - Avoid chartjunk.
    - Avoid tombstoning.
    - Leave at least three lines in a column before beginning a new heading and at least three lines following a new heading at the bottom of a column.
    - Avoid widows and orphans.

7. Use typographic devices—numbered lists, bulleted lists, boxes, shading or tints, and colors—to emphasize key points.

8. Consider the impact of serif and sans serif typefaces.

9. Generally use 10- or 12-point type for workplace documents. Use 12- or 14-point type for headings. Use 18- or 24-point type for transparencies.

10. Cautiously use type styles—CAPITALIZATION, SMALL CAPS, **boldface,** *italics*—to influence readers and signal emphasis.

11. Make Web sites effective by designing a consistent grid and avoiding simply dumping material on the site.

Individual and Collaborative Assignments

1. **Choose the appropriate format for a document.** Four common presentation formats are explained in this chapter:

   - verbal presentation alone in paragraph format
   - verbal presentation with visuals
   - visual presentation with verbal explanations
   - visual presentation alone

   Choose one of these formats for each of the following situations and explain your choices:

   - Instructions for first-aid emergency
   - Preparation of a car for repainting
   - Explanation of a solution for a manufacturing problem
   - Presentation of computer printer components
   - Application of fertilizer to golf course greens

2. **Evaluate effective page design in a technical document.** Work with a small group of classmates in your academic discipline or a related one.
   (a) Based on what you have learned in this chapter and your own observations of page design, create a rubric that you can use to evaluate several documents.
   (b) Look for examples of page design in technical documentation and evaluate several of them.
   (c) Choose a page that is a particularly good example of effective page design and discuss the elements that make the page design effective and appealing.
   (d) Choose a page that is difficult to read because of poor design or poor visuals and redesign the layout of that page.

3. **Assess the differences between print and online journals.** Work with a group of classmates who share your major or a related field of study.
   (a) Search on the Web for online academic journals in your field.
   (b) Locate the corresponding print journal in your library.
   (c) Evaluate the differences between the two versions of the journal. Write your findings in a memo to your instructor.

4. **Transfer a print document to the Web.** As you have learned in this chapter, online publication of existing print documents involves different design and organizational considerations. Use an existing print document that you have already completed for this class or another class. Change the format, design, and organization of your document and put it on the Web.

Write a memo to your instructor in which you detail the changes that you made in your print document in order to make it Web accessible.

5. **Evaluate the effectiveness of the design of a technical Web site.** Locate several Web sites that deal with technical information in your field of study. Compare the effectiveness of the design of these Web sites.

(a) Use (and modify) the rubric you created in Assignment 2 or use (and modify) the following rubric. Consider the following questions:

- Which presentation formats are most popular in Web-based documents?

- Why do you think this is so?

- What suggestions do you have for technical communicators designing Web-based documents?

(b) Present your findings and your final rubric in a memo to your classmates.

Web Site Features[15]	1 Excellent	2 Acceptable	3 Weak	4 Unacceptable
Content				
1. Current				
2. Accurate and error-free				
3. Verifiable				
4. Reliable				
5. Research-based				
6. Sources listed				
7. Contact information provided (other than e-mail)				
Context				
1. Sponsorship and affiliation are evident				
Purpose (.org, .gov, .edu, .com, .net)				
1. Inform				
2. Persuade				
3. Sponsorship and affiliations visible				
Audience				
1. Reader benefits obvious				
2. Matches level of interest and education				
Organization				
1. Clear navigation				
2. Information no more than three clicks from entry page				
3. Bulleted or numbered lists				
4. Relevant links				
Visuals				
1. Relevant				
2. Concise				
3. Consistent				
4. Aid navigation				
Design				
1. Maximum download time—ten seconds				
2. Arrangement of headings aid navigation				
3. Effective use of white space				
4. Consistent background				
5. Appropriate for rhetorical situation				

Intertext

Collaboration Revolutionizes Design Process[16]

COLLABORATIVE DESIGN and manufacturing tools, formerly the sole domain of industrial giants such as Ford and Boeing, will soon be available to smaller companies thanks to a new generation of emerging Web-based design tools and services.

Collaborative design software is revolutionizing product design, reducing time-to-market costs, and reshaping the kinds of products that are ultimately created.

Boeing, Ford, Kodak, MacNeal-Schwendler, and Structural Dynamics Research, for example, formed the Technology for Enterprisewide Engineering consortium three years ago to understand ways to design, test, and market products using the Internet as the enabling tool for real-time collaboration with suppliers and partners.

"The consortium looks at everything from 'What is work?,' 'Who is an employee?,' and 'Why do we need a building?'" said Robert Carmen, program manager for enterprise technologies at Boeing, in Seattle.

Now application service providers (ASPs) are taking hold of that concept and extending it to the Fortune 1000 and beyond. Start-up Alibre will launch its distributed design service in which companies will share mechanical-design software over the Internet.

The company, founded by former Micrografx CEO Paul Grayson, will offer a subscription-based service, eliminating the need for large capital outlay and giving smaller companies access to big-league design packages.

Also, AristaSoft will kick off an ASP service for small and midsize high-tech companies that will include tools to support cross-company product development efforts by the end of the year. For many companies, the emergence of these types of tools and services can change the way they do business.

"A lot of the small guys would like to sell parts to one of the Big Three automakers, but they can't afford to keep up the Web-based approach," said Don Rathbun, staff engineer at AlliedSignal, in Kansas City, MO. "But if they could use a service, they could sell parts to Ford."

New ways of looking at business processes recently allowed Boeing to identify a world-class engineer at Texas Instruments who had 20 years of experience using Parametric Technology's ProEngineer CAD software. Using collaborative tools, the engineer remained at his desk while giving Boeing 10 percent of his work time for the company's project. "We went from 1,600 to six parts for the design. We would never have come up with this design without him," Carmen said.

As a result of such initiatives, the prospect of a Ford car and a Volvo station wagon sharing parts is now a distinct possibility. "Ford just acquired Volvo. To reduce overall cost of development, Ford would like to stage a Volvo and Ford on the same platform, possibly use the same [body]. They are trying to understand where they can save money, rather than having two [design] teams," said Ken Versprille, program manager of the design, creation, and validation program at D. H. Brown Associates, in Port Chester, N.Y.

Web collaboration starts before the design team assembles, according to Roger Moorehead, program manager at Lockheed Martin Fire and Missile Control, in Bethesda, MD. Lockheed Martin uses NexPrise ipTeam Web-collaboration software in the procurement process.

"We normally issue an RFP [request for proposal] with terms and conditions, design drawings, and performance specs, which amounts to 500 to 600 pages of data. With online, there are no duplications, and the subcontractor doesn't have to redistribute. He merely grants them access through ipTeam, Moorehead said.

But sharing information among a group of partner companies—some of which may be collaborators in one field and competitors in another—requires a secure "neutral zone" somewhere outside corporations' own networks.

In step with advances in collaboration software, growing network capacity and improved security technology are allowing enterprises to shake hands while keeping data confidential.

Because it links up with its partners over a private WAN, Boeing set up a pair of firewalls at the edge of its network and placed its Nexprise server between them. The outer firewall admits only authorized users who need to collaborate with Boeing. At the same time, the inner firewall keeps those collaborators away from Boeing's own departments.

Companies such as Boeing and Lockheed Martin typically license the collaborative software and give it to their suppliers. But many smaller companies can't afford to buy the software and set up their own networks. Service providers are joining in with companies such as Alibre and AristaSoft to make collaboration tools more widely available and affordable.

Qwest, MCI WorldCom's UUNet division, and other network providers are setting up hosting facilities that can include a secure site for collaboration. AristaSoft will base its services at data centers run by Covad and Digital Island, and Alibre is running a pilot program using data centers run by Qwest.

"A lot of the smaller innovators you may want to collaborate with on a proprietary EDI [electronic data interchange] network may not be able to afford the infrastructure required," said Kneko Burney, an analyst at InStat, in Scottsdale, Ariz. "These outside services are making collaboration affordable for a new generation of smaller, growing companies."

9

Using Visual Forms

Visuals not only attract attention and create appeal, but they also have benefits in specificity, cognitive processing, and learning.

- Can be more specific than text
- Can be processed more easily than text
- Can be processed more quickly than text
- Help readers learn

Incorporating Visuals

Visual/Verbal Combinations. You should consider the value of effective, well-designed visuals in these situations:

- When readers' understanding of the technical content is limited
- When speed is important and reading text would slow the process
- When the process is more clearly illustrated visually

Adapting Visuals to Audiences. Visuals can be adapted to different audiences—in complexity of content, presentation, color, and size.

Conventions in Referencing and Placing Visuals. You need to consider textual reference, labeling, and placement.

Conventions in Using Color

You need to learn cautions against the misuse of color, suggestions about the appropriate use of color, and factors in using color for online documents.

Visual Functions

Organize Numeric or Verbal Data. Generally, tables display data identifying the characteristics of ideas, objects, or processes.

Show Relationships. Graphs—including line graphs, scatter graphs, pie graphs, bar graphs, and pictorial graphs—display relationships between two or more sets of data.

Present Chronology, Sequence, or Process. Charts can represent the components, steps, or chronology of an object, mechanism, organism, or organization. The most common charts include block components charts, organizational charts, and flowcharts.

Illustrate Appearance, Structure, or Function. Diagrams illustrate the complex physical components and structures of objects, mechanisms, or organisms. Drawings and photographs depict the actual appearance of an object, mechanism, or organism.

Identify Facilities or Locations. You use maps and photographs to display geographic information and topographic, demographic, agricultural, meteorological, and geological data. You also use Web site maps.

Technical visuals are not a recent addition to technical communication. Leonardo da Vinci is only one of many scientific investigators who have produced a wide variety of technical art. Leonardo da Vinci's work—reproduced on the cover and the section dividers of this text—exemplifies the accuracy and attention to detail found in effective technical visuals.

Like Leonardo da Vinci's fifteenth- to sixteenth-century visuals, those in contemporary technical documents should have a specific purpose and convey specific content. Why use visuals instead of text or in addition to text? Beyond attracting attention and adding appeal, visuals strengthen your documents in other ways.[1]

- *Visuals can be more specific than text.* The *word* "tugboat," for example, could represent anything from "Tony Tug" in a children's story to barge tugs, but a *visual* of a specific tugboat is easily identifiable.

- *Well-designed visuals can be processed more easily than text.* Visuals can be particularly effective when dealing with numeric data. Consider the following text and the corresponding information in a graph. While the text presents precise numbers, the graph makes grasping the overall trend in the figures far easier. Most readers are better able to process and remember trends presented in graphs and charts.

In what situations might visuals be distracting or minimally helpful to a reader?

⬥ TEXT EXAMPLE

Staff growth. In the past four years, our staff size has changed. For full-time staff, numbers have changed from 24 in 1997 to 26 in 1998 to 29 in 1999 to 30 in 2000. For temporary staff, numbers have changed from 5 in 1997 to 6 in 1998 to 8 in 1999 to 7 in 2000.

⬥ GRAPH EXAMPLE

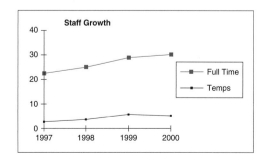

- *Visuals can be processed more quickly than text.* Visuals can be processed at a glance, in as little as one-third of a second (although obviously more time is required to get the full meaning of a complex chart), while text must be consciously scanned.

- *Visuals help readers learn.* Readers who are given documents containing visuals consistently comprehend and retain information better than readers given only text. On average, readers who are given documents containing text and visuals learn 36 percent more than those given text-only documents.

Given these benefits, visuals can be extraordinarily important in increasing the accessibility and usability of your documents. However, you also need to understand the parameters in which you're operating. For example, how much can you alter and adjust a visual in order to make your point—say, for example, changing the color on a photo or shifting the scale on a graph? The ethics sidebar on the next page addresses some of the issues involved in deciding whether manipulation of a visual is ethical or unethical. (The Intertext at the end of the chapter addresses additional ethical considerations in using visuals.)

This chapter is separated into two main sections: The first discusses factors that influence your decisions about incorporating visuals into a document; the second identifies specific functions of visuals you can choose.

Incorporating Visuals

In what situations might visuals be more appropriate and useful than words for conveying technical information?

This section of the chapter focuses on making choices about verbal/visual integration, adjusting visuals for different audiences, knowing when to choose visuals instead of text, and using color appropriately in visuals.

Visual/Verbal Combinations

In technical communication, visuals work by themselves and in combination with text to create stories for readers. While visuals should make sense by themselves, they should also illustrate, explain, demonstrate, verify, or support the text. In deciding about appropriate visual/verbal combinations, you can choose from several choices, displayed in the thumb-nail sketches in Figure 9.1.

You need to select visual/verbal combinations that most effectively communicate to readers. In many situations, visuals are more efficient than words. For example, a troubleshooting manual could begin with a verbal table identifying the problems along with analyses and solutions. Such a table would be

"With No Sacrifice to Truth": Ethics and Visuals

Consider this scenario:

> You are working on a report that includes illustrations and photographs. Reviewing the photographs, you find certain important details are hard to see. To draw out these details more, you use visual design software to alter the intensity and hues to make the colors richer. The revised photos seem more appealing.
>
> After you turn in the report, however, your supervisor calls you, claiming you unethically manipulated the photos. You defend yourself, arguing that the changes were artistic and didn't fundamentally alter the truth of the photographs. But your supervisor's response makes you wonder: Did you create unethical photos?

Are changes in intensity or color hues unethical manipulation of visuals? The editors of *Time* magazine didn't think so, at least not in the summer of 1994. That summer, the nation was captivated by the O.J. Simpson murder trial. After Simpson's arrest in June, both *Time* and *Newsweek* used versions of Simpson's police mug shot on their covers. *Time's* version, however, drew public criticism because the photo had been altered. The image, referred to by *Time* as a photo-illustration, artificially darkened Simpson's face although it still looked like the official police mug shot.[2]

Critics argued that the altered photo was racist, making Simpson look more menacing, especially when compared to *Newsweek's* nearly identical but unaltered cover. *Time's* managing editor, James Gaines, replying to the criticism, argued that the changes "lifted a common police mug shot to the level of art, with no sacrifice to truth." While Gaines recognized that "altering news pictures is a risky practice," he stated that "every major news outfit routinely crops and retouches photos to eliminate minor, extraneous elements, so long as the essential meaning of the picture is left intact."

How could you alter a visual without deceiving the audience?

But was the "essential meaning" intact? Not according to researcher Donna Kienzler, who identifies the altered photo as unethical. Kienzler believes the image is unethical because readers did not immediately know that the image had been altered. Kienzler argues that the altered image should be seen as art, which "filters reality" (180), and not as truth. The acknowledgment that the photo had been altered was not placed on the cover; such an acknowledgment was, instead, placed on the contents page. According to Kienzler, placing the acknowledgment within the magazine violated the "readers informed consent to be persuaded by art, rather than themselves evaluating a photograph" (180).[3]

To avoid creating unethical visuals, Kienzler offers some questions we can ask ourselves as we work with documents:

- What are possible consequences of our visuals?
- How would we feel if we received the visual?
- What would the world be like if everyone used these visual techniques?

Do you agree with Kienzler that the altered Simpson photo was unethical? Is any alteration an unethical manipulation? Where do you draw the line?

far more useful than a series of paragraphs detailing potential problems. You should consider the value of effective, well-designed visuals in the following situations:

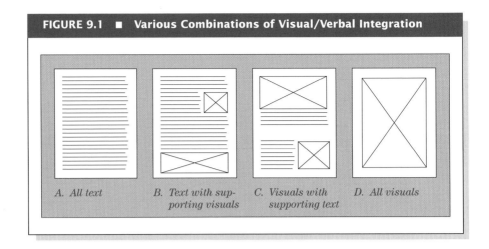

FIGURE 9.1 ■ **Various Combinations of Visual/Verbal Integration**

A. All text *B. Text with sup- porting visuals* *C. Visuals with supporting text* *D. All visuals*

- When readers' understanding of the technical content is limited

- When speed is critical, and reading text would slow the process

- When the process is more clearly illustrated visually

Some concepts or processes are so complex that one visual is insufficient. The series of visuals in Figure 9.2 all help to illustrate the uses of the Fabry-Perot Fiber-Optic Temperature Sensor published in *NASA Tech Briefs.* This photonic temperature sensor monitors and controls temperature in highly sensitive areas—aircraft engines, conventional power plants, industrial plants—where electronic temperature sensors pose a sparking hazard.

- Figure 9.2a shows a cutaway view of the sensor head that is clearly labeled with noun phrases, while arrows point to specific components. Cross-hatching distinguishes the nickel-alloy sheath from the Fabry-Perot interferometer that it holds.

- Figure 9.2b diagrams the entire sensor system; the blue arrow indicates the placement of the sensor head. A source of white light flows into one of the pair of optical fibers (represented by black lines) that flow into (and out of) the fiber-optic coupler, to the fiber-optic connector, and finally to the sensor itself. Shading, spot color, and labels distinguish one component from the other.

- Figure 9.2c depicts a reflected light spectrum that is characteristic of the temperature in the sensor head. The colored line of this line graph is easily discernible against the white background.

Taken together, this series of visual aids tells a complete story of a particular piece of hardware, the system it connects to, and the work that it does.

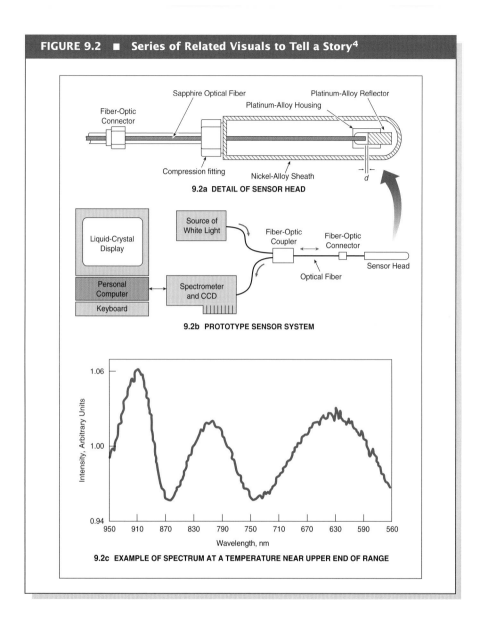

FIGURE 9.2 ■ Series of Related Visuals to Tell a Story[4]

9.2a DETAIL OF SENSOR HEAD

9.2b PROTOTYPE SENSOR SYSTEM

9.2c EXAMPLE OF SPECTRUM AT A TEMPERATURE NEAR UPPER END OF RANGE

Adapting Visuals to Audiences

Visuals can be adapted to different audiences—in complexity of content, presentation, and sometimes color and size. Readers who are not experts may need more frequent and simple visuals than experts. Nonexperts also may not understand visual conventions that experts readily recognize, so they may need additional explanations beyond the titles, legends, and captions that experts understand. For example, whereas an expert knows that the bars in a histogram represent ranges of data, nonexperts may need to have this explained.

What's the difference between "dumbing down" and adapting to the audience?

FIGURE 9.3 ■ Visual in Magazine for General Readers[5]

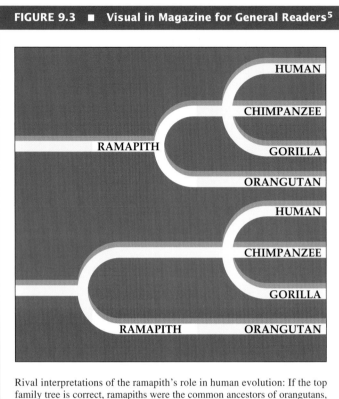

Rival interpretations of the ramapith's role in human evolution: If the top family tree is correct, ramapiths were the common ancestors of orangutans, African apes, and humans. An alternative interpretation, below, has ramapiths ancestral only to orangs. In this view, the common ancestor of humans and African apes remains unknown.

FIGURE 9.4 ■
Visual in Journal for
Professionals[6]

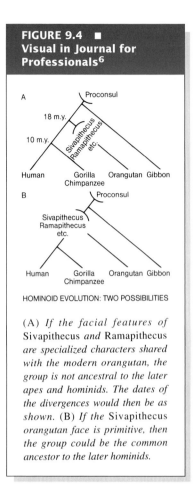

HOMINOID EVOLUTION: TWO POSSIBILITIES

(A) *If the facial features of* Sivapithecus *and* Ramapithecus *are specialized characters shared with the modern orangutan, the group is not ancestral to the later apes and hominids. The dates of the divergences would then be as shown.* (B) *If the* Sivapithecus *orangutan face is primitive, then the group could be the common ancestor to the later hominids.*

Figures 9.3 and 9.4 illustrate one way that the same information can be adapted to two very different audiences. Both figures were published by the American Association for the Advancement of Science; both are about the same discoveries and hypotheses in the study of human evolution. Figure 9.3 is from a monthly magazine for educated nonexperts interested in science. Figure 9.4 is from a weekly journal that updates professionals in science about new research.

Conventions in Referencing and Placing Visuals

Virtually all visuals have widely accepted conventions that accompany their use. Although you may sometimes choose to ignore a specific convention for good cause in a particular situation, generally you should follow these guidelines, which will help you to reference, label, and place visuals in ways that will be most useful to readers.

Textual Reference.   As a general practice, you should refer to visuals in the text, rather than simply including visuals and expecting readers to see them and connect them to the appropriate section of the text. Simply put, do not assume that readers will check a visual unless you refer to it. In your text reference, include adequate information, such as the figure number and title.

Textual references can be accomplished in several ways, as embedded references in sentences or as parenthetical references:

- "The incision should be made just above a joint with a bud, as illustrated in Figure 2: Grafting."

- "The effectiveness of the antitoxins tested is presented in Figure 4: Antitoxin Response."

- "Table 5 shows the rapid increase of gas prices during a five-year period."

- ". . . (see Table 3)."

You can also suggest the particular focus or interpretation you expect readers to apply when examining a visual. Without an explanation describing the significance of a visual, readers may not understand its purpose.

Describe how you would counter this statement: "The visual is right there on the page. I'll insult my readers if I not only tell them to look at the visual but also tell them what to pay attention to."

Labeling.   Complete and accurate labeling of visuals makes them much easier to use. Complete labeling includes identification, title, and caption.

- **EXAMPLE** ——— *identification* ——— *title*

Table 1: Worker Fatigue Using Wire Cutters
Worker fatigue was compared using three different models of
ergonomic cutters during a two-week period. ——— *caption*

The following conventions are generally followed to help readers locate, interpret, and verify visuals the way you intend:

- If a formal report has more than five visuals or includes visuals that readers would need to access independently from the text, include a list of figures or list of tables at the beginning of the document.

- Include the complete dimensions of objects in each visual, making sure to specify the units of measure or scale.

- Whenever possible, spell out words rather than using abbreviations. If abbreviations are included, use standard ones and include a key.

- Identify the source of the data as well as the graphic designer.

Placement.   Generally, place visuals as close as possible following the text reference. Surround visuals with white space to separate them from the text of the document.

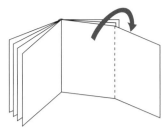

Fold-Out Page for Visual

If a visual requires an entire page in a document that's printed on both sides of the paper, you should try to locate the full-page visual on the page facing the text reference and discussion. If a visual requires an entire page in a document printed only on one side of the paper, you should try to locate the visual on the page following the text reference. Visuals that readers need to refer to repeatedly can be placed near the end of the document. For example, they can be located after the final text reference or in the first appendix on a fold-out page, as shown in this thumbnail sketch.

Conventions in Use of Color

With the wide availability of relatively inexpensive color printers and of color photocopiers, color in technical documents is commonplace. This section is concerned not with decorative color but with functional color—color that adds to the meaning of visuals or helps readers interpret them. (Chapter 8 discusses some of the ways that functional color adds value to text. Chapter 18 suggests ways that color can be used in your presentation visuals.) Color can be an extraordinarily powerful tool to help writers create more effective visuals, but it can also be misused. This section—and the examples that follow—first provides cautions against misuse and then offers specific suggestions about appropriate use of color.

Cautions Against Misuse of Color

Because color is so easy to use, the temptation to overindulge is great. These are some of the problems to avoid:

- *Overuse of decorative color.* Using color simply as decoration contradicts the basic premise that color in technical documents should be functional. Color should be associated with meaning or function so that when readers see a color used in a particular document, it triggers appropriate associations: For example, "The printout of the stress test shows the weak spots in red, the questionable spots in yellow, and the unstressed parts in shades of blue and green." Or, "The troubleshooting guide for each section is signaled with a red strip on the edge of the page so these pages are immediately identifiable."

- *Too much color.* Using too many colors, too much color, or inappropriate color distracts or annoys readers. Select a few colors rather than trying to pack in as many as possible. Similarly, the intensity of the color should match the context, purpose, or audience. For example, an industrial catalog for laboratory safety supplies can appropriately use seven colors in a table that matches them to OSHA and ANSI color-coded safety guidelines, but in most tables using that many colors would be unnecessary and, therefore, inappropriate.

- *Cultural insensitivity.* Violating cultural expectations can mean that the use of color contradicts the expectations in either the workplace culture or the broader social culture. For example, in industry day-glo orange is usually used in small triangles to signal warnings, so readers of an instruction manual for a precision lathe might feel disconcerted if all the manual's headings were in day-glo orange.

Suggestions for Appropriate Use of Color

Used effectively in visuals, color can help readers deal with factors such as consistency, emphasis, and organization.[7] Most documents are printed in one color—black—on white paper. Some documents have a second color added; in this book, the second color is green—specifically, Pantone or PMS 336. (Pantone is one of four major systems that graphic designers and printers use for naming colors.)

In most of the print documents you produce, cost and time will dictate that you use a single color (black) or use black and a second color selected to increase the appeal and accessibility of the document. Sometimes, however, the content, context, purpose, or audience require that you produce four-color documents, as this section of the text. So, the rest of the discussion in this section focuses on some of the important uses of four-color visuals.

Color is produced differently on paper and on a screen. The differences involve the colors themselves as well as the way they combine to create images.[8]

- Color on paper is produced by combining four inks (CMYK: cyan, magenta, yellow, and black). Each of the four colors is printed individually; that is, a page is passed through the printing press four separate times, one time for each color. A balanced combination of these four colors produces visuals like those in the color section.

- Color on a computer screen is produced by combining three colors (RGB: red, green, and blue). These three colors make up all colors on a computer monitor. All three colors at 100 percent of their value make white. The complete absence of all three makes black. Various percentages of each make up 16.7 million colors, although the Web-safe browser palette consists of 216 colors.

Whether you're creating print or Web visuals, you'll use a color palette, a group of colors used for graphics. You have no color limitations for print documents, but different computer platforms use different color palettes. Both Macs and PCs have 256 colors in their system palettes, but only 216 of them are the same. So you should use the Web-safe color palette (216 colors) common to both Windows and Mac computers, shown in Figure 9.5. It's also the safest for

FIGURE 9.5 ■ Color Chart[9]

000000	003300	006600	009900	00CC00	00FF00
000033	003333	006633	009933	00CC33	00FF33
000066	003366	006666	009966	00CC66	00FF66
000099	003399	006699	009999	00CC99	00FF99
0000CC	0033CC	0066CC	0099CC	00CCCC	00FFCC
0000FF	0033FF	0066FF	0099FF	00CCFF	00FFFF

330000	333300	336600	339900	33CC00	33FF00
330033	333333	336633	339933	33CC33	33FF33
330066	333366	336666	339966	33CC66	33FF66
330099	333399	336699	339999	33CC99	33FF99
3300CC	3333CC	3366CC	3399CC	33CCCC	33FFCC
3300FF	3333FF	3366FF	3399FF	33CCFF	33FFFF

660000	663300	666600	669900	66CC00	66FF00
660033	663333	666633	669933	66CC33	66FF33
660066	663366	666666	669966	66CC66	66FF66
660099	663399	666699	669999	66CC99	66FF99
6600CC	6633CC	6666CC	6699CC	66CCCC	66FFCC
6600FF	6633FF	6666FF	6699FF	66CCFF	66FFFF

990000	993300	996600	999900	99CC00	99FF00
990033	993333	996633	999933	99CC33	99FF33
990066	993366	996666	999966	99CC66	99FF66
990099	993399	996699	999999	99CC99	99FF99
9900CC	9933CC	9966CC	9999CC	99CCCC	99FFCC
9900FF	9933FF	9966FF	9999FF	99CCFF	99FFFF

CC0000	CC3300	CC6600	CC9900	CCCC00	CCFF00
CC0033	CC3333	CC6633	CC9933	CCCC33	CCFF33
CC0066	CC3366	CC6666	CC9966	CCCC66	CCFF66
CC0099	CC3399	CC6699	CC9999	CCCC99	CCFF99
CC00CC	CC33CC	CC66CC	CC99CC	CCCCCC	CCFFCC
CC00FF	CC33FF	CC66FF	CC99FF	CCCCFF	CCFFFF

FF0000	FF3300	FF6600	FF9900	FFCC00	FFFF00
FF0033	FF3333	FF6633	FF9933	FFCC33	FFFF33
FF0066	FF3366	FF6666	FF9966	FFCC66	FFFF66
FF0099	FF3399	FF6699	FF9999	FFCC99	FFFF99
FF00CC	FF33CC	FF66CC	FF99CC	FFCCCC	FFFFCC
FF00FF	FF33FF	FF66FF	FF99FF	FFCCFF	FFFFFF

cross-browser compatability because it produces the most consistent colors on different platforms with different browsers.

Even though the discussion of the following examples emphasizes a particular use of color for each visual, in practice, most well-designed color visuals use color to accomplish multiple purposes. Whenever color is used in technical documents, it should be an integral part of the information that readers need. These are among the most important purposes:

- Attract attention

- Enable accurate identification

- Show structure or organization

- Highlight components and their process or movement

- Aid comprehension

- Influence interpretation

Attract Attention.   Color can attract readers so that they are drawn toward the topic. Figures 9.6a and 9.6b show a German brown trout in two versions. The technical illustrator, Dean Biechler, created the color version (Figure 9.6a) for the folder cover for a series of fact sheets produced by the Coldwater Stream Program of the Iowa Natural Heritage Foundation. The strong color drawing on the cover attracts attention. The fact sheets focus on conservation and resource management. Biechler created the black-and-white version (Figure 9.6b) for one of the fact sheets. (This black-and-white version was also used on the Coldwater Stream Program t-shirt.)

The color not only attracts attention but also assures accurate identification and provides contextual details important to those who provided financial and editorial support for the program—the REAP (Resource Enhancement

In what situations might black-and-white drawings or photos be more appropriate and more useful than color?

FIGURE 9.6a ■ Color Drawing of Fish[10]

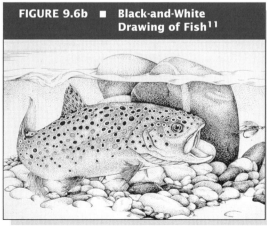

FIGURE 9.6b ■ Black-and-White Drawing of Fish[11]

and Protection) Conservation Education Program, the USDA Soil Conservation Service, and the Iowa Department of Natural Resources.

Enable Accurate Identification.   A second purpose for using color is to help readers focus on critical features of the object. Figure 9.7 represents the human lymphoid system. Color is useful in this drawing in several important

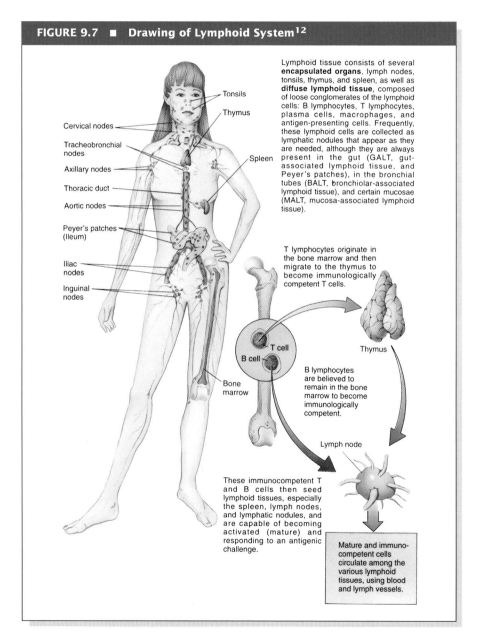

FIGURE 9.7 ■ Drawing of Lymphoid System[12]

Tonsils

Thymus

Cervical nodes

Tracheobronchial nodes

Spleen

Axillary nodes

Thoracic duct

Aortic nodes

Peyer's patches (Ileum)

Iliac nodes

Inguinal nodes

Lymphoid tissue consists of several **encapsulated organs**, lymph nodes, tonsils, thymus, and spleen, as well as **diffuse lymphoid tissue**, composed of loose conglomerates of the lymphoid cells: B lymphocytes, T lymphocytes, plasma cells, macrophages, and antigen-presenting cells. Frequently, these lymphoid cells are collected as lymphatic nodules that appear as they are needed, although they are always present in the gut (GALT, gut-associated lymphoid tissue, and Peyer's patches), in the bronchial tubes (BALT, bronchiolar-associated lymphoid tissue, and certain mucosae (MALT, mucosa-associated lymphoid tissue).

T lymphocytes originate in the bone marrow and then migrate to the thymus to become immunologically competent T cells.

T cell

B cell

Bone marrow

Thymus

B lymphocytes are believed to remain in the bone marrow to become immunologically competent.

Lymph node

These immunocompetent T and B cells then seed lymphoid tissues, especially the spleen, lymph nodes, and lymphatic nodules, and are capable of becoming activated (mature) and responding to an antigenic challenge.

Mature and immuno-competent cells circulate among the various lymphoid tissues, using blood and lymph vessels.

ways. First, color helps readers to identify key features of the lymphoid system by highlighting two kinds of lymphoid tissues. By drawing the diffuse lymphoid system in green (obviously not the true color of the lymphoid system), the artist immediately draws readers' attention to this key feature. The artist did not select blue or red to represent the lymphoid system because these are colors conventionally used to represent arteries (red) and veins (blue). Despite the fact that the encapsulated organs are also in color, they are de-emphasized when compared to the green diffuse lymphoid system. Second, the artist uses other colors, as well as colored arrows, to represent the development and maturation of the T lymphocytes and the B lymphocytes in the detail drawing in the lower right-hand corner. Finally, the artist uses the green to highlight the relationship between the primary illustration and the detail drawing. Because green is used to represent the lymph node in the detail drawing, readers are likely to recognize that this information is directly related to the green lymph nodes in the primary drawing.

Show Structure or Organization.   A third purpose for color is that it enables readers to better understand the structure displayed in the visual. It can also organize those parts, chunking them so that readers can more easily see critical relationships. Information of a similar type is presented in the same color so that readers immediately see the likenesses and, thus, more easily understand and recall information.

Figure 9.8 shows a computer-generated stress analysis of a tooth from the front of a tractor bucket. Test engineers at John Deere first drew the tooth, then used a computer modeling system to apply loads at the positions and from the directions the tooth would be stressed in actual situations. The system then calculated the stresses that would occur on the tooth. Changes in color show regions of stress: dark blue shows the lowest levels of stress, then light blue,

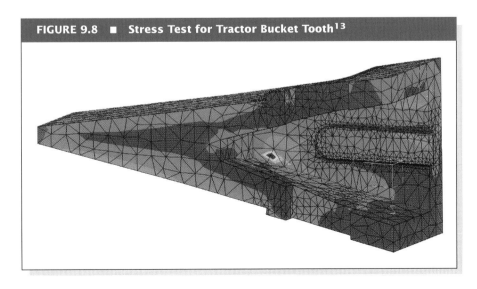

FIGURE 9.8 ■ Stress Test for Tractor Bucket Tooth[13]

green, and orange show successively higher levels of stress. Red shows the highest level.

Highlight Components and Their Function or Movement.   A fourth purpose of color shows readers a path for moving through a visual. Color itself can signal a change. Or, color can draw attention to the nature and direction of the change. Consistency in the use of color helps readers track the changes an object or organism goes through during a process.

Figure 9.9 shows a computer model created by AmTec Engineering in Bellevue, Washington, using software called TecPlot. The figure is a 3D depiction of flow over an airfoil (airplane wing), which is useful for aeronautical engineers who want to increase the stability and efficiency of airfoils they are designing or analyzing. The model shows an airfoil, the air flow around the airfoil, and a computational grid (only the last plane of this green grid shows) for analyzing the flow. The model enables aeronautical engineers to collect and analyze huge sets of data as they create visualizations that depict, for example, air pressure, velocity, and vorticity. The colored ribbons display more than the path of the air; they show how the flow twists in finite-width bands that rotate according to the vorticity—that is, how the flow twists. In the figure, you can see a flow separation, evident by the ways the ribbons flow up and over the top.

Aid Comprehension.   A fifth purpose for color is to make an image easier to understand. For example, the photographs taken by cameras on the Hubble Space Telescope have often been translated into color images to aid comprehension.[15]

- Some Hubble data are originally translated into black-and-white photos. Scientists arbitrarily choose "false colors" to replace shades of gray because people can more easily see the details depicted in color.

- Some data are originally captured in color; then scientists enhance or intensify selected colors to emphasize particular features.

- Some data are captured in true color by taking photographs through separate red, green, and blue filters and then combining the images into a realistic photograph.

The eerie, dark, pillar-like structures in Figure 9.10 are actually columns of cool interstellar hydrogen gas and dust that are also incubators for new stars. The pillars protrude from the interior wall of a dark molecular cloud like stalagmites from the floor of a cavern. They are part of the "Eagle Nebula" (also called M16—the sixteenth object in Charles Messier's eighteenth-century catalog of "fuzzy" objects that aren't comets), a nearby star-forming region 7,000 light years away in the constellation Serpens.

The picture was taken with the Hubble Space Telescope. The color image is constructed from three separate images taken in the light of emission from different types of atoms. Red shows emission from singly ionized sulfur atoms.

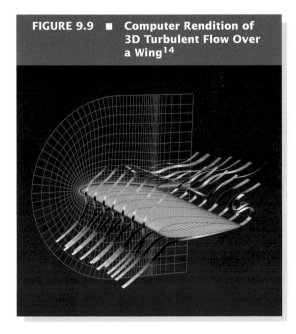

FIGURE 9.9 ■ Computer Rendition of 3D Turbulent Flow Over a Wing[14]

FIGURE 9.10 ■ Pillars of Creation in a Star Forming Region[16]

Green shows emission from hydrogen. Blue shows light emitted by doubly ionized oxygen atoms.

Influence Interpretation.   A final purpose for color is its ability to influence the way viewers interpret information in visuals such as phase diagrams, which are familiar to chemists, physicists, chemical engineers, and materials scientists.

Phase diagrams are important for the design of chemical separations equipment such as absorbers and distillation columns. These diagrams show the phase behavior of a complex system at a glance and often eliminate the need for in-depth study of detailed, numerical equilibrium data. For example, the phase diagrams in Figure 9.11 were produced at Iowa State University using *Animate*, an interactive computer-graphics program for the study of multicomponent, fluid-phase equilibria.

Phase diagrams for fluid mixtures containing four chemical species (quaternaries) use tetrahedral models to show the results of boiling or condensation. In the computer-generated drawings in Figure 9.11, the pure components A (acetonitrile), B (benzene), C (ethanol), and D (acetone) are designated by the vertexes of the tetrahedron, while all intermediate quaternary mixtures are located in the space within. The compositions of boiling liquids are shown by the red surfaces, and those of condensing vapors are shown in green, with the specific, red-green pairs that coexist together (that is, in equilibrium) connected by tie-lines, several of which have been drawn in white.

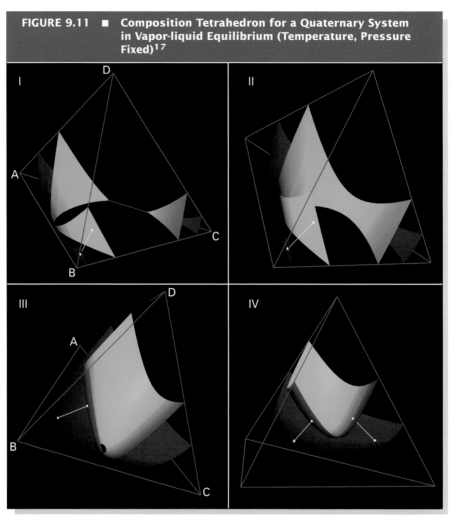

FIGURE 9.11 ■ Composition Tetrahedron for a Quaternary System in Vapor-liquid Equilibrium (Temperature, Pressure Fixed)[17]

The software was written by Eric Cochran and Professor Kenneth R. Jolls, ISU Chemical Engineering Department, and the sequence was designed by Chad Sanborn, ISU Engineering Publication and Communication Services.

In the series of images I–IV, the movements of the surfaces—both through the tetrahedron and also relative to one another—show how the equilibrium compositions change in response to increasing fluid pressure while the temperature remains fixed. The rotation of the model itself lets viewers study the diagram from all angles.

Color in Designing Online Documents

In print documents, color can be a valuable, or even essential, element. Color is just as important (and is perhaps even expected) in many online documents.

Because color is produced differently on a screen than it is on paper, technical communicators must think about it differently. Onscreen colors, like paper colors, are affected by the environment in which you view them—the reflections off the monitor face, the light in the room, and the combinations of colors on the screen all affect the way you see onscreen colors, and the effects work differently than on paper documents.

Because of the variations in the ways viewers interpret onscreen colors, you need to consider color—and viewers' reactions to it—when you're designing online documents.

- Will the document be viewed on a screen of lower or higher resolution than the one you're using? If so, you must consider whether the viewers' graphics will look grainy or poorly defined.

- Will the document be viewed in a room with bright lights (such as in a fluorescent-lit office?), or dim lights (such as in a private home)? The reflections from the screen can have a major impact on how color is perceived.

- Will the document be printed? If so, the differences between screen color and paper color must be considered. If readers might print the document without color, you should look at black-and-white hard copy to see if what you thought was functional color becomes a gray blob when viewed in black and white.

What additional questions could be important in your decision about using color in online documents?

Visual Functions

Visuals of different types—tables, graphs, diagrams, charts, drawings, maps, and photographs—fulfill one or more functions in technical documents. Six major functions of visuals are the focus of this section:

- Organize numeric or verbal data (for example, tables and diagrams).

- Show relationships among numeric or verbal data (for example, tables, graphs, and diagrams).

- Define or explain concepts, objects, and processes (for example, drawings, photographs, and diagrams).

- Present chronology, sequence, or process (for example, line graphs, flow charts, organizational charts, and milestone charts).

- Illustrate appearance or structure, which may include describing objects or mechanisms (for example, drawings, photographs, maps, and diagrams).

- Identify facilities or locations (for example, maps, charts, schematics, and blueprints).

Locate a figure in this textbook that is particularly useful in helping you understand the information it conveys. Share your preference in class. Note distinct preferences that different readers have.

Function 1: Organize Numeric or Verbal Data

Numeric and verbal information identifying the characteristics of ideas, objects, or processes can be displayed in tables. The rows and columns of a table provide a system for classifying data and showing relationships that would be confusing if presented only in sentences and paragraphs.

While the information in a table is usually organized in a way that gives readers the sense they can reach their own interpretations, the display itself shapes these interpretations. For example, readers are influenced by the sequence of the rows and columns, by the column and line heads, by the inclusion of footnotes, and so on. The text accompanying a table should discuss the information in a table, providing readers with a direction for their interpretation.

If the data in a table are self-contained and self-explanatory, they are usually boxed as well as surrounded with white space to set them apart from the text. Such tables are labeled with a number and a title. Conventions that have been established for designing an effective table are listed here and illustrated in Figure 9.12.

- Place columns to be compared next to each other.

- Round numbers if possible.

- Limit numbers to two decimal places.

- Align decimals in a column.

- Label each column and row.

- Use standard symbols and units of measure.

FIGURE 9.12 ■ Model Format for Tables

Model of an Effective Tabular Format

Subtitle is an Optional Addition

rule

identifies horizontal line of data

rule

Stub	Multiple Column Head		Single Column Head	Single Column Head
	Subhead[a]	Subhead[b]		
Line Head	ww.w	xxx.x	y.y	zzz.z
Line Head	www.w	x.x	yy.y	zzz.z
Line Head	w.w	xx.x	yyy.y	z.z
Line Head	www.w	xx.x	yy.y	zz.z

rule

Column
Average

rule

[a]Footnote
[b]Footnote

- Use footnotes for headings that are not self-explanatory.

- Present the table on a single page whenever possible.

Less formal tables are integrated into the text. These shorter tables depend directly on the surrounding text to provide a context for the data. They are not numbered or titled, but they usually do have clear row and column headings.

Numeric Tables That Organize Data.   In addition to their obvious organizational benefits, tables can present large amounts of numeric data in an accessible format that takes far less space than would the verbal presentation of the same information, as in Figure 9.13, which shows body weight and blood alcohol percentages. The same information presented in a paragraph would be difficult to follow and would force readers to work unnecessarily hard to get the information.

Tables can also use visual cues to help readers understand how to interpret the data. For example, Figure 9.13 effectively uses shading to help readers interpret the connection between alcohol consumption and intoxication and, thus, make an informed decision about safe driving. Originally printed on a business card, this table is designed for people to carry in their wallets or pockets for quick reference.

Verbal Tables That Organize Data.   Although tables generally present numeric data, the tabular format is also appropriate for some primarily and even completely verbal material. Verbal tables can be economical and effective. Explaining the information in Figure 9.14 in sentences and paragraphs would be time-consuming, and the resulting text would be difficult to read. The columns

FIGURE 9.13 ■ Table with Visual Cue for Interpreting Data[18]

KNOW YOUR LIMITS

CHART FOR RESPONSIBLE PEOPLE WHO MAY SOMETIMES DRIVE AFTER DRINKING!

APPROXIMATE BLOOD ALCOHOL PERCENTAGE

Drinks	Body Weight in Pounds								
	100	120	140	160	180	200	220	240	Influenced
1	.04	.03	.03	.02	.02	.02	.02	.02	Rarely
2	.08	.06	.06	.06	.04	.04	.03	.03	
3	.11	.08	.08	.07	.06	.06	.06	.05	
4	.15	.12	.11	.08	.08	.08	.07	.06	
5	.19	.16	.13	.12	.11	.09	.09	.08	Possibly
6	.23	.19	.16	.14	.13	.11	.10	.09	
7	.26	.22	.19	.16	.15	.13	.12	.11	
8	.30	.25	.21	.19	.17	.15	.14	.13	Definitely
9	.34	.28	.24	.21	.19	.17	.15	.14	
10	.38	.31	.27	.23	.21	.19	.17	.16	

Subtract .01% for each 40 minutes of drinking
One drink is 1 oz. of 100 proof liquor, 12 oz. of beer, or 4 oz. of table wine.

SUREST POLICY IS...DON'T DRIVE AFTER DRINKING!

Multiple column heads help readers chunk appropriate information.

Two visual cues— the shading and the right-hand column indicating the level of influence—make the table easier to read.

FIGURE 9.14 ■ Verbal Information Organized in a Table[19]

MEET THE BUGS

Name	Possible Symptoms (from most to least common)	Foods that Have Caused Outbreaks	How Soon it Typically Strikes	How Soon it Typically Ends
Campylobacter (bacteria)	diarrhea (can be bloody), fever, abdominal pain, nausea, headache, muscle pain	chicken, raw milk	2 to 5 days	7 to 10 days
Ciguatera (toxin)	numbness, tingling, nausea, vomiting, diarrhea, muscle pain, headache, temperature reversal (hot things feel cold and cold things feel hot), dizziness, muscular weakness, irregular heartbeat	grouper, barracuda, snapper, jack, mackerel, triggerfish	within 6 hours	several days (neurological symptoms can last for weeks or months)
Clostridium botulinum (bacteria)	marked fatigue; weakness; dizziness; double vision; difficulty speaking, swallowing, and breathing; abdominal distention	home-canned foods, sausages, meat products, commercially canned vegetables, seafood products	18 to 36 hours	get treatment immediately
Cyclospora (parasite)	watery diarrhea, loss of appetite, weight loss, cramps, nausea, vomiting, muscle aches, low-grade fever, extreme fatigue	raspberries, lettuce, basil	I week	a few days to 30 days or more
E. coli O157:H7 (bacteria)	severe abdominal pain, watery (then bloody) diarrhea, occasionally vomiting	ground beef, raw milk, lettuce, sprouts, unpasteurized juices	I to 8 days	get treatment immediately
Hepatitis A (virus)	fever, malaise, nausea, loss of appetite, abdominal pain, jaundice	shellfish, salads, cold cuts, sandwiches, fruits, vegetables, fruit juices, milk, milk products, infected food handlers	10 to 50 days	I to 2 weeks

in Figure 9.14 are clearly labeled. The rows are presented in alternating shades so that readers can easily see related information.

Function 2: Show Relationships

Relationships between two or more sets of data can be displayed using several types of visuals, but the most frequently used types are *graphs.* Graphs include line graphs, scatter graphs, pie graphs, bar graphs, and pictorial graphs.

What graphs are most commonly used in your discipline or profession? What are ways to distort data with these graphs?

Sometimes the relationships are emphasized by the use of color. One technique, called *field stepping*, uses increments of color—for example, ranging from a pale, light background color at the bottom of a line graph to a brighter, more saturated color at the top of the graph so that the peaks of the lines stand out more vividly against the bright color. A similar technique called *field ramping* shades the background from left to right, again, to provide a greater contrast with the lines.

Line Graphs. Line graphs show the relationship between two values represented by intersecting values projected from the *abscissa* (horizontal) and *ordinate* (vertical) axes on a coordinate grid. Line graphs usually plot changes in quantity, showing the exact increases and decreases over a period of time— minutes, days, decades, or centuries—or other quantifiable variables. Line graphs are one of the most commonly used forms of displaying relationships, so most readers are familiar with them. In constructing line graphs, these conventions are usually followed:

- Use the horizontal axis to depict time, some event occurring over time, or some other quantifiable variable.

- Limit the number of lines on a graph to those easily interpreted by readers.

- When using more than one line, differentiate the lines by design or color, or use a key or label to identify each line.

- Add notes or labels to make information clear to readers.

- Keep the vertical and horizontal axes proportionate.

The line graph in Figure 9.15 shows the differences in absorption properties for various wavelengths. Scientists can better determine the range of medical benefits of diode laser technology by understanding these properties. The primary information in Figure 9.15 comes from lines differentiated by color: diode laser is purple, protein is yellow, hemoglobin is red, melanin is black, and water is green; thus, you are able to read and interpret the graph easily. Although the color and thickness of the grid lines (running vertically and horizontally) allow you to accurately pinpoint absorption coefficients, the grid lines themselves do not detract from the message of the graph.

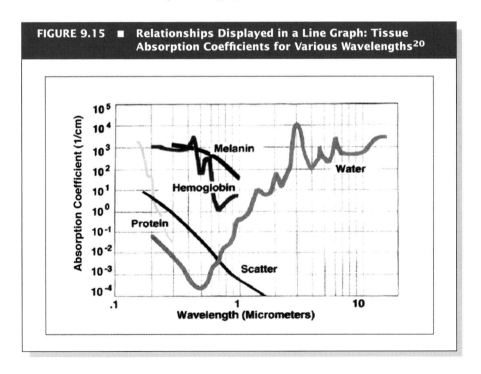

FIGURE 9.15 ■ Relationships Displayed in a Line Graph: Tissue Absorption Coefficients for Various Wavelengths[20]

Scatter Graphs. Scatter graphs use single, unconnected dots to plot instances where two variables (one on each axis) meet. Usually, scatter graphs are plotted on graphs where the x-axis (horizontal) and y-axis (vertical) are proportionate. However, if the range of data is very large, the data can be charted logarithmically to show more clearly the direction of the correlation.

The pattern of the dots expresses the relationship between variables, as illustrated in Figure 9.16. If the dots are randomly scattered, the two variables have no correlation. If the dots are primarily on a diagonal running from the lower left to the upper right, the correlation is positive. If the diagonal runs from the upper left toward the lower right, the correlation is negative.

The correlation between the variables is sometimes highlighted by shading an area on the graph. However, the significance of the correlation must also be discussed in the text. Because interpreting scatter graphs is often difficult, their use is generally limited to professional and expert audiences.

Pie Graphs. Pie graphs—also called pie diagrams, pie charts, percent graphs, or divided circle graphs—emphasize the proportionate distribution of something, frequently money or time. Pie graphs are 100-percent graphs, where each percent represents 3.6 degrees of the circle, as shown in Figure 9.17. Even though software gives you great flexibility in the way you construct pie graphs, following these conventions makes them easier for readers to understand:

- Slices of the pie are arranged from largest to smallest, starting at "noon" and moving clockwise.

- Slices of the pie are colored from darkest to lightest, starting at "noon" and moving clockwise.

Adding a plot curve and using two colors, one for summer rates and the other for winter rates, helps readers see the relationship between the variables.

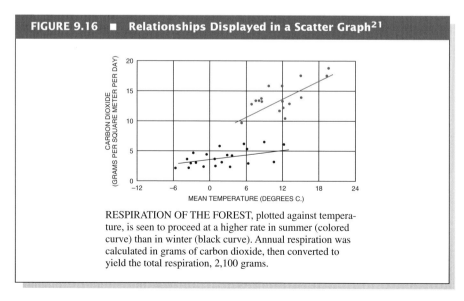

FIGURE 9.16 ■ Relationships Displayed in a Scatter Graph[21]

RESPIRATION OF THE FOREST, plotted against temperature, is seen to proceed at a higher rate in summer (colored curve) than in winter (black curve). Annual respiration was calculated in grams of carbon dioxide, then converted to yield the total respiration, 2,100 grams.

The clear caption helps readers interpret the information in the graph.

FIGURE 9.17 ■ Relationships Displayed in a Pie Graph[22]

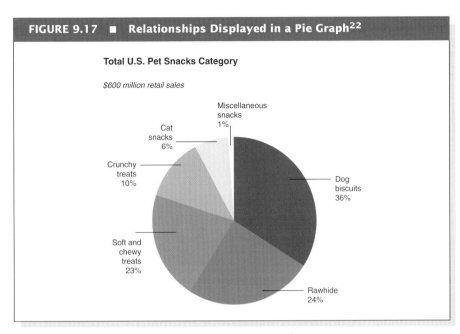

Total U.S. Pet Snacks Category

$600 million retail sales

Miscellaneous snacks 1%

Cat snacks 6%

Crunchy treats 10%

Dog biscuits 36%

Soft and chewy treats 23%

Rawhide 24%

This graph follows conventions:
- *No more than six items are displayed.*
- *Segments move from largest to smallest.*
- *Segments are shaded from darkest to lightest.*

Pie graphs can make a striking visual display, but the significance of the presented information must be discussed in the accompanying text. Pie graphs are popular attention-getting devices that focus the reader's attention for examining more detailed data. However, they are generally unsuitable for the comparison of more than five or six items; the primary problem is the impossibility of comparing areas. Additionally, the visual difference between areas representing similar percentages is minimal.

Bar Graphs.   Bar graphs can show several kinds of relationships, including comparisons, trends, and distributions. Like line graphs, bar graphs are drawn from a series of values plotted on two axes, but the values are represented by vertical or horizontal bars instead of points joined by a line. Because each bar represents a separate quantity, bar graphs are especially appropriate when the data consist of distinct units, such as tons of grain or megawatts of hydroelectric power produced over a specified period.

Commonly used bar graphs include a simple bar graph, subdivided bar graph, and subdivided 100-percent bar graph. Figures 9.18, 9.19, and 9.20 illustrate how the same data plotted on these three kinds of bar graphs can create quite a different appearance for readers.

Other variations of bar graphs—subdivided 100-percent area graph, multiple bar graph, sliding bar graph, and floating bar graph, shown in Figures 9.21, 9.22, 9.23, and 9.24—are appropriate for somewhat more complex displays of information.

In the *simple bar graph* in Figure 9.18, all bars represent the same type of information, so the differences are stressed. The same guidelines apply to any bar graph:

- Make bars the same width.

- Make the space between bars one-half the bar width.

- Label each bar.

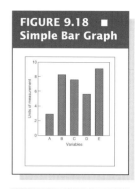

FIGURE 9.18 ■
Simple Bar Graph

In the *subdivided bar graph* in Figure 9.19, each bar is subdivided to represent the magnitude of different components. Parts are differentiated by shading or crosshatching. Although the total magnitude of each bar can be compared, as in a simple bar graph, the individual components are not easily compared.

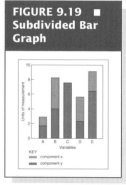

FIGURE 9.19 ■
Subdivided Bar Graph

In the *subdivided 100-percent bar graph* in Figure 9.20, each bar extends to 100 percent, and the components of the bar are separated by percentage. Unlike simple bar graphs and subdivided bar graphs that enable you to compare total magnitude, subdivided 100-percent bar graphs enable easy comparison of the individual components.

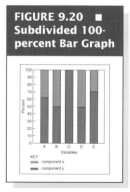

FIGURE 9.20 ■
Subdivided 100-percent Bar Graph

Figure 9.21 illustrates a variation of a subdivided 100-percent bar graph—a *subdivided 100-percent area graph*. Imagine a series of 150 bars, each extended to 100 percent and each bar subdivided to show the percentage of, say, types of fuel used during one year. The bars are then pushed together so the overall effect is a continuous line for each category. The area under each bar is shaded to make the distinctions clear.

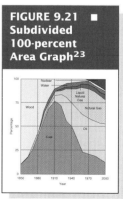

FIGURE 9.21 ■
Subdivided 100-percent Area Graph[23]

Part II: Developing the Communicator's Tools

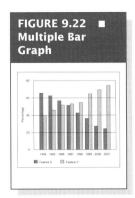

FIGURE 9.22 ■
Multiple Bar
Graph

A *multiple bar graph* groups two or more bars to present the magnitude of related variables. The example in Figure 9.22 compares "Feature X" and "Feature Y" over an 8-year period.

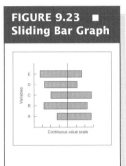

FIGURE 9.23 ■
Sliding Bar Graph

The bars in the *sliding bar graph* in Figure 9.23 move along an axis that is usually marked in opposing values (active/passive, hot/cold) that extend on either side of a central point, such as values on a temperature scale.

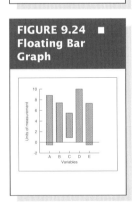

FIGURE 9.24 ■
Floating Bar
Graph

The *floating bar graph* in Figure 9.24 has bars that "float" in the area above the x-axis, which may extend below zero.

Pictorial Graphs.   An adaptation of the bar graph, called a *pictorial graph*, uses actual symbols to make up each bar. Each symbol (*isotype*) represents a specific number of people or objects. Pictorial graphs are very appealing and are widely used with many audiences. Problems arise, however, when depicting fractions (see Figure 9.25). Following these guidelines when creating pictorial graphs generally avoids problems:

- Round off numbers to eliminate fractions.
- Make all symbols the same size and space them equally.
- Select symbols that are clearly representative of the object.

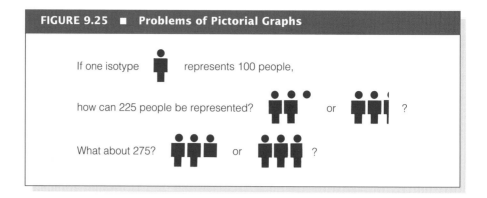

FIGURE 9.25 ■ Problems of Pictorial Graphs

If one isotype represents 100 people,

how can 225 people be represented? or ?

What about 275? or ?

Another version of a pictorial graph uses single isotypes of different sizes to represent the quantity or magnitude of each variable, as shown in Figure 9.26. In this graph, the increasing number of children allowed in daycare groups is represented by successively larger isotypes representing children in each age group. Such a graph is appropriate for attracting reader attention, but it should not be used to present technical data. (See the Intertext about distorting visuals that follows this chapter.)

Function 3: Define Concepts, Objects, and Processes

How does your discipline or profession use visuals for definition?

Visuals can be exceedingly valuable as definitions. The drawings of types of screw heads in Figure 9.27 are more efficient and useful than verbal descriptions. Visuals can illustrate details that are difficult to describe verbally, such as the types of heads and slots on the top of screws. Additionally, the angle of

While the isotypes here are proportional, they cannot themselves logically represent group size.

The graph works not because the isotypes represent the size of day care groups but because the isotypes are engaging and encourage readers to look more carefully at the information.

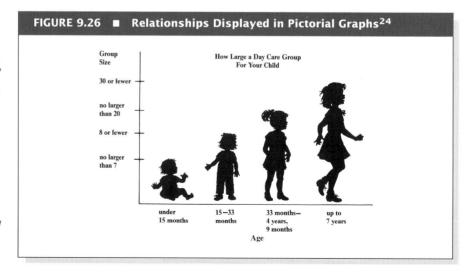

FIGURE 9.26 ■ Relationships Displayed in Pictorial Graphs[24]

FIGURE 9.27 ■ Visual Definition of Screws[25]

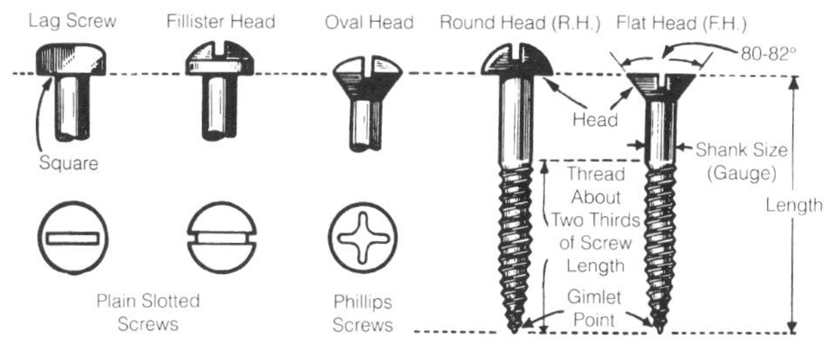

Simply by referring to the visual, a reader can correctly identify the various kinds of screws that are illustrated.

The proportions—head, shank, and thread—are easier to display visually than verbally.

a flathead screw is easily depicted in a drawing. Explaining the same information in a verbal definition would not be nearly as effective.

Figure 9.28 shows two biological classification systems: a functional hierarchy and a taxonomic hierarchy. The figure reinforces the point that while the

FIGURE 9.28 ■ Relationships Displayed in a Line Graph[26]

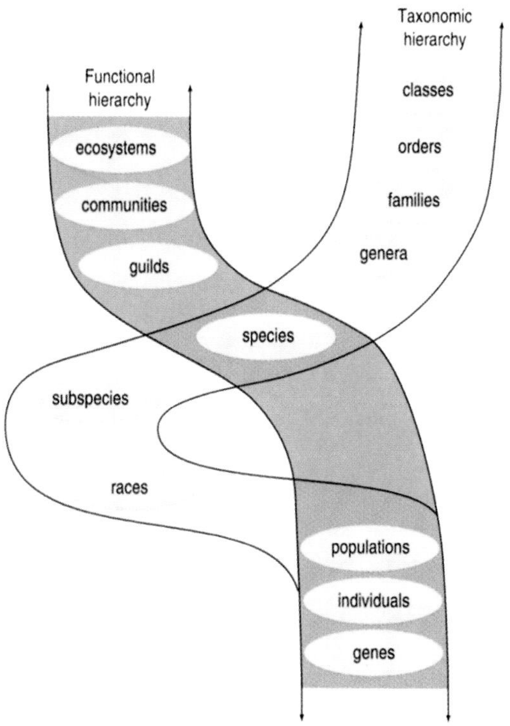

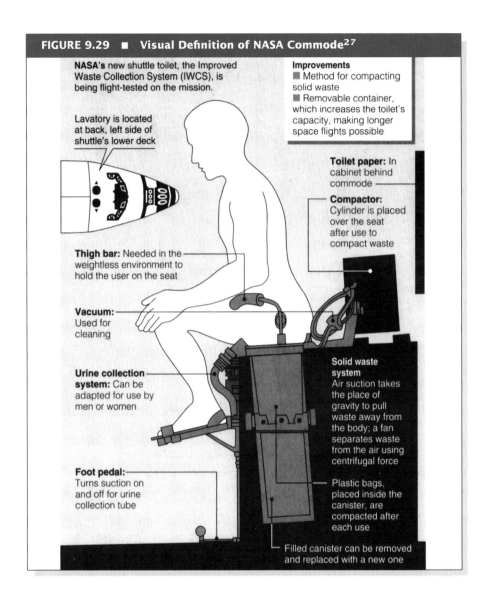

FIGURE 9.29 ■ Visual Definition of NASA Commode[27]

NASA's new shuttle toilet, the Improved Waste Collection System (IWCS), is being flight-tested on the mission.

Improvements
■ Method for compacting solid waste
■ Removable container, which increases the toilet's capacity, making longer space flights possible

Lavatory is located at back, left side of shuttle's lower deck

Toilet paper: In cabinet behind commode

Compactor: Cylinder is placed over the seat after use to compact waste

Thigh bar: Needed in the weightless environment to hold the user on the seat

Vacuum: Used for cleaning

Solid waste system Air suction takes the place of gravity to pull waste away from the body; a fan separates waste from the air using centrifugal force

Urine collection system: Can be adapted for use by men or women

Foot pedal: Turns suction on and off for urine collection tube

Plastic bags, placed inside the canister, are compacted after each use

Filled canister can be removed and replaced with a new one

two systems use unique terms to categorize biological material, the terms *species, populations, individuals,* and *genes* are common to both systems.

The similarity and differentiation are elegantly and simply communicated through the use of color and a nested arrangement. The colors used for each hierarchy—blue and yellow—combine to form green when the hierarchies overlap. The nested arrangement of the blue functional hierarchy with the yellow taxonomic hierarchy allows you to immediately grasp what terms are unique to and what terms are shared by each hierarchy.

Visuals may be more appropriate than text when readers need a definition of an unfamiliar or complex object or process. Figure 9.29 provides a good example.

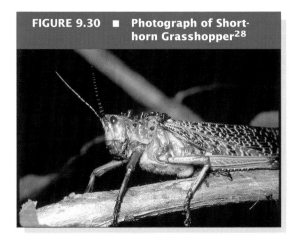

FIGURE 9.30 ■ Photograph of Short-horn Grasshopper[28]

FIGURE 9.31 ■ Photograph of Wasp Moth[29]

In this visual, the toilet on the space shuttle is explained clearly, with a discrete, nongender-specific human figure that helps readers understand how the system works. Readers' comprehension can sometimes be faster and more complete when visuals illustrate overall concepts as well as details.

Color is important in visually defining certain objects and organisms. For example, color patterns help to identify insects and to distinguish between insects that look identical except for color patterns, particularly butterflies. Figures 9.30 and 9.31 show two brilliantly colored insects that are identified in large part by their color. Figure 9.30 is a photograph of a common short-horn grasshopper (Phymateus saxosus) that entomologist and photographer Tom Myers took when he stopped along a roadside in Madagascar. The particular combination of colors is unique to grasshoppers in Madagascar. Figure 9.31 is a photograph of a wasp moth (Orcynia calcarata) that Myers took while in French Guiana. The black and yellow of this moth mimics the coloration of a wasp, warning away birds and other predators. Myers's photographs are frequently published in magazines, but he also uses them in presentations about rainforest insects to professional conferences and school and community groups.

Function 4: Present Action or Process

Visuals are particularly appropriate for action views and processes. While the visuals vary widely according to the process being presented, actions are particularly easy to depict in a sequence, and processes are easy to depict in various kinds of charts.

Action Sequences.   Figure 9.32 shows the breach of a whale, with arrows showing the direction it takes at each stage of the breach. Because of the sequence of five drawings and the arrows to indicate the direction of the movement, this drawing enables readers to understand the breach without referring to the text. The visual tells a story by itself.

How does your discipline or profession visually present actions or processes?

FIGURE 9.32 ■ Drawing Showing Action: Whale Breaching[30]

Charts. Charts can represent the components, steps, or chronology of an object, mechanism, organism, or organization. The most common charts are block charts, organizational charts, and flowcharts.

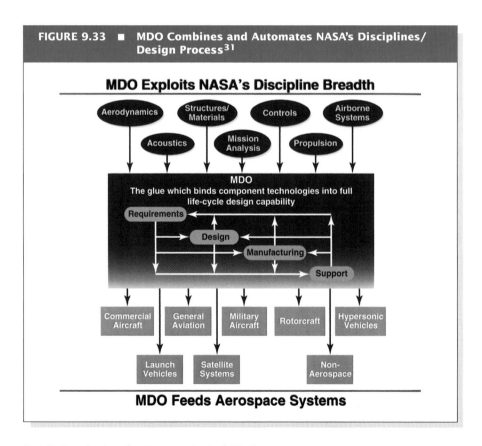

FIGURE 9.33 ■ MDO Combines and Automates NASA's Disciplines/ Design Process[31]

A *block chart* (also called block diagram or classification chart), illustrated in Figure 9.33, uses blocks to represent the components or subdivisions of the whole object, system, or process. This example uses shapes, colors, and arrow placement to illustrate the components of Multidisciplinary Design Optimization (MDO)—a computer software analysis procedure used to streamline the complicated aircraft design process.

At top, the purple ovals represent the various disciplines—for example, aerodynamics and acoustics—necessary to aircraft design. At center, the ovals and arrows combine to illustrate the cyclical and complex design process. The MDO networks all of these disciplines throughout each phase of this process. At bottom, the green boxes depict the variety of aircraft products—commercial aircraft, launch vehicles, etc.—that can be designed.

Figure 9.33 uses both arrows and color to draw your eyes from the top of the block diagram to the bottom, while the use of a gradient purple color in the center box also draws your eyes from the top of the center box to the bottom. The purple arrows against the white background lead your eye from the purple ovals through the center box to the green "aircraft products" boxes.

An *organizational chart* portrays the hierarchy of an organization by putting each position in a separate block, as in Figure 9.34. The chart shows the vertical

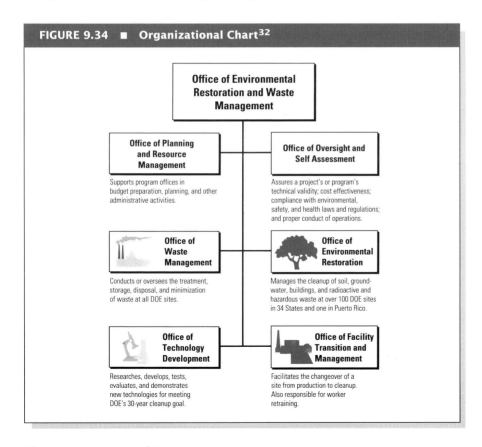

FIGURE 9.34 ■ Organizational Chart[32]

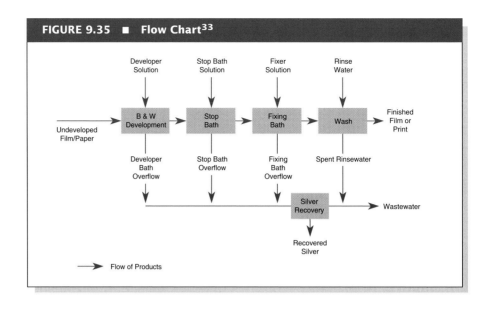

FIGURE 9.35 ■ Flow Chart[33]

Developer Solution

Stop Bath Solution

Fixer Solution

Rinse Water

Undeveloped Film/Paper

B & W Development

Stop Bath

Fixing Bath

Wash

Finished Film or Print

Developer Bath Overflow

Stop Bath Overflow

Fixing Bath Overflow

Spent Rinsewater

Silver Recovery

Wastewater

Recovered Silver

→ Flow of Products

and horizontal relationships in the U.S. Department of Energy's Office of Environmental Restoration and Waste Management. In addition to the bare-bones information, the chart also provides icons and brief descriptions of the responsibilities associated with each office.

A *flowchart* (also called a route chart), shown in Figure 9.35, depicts the sequence of steps in a process, in this case the development of black-and-white photographic film. Such charts sometimes indicate the amount of time each step takes. The shaded boxes help highlight the steps in the process, and the colored arrows help readers follow the sequence.

Function 5: Illustrate Appearance, Structure, or Function

How does your discipline or profession visually depict parts of objects, mechanisms, or organisms?

Physical characteristics are often easier to present visually than verbally. Diagrams and drawings are especially effective ways to show the parts of objects, mechanisms, or organisms—and the relationships among those parts. Only the parts readers need to know about are represented.

Diagrams. *Diagrams* illustrate the complex physical components and structures of objects, mechanisms, or organisms. Indeed, they are often easier to understand than photographs or representative drawings because the reader is not distracted by unnecessary details. The diagram in Figure 9.36 shows a system comprised of a motor, heat exchanger, tank, and valves used to cool the space shuttle's cryogenic liquid rocket propellants. The system works to continuously circulate warmer cryogenic liquid with subcooled liquid.

Color distinguishes the warmer liquid (dark purple) from the cooler liquid (light purple), while the blue arrows signal the direction of the flow. The white

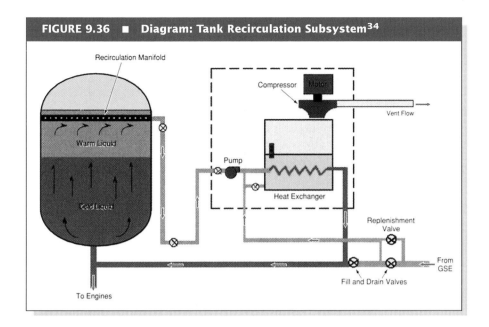

FIGURE 9.36 ■ **Diagram: Tank Recirculation Subsystem**[34]

outlines of these blue arrows make them easier to distinguish. The green of the heat exchanger also helps to illustrate the flow of liquid through it. While the diagram's components are clearly labeled, a consistent use of color enables you to easily identify the valves (yellow) and the motor and pump (red).

Drawings.   *Drawings* depict the actual appearance of an object or organism. Unlike a photograph, a drawing can delete details and emphasize more important portions. Drawings are appropriate when you want to focus on specific characteristics or components of a subject. A drawing does not have to be complicated to be effective. Figure 9.37 shows just how well a simple drawing can illustrate an abstract concept.

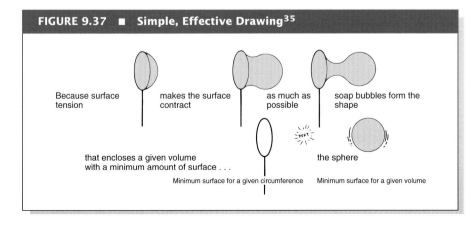

FIGURE 9.37 ■ **Simple, Effective Drawing**[35]

Various components and aspects of objects, mechanisms, and organisms can be shown by different drawing views. Drawings that a technical professional might refer to include perspective drawings, phantom views, cutaway views, exploded views, and action views.

Figure 9.38 shows a three-dimensional view of the Nebula GNX car. This drawing was produced using a special CAD software that allowed the user to create realistic images of a variety of different shapes and surfaces. While Figure 9.38 shows a three-dimensional view, the view itself is not realistic—that is, the play of light and shadow on the car allows you to see both the outlines of the car's exterior and the shape of the car's engine and frame.

The car's exterior is deep red, while its interior is a shadowy, gunmetal gray. The car's frame and suspension is yellow, a color picked up in parts of the engine (including the Nebula GNX logo on the engine itself). The yellow and red emphasize the engine and immediately draw your eyes to this area.

The versatility of drawings is demonstrated in a book for farriers. The series of three drawings in Figure 9.39 shows an external view—a representational drawing—of a hoof, followed by a phantom view and a cutaway view to reveal

FIGURE 9.38 ■ Drawing[36]

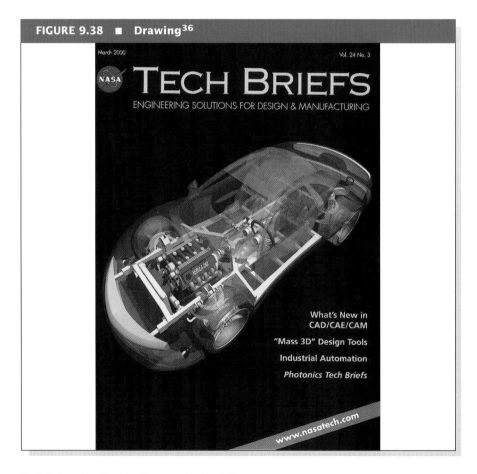

March 2000   Vol. 24 No. 3

NASA TECH BRIEFS

ENGINEERING SOLUTIONS FOR DESIGN & MANUFACTURING

What's New in
CAD/CAE/CAM

"Mass 3D" Design Tools

Industrial Automation

Photonics Tech Briefs

www.nasatech.com

FIGURE 9.39 ■ External View, Phantom View, and Cutaway View[37]

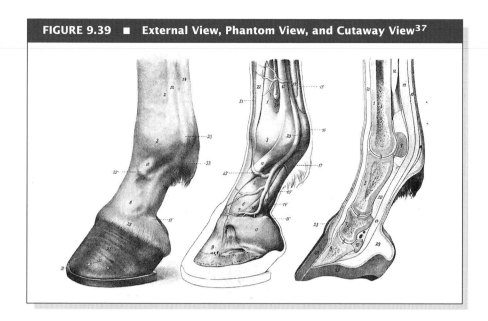

the internal structure. Because these drawings have the same scale and are placed close together, you can easily make comparisons.

Another common type of technical drawing is an exploded view, illustrated in Figure 9.40. An exploded view shows an entire mechanism or organism by

FIGURE 9.40 ■ Exploded View[38]

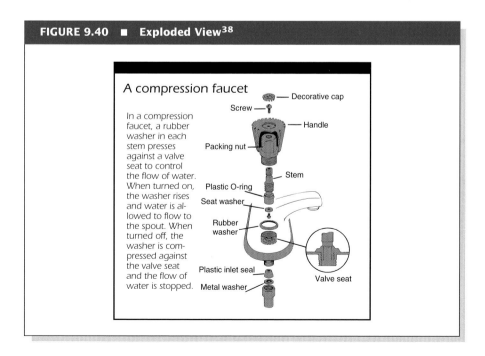

A compression faucet

In a compression faucet, a rubber washer in each stem presses against a valve seat to control the flow of water. When turned on, the washer rises and water is allowed to flow to the spout. When turned off, the washer is compressed against the valve seat and the flow of water is stopped.

Decorative cap
Screw
Handle
Packing nut
Stem
Plastic O-ring
Seat washer
Rubber washer
Plastic inlet seal
Metal washer
Valve seat

separating (exploding) the whole to provide a clear view of each component. Exploded views are useful as part of an overall description of a mechanism or organism, but they are most frequently used in assembly and repair manuals. Your understanding of the compression faucet in Figure 9.40 is increased by the clear labels next to the appropriate parts and the concise process explanation of the way the faucet works.

Function 6: Identify Facilities or Locations

How does your discipline or profession use maps and photographs?

Identifying facilities and locations traditionally meant maps and photographs. Now, however, *map* also refers to a navigational tool used on the Web, and workplace photographs are made as often with digital cameras as with traditional film cameras.

Maps.   Geographic information is displayed on maps (called charts, not maps, for air or water). To many people, maps mean road guides. But maps can also display topographic, demographic, agricultural, meteorological, and geological data. And now, maps also refer to Web sites, providing users with an overview of the electronic terrain.

Maps show features of a particular area, such as land elevation, rock formations, vegetation, animal habitats, crop production, population density, or traffic patterns. Statistical maps can depict quantities at specific points or within specified boundaries. Data can be presented on maps in a number of ways: dots, shading, lines, repetitive symbols, or superimposed graphs.

Figure 9.41 shows a map that identifies patterns of protein and oil content in soybeans grown in various regions of the United States. The text accompanying this figure explains that "Southern soybeans contain about 1.5 percent more protein and about the same amount of oil as western corn belt soybeans. Although specifics are not well-known, day length and growing season are often given as reasons for these differences." The shaded sections make the regions distinct.

Another kind of map is presented in Figure 9.42, which shows a computer model—a map—that depicts possible underground paths of water flowing toward the Columbia River in the state of Washington. This ground water may contain contaminants leaking from tanks at the Hanford Reservation, tanks used to store waste radioactive materials from the manufacture of nuclear weapons. Tracking the ground water helps the U.S. Department of Energy establish the severity of the problem, determine concentrations and radioactivity of contaminants, and show the feasibility of slowing the movement of the ground water toward the Columbia River.

The computer model, designed by Michael Connelly, a geophysicist who works at Bechtel-Hanford, Inc., in Hanford, Washington, uses color to help viewers interpret the information. The map model shows the bottom and top boundaries of the region being studied and modeled: (1) The purple mountain depicts the impermeable layer of bedrock far underground. (2) The yellow grid (only the top plane of which shows on the model) depicts the actual ground level. Ground water can flow between purple mountain and yellow grid.

FIGURE 9.41 ■ Map Showing Regional Distinctions[39]

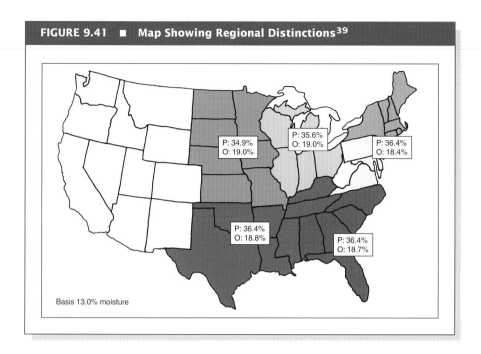

P: 34.9%
O: 19.0%

P: 35.6%
O: 19.0%

P: 36.4%
O: 18.4%

P: 36.4%
O: 18.8%

P: 36.4%
O: 18.7%

Basis 13.0% moisture

Web site maps are important navigational tools for users. Like maps for physical locations, Web site maps tell users what places are present on the Web site, give a general sense of where these places are in relation to each other, and point the direction for getting there. At a minimum, effective site maps (a) provide an overview of the site architecture—that is, the framework that

FIGURE 9.42 ■ Computer Rendition of an FEM Surface Grid[40]

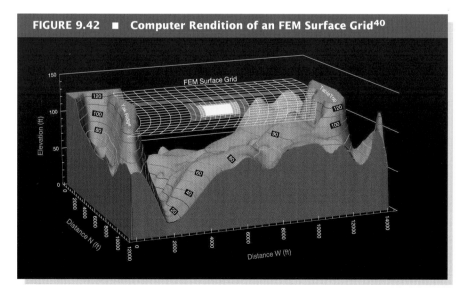

FEM Surface Grid

Elevation (ft)

Distance N (ft)

Distance W (ft)

FIGURE 9.43 ■ Web Site Map[41]

Intranet View by Department

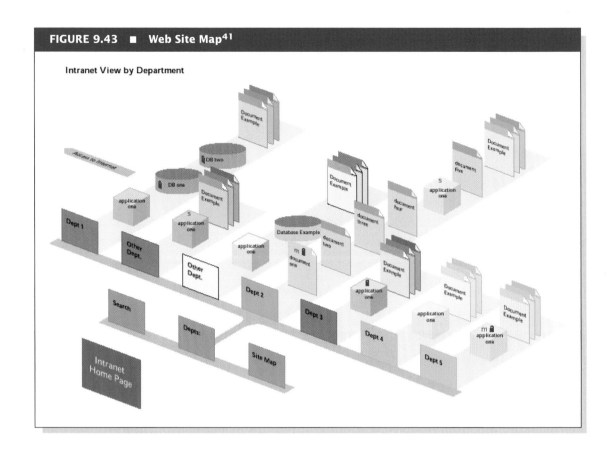

structures the content and (b) give users navigational cues that let users know where they are in relation to the rest of the site. Figure 9.43 presents an effective site map.

Photographs. Because a photograph displays an actual view of a subject, it's appropriate when you want to emphasize realism, particularly showing the natural features of a setting. However, even though photographs accurately depict locations, they often show too much detail. For this reason, callout arrows (small arrows superimposed on a photo) can be used to draw attention to main features.

Also, when a photo is printed, its appearance can be altered so that the primary subject is visually more prominent than the background, thus giving emphasis that is not possible if the photo is printed normally. Photos can also be reduced, enlarged, or cropped to emphasize a particular portion of the subject.

Virtually every state has both public and private photo archives that contain thousands and in some cases millions of aerial photographs that provide a

FIGURE 9.44 ■ Aerial Photograph from Low-Flying Airplane[42]

complete record of features in the state. Routinely taken, aerial photos record various kinds of information:

- Agricultural information (crop data, erosion management, forestry management)

- Municipal information (property lines, utilities, streets)

- Transportation information (major and minor roads and highways, bridges, waterways, traffic patterns, railroads, airports)

Figure 9.44 is an aerial photograph (from a low-flying airplane; similar photographs are taken from high flights in airplanes and from satellites). It shows a water treatment facility and county maintenance shed. The hydrogeologist who used this photo wanted confirmation of land features and building locations as he tracked an underground hazardous waste spill.

Another kind of photograph is presented in Figure 9.45, which shows four views of the Long Valley region of California using synthetic aperture radar (SAR) technology. SAR allows all-weather mapping of topographic and geographic features of land surfaces. The four views illustrate different SAR processing steps (clockwise from upper left): the initial SAR image, the interferogram, the perspective view, and the contour map.

FIGURE 9.45 ■ **Satellite Maps**[43]

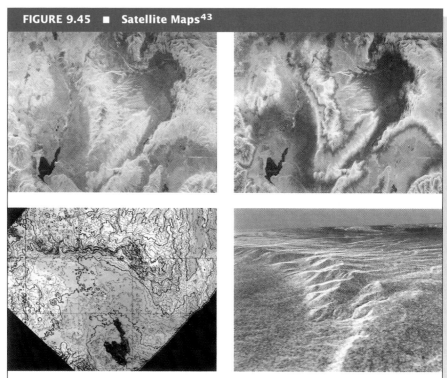

Figure 10-1. Long Valley region of east-central California acquired by SIR-C/X-SAR interferometer, illustrating processing steps from SAR image (upper left) to interferogram (upper right) to contour map (lower left) to perspective view (lower right).

Color is important in each of these views: The *initial SAR image* uses white, black, and gray shadow to illustrate the features of the land; the *interferogram* uses a range of colors—violet, yellow, blue, and green—to highlight these surface features. The *contour map* relies on shades of green, yellow, and gray to highlight land surfaces, and black contour lines further distinguish these features. The *perspective view* relies more heavily on light and shadow—rather than contrasting colors—to distinguish the features of the land surface.

End-of-Chapter
Recommendations for Technical Communicators

1. Choose visual/verbal combinations—all text, text with visual support, visuals with textual support, or all visuals—that are appropriate for your purpose and audience.

2. Use well-designed visuals when readers' understanding of the technical content is limited, when speed is of the utmost importance and reading would slow the process, and when the process is more clearly illustrated visually.

3. Choose visuals when you want to show relationships among the data, define certain mechanisms and processes, and illustrate unfamiliar information.

4. Follow standard conventions in using visuals:
   - Place visuals as close as possible following the text reference.
   - Accurately label each visual.
   - Include complete dimensions of objects in each visual.
   - Use standard abbreviations and include a key.
   - Surround the visual with white space.
   - Include a complete textual reference.
   - Include a list of figures if you have five or more visuals in a document.
   - Identify the source of the data as well as the graphic designer.
   - Specify the focus or interpretation you want readers to apply.

5. Consider using color to accomplish these purposes:
   - Attract attention.
   - Enable accurate identification.
   - Show structure or organization.
   - Highlight components and their function or movement.
   - Influence interpretation.

6. Organize numeric or verbal data in tables.

7. Show relationships by using graphs—line graphs, scatter graphs, pie graphs, bar graphs, and pictorial graphs.

8. Define concepts, objects, and processes by using drawings.

9. Present chronology, sequence, or process by using drawings and charts—block components charts, organizational charts, or flow charts.

10. Illustrate appearance, structure, or function by using diagrams or drawings.

11. Identify facilities or locations by using maps and photographs.

Individual and Collaborative Assignments

1. **Design a table.** Conduct the appropriate research and then design a speed comparison table that presents the equivalents for kilometers per hour, miles per hour, and knots per hour. For whom would this comparison table be useful?

2. **Transform a pictorial graph.** The following pictorial graph[44] shows the per-capita income disparity for developing, transition, and well-developed countries. Well-developed countries (such as Canada, the United States, Japan, and Israel) show the greatest per-capita income disparity over a 30-year period. That is, over the next 30 years, the rich will become richer while the poor will become poorer. Design another visual depiction of this information. Identify the audience and purpose of your visual.

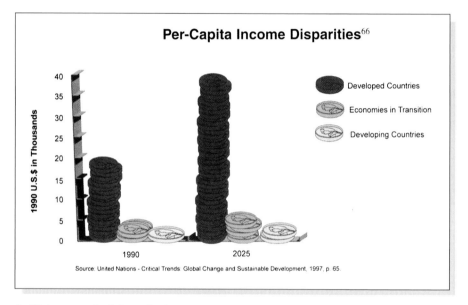

3. **Write a verbal description based on visual information.** Refer to the flowchart in this chapter (Figure 9.35). Write a description of the process based on the information in the visual. Make sure the information is accurate. After you have completed the paragraph, examine it to identify the textual features you used to help readers follow the process.

4. **Transform a bar graph.** The following subdivided 100-percent bar graph shows the proportions of saturated, polyunsaturated, and monounsaturated fatty acids in different vegetable oils.[45] All dietary fats comprise mixtures of fatty acids, but lower amounts of saturated fatty acids (like those found in sunflower and safflower oil) are healthier for your body than saturated fatty acids. Develop two additional ways to depict this same information. Identify the audience and purpose of your visuals.

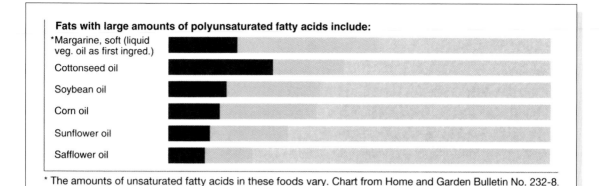

Fats with large amounts of polyunsaturated fatty acids include:

*Margarine, soft (liquid veg. oil as first ingred.)

Cottonseed oil

Soybean oil

Corn oil

Sunflower oil

Safflower oil

* The amounts of unsaturated fatty acids in these foods vary. Chart from Home and Garden Bulletin No. 232-8, *Foods and Planning Menus*, USDA, Human Nutrition Information Service.

5. **Evaluate a published visual.** (a) Select a published visual and examine it according to the following criteria:

   - Is the appearance appealing?

   - Is the accompanying description/discussion complete?

   - Is the type of visual appropriate for the data and purpose?

   - Is the presentation free from distortion?

   (b) Use this and other criteria that you establish to create a rubric for evaluating the effectiveness and accuracy of visuals.

6. **Assess a visual.** (a) Read this explanation of the following visual. It is used in veterinary classes to show changes to blood as it moves through a capillary. In capillaries (the smallest blood vessels of the body), bright red blood containing oxygen loses oxygen to the tissues and turns slightly blue. Blood then goes back to the heart and on to the lungs where it is oxygenated and turns red again.
   (b) Explain whether the use of color is effective. Is it necessary?

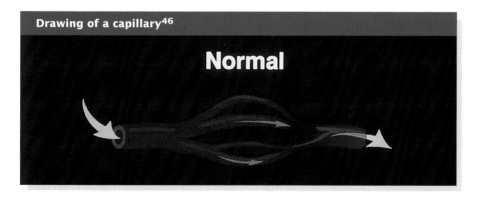

Drawing of a capillary[46]

Normal

7. **Revise a document by adding visuals.** Select a document that you have previously completed (perhaps in this course, perhaps in another course, perhaps in the workplace). Revise it using appropriate visuals to clarify or support the points you made in the document.

8. **Analyze the use of visuals on a Web site.** Visit the following Web sites:
   <www.pbs.org/wgbn/nova/>
   <www.discover.com>
   <www.nationalgeographic.com>
   <http://cfa-www.harvard.edu/>
   <http://www.si.edu/activity/planvis/museums/i-nasm.htm>

   (a) Use (and modify) the rubric you created in Assignment 5 and evaluate two of the Web sites according to those criteria. Consider the following questions:

      ■ Do the visuals effectively and accurately explain or enhance the text?

      ■ Are visuals used for navigational cues? Are they effective?

      ■ What are some positive attributes of Web site visuals?

      ■ What are some negative attributes of Web site visuals?

      ■ What suggestions do you have for Web site technical communicators regarding the use of visuals?

   (b) Prepare your analysis in a five-minute oral presentation in which you display selected screen captures from the Web sites to illustrate your points.

Intertext

Avoiding Distortion and Misuse of Visuals

B ecause visuals can distort a reader's perception of the material, you must learn how to avoid unintentionally misrepresenting information. Sometimes avoiding distortion rests with the data collection; other times it's with the presentation.

Careless Data Collection

Several traps that can cause you to distort your data are easily avoided. Positive responses to the following questions will let you know collection of the data has not distorted the information:

1. Is the random testing sample sufficiently large? A nonprescription medication that relieves pain in 90 percent of the users sounds impressive, but the results don't mention that only 10 people were in the sample.

2. Have questions been designed to elicit unambiguous responses? Do questions address all relevant aspects of the topic?

3. Have all of the available data been recorded? Have all data been included, even that which is unfavorable?

4. Are the data measuring what is claimed to be measured?

5. Are the cause–effect relationships logical? Does A logically result in B, or is the sequence of A and B merely coincidental?

6. Are measures of central tendency used correctly? For example, imagine that production runs of 100 during a given week result in rejection rates of 1, 2, 2, 2, 3, 5, 7, 8, 8, 19, 27—what is the average rate of rejection? The *mean* is 7.6, the *median,* 5, and the *mode,* 2. What can be said about the rejection rate? To be accurate, identify which measure of central tendency you're using. Know the difference between these measures of central tendency, then select the most appropriate one:

   - *mean* (arithmetic average)   the numerical result obtained by dividing a sum by the number of quantities added

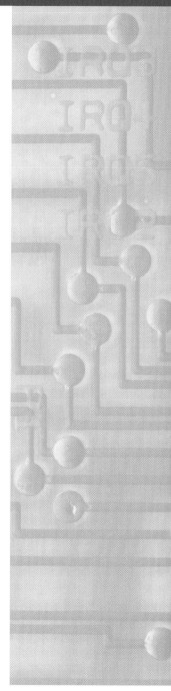

- *median*   the middle number in a series containing an odd number of items or the number midway between the two middle numbers in a series containing an even number of items
- *mode*   the value or number that occurs most frequently in a series

Inaccurate Data Presentation

Even if you have collected accurate and complete data, the manner of presentation can be distorted. Following are a few general observations about ways to avoid confusion or misrepresentation of data. Then suggestions about some common problems encountered when constructing graphs are discussed.

Selecting the appropriate type of figure is important. Think of the purpose of the figure, and then select the type that most effectively conveys the significant information. For example, a line graph showing the increases in sales during the last fiscal year is better suited for an annual report than is a table detailing the sales totals in each department for each month.

Percentages can distort information. Imagine that a monthly report from a group leader concludes that although production was down 30 percent during the first week of the month, it was up 10 percent during the next three weeks, so nothing was lost.

■ EXAMPLE

week 1: 30% decrease, from 100 widgets/hour to 70 widgets/hour

week 2: 10% increase, from 70 widgets/hour to 77 widgets/hour

week 3: 10% increase, from 77 widgets/hour to 84.7 widgets/hour

week 4: 10% increase, from 84.7 widgets/hour to 93.17 widgets/hour

Although the percentages are correct, the conclusion that "nothing is lost" is wrong, as simple calculations show. A careful writer makes sure the percentages and numbers match the conclusions.

Extending or projecting data cannot always be done merely by multiplying or dividing the numbers. For example, a company with 100 employees is not necessarily twice as productive as a company with 50 employees. Other variables besides the number of employees affect the productivity of a company. When extending or projecting data, consider all of the variables involved.

Two types of graphs often unnecessarily distort data: line graphs and pictorial graphs. Following several standard practices eliminates most problems. Constructing an accurate line graph that does not manipulate or distort information requires attention to several aspects of the graph's construction:

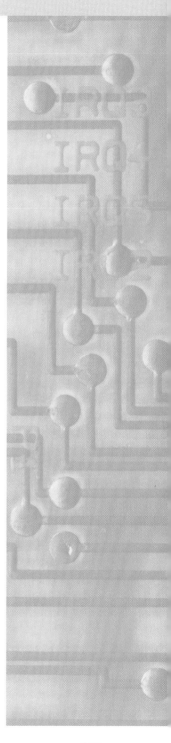

- Begin the quantitative scale (usually the *y*-axis) at zero. "Suppressing" the zero prevents the reader from seeing the complete proportion of the graph.

- Differentiate lines on a graph by varying the type of line used. (Note the caution about misusing color. If the graph is photocopied, the color isn't reproduced, and thus the differentiation is lost. Professional printing costs escalate rapidly when color is added to a document because each added color means an additional press run.)

- Do not change the proportion of the grid by distorting the relationship between the vertical and horizontal scales. (See Figure I.1 for specific examples.)

    Figures I.1A–F all plot the same data points (12, 16, 8, 10, 20, 18) during a 24-hour period. Figure I.1A accurately displays the data. Figures I.1B–F display various types of distortion that result from manipulating the *x*- or *y*-axis. Such manipulation can mistakenly lead the reader to believe that the changes displayed on the graph are more or less significant than they really are.

Even though a pictorial graph is designed for the impact it will make on general readers, it must still be accurate. Its accuracy depends on two primary factors:

- Avoid using fractions of isotopes (the symbols on a pictorial graph).

- Use isotypes of the same size for the same graph. Changing more than one dimension of pictorial representations—for instance, width as well as height—alters the meaning of the isotype. For example, Figure I.2 has a $\frac{1}{2}$-inch figure representing the 500 workers employed by company X in 1980, whereas the second isotype, a 1-inch figure, represents the 2,000 workers employed in 1990. The problem is that a 2-inch figure is more than four times the size of a $\frac{1}{2}$-inch figure, just as a 6-foot man is more than four times larger than a $1\text{-}\frac{1}{2}$-foot toddler.

To determine whether your visual presentation of information could mislead readers, ask yourself the following questions:

- Does the visual clarify, explain, or support the text?
- Will the reader know the source of the data? Is the source authoritative?
- Is the sample for collected data randomly selected?
- Are all of the necessary collected data included?
- Are irrelevant data omitted?
- Is the visual completely labeled: number, title, caption?
- Are variables and scales accurately labeled?
- Is the quality of the visual—its design and presentation—the highest possible?
- Is the visual easy to understand?
- Does the conclusion logically follow from the data?

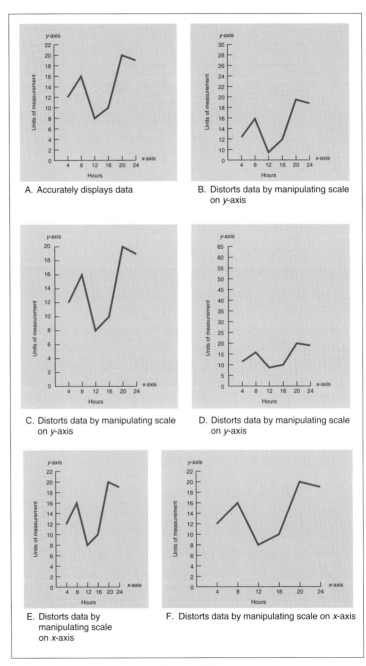

Figure I.1
Manipulation of Data on Graphs

322

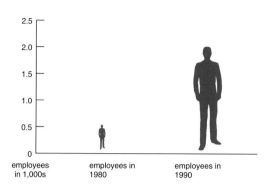

Figure I.2
Incorrect Use of Isotypes

- Does the text refer to and discuss the visual?
- Is the significance of the information in the visual clear?

If you can respond positively to these questions, you can be fairly sure your visual is appropriately used.

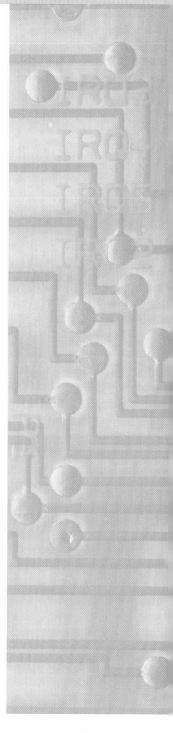

Understanding the Communicator's Strategies

10

Creating Definitions

CHAPTER 10 IN BRIEF

An effective definition explains an unfamiliar term using vocabulary and concepts within your readers' grasp. You can tailor a definition for different audiences by adjusting details, vocabulary, and types of examples and explanations.

The Need for Definitions

Inadequate definitions may cause problems for readers. When definitions are not used at all, readers may become confused by multiple meanings, complexity of meanings, technical jargon, and symbols.

Construction of Definitions

Definitions are a valuable writing tool because they answer questions readers have or could have before the readers verbalize them. Definitions generally fall into four categories:

- Informal definitions are particularly useful for technical communicators: synonym, antonym, stipulation, negative, analogy, and illustration.
- Formal definitions (*species = genus + differentia*) are valuable for identifying the broad category to which a term belongs as well as its distinctive characteristics.
- Operational definitions summarize or outline the primary steps involved in a function, usually in chronological order.
- Expanded definitions take many forms, with each form providing a different kind of detailed information: etymology, history, and examples.

Placement of Definitions

Writers of technical material have four basic choices for placing and incorporating definitions although the choices are not mutually exclusive:

1. glossary
2. information notes
3. incorporated information
4. appendix

Not only do the meanings of words change but new words come into our language. For example, in helping readers to understand the meaning of *hypertext*, a word that has recently entered our common academic and workplace vocabulary, you could use many forms of definition. The following brief explanation of hypertext incorporates many of the types of definition that you'll read about in this chapter.

Synonym

Operational definition

Negative definition (contrast; what it is not)

Historical note

Formal definition

Examples

Analogies

Stipulation

Hypertext also called HYPERLINKING, involves linking related pieces of information by electronic connections in order to allow a user easy access between them. Hypertext is a feature of some computer programs that allows the user of electronic media to select a word from text and receive additional information pertaining to that word, such as a definition or related references within the text. In the article "whale" in an electronic encyclopedia, for example, a hypertext link at the mention of the blue whale enables the reader to access the article on that species merely by "clicking" on the words "blue whale" with a mouse. The hypertext link is usually denoted by highlighting the relevant word or phrase in text with a different font or colour. Hypertext links can also connect text with pictures, sounds, or animated sequences.

Hypertext links between different parts of a document or between different documents create a structure that can accommodate direct, unmediated jumps to pieces of related information. The treelike structure of hyperlinked information contrasts with the linear structure of a print encyclopedia or dictionary, for example, whose contents can be physically accessed only by means of a static, linear sequence of entries in alphabetical order. Hypertext links are, in a sense, text cross-references that afford instant access to their target pieces of information. Such links are most effective when used on a large array of information that is organized into many smaller, related pieces and when the user requires only a small portion of information at any one time. Hypertext has been used most successfully by the interactive multimedia computer systems that came into commercial use in the early 1990s.[1]

When you prepare technical documents, you need to define critical terms, using vocabulary and concepts within the reader's grasp. You can tailor a

Chapter 10: Creating Definitions

definition for different audiences by adjusting details, vocabulary, and types of examples and explanations. This chapter discusses the need for definitions, examines the construction of various types of definitions, and presents specific places to use definitions in various documents.

The Need for Definitions

Inadequate or missing definitions cause a variety of problems. Readers may become confused by multiple meanings, complexity of meanings, technical jargon, and symbols.

Multiple Meanings

Some words have multiple meanings—different definitions for the same word—that might mislead readers. The definition of even simple terms sometimes changes entirely when the term is applied in a different field. For example, a biologist, geologist, and naval gunner would probably react differently to the everyday word *focus:*

- In biology—the localized area of disease or the major location of a general disease or infection[2]

- In calculus—one of the points that, with the corresponding directrix, defines a conic section[3]

- In earth science—the location of an earthquake's origin[4]

- In photography—the adjustment of a camera lens to a particular image to ensure a sharp and clear picture[5]

- In physics—the small area of a surface that light or sound waves converge upon[6]

- In naval gunnery—the rotation and elevation of a gun to accurately hit a target[7]

Indeed, definitions are frequently necessary even for common words if their meaning may be ambiguous or unclear. Examples include such words as *limit, base, traverse, positive, stock,* and *cover.*

What problems might occur if you introduce and define key terms near the beginning of a training manual and then throughout the manual substitute a variety of synonyms for these key terms to add some variety to your writing?

One of the largest groups of technical readers—nonexpert professionals—is often victimized by multiple meanings. Imagine a manager with a background in agronomy reading a memo from a graphic artist that includes the phrase "insufficient crop." The context may make the meaning clear, but only after a moment or two of hesitation. To eliminate problems caused by multiple meanings, assess your audience and decide whether any of your terms has a meaning that readers might think of before discerning the intended technical definition. If readers might be confused, include an unobtrusive parenthetical definition.

Part III: Understanding the Communicator's Strategies

Complexity of Meaning

Definitions can be simple or detailed, depending on the intended reader. The following two definitions of *volt* illustrate a range of complexity. The first definition comes from a general dictionary like those in public schools and homes; the second comes from a technical dictionary.

- volt—standard unit of electromotive force; after Alessandro Volta, an Italian electrician[8]

- volt—the derived SI unit of electric potential defined as the difference of potential between two points on a conducting wire carrying a constant current of one ampere when the power dissipated between these points is one watt. Also the unit of potential difference and electromotive force. 1 volt = 108 electromagnetic units. Symbol V (= W/A). Named after Alessandro Volta (1745–1827).[9]

This first definition would satisfy most general readers.

The second definition requires some technical knowledge because of the vocabulary (for example, ampere, watt, electromagnetic units), kind of details, and amount of information.

Your decision to include definitions in a document depends on your assessment of both the intended audience and the situation. Once you make the decision to define a term, you need to determine the amount of detail and the appropriate complexity of the definition. You need to decide what information is needed to understand the term in the context of the document.

Technical Jargon

Definitions are frequently needed when technical rather than everyday terms are used. You should assess whether readers are familiar with the terms; if so, no definitions are necessary. As the Snoopy cartoon shows, you can easily misjudge the level of technical information an audience can handle.[10]

The following paragraph contains technical vocabulary that the writer could be fairly certain the intended readers already know; the magazine is a trade publication for the plastics industry, and the intended readers are professionals knowledgeable about plastics. The specialized technical terms, italicized here, were not italicized in the original.

Ratios are indexed via a *digital thumbwheel*. *Reinforcement* is loaded into the emptied tank (by means of a *positive vertical auger conveyor*) and activated to achieve a uniform density; *polyol* is then added from bulk storage tanks and mixed with *reinforcement*. With initial production now under way, no requirement for *heat-tracing* of mixing tanks has been observed, and this is probably due to the effective but *essentially shearless mix action* of the *orbital auger principle* employed.[11]

Under what circumstances and in what types of documents might a writer take the time and effort to define terms for readers who have technical expertise?

Sometimes, however, technical terminology unfamiliar to the readers is necessary. For instance, a process may be introduced that requires a technical explanation employing new terms. In such cases, the writer should define the terms. The following excerpt, from a short article about safety precautions neces-

---

FIGURE 10.1 ■ Incorporated Definitions[12]

FINISH/FLATNESS CONCEPTS

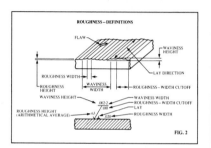

FIG. 2

SURFACE FINISH

The surfaces produced by machining and other methods of manufacturing are generally irregular and complex. Of practical importance are the geometric irregularities generated by the machining method. These are defined by height, width and direction, and other random characteristics not of a geometric nature.

The general term employed to define these surface irregularities is *surface texture,* the repetitive or random deviation from the nominal surface (Figure 1) that forms the pattern of the surface. It includes roughness, waviness, lay, and flaw.

- Roughness consists of fine irregularities in the surface texture produced by the machining process (Figure 2).
- Waviness is the widely spaced component of surface texture. It has wider spacing than roughness (Figure 2). It results from cutting tool runout and deflection.

FIG. 1

- Lay is the direction of the predominate surface pattern and it is determined by the machining process used in producing the surface (Figure 2).
- Flaws are irregularities that occur at scattered places, without a predetermined pattern. They include cracks, blow holes, checks, ridges, scratches, etc. (Figure 2).

Roughness is defined as the arithmetical average (AA) deviation of the surface roughness expressed in microinches from a mean line or roughness centerline (Figure 3). AA has been adopted internationally and is often referred to as CLA or c.l.a. (centerline, average). Many instruments still in use employ an average deviation from the roughness centerline, which is the root mean square average (RAMS) deviation of surface roughness, also expressed in microinches. RMS, while used frequently, has actually been obsolete since

---

sary to protect workers who use industrial robots, defines the unfamiliar term *dwell-time.*

Perhaps the most dangerous condition exists when people are unaware of a robot's *dwell-time.* (Dwell-time is the temporary period of inactivity between motions.)

Figure 10.1 illustrates longer definitions incorporated into an informational sales brochure for *diamond laps,* instruments used to make metal surfaces flat. The definitions are given credibility because they are taken from *Machining Data Handbook,* a standard machinists' reference book. The company includes

---

FIGURE 10.1 ■ Incorporated Definitions *(continued)*

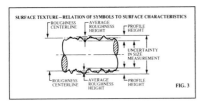

Type of Surface	Roughness Height (Microinches)
Honed, lapped, or polished	2
	4
	8
Ground with periphery of wheel	4
	8
	16
	32
	63
Ground with flat side of wheel	4
	8
	16
	32
	63
Shaped or turned	32
	63
	125
	250
	500
Side milled, end milled or profiled	63
	125
	250
	500
Milled with periphery of cutter	63
	125
	250
	500

about 1950. Roughness measuring instruments calibrated for RMS will read 11 percent higher, on a given surface, than those instruments calibrated for AA. The difference is usually much less than the point-to-point variations on any given machined surface.

The commercial ranges of surface roughness produced by various machining processes are shown in the table. A range of finishes can be obtained by more than one process; however, the selection of a surface finish involves more than merely designating a particular process. The ability of a process operation to produce a specific surface roughness or surface finish depends on many factors. In turning, for example, the surface roughness is geometrically related to the nose radius of the tool and the feed per revolution. For surface grinding, the final surface depends on the type of grinding wheel, the method of wheel dressing, the wheel speed, the table speed, cross feed, down feed, and the grinding fluid. A change in any one of these factors may have a significant effect on the finish of the final surface produced.

the definitions to educate its customers about the comparative benefits of its product.

Symbols

Technical language can be nonverbal, as in the symbolic language of mathematics, chemistry, and physics. For example, the equation explaining conservation of matter and energy ($E = mc^2$) is completely understandable to a physicist and, in fact, to most physics students who would know that E = energy, m = mass, and c = velocity of light, and could translate the symbolic statement into a verbal statement. Yet the symbols might be confusing even to highly educated people not trained in physics or a related field.

Simply defining the symbols is not sufficient to ensure that nonexperts comprehend the content of either the symbolic or verbal statement. Clearly, the definitions you construct need to do more than identify the unfamiliar terms. You must consider your readers' knowledge and adjust the definition to the appropriate level. These definitions illustrate two of the possibilities:

- $E = mc^2$ means that *energy* is equivalent to *mass* times the square of the constant velocity of light.

- $E = mc^2$ means mass-energy is conserved. The energy produced directly from the loss of mass during a nuclear fission or fusion reaction is equal to that mass loss times the square of the constant velocity of light.

You need to understand the concepts behind the symbols in order to provide an explanation appropriate for the readers' education and experience.

Construction of Definitions

Effective definitions answer questions readers have—or could have—*before* the readers verbalize them. Recognizing the nature and variety of possible questions helps you construct your definitions, recognize when a definition is appropriate, and determine the effectiveness of existing definitions when editing. After the initial "What is it?" you can ask yourself some common questions:

Physical Characteristics	■ What does it look like?
	■ What are its physical features?
Comparison	■ How is it classified?
	■ What is it similar to?
	■ How does it differ from similar objects (theories, procedures, situations)?

Parts/Whole	■ What are its distinguishing characteristics?
	■ What are its components (structural parts and functional parts)?
Function	■ What does it do?
	■ How does it work (function, operate)?
Operation	■ Who uses it?
	■ What are examples of its use?
	■ What is its value?

A variety of techniques aid you in answering these questions when constructing definitions, which generally fall into four categories: formal, informal, operational, and expanded.

Formal Definitions

Because dictionaries use formal definitions in many entries, people often believe that is the only way to define a term—identifying the broad category to which a term belongs as well as its distinctive characteristics. As a writer, you may be expected to construct clear and accurate formal definitions for new products and processes when no definition exists and for existing products and processes when current definitions are inadequate. The format of formal definitions is always the same.

Species	*equals*	*Genus*	*plus*	*Differentia*
term being defined		class or category to which the term (species) belongs		distinguishing characteristics that differentiate this species from other species in the same genus

A simple example illustrates the structure and demonstrates the application of guidelines that you should follow when constructing effective formal definitions.

Species	*equals*	*Genus*	*plus*	*Differentia*
A robin	is	a bird	with	a red breast and yellow beak.

You should make the genus as narrow as possible. A robin is a bird, but can the category be more specific? Yes. A robin is a type of thrush, so the formal definition can be revised.

Species	*equals*	*Genus*	*plus*	*Differentia*
A robin	is	a thrush	with	a red breast and yellow beak.

You should make the differentia as inclusive as possible to eliminate the possibility of mistakenly identifying one species with another. Do robins have additional characteristics that differentiate them from other thrushes? Again, yes. A robin has a distinctive black back and wing tips. A more complete formal definition for robin can be constructed:

Species	*equals*	*Genus*	*plus*	*Differentia*
A robin	is	a thrush	with	a red breast, yellow beak, and black back and wing tips.

The need to construct your own formal definitions arises when dictionary definitions are inadequate or nonexistent. The following example of a formal definition was constructed for a specific report. Formal definitions answer questions such as these: How is it classified? How does it differ from similar objects? What distinguishes this from related objects? What are the identifying characteristics? Notice that in this example, the genus is purposely kept narrow and the differentia are inclusive.

Species	*equals*	*Genus*	*plus*	*Differentia*
Hypertext	is	electronically linked pieces of information	with	connections that allow users easy access between them.

Informal Definitions

Informal definitions tend to be the type we insert in communication without realizing that we're defining a term. We integrate informal definitions casually and comfortably and frequently out of necessity into our normal writing and speech. The six types of informal definitions presented in Figure 10.2 are particularly useful for technical communicators: synonym, antonym, negative, stipulation, analogy, and illustration.

Three of these types of informal definitions—stimulation, analogy, and illustration—deserve additional discussion because they are so useful in technical documents and presentations. These informal definitions are especially good at providing readers with information to differentiate the term from similar ones. For example, the following definition begins by providing a synonym, presenting an additional definition, and then offering an example to help readers understand the concept of "domain name." But perhaps the most helpful part of the definition is the set of the stipulations of specific extensions for particular situations. The stipulations are what readers are likely to remember.

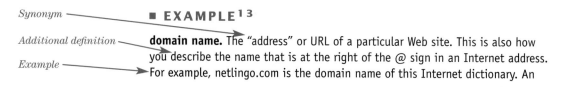

Synonym

Additional definition

Example

■ **EXAMPLE**[13]

domain name. The "address" or URL of a particular Web site. This is also how you describe the name that is at the right of the @ sign in an Internet address. For example, netlingo.com is the domain name of this Internet dictionary. An

FIGURE 10.2 ■ Types of Informal Definitions

Term	Definition	Examples	Comment
Synonym	A word that means essentially the same thing as the original term is a synonym.	microbe = germ helix = spiral Corrugated paperboard is the technical term for what is popularly known as cardboard. The bellows in a thermostatic element is made of a paper-thin, hardened (heat-treated) copper to make it strong, elastic, and corrosion resistant.	Synonyms usually answer such questions as "What is it similar to? What do I know that it resembles?"
Antonym	A word that is opposite in meaning to the original term is an antonym.	deviating - direct indigenous - foreign	Antonyms answer the obvious question, "What is the opposite?"
Negative	Explaining what something is *not* provides readers with useful information.	Machine rivets, usually made from metals such as aluminum or titanium, are unlike the rivets used in iron work in that they do not need to be heated before insertion.	Negatives respond to such questions as "What similar things should I not equate with this object? What similar things might mislead me?"
Stipulation	Stipulative definitions specify the meaning of a term for a particular application or situation.	When the term x [not necessarily mathematical, just any term] is used in this paper, it means . . .	Stipulations respond to such questions as "What are the limitations of use?"
Analogy	An analogy directly compares the unfamiliar to the familiar to identify major characteristics of the unfamiliar term.	A kumquat is a citrus fruit about the size and shape of a pecan. The skin is much thinner than that of a tangerine, and entirely edible. When fully ripe, the kumquat is a motley orange-green, much like an unprocessed orange.	An analogy responds to the same questions as a synonym: "What is this similar to? What related object has characteristics I'm already familiar with?"
Illustration	An actual drawing or diagram can illustrate a term.	[diagrams, drawings]	Visuals respond to the question, "What does it look like?"

organization called InterNIC registers domain names for a small fee and keeps people from registering the same name. Most recently, more domain names will be allowed due to new suffixes coming out:

Stipulations

.arts for arts and cultural entities
.firm for business
.info for information services
.non for individuals
.rec for recreation and entertainment
.store for merchants
.web for Web services

Analogies are a particularly powerful technique to explain unfamiliar concepts or objects, especially for audiences that lack expert knowledge of the topic because they link the familiar and the unfamiliar. The following example begins with a visual display of how the word *modem* was coined and then provides a formal definition. The analogy that follows, though, is probably what will help readers unfamiliar with what a modem does remember its primary function.

■ EXAMPLE[14]

modem (MOdulator, **DEM**odulator) ←——————— *Illustration using typography*

Formal definition → A device that you connect to your computer and to a phone line that allows the computer to talk to other computers through the phone system. Basically, modems do for computers what a telephone does for humans. Generally, there ——— *Analogy* are three types of modems: external, PC Card, and internal.

An actual drawing or diagram can illustrate a term. In many cases, a visual definition is far more efficient and accurate—and easier for the audience to understand—than a verbal definition. In Figure 10.3, annotated drawings accompany a definition so readers can readily understand the explanation of the terms *capillary attraction* and *capillary repulsion*.

FIGURE 10.3 ■ Illustration to Increase Rapid Comprehension[15]

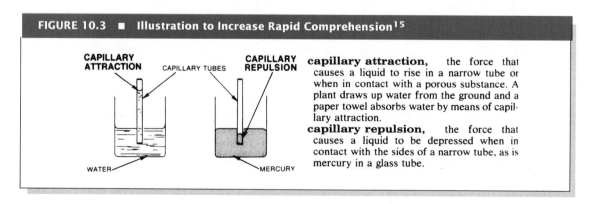

capillary attraction, the force that causes a liquid to rise in a narrow tube or when in contact with a porous substance. A plant draws up water from the ground and a paper towel absorbs water by means of capillary attraction.

capillary repulsion, the force that causes a liquid to be depressed when in contact with the sides of a narrow tube, as is mercury in a glass tube.

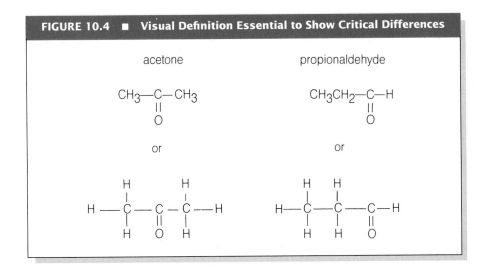

FIGURE 10.4 ■ Visual Definition Essential to Show Critical Differences

acetone

CH_3-C-CH_3
         $\|$
         O

or

propionaldehyde

CH_3CH_2-C-H
             $\|$
             O

or

Sometimes, visual definitions are not merely desirable but essential. For example, both acetone and propionaldehyde molecules contain three carbon atoms, six hydrogen atoms, and one oxygen atom. Although each molecule has the same number and kind of atoms, they are arranged differently, resulting in two compounds with different characteristics. The chemical formulas in Figure 10.4 state the differences verbally, but the addition of the diagrams brings those differences into focus.

Whatever the reason for using illustrations, the visuals respond to the question, "What does it look like?"

Operational Definitions

The term *operational definition* means different things to different technical professions. For example, for experimental researchers, operational definitions specify the activities (the operations) that researchers use to measure a variable. In contrast, for engineers, operational definitions specify the functions or workings of an object or process. In fact, although these two uses of operational definition are different, they both depend on a definition to identify the key steps that make up a process either to clarify the process or to measure it.

Situations that lend themselves to operational definitions require answers to questions such as these: How does it work? How can I measure or test it? How can I determine if its function is successful? What are the steps in its operation?

An operational definition summarizes or outlines the primary steps involved in the function, usually in chronological order. An effective operational definition can form the basis for a detailed process explanation (see Chapter 12). Whereas an operational definition usually outlines the major steps in a procedure, a process explanation provides specific details of each step, often describing

Chapter 10: Creating Definitions

the relationships between steps as well as offering theoretical background. The following example shows how useful an operational definition can be when defining a term.

■ **EXAMPLE**

Why is a formal definition a useful way to begin? Why is identifying the physical structure useful? Where does the actual operational definition start? What are the primary steps in this process? How could you illustrate this process?

A thermostatic element with a remote bulb is a temperature-sensitive instrument that converts a temperature change into a mechanical force. The instrument consists of three copper parts (bulb, capillary tube, and bellows) soldered together, with a liquid sealed inside. The bulb contains liquid that turns to a gas when heated. Since the gas requires more volume per unit weight than the liquid, the pressure in the bulb increases, forcing gas through the capillary tube and into the bellows. This increase in the volume of gas causes the bellows to expand. Just the opposite happens when the bulb is cooled. This loss of heat in the bulb causes some of the gas in the bulb to condense into its liquid state. Since the liquid has a much smaller volume per unit weight, the pressure drops, which pulls gas back from the bellows. A decrease in the volume of gas in the bellows causes the bellows to contract.[16]

Sometimes operational definitions move beyond specifying physical features or processes. The ethics sidebar on the next page discusses definitions of acceptable professional behavior—that is, codes of conduct. Virtually every profession has a code of conduct that you should read and consider. In the workplace, you'll also find operational codes of conduct in an organization's policy manuals, which define activities and behaviors—legal and ethical.

Expanded Definitions

Expanded definitions explain and clarify information. They also maintain readers' interest and make a document usable for a wider audience. In fact, many of the documents you prepare will contain expanded definitions. What are the most common forms of expanded definitions? Etymology. History. Examples. To determine which form is most appropriate to use in a particular situation, you need to analyze both the reader and the task.

- Presenting the *etymology* (the linguistic origin) of a term is appropriate for general readers who appreciate high-interest material.

- The *history* of a term is also appropriate for general readers; even readers with technical expertise may need recent historical information.

- Relevant *examples* have value for all audiences.

Etymology.   Etymologies anticipate questions such as these: How did this object get its name? How old is this word? Where did this word come from? What are the historical precedents of this word? Presenting the linguistic origin of a term sometimes gives insight into its current meaning(s). Etymological information is found in dictionaries or in research books specializing in etymolo-

Professional Codes of Conduct

Many professional organizations provide their members with ethical guidelines, sometimes referred to as codes of conduct—that is, definitions of what constitutes acceptable professional behavior. Codes of conduct have many purposes, including providing members of professional organizations with possible responses to ethical dilemmas. Codes of conduct also help build the credibility of the organization (and its profession) to the outside community.

A useful code of conduct for technical professionals is The Society for Technical Communication (STC) Code of Conduct, available at this Web address:

http://www.stc-va.org/code.html

This code separates conduct into six categories: legality, honesty, confidentiality, quality, fairness, and professionalism. The STC code, like almost all professional codes of conduct, is designed to influence the way technical communicators act both toward others within their profession and toward those outside the profession. For example, the STC code of conduct requires that its members "avoid conflicts of interest in fulfilling our professional responsibilities and activities." If a conflict of interest does arise, STC members are expected to "disclose it to those concerned and obtain their approval before proceeding."

An online listing of codes of conduct, sponsored by the Illinois Institute of Technology Center for the Study of Ethics in the Professions, is available at this Web address:

http://csep.iit.edu/codes/codes.html

Are you aware of a code of conduct in your field of study? Should you be? How much of a code of conduct is common sense? Codes of conduct do not always clearly indicate how or even if an organization will enforce the code. How should codes of conduct be enforced? Can they be? Should codes of conduct be viewed as rigid rules or as advice?

What would you include in an operational definition of professional conduct for a new organization?

---

gies. In a dictionary entry, this information is most frequently presented in abbreviated form inside square brackets. Every dictionary contains a page near the front of the volume explaining its abbreviations.

Etymologies are a useful part of a definition if knowledge of the original meaning increases your readers' understanding of the modern meaning and usage. Such explanations are particularly appropriate if you are writing for general audiences, although etymologies also add interest to definitions for more technical audiences. The following example demonstrates how etymologies can be used effectively as a technique for definition.

■ EXAMPLE

The word rivet comes from the Vulgar Latin word *ripare,* which means to make firm, or from the Middle French words *rivet* or *river,* which means to clinch.[17]

History.   Presenting historical background about the development and use of the subject puts the current meaning into perspective. History can cover several thousand years (if the subject is chemistry and begins at least as early as the magicians in the pharaohs' courts) or decades (if the subject is lexan, which was invented in the 1960s). The use of historical background anticipates questions such as these: What are the subject's origins? How long have such objects (concepts) existed? How has the history affected modern development? How were the original objects (concepts) different from modern ones? The following example shows how history can be used.

■ EXAMPLE

The process of making carbon black, though obviously not as sophisticated as the technology used today, has been known for a very long time. Records show that carbon black was made in China about 3000 B.C., and records indicate that China began exporting carbon black to Japan about A.D. 500. The original process used by the Chinese consisted of burning purified vegetable oil in small lamps with ceramic covers. The smoke would gather on the cover; thus, deposits of carbon black would be on the covers and would have to be scraped off.

Commercial production of carbon black has been taking place in the United States for over 100 years. In the earlier days, it was used primarily as a pigment (powdered coloring), but as technology improved and expanded, so did the uses of carbon black. Prior to 1870, the only commercially produced blacks were made by the lampblack process, which is a process similar to that of the Chinese.

In approximately 1912, researchers discovered that carbon black has good reinforcing properties in rubber. With this discovery, carbon black production went from a small volume pigment to a large volume industrial chemical used in rubber products, particularly tires.

Because of the increased need, new methods of production were introduced. Thermal black and acetylene black processes were tried and in some locations are still in use. In the early 1940s, the oil furnaces process was invented; today this process accounts for nearly all of the world's production of carbon black because it is the most efficient of all the processes.[18]

Examples. Using specific examples to illustrate the application of a term effectively expands a definition. Defining a concept with an example can be particularly effective, as in the following example taken from a sidebar, "Rayleigh-Taylor Instability and ICF," for an article, "Diagnostics for Inertial Confinement Fusion Research," in *Energy and Technology Review*, a publication of Lawrence Livermore National Laboratory.

■ EXAMPLE

We are all familiar with the Rayleigh-Taylor instability. Consider, for example, what happens if a layer of water is carefully laid on top of a lower-density liquid, such as alcohol, in a container. The heavier water will find its way through the lighter alcohol to the bottom of the container if the container is disturbed. The mechanism that initiates this fluid interchange is the Rayleigh-Taylor (RT) instability: fingers of the heavier fluid start poking into the lighter fluid, and bubbles of the lighter fluid rise through the heavier fluid until eventually the interchange is complete.[19]

Placement of Definitions

Writers of technical material have five basic choices for placing and incorporating definitions, although the choices are not mutually exclusive:

- glossary

- information notes and sidebars

- incorporated information

- appendixes

- online help

Where are definitions placed so they are most convenient for you as a reader? Where are you most likely to use them? Where are they least obtrusive?

Glossary

A glossary is a minidictionary located at the beginning or end of a technical document. A glossary at the beginning is particularly useful when readers are unfamiliar with the information and must know the terminology in order to comprehend the document. The disadvantage of an initial glossary is that without having read the document, readers may lack a frame of reference and may not be able to judge which terms to focus on. A glossary at the end of a document provides definitions and explanations readers can refer to as they need the information. When a terminal glossary is used, the terms should be marked in some way (boldface, italics, asterisks) as they occur in the body to let readers know that the definition is in the glossary.

■ EXAMPLE

The **seat gaskets** are first removed from the plug . . . .

_____

All boldface terms are defined in the Glossary beginning on page 11.

Individual entries can employ many of the forms of definition: formal, informal, operational, or expanded. Figure 10.5 shows an excerpt from a glossary in a *Dell Computer User's Guide.* Like most workplace documents that use definitions, this glossary does not restrict itself to one kind of definition; instead, it incorporates a variety of types of definitions to address the readers' anticipated needs.

Information Notes and Sidebars

Readers may need extended information that interrupts the flow of the text if it's included in the main discussion. Presenting this information as information

FIGURE 10.5 ■ Glossary Entries from a Computer User's Guide[20]

Cross references help readers locate information.

Frequently used abbreviations are explained.

The diagrams help readers understand the explanations in the glossary entries.

dBA
Abbreviation for adjusted decibel(s).

DC
Abbreviation for direct current.

device driver
A device driver allows the operating system or a program to interface correctly with a peripheral, such as a printer or network card. Some device drivers—such as network drivers—must be loaded from the **config.sys** file (with a **device=** statement) or as memory-resident programs (usually, from the **autoexec.bat** file). Others—such as video drivers—must load when you start the program for which they were designed.

diagnostics
See **diskette-based diagnostics** and **embedded diagnostics**.

DIN
Acronym for *Deutsche Industrie Normenausschuss.*

DIP
Acronym for dual in-line package. A circuit board, such as a system board or expansion card, may contain DIP switches for configuring the circuit board. DIP switches are always toggle switches, with an ON position and an OFF position.

DIP Switches

Frequently used acronyms are explained.

directory
Directories help keep related files organized on a disk in a hierarchical, "inverted tree" structure. Each disk has a "root" directory; for example, a C:\> prompt normally indicates that you are at the root directory of hard-disk drive C. Additional directories that branch off of the root directory are called *subdirectories*. Subdirectories may contain additional directories branching off of them.

Directory Hierarchy

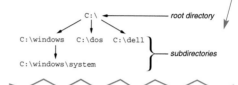

video adapter
The logical circuitry that provides—in combination with the monitor or display—your computer's video capabilities. A video adapter may support more or fewer features than a specific monitor offers. Typically, a video adapter comes with video drivers for displaying popular application programs and operating environments in a variety of video modes.

On most current Dell computers, a video adapter is integrated into the system board. Also available are many video adapter cards that plug into an expansion-card connector.

Video adapters can include memory separate from RAM on the system board. The amount of video memory, along with the adapter's video drivers, may affect the number of colors that can be simultaneously displayed. Video adapters can also include their own coprocessor chip for faster graphics rendering.

The importance of terms is explained.

The formal definition here is elaborated to address questions that users might have.

notes or sidebars gives readers the option of reading the additional information if they need it.

Information notes can be placed on the bottom of a page or collected at the end of a document along with source or reference notes. Information notes may simply define a term or concept. Such notes also give writers the opportunity to provide examples, to cite related studies, to explain tangential concepts, to present possible explanations, and so on. Technical reports for decision making usually restrict themselves to information notes that offer brief definitions or explanations since readers usually have little time. Technical documents for research or academic purposes may include more detailed information notes for readers who might want to investigate an idea in greater depth.

Sidebars usually provide more elaborated information than bottom-of-page or end-of-document notes. The sidebar and accompanying illustration in Figure 10.6 are taken from an article about balloon angioplasty in the *Harvard Health Letter*. This newsletter, published by the Harvard Medical School, says its overall goal is

---

FIGURE 10.6 ■ Illustrated Sidebar from a Health Newsletter[21]

WHAT TYPE OF BLOCKAGE?

Physicians use *coronary angiography* to determine the location, size, shape, and to some degree the composition of atherosclerotic lesions that narrow the coronary arteries. This information helps predict who is a good candidate for balloon angioplasty, who is likely to have a better result with a more specialized procedure, and who should go straight to coronary artery bypass graft surgery.

A popular classification system devised by the American College of Cardiology and the American Heart Association divides blockages into three categories. (*See illustration.*)

Type A: These are simple lesions in easily accessible locations that are concentric, less than 10 mm long, and contain little or no calcium and no clots. They are ideal for treatment with balloon angioplasty.

Type B: These somewhat complex, irregular narrowings are 10–20 mm long, with moderate-to-heavy calcification and some *thrombus* (clot), and are situated in a bend or vascular junction. Balloon angioplasty is slightly less likely to restore blood flow and slightly more likely to have complications.

Type C: This category includes heavily calcified lesions, total blockages more than three months old, and narrowings located in a sharp turn or in a deteriorated bypass graft. The success rate for balloon dilation is significantly lower so bypass surgery, stenting, or atherectomy may be a better choice.

Balloon angioplasty is most successful for patients who are male, less than 70 years old, with normal left ventricular function (pumping ability), who have no more than two blocked arteries and no history of diabetes, heart attack, or bypass surgery.

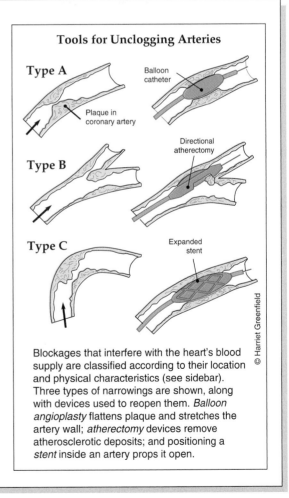

Blockages that interfere with the heart's blood supply are classified according to their location and physical characteristics (see sidebar). Three types of narrowings are shown, along with devices used to reopen them. *Balloon angioplasty* flattens plaque and stretches the artery wall; *atherectomy* devices remove atherosclerotic deposits; and positioning a *stent* inside an artery props it open.

---

to "interpret medical information for the general reader in a timely and accurate fashion." The sidebar defines the categories of blockages that occur in arteries. The accompanying illustration helps readers visualize both the blockages and the tools surgeons use to unclog arteries.

Incorporated Information

Frequently, definitions can be incorporated into sentences without the distraction of glossary entries or information notes. The following examples illustrate several ways to punctuate definitions that you incorporate into sentences.

■ EXAMPLES	COMMENT
Computers carry out all computations using binary (base 2) arithmetic, which involves rapidly manipulating strings of bits according to fixed rules.	Incorporated information can be separated by parentheses.
Because of the nature of computer storage procedures, a byte is the amount of storage space needed to represent a character (i.e., a numeral, letter, symbol, or blank).	
It's usual at the end of each day to create backup files—duplicates of the updated records—as a safeguard against loss or damage of magnetic disks. . . .	A definition can be separated by an *-em dash* (which looks like this—) as opposed to two hyphens (which look like this - -).
This basic procedure—calling up programs and files by following a "menu" sequence, and entering data or commands—is commonly used in business tasks.	
Two basic kinds of hard disks are available: packs, which consist of several platters in a removable case, and cartridges, which usually contain one platter.	Incorporated definitions can be separated by commas.
A modem, a device that couples a computer or terminal to a telephone line, is used for long-distance data transmission.	

Appendixes

Lengthy documents intended for readers with widely varying backgrounds often have difficulty appealing to the entire range of readers. For example, nonexperts can be confused if the document jumps into the subject without sufficient explanation. Technical experts can be bored or even offended if the documents include too much elementary material. One way to resolve this dilemma is to include appendixes that provide both operational and expanded definitions of critical concepts. Readers already familiar with the material glance at the reference to the appendix in the text and continue reading, virtually uninterrupted. Readers who need to review the background material appreciate the detailed, illustrated definitions and discussions.

Online Help

More and more software companies provide users with critical information electronically via online help systems rather than in print manuals. Online help systems are designed to provide users with information immediately—and in several different formats. For example, the word processing program used to prepare the manuscript for this textbook has a "balloon help" option; when activated, it provides the user with a callout that includes brief definitions and explanations of many features and functions on the computer desktop.

In addition to the balloons, this same software has a number of other online help features, typical of most software:

- an alphabetic index of all help topics available to users of this software

- a list of frequently used topics that often saves time

- on onscreen box that provides hints and wizards (shortcuts to common practices)

- a searchable database to answer questions

Virtually all of these online help options include various kinds of definitions to assist users who are confused or stuck.

End-of-Chapter
Recommendations for Technical Communicators

1. Tailor definitions for different audiences by adjusting technical details, technical vocabulary, and types of examples and explanations.

2. Recognize that some words have multiple meanings that might mislead readers and, thus, need definitions.

3. Determine the amount of detail and appropriate complexity of the definition by considering what information is needed to understand the term in the context of the document.

4. Use undefined jargon and symbols only when you are sure that your readers will understand them. Otherwise, define jargon and symbols or, better yet, minimize their use with nonexperts.

5. To construct effective definitions, ask yourself questions that you imagine readers asking: What is it? What is it similar to? What does it look like? What are its features? How is it classified? What does it do? How does it work (function, operate)? What are examples of its use?

6. Learn to incorporate a variety of *informal definitions*—synonym, antonym, stipulation, negative, analogy, and illustration—into your writing.

7. Learn to construct and use the rigorous structure of *formal definitions:*

    species = genus + differentia.

8. Learn to construct and use *operational definitions* for summarizing or outlining the primary steps involved in a function.

9. Learn to construct and use various kinds of *expanded definitions:* etymology, history, and examples.

10. Incorporate definitions in your texts in any of these ways:
    - glossary
    - information notes and sidebars
    - incorporated information
    - appendixes
    - online help

Practicum

Learning about Big Creek Forestry

Big Creek Forestry is a small consulting firm located outside of Marquette in Michigan's Upper Peninsula. The business is a sole proprietorship, owned and operated by Christopher D. Burnett. His business works either independently or in subcontracting arrangements with other qualified consulting foresters. Of the two current subcontractors, one is a Ph.D. candidate in forestry at Michigan Technological University, the other has an M.S. in forestry and is employed full-time in the computer industry. Both plan to work extensively with the business when their current commitments are completed.

The primary mission of the business is to help nonindustrial, private, forest (NIPF) landowners conduct timber harvests that are environmentally, socially, and economically sustainable. A distinctive feature of the consulting forestry business is that it involves clients (i.e., landowners) as well as customers (i.e., loggers). In short, Chris Burnett's job is to assess clients' land ownership objectives, determine the capability of the land to meet those objectives, design timber harvests that will further his clients' objectives, and negotiate timber sale contracts with reputable loggers.

Although Big Creek Forestry's clientele is diverse, including resident and absentee landowners, most of its clients own forested land primarily for recreational purposes. Nevertheless, real estate purchase prices, property taxes, and other land ownership costs lead many such landowners to consider harvesting timber so the land will "pay for itself." From the landowner's viewpoint, the main problem is usually fear of what the land will look like after logging and fear that they will not receive a fair price for the harvested wood.

The most interesting recent development in the business is that Big Creek Forestry is about to become the first SmartWood Certified Resource Manager in Michigan (see *www.smartwood.org* and *www.fscoax.org* and associated links for background on the certified wood movement). In brief, this means that wood harvested under the supervision of Big Creek Forestry can be labeled in the marketplace as originating from a sustainably managed forest, somewhat analogous to the labeling of organic food. In many parts of the world, consumers are demanding that the wood used to make the products they buy have such "green labeling," and they are willing to pay higher prices for such products. Ultimately, price premiums for environmentally friendly wood products should "trickle down" to forest landowners and thereby encourage good forestry practices.

One of the biggest challenges currently facing the business is obtaining access through adjacent properties for bringing in logging equipment and for hauling out harvested wood. Chris hopes that becoming certified will help assure adjacent landowners that they and their land will be treated with respect.

Introducing SmartWood

As sole proprietor, Chris' job of running Big Creek Forestry includes everything that must be done to run a small business (e.g., recruiting work, accounting, emptying the waste basket) in addition to the technical work for clients. The majority of his technical work includes writing forest management plans, locating property boundaries, marking the trees to be cut, and supervising logging. The assignment below deals with Big Creek Forestry's move into the realm of certified wood. The task combines educating forest landowners about the concept of certified wood and recruiting additional work for the business.

Becoming a SmartWood Certified Resource Manager involves several steps: *screening* (telephone interview), *scoping* (half-day office and field visit by project coordinator), *field assessment* (two-day office and field visit by interdisciplinary team), *assessment findings and peer review, certification decision,* and *annual field audits.* Big Creek Forestry has successfully completed the first three steps and expects to be certified in the near future. Once the business is certified, individual properties may then become part of the Big Creek Forestry's Smart-Wood Group by meeting two main criteria. First, the property must have a ten-year forest management plan that meets the criteria of the Forest Stewardship Council (FSC, the international agency that certifies SmartWood and other certifiers). Second, the property owner(s) must sign a Long-Term Forest Management Agreement stating that they (1) understand the certified wood concept, (2) will manage the land in question according to the approved plan, (3) intend to continue such management over the long term (50–100 years), and (4) will promptly notify Big Creek Forestry if deviations from the plan are made.

Reviewing a Mission Statement

The following document is a draft of the Big Creek Forestry Mission Statement being developed as part of the certification process and destined for the business's Web site. It is essential that the gist of this statement be communicated to prospective SmartWood Group participants to help convince environmentally oriented landowners that there is a type of forestry that would further their interests.

Assignment

Until recently, certified forestry was limited to operations (primarily forest industries) that own large tracts of land. This approach excluded the many NIPF landowners who, as a group, control the majority of the land in many

MISSION STATEMENT
BIG CREEK FORESTRY

Worldview—The mission of Big Creek Forestry is to help bring the management of nonindustrial, private forests (NIPF's) into harmony with native ecosystems. We believe the relationship between humans and the rest of nature should be a reciprocal, mutually beneficial one. Given our species' ecological role as consumers, humans need to harvest timber and other woodland products in order to survive and prosper. Conversely, humans have a critical, creative role to play in the survival of our fellow organisms and the ecological health of the Earth. To achieve these goals, we must balance issues of economic productivity, ecological health, and societal values.

Economic Productivity—Market factors that are largely outside the control of private woodland owners often have an over-riding influence on the nature of timber harvesting on private lands. Big Creek Forestry's economic mission is to strengthen the position of NIPF owners in relation to the rest of forest industry so that management decisions can be based more on landowner interests and ecosystem health than on industrial demand for raw material.

Ecological Health—The ecosystems that support us are inconceivably complex, constantly evolving, and vulnerable to certain disturbances. Although land management activities are generally thought of in terms of how they affect ecosystem structure (e.g., size and spacing of trees), understanding how our actions affect underlying ecological processes is more important in the long run. Thus, Big Creek Forestry's ecological mission is to promote "naturalistic" management practices that minimize disturbance of locally evolved nutrient cycles, hydrological regimes, organism movement patterns, and other ecological processes. Due to our limited understanding of ecosystem dynamics (including human factors), all management actions should be conceived of as working hypotheses or informal experiments, rather than as "the scientifically correct way."

Societal Values—Because timber is a long-lived, slow-growing crop that has considerable market value before it reaches biological or economic maturity, great restraint is required to prevent short-term interests from overriding greater long-term values. And despite the fact that non-timber values can be difficult to quantify, these other values (e.g., water supply, natural beauty, recreation) often outweigh timber values. Furthermore, the value of a woodland is not just a matter of what is on that piece of land. For example, the wildlife and recreational value of a woodland depends, in large part, on that woodland's context in the larger landscape. Similarly, the economic value of the timber on a property can be greatly influenced by its position in the human community. On the downside, access disputes between neighbors can greatly decrease timber values. On the upside, cooperation among landowners (e.g., access routes, marketing pools) can greatly increase timber values. Thus, Big Creek Forestry's social mission is to encourage landowners to make land management decisions in light of long-term (i.e., multigenerational) and community (i.e., landscape-level) values.

regions. Thus, the basic problem is to develop a collective land base for Big Creek Forestry's SmartWood Group. Without long-term commitments from landowners, certified wood cannot be produced. You have two tasks: to write a letter and to create a landowner agreement form.

1. **Write a letter to landowners.** Your first task is to write a letter to NIPF landowners introducing the concept of certified wood and inviting them to become part of Big Creek Forestry's SmartWood Group. Such an introductory letter cannot be expected to answer all the questions that will arise, but it should make landowners familiar with the concept of certified wood, explain the advantages of participation (economic and ethical), and encourage them to respond to the invitation.

   While the letter should conform to workplace conventions as far as format, the content should be informative, the tone friendly, and the language should be accessible because, for most recipients, the letter will be their first exposure to the concept of certified wood. A good first impression is important from multiple viewpoints. From an *environmental viewpoint*, landowners should become producers of certified wood because certified forestry operations utilize state-of-the-art practices in terms of protecting soil, water, and wildlife. From a *business viewpoint*, Big Creek Forestry has already spent a substantial amount of time and money to become certified, and annual audit costs will be incurred. To recoup these costs, more consulting contracts are needed, especially with clients who have strong environmental ethics. And from a *community viewpoint*, certified forestry operations are more likely than conventional operations to support local economies (social criteria are part of the certification process).

   The letter should not exceed two pages in length. It should present the concept of certified wood briefly and clearly, without technical jargon. The tone should be upbeat, but not hyper, about this new opportunity for landowners. The visual presentation should be professional. The letter should close with a friendly offer of further information about becoming a certified wood producer or about any other forestry issues.

2. **Create the Landowner Agreement form.** Once NIPF landowners agree to participate in Big Creek Forestry's SmartWood Group, they will need to sign a Long-Term Forest Management Agreement form. Your second task is to design this form. This form must provide a place for the clients to indicate that they (a) understand the concept of certified wood, (b) will manage the specified land according to the approved plan, (c) intend to continue such management over the long term (at least 50–100 years), and (d) will promptly notify Big Creek Forestry if they deviate from the plan in any way.

   The form is not a legal document, but it should reflect the current philosophy in creating legal documents by using plain language—that is, the form should be easy to understand rather than riddled with difficult or obscure legalese.

The form should not exceed one page in length. When the form is printed, it will need to be on NCR (no carbon required) paper with three copies— one for the client, one for Big Creek Forestry, and one for SmartWood.

Christopher D. Burnett is the owner (sole proprietor) of Big Creek Forestry in Marquette, Michigan. Chris has a B.S in forestry (Syracuse) and a Ph.D. in ecology (Boston University). His major job responsibilities are to recruit work, keep records, write reports, conduct field work, and participate in the continuing education of his clients. He believes that foresters, ecologists, and other professionals in the management of natural resources need to be effective, skillful writers and speakers as they address important environmental improvement/protection issues.

Individual and Collaborative Assignments

1. **Identify types of definitions.** Read the following examples and identify each type of definition. Some of the examples have more than one type of definition embedded. Discuss the appropriateness of each definition for the audiences.

(a) From a teacher's manual: The word for chemistry comes from the Middle East; long ago the sacred name for Egypt was *Chemia*, which means black and probably referred to the fertile black soil of the Nile valley. In those ancient times almost any kind of change was mysterious, such as the change of wood to ash when it burns, or the transformation of sand into glass. Men who understood how to make some things change were considered to be magicians (at least we might call them that today). From their mysterious abilities to cause changes, the word for the study of change was derived.[22]

(b) From a dictionary: chemistry—The study of the composition of substances and of the changes of composition which they undergo. The main branches of the subject are inorganic chemistry, organic chemistry, and physical chemistry.[23]

(c) From a Web site defining network terms: Hypertext—A system of writing and displaying text that enables the text to be linked in multiple ways, to be available at several levels of detail, and to contain links to related documents. The term was coined by Ted Nelson to refer to a nonlinear system of information browsing and retrieval that contains associative links to other related documents.[24]

(d) From a technical report: The reduction in speed of the steam turbine engine is necessary to achieve efficiency. The efficient speed for operating the turbine is higher than the speed of the shaft. The transmission of your automobile functions similarly by converting a high engine speed to a lower wheel speed.

(e) From an international journal, *Progress in Lipid Research*, in an article about lipid barriers in biological systems: The current model views the mammalian stratum corneum as a two-component system ("bricks and mortar") consisting of protein-rich cells (bricks) embedded in a lipid matrix (mortar), with these intercellular lipids being primarily responsible for the integumental water barrier.[25]

(f) From a Web site defining network terms: Search engine—A program that acts like a library card catalog for the Internet. Search engines attempt to help a user isolate desired information or resources by searching for keywords that the user specifies. The method for finding this information is usually done by maintaining an index of Web resources that can be queried for the keywords or concepts entered by the user. The index can be built from specific resource lists or created by Web wanderers, robots, spiders, crawlers, and worms. From the Net surfer point of view, search engines can be quite tiresome and not very fruitful if you don't know how to use them correctly. Different engines are good for different kinds of searches. It's a good idea before using a search engine to read the help section of the engine's Web site to see what the best way is to optimize your results.[26]

2. **Determine three levels of definitions for the same term.** Work with a classmate who is in the same discipline or field (if possible) and identify a concept or term that you would like to research. Check dictionaries, texts, encyclopedias, handbooks, professional journals in the reference and periodical section of your library, and various Web sites. Make copies of the definitions you select, and document your sources, using the appropriate formats from the Usage Handbook. Identify the major distinctions among the various definitions, and evaluate the effectiveness of each definition for the intended audience. Prepare a brief oral report for your classmates.

3. **Incorporate definitions into a document.** Imagine that your audience, managers of small businesses, needs some elementary information about computers. You are revising a newsletter article dealing with computer basics that will contain a complete glossary at the end of the article, but you believe that brief definitions should be incorporated into the article itself so the readers don't have to regularly check the glossary while they're reading. Rewrite this basic paragraph, incorporating the following definitions (or parts thereof) as you believe is appropriate for the audience.

Every computer system has two types of components, hardware and software. Most visible is the hardware, typically a central processing unit (CPU) and peripheral equipment. Less visible, but usually even more critical is the software. Too often computer buyers and sellers focus on stylish, competent-looking hardware, rather than on the software that determines what a system can or can't do for a particular business. Another often overlooked expense is the backup storage equipment that generally is needed in addition to basic system components.

- *Backup storage.* Copies of data files, used as a safeguard against damage or loss.
- *Computer system.* A computer plus software plus one or more pieces of peripheral equipment.
- *CPU (central processing unit).* The part of a computer that performs calculations and processes data according to the instructions specified by the software. CPU is sometimes used interchangeably with computer. See also microcomputer.
- *Hardware.* The computer itself or any item of peripheral equipment.
- *Peripheral equipment.* Input-output and data storage devices: printers, keyboards, CRTs, remote terminals, and tape and disk drives.
- *Software.* The programs, or instructions, that tell the computer how to respond to specific user commands.[27]

4. **Identify audiences for a document that uses definitions.**
   (a) Carefully read the following paper, "The Fugue."

The Fugue[28]

A fugue is a polyphonic form of music that is most easily recognized by several reappearances of a short melodic theme. Fugues are usually written in from two- to five-part harmonies. Each part blends with the other parts to form harmony, but it is also a melodic line as well. This characteristic of a fugue makes it unique. Writing a short melody with simple harmony is easy; however, if the supporting parts do not form a melody very similar to the melodic theme first stated in the fugue, then the composition cannot be called a fugue.

A fugue is similar to a canon or a round, but a canon usually has only two parts that are always exactly alike. One part begins the canon and the second part enters later, duplicating the first. An example of a canon is shown in Figure 1.

Figure 1 *Canon*

(By the way, can you name that tune?)

The fugue, however, always has the second part entering in a different key. This new key is called the dominant key and is five tones higher than the original key, the tonic key. (See Figure 2.)

Figure 2 *Tonic-Dominant Relationship*

There are, then, two important characteristics of a fugue:

1. The melodics are imitative.
2. The imitation occurs in related keys.

The fugue is commonly divided into three distinct sections: exposition, development, and stretto.

The exposition consists of the statement of the melodic theme and its answer in the dominant key. These statements and answers may occur several times, depending upon the number of parts written into the composition. Most frequently, fugues are written in four parts and require two statements and two answers.

The development is the most exciting and improvisational part of the fugue. Indeed, the fugue is so-named because of the action within the development. Fugue is derived from the Latin *fugere,* meaning to flee or run away. The development runs away from the straightforward statements and answers of the exposition and adds color and variety to the composition. The development uses the following techniques to achieve interest:

1. Countersubject—playing a new theme with the original theme
2. Augmentation—playing the theme more slowly
3. Diminution—playing the theme more quickly
4. Inversion—playing the theme upside down

The stretto section of the fugue is a restatement of the original theme by all the parts. They often overlap unexpectedly and reach a climax to provide a dramatic end to the fugue.

The fugue was a popular form of composition during the Baroque era. Most of the major composers have written fugues or parts of fugues in larger compositions. However, Bach remains the most famous and prolific writer of fugues.

    (b) Marginally annotate to identify all the types of definition the writer uses.

    (c) Identify probable audiences for this paper.

5. Identify an audience, context, and purpose.

    (a) Carefully study the diagram, titled "It Does a Body Bad," that defines immediate and long-term effects of stress.

    (b) Identify audiences for whom this presentation would be appropriate and effective; what would be possible context(s) and purpose(s)? Then identify inappropriate or ineffective contexts, purposes, and audiences.

    (c) Describe (and, if appropriate, do thumbnail sketches of) other ways to define the psychological effects of stress.

IT DOES A BODY BAD

■ **These are some** immediate and long-term effects of stress. If long-term symptoms persist for more than a few weeks and interfere with your ability to work or perform normal daily activities, see a physician:

Brain

Instant: Hypothalamus and pituitary glands, which stimulate other organs and release stress hormones (primarily adrenaline, cortisol and norepinephreine), kick in.
Long-term: Mental and emotional problems, including insomnia, depression, anxiety, personality changes, irritability, sleeping problems, exhaustion.

Face/Head

Instant: Face "flushes" as blood flow increases.
Long-term: Muscles in the head, neck, jaw can tighten, causing chronic headache, neck ache, jaw pain, tics.

Lungs/Breathing

Instant: Lungs speed up to take in more air and deliver more oxygen to muscles, producing a breathless feeling.
Long-term: Stress can worsen chronic lung problems, such as asthma or emphysema.

Muscles

Instant: Muscles become more efficient and stronger, sometimes producing seemingly superhuman strength, speed, reaction.
Long-term: Muscle aches, soreness, pain, tension, upper and lower back, shoulder, neck problems.

Kidneys

Instant: A rush of anti-diuretic hormone (adh), decreased blood supply and tightened muscles decrease urine output and temporarily shut down the kidneys. Defecation and urination are prevented.
Long-term: Diarrhea or uncontrolled urination may occur as muscles relax, blood supply increases and hormones level out.

Senses

Instant: Pupils dilate. Smell is heightened.

Salivary glands

Instant: Salivary glands stop secreting saliva, making the mouth feel dry.
Long-term: Mouth ulcers, sores.

Heart

Instant: Heart pumps more blood to muscles, heart rate increases, producing a pounding, fluttering feeling in the chest. Blood pressure increases.
Long-term: Heart disease, heart attack, and high blood pressure.

Liver

Instant: Releases more sugar into the blood to provide muscles with instant energy. May also release more cholesterol into the blood.

Stomach/Digestive system

Instant: Stomach secretes more acid, producing a feeling of "butterflies" or gurgling. Digestion shuts down temporarily.
Long-term: Ulcers, colitis, irritable bowel syndrome, gastritis, heartburn.

Skin

Instant: Skin turns pale as blood is drawn toward internal organs. Palms and feet sweat to cool the body.
Long-term: Outbreaks of rashes or other skin problems, including eczema, psoriasis, hives.

Blood

Instant: Blood clotting mechanisms improve with stress.

SOURCES : *The Complete Manual of Fitness and Well Being* (Reader's Digest; 1984); Dr. Howard Schertzinger Jr., of Queen City Sports Medicine Rehabilitation; The American Institute of Stress, Yonkers, N.Y.

GANNETT NEWS SERVICE

6. **Write a paper incorporating definitions.**
   (a) Work with a classmate who is in the same discipline or field (if possible) and identify a concept or term that you would like to define.
   (b) Write a multiparagraph paper incorporating various forms of definitions for that single term. Your paper should resemble the samples in Assignments #3 and #4. Make sure to include visuals if they are appropriate for illustrating or clarifying the term. Document any sources used in preparing the paper.

7. **Analyze definitions.** Visit the following Web site <www.search.eb.com>
   (a) Choose a term from your discipline and search for it in the *Encyclopedia Britannica* and *Merriam-Webster's Collegiate Dictionary.*
   (b) Identify additional Web sites that provide useful definitions of your term.
   (c) Create a rubric that lists the criteria for analyzing the effectiveness of each definition; use your rubric to identify the different purposes and audiences to assess each definition.

Intertext

Sexual Harassment Training: Truth and Consequences[30]

Go to a sexual harassment training program. Whether the facilitator is a lawyer, an HR [human resources] professional, or a diversity consultant, you'll probably hear that harassment is in the eyes of "the reasonable woman." The reasonable woman is a staple of harassment programs, but it's not the law. That is just one of several common mistakes made by sexual harassment trainers.

Going by the reasonable woman standard. The "reasonable woman standard" was established by the Ninth Circuit Court of Appeals, and the concept quickly spread. In 1993, when the U.S. Supreme Court ruled on *Harris v. Forklift Systems,* the case had been previously decided by the lower courts using the reasonable woman standard. But the Supreme Court decided the case based on a reasonable person. Since then, all of the circuit courts have returned to the reasonable person standard. That shift helps to explain why the definition of what constitutes harassment has narrowed in recent years. Since Harris, the federal courts of appeals have defined sexual harassment in 62 cases.

In virtually every case in which harassment was found, there was a sexual battery. In the cases in which there was no touching, harassment was found only when the plaintiff was repeatedly slandered, frequently publicly humiliated,

constantly subjected to sexist slurs, or propositioned on an almost daily basis.

Here are some examples of behavior that was held not to be harassment:

- A man frequently called a woman "bitch."
- A woman was told she had been voted the "sleekest ass" in the office.
- A manager pantomimed masturbation to his secretary.
- A woman was told to "bring your buns over here."

The Court of Appeals ruled that those incidents were not harassment because they were not "severe and pervasive" and therefore did not create a hostile environment under the reasonable person standard. In fact, a number of appellate courts are now using the "prime-time television standard." If you can hear it on TV, it's not harassment. Talk about setting a low standard!

Despite the clear message from the courts, most trainers say it is harassment to tell jokes, use endearments, or give compliments. That is not true. Jokes and endearments aren't even discussed in actual cases because they are trivial compared to the severe harassment many women endure.

Courts have found that women have been raped on the job, been forced to masturbate their supervisors, and seen men expose themselves. That is sexual harassment. It is behavior so offensive that any reasonable person, male or female, would agree that it should be illegal.

Stating the trainer's values as "the law." One trainer I know is extremely offended by swearing in the workplace. Most of his life he worked for a school, and people there did not swear. When he started working for a large company, he was embarrassed by the language that his co-workers used. When he taught harassment programs, he emphasized that swearing was harassment.

Swearing may be personally offensive to many people, but no court of appeals since the *Harris* case has held that it is harassment. For example, in *Carr v. Allison Turbine,* the Seventh Circuit ruled in a case in which an employee was clocked using the F word 50 to 60 times in a 10-minute period. The court said the purpose of the law is not to clean up language in the workplace but to prohibit discrimination. Because the employee cursed whether or not women were present, his cursing wasn't discriminatory and, therefore, not illegal.

That same logic was adopted by the U.S. Supreme Court in 1998 in *Oncale v. Sundowner,* a case that involved male-on-male harassment. The Court said behavior that meets the "both sexes test" is not harassment. If men and women are treated the same in similar contexts, it's not illegal sexual harassment because the behavior isn't discriminatory. Thus, dirty jokes can't be sexual harassment because men (and women) tell them to men and women.

It is possible that much of the behavior commonly thought to be harassment—displaying nude pictures, bragging about sexual prowess, asking about someone's sex life—may be determined by future courts in some contexts to meet the both-sexes test and, therefore, to be legal. Does that mean that employers must allow such behavior? Of course not. Companies can set their own standards as high as they want, as long as they communicate those standards to everyone.

The trainer who was offended by swearing worked in a company that didn't prohibit swearing, nor would it ever adopt such a policy. In that kind of environment, it's certainly appropriate for a trainer or worker to state his or her personal discomfort with swearing, to ask others to be considerate, and for others to moderate their swearing in response. But in such environments, for the trainer to define his or her personal values as harassment is not consistent with corporate policy or a correct statement of the law.

It is important for trainers to stay current with the law and to distinguish clearly between behavior prohibited by law, behavior prohibited by employer policy, and behavior the trainer finds personally offensive.

Making assumptions about women (and men). One of the insidious side effects of the reasonable woman standard was that it encouraged trainers to make assumptions about women and men. The reasonable woman standard is based on the assumption that men and women have different life experiences and will interpret behavior differently. Obviously, we all have different life experiences, and we all interpret behavior differently. But in 17 years of conducting sexual harassment training, one thing I've learned is that how people perceive sexual behavior at work is entirely unpredictable based on gender.

Once, I facilitated a sexual harassment prevention program for a utility company. Three employees—a 50-ish white woman, a 30-something white man, and a black man in his 20s—were completing an exercise. I wandered by and glanced over their shoulders. In answer to one of the questions, they had noted that one of them liked to hear ethnic jokes at work, one liked to hear dirty jokes, and one liked both dirty and ethnic jokes.

Presumably, the so-called reasonable woman doesn't like dirty jokes, so that must mean that the woman in the group liked ethnic jokes. Other assumptions could be made about the men based on their gender and race. When it came time for them to share their answers, it turned out that the black man liked ethnic jokes. The white man didn't, but he liked dirty jokes. And the woman? She liked both! The lesson is that trainers shouldn't make sweeping statements about what women or men like or don't like. Some people feel one way, and some another. That's more inclusive, and more honest.

Using false statistics. In many harassment programs, facilitators talk about the cost of sexual harassment. They say that more and more multimillion-dollar suits are being filed and that juries are awarding millions. That's true, but it's not the whole truth. In fact, plaintiffs lose about half of the cases that are decided in trial courts. When they win, they usually get a small award. If they get a huge award, inevitably it is reduced.

- A few years ago, Wal-Mart made the news because of a jury verdict for $50 million. What didn't make the news was that the trial judge reduced the verdict to $5 million. And what certainly didn't make the news was that the Court of Appeals reduced it to $350,000.

- In 1998, there were 16 state and federal sexual harassment jury verdicts that were appealed to U.S. higher courts. (Yes, 16 in the entire United States.) The average jury award in the federal cases was $92,000. The range was from $1 to $225,000. There was one reversal and one reduction, but the average award on appeal was a bit higher, $96,300.

- Of the five state court cases, the average jury verdict was a whopping $1.8 million. Two verdicts were reduced, but the average award on appeal was still $1 million. However, if you throw out the million-dollar awards in California and New York, the average award has been $121,000—not much more than in the federal cases.

One hundred thousand dollars is still big money, and the employers pay the attorneys' fees. But let's be honest: Multi-million-dollar verdicts are rare, and million-dollar awards are almost nonexistent. Sure, there are million-dollar settlements, but they're often not paid in the end. Harassment cases are expensive and should be prevented. But the way to do that is not by exaggerating the magnitude of the risk.

Scaring people into compliance. Look at almost any harassment video and you'll see grim-faced experts threatening dire consequences to sexual harassers, even implying that they can go to jail. Much of illegal harassment is also sexual battery and does cross the line into criminal behavior. But sexual harassment training can't reach people who have criminal minds, and trying to scare everyone else into compliance creates a backlash. Most people want to do the right thing and create a respectful workplace. One of my clients hired a law firm to train its employees. The lawyers made every mistake possible. They tried to scare the men by saying that everything and anything was harassment if a woman perceived it as such.

The result? Men stopped talking to women. Women filed complaints for everything and anything. Men filed counterclaims. Two years later, the company realized that its workforce was more divided than ever. Employees were spending an inordinate amount of time processing personality conflicts disguised as harassment complaints. So, the company brought [a company] in to teach a program on creating a respectful workplace.

How do trainers define a respectful workplace? We don't. Once we've defined the boundaries of the law and the policy, we have to let reasonable people decide for themselves what kind of workplace environment they want.

An in-house lawyer told me what typically happens on his company's e-mail bulletin boards. He said, "If people post For Sale on the wrong bulletin board, they get 10,000 flames, and they never do it again. But if people post tasteless jokes, HR gets 10,000 complaining e-mails. If people just flamed [sexual] offenders, they'd stop immediately. Peer pressure is much more effective than a warning from HR."

Historically, harassment training has emphasized reporting problems to Human Resources. People should go to HR when they experience truly hostile behavior. But in cases of behavior that makes people uncomfortable but isn't illegal and doesn't violate employer policy, we should encourage workers to speak up, communicate their boundaries, and ask co-workers to modify their behavior out of respect.

If that doesn't work, people have the right to move on to workplaces where they will feel more comfortable. They don't have the legal right to demand that everyone conform to their standards. The workplace is made up of diverse people, so a respectful workplace seeks to balance different needs. Having everyone walking on eggshells to avoid offending one super-sensitive person does not create a respectful workplace for anyone.

Men and women can be driven apart by prevention programs that try to scare them into compliance. A better approach is to tell the truth about the law and appeal to people's good natures to set their own behavior at a high standard. Then, workplace relationships will be based, not on fear, but on mutual respect.

Resources

Preventing Sexual Harassment; A Fact Sheet for Employees (Washington, D.C: BNA Books (800.262.9699), 1999).

Darlene Orlov and Michael T. Roumell, *What Every Manager Needs to Know About Sexual Harassment,* New York: AMACOM (800.262.9699).

Rita Risser is the founder and president of Fair Measures, a training company whose five lawyers present corporate sexual-harassment training programs across the United States. She can be reached at 831.458.0500; rita@fairmeasures.com. For the legal research on which this article is based, see www.fairmeasures.com/print/report/index2.html.

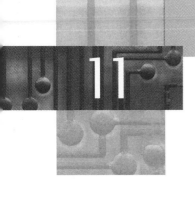

Creating Technical Descriptions

Defining Technical Description

Technical descriptions organize specific details about objects, substances, mechanisms, organisms, systems, and locations for an identified audience. Descriptions summarize physical characteristics, answering questions you expect your readers to have about the appearance, acceptability, and impact:

- What is it? How is it defined? By whom?
- What is its purpose? What is its importance or impact?
- What are the characteristics of the whole? What are within acceptable tolerances?
- What are its parts? What are within acceptable tolerances?
- How do the parts fit together? How do they work together? What defines effective function?

Using Technical Description

Technical descriptions usually appear as part of larger documents. The most common applications include observation notes, manuals and training materials, proposals and reports, marketing and promotional materials, and public information and education.

Preparing a Technical Description

Audience's Task. You need to make sure your technical description meets your readers' needs by answering their questions.

Components. You need to partition your subject into structural parts and/or functional parts.

Diction. The diction of a technical description should be precise so that the information is verifiable. You can achieve this precision by matching terms with audience needs, choosing accurate terms, and using appropriate metaphors.

Visuals. When preparing a technical description, you can choose from a variety of visuals: photographs or realistic drawings, topographic and contour maps, phantom views, overlays, schematics and wiring diagrams, cross-section maps, exploded views, blueprints.

Organization. A technical description almost always uses spatial order to give readers the clearest view of appearance and structure. The body of a technical description involves a part-by-part description arranged in order of location, assembly, or importance. The conclusion explains how the parts fit and function together.

Since the seventeenth century, scientists have been describing the moons of Jupiter—Io, Europa, Ganymede, and Callisto—though in nearly 400 years the level of detail has changed considerably. The inquiry started in 1610, when Galileo Galilei announced "the occasion of discovering and observing four planets, never seen from the very beginning of the world up to our own times, their positions, and the observations made during the last two months about their movements and their change of magnitude. . . ."

In his journal, Galileo carefully recorded his observations of the four satellites of Jupiter, establishing size as "greater than [another . . . that was] exceedingly small," luminescence as "very conspicuous and bright," and location as "deviated a little from the straight line toward the north."

> *January 11.* [My observations] established that there are not only three but four erratic sidereal bodies performing their revolutions round Jupiter. . . .
>
> *January 12.* The satellite farthest to the east was greater than the satellite farther to the west; but both were very conspicuous and bright; the distance of each one from Jupiter was two minutes. A third satellite, certainly not in view before, began to appear at the third hour; it nearly touched Jupiter on the east side, and was exceedingly small. They were all arranged in a straight line, along the ecliptic.
>
> *January 13.* For the first time four satellites were in view. . . . There were three to the west and one to the east; they made a straight line nearly, but the middle satellite of those to the west deviated a little from the straight line toward the north. The satellite farthest to the east was at a distance of 2' from Jupiter; there were intervals of 1' only between Jupiter and the nearest satellite, and between the satellites themselves, west of Jupiter. All the satellites appeared of the same size, and though small they were very brilliant and far outshone the fixed stars of the same magnitude.[1]

In the 1970s, these same four satellites were the object of intense scrutiny by NASA's *Voyager 1*, whose mission was to collect data about Jupiter's "miniature solar system," including the four Galilean satellites. In vivid contrast to Galileo's brief comments, in 1979 the *Voyager Bulletin* (a mission status report that regularly reported the discoveries of *Voyager 1*) described the Galilean satellites in considerable detail:

> Of all the satellites, Io generated the most excitement. As *Voyager 1* closed in on Io, the puzzle was why its surface, so cratered and pocked when viewed from a

distance, began to look smoother and younger as the spacecraft neared. . . .
But the mystery was solved with the discovery of active volcanoes spewing sulfur
160 km (100 mi) high and showering it down on the crust, obliterating the old
surface. Infrared data indicated hot spots at the locations of the plumes identified in the photographs, confirming the find. Io is undoubtedly the most active
known surface in the solar system, surpassing even the Earth.[2]

Now NASA's Space Science News Web site regularly reports on the descriptions coming from the Galileo project (Voyager's successor), noting that "since
the first volcanic plume was discovered by Voyager in 1979, Io has remained
under intense scrutiny." The generalizations of the 1970s are being replaced with
more detailed descriptions.

For a world dominated by fiery volcanoes, it's curious that Io is also very, very
cold. The ground just around the volcanic vents is literally sizzling, but most of Io's
surface is 150 degrees or more below 0°C. The moon's negligible atmosphere traps
little of the meager heat from the distant Sun. As soon as volcanic gases spew into
the air, they immediately begin to freeze and condense. The plumes of Io's sizzling
volcanoes are very likely made up of sulfur dioxide snow.[3]

Thus, you can see that descriptions have a long history. The excerpts from
Galileo's journal, from the *Voyager Bulletin*, and from the current NASA Space
Science News Web site illustrate several characteristics of description that
are discussed in this chapter. Most important, the descriptions include specific
details, presented in an organized manner to meet the needs of an identified
audience.

Defining Technical Description

Descriptions summarize physical characteristics, answering questions you
expect your readers to have about the appearance or composition of an object,
substance, mechanism, organism, system, or location. Regardless of a description's length or subject, it is characterized by verifiable information that responds
to assumed questions.

1. What is it? How is it defined? By whom?

2. What is its purpose? What is its importance or impact?

3. What are the characteristics of the whole? What is "normal" or "typical"?
   What are within acceptable tolerances or specifications?

   - What does it look like (size, shape, color)?

   - What are its characteristics (material or substance, weight, texture,
     flammability, density, durability, expected life, method of production
     or reproduction, and so on)?

*What additional
characteristics might
be important for
descriptions in your
professional field?*

Part III: Understanding the Communicator's Strategies

4. What are its parts? What is "normal" or "typical"? What are within acceptable tolerances or specifications?

   - What is the appearance of each part (size, shape, color)?
   - What are the distinctive characteristics of each part?

5. How do the parts fit together? How do they work together? What defines effective function?

Which of these questions are answered depends on the depth of detail required by the description. Complex descriptions clearly answer more questions.

Sometimes, technical description constitutes an entire document. However, in many situations a technical description is limited to a single segment of a longer document detailing many facets of a subject. Descriptions range from a few lines included in a one- or two-page memo to several paragraphs in a longer report. For instance, a description of equipment would be just one part of a report about monitoring airport noise that is interfering with animals in an adjoining wildlife refuge. Or the description of equipment would take up one section in a proposal to purchase a new X-ray machine.

Do technical descriptions matter? Do they have any impact beyond providing accurate information about physical features? The sidebar on the next page shows that descriptions—if inadequately presented and explained—may cause readers to underestimate their importance or even neglect them entirely. Sometimes the results can be deadly.

Using Technical Description

How do you know when to use a technical description? You can decide whether to include a description and what kind of details to incorporate by examining the context, purpose, and task of your document.

- Will the description help accomplish your purpose of providing information, persuading the reader, or helping the reader complete a task?
- Will a technical description help the reader accomplish the task of gathering information, making a decision, or completing an action?
- Will a technical description help prevent problems?

The following discussion identifies and illustrates some common applications for technical descriptions: observation notes, reference and training manuals, reports and proposals, marketing and promotional materials, and public information and education.

Observation Notes

Many situations require accurate first-hand descriptions, particularly in medicine, field study, and scientific research. The technical expert observes, selects,

"The decision was flawed": Ethical Responsibility and the Challenger Explosion

One of the most tragic accidents in NASA history was the space shuttle Challenger explosion in 1986. The explosion occurred when fuel leaked out of the fuel tanks and mixed with engine exhaust. The leaks were traced to defective seals, called O-rings, on the fuel tanks. During launch, the O-rings were charred by the hot engines enough that they allowed fuel to leak out.

Researcher Paul Dombroski[4] believes the explosion occurred in part because of an ethical failure of the technicians and administrators involved to act on the information they had and not from a lack of information about the O-rings. Technical descriptions of the fuel tanks, written after each previous shuttle flight, revealed that the O-rings were being charred during launch. Although technicians and administrators knew the O-rings were burned, the burning was described in the reports as "allowable erosion" and "acceptable risk." While some engineers questioned these descriptions (and the integrity of the O-rings) the night before the launch, these engineers were unable to provide strong enough arguments to persuade administrators to cancel the launch. The technical descriptions were not in question; everyone agreed that O-rings were charring. However, the contextual pressures to launch influenced the way that technical information was interpreted. The O-rings were deemed safe enough, and seven lives were lost.

Dombrowski uses this example to indicate that technical professionals cannot necessarily rely on conventional procedures to deal with ethical dilemmas. Technical professionals must recognize when the information in a document is not enough—even when it is entirely accurate. They should be willing to take personal responsibility to make sure they have done all that is possible to convey the full picture and explain the implications of descriptions that would otherwise go unnoticed

How could you write a description that would be sure to get the attention of managers who needed to know the information for decision making?

If you were in a similar situation, with millions or even billions of dollars and lives on the line, could you follow Dombrowski's advice? Could you have the ethical strength to speak up? How would you do it?

and records relevant data, often employing abbreviations and jargon specific to the field. The initial purpose of observation notes is to maintain an accurate record. Later, the notes can be extended or transcribed so others can read them, or they can be used as the basis for a more formal document.

The *Manual of Pediatric Therapeutics*, a reference volume for pediatric practitioners, outlines the criteria for immediate evaluation of the newborn. This evaluation, based on observation by the medical professional, provides a detailed physical description of the newborn. The excerpt in Figure 11.1 provides information for the delivery room observation and evaluation.

Reference and Training Materials and Manuals

Most manuals include a technical description of the mechanism or system that the manual deals with. The description usually appears in one of the manual's early sections, often providing a general overview, followed by more detailed information. The technical description introduces the user, operator, technician,

I. EVALUATION OF THE NEWBORN

A. **Delivery room.** Immediate assessment of the newborn infant by the Apgar scoring system should help to identify infants with severe metabolic imbalances. At 1 and 5 minutes after delivery (the times at which feet and head are both first visible), the infant is to be evaluated for five signs, namely, *heart rate, respiratory effort, muscle tone, reflexes,* and *irritability* and *color* and given a rating of 0, 1, or 2 (as defined in Table 5-1). In the extremely compromised infant, prompt and efficient resuscitation is far more important than his exact Apgar score.

TABLE 5-1

Apgar Score *(Score infant at 1 and 5 minutes of age)*

Sign	0	1	2
Heart rate	absent	slow, less than 100	100 or over
Respiratory effort	absent	weak cry, hypoventilation	crying lustily
Muscle tone	flaccid	some flexion, extremities	well-flexed
Reflex irritability	no response	some motion	cry
Color	blue, pale	blue hands and feet	entirely pink

or repair person to the physical characteristics of the mechanism or system. Technical descriptions in manuals are usually accompanied by a variety of visuals: the entire mechanism or system, exploded views, blowups, and phantom and cutaway views of individual parts and subparts.

Work-study students and new employees often need descriptions of the mechanisms and systems with which they'll work. Short technical descriptions orient both students and employees as part of their initial training. The description in Figure 11.2 of a circular inspection mirror is used to introduce a basic piece of inspection equipment.

Proposals and Reports

If a description helps a reader to understand and approve a proposal, it should be included. This type of description gives an overview and then provides details appropriate for the primary reader(s). For example, a proposal from a manager of research and development (R&D) to the company comptroller about an equipment purchase would logically include a description of the equipment. However, the description would not be detailed because the equipment's technical specifications and capabilities are not relevant for the reader. If secondary readers for the same proposal are familiar with R&D operations, an appendix could discuss technical details. In contrast, a proposal to a state's environmental control commission from a local community to preserve a wetlands area would include a detailed description of the geographic area as a main part of the proposal. The members of the commission would need the details to make an informed decision about the validity of the preservation plan.

FIGURE 11.2 ■ Technical Description Used for Training

CIRCULAR INSPECTION MIRROR[6]

A circular inspection mirror is a tool used when visually inspecting general electrical and mechanical equipment for production flaws. The tool's appearance is similar to a hand mirror used by a dentist to inspect teeth, with one exception: the mirror swivels separately from the handle.

The inspection mirror shown in Figure 1 consists of three main parts: mirror, handle, and universal swivel joint. The mechanics incorporated in the swivel design allow a complete 360° spherical positioning of the mirror with no movement of the handle.

Using the circular inspection mirror helps a person observe areas that, because of the angled displacement within the unit, are normally hidden from view.

The $1\frac{1}{8}$"-mirror reflects identical size figures. The mirror's durable stainless steel casing adds $\frac{1}{8}$" to the overall diameter, making the total diameter $1\frac{1}{4}$".

Attached by spot welding to the inside of the casing back is a small stem extending $\frac{3}{8}$"

and concluding in the form of a round bearing. This bearing is positioned inside a two-bearing universal joint.

The simple universal joint uses two encloser plates held together by a nut-and-screw combination. Impressed in the plates are four concave pockets that prevent the bearings from leaving the joint, but allow maximum rotation to the attached handle or mirror. By tightening and loosening the screw, an operator can adjust the mirror to the desired tension.

Also located inside the universal casing and opposite the bearing attached to the mirror is the second bearing, which connects to a hard tempered-steel rod approximately 6" in length. The rough surface of the metal is covered for 3" with plastic orange insulating material that protects the user from electrical shock and possible electrocution.

An additional feature of the circular inspection mirror is a pocket clip, located toward the middle of the handle, which allows the tool to be carried in a shirt pocket like a pen.

FIGURE 1
Circular Inspection Mirror

Several types of reports incorporate descriptions. For example, a report about changes in the work flow in an assembly area because of new automatic insertion equipment could logically include a description of this equipment. A supervisor writing to the division manager would emphasize features of the equipment that have affected the work flow. Generally, any report justifying or recommending acquisition or modification of equipment or facilities will include a description.

Marketing and Promotional Pieces

Technical descriptions in marketing materials are usually both informative and persuasive. Positive (and, of course, subjective) terms are often incorporated into the initial description. The information presents an overview, identifying major components and characteristics. Additional information is often condensed on specification sheets (specs). Promotional and marketing materials frequently include visuals that first display the entire object or mechanism and then highlight its special features. For example, an ad for Pen Engineering and Manufacturing Corporation (PEM) displays a photo of a Coleman lantern, along with two smaller inserts. The first insert is a cutaway view of the lantern's mixing chamber assembly; the second is a photo of the PEM self-clinching stud, which is used in the assembly. The ad copy and the small inserts both describe the self-clinching stud, the actual focus of the ad.

Public Information and Education

Much of the technical and scientific information presented to the public in newspapers and general-interest magazines includes a substantial amount of description, simply because people need to know *what* something is before they make decisions about its value. Sometimes the presentation of this information follows the same general organization as presentations in more technical documents (that is, text supported by visuals). At other times, though, the presentation to general readers uses a small amount of text to support dramatic visuals.

Preparing a Technical Description

To prepare a technical description, you need to identify the audience and task, determine the components, choose precise diction, design effective visuals, and select an appropriate format.

Audience's Task

Technical description should address the intended audience. The only way for you to make sure the description meets your readers' needs is to conduct a careful audience analysis to determine their purpose in reading the document and identify the questions they expect to have answered. You may find talking with representatives of the actual users very productive. At this stage, you should ask several questions:

- Why do readers want or need the information? What is their task? In what ways will the information be important?

- Do they need information in order to understand more detailed discussion that follows? Do they need to make a decision?

What additional questions might be useful to anticipate?

- Are readers interested in a general overview or a detailed description?

- What details do the readers need: Dimensions? Materials? Assembly? Function? Capabilities? Benefits?

Giving insufficient information leaves readers with unanswered questions, but be equally wary of including unnecessary information; you may obscure facts you want to convey.

As you prepare a technical description, select information that responds to the audience's probable questions. The more removed the reader is from actually using the information in the description, the more general it can be. For example, the excerpt from the *Voyager Bulletin* at the beginning of this chapter is easy to read despite the inclusion of specific data; the readers of this status update report are generally interested nonexperts, not astrophysicists or aerospace engineers. Precisely identifying the audience also helps you decide on such crucial aspects of the description as components, diction, visuals, and format.

Components

Before you can describe something, you must separate it into parts or components because the description emphasizes the physical characteristics of each part. But people's concepts of *part* differ greatly. For instance, should the Jovian moon Io be separated according to elements, geologic structures, or electromagnetic fields? Or consider mechanical engineers asked to specify the number of parts in a simple house key. The answers ranged from 1 to 27, with the mode (the number occurring most frequently) being 5. Their answers differed because they did not define *part* in the same way. You can easily see that how you partition something depends on your purpose as the writer and on the background and task of the audience.

Components can usually be separated into structural parts and functional parts.

What other items have distinct structural and functional parts? What are the structural and functional parts of a fiberglass sailboat hull? A screw driver? A tailpipe?

- *Structural parts* comprise the physical aspects of the device, without regard to purpose. For example, a simple house key is made of a single piece of metal.

- *Functional parts* perform clearly defined tasks in the operation of the device. Although the key has a single structural part, it has multiple functional parts.

Applying your knowledge about the audience can help you decide whether one method of separating an object into its parts is more appropriate than another. Thinking about the audience and the purpose for writing the description also helps you decide whether you need to describe all the parts or only some of them.

Diction

The diction of a technical description should be precise, so that the information is verifiable. You can achieve this precision in three ways: choose the most

Part III: Understanding the Communicator's Strategies

specific terms appropriate for your audience; choose technically accurate terms; and consider the value of metaphor to convey descriptions.

Audience-appropriate Terms.   Whether you select general or specific terms depends on the needs of your audience. Generally, nonexperts need accurate information, but they do not require extraordinary detail. Readers with more technical background need more technical details. For example, a general description of a lawn mower might appear in an advertising flyer from a chain store sent in a mass mailing to all residents in an area. A more detailed description could be in a product brochure that sales reps could use to explain the mower's specifications to interested customers. Figure 11.3 presents two lawn mower descriptions that illustrate how characteristics can be described using general or specific diction, depending on audience needs.

Accurate Terms.   A second way for a writer to ensure precision is to use the most accurate terms available. For example, many writers can more accurately differentiate two- and three-dimensional objects. How often have you heard someone mistakenly refer to a ball as round instead of spherical or a box as a square rather than a cube? These geometric shapes—sphere/circle, cube/square, cone/pyramid/triangle—are commonly misnamed.

What other terms have you heard people misuse?

Not only is careless diction inaccurate, but it also causes confusion for readers. For example, if a three-dimensional object is described as triangular, how will the reader know if the solid form is really a cone or a pyramid? Figure 11.4 reviews the terminology of geometric shapes. You can use these terms for these figures, solids, and surfaces if your audience is familiar with them. If your audience is unlikely to know these terms, you may need to define the term or use a diagram.

FIGURE 11.3 ■ Gaining Precision in Technical Descriptions		
General Abstract Terms		**Specific Concrete Terms**
dependable mower	(specify brand)	Briggs and Stratton
powerful	(specify amount)	4 cycle, 3 1/2 HP
self-propelled	(specify type)	rear-wheel belt-to-chain drive
wide blade	(specify size)	21" blade
adjustable height	(specify variation)	7 positions, 1-3"
powerful, dependable, self-propelled mower with wide blade adjustable to cut different heights		Briggs and Stratton mower with 4-cycle, 3 1/2 HP engine; self-propelled by rear-wheel belt-to-chain drive; 21" blade; 7 cutting heights from 1-3"

What other details might be important to technical experts?

FIGURE 11.4 ■ Geometric Shapes[7]

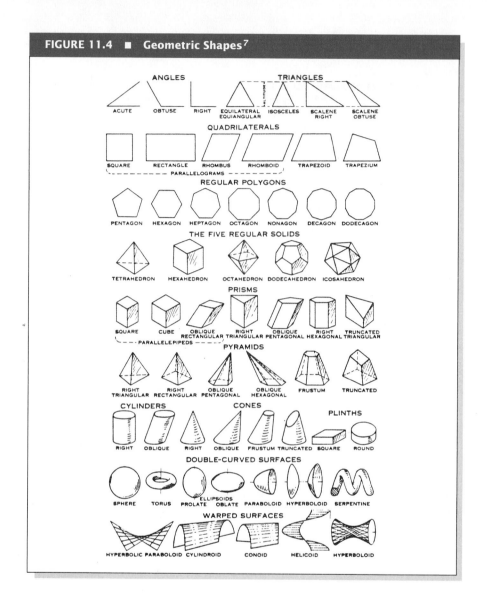

Figurative Language. A third way to ensure precision is to consider whether figurative language such as *metaphors*, *similes*, and *analogies* will give readers a clear description. The example in Figure 11.5 is taken from the trade magazine *Air & Space*, a publication read by aerospace engineers. The example presents a technical description of a microelectromechanical system (MEMS) that embeds both verbal and visual metaphors. The visual metaphor uses a playing card to illustrate the size of the MEMS in relation to the stealth aircraft that uses it. The language includes not only metaphors (e.g., "smart cars," "radar signatures"), but also similes (e.g., "like a spoiler," "flap-like

FIGURE 11.5 ■ Visual and Verbal Metaphor in Technical Text[8]

SMALL BUT *VERY* SMART

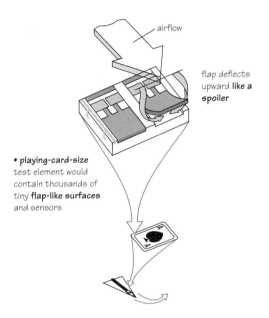

airflow

flap deflects upward **like a spoiler**

• **playing-card-size** test element would contain thousands of tiny **flap-like surfaces** and sensors

Smart is an engineering buzzword . . . ; there are smart cars, smart highways, smart bombs, smart TVs, and, if a group of University of California at Los Angeles and Cal Tech researchers can work it out, smart wings.

These scientists and engineers have developed a "microelectromechanical system" that, instant by nano-instant, alters the airflow over a wing to maintain laminar flow. Whenever microscopic sensors detect the changes in airflow that foretell an incipient burble, minute tabs that function as tiny spoilers bend upward into the airflow to create counter-burbles that cancel out the boundary layer separation.

Microelectromechanical systems—let's henceforth revert to the official acronym MEMS—include devices (flaplets, in this case) so small that thousands of them can be built into microchips that also house the controlling sensors as well as the actuators that activate the surfaces themselves. (We're talk-

ing *way* tiny here: Think of sequins too small for a Barbie doll's cocktail dress. The UCLA/Cal Tech team foresees important uses for a version of the system implanted in the human body to detect and correct the adverse blood flow that can lead to arterial clotting, among other things.)

If you have doubts about systems nearly as delicate as butterfly wings surviving on an airliner in today's air transportation environment, it helps to understand that the research project is largely driven by the needs of future military aircraft. For stealthy airplanes, MEMS arrays that maintain laminar flow could also be used as substitutes for conventional movable control surfaces, which can create radar signatures when they're deflected. Deflect a bunch of MEMS on one wing or the other, say, and considerable lift asymmetry can be created, literally invisibly, rolling the airplane just the way an aileron would.

How effective is the visual metaphor of a playing card to illustrate the relative size of MEMS?

What specific examples of metaphoric language—metaphors, similes, and analogies—can you identify in this article?

How does the metaphoric language help readers understand the features of MEMS?

surfaces," "as delicate as butterfly wings") and analogies (e.g., "sequins too small for a Barbie doll's cocktail dress").

Visuals

Precise visuals are as important in effective technical descriptions as is precise diction. Visuals enable readers to form a mental image of the subject being described. Of course, all visuals should be labeled and titled and referred to in the text. Dimensions are usually more appropriately presented in visuals so the text is not cluttered or difficult to read.

In organizing a typical technical description of a mechanism, you could have an introductory section with a drawing or a photograph that shows the overall features. In organizing the rest of the description, you could use detailed views, perhaps phantom or cutaway views, to show the location of parts and then enlarged drawings, which could be placed adjacent to the text that describes them. Figure 11.6 suggests that different types of visuals can be used to illustrate the exterior, the interior, and individual components as they relate to the whole. (Chapter 9 discusses visuals in more detail.)

Writers and designers frequently decide to use more than one visual in combination to convey information to readers. For example, readers of an article

What kinds of visuals have you seen used in technical descriptions?

FIGURE 11.6 ■ Visuals for Technical Descriptions	
Purpose of Visual	**Selected Visual to Use in Technical Descriptions**
visuals to give readers a visual overview	◆ photographs ◆ realistic drawings ◆ topographic or contour maps
visuals for interior components, to give readers an image of the way the parts fit together	◆ phantom views (drawings that depict an exterior surface as transparent so the inside structure can be viewed) ◆ schematics and wiring diagrams ◆ cross-section maps
visuals for individual parts in relation to the whole, to give readers an image of each individual component	◆ exploded views (drawing that separates all the components and displays them in the proper sequence and relationship for assembly) ◆ cutaway view (drawing that slices a section out to show a full or partial cross-section) ◆ blueprints ◆ photographs or drawings of individual parts

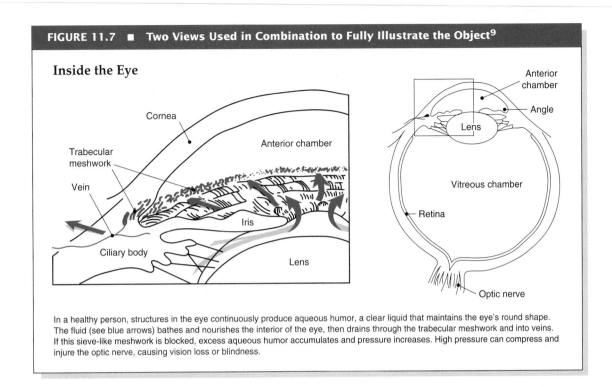

FIGURE 11.7 ■ Two Views Used in Combination to Fully Illustrate the Object[9]

Inside the Eye

Cornea

Anterior chamber

Trabecular meshwork

Vein

Iris

Ciliary body

Lens

Anterior chamber

Angle

Lens

Vitreous chamber

Retina

Optic nerve

In a healthy person, structures in the eye continuously produce aqueous humor, a clear liquid that maintains the eye's round shape. The fluid (see blue arrows) bathes and nourishes the interior of the eye, then drains through the trabecular meshwork and into veins. If this sieve-like meshwork is blocked, excess aqueous humor accumulates and pressure increases. High pressure can compress and injure the optic nerve, causing vision loss or blindness.

about glaucoma in the newsletter the *Harvard Health Letter* need to know how a healthy eye is constructed in order to understand how glaucoma affects vision. Figure 11.7 shows a cross-section of an eye and then shows an enlargement of a segment of that cross-section. The cross-section shows the basic structure; the enlargement shows how these structures work. The caption explains to readers how they can interpret the drawings.

Organization

When preparing a technical description, you have to make decisions about the sequence of information. Writers conventionally organize technical descriptions in spatial order to give readers a clear view of appearance and structure. Occasionally, writers use chronological order, describing the components in order of assembly, or use priority order, describing the components in order of importance. Figure 11.8 outlines a conventional sequence of information you can use to plan a detailed technical description.

Technical descriptions should have a title if they are printed as a separate document and a section heading if they are incorporated into one section of another document.

FIGURE 11.8 ■ Planning a Technical Description

Title

1.0 Define the object (or substance, mechanism, organism, system, or location) in the introduction.
    1.1 Define the object. Identify whose perspective the definition is from.
    1.2 Identify the purpose of the object. Indicate the importance or impact of this purpose.
    1.3 Describe the characteristics of the whole. Indicate acceptable tolerances or specifications.
    1.4 Present a visual that provides an overall view of the object.
    1.5 Identify the parts of the object.

2.0 Present a part-by-part description arranged in order of the parts' assembly, location, or importance.
    2.1 Describe part one.
        2.1.1 Define the part.
        2.1.2 Identify the purpose of the part.
        2.1.3 Describe the general appearance of the part (including a visual if it's useful).
        2.1.4 Describe the characteristics of the part. Indicate acceptable tolerances or specifications.
            2.1.4.1 Identify the general shape and dimensions.
            2.1.4.2 Identify the material type and characteristics (color, flammability, optical properties, solubility, density, conductivity, magnetism, and so on).
            2.1.4.3 Identify the surface treatment, texture.
            2.1.4.4 Identify the weight.
            2.1.4.5 Identify the method of manufacture.
            2.1.4.6 Identify the subparts of part one.
        2.1.5 Describe its attachment to other parts.
    2.2 Describe part two.
        . . . and so on

3.0 Conclude the description.
    3.1 Explain how the parts fit together.
    3.2 Explain how the parts function together. Explain what criteria are used to establish effectiveness.

What visuals would be appropriate for various sections of a technical description?

The introductory section usually begins with a definition suitable for the intended audience. The definition can include or be followed by a statement of the purpose or function of the document, as in this example:

■ **EXAMPLE**

As the new owner of a wood-burning stove, you should be familiar with its structure and components. This information will help you safely maintain your stove as a supplemental source of home heat.

The introductory material presents an abbreviated version of the description. It includes characteristics of the whole: overall shape and major dimensions, primary color and texture, and any distinctive aspects. A photograph or realistic drawing often supplements this overall description. The final part of the introductory section partitions the whole into its major parts, in the order they will be described. This partition can be illustrated with an exploded or cutaway view.

To appeal to a particular audience, you may incorporate into the introductory material elements that increase reader interest and background knowledge but do not add substantively to the technical content. Keep in mind that expert readers are usually annoyed by the inclusion of what they consider extraneous information. However, if you are writing for a general or nonexpert audience, consider some of these elements that may add interest or appeal to the introductory section:

- *Background information:* What is the history? What are current developments?

- *Parts–whole relationships:* Where does the object fit in relation to similar ones?

- *Qualitative distinctions:* What separates it from similar objects?

The body of a technical description involves a part-by-part description arranged in order of location, assembly, or importance. Each section of the body follows the same format. Initially, the part, and sometimes its purpose, is defined. Then a description of the general appearance of the part, including shape, major dimensions, and material, follows, often accompanied by a visual presenting detailed dimensions. The outline in Figure 11.8 identifies additional characteristics that are relevant for some audiences. Specifics are added according to the needs of the audience.

■ EXAMPLES

An architect designing a passive solar house would want information about surface treatments, optical and insulating properties, and weights of specially treated glass.

An interior designer would be more concerned with color and texture. Both would be interested in subparts and methods of attachment to other parts.

The conclusion explains how the parts fit and function together. Just as you can stimulate reader interest in the introduction, you can also create a more lively conclusion by including some of these elements:

- *Applications:* How is it used?

- *Anecdotes or brief narratives:* Who uses it?

- *Advantages/disadvantages:* What are the benefits and/or problems?

Often a technical description does not have a concluding section, but simply ends when the last part has been fully described.

End-of-Chapter
Recommendations for Technical Communicators

1. Summarize physical characteristics by answering questions you expect your readers to have about the appearance or composition of objects, substances, mechanisms, organisms, systems, or locations.

2. Decide what kind of details to incorporate by examining the purpose and task of your document.

3. Learn common applications of technical descriptions: observation notes, manuals and training materials; proposals and reports, marketing and promotional materials; and public information and education.

4. Conduct a careful audience analysis to determine your readers' purposes in reading the technical description and to identify the questions they want answered. Select information that responds to the audience's probable questions.

5. Separate your subject into parts or components because technical descriptions deal with physical characteristics of each part, usually emphasizing either structural parts or functional parts.

6. Use precise, concrete, accurate terms, and, if appropriate, metaphors, similes, and analogies.

7. Select appropriate visuals, choosing photographs or realistic drawings, topographic and contour maps, phantom views, overlays, schematics and wiring diagrams, cross-section maps, exploded views, and blueprints.

8. Usually begin your introductory section with a definition suitable for the intended audience, followed by a statement of the purpose or function of the document.

9. Develop the body of the technical description with a part-by-part description arranged in order of location, assembly, or importance. Use the same format for each subsection.

10. Conclude with an explanation of how the parts fit and function together.

Practicum

The Boeing Company

The Boeing Company is the largest aerospace company in the world, with its heritage mirroring the history of aviation. It is the world's largest manufacturer of commercial jetliners and military aircraft and the nation's largest NASA contractor. In terms of sales, Boeing is the largest U.S. exporter. Total company revenues for 1999 were $58 billion.

Boeing is a company that is continually expanding its products and taking advantage of new technologies—from creating new versions of its family of commercial airplanes to developing new aircraft for the U.S. military, from building launch vehicles capable of lifting more than 14 tons into orbit to improving communications for people around the world with an advanced network of satellites.

The global reach of the company includes customers in 145 countries, employees in more than 60 countries, and operations in 27 states. Worldwide, Boeing and its subsidiaries employ more than 190,000 people—with major operations in the Seattle-Puget Sound area of Washington state; Southern California; Wichita, KS; and St. Louis, MO. Boeing is organized into four major units: Commercial Airplanes, Space and Communications, Military Aircraft and Missiles, and Shared Services.

Information Systems and Software Maturity

Each of these major units includes an Information Systems (IS) group that supports computing technologies and software programs specific to its products and services. These groups write and modify software for embedded systems (factory machines and flight deck), manufacturing applications, engineering (design and fleet support), business applications (finance, human resources and procurement), and general office use (intranet and desktop). Since all of these systems either directly or indirectly impact Boeing products (commercial and military airplanes, missiles, satellites), high quality and reliable systems are paramount.

All Boeing IS groups work toward improving software development and maintenance processes to meet the required quality and reliability goals. One way to improve software processes is to look at a group's software development level of "maturity." A widely accepted measure of software process maturity is the SEI-CMM^{SM} (Software Engineering Institute—Capability Maturity Model) developed at Carnegie Mellon University.

This model has levels from Initial (CMM Level 1) to Repeatable, Defined, Managed, and Optimizing (CMM Level 5). Level 1 software organizations are the most common, and their results are typically unpredictable and poorly controlled. Successes from groups at this level are often determined by an individual "star" performer or intense rework on initial efforts. Level 2 organizations exhibit more "maturity" in that they can repeat previously mastered tasks and meet key process areas: requirements management, software project planning, software project tracking and oversight, software quality assurance, software configuration management, and software subcontract management. Simply reaching a designation of Level 2 can take an organization years of concentrated effort; each increasing level requires more time and dedication. Only a handful of software development groups in the world have reached Level 5.

Boeing's Software Development Methodology

Boeing uses a consistent software development methodology, Productivity Plus from DMR Consulting, across the company. This methodology is adapted to the needs of individual projects because the nature of each project (for example, new development vs. maintenance, Web vs. client/server, etc.) determines the set of deliverables that should be produced. (The methodology calls out over 100 potential deliverables!) The general methodology has five major roughly sequential sections for each phase in the software lifecycle:

- opportunity evaluation

- preliminary analysis

- system architecture

- functional design

- system construction

Each section builds on decisions made earlier in the software development lifecycle. Questions about scope and funding are addressed first; questions about design and implementation are made after the "opportunity" has been established. By using this methodology consistently, organizations document and repeat their processes. This standard approach in turn helps organizations improve their maturity level because they are demonstrating "repeatability."

The software development methodology used at Boeing and SEI-CMM complement each other in several key intersections, one of which is identifying requirements. Developing a system that meets user and business requirements is difficult if those requirements are not well defined. The software development team must find out who can contribute requirements (any user of the target system, their manager, the company's financial officer, etc.) and whether those requirements are feasible, complete, and testable. Requirements should be reviewed carefully so that problems can be identified, and all impacted groups can be notified early in the development process.

System requirements feed the project plan, schedule, and communication with associated systems. Requirements may be grouped to form interim system releases or be large enough to warrant a separate release. In addition, changes to requirements can then be tracked against a baseline so changes are made only after careful evaluation and corresponding business rationale.

Innovation at Boeing: Web-based Ordering

The Boeing Company used this methodology and continually gathers new requirements for their Web-based system that allows customers (airline customers, in this case) to order spare parts. Electronic, customer-driven ordering systems can increase accuracy and speed for orders, decrease order flowtime, and help customers resume normal operations faster. The Boeing Web-based system allows users to complete these tasks:

- View up-to-date part information such as prices, availability, and interchangeability.

- Enter a new purchase order, change an existing purchase order, or check the status of orders.

- Request a price quote or view existing price quotes.

- Track shipments all the way to customer destinations.

First released in 1996, the Boeing PART Page[10] (shown on the next page) has demonstrated phenomenal growth and acceptance with airline customers. In 1999, over $400 million in spare parts were sold via this site to airline customers around the world.

Assignment

You have just accepted a position at Theta Manufacturing and have been asked to develop the next version of their Web-based system for customer parts ordering. Theta Manufacturing's current system was a big step forward in technology when it was first created, but now the site needs the additional functionality that can be gained with the following enhancements:

- Offer purchase orders as a payment method in addition to credit cards.

- Provide a warning about long lead-time orders if a part will take several weeks to arrive.

- Display multiple image sizes so customers can "zoom in" and see more detail about the item they're selecting.

- Associate the price for an item along with the description of an item in the customer's shopping cart.

- Categorize parts in groups so customers can quickly find their desired item.

The following text appears within the browser window image:

Netscape: The Boeing PART Page

Back | Forward | Reload | Home | Search | Netscape | Images | Print | Security | Stop

Netsite: http://www.boeing.com/assocproducts/bpart/partpage/ — What's Related

BOEING PART Page

BOEING

associated products
and services

Introducing the Boeing PART
Page

More Information

The information you need, when you need it.

We are pleased to announce a new way for you to research and order parts from Boeing Spares.

To provide more value and better service to our customers, we have developed a way to use the sophisticated technology of the World Wide Web to give customers direct access to our extensive part information and ordering system. You can now order parts and view part information through a new World Wide Web site called the Boeing Part Analysis & Requirement Tracking (PART) Page.

Through the Boeing PART Page, current data such as part inventories, prices, part interchangeability and purchase order status are at your fingertips.

The system is simple and accessible to any authorized Boeing customer.

Features | Benefits | Customer Requirements | To Get Started

Technical Data Products and Services (TDPS)

Boeing Home | Associated Products & Services
Copyright © 2000 The Boeing Company - All rights reserved.

- Provide a search mechanism to back up the categorization and provide more ways to find items.

Your assignment is to develop a summary of these requirements that includes information about how these requirements will be incorporated into the new Web-based parts system. The information in your report will be used by other Theta Manufacturing team members for project plans, communication with external groups, and as a reference along the development cycle. You need to complete the following tasks for your deliverable:

- Develop a cover page with your company's logo, document title (Requirements Summary), and date.

- Take into account who might need to approve this document: The project leader? A user representative? Other key project members? Leave space for signatures for their review and acceptance of the document.

- Provide a table of contents so readers can skim the major sections.

- Write a brief overview of the modifications—about one paragraph per item.

- Use the rest of the report to describe in detail each one of the requirements and corresponding modifications that it will require. Use a short version of the requirement as a section title and use one page per requirement with the following sub-sections:

  - Summary—a sentence or two on the requirement (this will be very similar to what you wrote for the overview)

  - Detail—what needs to change on your Web site to accommodate this new requirement? Will you need to work with other groups to make the changes (for example: your company's accounting department for the purchase order requirement or receiving department for the lead-time information)? Do you need to tie in additional computing resources (databases, external software)? Each of these should be mentioned.

You might want to look at other company Web sites to get ideas about how these modifications could look on your pages. You won't need to describe in detail how to implement these changes, but should provide references to URLs if they have features you'd like to imitate.

References

For more information on The Boeing Company, see <http://www.boeing.com> or you can go directly to the Boeing PART Page (illustrated on the previous page) to learn more about this Web-based system for customer parts ordering.

For more information on SEI-CMM see <http://www.sei.cmu.edu/>

Janet Renze is a Systems Analyst currently working on client/server software projects. She is responsible for gathering requirements for future releases, coordinating user focals for screen design and acceptance testing, developing functional specifications, and supporting integration issues with other corporate systems.

She has over 10 years of computing experience in training, Web development, testing, analysis, and technical support. After three years at The Boeing Company, Janet recently moved to HomeGrocer.com, an online grocer and home delivery company based in Seattle, WA.

Janet has a B.A. in Music and an M.A. in Business and Technical Communication from Iowa State University. You can contact her at jlrenze@yahoo.com.

Individual and Collaborative Assignments

1. **Identify parts for analysis.** (a) Identify ways to describe the following subjects. Each can be separated into a number of different parts or subsystems. (b) Add one subject from your own profession to each category and identify its parts or subsystems, too.

   Example. An organism such as a wolf can be separated in a number of ways. Some ways include by cellular composition, by categories of fluids such as blood, by categories of systems such as muscles, by categories of physical functions such as reproduction and respiration, and by categories of ecological functions such as controlling the elk population.

Subject	Example	Parts or systems
Objects	◆ golf ball ◆ screw	
Mechanisms	◆ carbon monoxide detector ◆ kidney	
Substances	◆ granola ◆ ocean water	
Systems	◆ immune system ◆ workflow in office	
Organisms	◆ decathlon athlete ◆ experimental variety of corn	
Locations	◆ site of a new building ◆ protected wetland	

2. **Distinguish between structural and functional parts.** Identify the structural and functional parts for one column of the following items. Both word lists and diagrams will help you identify the distinctions.

AAA battery	comb	hand saw	pocket lighter
ballpoint pen	field daisy	light bulb	pocket knife
baseball	flashlight	magnet	scissors
candle	hand saw	pinecone	zipper

3. **Choose appropriate diction for specificity.** Some descriptions might be inappropriate because they're negative or vague.
   (a) Under what circumstances might the following descriptions be inappropriate? Suggest possible alternatives that would provide more detailed and accurate descriptions.

- fat patient
- complicated step
- sharp angle
- fast photocopier
- fast microprocessor
- cheap replacement part
- hard surface
- recent decision
- easy-to-assemble desk
- cold weather

(b) What other general description terms can you think of that might be inappropriate? In what circumstances?

4. **Consider audience needs.** Imagine that you work for a company that manufactures modular houses and sells directly to individual customers. Several publications are being prepared, and you have been assigned responsibility for creating descriptions of the modular houses. How would you identify the parts of the modular houses for the following audiences?

- government agency with information about fuel-efficient construction methods
- production-line manager
- architect
- lumber wholesaler
- municipal wiring and/or plumbing inspector
- prospective homeowner

5. **Choose visuals for certain descriptions.** Several kinds of visuals are described in this chapter. Which would be appropriate to incorporate into a description of each of the following items? What would make one kind of visual more appropriate than another kind for each item—considering, for example, context, purpose, and audience?

- apple—from bud to harvest
- checkwriter
- paint sprayer
- computer mouse
- crankshaft
- espresso coffee maker
- gas well
- human leg
- Mechineck (toy creature whose neck extends and head turns when a lever in back is pressed)
- mint: catnip, spearmint, peppermint, applemint
- proposed condominium complex
- reclining chair or geriatric chair
- septic tank and leach field
- silicon chip
- snow blower
- sprocket gears (as on a bicycle)

6. Analyze technical descriptions.

(a) Bring two examples of technical descriptions to class. If possible, locate one description in a U.S. publication and the other description from a publication outside the United States.

(b) Work with classmates in a small group to conduct a preliminary analysis of two of the technical descriptions your group brought in, considering at least these points:

- *Context.* What assumptions seem to have been made about the context in which the descriptions will be used?

- *Audience.* For what audience is each intended? Has the writer accurately analyzed the audience(s)?

- *Visuals.* Are the visuals appropriate and helpful? Are additional visuals needed? Do the visuals differ in descriptions from different cultures?

- *Format.* Does the format make the descriptions easy to read? Does the form differ in descriptions from different cultures?

(c) Based on your preliminary analysis, create an evaluation rubric that shows how you've incorporated the criteria discussed above and other criteria that you and your classmates have determined are helpful in analyzing and assessing technical descriptions. Refer to the rubric template in the Usage Handbook as a starting place; modify this template as necessary.

(d) Test and refine the new rubric by using it to conduct a complete analysis and evaluation of at least two other descriptions you and your classmates brought in.

(e) Give a brief oral presentation to the class about the criteria you selected and the assessment of one of your group's descriptions.

7. Analyze a Web-based technical description.

(a) Visit the following Web sites:

<http://www.sdinfo.com/volume_1_1/v1n1cds.html>
<http://www.sonicstudios.com/dsm.htm>
<http://www.medmedia.com/orthoo/25.htm>
<http://www.medexpert.net/medinfo/angiogra.htm>
<http://www.west.net/~eyecare/myopia.html>

(b) Use (and appropriately modify) the rubric you created in Assignment 6 to analyze and evaluate the technical descriptions you find at these Web sites.

8. Write a technical description.

(a) Select an object, mechanism, substance, organism, or location from the following lists, or choose another subject that relates to your field:

Objects	Mechanisms	Substances
electrical cable	cider press	photographic developer
drill bit	pool filter	acetylene
shotgun shells	spinning reel	baking powder
contact lenses	spinning wheel	baby food
mallet	camera lens	blood sample
gable roof	combination lock	measles vaccine
computer chip	solar panel	yogurt
polarizing filter	smoke alarm	plant fertilizer
photographic film	semicircular canals	effluent
golf club	transit	cough medicine

Systems	Organisms	Locations
respiratory system	termites	a harbor mooring
photovoltaic system	dolphins	cross section of well site
braking system	tape worms	R&D section of a plant
electronic auto	algae	forest marked for logging
inspection system	chickens	layout for vegetable garden
planetary system	yeast	geologic fault
H/AC system	mosquitoes	archaeological excavation
irrigation system	foxgloves	traffic cloverleaf pattern
photocopying machine	pumas	underground storage tank
scrubber for contaminants	protozoa	runway grid for airport

(b) Modifying the format outlined in Figure 11.8, write a description that appropriately considers context, audience, and purpose of your description.

(c) After writing your description, work in a small group to compare and contrast it with those written by other students. Examine the organization, selection of details, adjustment for audience, and use of visuals. Explain your reasons for the choices you made in designing and developing your description.

Intertext

Cross-cultural Communication: Is It Greek to You?[11]

With the internationalization of today's marketplace, U.S. businesses are starting to market their products outside the United States. These companies tapping into the overseas market are often faced with unforeseen obstacles and roadblocks that arise from difficulties in communicating in foreign languages and with foreign cultures.

Unfortunately, many U.S. companies do not demand the same quality from translated product literature as they do from their native-tongue literature. This double standard is developing not from a lack of interest in international markets, but rather from monolingual executives making decisions that require bilingual competency.

Marketing and product information managers who have very little knowledge of their target audience and its language are often responsible for approving translated materials. Since a monolingual person has no basis on which to judge the quality of a translation, cost often becomes the driving force.

Many errors in communication may go unnoticed until after a product hits the shelf. Undetected inaccuracies in product information not only can be devastating to sales, but may also have legal implications. Clearly, some careful planning is required before selling a product abroad.

Ignorance Is Not Always Bliss

Although outside translation services are readily available, their services alone do not always satisfy a company's translation needs. Translators from outside services do not attend product marketing meetings, usually have very little technical knowledge about the product, and may be unaware of a client's corporate standards. Unless a company makes a genuine effort to include them in key meetings and inform them of important issues, outside translators do not see the "big picture."

Marketing executives often find themselves at the mercy of a translation service. They rely on outside translators not only to translate product materials, but also to accurately interpret technical information and to convey an appropriate implied marketing message through the style and tone of writing. This approach is like a company hiring a writer with no specific product expertise to develop marketing literature, manuals, and training materials without assistance from marketing and technical experts.

Manufacturers of products that must adhere to certain safety or regulatory standards have additional concerns. These companies typically require their legal departments to make sure that safety issues are appropriately handled in product literature. Lawyers review documents for adherence to the American National Standards Institute (ANSI) standards for hazard alert messages. They may also require approvals from agencies like the FCC or UL.

Unfortunately, translated documents do not have to adhere to ANSI standards, and FCC and UL approvals carry little weight overseas. Depending on the product and the country in which it is being marketed, varying safety and regulatory requirements must be met. Companies that overlook the legal implications of marketing their products overseas may be exposing themselves to the high risk of lawsuits stemming from incidents of product malfunction or misuse.

You're Not in Kansas Anymore

Companies that want to succeed in marketing their products across cultural boundaries clearly need to break through the communication barrier. To compete successfully in an international business environment, marketing executives need to learn about the language, culture, and values of the people in a foreign market.

Depending on its size and resources, a company can assimilate a foreign culture into its product marketing campaign in a variety of ways. Smaller companies can utilize bilingual employees who are currently on their staff or hire a translator to act as a bilingual consultant. Larger companies may find it appropriate to organize an entire bilingual marketing department consisting of both native English speakers and native speakers of the foreign language.

Although they may not be bona fide marketing experts, bilingual staff members can serve as an informative market focus group. They can help to reposition the mindsets of American marketing experts, whose instincts are driven by the American market. Bilingual staff members can voice some of the questions and concerns of people from the foreign country, and marketing experts have the opportunity to try out their advertising ideas on a bilingual test group. This dynamic exchange leads to the development of advertising ideas that promote both the corporate marketing strategy and product acceptance by the target audience.

Bilingual staff members can help improve a cross-cultural marketing campaign by—

- **Identifying product features and capabilities that will appeal to the target audience.** For example, a country with a widely educated, technically oriented population may be influenced by a superior product design and better performance. A country that is suffering from a slow economy may be more interested in value, durability, and reliability. Of course, real life is not as simple as these examples. A native of a country can draw attention to the more subtle preferences and values of a culture.

- **Being sensitive to the social and political beliefs of a foreign country.** A company entering a new foreign market needs to know what types of behavior are considered socially correct or incorrect. In the U.S., for example, whether a person smokes or wears a fur coat may make an unintentional and possibly undesirable political statement. In a foreign country, smoking may not have the stigma that Americans attach to it, but drinking alcoholic beverages or wearing shorts might be considered improper. It is also important to be informed of product boycotts, trade embargoes, or widespread strikes that are being staged in a country. If railroad workers in a foreign country are on strike, for example, a company may be well advised to ship its products by truck.

- **Selecting photos, art, and other visual images that are directed toward the target audience.** Marketing literature is more persuasive when it reflects the values of the customers that it is trying to attract. Advertising mascots and models should be carefully chosen to ensure that they are conveying what is considered a desirable look and image by people of the country. For example, a model with large, bulging arm muscles may be considered attractive and desirable in one country but may look like a genetic freak in another country.

- **Flagging humor that may be misunderstood or considered distasteful to people of a foreign country.** Although humorous advertising can be very effective, it should be funny to the people who are reading or listening to it. Idiomatic expressions and plays on words are particularly dangerous in translations.

- **Developing a "personality" for your product that will be well received by the target audience.** Bilingual staff members can identify product "personality traits"—such as being macho, free-spirited, dignified, or snobbish—that may be desirable in a foreign culture.

The Truth, the Whole Truth, and Nothing but the Truth

If a company is fortunate enough to already have bilingual employees on its staff, these employees may be valuable resources for verifying technical product information in translated literature. Another alternative is to educate bilingual consultants about a product through sales and service training sessions and the company's native-tongue literature.

Depending on the size and scale of a project, bilingual staff or consultants may be responsible for developing product literature themselves or may supervise the efforts of an outside translation service. Since bilingual staff members are familiar with technical product details and the company's marketing strategy, they can proofread translations for technical correctness and consistency with corporate standards. This review process helps to ensure not only that product literature is accurate, but also that it conveys the desired product image.

Bilingual staff members can improve the quality of translated product literature by—

- **Verifying spelling and word hyphenation in documents.** If a foreign-language word processor is used, this task is greatly simplified. As any writer can attest, however, electronic spell checkers have their limitations and cannot replace a human proofreader. Documents that are not produced on a foreign-language word processor designed specifically for the language used in the document need to be reviewed with extra care for spelling errors and typos. Since the rules for hyphenating

English text are often different from those of a foreign language, hyphens that are automatically generated by word-processing software need to be closely checked.

- **Removing regional dialects from a translation.** An issue that commonly needs to be addressed with French translations is whether to use Canadian or Parisian French. While this decision depends on the particular circumstances, a translation that tries to avoid use of strictly Canadian or strictly Parisian phrasing is most desirable and can be used in either Canada or France. A bilingual staff member can help to internationalize translated literature by ensuring that the purest form of a language is used. Although this might not have an immediate impact, a company that markets a product in Canada may later decide to market a product in France.

- **Coordinating and standardizing translations.** On large projects where more than one translator is used, a bilingual staff member needs to verify that certain key words are translated consistently throughout different pieces of literature. Depending on the product, a company may choose to translate control panels, product decals, and other labels that are placed directly on a product. In this case, a bilingual staff member needs to coordinate the translations so that manuals agree with other extraneous written material. For example, the words used for "on" and "off" in an operator's manual should be the same words that appear on the control panel.

- **Ensuring that the proper language form is being used.** Foreign languages often have two or more ways of saying the same thing. One form is usually considered more polite and formal than the other. Depending on the target audience and the image a company wants to project, a bilingual staff member will ensure that translations use appropriate pronouns and verb forms.

Because laws and regulations can vary significantly in foreign countries, a lawyer who practices in the country where the product is being marketed should thoroughly review all translations. This lawyer should review the literature for compliance to the safety, regulatory, health, and environmental standards of the country. A lawyer can also help develop boilerplate statements that can be reused for similar products being marketed overseas. These boilerplate statements may include hazard alert warnings, warranty terms, and disclaimers.

Riding Off Into the Sunset

Although no marketing strategy can guarantee success, a carefully planned cross-cultural marketing campaign helps to minimize obstacles that arise from communication problems. An advertising strategy that specifically targets the needs and values of an overseas audience will get a product noticed. Accurate and thorough product literature will help customers get the most out of a product. In short, a company that takes its translated materials seriously will be taken seriously by its markets abroad.

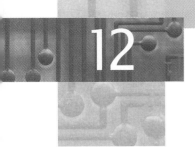

12

Creating Process Explanations

CHAPTER 12 IN BRIEF

Defining Processes

The most obvious characteristic of process explanations is that they explain sequential actions in chronological order. Process explanations don't focus on the details required to complete a task; instead, they introduce a process by providing an overview.

Using Process Explanations

Process explanations usually appear as part of larger documents. The most common applications include manuals, orientation and training materials, marketing and promotional materials, and public information and education.

The sequence is technical description, process explanation, benefits or advantages. If you follow this common sequence, your readers will learn what a mechanism is, then how it works, and finally why it's useful.

Preparing Processes

Audience and Purpose. Identifying your audience and its task for reading a document helps you prepare a process explanation.

Identification of Steps. An essential part of preparing process explanations involves listing the steps of the action.

Visuals. You can choose from several visuals to illustrate the sequence of a process. The most common visuals are flowcharts, but you can also use time lines, schedules, single drawings showing each element in a process, time-lapse photographs, drawings with overlays of changes, drawings showing the final product, and sequential drawings.

Diction. Your choice of active or passive voice is influenced by the audience and purpose of the process.

Organization and Format. Processes are chronological, often using headings to distinguish the major steps.

Examining a Process Explanation

One short process explanation about creating low-cost roofing materials is annotated and discussed.

Process explanations play an important role in technical communication—providing information about the sequence of steps in any action, from blood donation to operation of a jet engine. Generally, process explanations (also called process descriptions) provide an overview or background, regardless of readers' specific tasks.

Because some managers read process explanations to help them make purchasing decisions, marketing brochures frequently contain such explanations. Supervisors often read process explanations, like those in many manuals, to gain an understanding of a process they're responsible for but don't actually do. Technicians and operators are usually encouraged to read a process explanation before following the directions to actually conduct a process. General readers find that process explanations satisfy their curiosity about many things—how wine is made, how hurricanes are tracked, how oil wells are drilled.

Defining Processes

Process explanations explain sequential actions to readers who need enough details to understand an action or process, but not enough to necessarily enable them to complete it. The following example of one step in a mechanical inspection process illustrates the difference between a process explanation and directions (which you'll read more about in Chapter 15). The process explanation identifies the general nature of the task; it is valuable precisely because it provides an overview rather than focusing on the details. In contrast, this step of the directions that enables a mechanical inspector to complete the task is very specific.

■ **EXAMPLE**

Process Explanation
A mechanical inspector initially ensures that the labels on the packages are correct.

Directions
Ensure that the computer-printed label contains all of the following information:
a. customer contract number
b. contract annex and line item
c. part number
d. nomenclature
e. NSN (national stock number)
f. quantity
g. date packaged
h. serial number (if applicable)

Accurate, accessible processes are a large part of what makes an organization function safely and legally. When the processes are inaccurate or inaccessible, problems arise. Most organizations work diligently to keep processes accurate and up to date; in fact, many organizations have built-in reviews to assure that all processes are current. However, some organizations have flawed processes—sometimes accidentally, sometimes purposely—that put people at risk. When an organization ignores such problems, some people believe they have an ethical, professional responsibility to make the problem public. These whistleblowers, now protected by law, make the workplace safer for everyone, but usually at great cost to themselves. The ethics sidebar on the next page addresses the risks and benefits of whistleblowing.

Using Process Explanations

Process explanations often appear in the same kinds of documents as technical descriptions. You can decide whether to include a process explanation and what kind of details to incorporate by examining the purpose and task of your document. Will the process explanation help accomplish your purpose? Will it help the reader understand the process? The following discussion identifies and illustrates some of the common applications of process explanations: manuals, orientation and training materials, marketing and promotional materials, and public information and education.

Manuals

Manuals—whether print documents or online help systems—frequently use this sequence of information, especially in an introductory section:

- *Technical description:* what a mechanism is

- *Process explanation:* how it works

- *Benefits or advantages:* why it's useful

This sequence is a particularly important part of the documentation accompanying new equipment that may be unfamiliar to either the user or manager.

An effective process explanation appears in Figure 12.1, an excerpt from the System Manager's Reference Manual for the ATEX text-processing system. This excerpt from the beginning of the manual reviews the editorial and production processes for system managers and identifies the ways the ATEX system changes these processes.

Orientation and Training Materials

Although managers frequently appreciate simple, straightforward process explanations, students may need more detailed information because they are often expected to understand the reasons behind a sequence of actions—even

Whistleblowers: Ethical Choices and Consequences

Dealing with the consequences of an ethical conflict can be difficult, especially when the conflict arises because of a difference between an employee's personal values and an organization's goals. Some technical professionals, faced with workplace situations they find unethical, decide their only viable option is to reveal corporate secrets to the public. These professionals, referred to as whistleblowers, jeopardize their career and personal safety because they believe the public's right to know supersedes corporate obligations.

Whistleblowers are employees who for ethical, legal, or financial reasons publicly expose a company's internal secrets. Movies like *The China Syndrome* (1979), *Silkwood* (1983), and *The Insider* (1999) dramatically indicate the extreme repercussions some whistle blowers have faced. In these movies and in the actual situations on which these movies were based, the whistleblowers lost their jobs, found their careers finished, and faced personal assaults. While these movies dramatized extreme examples, many whistleblowers deal with less dramatic but still very important issues. Beyond the probable loss of a job, many whistleblowers have a difficult time getting hired at other companies and often must change careers.

So, faced with these negative consequences, why would a technical professional choose to be a whistleblower? Legal regulations provide one answer. A technical professional has a legal obligation to inform the public of potential harm. Researcher Carolyn Rude refers to this legal obligation as the "duty of due care":

> Technical communicators could be negligent, legally and ethically, if they knew that a product being documented could be hazardous, knew of the responsibility to provide clear instructions and adequate warnings but did not make an effort to do so, or to investigate hazards in the use of the product. (p. 179)[1]

Legal requirements are not the only factor behind the decision to become a whistleblower. Technical professionals also respond from a sense of responsibility to the community. Or they should, at least according to reporter Todd Crowell of the online news service *Asia Now*. Crowell believes whistleblowers "can be the catalysts for needed change" in a company.[2] Crowell believes that a whistleblower could have prevented Japan's worst nuclear power plant accident. Workers at the plant used an unauthorized operations manual that sacrificed safety for expedience; using this manual, employees accidentally set off a uranium chain reaction in 1999 that killed one worker and exposed hundreds of citizens to dangerous levels of radiation. Crowell believes the accident could have been avoided if someone had been willing to expose the improper procedures being used.

How would you write a process explanation for a process with potentially harmful aspects?

Making the decision to reveal company secrets is not easy, and it does not come without consequences. However, the consequences of not revealing information can be equally troubling. Would you be able to face the potential scorn and repercussions of being a whistleblower? Would you be compromising your personal ethics to keep information secret you felt the public should know? How do you make such a difficult ethical decision?

when the information is just a summary. The illustrated summary of a natural process in Figure 12.2 is given to students in a seminar about bog formation; the article contains terminology, definitions, and explanations that make the material inappropriate for readers interested in more general information.

The writer makes a number of assumptions about his readers' background knowledge but still adheres to the format of an effective process explanation.

FIGURE 12.1 ■ An Effective Process Explanation[3]

INTRODUCTION

The excerpt begins by briefly identifying the physical components of the system.

The goal of the system is defined.

A summary of the process precedes more specific information.

The process provides for input by writers, editors, and reviewers.

. . . The ATEX system consists of a unique combination of specific hardware and software products that provide its users with full electronic text processing capabilities. The goal of the ATEX system is the same as that of a non-electronic system, but ATEX allows the editorial and production processes to function faster and more efficiently. The emphasis here is on processing; the ATEX system accepts letters, numbers, words, and sentences from many different sources simultaneously and stores them for easy, repeated access. This means that text can be entered into the system once and manipulated any number of times. Thus, once a writer's story is in the system, he/she can modify it as often as desired; when finished, the text can be passed electronically to his/her editor. The editor, in turn, may use a video display terminal (VDT) to read and modify/correct the text, then use the system to send it either back to the writer for further work, or on to the reviewers or analysts (who, in turn, can manipulate the text and return it electronically to the editor). When the text is ready, the ATEX system allows people in either the editorial or production phases to format it as desired and send it out to a device (either a phototypesetter or printing terminal) that produces printed pages or galleys. Figure 1-2 shows the general flow of text through the system.

FIGURE 1-2

Copy Flow with an ATEX System

The process is summarized in the figure.

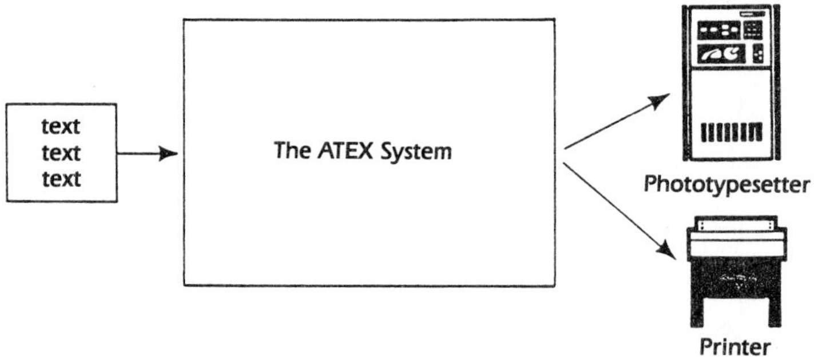

text text text → The ATEX System → Phototypesetter

Printer

He begins with a broad definition of a bog before summarizing the sequence of its development; however, because he assumes that readers have some prior knowledge, he does not define all technical terms. The writer uses chronology to explain the development but also orients readers with precise spatial references.

Marketing and Promotional Materials

Some actions are far easier to delineate than bog development. For instance, Figure 12.3 presents an example written primarily for professionals; it explains

FIGURE 12.2 ■ Illustrated Summary of a Natural Process[4]

BOG DEVELOPMENT

The characteristic bog develops over several thousand years in a relatively deep glacial depression, a "kettle," which is either poorly drained or has no outlet. Water is gained through precipitation alone and is lost by evapotranspiration. As flow through the pond in the depression is sluggish or nonexistent, there is no source for minerals, and the bog water is deficient in nearly all major plant and animal nutrients, especially nitrogen. Certain plants, particularly Sphagnum moss, may dominate the lower levels of vegetation, crowding out less well-adapted species. The Sphagnum also withdraws nutrients from the water, replacing them with acids. Bog water is, thus, acidic—especially beneath the Sphagnum-dominated zones.

Bog succession begins as horizontal growth over the surface of the water, since the bottom is generally too deep near the shore to allow plants to root as in a typical marsh or swamp. This lateral growth forms a dense mat of intertwining stems that supports all further growth. This mat characteristically grows out over the water, closing in on the pond center from all sides and eventually covering all open water. As there is still water beneath the mat,

the mat is essentially floating; though it will generally support the weight of a person, the person gets the feeling that the earth is trembling. From this phenomena stems the term "quaking bog."

Growth proceeds upon the mat as vegetation builds up vertically, the accumulating mass forcing underlying vegetation downwards and below the static water level. This plant matter decays slowly, if at all, because the acidity of the water coupled with its coldness (it is, after all, well insulated from the warmer air above) inhibits bacterial action that causes decomposition. Thus, the basin becomes filled with partially decayed vegetation, and the mat eventually supports trees, which grow first over the landward, more "grounded" parts of the bog. Trees will advance out over the mat as the depression becomes filled, ultimately closing over the original open bog altogether. At this stage, the old bog may be difficult to recognize, though for some time to come, the acidity of the soil dictates which plants may survive there and which may not. The accompanying figure shows the cross section of a typical bog.

Explanations help readers understand the origin of common terms such as "quaking bog" and phenomena such as the high level of acidity of bog water.

The chronology of the process is clearly signaled to readers by phrases such as "succession begins" and "growth proceeds."

FIGURE 1
Cross Section of a Typical Bog

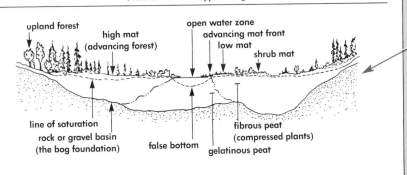

The diagram illustrates each of the main elements identified in the text.

As you read the article on bog development, identify the technical terms that are not defined. Explain whether the lack of definitions hinders your understanding.

the operation of a thermal inkjet cartridge for computer printers. This example provides a good illustration of the way in which process explanations are often embedded in longer pieces of writing.

The process explanation makes more sense in the context of complete information. In this case, the first five paragraphs provide an overview that defines, describes, and illustrates the printer, identifying the critical components that readers need to know in order to understand how the process of firing a drop of ink works. The overall definition and description are followed by two paragraphs that identify the sequence involved in firing a drop of ink. The concluding three paragraphs deal with ways in which the process can be controlled to produce high-quality printing.

Public Information and Education

Readers of general-interest publications such as daily newspapers or Web sites are often interested in technical information, but they may not have the experi-

---

FIGURE 12.3 ■ Process Explanation of How a Thermal Inkjet Cartridge Works[5]

THERMAL INKJET REVIEW, OR HOW DO DOTS GET FROM THE PEN TO THE PAGE?

These initial paragraphs provide an overview that defines this type of printer, illustrates its critical parts, and explains their purpose and importance.

In its simplest form, an inkjet device consists of a tiny resistor aligned directly below an exit orifice. Ink is allowed to flow into the resistor area, and when the resistor is heated, the ink on the resistor essentially boils and forces a tiny droplet of ink out of the aligned orifice. This is called firing the nozzle.

A cross-sectional view of a single inkjet nozzle is shown in Fig. 1. On the floor of the firing chamber is a resistor. This resistor is patterned onto a silicon substrate using conventional thin-film fabrication procedures. Leads are connected to the resistor through the thin-film substrate. These leads ultimately travel out to the flexible circuit on the body of the print cartridge, through which a voltage can be applied across the resistor. The resistor is the heart of the thermal inkjet device, and the size of the resistor is the primary factor governing the volume of the ejected droplets.

The walls of the firing chamber are made up of a photosensitive polymer. This polymer serves to define the walls of the firing chamber and deter-

FIG. 1.

An exploded cross-sectional view of a single inkjet nozzle

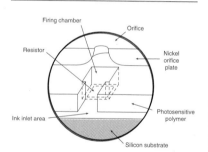

mines the spacing between the resistor surface and the orifice. The thickness of this photosensitive barrier and the dimensions of the firing chamber are critical to the production of a well-formed droplet.

The photosensitive polymer also defines the dimensions of the inlet area to the firing chamber. Ink enters into the firing chamber

---

ence or expertise to understand complex explanations. Instead, they need simple and appealing explanations. Depending on the subject and the audience, these explanations can be largely visual or largely textual.

Figure 12.4 is a primarily visual presentation that explains how acid rain is formed. Although the term acid rain is familiar to most people, the complex natural process by which it is formed is not. Figure 12.4 simplifies the process with a drawing that includes the major elements of the cycle of acid rain formation and provides an explanation appropriate for its intended audience.

Preparing Processes

In preparing a process explanation, you need to consider the audience and purpose, identify the steps in the process, select or design visuals, and organize information.

FIGURE 12.3 ■ Process Explanation of How a Thermal Inkjet Cartridge Works[5] *(continued)*

through this inlet area. Like the barrier thickness, the inlet dimensions greatly affect the characteristics of the ejected droplet.

Finally, a gold-plated nickel orifice plate sits on top of the barrier. An orifice is formed in this plate directly above the firing chamber. This orifice hole is formed using an electro-forming process. The diameter of the orifice has a direct bearing on the volume and velocity of the ejected droplets.

To fire a drop, a voltage pulse is applied across the resistor. This pulse is typically very short, on the order of 2 to 5 microseconds in duration. The voltage pulse causes the resistor to heat up, temporarily bringing the resistor surface to temperatures up to 400°C. Heat from the resistor causes ink at the resistor surface to superheat and form a vapor bubble. Formation of this vapor bubble is a fast and powerful event, and expansion of the bubble forces some of the ink in the firing chamber out of the orifice at velocities of typically 10 meters per second.

By the time a droplet is ejected, the resistor has cooled down and the vapor bubble has collapsed. Through capillary forces, more ink flows into the firing chamber through the inlet area, thus readying the system for the firing of another

droplet. The frequency at which the printhead can repeatedly fire droplets is determined by several factors including the inlet dimensions, the barrier thickness, and the fluid properties of the ink.

The device described above is essentially a droplet generator. The device designer has a fair amount of control over the characteristics of the ejected droplets. For example, the volume of the ejected droplet can be controlled by changing the size of the resistor—bigger resistors give droplets of larger volumes. In addition, the diameter of the orifice can be used to control droplet volumes. Droplet velocity is also controlled primarily by the diameter of the orifice.

The frequency at which droplets are ejected can be controlled by altering the size and shape of the barrier and by changing the rheological properties of the ink. . . .

Droplet characteristics, as they relate to print quality on the media surface, can be optimized through careful control of orifice profiles and resistor/orifice alignment. . . . Ink properties such as surface tension, viscosity, and thermal stability all play important roles in the production of useful droplets.

The explanation of the process of firing a drop of ink is embedded in the overall document.

The concluding paragraphs discuss the effect that the process has on the product.

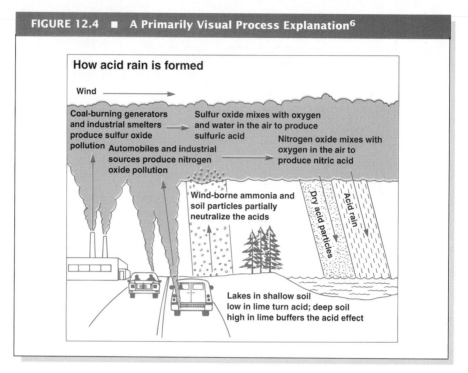

FIGURE 12.4 ■ A Primarily Visual Process Explanation[6]

How acid rain is formed

Wind

Coal-burning generators and industrial smelters produce sulfur oxide pollution

Automobiles and industrial sources produce nitrogen oxide pollution

Sulfur oxide mixes with oxygen and water in the air to produce sulfuric acid

Nitrogen oxide mixes with oxygen in the air to produce nitric acid

Wind-borne ammonia and soil particles partially neutralize the acids

Dry acid particles

Acid rain

Lakes in shallow soil low in lime turn acid; deep soil high in lime buffers the acid effect

Arrows signal the sequence of the process.

Each major step in the process is identified, but few details are provided.

Readers will relate to the easily identified elements such as cars and exhaust, factories and smoke stacks.

Clear causal relationships are identified.

The visual elements reinforce the information in the text.

Active voice is appropriate here.

Explain whether simplified process explanations such as the one about acid rain in Figure 12.4 should be avoided because they may mislead readers by omitting key information.

Audience and Purpose

Identifying your audience and their purpose for reading your document helps you to prepare a process explanation. Most readers, including professionals, are initially interested in an overall explanation of an action rather than the precise details necessary to complete that action. You need to ask not only who is going to use the process explanation and why, but you also need to know the circumstances under which they're likely to need such an explanation.

Identification of Steps

An essential part of preparing process explanations involves listing the steps of the action. If the time needed for each step or the time between steps is important, it too should be recorded. The sequence of steps forms the basis for the process explanation and also aids in designing visuals. For example, a common procedure in a hospital pediatrics unit is setting up a croup tent, which aids infants and children in breathing by providing an enclosed tent with moist, oxygen-enriched air. Both parents and young patients demonstrate anxiety about the tent, but parents seem to calm down (and thus the children relax) after they read an explanation about what the croup tent does, how it is set up, and how it operates. The brief outline in the following example identifies the basic steps you could use to prepare a process explanation.

■ **EXAMPLE**

1. Defining a croup tent

2. Setting up a croup tent
   a. Metal frame attached to crib
   b. Canopy placed over the frame
   c. Water bottle filled and attached to frame
   d. Ice placed in chamber
   e. Valve inserted and hoses attached

3. Operating a croup tent
   a. Oxygen flow turned on to prescribed level
   b. Oxygen forced through water
   c. Oxygen enters tubing and passes through ice
   d. Moist, cooled oxygen enters tent

Visuals

You can choose from several visuals to illustrate the overall sequence of a process. Most common are flowcharts that give a visual overview, in the same way that the introductory section of the text defines the action and identifies the major steps. Other visuals that provide an overview of the entire sequence are time lines and schedules.

A drawing can effectively show each element in a process, as in the cross section of a bog accompanying Figure 12.2. More common, though, are step-by-step changes that can be illustrated in a variety of ways: time-lapse photographs, drawings with overlays of changes, and drawings showing the final product. One other way is to use sequential drawings, as in Figure 12.5, which shows eight steps in the deployment of a satellite, from launch through to the final operational position. In this example, the steps in the action view are accompanied by very brief captions that are supplemental rather than essential; the drawing can stand alone.

Diction

The audience and purpose of your process explanation affect the language you use. One of your most important decisions is whether to select active or passive voice. Basically, if you want to emphasize the operator, the doer of the action, or the activating agent, use active voice. However, if you want to emphasize the recipient of the action or if the person doing the action is insignificant or unimportant, use passive voice. Figure 12.6 summarizes these key factors in making a decision and provides examples. (See Chapter 13 and the Usage Handbook for more details about active and passive voice.)

Organization and Format

Processes are chronological, often using headings to distinguish the major steps. Section headings and subheadings help readers by signaling the movement from

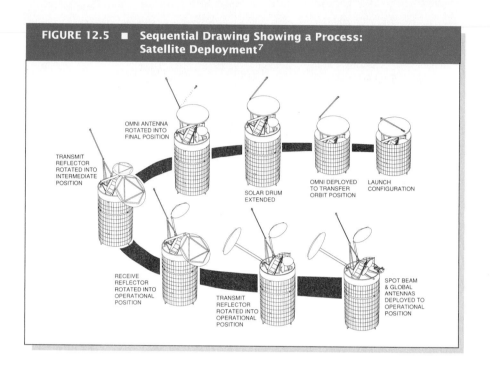

FIGURE 12.5 ■ Sequential Drawing Showing a Process: Satellite Deployment[7]

OMNI ANTENNA ROTATED INTO FINAL POSITION

TRANSMIT REFLECTOR ROTATED INTO INTERMEDIATE POSITION

SOLAR DRUM EXTENDED

OMNI DEPLOYED TO TRANSFER ORBIT POSITION

LAUNCH CONFIGURATION

TRANSMIT REFLECTOR ROTATED INTO OPERATIONAL POSITION

RECEIVE REFLECTOR ROTATED INTO OPERATIONAL POSITION

SPOT BEAM & GLOBAL ANTENNAS DEPLOYED TO OPERATIONAL POSITION

one part of the process to the next. Processes follow a format, summarized in Figure 12.7, that can be varied according to audience needs. The less expert the audience, the less complex the information should be. However, less-informed

FIGURE 12.6 ■ Active or Passive Voice in Process Explanations

	Use active voice. . .	Use passive voice. . .
when the action involves a person and . . .	. . . you want to emphasize the operator or doer of the action	. . .you want to emphasize the recipient of the action, *or* . . .the person doing the action is insignificant or unimportant
■ EXAMPLES	Dr. Hunt attended a seminar to learn about new techniques for treating kidney disease.	The marathon runner was treated for dehydration by the doctor on duty in the emergency room.
when the action does not involve a person and . . .	. . .you want to emphasize the activating agent	. . .you want to emphasize the recipient of the action
■ EXAMPLES	Torrential rains weakened the dam.	The machine was activated by the automatic timer.

Title

1.0 Identify the process in an introduction.
  1.1 Define the process.
  1.2 Identify purpose or goal.
  1.3 *Optional:* Identify the intended audience and the purpose.
  1.4 *Optional:* Explain background needed by the intended audience.
  1.5 *Optional:* Identify the relevant parts, materials, equipment, ingredients, and so on.
  1.6 *Optional:* Design a flowchart or other visual to provide an overview.
  1.7 Enumerate the major steps.

2.0 Present a step-by-step explanation of the process in chronological order, including cause-and-effect explanations as necessary.
  2.1 Explain step one of the process.
    2.1.1 Define step one.
    2.1.2 Present the purpose or goal of step one.
    2.1.3 *Optional:* Identify the necessary parts, materials, equipment, or ingredients for step one.
    2.1.4 *Optional:* Illustrate step one.
    2.1.5 Present chronological details of step one, including any substeps.
    2.1.6 *Optional:* Present chronological details of the substeps if they're relevant to the audience.
    2.1.7 *Optional:* Explain the theory or principle of this step's operation or function if it's relevant to the audience.
    2.1.8 Explain how this step relates to the next step.
  2.2 Explain step two . . .

3.0 *Optional:* Present a conclusion if it will increase the reader's understanding of the sequence, its theory, or applications.
  3.1 Summarize the major steps only if the action is long and/or complex.
  3.2 Discuss the theory or principle of operation if it has not already been incorporated in the primary discussion.
  3.3 Explain applications if they're not self-evident.

nonexperts often need careful explanations, which may take more space than the highly technical explanations appropriate for experts. You notice that a number of the parts are optional—included or not depending on the audience's needs.

Examining a Sample Process Explanation: Developing Low-Cost Roofing Materials

When Nilsa Cristina Zacarias was the Coordinator of the Research Division of the Appropriate Technology Center (CTA: Centro de Tecnologia Apropiada) in Asuncion, Paraguay, she wrote a process explanation as part of a final report to a German agency. This agency had funded a pilot project to develop building materials that low-income people in rural areas of a developing country could make and install themselves.

The logging industry in Paraguay's forests produces a great deal of sawdust, which is considered waste. One of Nilsa's colleagues, a researcher in CTA's laboratory, was supported by the International Development Research Center in Canada to develop an ecologically sound, low-cost material that could be used to make roof material. Nilsa field tested this process to determine if it could be used in an actual community. Figure 12.8 shows one of Nilsa's early drafts of this process explanation, with comments about things that she wants to change in her revision.[8]

Nilsa knew that her readers weren't going to complete the process themselves, but she wanted them to understand it. Because her process explanation was part of a much longer report, Nilsa wanted to keep this section brief and easy to read while emphasizing the economic and ecological goals expected by the funding agency. She decided that using a modified outline structure would make the process easy for readers to skim quickly (Figure 12.9). She decided that passive voice would be appropriate since her emphasis was on the process

---

FIGURE 12.8 ■ Preliminary Draft of Process Explanation

BUILDING WITH SAWDUST PLATES *Add an introductory paragraph.*

Make wording of headings and steps parallel.

Three major steps are necessary to build with sawdust plates: 1. treating the sawdust, 2. fabricating the plates, and 3. placing the plates. *List steps to help them stand out.*

1. Treatment *ing the sawdust*

   Sawdust is submerged into boiling water treated with 2% ferric sulfate for 10 minutes. Then the sawdust is passed through a strainer and rinsed with cold water. Finally it is placed on a clean surface to dry.

2. Fabrication *ing the plates*   *(cement: sawdust)*

   First the sawdust and the cement are mixed with 1:7 proportion. Water is added until the mixture gets a determined level of plasticity. Second, this mixture is poured into wood molds and floated for getting a flat surface with a wood or steel float. This procedure is fast, but it has to be conducted with a smooth pressure. After fabrication the plates could be lifted and put into storage for the drying process.

   How long?

3. Placement *ing the plates*

   How the plates are placed over the roof and fastened with bolts to the wooden structure. The plates are painted with a white, waterproof paint to protect the surface against the rain and sun.

Separate each major step to make the process easier to read.

FIGURE 12.9 ■ **Revision of Process Explanation Using an Outline Structure**

BUILDING WITH SAWDUST PLATES

Fabricated sawdust plates are an inexpensive alternative building material for low-cost roof construction. These plates are fabricated by mixing sawdust (waste from the logging industry) with cement and water. After the plates are fabricated, they can be used to insulate abnormally high roof temperatures from the interior rooms.

Introductory paragraph situates the process for readers.

Three major steps are necessary to build with sawdust plates:

1. treating the sawdust.
2. fabricating the plates, and
3. placing the plates.

Listing steps makes them easier to read.

1. **Treating the sawdust**
   - To avoid having the sawdust rot it is submerged into boiling water treated with 2% ferric sulfate for 10 minutes.
   - Then the sawdust is passed through a strainer and rinsed with cold water.
   - Finally it is placed on a clean surface to dry.

Rationale for step helps readers understand the process.

Text is more coherent when steps and section headings are parallel.

2. **Fabricating the plates**
   - First the sawdust and the cement are mixed with 1:7 proportion (cement:sawdust). Water is added until the mixture gets a determined level of plasticity.
   - Second, this mixture is poured into wood molds and floated for getting a flat surface with a wood or steel float. This procedure is fast, but it has to be conducted with a smooth pressure.
   - After 12 days of fabrication the plates can be lifted and put into storage for the drying process.

Clarifying substance for each proportion reduced ambiguity.

Specifying time helps readers better understand the fabrication process.

Identifying the substeps in the process makes the simplicity of the process immediately apparent.

3. **Placing the plates**
   - The illustration shows how the plates are placed over the roof and fastened with bolts to the wooden structure.
   - The plates are painted with a white, waterproof paint to protect the surface against the rain and sun.

Adding an illustration helps readers understand how the plates are attached to the existing roof.

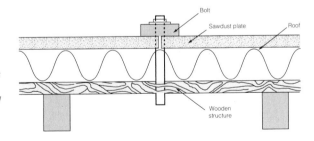

rather than the people completing the process. She also knew that including a figure would help readers visualize the way sawdust plates were attached to a roof. Although her explanation of building sawdust plates has few details, it follows the basic structure of more elaborated process explanations.

End-of-Chapter
Recommendations for Technical Communicators

1. Use process explanations to present an overview of the sequence of steps in any action or process.

2. Decide whether a process is better explained visually or verbally—or both.

3. Become accustomed to using the common sequence—technical description, process explanation, benefits or advantages—so that your readers will learn what a mechanism is, then how it works, and finally why it's useful.

4. Identify your audience and its task for reading the process explanation.

5. List the steps of the action.

6. Choose from several visuals to illustrate the overall sequence of a process: flow charts, single drawings showing each element in a process, time-lapse photographs, drawings with overlays of changes, drawings showing the final product, and sequential drawings.

7. Use active voice unless you have a good reason not to.

8. Organize your process explanation chronologically. Consider the value of headings to distinguish the major steps.

Practicum

Lockheed Martin

Background

Lockheed Martin is a multinational corporation with headquarters in Bethesda, Maryland. It has facilities across the United States and in more than 50 other nations and territories. The corporation was formed in 1995 with the merger of Lockheed and Martin Marietta. In subsequent years, it has merged with more than a dozen other companies to form one of the largest aeronautics, space, systems integration, and technology services corporations in the world. It conducts approximately 50% of its business with the U.S. Department of Defense, 20% with NASA and other government agencies, 20% with international customers, and 10% with domestic commercial customers.

Naval Electronics and Surveillance Systems-Eagan (NE&SS-Eagan) in Eagan, Minnesota (the setting for this practicum), develops real-time command, control, and communication systems and general-purpose military computers for aircraft, surface ship, submarine, and ground applications.

Lockheed Martin continues to be an industry leader in advancing the maturity of processes it uses to accomplish work. Companies that use mature processes are widely recognized for their effectiveness in lowering risk, their cost-effective solutions for developing products, and their delivery of services. NE&SS-Eagan has been assessed at high maturity levels for its software development, hardware development, and systems engineering processes.

Scenario

Let's say that Lockheed Martin NE&SS-Eagan has recently hired you to work on one of its projects. You will be doing software development and systems engineering for a communication network that will go on board an amphibious transport ship. One part of your orientation to the company is a process awareness class that you take during your second day of work. In the class you learn that peer reviews are an important part of the engineering work at the company. In a peer review, engineers who did not develop the item critique it according to predetermined criteria. To your surprise, the very next week you are invited to the peer review of a requirements document for your project. You suspect, from the number of people at the peer review and the amount of time spent, that peer review is not only important to the company in general but also to the specific work being done on your project. Your suspicions are confirmed in a conversation with the project manager.

An e-mail from the project manager is waiting for you when you arrive at work the next morning. The message asks you to drop by his desk some time between 10:00 and 10:30 when he'll be between meetings. You "drop by" promptly at 10:00.

"How are things going?" the project manager asks.

You describe the round of orientation activities and training that kept you occupied for the first week. You also mention the peer review you attended yesterday.

"What did you think of it?" the manager asks.

"It seems like a lot of people put in a lot of time," you reply.

"Exactly! Do you think we are using our time wisely?" The manager leans back in his chair. "This is a new project, and I want us to get off on the right foot. Are we looking at the right things in our peer reviews—the things that are going to make a difference to our customers? *And* are we doing it cost effectively?"

The manager bends forward and shuffles through a messy looking pile of papers on the corner of his desk. "Here." He slides the papers shown in Figures 1 and 2 in front of you. "They use these on a couple of projects around here." You must have a blank look on your face as you quickly try to scan the papers because he adds, "They're checklists. You see, that's what I figure we need, a really good checklist to flesh out our peer review process. We need something to keep us on track so that we cover all the important stuff and don't waste time on what isn't important. I've been meaning to look into this myself. I feel it's really important. We'll start with a checklist for document peer reviews. What do you say?"

You wonder what you can say. "Sure," you reply.

"Great!" The manager beams. "By the way, I don't really care much for either of those." He nods at the two checklists lying side by side on the desk. "I guess they work all right for the projects that use them. But the requirements product checklist is pretty vague if you ask me. The people on that project are very experienced at making processes; they probably only need a few reminders of what

---

FIGURE 1 ■ One Example of a Peer-Review Checklist

Software Requirements Product Checklist

_____ 1. Structure, style, and content of document conforms to the project-defined style in the Software Requirements Specification Style Guide
_____ 2. System context is appropriately explained in the overview
_____ 3. Software requirements are written at an appropriate level of detail
_____ 4. Specification is understandable to the customer, designer, and tester
_____ 5. All sections are devoid of TBDs (To Be Determineds)
_____ 6. Terminology is consistent with other project documents
_____ 7. Specification does not conflict with other accepted specifications
_____ 8. Interface requirements are sufficient to address the subsystem interface (input and output) requirements
_____ 9. Software requirements are responsive to subsystem design constraints
_____ 10. Software requirements are sufficient to satisfy the subsystem requirements allocated to software

---

they're supposed to do. But we're rookies." He grins at you. "We're going to need something more specific than that."

"As for the other one . . . , well, I want clean documents but I don't want us wasting everyone's time looking for editorial problems in a peer review. That should be taken care of ahead of time by the document producer. It's just plain

---

FIGURE 2 ■ Another Example of a Peer-Review Checklist

Document Editorial Checklist

Document Title	
Producer	
Editorial Checker	
Date Checklist Completed	

		✓ yes
1	Exhibit correct spelling (run spell-check), grammar (e.g., missing or repeated words, agreement between subject and verb, verb tense, use of "i.e." and "e.g."), capitalization, and punctuation (watch for double or no periods)?	
2	Reference items by their correct titles and reference numbers?	
3	Have consistent spacing and margins?	
4	Use a consistent font for the document body?	
5	Have consistent capitalization and punctuation on bullets?	
6	Use a consistent listing format (e.g., outline style with numbers and/or letters or bullets?	
7	Spell out the first use of an acronym and refer to the term by its acronym thereafter?	
8	Contain all references in the Reference List with proper titles, document numbers and dates?	
9	Contain all acronyms in the Acronym List?	
10	Correctly order all paragraphs, figures, and tables by number?	
11	Refer to each figure and table in the text?	
12	Contain no orphaned figure or table titles (i.e., the title is not on a different page than the figure or the table)?	
13	Contain no figures split over a page boundary or tables split over page boundaries that do not contain headers on each page segment of the table?	
14	Refer to any applicable Problem/Change Reports in the Record of Change or Document Revision History?	
15	Adhere to the proper customer or project document template?	
15a	Have a properly formatted title page (including the correct document title and last-saved date)?	
15b	Have properly formatted page headers (including a number assigned by Configuration Management and the proper revision designation?	
15c	Have properly formatted page footers (including page numbers formatted appropriately for the part of the document in which they occur)?	

---

good workmanship to turn out a document that uses proper grammar and punctuation." He pauses and, as if on cue, his phone rings. He picks it up and starts talking. A sentence or two later he puts his hand over the receiver. "This is going to take a while. Take a crack at the checklists. We'll talk later, maybe the middle of next week. I'll take a look at what you've got then."

That's it. You walk out of the manager's office, a couple of pieces of flimsy paper in hand (Figures 1 and 2).

Assignment

Well, the assignment is pretty obvious, isn't it? The project manager wants you to come up with a checklist to use in the process of peer reviewing documents. But when you start to put pencil to paper, you quickly realize that you have only a vague idea of how to proceed. What had seemed like a simple, direct task when he had talked about it now seems vague and confusing on closer examination, especially when you try to make sense of the two very different examples.

Sarah, who sits at the desk across the aisle from you and who has been with the company for nearly three years, notices that you look perplexed. "What you need is a plan of attack for coming up with the checklist," she says. "I'd suggest writing an approach paper that you can use when you talk to the boss about what you're doing next week. You can use it as a way to make sure that he and you are thinking along the same lines."

You give her a puzzled frown.

"An approach paper isn't very complicated," she adds helpfully. "It can have any format, but often around here they look a lot like expository papers you'd write in school with headings. They have an introduction giving a brief summary—or thesis, you could say—of your plan (process) for developing the checklist, a body that details your plan and explains why you will do the things you propose, and a conclusion that summarizes how the details are going to be brought together to result in the final checklist. You probably want to include a schedule, too."

And so, on Sarah's advice, we come to your assignment for this practicum—which you'll find is the first, vital step in doing many tasks on your project in the future. Your assignment is not to produce a checklist but to come up with a plan of attack in the form of an approach paper for producing a checklist.

Of course, there isn't one single approach to the process of developing a checklist. What is important is that you take into consideration that a checklist is a means of communication, especially for the people participating in the peer review. Your approach paper should cover at least these topics:

- *Assumptions.* List what you know about the checklist task from what the project manager has told you and the examples he has given you.

- *Holes in your knowledge base.* List what you need to know about the checklist task that you don't already know, including the relevant audiences for and the purposes of the checklist.

- *Plans for filling the holes in your knowledge base.* Describe how you are going to go about finding the information you need; include backup plans in case one method of filling a hole doesn't work or doesn't work well enough.

- **Plans for developing the checklist itself.** Describe when and how you will put together the checklist. How will you verify that it does what you intend it to do?

- **Schedule.** Outline the time you think it will take for the whole checklist task, including filling the holes in your knowledge base and coming up with the checklist itself.

- **Reasons.** Throughout your approach paper you should note the reasons that justify your approach.

That's it. Remember how concerned the project manager seems to be with cost. He wants you to come up with a "good" checklist in as little time as possible. Your approach should reflect that concern.

Kari Kruempel is a software engineer at NE&SS-Eagan. She has worked there since 1976. Recently she helped prepare NE&SS-E for the successful completion of several process assessments. She holds a B.S. degree from the University of Minnesota in mathematics and English and an M.S. in mathematics from the University of Wisconsin-Milwaukee. She is currently working on a Ph.D. at the University of Minnesota in Rhetoric, Scientific, and Technical Communication.

Kari Kruempel believes that one of the most difficult transitions to make from the classroom to the workplace is realizing how to apply concepts from a structured classroom environment to the often vague, sometimes confusing workplace environment. In discussing this practicum, she said, "Concepts learned in school can be invaluable in solving workplace problems, particularly communication problems. The challenge is to be creative enough first to recognize the connections between the two environments and second to apply and mold to the specific situation learning gained in school."

For more information about the Lockheed Martin corporation, visit <http:\\www.lmco.com\>

Individual and Collaborative Assignments

1. **Analyze a brief process explanation.** What features of the following sentence quality it as a process explanation?

   Routine maintenance involves changing the filter when it's dirty and making sure the heat exchanger and smoke pipe are clear of accumulated creosote.

2. **Summarize a process explanation.**
   (a) Read the following excerpt from a Web site about ongoing research to investigate the moons of Jupiter, one of which is Io (see the opening of Chapter 11 for a description of Io).
   (b) After reading the passage (and, if you want, checking the Web site for additional information: http://www.spacescience.com/newhome/headlines/ast04oct99_1.htm), compose a one- to two-sentence process explanation about Direct Simulation Monte Carlo as a way to learn more about Io. In order to do a summary, you need to clearly identify the steps in the process.

   . . . [Researchers] at the University of Texas . . . have been working for years on computer simulations of Io's volcanic plumes. Using a technique called Direct Simulation Monte Carlo [DSMC], they send computerized test particles blasting out of a model volcanic vent. The University of Texas program tracks the motion of ejected molecules taking into account intermolecular collisions, energy input from the Io torus, and energy lost to infrared radiation. By varying the size of the vent, the temperature and velocity of the ejected gas, and the temperature of the surrounding terrain they can match the appearance of their computerized plumes with the ones photographed by NASA space probes. Sometimes this leads to new insights about the fluid dynamics and physics of Io's volcanoes.

   In one of the University of Texas [simulations] . . . , gas erupts from a vent at 2.7 times the velocity of sound into Io's tenuous atmosphere. The ejecta soar to a height of about 120 km. Much of the material lands about 150 km away where it hits the ground and bounces. Just before it hits the surface, the gas passes through a shock wave and heats up to 200–300 K. . . .[9]

3. **Evaluate a process explanation.**
   (a) Read the following explanation about the operating process of a hydrogen/oxygen torch ignitor.
   (b) Identify the probable audience(s).
   (c) Evaluate all aspects of the process explanation, including the effectiveness of the organization, the visual, and the language choices (voice, person, mood).
   (d) Create a rubric that identifies the criteria for assessing the effectiveness of this process explanation.

HYDROGEN/OXYGEN TORCH IGNITOR[10]
This reliable device can be used to ignite a variety of fuels.
Lewis Research Center, Cleveland, Ohio

The figure illustrates a hydrogen/oxygen torch ignitor that is reliable and simple to operate. This device is the latest in a series of such devices that have been used for more than 20 years to ignite a variety of fuel/oxidizer mixtures in research rocket engines. The device can also be used as a general-purpose ignitor in other applications, or as a hydrogen/oxygen torch.

The operation of this device is straightforward. Hydrogen and oxygen flow through separate ports into a combustion chamber in the device, where they are ignited by use of a surface-gap spark plug. The hot gases flow from this combustion chamber, through an injector tube, into the larger combustion chamber that contains the fuel-oxidizer mixture to be ignited.

The pressures and flows of hydrogen and oxygen are adjusted to obtain a pressure of about 135 psig (gauge pressure of 0.93 MPa) in the combustion chamber during operation. The pressures and flows are also adjusted for an oxidizer/fuel ratio of 40 to obtain a combustion temperature of 2,050 K, which is low enough that there is no need to cool the combustion chamber if the operating time is short enough.

Some of the flow of hydrogen is diverted to the annular space surrounding the injector tube to cool the injector tube. The rate of this cooling flow is chosen so that when it mixes with the hot gases at the outlet of the injector tube, the resulting oxidizer/fuel ratio is 5. The resulting flame at the outlet is about 12 in. (about 30 cm) long and its temperature is about 3,100 K.

The Hydrogen/Oxygen Torch Ignitor can be used as a general-purpose ignitor or as a hydrogen/oxygen torch.

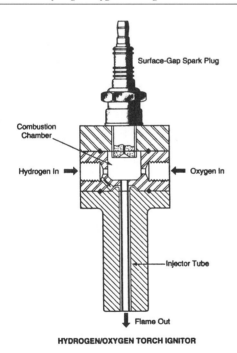

HYDROGEN/OXYGEN TORCH IGNITOR

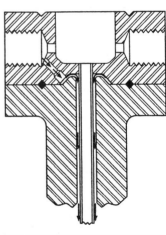

DETAIL SHOWING COOLING FLOW OF HYDROGEN
ALONG OUTSIDE OF INJECTOR TUBE

4. **Write a process description.** Select one of the topics below or choose one in your field/discipline. Identify the intended audience and specify the purpose of the description. Analyze the audience to determine the use of (a) active or passive voice, (b) first, second, or third person, (c) relevant visuals, and (d) headings and subheadings.

birth of a calf or foal	installation of a wood-burning stove
breeding of genetically pure laboratory animals	inventory control (FIFO)
	maintenance of a spinning reel
creation of a silicon crystal	manufacture of carbon fibers
depreciation	operation of a laser
design of a dietary program	operation of a rotary engine
development of hybrid varieties of corn	operation of a septic tank, leach field
	operation of a transit
energy audit of house	packing a parachute
extrusion of polymer parts	refinishing of a piece of furniture
fabrication of metal optics	regeneration of tails in lizards
formation of a weather front	self-regulated pain control (e.g., biofeedback)
formation of kidney stones	test/inspection procedure
formation of plaque on teeth	thermal aging process
grafting of plants	welding or brazing

5. **Design a visual to depict a process.**
   (a) Identify the intended audience and specify the purpose of the process that you can present in a visual (the way Figure 12.4 explains acid rain). Design the visual so that it is both accurate and appealing. Consider some of the topics listed in the preceding list.
   (b) Write a direct, brief caption that explains and supports the visual.

6. **Evaluate a Web-based process explanation.**
   (a) Visit the following Web sites:
       <www.colgate.com/Smiles/FAQ/procedures-2.html>
       <www.colgate.com/Smiles/FAQ/procedures-3.html>
       <www.colgate.com/Smiles/FAQ/procedures-4.html>
       <www.howstuffworks.com> (choose a procedure to evaluate)
   (b) Evaluate the process explanations by considering whether the information is effectively organized (including whether the site is navigable), how visuals are used, and what language choices are effective (or ineffective).
   (c) Create a rubric to identify the criteria you'll use for evaluating these process explanations.

Intertext

The Changing Face of Sexual Harassment[11]

Current Standards and New Developments

Sexual harassment is among the most prominent civil rights issues in the workplace. More than 15,500 sexual harassment charges were filed with the Equal Employment Opportunity Commission or state agencies in fiscal 1998, compared to about 10,000 complaints of racial harassment. Moreover, one of the most prominent features of harassment cases these days is the concept of "tangible employment action." But do you know what it is and why it is important? It is imperative that human resources managers thoroughly understand the legal concepts that are the basis of harassment litigation, so that they can create policies that help keep their companies out of court.

Supreme Court Justice Anthony Kennedy described a tangible employment action as "hiring, firing, failing to promote, reassignment with significantly different responsibilities or a decision causing a significant change in benefits."

The developing concept of "tangible employment action" recently led to the creation of an employer's defense against claims of harassment, where a hostile environment has been created, but no tangible employment action has occurred.

'98 Supreme Court Decisions Have Major Impact

Rulings in some cases the Court considered last year may alter the landscape of harassment. The concept of tangible employment action was important to *Burlington Industries v. Ellerth,* in which Kimberly Ellerth's harasser threatened to take steps against her if she didn't comply with his wishes. Since he never carried out the threat, Ellerth's employment status was not negatively affected. However, her harassment was severe and pervasive, and Burlington was held liable for that instead.

Severe and pervasive harassment, with an absence of tangible employment action, also characterized a case decided the same day—*Faragher v. City of Boca Raton.* In that case, lifeguard Beth Faragher had been repeatedly harassed by two male supervisors for several years. She complained to other beach supervisors, but to no avail. Attorneys for the city argued that she had not complained to authorities at a high enough level. This defense laid the foundation for another key concept the Court stressed: "vicarious liability."

Under the concept of vicarious liability, an employer may be liable for harassment if it is committed by anyone present in the workplace—including co-workers, customers, or vendors—if it is brought to the attention of any manager or supervisor.

In effect then, the Court held that employers are liable for harassment by anyone present in the workplace, if they knew or should have known of the harassment. And, even more important, employers are liable for harassment by all supervisors, whether the employer knew of it or not.

In the wake of these decisions, lower courts promptly began to apply the key concepts that emerged to all types of workplace harassment—not only offensive behavior based on gender, but also such behavior based on sexual orientation, race, ethnic or national origin, age, religion or disability. For the most part, the concepts apply in the same way across the board, and employers must meet the same standards to avoid liability for harassment arising from any of these characteristics.

How Can We Defend Ourselves?

In the *Ellerth* and *Faragher* decisions, the Court issued a specific description of how employers can defend themselves against claims of supervisory harassment.

The employer defense established by the Court exists if the supervisor's harassment does not result in a tangible employment action (that is, firing, failure to promote, and so forth):

First, the justices said, the company must show that it exercised reasonable care to prevent and correct any harassment. For example, there must be an anti-harassment policy and a complaint procedure in place, and all employees must be aware of it. The employer must promptly and effectively address all complaints of harassment.

Second, the complaining employee must "unreasonably" fail to take advantage of the procedure. Thus, the person being harassed must neglect to follow the employer's procedure for promptly reporting a problem to a supervisor or manager.

The difficulty with the second aspect of a proper employer defense is that it depends on something the company can't control—the employee's failure to take advantage of a harassment-prevention policy. In this regard, employment-law attorneys have suggested that an employee can probably wait as much as three months after harassment occurs to file a complaint, but his or her case is likely to fail if a year or more passes without reporting the problem.

Although timing is relevant, the courts have not relied as heavily on this factor. Instead, they have focused on the severity of the harassment, the effectiveness of the employer's policy and its distribution, and whether the employer moved quickly and effectively to address and correct harassing behavior. Typically, the courts have reasoned that an employer should investigate a complaint of harassment within two days of receiving it.

Who Is a Supervisor? When Is That Person Liable?

Just how far a company must go to avoid a guilty verdict in a harassment case is the subject of comprehensive guidance issued recently by the EEOC. The agency was also quick to emphasize that the standards apply to harassment based on any protected characteristic—age, religion, disability, and so forth, as well as gender.

The EEOC's straightforward definition of a supervisor is anyone who can take tangible employment action against the worker or who can direct his or her daily work activities. A company can be liable, the guidance points out, for harassment, even by someone who is not in the chain of command of the lower-level employee—in other words, harassment by somebody else's boss.

Individual liability, or a particular supervisor being found guilty and assessed a penalty that he or she must pay, is highly unlikely. Nearly every court has ruled that only companies, not individuals, can be held responsible for harassment under Title VII of the Civil Rights Act. Be aware, however, that an increasing number of state laws are allowing individual liability for supervisors who harass their employees.

The EEOC's guidance makes clear that the decision will always go against the employer if the harassment led to a tangible employment action, such as failure to promote or termination. Even when no tangible employment action is taken, the company may be liable if it didn't try hard enough to prevent the harassment from occurring in the first place or to correct it once it did happen.

How Must Companies Investigate Harassment Claims?

The EEOC's new enforcement guidance on harassment by supervisors, which is available at www.blr.com (in the HR Resources and Documents Center), recommends a variety of steps to take in investigating a harassment complaint.

The guidance includes detailed lists of questions to be asked of the complainant, the accused person, and witnesses or other third parties.

EEOC's enforcement guidance suggests the following questions—tailored to the particular facts of the complaint—be asked during a complaint investigation:

For the Complainant—Who, what, when, where, and how:

- Who committed the alleged harassment?
- What actually occurred or what was said? When did it occur? Is it ongoing?
- Where did it occur? How often did it occur? How did it affect you?

Employee reaction:

- What response did you make when the incident(s) occurred or afterward?
- Effect of harassment: Has your job been affected in any way by the harasser's actions?

Collecting relevant information from other sources:

- Was anyone present when the harassment occurred? Did you tell anyone about it?
- Did anyone see you immediately after episodes of harassment?

Determining a pattern of harassment:

- Do you know whether anyone complained about harassment by that person?
- Are there any notes, physical evidence, or other documentation regarding the incident(s)?
- How would you like to see the situation resolved?
- Do you have any other relevant information?

For the alleged harasser:

- What is your response to the allegations?

- If the harasser claims that the allegations are false, ask why the complainant might lie.

- Are there any persons who have relevant information?

- Are there any notes, physical evidence, or other documentation regarding the incident(s)?

- Do you have any other relevant information?

For third parties:

- What did you see or hear? When did this occur? Describe the alleged harasser's behavior toward the complainant and toward others in the workplace.

- What did the complainant tell you?

- When did she or he tell you this?

- Do you have any other relevant information?

- Are there other persons who have relevant information?

After the investigator has made the proper inquiries, it may also be necessary to make credibility determinations if there are conflicting versions of events. In its enforcement guidance, the EEOC lists some factors to consider when making a credibility determination, including:

- Is the testimony believable on its face? Does it make sense?

- Did the person seem to be telling the truth or lying?

- Did the person have a reason to lie?

- Is there witness testimony (eyewitnesses, people who saw the person soon after the alleged incidents, or people who discussed the incidents with the complainant around the time the incidents occurred) or physical evidence (written documentation) that corroborates the complainant's testimony?

- Does the alleged harasser have a history of harassing behavior?

The EEOC warns that although the above questions are helpful in establishing credibility, no one factor should be used to make a final determination. For example, the fact that there are no eye witnesses to the alleged harassment does not automatically make the complaint unbelievable, since harassment often occurs behind closed doors.

Finally, the EEOC's new guidance outlines methods of reaching a determination regarding a claim of harassment; assuring all parties that immediate and appropriate corrective action will be taken; and taking other preventive and corrective measures against unlawful harassment.

This article was prepared by Susan E. Long, J.D., managing editor at Business & Legal Reports, Inc., Madison, Conn., and Catherine G. Leonard, Gomez & Leonard Marketing, East Haven, Conn.

13 Ensuring Usability: Testing, Revising, and Editing

CHAPTER 13 IN BRIEF

Testing, revising, and editing are critical to the success of your documents.

Document Testing

The term *document testing* refers to a cluster of techniques used to assess the technical and textual accuracy, appropriateness, and appeal of a document.

Procedures for Document Testing. A critical part of planning involves building in the time for testing and a budget to support that testing.

Categories of Document Testing. Three categories of document testing are distinguished by the way in which the information is collected and by the nature of the feedback: text-based, expert-based, and user-based testing. Information from testing can be used to revise and edit your documents.

Revising

Revising is a global function involving both complex, interrelated factors.

Redesigning Documents. Substantive revision generally focuses on overall factors such as organization of information, logic, tone, selection and placement of support, design of document, and selection and placement of visuals.

Revising for Plain Language. Five particular problems often afflict technical documents—density, violation of given-new constructs, overdependence on passive voice, inappropriate verb mood, and inappropriate choice of person.

Editing

Editing, a concern with conventions and consistency, improves a document's technical or textual accuracy, as well as its appropriateness and appeal to readers.

Four areas need a final check before a document is complete: concrete details, directness, positive phrasing, and wordiness.

Examining Revision and Editing Decisions

Revising and editing a report make it more accessible to readers.

Testing, revising, and editing are critical to the success of your documents. Although these three processes often overlap and definitions vary slightly from expert to expert and company to company, their fundamental purposes remain the same: to create documents that are accurate and appropriate.

- *Testing* refers to a variety of techniques for assessing documents.

- *Revising* refers to the process of changing overall (or global) elements of documents.

- *Editing* refers to (1) changing specific (or local) elements of documents and (2) managing administrative details necessary for publication of documents.

Document Testing

The term *document testing* refers to a cluster of techniques used to assess the technical and textual accuracy, appropriateness, and appeal of a document. The information obtained from document testing helps you revise and edit documents.

Procedures for Document Testing

Everyone involved in the creation of technical documents—writers, technical experts, managers, designers, editors—agrees that testing documents takes time. The benefits, though, are undeniable because a well-planned document testing program can provide invaluable information for revising and editing a document. Successful document testing looks for problems that you haven't recognized so that they can be eliminated; testing a document that has flaws you've already identified wastes time and energy.

This section suggests generic preliminary steps for conducting document testing. You need to modify them to fit the needs of specific situations. The goal of all testing is to help produce a better document, one that accomplishes its intended purpose with the identified audience.

1. ***Goals.*** Establish the goals for your testing. What do you want to find out? Ways to reduce time on task? Increase accuracy? Reduce calls to the helpline?

2. *Criticality.* Assess the importance of the document you plan to test and decide what kind of testing feedback you need. For example, a new computer manual probably needs text-based, expert-based, and user-based testing. However, that would be excessive for a monthly progress report.

3. *Constraints.* Identify the constraints that you have to work with. Those typically include available expertise (someone to conduct and interpret the tests), time, and budget.

4. *Schedule.* Build the time for testing into the project schedule, and provide for that testing in the project's budget. Establish a schedule that, if at all possible, includes testing of different kinds as an ongoing part of the project.

5. *Involvement.* Explain the purpose and procedures of document testing to all key personnel on the project so that they understand the goals and cooperate with the testing.

6. *Maintenance.* Determine how the test results will be used as part of the development and revision process.

Document testing should not be limited to instructions and manuals. Many other documents benefit from careful testing—for example, form letters, advertising copy, product descriptions, spec sheets, and standard sections of proposals (such as the boilerplate sections about the organization). And do not limit testing to the verbal sections of a document; test other components as well, including visuals and the overall design. Your goal is to determine the effectiveness of a document for its intended audience.

The three categories of document testing are distinguished by the way the information is collected and by the nature of the feedback.[1] Figure 13.1 identifies three categories of testing: text-based, expert-based, and user-based testing.

Text-Based Testing

Text-based testing usually concentrates on the words and sentences of a document. Traditionally, people doing this kind of testing examine local-level features of a document and then draw conclusions about factors such as the

FIGURE 13.1 ■ Approaches to Document Testing[2]		
Text-Based Testing	**Expert-Based Testing**	**Reader-Based Testing**
◆ Guidelines and maxims	◆ Peer review	◆ Concurrent tests
◆ Checklists	◆ Technical review	◆ Retrospective tests
◆ Readability formulas	◆ Editorial review	
◆ Computer programs to assess structure and style	◆ Document design review	

document's reading level and use of language. Text-based testing includes a variety of guidelines and checklists, as well as readability tests and computer programs to assess structural and stylistic features (for example, types of sentences or active versus passive voice).

These tests are useful for identifying specific errors and for establishing the presence or absence of common text features. While quick and inexpensive text-based testing reminds writers about things they need to check, such tests do have drawbacks.

- Checklists usually provide generalized information without criteria for assessing how effectively a feature has been used in a document.

- Some text-based testing reports quantitative information without any indication of whether that feature is appropriate in a document or situation.

- Text-based testing does not assess the technical accuracy of a document.

- Text-based testing does not indicate how actual readers will respond to a document.

Despite its obvious limitations, text-based testing can help assess a whole range of local-level factors—from spelling to consistent terminology, from punctuation to sentence structure, from capitalization to grammar, from documentation to local coherence. Writers have a difficult time seeing their own errors, so this kind of testing can be very helpful.

Can you think of any circumstances in which text-based testing alone would be sufficient?

Expert-Based Testing

A second kind of testing, *expert-based testing*, includes several kinds of reviews: formal and informal peer reviews, technical reviews, editorial reviews, and document design reviews. Expert-based testing is particularly useful not only for assessing the technical accuracy of a document, but also for selecting supporting evidence and for identifying the level of detail for the intended audience. Recent workplace research supports the practice of using several kinds of experts in testing. The expert testing of a user manual accompanying impendance spectroscopy software for a multinational market is an example. Investigation of the testing indicated that the manual benefited from review by three kinds of experts: experts in engineering, in information design, and in nonnative readers of English.[3]

Many large companies and agencies have formal review boards that read every publication that goes out of the company—to ensure technical accuracy but also to ensure that writers are not unintentionally giving away proprietary information (that is, guarded or secret information such as production processes). Such committees are also sometimes charged with ensuring that documents adhere to the organization's policies and practices regarding publication, which might include anything from checking the correct bibliographic format to assuring that the documents are coherent.

Formal review is also a process that is mandated by some organizations—a sequence or cycle that documents go through to be assessed for consistency and appeal in format and design. Documents may move from a technical writer or editor to a subject expert and then back two or three times, or perhaps a dozen or more times. Similarly, a document may move between an editor and a graphic designer many times. In many organizations, documents cycle through a review–revise–review sequence several times, with different reviewers at different levels in the organization who identify problems with the documents' textual and technical accuracy.

Informal expert-based testing doesn't follow a rigid process. Rather, informal expert-based testing generally means stopping by the office of a colleague and saying, "Sandy, I'd appreciate it if you had the time to read through this to check _____." And, you fill in the blank to ask for a review of technical content, language use, logic of your argument, presentation of the information, and so on. As you develop a major document, you may see that it receives dozens of these informal reviews by various kinds of experts.

What would you include as essential components of an expert-based testing program?

Although experts can examine both specific and overall features of a document, they cannot predict how actual users will respond, largely because they know so much more than people who will read the document. However, feedback from experts is important because they can identify areas that need improvement in the consistency, accuracy, coherence, completeness, and appeal of the verbal and visual aspects of a document. Revision and editing are much easier when you have expert feedback.

User-Based Testing

Because text-based testing and expert-judgment testing aren't sufficient, *reader-based* or *user-based testing* gets information about the document directly from the users. Revising based on reader feedback is so important that the U.S. government urges federal departments and agencies to user-test their documents.[4]

Information can be collected from readers as they read and use a document (which is called *concurrent testing*) or after they have finished reading it (which is called *retrospective testing*). Generally, writers have their choice of two kinds of *concurrent testing*.

- One kind of concurrent testing involves watching readers' behavior as they perform a task. As you observe the users, you can observe places in the document where they have difficulty following the instructions. For example, you can observe the amount of time or apparent ease (or difficulty) they have in locating information or performing individual tasks or sequences of tasks. You can keep notes on any number of factors—from the number and type of errors they make to their attitudes while using the document.

- Another kind of concurrent testing asks readers to read and think aloud—that is, not only to read the document aloud but also to say aloud all their comments, reactions, and opinions. You can tape-record their comments as they use a document. By reviewing the tape, you can identify specific places in the document where information is confusing to users.

If you conduct user-based testing with several individuals, you may begin to see patterns of problems signaling areas in the document that need possible revision and editing. The problem with concurrent testing is that it is time-consuming and expensive and requires trained testers. The advantage is that the writer has feedback directly from actual users.

Retrospective testing includes such methods as questionnaires, interviews, focus groups, and reader-feedback cards. Although retrospective testing does provide information from actual users, it should be used cautiously because readers' memories are not necessarily accurate, and the information they provide is often vague.

Why is user testing often considered the most important kind of document testing?

Despite the problems of user-based testing, it provides very valuable information. Using this feedback, you can revise and edit documents so that they are more useful for the intended audience.

General Observations About Testing

When you have access to information from several kinds of testing, you will be able to make changes to documents that improve their technical and textual accuracy. Perhaps more important, you will be able to make changes so that the document is more accessible, appealing, and relevant for your intended audience. When you create a testing plan for an important document, try to include text-based, expert-based, and user-based testing because each type provides a different kind of feedback that you can use to improve document quality.

Document testing is time consuming; thus, an organization must make a commitment to testing as part of a process or production schedule. Waiting until the final draft is completed to do some kind of testing usually means that there's not enough time to incorporate the necessary changes recommended by the testing. Testing documents early increases the chances that changes can be incorporated in the document. As the value of testing is becoming more widely recognized, more organizations are employing some kind of testing as part of the revision process. Generally, the feedback from various kinds of testing enables you to improve documents enough to merit the extra time and expense.

Revising

This section of the chapter focuses on two levels of revision—*global revision* (redesigning and reorganizing the overall document) and *local revision* (revising individual paragraphs and sentences). Both kinds of revision depend on thinking of chunks of text rather than individual words and phrases. The information for making revisions can come from various kinds of document testing.

Redesigning Documents

The organization and format of a report have a strong impact on the reaction of readers. Figures 13.2 and 13.3 are different versions of the same memo report

FIGURE 13.2 ■ Report Without Careful Design of Information

Add headlines and subheadings to help readers identify issues and recommendation.

MEMO

Add job titles

To: Charles Malatesta,

From: Tom Mansur *T.M.*

Subject: Purchase and installation of automatic roll-up doors

Date: September 27, 20—

Make subject line more specific

#Reorder sections to create a stronger argument. (see numbers)

Overview of unacceptable conditions

① The R&D Model Shop moved to its current location—next to the rear shipping and receiving dock of the Colebrook facility—15 months ago. Since then, we have been subjected to excessive heat in summer and extreme cold in winter. Most of the day the loading doors are open, and the heat or air conditioning is lost through the two connecting doorways. This is both expensive and a health risk.

⑤ *Previous attempts to solve the problem.*

Swinging Metal doors:
One attempt to control the temperature was swinging metal doors, which kept out the weather but were dangerously noisy. These doors banged loudly against the chain link fence outside. Machinists would jump at the sound, presenting the danger of severed fingers. Eventually these doors were knocked off their hinges, leaving us no protection from the outside elements.

Plastic Flap Doors:
We next installed clear plastic strip doors, which flap in the breeze and offer no protection from extreme temperatures. They also present a safety risk to fork truck drivers, in that the flexible strips swing down from the fork truck extensions and slap the drivers on the face and arms.

② *Background on current problems*
Personnel Concerns:
(expand!)

Cost of Lost Energy:
The approximate cost of the lost heat and air conditioning is $5,970.00 per year. (See attached cost breakdown) In human terms, in the summer when the air conditioners are on, we are sweating; in the winter when the heaters are blowing, we are shivering. These conditions are unacceptable.

Energy Loss:
(add info)

Recommendation for Automatic Garage Doors

③ We, therefore, recommend the purchase and installation of two electric garage doors with both wall-mounted and pull-chain openers. These doors would be equipped with pneumatic safety stops at the bottom to prevent injury. In compliance with the fire safety egress requirements, we recommend the installation of two regular doors, with pneumatic closers, as common entry/exit ways. The total cost to purchase and install the equipment to correct the situation is $4,262.00. This would account for $1,708.00 in savings at the end of one year. Please refer to the attached estimates for prices of the garage doors and regular doors. Refer also to the attached building layout that identifies the recommended locations of the proposed doors.

④ *Financial Evidence*

Purchase and Installation Costs:

Potential Savings:

Discussion

⑥ We need these doors now, since winter is rapidly approaching. *(Expand!)*

TM/db

Attachments

FIGURE 13.3 ■ **Revised Report with Careful Design of Information**[5]

MEMO

To:	Charles Malatesta
	Plant/Facilities Administration
From:	Tom Mansur *TM*
	R&D Model Shop Group Leader
Subject:	Justification for the purchase and installation of
	automatic roll-up doors for the R&D Model Shop
Date:	September 27, 20—

A detailed subject line helps orient the reader to the purpose of the memo.

Overview of Unacceptable Conditions

The R&D Model Shop has been in the Colebrook facility, zone 5 (see Figures 1 and 2), for 15 months, adjacent to the shipping and receiving dock. The dock's loading doors are open approximately 8–10 hours a day, so the heat or air conditioning escapes from the R&D Model Shop through the two connecting doorways. The Model Shop machinists are exposed to excessive heat during the summer and extreme cold during the winter.

Establishing the problem— the seriousness and the background—helps the reader see the need for immediate action.

Background on Current Problems

This situation poses personnel concerns as well as energy losses, both of which are influential in analyzing and addressing the current problem.

Personnel Concerns: Machinists working in the R&D Model Shop are exposed to temperature extremes for up to 10 hours a day, causing discomfort and decreasing resistance to colds and flu. Employee satisfaction with the working conditions is low, influencing shop productivity. Additionally, use of sick days by R&D Model Shop employees has increased 7% since we moved to the Colebrook facility, costing the company money.

Energy Loss: Because the loading dock is open to the outside for up to 10 hours a day, the energy expended to heat or air condition the R&D Model Shop is wasted.

Reordering of sections clearly establishes and labels the problems before making a recommendation that addresses the identified problems.

Specific headings and subheadings ease reading.

Recommendation for Automatic Garage Doors

The purchase and installation of two electric garage doors with both wall-mounted and pull-chain openers would eliminate the problem with temperature extremes. These doors would be equipped with pneumatic safety stops at the bottom to prevent injury. In compliance with the fire safety egress requirements, two regular doors (with pneumatic closers) would be installed as common entry/exit ways.

Financial Evidence

This recommendation for automatic garage door openers takes three financial factors into consideration

Cost of Lost Energy: The cost of BTU loss in zone 5—based on heating and air conditioning expenses for the last fiscal year and cost formulas (see Figures 3, 4, and 5)—is approximately $5,970.00.

Purchase and Installation Costs: The total cost to purchase and install the equipment to correct the situation is $4,262.00, based on quotations from Dempsey Door Company and Jackson Lumber Company. (See Figures 6 and 7.)

Potential Savings: The payback period would be less than one year.

Estimated annual cost of problem	$5,970.00
Estimated cost of solution	−4,262.00
Savings the first year	$1,708.00

All the financial information is chunked and labeled so that the implications are easy to see.

The recommended solution would account for more than $1,708.00 in savings at the end of one year. Please refer to the attached estimates for prices of the garage doors and regular doors. Refer also to the attached building layout that identifies the recommended locations of the proposed doors.

Reviewing the previous attempts reminds the reader that the problem is long term and that various solutions have been tried.

Previous Attempts to Solve the Problem

The two previous attempts to address the problem have not been successful.

Swinging Metal Doors: Swinging metal doors were in place for the first six months that the R&D Model Shop was in the present location. They kept out the weather but were dangerously noisy. When fully loaded fork trucks passed through, these doors banged loudly against the chain link fence that surrounds the shop. Machinists in the area would jump at the sound, presenting the danger of severed fingers or worse, not to mention the rattled nerves. The constant traffic of fork trucks eventually knocked these doors off their hinges.

Plastic Flap Doors: The swinging metal doors were replaced with clear plastic strip doors. These doors flap in the breeze and actually provide no protection at all from extreme temperatures. They also present a safety risk to fork truck drivers. As the fork trucks move through the doorway, the flexible strips swing down from the fork truck extensions and slap the drivers on the face and arms.

Figures, which provide supplementary information, are attached if the reader needs to check any details.

The figures that accompanied the original report are not included here.

Discussion

Implementing the recommendation in this report will benefit both the R&D Model Shop employees as well as the Colebrook operation in general. The comfort of the work environment and job satisfaction will increase for employees in the R&D Model Shop. Sick time should decrease. The impact on the heating and air conditioning expenses should be felt almost immediately.

This report has been approved by Raphael Calvo, Manager of the R&D Model Shop, and Max Freeport, Director of Colebrook Operations.

So that work can begin immediately, a working print (Figure 8) and the completed work request form (Figure 9) are attached.

The brief discussion acts as a conclusion that reminds the reader about benefits that are gained if the recommendations are followed.

requesting that automatic garage doors be installed in a shop area constantly exposed to harsh weather. Both reports were accompanied by several attachments that are not included here. In the first version of the report (Figure 13.2), readers have to work too hard to get the information they need. This version has been marked for the following revisions:

- Add headings and subheadings.

- Reorder sections.

- Elaborate in some places, especially about personnel problems and energy losses.

- Add expected conventions (for example, the writer's initials and a more specific subject line).

The second version of the report (Figure 13.3) is far easier to read because of its headings, organization, details, and adherence to conventions—in other words, a general awareness of readers. Probably the most obvious difference between the two versions is that Figure 13.3 provides design cues in the form of headings and subheadings that save readers time and energy in understanding the relationships among the various sections of the memo. Equally important, though, is that the information in Figure 13.2 has been reorganized and chunked so that it is easy to follow the writer's argument. A third major difference is that financial details are given special attention by being separated from the rest of the text. Another difference is that readers are reminded of the benefits that accrue if the recommendations are followed.

If the information in a document is accurate and complete, why does a writer need to revise the document so that it's accessible and adapted to the audience?

Revising for Plain Language

Plain language is more than a good idea; it's a presidential order. In 1998, President Clinton signed a "Memorandum for the Heads of Executive Departments and Agencies" about plain language in government writing:

> The federal government's writing must be in plain language. By using plain language, we send a clear message about what the government is doing, what it requires, and what services it offers. Plain language saves the government and the private sector time, effort, and money. . . . Plain language documents have logical organization, easy-to-read design, [and these language features]:
>
> - common, everyday words, except for necessary technical terms
>
> - "you" and other pronouns
>
> - the active voice
>
> - short sentences[6]

Explain whether you believe all states should have their own plain language laws that apply to state regulations and publications, insurance policies, mortgage and rental agreements, and so on.

Plain language communicates information—even very complex information—so that it makes sense to most people.[7] Although no legal definition of plain language exists, many experts in both law and technical communication agree that it has a number of characteristics in addition to those identified in President Clinton's memorandum:

- Straightforward language that eliminates unnecessary or inappropriate formalisms ("wherefore," "whereas"), archaic expressions ("herein," "thereof"), redundancies ("consent and agree," "each and every"), and Latin words

- Strong verbs that eliminate nominalizations ("classify" rather than "classification")

- Direct language that eliminates wordiness[8]

The federal agency charged with helping departments and agencies use plain language—Plain Language Action Network (PLAN)—says that "People should be able to understand what we write the first time they read it, especially materials that tell people how to obtain benefits or comply with requirements."[9] As part of their effort to help federal departments and agencies produce clear, enforceable regulatory documents, the Office of the Federal Register offers a guide to legal writing that you might find interesting to check out on this Web site: http://www.nara.gov/fedreg/dldhome.html#top. A related Web site established to assist people prepare plain-language documents provides some specific examples of the kinds of technical documents that should follow these plain language guidelines:

Explain why you agree or disagree with this statement: Plain language is the result of lower standards in education and increased inability to use our own language. It's essentially "dumbing down."

- An OSHA publication explaining safety requirements for factories

- A Bureau of Land Management publication explaining how to adopt wild horses

- A Social Security Administration pamphlet explaining how to apply for survivor's benefits[10]

The basic question still exists: Does plain language really make a difference? One dramatic situation serves as an example of the way complex technical language can affect people's lives: Recently, the U.S. Court of Appeals for the Ninth Circuit heard a case between Maria Walters versus the United States Immigration and Naturalization Service (INS).

The court found that certain government forms were so difficult to read that they violated due process requirements that people be given "notice" of possible legal actions against them, and of the legal consequences of their own actions. In brief, the Ninth Circuit Court of Appeals found that aliens subject to deportation based on INS charges that they committed document fraud did not get due process. The forms used by INS to tell the plaintiffs that they might be deported did not "simply and plainly communicate" legal consequences to the plaintiffs. The court ordered INS to redo the forms to communicate better. The court also ordered INS to refrain from deporting any alien whose case had been processed using the deficient forms.[11]

How else can plain language make a difference? Which of these pairs of sentences would you prefer to read? Which would you prefer to write?

When the process of freeing a vehicle that has been stuck results in ruts or holes, the operator will fill the rut or hole created by such activity before removing the vehicle from the immediate area.	*or this* . . .	If you make a hole while freeing a stuck vehicle, you must fill the hole before you drive away.
The Secretary of the Interior may, in specific cases or in specific geographic areas, adopt or make applicable to off-reservation Indian lands all or any part of such laws, ordinances, codes, resolutions, rules or other regulations of the State and political subdivisions in which the land is located as the Secretary shall determine to be in the best interest of the Indian owner or owners in achieving the highest and best use of such property.	*or this* . . .	We may apply state or local laws to off-reservation lands. We will do this only if it will help the Indian owners make the best use of their lands.[12] http://www.plainlanguage.gov/cites/page1.htm

The remainder of this section focuses on five particular problems that often afflict technical documents—density, violation of given-new constructs, overdependence on passive voice, inappropriate verb mood, and inappropriate choice of person. These are all problems that tend to affect the entire document rather than a sentence or two. Eliminating these problems, which helps create effective plain-language documents, requires attention to the audience for and purpose of the document. (Some of the other problems that reduce the plain language effectiveness of technical documents are addressed in the editing section, the next major section of the chapter following this discussion of revision.)

Density.   Sometimes a paragraph appears to focus on a single topic and has appropriate sentence structure, yet is difficult to read. Such a paragraph can suffer from density; the ideas are packed so tightly that connections are omitted, and readers have trouble following the reasoning. Several techniques can help you reduce the density in your writing:

Suggestions about verbal elements

- Separate information into several sentences rather than a few very long sentences.

- Develop important points in separate paragraphs.

- Add examples and explanations to illustrate points.

FIGURE 13.4 ■ Dense Paragraph

Separate
each chunk
into sentences
to give equal
emphasis to
each point.

Too much new
information in
each sentence.

A robot hand can perform rapid, small motions by human-like finger actions—
independently of its manipulator arm, be attachable to many different manipulators
without any modifications to the arms, and has the potential as a prosthesis for humans.
The hand employs three opposed fingers, each one with three joints and a cushioned tip
on the outer segment, controlled by four sheathed cables running to motors on the
forearm. The motor drives on the forearm impose no loads on the hand actuators, and the
drives are more easily accommodated on the forearm and have a much smaller effect on
its response than they would if located on the hand. The robot-hand fingers can provide
more than three contact areas since more than one segment per finger can contact an
object; thus, the robot hand can move objects about, twist them, and otherwise
manipulate them by finger motion alone.

Separate
into paragraphs
to reduce density.

Add a figure
so readers can
visualize the
robot hand.

- Use direct diction.
- Add transitions within paragraphs and between paragraphs and sections of a document.

Suggestions about visual elements

- Use headings and subheadings to identify key sections.
- Illustrate objects and concepts to aid understanding.
- Use selected visual devices to highlight key ideas: lists, bullets, tables, underlining, italics, boldface.

In Figure 13.4, the information in the paragraph is so dense that readers have trouble absorbing it. The sentences are long and wordy, with few transitions to establish relationships among the ideas; in some places, additional information is needed. Revision of this paragraph in Figure 13.5 uses some of the devices recommended above—writing shorter sentences, separating information into several paragraphs, adding a clarifying figure, and including transitions to signal relationships.

One of the interesting things about the revision of the robot hand paragraph is that the changes have more to do with organization of information than with adherence to mechanical or grammatical conventions. The improvements were triggered largely by the writer's asking what could be done to make the information more accessible to readers.

FIGURE 13.5 ■ Revision of Dense Paragraph[13]

Applying given–new principle places "hand" in the subject position.

A robot hand currently under development performs rapid, small motions by human-like finger actions—independently of its manipulator arm. Without modification, the robot hand attaches to many different arms. The hand even has the potential as a prosthesis for humans.

As shown in the figure, the hand employs three opposed fingers. Each has three joints and a cushioned tip on the outer segment. Each finger is controlled by four sheathed cables running to motors on the forearm.

The new hand eliminates some problems with previous designs. Its motor drives are on the forearm (rather than on the hand itself), where their weight and inertia impose no loads on the hand actuators. The drives are more easily accommodated on the forearm and have a much smaller effect on its response than they would if located on the hand.

The topic of the paragraph (eliminating problems) is placed first.

The use of an analogy—comparing the robot hand to a human hand—helps readers understand key distinctions.

Like the fingers on the human hand, the robot-hand fingers provide more than three contact areas since more than one segment per finger contacts an object. Thus, like the human hand, the robot hand moves and manipulates objects by finger motion alone.[3]

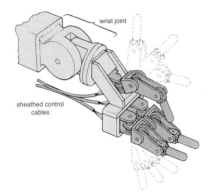

wrist joint

sheathed control cables

A figure helps readers visualize the robot hand.

Given-New Analysis.

A second problem arises when documents aren't coherent—that is, one idea doesn't logically or clearly relate to the following idea; the connections simply aren't obvious to readers. This problem often occurs when a writer presumes too much about the readers' prior knowledge. In these situations, a writer forgets (or neglects) to include background and connecting information that readers need.

One way to ensure that you have provided readers with the cues they need is to use *given-new constructions*, which strengthen the coherence of a document. In such constructions, new information is connected to what readers already know, either from background knowledge or from immediately preceding reading. Given-new analysis aids revision by providing a quick, effective way to spotlight the new information you have introduced. These are three of the many variations of given-new that are possible, with A, B, C, and so on representing pieces of information:

■ **EXAMPLE 1**[14]

sentence	given-new	
(1)	given A: new B	(1) The *ink* of a squid [A] is *brown or black viscous fluid* [B], which is contained in a reservoir. (2) The *ink* [A] is *ejected through the siphon when a squid is alarmed* [C]. (3) This *ink* [A] not only forms an *effective screen* behind which the animal can escape [D], but it [A] contains *alkaloids that paralyze the olfactory senses of the enemy* [E].
(2)	given A: new C	
(3)	given A: new D	
	given A: new E	

■ **EXAMPLE 2**

sentence	given-new	
(1)	given A: new B	(1) All *squids* [A] propel themselves by *taking in and forcibly expelling water* from the mantle cavity through the siphon [B]. (2) The *force and direction of the water expelled* [B], plus the undulation of the fins and body, determine the *direction and rapid movement* [C] of the animals. (3) The *rapid movement* [C] is always in the opposite direction of the *water ejected from the siphon* [D]. (4) The *ejection of the water* [D] also *oxygenates the gills,* located in the mantle cavity [E].
(2)	given B: new C	
(3)	given C: new D	
(4)	given D: new E	

■ **EXAMPLE 3**

sentence	given-new	
(1)	given A: new B	(1) The unusual *coloration* [A] of squid is caused by the presence of *integumental pigment cells* [B]. (2) These *cells, called chromatophores* [B], contain red, blue, yellow, and black *pigment* [C]. (3) *Coloration* [A] is specific to each species [D]. (4) The *chromatophores, color cells,* [B] are controlled by muscles that expand or contract in relation to visual or olfactory stimuli, thus *changing the color of the animal* [E].
(2)	given B: new C	
(3)	given A: new D	
(4)	given B: new E	
(5)	given B: new F	(5) The *pigment cells'* [B] release of color into the flesh of a dead animal indicates the *onset of spoilage* [F].

Active and Passive Voice. A third problem that readers sometimes have results from writers' inappropriate use of voice. Your selection of active or passive voice depends on the subject, the purpose and focus, and the audience.

Active voice emphasizes the doer of the action (sometimes called the agent) and de-emphasizes the receiver, which is appropriate in most situations. Such emphasis is appropriate when readers are more interested in the doer or in the action itself than in the receiver or result of the action. Material presented in active voice is also more interesting to read, in part because the subject of the sentence is responsible for the action. Active voice is more direct; readers do not have to work as hard to figure out who does what. Active voice is less wordy because the "to be" verb form necessary to create a passive construction is omitted. In general, you can use active voice unless you have a specific reason not to.

Although you might not think a great deal about active and passive voice while you're drafting a document, voice becomes more important during revision. The agent (the doer) in active voice does not always have to be a person, or even a living organism, as the following example illustrates.[15]

■ EXAMPLE

Solid-state computer scanners maintain a file of fingerprints. When a fingerprint is put into the file, the computer scanner identifies the characteristic "points" of a fingerprint (up to 150 points, though only 12 are needed for legal identification) and then converts them to a series of numbers that are stored on a computer disk file. When a fingerprint from a crime scene is digitized in a similar manner, the scanner attempts to match the "numbers." Each disk drive stores up to 90,000 fingerprint cards, each card with 10 prints. The computer can riffle through 1,200 such points every second. The computer can increase arrest rates based on fingerprints 10 to 15 percent above the current levels.

In this example, the agent is the computer scanner, which can maintain a file, identify characteristic "points," convert them for storage, and, later, match the numbers. Passive voice has appropriate uses. When the receiver is more important than the agent, passive voice is appropriate. In this following example, the agent ("by Hollywood") is less important than the concept ("the fingerprint").

Passive voice   The fingerprint is overrated by Hollywood lore as a way to catch criminals.

Passive voice is also appropriate when the agent is unknown or insignificant.

Passive voice   Fingerprints are collected only between 25 and 30 percent of the time, even though they are usually the most prevalent form of physical evidence at the scene of a crime.

In this sentence the agent is not identified—"Fingerprints are collected [by unknown detectives] only between 25 and 30 percent of the time"—so passive voice is not only appropriate but necessary.

When you are deciding whether to use active or passive voice, consider your purpose and audience. If you want the focus to be on the receiver of the action (rather than on the agent), then use passive voice. If, on the other hand, you want to emphasize the agent, then use active voice.

Passive voice masks or minimizes the agent of action and emphasizes the receiver of the action.	**Active voice** emphasizes the agent of action.
Argon lasers and household "Super Glue" are now used by some dactylography experts to collect fingerprints. A small, highly concentrated, single-wavelength light beam is produced by the laser. Fluorescence is induced by the laser in such fingerprint chemicals as riboflavin. Prints—even old ones—can be lifted from paper, something that has been impervious to traditional dusting, by the laser. The benefits of "Super Glue" were discovered by accident. The fumes from the glue interact with the amino acids and outline the print. A fingerprint is raised and preserved by "Super Glue" on just about any surface. The glue is used on surfaces such as skin, plastic, coarse metal, and leather.	Some dactylography experts now use argon lasers and household "Super Glue" to collect fingerprints. The laser produces a small, highly concentrated, single-wavelength light beam that can induce fluorescence in such fingerprint chemicals as riboflavin. The laser can lift prints—even old ones—from paper, something that has been impervious to traditional dusting. Experts discovered the benefits of "Super Glue" by accident. The fumes from the glue interact with the print in a way that raises and preserves it on just about any surface, including skin, plastic, coarse metal, and leather.

Verb Mood.   Mood refers to the characteristics of verbs that convey a speaker's or writer's attitude toward a statement.

- Indicative mood states facts or opinions or asks questions.

fact	Nurses use a rectal thermometer to take a baby's temperature.
opinion	Babysitters prefer a thermometer strip rather than a rectal thermometer to take a baby's temperature.
question	Why should babysitters use a thermometer strip to take a baby's temperature?

- Imperative mood expresses commands or gives a direction.

command	(You) Use a rectal thermometer to take a baby's temperature.
direction	(You) Get a thermometer from the drawer labeled "Thermometers" in Utility Room II.

- Subjunctive mood expresses recommendations, wishes, conjectures, indirect requests, and statements of conditions contrary to fact.

recommendation	When children are hospitalized, it is important that parents be with them. [not *are*]

wish	I wish the clinic were able to provide more well-baby classes. [not *was*]
conjecture	If the budget were not cut, we would have electronic thermometers. [not *was*]
indirect request	If the rectal thermometer were to break, a baby could be seriously injured. [not *was*]
condition contrary to fact	The parent asked if the examination were almost over. [not *was*]

Because process explanations deal with observable, verifiable information, they are written in indicative mood. But you also need to be able to recognize and use imperative mood (especially for directions) and subjunctive mood (useful in correspondence and reports).

Person. Choosing among first, second, or third person depends on the purpose and audience of the document. First person (I, we) is correct if, for example, you are narrating the events in a sequence in which you were involved. If your role in the action was significant, the use of first person emphasizes this. Second person (you) is usually reserved for directions since readers are being directed to complete a particular action. Third person (he, she, one, it, they) is most common, allowing you to emphasize the sequence of action rather than yourself or the readers.

Why do you think that many technical documents have traditionally been written in third person, with no use of "I"?

The five problems discussed in this section—density, violation of given-new constructs, overdependence on passive voice, inappropriate verb mood, and inappropriate choice of person—are by no means the only ones that give readers difficulty. However, they are common problems, and if you eliminate them from your own documents, you will have made substantial progress in creating reader-based documents.

Editing

Most people think of editing as having to do with correctness—avoiding errors in mechanics and grammar. You might find a more useful approach is to think of editing as *adhering to conventions* and *assuring consistency*. Conventions are what a particular group of people agrees is acceptable, expected usage. Consistency involves assuring that a document conforms to those agreed-on conventions. Conventions differ from country to country and from company to company. Skillful editors seldom make absolute decisions; instead, they make situated, contextualized decisions. So in the United States, *color* is conventional; in much of the English-speaking world outside the United States, *colour* is conventional.

If "correctness" is often a matter of conforming to conventions, why do people make such a big deal about not following these conventions?

When readers have difficulty understanding sections of a document, you can determine whether the text has any of the specific problems discussed in this section of the chapter—problems dealing with usage at the level of words and phrases. Following the guidelines suggested here will also help you create effective plain language documents.

Editing is designed to improve a document's technical or textual accuracy as well as its appropriateness and appeal to readers. The term *editing* as it is used in this text refers to four functions that describe nine levels of edit identified in Figure 13.6. These functions, which typically take place in the final stages of preparing a document, help writers adhere to conventions and assure consistency.

In some organizations *content accuracy* is the responsibility of the writer, in others it is the responsibility of an editor, and in still others writers and editors act as safety checks for each other. There is not much point to completing any other level of edit until the content accuracy is established. Individuals who assume this responsibility need to have a good grasp of the technical information.

Design review typically includes assuring the consistency of all elements of design—from "macro" elements, such as assuring the same font type, style, size, and placement of headings, to details, such as assuring that numbers of figures and their textual references match. Individuals who assume this responsibility need to understand the general principles of document design as well as have a keen eye for inconsistencies in mechanical details.

Proofreading encompasses a broad range of responsibilities, including those most typically considered editing. All of the problems and errors in numeracy and language use fall into this category. Individuals who proofread documents

FIGURE 13.6 ■ Functions of Editing and Levels of Edit[16]	
Functions of Editing	**Levels of Edit**
Content Accuracy	◆ Substantive edit reviews the content for accuracy and organization.
Design Accuracy and Consistency	◆ Format edit establishes consistency in "macro" physical elements such as headings, fonts, page design.
	◆ Integrity edit matches text references to corresponding figures, tables, references, footnotes, and appendixes.
Proofreading for Conventions	◆ Mechanical style edit establishes consistency in "micro" physical elements such as symbols, citations, and numerical copy.
	◆ Screening edit corrects language and numerical errors.
	◆ Language edit changes grammar, punctuation, usage, and sentence structure to meet conventions.
Administrative Tasks	◆ Policy edit ensures that institutional policies are enforced.
	◆ Clarification edit provides clear instructions to the compositor and graphic artist.
	◆ Coordination edit deals with the administrative aspects in publishing technical documents.

need to have a thorough command of language appropriateness as well as the skill and sensitivity to create reader-based documents.

Some writers try to decrease their editing/proofreading burden by using software tools to flag potential problems in style, mechanics, and usage. Some word-processing software (for example, Microsoft Word) comes with a built-in editor—a spelling and grammar checker that catches glaring problems. However, software tools cannot guarantee that a document will be error-free or that it will communicate effectively with its audience. Writers should never depend on software tools to identify all the errors in a document. Writers should consider the following benefits and limitations of software tools for editing.[17]

Benefits	*Limitations*
Software can identify:	Software cannot identify:
■ misspelled words	■ correctly spelled words used the wrong way
■ passive voice	■ inconsistent writing styles
■ complex sentences	■ confusing sentence structures
■ wrong part of speech	■ what the audience needs to know
■ redundancy	■ every grammar/mechanical problem
■ potentially difficult wording— based on word and sentence lengths only	■ poorly organized documents
■ slang/colloquialisms	■ missing or faulty information
■ potentially sexist language	■ potentially offensive ideas
■ negative wording	■ how a document will be used

Finally, a number of *administrative responsibilities* are often considered editorial tasks. An individual who assumes these responsibilities needs to be familiar with corporate policies, understand the production and publication processes, and be a skillful manager of people and tasks.

These nine levels of edit are functions that in a small organization may be performed by a single individual. In very large organizations, several people may be responsible for these editing functions. However, whether one person or several are responsible, they complete the functions in several passes through a document. No editor tries to look for everything at the same time. So, for example, an editor who is doing a substantive edit for content accuracy typically ignores the other areas. Similarly, an editor who is checking for consistency in headings or documentation tends to set other problems aside temporarily.

Your responsibilities as an editor are not always clear-cut. Although you often have rules and guidelines to follow (e.g., Are there problems in punctuation? Is all the documentation correct?), an even bigger part of your editorial role requires judgment. You may make recommendations to a writer based on the response

Which of the nine levels of edit are you skillful at? Which of these levels of edits would help you be successful in your career?

you imagine readers will have. Rather than having a rule to enforce, you'll ask, "Is the document easy to read? Is the document easy to understand?"

The discussion in the remainder of the chapter identifies four areas that are often proofreading problems for writers—areas that need a final check before a document is complete: concrete details, directness, positive phrasing, and the elimination of several kinds of wordiness.

Use Concrete Details

Concrete words that refer to tangible objects are usually easier for your readers to understand than abstract words. Thus, you can generally make your writing more precise if you use specific details and examples. An effective technique for reducing abstract writing is to insert specific details in place of vague or general statements. The list in Figure 13.7 identifies some of the questions you can ask yourself as you edit a document to make abstract statements precise and concrete, to make your statements quantifiable and verifiable.

Use Direct Language

Why might a writer purposely obscure meaning in writing?

Indirect language often results from inappropriate attempts to be formal or to use inflated language or abstract language. In general, direct language is better. Direct language is typically plain and simple. However, no word is inherently right or wrong until you take the context, audience, and purpose into account. For example, the word *feel* would be appropriate in a pamphlet for women on breast self-examination that stated, "If you feel your breast tissue and detect a lump, contact your doctor." However, in a document for medical personnel, *palpate* would be a better choice than *feel*.

FIGURE 13.7 ■ Selecting Concrete Details

Abstract Information		Concrete Details
important client	Who?	Jean Thompson, PPI president
a new development	What?	developed a blight-resistant chestnut
schedule early	When?	schedule before 9 a.m.
ideal location	Where?	Southfield, MA
a substantial profit	How much?	a 37 percent profit
a broken part	Which one?	a broken camshaft
limited leg mobility	What percentage?	lift her leg 40 percent of normal extension
high-temperature environment	What degree?	up to 2,000°F
a small wingspan	What size?	a 7.0-mm wingspan
few changes in the procedure	How many?	three changes in the procedure
corrosion-resistant metal	What kind?	stainless steel

One way to be direct is to use straightforward terms. The revision of the following sentence substitutes simple language for needlessly ornate language. (Refer to the Usage Handbook, Section 1.3, for additional examples.)

Inflated Language	**Revised: Direct Language**
Your conceptualization of our aggregate capability may enhance our marketing position.	Your ideas about our capability may improve our marketing.

Another guaranteed shortcut to improved writing involves changing abstract nouns into verbs. One example is listed below, but many others appear in technical documents. If you change abstract nouns back to verbs and delete words that add little to the meaning, you'll greatly improve your writing. (Refer to the Usage Handbook for additional examples.)

Abstract Language	**Revised: Direct Language**
The judge provided the required authorization for the search.	The judge authorized the search. "Authorize" identifies the action.

Use Positive Phrasing

Effective writers often employ positive phrasing for several reasons. Psychologists and linguists know that readers and listeners understand positively phrased sentences more quickly and accurately than negatively phrased sentences, which the human brain takes slightly longer to process. Also, positive phrasing generally is more direct and appealing because eliminating negatives eliminates words.

The most obvious negative words, which include *no, not, none, never,* and *nothing,* are added to a positive sentence to negate the idea. When you edit, consider replacing a negative word with a less overtly negative term, often an antonym for the word in the "not" phrase:

not many	→	few
do not accept	→	reject
do not succeed	→	fail

Other negative words are created by adding a common negative prefix to a word. The words with the prefixes are more indirect; they're less overtly negative. However, when you want to emphasize a negative point, use *not:*

inefficient	→	not efficient
impossible	→	not possible
unreliable	→	not reliable

While one negative word or phrase only slightly delays a reader, multiple negatives significantly decrease reading speed and inhibit comprehension. Also, possible confusion results from multiple negatives. The following sentences illustrate how replacing negative wording with positive wording lessens the chances of confusion arising from multiple negatives.

Negative Phrasing	More Positive Phrasing
The production-line changeover will not be ready on time.	The production-line changeover will be delayed.
The manager could not approve the decentralization of the tool crib because there would be no inventory control or centralized maintenance checks.	The manager denied decentralization of the tool crib because it provides a regular inventory control and maintenance check.

In some situations, however, you'll find that positive phrasing is inappropriate because it is not emphatic enough. The following set of directions presumes that many users will do the wrong thing unless specific *do not's* are presented.

■ EXAMPLE

Failure to follow standard procedures in using a disk will have detrimental results. Follow these guidelines:

- Do not turn drive on or off with disk in the drive.

- Do not bend disk.

- Do not touch disk surfaces with fingers or objects.

- Do not store disk out of protective envelope.

- Do not expose disk to heat, magnets, or photoelectric beams.

In what situations might you choose to word directions positively? Negatively?

Such phrasing cautions computer operators to treat disks carefully. Although the wording is negative, experience has led manual writers to realize that some readers ignore cautions that use positive wording.

Eliminate Wordiness

Wordiness can make your writing difficult to understand because readers are forced to plow through unnecessary words to read essential information. Your readers may lose patience. The most effective way to reduce wordiness is to avoid redundancy—the unnecessary repetition of concepts, words, or phrases. Sometimes readers cannot discern the point because it is hidden underneath layers of language. At other times redundancy is so annoying or time consuming that readers give up without completing a document.

The memo in Figure 13.8 has numerous instances of redundancy. Section manager Catherine Saunders typed the memo directly into her word processor and read a copy after it was printed. When she proofread her draft, she was appalled by its redundancy, which she eliminated by crossing out unnecessary terms and making minor changes in wording. Figure 13.8 shows the editing she did on her memo. Producing a new copy constituted very little work on her word processor; within a few minutes, she printed the revision (Figure 13.9).

You may encounter several redundant elements that you can edit out of the final drafts of technical documents—modifiers similar to those in Ms. Saunders' first memo.

Redundant Pairs.   Some common terms contain two words, both of which mean the same thing. Some writers use such redundant pairs to give their writing what they think is an air of elegance. Because both terms mean the same thing, only one is necessary. You could appropriately write *first* or *foremost*, but using both terms is repetitive. Sometimes, as in Ms. Saunders's memo, neither term is necessary because there is only one stated goal. Some other common redundant pairs include "null and void" and "final and conclusive." (Refer to the Usage Handbook, Section 1.4, for additional examples.)

Redundant Modifiers.   Phrases in which one term implies the other are known as redundant modifiers. For example, "collaborate" implies "together," so "collaborate together" is redundant. Some other common redundant modifiers include "initial preparation" and "most unique." (Refer to the Usage Handbook, Section 1.4, for additional examples.)

Ms. Saunders's memo contains the phrase "high degree of expertise of the consultant brought in," which has three redundant features. A consultant is assumed to have expertise and is also brought in from outside the company; saying a consultant has expertise and is brought in is doubly redundant. Also, expertise assumes a high degree of competence; repeating "high degree" is unnecessary.

Redundant Categories.   When one term in a phrase is in the general category to which the other term belongs, it's known as a redundant category. For example, the expression *bitter taste* is redundant because bitter is one of four tastes; the word *bitter* is sufficient. In Ms. Saunders's memo, the initial "a.m." implies the category stated in the second term, so "morning" is unnecessary. You could appropriately write "at 10 a.m. Tuesday" or "at 10:00 Tuesday morning." Some other common redundant categories include "reliability factor" and "red in color." (Refer to the Usage Handbook, Section 1.4, for additional examples.) The following examples show how eliminating redundant categories makes sentences less wordy.

Redundant	Improved
The reliability factor of the equipment was guaranteed.	The equipment's reliability was guaranteed.

Revise Noun Strings

Your writing can be improved by eliminating noun strings, a series of two or more nouns in which the first nouns modify the later ones. For example, in the string "circulation pump filter," both circulation and pump modify filter. Noun strings are distinguished by the absence of both apostrophes and connecting words that show relationships (such as *of, for, in*).

FIGURE 13.8 ■ Redundant Memo

MEMO

August 3, 20—

To	Production Supervisors
From	Catherine Saunders *CS*
Section	Manager
Subject	Staff Meeting

~~2~~ ~~The~~ staff meeting ~~will start at~~ 10 a.m. Tuesday ~~morning~~, August 6, in Conference Room 317 ~~on the third floor.~~

~~2~~ ~~First and foremost, our~~ primary goal ~~of the meeting will be~~ *it's* to reach a consensus ~~of~~ ~~2~~ ~~opinion~~ about the best way to ~~utilize~~ *use* ~~the high degree of expertise of~~ the consultant ~~we~~ *'s advice* ~~2~~ ~~brought in. The consultant advised us about future plans for implementing new state~~ ~~2~~ ~~of the art developments in~~ *about* production techniques.

determine the priorities for changes to
At this ~~point in~~ time, we must ~~prioritize in order of importance those basic and funda-~~ ~~2~~ ~~mental changes we believe are most important to modify in~~ our production system.

You'll run into problems if you use noun strings, particularly when the reader is unable to determine exactly how the nouns relate to each other. Strings that are only two words long seldom present difficulties. For example, *data analysis* is easily understood; saying "the analysis of data" is unnecessary. When the strings are three words long, the reader can usually figure out what is meant, but reading may be slowed slightly. When the strings reach four words, extra time is required to figure out the relationship among words. Although your reader probably will accurately interpret the string, this takes unnecessary time and effort, which may distract and annoy the reader. Strings that are five or more words long are open to multiple interpretations and can be indecipherable. The reader may never guess exactly what you intended.

Noun Strings	Revision
standardization blending	controller that standardizes blending
test module specification review	the specifications review for the test module
scanner head motion control	control of the scanner head's motion

Revisions of noun strings usually require additional words to clarify the relationships; however, these extra words eliminate ambiguity.

FIGURE 13.9 ■ Revised Memo

MEMO

August 3, 20—

To	Production Supervisors
From	Catherine Saunders *CS*
Section	Manager
Subject	Staff meeting
	10 a.m., Tuesday, August 6,
	Conference Room 317

Our goal is to reach a consensus about the best way to use the consultant's advice about production techniques.

At this time, we must determine the priorities for changes to our production system.

The issues of conventions and correctness addressed in this chapter are often more difficult to apply in workplace situations, which are nearly always complicated by politics and personalities. The ethics sidebar on the following page addresses some of these complications, which often force writers and editors to make difficult decisions. The sidebar suggests that identifying the values that are in conflict will aid decision making.

Examining Revision and Editing Decisions

Figure 13.10 shows the first few pages of a draft of a feasibility report (pages 454–458). This particular report evaluates two anchor bolts and recommends one for the company. Suggestions for revision and copyediting are marked on this draft. Marginal annotations comment on some of the other problems with the draft. Figure 13.11 shows the final revised and edited version of the same report (pages 459–468).

To assess the effectiveness of this document, you need to know about the purpose of feasibility reports—to advocate the best solution to a problem—and their structure. The introduction of the report usually gives an overview of the

Author, Audience, and Company: Ethics and Technical Editing

Imagine a technical editor in the following scenario:

> You are a technical editor, working for a software development company. As you edit the draft of a manual for the company's newest product, you realize that large sections are very technical, making them unclear and difficult to understand. When you talk to the writer, a programmer, you find her very reluctant to revise the manual; she argues that the technical information, as it is written, is necessary. The deadline for the manual is looming; you have little time to revise the manual without the writer's help.

What are the technical editor's responsibilities in this situation? As this scenario indicates, technical editors, because of their unique position in the document production process, must balance obligations to several different groups. First, they have an obligation to the audience to ensure that documents are clear and accurate. Second, they are expected to safeguard the employer's reputation and protect them from legal liabilities. Finally, they have to respect the author's intellectual independence, especially if the editor is not an expert in the subject. In most situations, each of these different obligations work toward a collective goal—clear, accurate, professional documents.

When these obligations do conflict, however, the editor is faced with an ethical dilemma: to which group do they have the greater responsibility: author, audience, or employer? For example, in the situation above, the editor faces several different ethical obligations:

- *To the audience*—they expect the manual to be clear and readable but also expect it to be technically accurate
- *To the author*—she is an expert on the product but may not appreciate the audience's lack of technical expertise
- *To the employers*—they could lose money if the product is delayed but could also suffer if the documentation is inaccurate or misleading

There is not one simple solution to this situation. Researchers Lori Allen and Dan Voss, however, provide a process that allows editors to at least clearly identify the values that are in conflict.[18] The outline of their process includes parenthetical notes about ways in which each step fits the scenario in this sidebar.

- Define what is at issue (producing a clear text) and the groups involved (audience, author, and employer)
- Determine the different groups' interests (clarity, experience, profit)
- Identify the relevant values (usability, integrity, capitalism)
- Determine the values that conflict (usability vs. integrity, capitalism vs. usability)
- Determine which value has greater importance (usability)
- Resolve the conflict for that value (require the writer to revise the document)

Requiring the writer to revise the document is one possible resolution for this dilemma. If the greater value is capitalism, then the ethical decision may be to improve as much of the quality of the manual as time allows. No matter which they choose, editors should heed Allen and Voss's final point: Editors carry a greater ethical responsibility because they are experts with language. Editors have the great advantage of looking at a situation from different perspectives, but that advantage comes with weighty ethical responsibilities.

How would you edit a poorly written technical document that the author does not want altered?

Reread the scenario at the beginning of this sidebar. Using Allen and Voss's six-step process, how would you resolve this conflict? What value(s) would you privilege?

feasibility study (the work that results in the report) by briefly stating the purpose of the study, describing the problem being investigated, and presenting the scope of the report. An optional background section—included when the audience is not likely to be familiar with the situation that necessitated the feasibility study—can contain information such as the history of the problem, the possible long-range impact of not correcting the problem, and relevant work that has already been done in the field.

The criteria and solutions sections are the most important. The criteria allow readers to evaluate the various solutions fairly, so their selection is important. Some of the following criteria are often used:

- cost of purchase, installation, maintenance

- ease and frequency of servicing

- ease of operation

- training required

- performance specifications

- dimensions

- compatibility with existing systems

- flexibility for expansion

- environmental impact

Writers should select only criteria that identify significant differences in the solutions, and the solutions offered should be feasible. Including impractical or weak solutions as a way to make a preferred solution look better borders on the unethical and can destroy the credibility of the entire document.

The final section of a feasibility report incorporates the conclusions and recommendations. These sections may be presented separately or together; in either case, the points are often bulleted or enumerated. Sometimes the conclusions in a feasibility report present both advantages and disadvantages of each solution, synthesizing rather than just summarizing the information. The recommendations identify the best solution based on the criteria used in the feasibility study. The recommendations should be clear, precise, unambiguous, and logical.

As you read the draft in Figure 13.10 and the final report in Figure 13.11, consider both global revisions (redesigning and reorganizing the report) and local revisions (revising paragraphs and sentences). Then consider the editing decisions that focus on word- and phrase-level usage that affect the report's accuracy as well as its appropriateness and appeal.

FIGURE 13.10 ■ Draft of a Feasibility Report Marked for Revision and Editing

EXPANSION ANCHOR FEASIBILITY REPORT

BY:
JOE MONTALBANO
ENGINEERING ASSISTANT II
JUNE 4, 20—

Lots of text in BOLD ALL CAPS is unnecessarily difficult to read.

PREPARED FOR:
~~MR.~~ NAYAN DESHPANDE
ENGINEERING SUPERVISOR
CIVIL ENGINEERING DEPARTMENT
GRAND GULF NUCLEAR STATION

The information on most title pages is centered.

Center

Don't use all caps for so much text.

DRAFT

FIGURE 13.10 ■ *Continued*

TABLE OF CONTENTS

Make "Criteria" and "Methodology" into level-1 heads and reverse their order.

Abstract

Introduction: Nonductile Expansion Anchors at GGNS 1

~~Background~~ 1

Criteria for Selecting Anchor Bolts 1

Methodology for Evaluating Anchor Bolts 1

Headings (which are also sections in the table of contents) should present content, not just section labels.

Conclusions 2

Recommendation 2,3

Use only the first page number of a section in the table of contents.

Discussion

    Description of the Bolt 3

    ~~Figures 1 & 2~~ 4

Inconsistencies and problems in the organization of a document often show up in the sequence of sections in the table of contents.

Criterion 1: Favorable Design Characteristics 3

Criterion 2: Ease of Installation 9

Criterion 3: Low Cost 10

Appendixes

Appendix A: Glossary 11

Appendix B: Comparison of Yield Forces and Maximum Pullout Forces . . . 12

Appendix C: Comparison of Shear Forces 13

Appendix D: Interview Questions 14

Appendix E: Survey Tabulation 15

Appendix F: Expansion Achor Preference Questionnaire 16

Provide names of the appendixes.

The changes in the table of contents should be reflected in the reorganization of the text and the retitling of the sections.

Works Cited 17

DRAFT

FIGURE 13.10 ■ *Continued*

1

(Add an abstract)

INTRODUCTION : Nonductile
Expansion Anchors
at GGNS

By convention, the first page of the main body usually doesn't have the page number on it.

~~1 Background~~

The nonductile expansion anchor has a long history of use at Grand Gulf Nuclear

Station (GGNS). The nonductile expansion anchor~~, which has been~~ used almost exclu-
                                          has been
sively ~~in~~ the Hilti Kwik Bolt anchor bolt. This wedge-type anchor is essential for instal-
                                          variety
lation of a wide vriety of components including conduit supports, pipe supports, instru-

ment supports, and ventilating and air conditioning supports.

Double spacing takes up an unnecessary amount of space. Space-and-a-half will maintain the ease of reading but save room as well.

~~1 However~~, replacement of the Hilti Kwik Bolt is required because the manufacturer
                                                        As a result,
recently discontinued production ~~of it~~. ~~Therefore~~, I conducted a search for a replace-
                                                    by
ment ~~anchor bolt. This search consisted of~~ evaluating ~~several types of~~ anchor bolts.
                                                                              two
~~they are~~ the Hilti Kwik Bolt II anchor bolt* and the Drillco Maxi-Bolt anchor bolt.*

Criteria for Selecting Anchor Bolts

I established three criteria that ~~best~~ describe the desired characteristics of the new

anchor bolt. ~~These criteria are listed~~ in order of importance.

- Favorable design characteristics

- Ease of installation

- Lowest cost

Readers may more easily follow the logic of the report if the general approach (the methodology) is presented before the specifics (the criteria for evaluation).

Methodology for Evaluating Anchor Bolts

In evaluating the Hilti Kwik Bolt II anchor bolt and the Drillco Maxi-Bolt anchor

————————

~~*See Glossary for definitions of terms.~~

All terms marked with an asterisk are defined in the Glossary in Appendix A on page 11.

What additional problems have you identified in this report?

DRAFT

FIGURE 13.10 ■ *Continued*

2

bolt, I used several methods of gathering information. The main method I used was of
reading vendor brochures, technical guides, and a technical standard. This provided a *information*
substantial amount of ~~information~~ *background* about the two bolt types. Also I gathered information *to engineers*
by distributing an expansion anchor preference questionnaire, and by interviewing an
engineer familiar with the two bolt types.

CONCLUSIONS

My
~~The~~ evaluation of the Hilti Kwik Bolt II and the Drillco Maxi-Bolt ~~produced~~ *led me to* the following ~~results~~ *conclusions*.

Generally single space the items in a list and double space between these items.

- In terms of design characteristics, the Hilti Kwik Bolt II has four of the most
  important ~~characteristics~~. The Drillco Maxi-Bolt has only one and it is the least
  important characteristic.
- In terms of ease of installation, the Hilti Kwik Bolt II satisfies both installation
  requirements. The Drillco Maxi-Bolt satisfies neither of them.
- In terms of lowest cost, the Hilti Kwik Bolt II satisfies this criterion because it
  is ~~was~~ at least 20 *percent* ~~cheaper~~ *lower* in cost than the Drillco Maxi-Bolt.

RECOMMENDATION

I recommend that the Civil Engineering Department approve the Hilti Kwik Bolt II for
future use at GGNC. This bolt *meets* ~~is suitable for use at GGNS because it adheres to~~ all the
established criteria, with the exception of load capacity. Although this bolt type does not
have the highest load capacity, it is acceptable. The load capacity is very similar to that

The word- and sentence-level editing makes the report easier to read.

DRAFT

FIGURE 13.10 ■ *Continued*

3

of the Hilti Kwik Bolt which was used at GGNS for a long time. *Repaginate to eliminate orphan.*

DISCUSSION

Make sure that the visual cues allow readers to easily and quickly distinguish between levels of headings.

Description of Bolts

The Hilti Kwik Bolt II and the Drillco Maxi-Bolt represent two different anchor designs with each having an ultimate tensile stress of 125,000 psi. The primary difference between the two bolts is the anchoring mechanism. The Hilti Kwik Bolt II has a wedge anchoring mechanism and is classified as a wedge anchor.* (See Figure 1.) Also it is a nonductile expansion anchor because of its nonductile failure characteristics. The Drillco Maxi-Bolt has a sleeve anchoring mechanism and is classified as a sleeve anchor.* (See Figure 2.) This anchor has ductile failure characteristics and is also called a ductile expansion anchor. *Insert Figures 1, 2 here*

Criterion 1:

Favorable Design Characteristics *) close up spacing*

listed here

The new anchor bolt must have five characteristics. They are in order of importance:

Incorporate critical figures and tables as close to the text reference as possible after the end of the paragraph.

- Largest assortment of bolt diameters and bolt lengths

- Minimum bolt embedment

- Minimum bolt spacing*

- Minimum free edge distance*

- Highest load capacity

(ital)

Eliminate unnecessary repetition by changing the first mention of the glossary to include references to all succeeding asterisks.

Hilti Kwik Bolt II. The bolt diameters for this bolt type range in sizes from $1/4$" to 1" in $1/8$" increments excluding $7/8$". Also each bolt diameter is available in at least two lengths. For example, the $1/2$" diameter bolt is available in $2^3/4$", $3^3/4$", $4^1/2$", and $5^1/2$" lengths. The large variety of sizes for this bolt type broadens the number of its applicable uses.

DRAFT

———

*See Glossary for definitions of terms.

*The choice to use **BOLD ALL CAPS** draws attention to the title. The brevity of the title makes **BOLD ALL CAPS** acceptable in this situation.*

The title clearly informs readers about the topic (expansion anchors) and the approach (feasibility).

EXPANSION ANCHOR FEASIBILITY REPORT

Joe Montalbano
Engineering Assistant II
June 4, 20—

The centered information in upper- and lowercase type is easy to read.

Prepared for
Nayan Deshpande
Engineering Supervisor
Civil Engineering Department
Grand Gulf Nuclear Station

FIGURE 13.11 ■ *Continued*

TABLE OF CONTENTS

The headings identify the content of each section rather than simply specify the section of the report—that is, Methodology for Evaluating Anchor Bolts rather than just Methodology.

ABSTRACT 1

INTRODUCTION: NONDUCTILE EXPANSION ANCHORS AT GGNS 1

METHODOLOGY FOR EVALUATING ANCHOR BOLTS 1

CRITERIA FOR SELECTING ANCHOR BOLTS 2

CONCLUSIONS 2

RECOMMENDATION 2

DISCUSSION

    Description of Bolts 3

    Criterion 1: Favorable Design Characteristics 3

    Criterion 2: Ease of Installment 6

    Criterion 3: Low Cost 7

APPENDIXES

    Appendix A: Glossary 9

    Appendix B: Comparison of Yield Forces and Maximum Pullout Forces . . 10

    Appendix C: Comparison of Shear Forces 11

    Appendix D: Interview Questions 12

    Appendix E: Survey Tabulation 13

    Appendix F: Expansion Anchor Preference Questionnaire 14

WORKS CITED 15

Page numbers are right justified.

Dot leaders help readers visually track from the topic to the page number.

The organization and typography of the table of contents match what appears in the report itself.

Only the first page number of a section is listed in the table of contents.

FIGURE 13.11 ■ *Continued*

1

ABSTRACT

The abstract should preview both the content and the organizational structure of the feasibility study.

This report presents the result of a feasibility study of two anchor bolts—the Hilti Kwik Bolt II and the Drillco Maxi-Bolt—and recommends the Hilti Kwik Bolt II for use at Grand Gulf Nuclear Station. The study evaluated both bolt types in terms of three criteria: design characteristics, ease of installation, and low cost.

INTRODUCTION: NONDUCTILE EXPANSION ANCHORS AT GGNS

The specific headings help readers anticipate the content to be discussed in each section.

The nonductile expansion anchor has a long history of use at Grand Gulf Nuclear Station (GGNS). The nonductile expansion anchor used almost exclusively has been the Hilti Kwik Bolt anchor bolt. This wedge-type anchor is essential for installation of a wide variety of components including conduit supports, pipe supports, instrument supports, and ventilating and air conditioning supports.

Replacement of the Hilti Kwik Bolt is required because the manufacturer recently discontinued its production. As a result, I conducted a search for a replacement by evaluating two types of anchor bolts: the Hilti Kwik Bolt II anchor bolt* and the Drillco Maxi-Bolt anchor bolt.*

The report uses first person ("I") because the individual engineer is making a recommendation. By using first person, he accepts responsibility for his recommendation.

Placing the Methodology before the Criteria helps readers understand the overall approach before they learn about the specifics.

METHODOLOGY FOR EVALUATING ANCHOR BOLTS

In evaluating the Hilti Kwik Bolt II anchor bolt and the Drillco Maxi-Bolt anchor bolt, I used several methods of gathering information. The main method was reading vendor brochures, technical guides, and a technical standard. This information provided a substantial amount of background about the two bolt types. I also gathered information by distributing an expansion anchor preference questionnaire to engineers and by interviewing an engineer familiar with the two bolt types.

Glossary terms are easy to identify because they're marked with an asterisk and clearly defined.

What additional strengths have you identified in this report?

*All terms with an asterisk are defined in the Glossary in Appendix A on page 9.

FIGURE 13.11 ■ *Continued*

2

CRITERIA FOR SELECTING ANCHOR BOLTS

I established three criteria, in order of importance, that describe the desired characteristics of the new anchor bolt:

*Bulleting
the criteria
helps readers
see their
importance.*

- Favorable design characteristics

- Ease of installation

- Low cost

CONCLUSIONS

*The conclusion
and recommen-
dation are put
up front so that
readers know
the critical
information
first. The
supporting
discussion
follows for
readers who
want more
information or
who want to
understand the
rationale for
the decision.*

My evaluation of the Hilti Kwik Bolt II and the Drillco Maxi-Bolt led me to the following conclusions.

- In terms of design characteristics, the Hilti Kwik Bolt II has four of the most important. The Drillco Maxi-Bolt has only one, and it is the least important.

- In terms of ease of installation, the Hilti Kwik Bolt II satisfies both installation requirements. The Drillco Maxi-Bolt satisfies neither of them.

- In terms of lower cost, the Hilti Kwik Bolt II satisfies this criterion because it is at least 20 percent lower in cost than the Drillco Maxi-Bolt.

RECOMMENDATION

I recommend that the Civil Engineering Department approve the Hilti Kwik Bolt II for future use at GGNS. This bolt meets all the established criteria, with the exception of load capacity. Although this bolt type does not have the highest load capacity, it is acceptable. The load capacity is very similar to the Hilti Kwik Bolt, which was used at GGNS for a long time.

DISCUSSION

In this section, I provide an overall description of the two different bolts and then discuss the three criteria that influenced my recommendation.

FIGURE 13.11 ■ *Continued*

3

Description of Bolts

The Hilti Kwik Bolt II and the Drillco Maxi-Bolt represent two different anchor designs,

each having an ultimate tensile stress* of 125,000 psi. The primary difference between

the two bolts is the anchoring mechanism. The Hilti Kwik Bolt II has a wedge anchoring

mechanism and is classified as a wedge anchor.* (See Figure 1.) Also it is a nonductile

expansion anchor because of its nonductile failure characteristics. The Drillco Maxi-Bolt

has a sleeve anchoring mechanism and is classified as a sleeve anchor.* (See Figure 2.)

This anchor has ductile failure characteristics and is also called a ductile expansion

anchor.

Figures 1 and 2 are proportional in size and placed side by side for fair and easy comparison. Note that both are referred to in the text.

FIGURE 1:	**FIGURE 2:**
Hilti Kwik Bolt II	Drillco Maxi-Bolt
Source: *Hilti Technical Guide*	Source: *Drillco Maxi-Bolt Brochure*

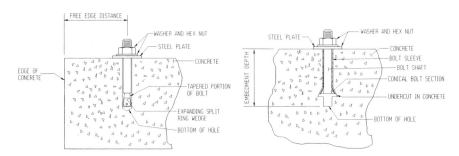

Criterion 1: Favorable Design Characteristics

The new anchor bolt must have five characteristics, listed here in order of importance:

Using a bulleted list to specify the favorable design characteristics helps readers know to look for in the assessment of each bolt.

• Largest assortment of bolt diameters and bolt lengths

• Minimum bolt embedment

• Minimum bolt spacing*

• Minimum free edge distance*

• Highest load capacity*

FIGURE 13.11 ■ *Continued*

4

Differentiating heading levels— on this page a level-3 heading—helps readers understand the hierarchical relationships in your discussion.

Hilti Kwik Bolt II. The bolt diameters for this bolt type range in size from $1/4$" to 1" in $1/8$" increments excluding $7/8$". Also each bolt diameter is available in at least two lengths. For example, the $1/2$" diameter bolt is available in $2 3/4$", $3 3/4$", $4 1/2$", and $5 1/2$" lengths. The large variety of sizes for this bolt type broadens the number of its applicable uses.

The bolt embedment is the portion of the bolt's overall length that is embedded in concrete (Standard 6). Each bolt diameter has a minimum embedment as indicated in Table 1. In comparing the embedment values given in Table 1, you will notice that the Hilti Kwik Bolt II has at least 33 percent shallower embedment than the Drillco Maxi-Bolt. Shallower embedments allow faster bolt installation.

Table 1 provides readers with an easy-to-read comparison that summarizes information. Note that the table is referred to in the text.

TABLE 1:

A Comparison of Embedments

Bolt Diameter (in.)	Hilti Kwik Bolt II Minimum Embedment (in.)	Drillco Maxi-Bolt Minimum Embedment (in.)
$1/4$	2	3
$3/8$	2	4.5
$1/2$	2.5	6
$5/8$	3	7.5
$3/4$	3.5	9.25
1	4.5	12.5

Source: Standard No. SERI-CS-03, "Standard for Design of Concrete Expansion Anchors"

Providing the citation for the information in Table 1 helps readers assess its credibility.

The bolt spacing and free edge distance represent minimum spacing requirements. These design characteristics are smaller for the Hilti Kwik Bolt II than the Drillco Maxi-Bolt. The smaller bolt spacing means the bolts can be installed close to each other. The small free edge distance means that the bolt can be located closer to the edge of a concrete structure. Instances where these design characteristics can be advantageous are on concrete walls or floors of the plant where there is limited room for additional items.

FIGURE 13.11 ■ *Continued*

5

Readers are referred to the attached appendixes, which increases the likelihood that they'll check that information.

The load capacity of the Hilti Kwik Bolt II is measured in terms of pullout force* and shear force.* For each bolt diameter, Appendix B shows the maximum pullout forces produced at the maximum embedment. Appendix C shows the maximum shear force for each bolt diameter. These two appendixes indicate that pullout forces and shear forces for the Hilti Kwik Bolt II are consistently lower than the yield forces and shear forces for the Drillco Maxi-Bolt. (The pullout forces and shear forces are also lower than for the original Hilti Kwik Bolt.) The lower forces mean that the Hilti Kwik Bolt II is not as strong as the other two bolts.

Drillco Maxi-Bolt. This bolt is available in the same bolt diameters as the Hilti Kwik Bolt II. But for each bolt diameter there are fewer alternate bolt lengths. The lengths of the bolts range from $4\frac{1}{2}$" for $\frac{1}{4}$" bolts to $16\frac{1}{2}$" for 1" bolts.

The embedments for the Drillco Maxi-Bolt are shown in Table 1 on page 4. The embedment for each diameter Drillco Maxi-Bolt is consistently larger than for the Hilti Kwik Bolt II. These deeper embedments are unfavorable because when bolts are installed in reinforced concrete, there is an increased probability of damaging or severing the reinforcing steel.

Like many paragraphs in this report, this paragraph uses given-new principles to provide coherence for readers.

The bolt spacing and the free-edge distance for this particular bolt type are dependent on bolt embedment. Because the embedment of the Drillco Maxi-Bolt is deeper than the Hilti Kwik Bolt II, it follows that the bolt spacing and free edge distance are larger. These larger spacing characteristics are a disadvantage because a larger area is required to produce the rated load capacity of the bolts.

The load capacity of the Drillco Maxi-Bolt is measured in terms of yield force* and maximum shear force. For each bolt diameter, Appendix B shows the yield force corresponding to the maximum embedment. Appendix C shows the maximum shear force for each bolt diameter. Both appendixes indicate that the yield forces and the shear

Like many paragraphs in this report, this paragraph uses a clear topic sentence to help readers anticipate what is coming in the next few sentences.

FIGURE 13.11 ■ *Continued*

6

forces of the Drillco Maxi-Bolt are consistently higher than the forces shown for the other two bolt types. The higher forces mean that this bolt type is stronger.

Conclusions about Design Characteristics. Based on the information provided for each design characteristic, I have made the following conclusions:

The conclusions are clearly labeled and formatted in a bulleted list so they are easy to distinguish from the rest of the text.

- The Hilti Kwik Bolt II has the largest assortment of bolt diameters and bolt lengths because it provides more alternate bolt lengths for each bolt diameter.

- The Hilti Kwik Bolt II has the desired minimum embedment characteristic because it requires a shallower embedment than the Drillco Maxi-Bolt.

- The Hilti Kwik Bolt II has the desired minimum bolt spacing and minimum free edge distance characteristic because this bolt type provides the smallest distance dimension.

- The Drillco Maxi-Bolt has a higher load capacity than the Hilti Kwik Bolt II.

The Hilti Kwik Bolt II is preferred in terms of design characteristics over the Drillco Maxi-Bolt because it satisfies four of the most important design characteristics. Its load capacity is only slightly lower than the Hilti Kwik Bolt.

A summary conclusion for criterion 1 removes any ambiguity that might have remained if the writer had simply presented the bulleted list of conclusions.

The same structure used to organize the information for criterion 1 is used here to organize the information for criterion 2: required features, compliance of Kwik Bolt II, compliance of Drillco Maxi-Bolt, and conclusion.

Criterion 2: Ease of Installation

Because of the anticipated high frequency of use of the new anchor bolt, it must meet the following installation requirements:

- Easy installation process

- Average installation time of less than 2 hours

Hilti Kwik Bolt II. The process of installing the Hilti Kwik Bolt II consists of three easy steps:

1. Drill a hole in hardened concrete.

2. Insert the bolt in the hole to the desired embedment.

3. Set the anchor by torquing the nut down.

FIGURE 13.11 ■ *Continued*

7

The installation process is so simple that it takes an average of only $1\frac{1}{4}$ hours with a few standard tools.

Drillco Maxi-Bolt. The installation of the Drillco Maxi-Bolt is a more involved, four-step process:

1. Drill a hole in hardened concrete.

2. Cut the undercut shape at the appropriate location in the hole.

3. Insert the bolt in the hole to the desired embedment.

4. Set the anchor by torquing the nut down.

This more involved process takes $2\frac{1}{2}$ hours and requires special tools such as the Maxi-Bolt undercutting tool and the Maxi-Bolt setting tool.

Conclusion about Installation. The Hilti Kwik Bolt II satisfies both ease of installation requirements, while the Drillco Maxi-Bolt does not satisfy either of them.

Criterion 3: Low Cost

The new anchor bolt must be the less expensive of the two bolt types being evaluated. Since the different bolt sizes are packaged in various quantities, I needed to determine a per unit cost for the Hilti Kwik Bolt II and the Drillco Maxi-Bolt. Table 2, which shows the per unit cost, indicates that for each bolt diameter the cost for the Hilti Kwik Bolt II is a minimum of 20 percent less than the Drillco Maxi-Bolt.

FIGURE 13.11 ■ *Continued*

8

Table 2, referred to in the text, summarizes the critical information about cost, in a display that is far more efficient and effective than using sentences. Whereas Table 1 came from a single source about industry standards, this table has been constructed by the author from two different sources, both of which are noted.

TABLE 2:

Cost Comparison

Bolt Diameter (in.)	Hilti Kwik Bolt II Cost[1]	Drillco Maxi-Bolt Cost[1]
1/4	$2.20	$2.65
3/8	3.05	4.00
1/2	4.30	5.55
5/8	5.10	6.35
3/4	6.15	7.40
1	7.50	9.45

[1]cost per bolt

Source: *Hilti Technical Guide* and *Drillco Maxi-Bolt Brochure*

Conclusion about Cost. Based on the available cost information presented in Table 2, I recommend the Hilti Kwik Bolt II.

Because the overall conclusions were presented near the beginning of the report, when the discussion of the criteria is completed, the report simply stops (with appendixes added).

The appendixes that accompanied the actual feasibility report are not included here.

End-of-Chapter
Recommendations for Technical Communicators

1. Build the time and budget to support document testing into your project schedules.

2. Create testing plans that incorporate text-based, expert-based, and user-based testing.

3. Use the results of document testing in revising and editing your documents.

4. When revising a document, consider factors such as organization of information, logic, tone, selection and placement of support, design of document, and selection and placement of visuals. Present information in plain language.

5. Check sentences and paragraphs for plain language by avoiding density, violation of given-new constructs, overdependence on passive voice, inappropriate verb mood, and inappropriate choice of person.

6. Learn to work through the various levels of edit when completing a document.

7. Make a final check for concrete details, directness, positive phrasing, and the elimination of several kinds of wordiness.

Practicum

Using Style Guides to Ensure Usability

I am an independent technical writing contractor working from my home office in Des Moines, Iowa. I started contracting after spending several years as a technical writer at CE Software, Inc. in West Des Moines, Iowa. CE Software is a small software company that develops Internet e-mail software as well as desktop automation utilities.

My last two years at CE Software were spent as the one and only technical writer. My experience as the lone technical writer enabled me to consolidate a wealth of experience into a relatively brief amount of time. While many technical writers spend a considerable portion of their careers learning about one stage of the documentation process, I was privileged to be responsible for the entire process.

When I started working for CE Software, I was one of four people on the document production team. After working at the company for two years, I *became* the document production team. When I emerged from a round of layoffs as the only technical writer, I quickly had to overcome several hurdles. I had to learn how to coordinate printing and production for all my manuals, manage documentation localization, create more efficient templates, copyedit my own writing, make my own style rules and much more. All this freedom may sound pretty good, but at moments this situation was scary. I was just beginning my career, and I was suddenly shouldering all the document production responsibilities for my entire company. I became accustomed to the life of a lone technical writer, but part of my job was frustrating—maintaining consistency in my writing.

The key to maintaining consistency in writing is developing a solid style guide.* That sounds easy until you actually try to do it. Eventually a style guide was half-heartedly developed after I joined CE's technical writing department, but it was very outdated and it spent too much time discussing material already covered in the *Chicago Manual of Style*. Additionally, as the only writer, I took quite a few liberties in changing the documentation templates, but I did not record those changes in the existing style guide because it was so time-consuming to edit and reprint. I usually just ignored updating and developing the style guide

---

*A style guide is a document that contains rules and guidelines. For example, Microsoft publishes the *Microsoft Manual of Style* for professionals who document Windows-based applications.

because I was the only writer. However, my decision to neglect the style guide eventually became a nightmare.

Scenario

I was working on a manual for a new product CE Software was releasing. After I began the project, I realized that a major manual revision for a different product line would coincide with my current project. This meant that I would have to hire a technical writing contractor to complete one of the manuals because I couldn't complete both manuals in the same time frame.

I found a contractor, and he—quite reasonably—asked for CE Software's style guide. I hurriedly updated what I could before I sent it to him, and then I returned my attention to the manual I was writing for my project.

Not much time elapsed before I started getting calls from the contractor asking me if he could change the way graphics were placed, use different fonts, change the footers, etc. I asked him why he wasn't following the style guide, and he said that the templates he received didn't follow the style guide, so he assumed that the style of the templates was negotiable. I knew the severe shortcomings of the style guide, and I didn't have time to micromanage, so I told the contractor to go ahead and make conservative changes to the templates as needed.

The contractor continued to require my attention throughout the project because he had no other reliable resources. He had already discovered that the style guide wasn't dependable, so he had to contact me to answer every question that the style guide should have answered. The end result: he was frustrated, I was frustrated, and both projects suffered unnecessary delays.

I recently updated the manual that the contractor completed during that project, and I was amazed at how long it took me to make the manual "match" existing CE Software documentation. I had to reorganize it, re-anchor all the graphics, change terminology, and adjust explanations that were not as task-oriented as CE's other manuals. All this took time that would have been better spent rewriting or updating the style guide before I sent the project to the contractor.

The problem here had nothing to do with the skill of the contractor. I have no doubt that the project would have been almost seamless had it not been for my inaccurate, incomplete style guide. The solution to this problem was obvious—I needed to make a commitment to recording my writing "rules" in the style guide.

Example

One example that illustrates the problems associated with not having an accurate style guide occurred toward the end of the project. I was hurriedly copy-editing the final draft submitted by the contractor when I noticed that he organized the manual differently than CE Software's other manuals. I asked him about it, and he indicated that he felt the current organization of the manual would be the most usable for CE Software's customers. He started the manual with the following chapters and sub-sections:

1) Introduction
2) Establishing Mail Directory Services
   a) Product Description
   b) Architecture Overview
   c) Product Features and Benefits
   d) Directory Synchronization
   e) Integration with Macintosh E-mail Services
3) Configuring Directory Services
   a) Installing the Software
   . . .

I missed what I considered to be an organizational problem in the first draft the contractor submitted because I was busy with my project; I assumed he would organize the manual in what I thought was the logical order of all CE Software manuals. I decided to look at the style guide to see if the organization of CE manuals was formally documented. Telling the contractor that he had to change the document because of the style guide would be much easier than asking him to change it because of what I preferred. This is what the style guide said about the topic of organization:

Front Matter

The front matter of a typical CE Software manual consists of four parts:

- an inside cover page that states the edition number
- the warranty
- the table of contents
- a "welcome" or "introduction" chapter that briefly explains how to contact CE Software

Middle Matter

The middle matter of the manual should highlight every feature in the software, explaining how to use it. Each chapter should be no longer than 25 pages.

The style guide made no mention of the fact that the installation chapter was to follow a brief overview chapter. Since we were on a tight timeline and we didn't want to pay the contractor for all the hours reorganizing the front matter of the manual would take, I allowed the manual to go to the printer without making any major changes.

About six months after the product was released, I got a message from a member of our technical support team asking when we were going to rewrite the directory service manual. The technical support representative then told me that customers didn't like the manual because it was too complicated. I asked the technical support manager if he'd heard similar complaints from customers, and he admitted that the manual was not well received by our customers.

When I sat down to rewrite the section of the style guide that addressed manual organization, this is what I wrote:

All CE Software manuals are organized in the same easy-to-follow way because our customers have grown accustomed to a specific organizational pattern. Since our customer base consists of small-to-medium-sized businesses that frequently do not have full-time network administrators, the documentation instructions must to be very clear and easy to understand. CE Software manuals include three main components: front matter, middle matter, and back matter.

Front Matter
The front matter of a CE Software user guide or administrator guide must contain:
- an inside cover page that states the edition number
- the license and limited warranty
- the table of contents
- a chapter entitled "Introduction" that briefly explains how to contact CE Software's technical support and customer service departments. This chapter must also explain how to use the documentation.

Middle Matter
The middle matter of the manual should highlight every feature in the software, explaining how to use it. Each chapter should be no longer than 25 pages.
- Chapter 1 should be entitled "Installing X" or "Getting Started," depending on the software being documented. It must provide instructions for installing and launching the software if there is not a separate installation guide.
- Chapter 2 should be entitled "Overview." It must offer a brief overview of the software, including pictorial representations of how the software works. The goal of this chapter is to familiarize users with the software interface and to guide the user through basic tasks.
- The remaining manual chapters should be organized in the order of the most necessary features. For example, a manual on e-mail should be organized into chapters on "Sending Mail," "Receiving Mail," "Setting Your Preferences," etc.

When I later updated this manual I organized the following chapters and sub-sections this way:

1. Introduction
2. Getting Started
   a. Installing X
      • Hardware Requirements
      • Software Requirements
   b. Launching X
3. Directory Service Overview
   a. Identifying Features and Benefits
   b. Learning How the Directory System Works
   . . .

Assignment

Create a scenario for which you need to write technical documentation. For example, imagine you work for a university, and you need to write a departmental directory that discusses a particular program of study, its faculty, and extracurricular activities available within that department.

Develop a style guide that the author of the departmental directory can use to create the directory. This department- or program-specific style guide should answer any stylistic questions that the author may have as he or she compiles the directory. Justify your decisions for what is included in the style guide and what users are expected to find using the *Chicago Manual of Style* or similar widely available style guides.

Determine the form of the style guide. It should be easy to update and easily accessible. For example, the style guide could be printed, based in HTML, based in Winhelp, or whatever else is appropriate as long as you can explain your choice.

Arricka Brouwer is a technical writer for TechnicalDocs.com, Inc. Her responsibilities include creating and updating technical documentation, coordinating printing and production, designing and conducting usability tests, converting documentation to portable document format and HTML for presentation on client Web sites, and developing and designing online help systems.

Arricka Brouwer believes that style guides are a critical resource for writers and other technical professionals. She says, "Style guides are not simply a collection of formulaic rules. They allow writers to make information consistent and accessible to a specific audience."

She has a B.A. in English with emphasis in Rhetoric and Professional Communication from Iowa State University. You can reach her at <abrouwer@technicaldocs.com>. Or check out her Web site at <http://www.technicaldocs.com>

Individual and Collaborative Assignments

1. **Determine the appropriate voice.** Work in a small group with your class-mates to determine whether you would use active or passive voice for each situation and audience listed below.

   Example
   A document about the grading of pearls could be written in active voice if the document is intended for trainees learning how to grade pearls because the focus should be on what the person does. However, the document could be written in passive voice if it's for customers who are more interested in the pearls than in the grader.

   (a) blood donation, for a potential donor
   (b) purification of water from sewage treatment plant, for an ecologist
   (c) grading of diamonds for jewelry, for a consumer
   (d) professional dry cleaning of antique clothing, for a dry cleaner
   (e) an operation, for a child in hospital for surgery
   (f) filing a claim, for a new insurance adjuster
   (g) a change in manufacturing procedures, for a customer
   (h) formation of sebaceous cysts, for patient with cysts
   (i) operation of a heat exchanger, for a homeowner

2. **Explain active and passive voice.** Carefully read the following two paragraphs. Explain the context, purpose, and audience that makes active voice appropriate for one paragraph and passive voice appropriate for the other.

   active voice   The neonatal nurse can decrease the chances that a newborn will suffer from cold stress by following several standard procedures. The nurse should monitor the baby's temperature regularly and should not bathe the baby until the temperature is stabilized. A careful nurse coordinates all medical procedures that expose the baby to cool air and will be certain to remove all wet bedclothes and diapers that cool the skin by evaporation.

   passive voice   A newborn will not suffer from cold stress if the neonatal nurse follows several standard procedures. The baby's temperature should be monitored regularly. The baby should not be bathed until the temperature is stabilized. A baby should not be exposed to cool air while undergoing medical procedures and should not be left with wet bedclothes or diapers that cool the skin by evaporation.

3. **Edit sentences for wordiness.** Work in a small group with your classmates. For each of the following sentences, prepare a less wordy revision. Explain

to your classmates why you think your revision is an improvement given the context, audience, and purpose that you envision.

- It has come to my attention that the lights in my office have not been working.

- Subsequent modifications will be disseminated to all users.

- The deterioration of her condition led to the determination that surgery was necessary.

- When the inspector did not accept this data, claiming it was unreliable, we were not so inefficient as to reject suggestions for alternative testing methods.

- A 35mm SLR (single lens reflex) camera is a camera (a light-tight box that uses a physical means of reproducing an image and a chemical means of preserving it) that uses film of 35mm width and allows the photographer to see the image to be photographed through a single lens, the one used to expose the film, rather than through a second one used only for viewing the image.

- A single-lens method of viewing the image to be photographed is preferable to the viewfinder or rangefinder method, in which the user "finds the view" through a separate lens because it eliminates the problem of parallax error, or not seeing precisely what will be photographed.

4. **Revise an explanation to eliminate density.** Read the following dense paragraph and revise it to make it more coherent. You may separate the material into shorter paragraphs, use lists, and add or delete material. This information was part of a memo informing employees about changes in procedures dealing with scrapped parts.

You may separate the material into shorter paragraphs, use lists, and add or delete material. This information was part of a memo informing employees about changes in procedures dealing with scrapped parts. Several steps must be taken to separate and stage inventory to be scrapped. The first step is to locate and stage all excess parts. The white tag on each part will identify the part as either EXCESS, GOOD or EXCESS, DAMAGED. Parts tagged EXCESS, GOOD should be staged in bin #020185. Parts tagged EXCESS, DAMAGED should be staged in bin #020186 for further sorting and staging by code. The code is etched into the frame of each part: 1A—defective consumable, 1B—unidentified damage, 1C—vendor return/unrepairable, 1D—identifiable damage. Parts labeled code 1A, defective consumable, are staged in bin #020188, to be automatically scrapped without further investigation. Parts labeled code 1C, vendor return/unrepairable, are staged in bin #020189; these parts can also be automatically scrapped. If a part is labeled code 1B, additional information is required. Code 1B parts should be visually examined for signs of damage such as broken chips or split jumper cables. Parts with observable damage should be placed on a skid in bin #020187. Parts with no observable damage should be hand carried to the Repair Center where each part will be tested to determine the extent of damage. Parts the Repair Center determines cannot be repaired are staged in bin #020187. Parts the Repair Center believes are repairable are placed in the Repair Stockroom and scheduled for repair. Parts labeled with code 1D are staged in bin #020190. When ten or more skids have accumulated, the manager should be notified to check the accumulated parts and fill out a justification form to scrap each part.

5. **Revise law to make more accessible.** Read the following state law explaining fishing regulations and then revise to clarify, while maintaining necessary information.[20]

Lake or Pond Partly in Another State. If, in the case of a lake or pond situated partly in this state and partly in another state, the laws of such other state permit fishing in that part thereof lying within such other state by persons licensed or otherwise entitled under the laws of this state to fish in that part of such lake or pond lying within this state, persons licensed or otherwise entitled under the laws of such other state to fish in the part of such lake or pond lying within such other state shall be permitted to fish in that part thereof lying within this state, and, as to such lake or pond, the operation of the laws of this state relative to open and closed seasons, limits of catch, minimum sizes of fish caught and methods of fishing shall be suspended upon the adoption and during the continuance in force of rules and regulations relative to those subjects and affecting that part of such lake or pond lying within this state, which rules and regulations the director is hereby authorized to make, and from time to time add to, alter and repeal.

6. **Revise using given-new structures.** Read the following paragraph.
   (a) Analyze to identify the current given-new structure, which will help you see why the paragraph is not coherent.
   (b) Revise the paragraph to more closely reflect given-new structures.
   (c) Identify the given-new structure of your revised paragraphs.

   (1) Hot Isostatic Processing makes metal more dense. (2) Dense metal is more durable. (3) Metal parts cannot be cast without unavoidable small cracks and air pockets. (4) Imperfections lead to wear and breakage. (5) These flaws can be eliminated with Hot Isostatic Processing. (6) The parts are heated in special units, then pressurized with gas to minimize flaws. (7) A controlled cooling process ensures that the parts retain their original shape. (8) Hot Isostatic Processing produces stronger parts, able to withstand greater pressures for a longer span of time.

7. **Use a software editing program.** Select a document that you have written that still needs careful editing—that is, you still need to clean up stylistic problems as well as eliminate errors in mechanics and usage. Then go to your school (or company) computer lab and select one of the software packages that does this kind of editing. Run the software program to identify problems

in style, mechanics, and usage. Make the corrections that you believe will improve your document.

8. **Evaluate a software editing program.** Write a review of the software you used in Assignment 7 in which you evaluate the effectiveness of the software. Prepare this review for publication in a local Society for Technical Communication newsletter so that other technical communicators and professionals who might use this software would have access to it.

9. **Conduct document testing.** Select a print or Web document that you are working on that would benefit from document testing. Prepare a report that includes these three parts:
   (a) Your best shot before document testing; that is, what you consider the very best you can do in preparing the document.
   (b) Document testing of the document. You must include at least one kind *each* of text-based, expert-based, and user-based testing. Identify the tests you selected (and justification for the selection), the test results, and an analysis/interpretation of the results.
   (c) The revision of your best-shot document based on the testing results and your analysis/explanation of the changes.

Intertext

Readability

Readability formulas reputedly assess a text's level of difficulty for readers' understanding. A variety of readability formulas are accessible and convenient; they are widely used in government, industry, and education, partly because of their availability on computer software. The question is whether they do what they claim.

How Readability Formulas Work

Readability formulas are based on the relationships between average word length (number of syllables per word) and average sentence length (number of words per sentence). The theory behind them states that both the higher the average number of syllables per word and the greater the average number of words per sentence, the more difficult the document is to read. The formulas yield a ratio between word length and sentence length that estimates a document's readability in one of two ways: level of difficulty (easy to difficult) and grade level (first grade to postgraduate study).

Problems in Using Readability Formulas

If you use readability formulas, be aware of their weaknesses and avoid restricting word choice or sentence structure inappropriately. Because readability formulas are based on a quantifiable ratio, several elements of writing are not adequately addressed, including variations in the scales themselves, overgeneralizations about word and sentence length, format, and content.

Sentence length can affect material's readability. Generally, shorter sentences are easier to read than longer ones; some reading experts assign levels of difficulty to sentence length, as the following examples show. The content in these sentences does not vary much in difficulty because all of the sentences are from the same article in *Aviation Week and Space Technology,* a magazine for professionals and experts in aerospace-related industries.

The cockpit instrumentation is well designed. (6 words)   *very easy, 8 words or less*

This aircraft is equipped with combined dual navigation and communication systems. (11 words)   *easy, 11 words*

All controls are within easy reach of the pilot and have readily discernible functions. (14 words)   *fairly easy, 14 words*

The DO 228 has easy access to cockpit seats by an optional door located on either side of the cockpit. (19 words)   *standard, 17 words*

The aircraft's fuel, electrical, deicing and starting systems controls are color coded and shown in clearly styled flow diagrams on the overhead panel. (23 words)   *fairly difficult, 21 words*

The front instrument panel is not cluttered, partly due to the large center console located between the pilots that contains most of the avionics controls. (25 words)   *difficult, 25 words*

Dornier's DO 228–200 commuter and utility twin turboprop offers operators a versatile-mission aircraft with short-field performance combined with excellent flight performance characteristics and easily maintained aircraft systems. (28 words)[21]   *very difficult, 29+ words*

Sentence length is only one factor in sentence difficulty. Sentences are not by themselves inherently difficult or easy to read. Readers' comprehension is affected by sentence length in combination with factors such as content complexity. The more difficult the content for individual readers, the lower their comprehension; similarly, the longer the sentence, the lower the comprehension. However, simple ideas in a long sentence may be easier to understand than difficult ideas expressed in a short sentence. When the content is difficult and readers' prior knowledge of the content is limited, it is particularly important to avoid long sentences that compound the difficulty in reading.

Just as critical as sentence length for ease in reading is variety of sentence lengths in the same article. An article or document with all of the sentences the same length quickly becomes repetitious and boring. Variation maintains readers' interest and increases comprehension. Although a single document might not have the tremendous variety shown in the previous examples, effective technical communicators generally try to vary sentence length.

Sentence type also affects readers' interest and comprehension. Simple sentences are often easier to understand than compound, complex, or compound-complex sentences because the relationships among the ideas are simpler. However, a series of simple sentences is not only boring but may not convey the relationships you intend; thus, readers are left to make independent and potentially erroneous interpretations.

Readability formulas do not consider difficulty of content. For example, a paragraph may be labeled "seventh-grade readability" because of relatively short words and sentences; however, a 12-year-old seventh grader would not necessarily be able to understand it. Highly technical or abstract material can have short words and sentences but ideas that are extremely difficult to comprehend.

For example, this sentence has only 15 words: "Boards with tight lines and spaces required reworking due to shorts caused by solder bridging." According to the reading scale above, the sentence falls between fairly easy and standard because most of the words are short and the sentence has a total of only 21 syllables. However, the terminology is unfamiliar to general readers, and the sentence is not easy to understand—despite formulas that indicate otherwise. Or consider what grade level you would assign for "I think; therefore, I am."

Another problem is that the formulas differ from expert to expert. (You'll find some common readability formulas at the end of this Intertext.) Lack of consistency leads to confusion because results from different formulas are not comparable. Readability formulas also ignore the important function of subordination in increasing comprehension. Writers recognize that for most readers, a series of short, separate sentences that treat all ideas equally may be more difficult to comprehend than sentences that have subordinate and main ideas clearly established. Two versions of the same information illustrate this point.[22]

■ EXAMPLE

A decayed woven linen robe was found in 1981. The robe dated from c. 1000 B.C.E. It is the oldest known piece of cloth found in Greece. The robe was found by a Greek-British excavation team. The team was digging on the island of Euboeoa. Euboeoa is about 40 miles from Athens.

■ REVISION

A decayed woven linen robe from c. 1000 B.C.E., the oldest known piece of cloth found in Greece, was unearthed in 1981 during a Greek-British excavation on the island of Euboeoa, 40 miles from Athens.

Although readability formulas indicate that the first version is easier to read, most adults prefer the second version because relationships are established clearly and repetition is eliminated.

Readability formulas equate short words with simplicity, without regard to word meaning or audience knowledge. However, shortness is not always a measure of reading ease, for short words do not necessarily have simple meanings. For example, *quark* and *erg*, although short, are more difficult words than *satellite* or *occupation*. And actually, some very long (and sometimes technical) words have a high recognition factor. For example, some multisyllable medical and chemical terms are easily and immediately recognized by all professionals in their respective fields. Likewise, a fourth grader recognizes the words *Mississippi* or *Massachusetts*. Such multisyllable, high-recognition words can give a false high grade-level equivalency (compared with the difficulty of the content) when evaluating readability for adult professionals.

Word length lessens in importance as a factor influencing comprehension if the words are familiar to the intended audience. Whereas some technical words are long and appear complex to the general reader, they are easily understood by experts in the field. In many cases the technical term is exactly the correct word; an explanation comprised of shorter, more recognizable terms would be less precise. The following sentence might not make sense to a general reader, but to a plastics engineer it is both accurate and easy to understand:

■ EXAMPLE

Polysulfones comprise a class of engineering thermoplastics with high thermal, oxidative, and hydrolytic stability, and good resistance to aqueous mineral acids, alkali, salt solutions, oils and grease.[23]

Finally, readability formulas do not consider document design. Closely spaced, small printing with little visual relief is more difficult and takes longer to read and comprehend—regardless of the content—than carefully designed, visually pleasing pages.

Restrained Use of Readability Formulas

Readability formulas can be useful tools—if applied properly and with other methods of assessing the suitability of writing for a particular audience. You can best determine whether material is understandable by giving it to representative readers in the intended audience. If these readers comprehend and act on the information, you can assume the information is appropriate.

Readability formulas can benefit technical writers by calculating whether all sections of a long report or a series of related manuals maintain a consistent level of difficulty. This is valuable when several writers are preparing separate sections of a lengthy report or a series of manuals. In addition, readability formulas may allow writers to tailor material for audience ability by identifying word and sentence length.

They also help writers identify and analyze reasons for the ineffectiveness of reports or manuals for specific audiences. Formula scores may show the material to be excessively difficult (thus ignored) or unnecessarily simple (thus boring and insulting).

As a writer of technical documents, you should choose words that readers comprehend. Use the simplest word that accurately and concisely conveys the meaning. Generally, if you have a choice between a short or a long synonym, choose the short one because readers comprehend it more quickly. Be concerned initially with accuracy and only secondarily with word length.

Readability Indexes and Formulas

This Intertext presents the methods to calculate two standard measures of readability: Flesch-Kincaid Formula and Fry Graph.

Flesch-Kincaid Formula.[24]   To determine grade level, use this formula: Multiply 0.39 by average number of words per sentence. Then add the product of 11.8 times the average number of syllables per word. Subtract 15.59 from that number to arrive at grade level.

$$\text{Grade level} = (0.39) \times (\text{average number of words/sentence}) + (11.8) \times (\text{average number of syllables/word}) - 15.59$$

Fry Graph.   To determine reading level, follow the seven steps and locate the two variables—average number of sentences and average number of syllables—on the accompanying graph. (See Figure I.1.)

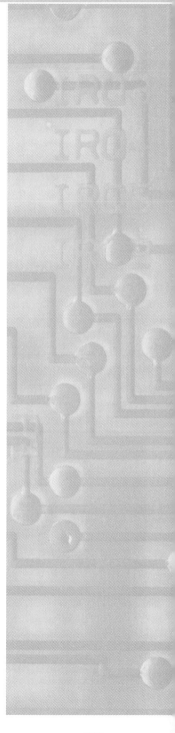

FIGURE I.1 ■ Fry Graph[25]

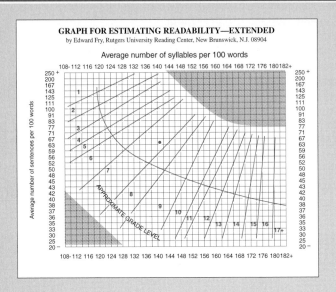

GRAPH FOR ESTIMATING READABILITY—EXTENDED
by Edward Fry, Rutgers University Reading Center, New Brunswick, N.J. 08904

Expanded Directions for Working Readability Graph

1. Randomly select three (3) sample passages and count out exactly 100 words each, beginning with the beginning of a sentence. Do count proper nouns, initializations, and numerals.
2. Count the number of sentences in the hundred words, estimating length of the fraction of the last sentence to the nearest one-tenth.
3. Count the total number of syllables in the 100-word passage. If you don't have a hand counter available, an easy way is to simply put a mark above every syllable over one in each word, then when you get to the end of the passage, count the number of marks and add 100. Small calculators can also be used as counters by pushing numeral 1, then push the + sign for each word or syllable when counting.
4. Enter graph with *average* sentence length and *average* number of syllables; plot dot where the two lines intersect. Area where dot is plotted will give you the approximate grade level.
5. If a great deal of variability is found in syllable count or sentence count, putting more samples into the average is desirable.
6. A word is defined as a group of symbols with a space on either side; thus, *Joe, IRA, 1945,* and *&* are each one word.
7. A syllable is defined as a phonetic syllable. Generally, there are as many syllables as vowel sounds. For example, *stopped* is one syllable and *wanted* is two syllables. When counting syllables for numerals and initializations, count one syllable for each symbol. For example, *1945* is four syllables, *IRA* is three syllables, and *&* is one syllable.

Note: This "extended graph" does not outmode or render the earlier (1968) version inoperative or inaccurate; it is an extension. (Reproduction permitted—no copyright)

PART IV

Completing Documents

14

Correspondence

CHAPTER 14 IN BRIEF

Correspondence, which includes all types of notes, memos, and letters as well as electronic mail and messages, provides a record of transactions.

Characteristics of Correspondence

Correspondence has features that distinguish it from other workplace communication. Correspondence, often more appropriate than telephone calls, has several modes of delivery from which communicators can select.

Domino Effect of Correspondence

Correspondence does not exist in a vacuum, nor does it have rigid format prescriptions.

Composing Letters, Memos, and Electronic Mail

Composing conventional, routine correspondence typically includes schema-driven planning and knowledge-driven planning.

Attitude and Tone. Some people form an opinion of your competence from the content and style of your writing.

- You can create a positive approach by using direct language.
- Readers respond well to a *you*-attitude rather than an *I*- or *we*-attitude. Focus on and emphasize the reader rather than yourself.
- Exclusionary language may be inaccurate, reflect badly on you as an individual, and convey a negative corporate image.

Audience. Readers are generally receptive to good news, so it is usually presented in *direct* or *descending order*. In contrast, readers are often resistant to bad news, so it is sometimes presented in *indirect* or *ascending order,* being easier to accept if readers have an explanation first.

Generally, letters are intended for external readers, whereas memos and notes communicate to internal readers. Electronic mail can be for internal or external readers.

Organization of Information. The content in any correspondence—directives, policy statements, or announcements; requests or inquiries; and responses—should be organized so that it can be read easily and quickly.

Format

Three formats are most commonly used for correspondence:

- standard block style letter
- standard modified block style letter
- memos with a "to/from/subject" heading

Visual Displays

Readers benefit greatly from visual devices that highlight, outline, or separate sections and identify main points.

C orrespondence includes all types of notes, memos, and letters as well as electronic mail and messages. Unlike face-to-face and telephone conversations, correspondence provides a record of transactions in business and industry that can be referred to and checked.

This chapter includes guidelines and examples that will help you prepare correspondence. You'll begin by reading about general characteristics of correspondence. Then you'll read a case that illustrates the *domino effect* of correspondence—one letter or memo generating a chain reaction of correspondence. Finally, you'll read about composing correspondence: following guidelines, using the appropriate attitude and tone, and responding to audience, organization, format, and visual displays.

Characteristics of Correspondence

This section focuses on the features of correspondence that distinguish it from other workplace communication, then suggests situations in which written correspondence may be more appropriate than telephone calls, and finally reviews modes of delivery from which communicators can select.

Distinctive Features of Correspondence

One way to distinguish correspondence from other technical communication is by its composing time. When preparing correspondence, you can usually save time by combining schema-driven planning and knowledge-driven planning. (Refer to Chapter 2 for a review of different kinds of planning.) You know your readers' expectations of format and tone; you also usually have a firm grasp of the content. As a result, much of your correspondence can be written fairly quickly, which is helpful since you will seldom have time for multiple revisions.

Another way to distinguish correspondence from other types of technical communication is by audience size. Many forms of technical communication, such as manuals, have large audiences, but correspondence is often directed to a particular person or a small group of readers with common interests. You can adjust language and content for that person or group. However, you should always be aware that business correspondence is seldom considered confidential; other people in the organization may read letters, memos, and e-mail messages that you write, even if they're addressed to one person.

Because correspondence usually responds to a current situation, most of it becomes outdated more rapidly than other forms of workplace communication. Although a correspondent may not have the responsibility of maintaining files, he or she should authorize a file clerk to discard or transfer to dead files correspondence that is no longer pertinent to current operations, keeping in active files only the correspondence for which an on-going record is needed.

Who should be responsible for each of the following document elements—the originator or the transcriber (secretary) of correspondence?

- *factual accuracy*
- *grammatical precision*
- *typographical correctness*
- *clear and tactful wording*
- *visuals, page layout*

Because correspondence is often prepared quickly, writers sometimes pay less attention to stylistic details and appropriate usage than in documents such as manuals, reports, or articles. However, you must always make sure that correspondence is accurate and unambiguous. Letters especially represent the organization to the public. Inattention to conventions in mechanics, grammar, diction, or organization reflects negatively on the organization's image, encouraging readers to think either that accuracy and details don't matter to the company or that the readers aren't important enough to merit attention to conventions. Ambiguous or inaccurate correspondence can sometimes cause liability problems for an organization in the event of a lawsuit.

Written Correspondence or Telephone Calls

A written document—whether paper or electronic—is sometimes more appropriate than a telephone call for these reasons:

- Establishing a permanent record
- Clarifying complex issues
- Guaranteeing precise, unambiguous phrasing
- Providing a corroborative record of a conversation
- Providing a reference for data
- Eliminating the necessity for direct interaction

Some activities—particularly those requiring no written record and not exceedingly complex—can be handled by telephone. Telephone calls may be more efficient than written correspondence for many kinds of routine business:

- Inquiring about costs, deliveries, specifications
- Responding to an inquiry
- Placing purchase orders (usually followed by written confirmation)
- Reminding colleagues about a meeting
- Thanking a colleague for assistance

Modes of Delivery

Once you've decided that a paper or electronic document is more appropriate for your situation than a telephone call, you must choose the mode of delivery.

Traditionally, external paper correspondence has been sent by first-class mail (arriving in one to five business days) or priority mail (arriving in one to three business days), and this is still the preferred mode of delivery for many formal documents, especially legal documents. But with the advent of overnight delivery, fax machines, and electronic mail, you will often need to make decisions about the mode of delivery based on urgency, cost, audience, and formality. Common electronic modes of delivery include fax machines ("fax" for "facsimile"), various kinds of asynchronous communication (including electronic mail—that is, e-mail; newsgroups; and electronic lists), and synchronous communication. (See Chapter 5 for more about synchronous and asynchronous communication.)

A *fax machine* lets you connect to another fax machine via telephone lines in order to send and receive copies of visual and verbal material. Benefits include accuracy coupled with speed (virtually instantaneous compared to days for "snail mail"). Faxed documents are particularly useful when the exact appearance of the original is critical, as it is with changes on blueprints for manufacturing or a signed addendum to a contract or a photograph used for identification.

Electronic mail (e-mail) lets you send and receive letters, memos, and other documents from one computer with e-mail software to another computer with compatible software. Benefits include speed, relative privacy, and convenience, especially for sending information to distribution lists. Although e-mail is perceived as a less formal communication method than snail mail correspondence, always begin your message with an appropriate salutation.

The rules of netiquette (introduced in Chapter 5) apply to all computer-mediated communication, including e-mail. *Netiquette*, a contraction of "network" and "etiquette," refers to the generally accepted guidelines of behavior for participating in computer-mediated communication. Keep in mind that electronic messages can be forwarded, printed, or permanently stored by any recipient. E-mail can also be misdirected, even when you are careful, so do not put something in an e-mail message that you would not want everybody to read.

Sending E-Mail Messages

- Include a brief and descriptive note in the Subject field. This makes for easier reading, storing, and searching at the other end.

- Check the To line of your e-mail message to confirm that you are responding to the appropriate person or persons.

- Cover only one topic per message. This makes it easier to reply, forward, or organize the archived, or saved, messages.

- Keep the message brief.

- Spell and use words with care. Careless use of language can detract from the content of your message.

- Write as if the whole world will read your message. Your mail may be forwarded with your name on it.

- Avoid using all caps. This is considered SHOUTING. Use upper- and lowercase text.

- Indicate the emotion, voice, or body language (tone) of your message by using text-based *emoticons*, hundreds of which exist:

:-)	smiley face, humorous intent, also :^)
;-)	wink, flirtatious
B^)	smiley in sunglasses, on vacation
:^>	sarcastic remark
:-(	frowny, unhappy about something

Receiving E-Mail Messages

- Indicate the content of the original message. This can be done by quoting pertinent portions often preceded with marks to indicate quotation, or by summarizing the subject. You do not need to copy the entire message.

- Reply to the sender if you receive a message intended for someone else.

- Delay response to a message that upsets you. Do not respond immediately; in any case, avoid *flaming*, that is, sending an angry or rude message.

- Determine unknown e-mail address by calling the person with whom you wish to correspond or using an electronic search function.

- Maintain an address file, since no central directory of addresses exists though many universities now publish e-mail addresses in school directories, and some have online directories that can be searched.

- Confirm that the recipient actually received your message by asking the recipient to acknowledge receipt.[1]

Another kind of correspondence—quite different from conventional memos and letters and even different from e-mail, which is generally directed to a specific individual or to an specific group of individuals—is asynchronous conversation in the form of newsgroups and lists. *Newsgroups* allow users to correspond by "posting" and "replying to" messages from other users. *Lists* transmit e-mail only to individuals who have subscribed to the list.[2] Both newsgroups and lists provide opportunities for correspondence to groups.

Newsgroup and List Netiquette

- Familiarize yourself with a newsgroup or list before you participate. Read the discussion in progress (called a *thread*) before posting replies.

- Avoid posting "Me Too" messages, where content is limited to agreement with previous posts. This just takes up bandwidth. Content of a follow-up post should exceed the quoted content.

- Send mail intended only for one person directly to that person. Post something to the newsgroup or list only when it will be of general interest to all participants.

- Respect a user's desire for anonymity. Do not use that person's real name online without permission. Some lists have vehicles for allowing you to post anonymously.

- Expect a slight delay in seeing your post when posting to a moderated group. The moderator may change your subject line to have your post conform to a particular thread. Therefore, if you post something and do not see it immediately, do not assume it failed and re-post it.

- Indicate that you sent or posted to multiple mailing lists or newsgroups with a message similar to the following "This message cross-posted to [names of mailing lists or newsgroups]."

- Recognize that anonymous postings are accepted in some newsgroups and lists and are disliked in others.[3]

Still another kind of electronic correspondence includes *Internet Relay Chats* (*IRC*), sites where users type messages to each other (chat) in real time (synchronous), which creates an online conversation. Most chat rooms have a particular topic that you're expected to focus on.[4]

Chat Netiquette

- Understand that listening, or *lurking*, is an acceptable practice. Many people commonly lurk before actually participating in chat to get to know the culture of the list group.

- Begin chat room participation with a general "hello." Greeting each member in a chat room is not necessary. Usually one greeting is enough.

- Respect signals from a chat room member that your commentary is unwelcome. People you do not know may not want to talk to you.

- Respect the guidelines of the group.

- Respect a user's desire for anonymity. Do not use that person's real name online without permission.[5]

If you follow netiquette guidelines, you can avoid a lot of problems—problems like those discussed in the ethics sidebar on the following page. Sometimes e-mail correspondence is less than careless; it is litigatable. The issues of privacy that are raised in this sidebar affect all of your e-mail messages.

Domino Effect of Correspondence

No piece of correspondence exists in a vacuum; a single message can trigger a series of letters, memos, and e-mail messages, as the organizational chain reactions illustrate in Figure 14.1 (Tele-Robics). As you read each letter, memo,

To Delete or Not to Delete: E-mail and Ethics

Consider the following actual e-mail exchange:

```
To: David Smith <dsmith@everycompany.com>
From: Laura
Message: Hi, David, Please destroy the evidence on the [litigation] you and
I talked about today. Thanks, Laura.
--------------
To: Laura
From: David
Message: Hi, Laura, Acknowledged your message and taken care of. Aloha,
David.
```

Consider another email sent to a co-worker:

```
Message: Did you see what Dr. [name omitted] did today? If that patient
survives, it will be a miracle.
```

These e-mails were recovered from computer hard drives by Electronic Evidence Discovery, a company specializing in e-mail retrieval.[6] Beyond being embarrassing, e-mails like these are often used in lawsuits. For example, in 1994, Nissan Motor Corporation fired two employees for receiving sexually suggestive e-mails. The court upheld the decision, accepting Nissan's argument that "the company owned the system and had the right to read anything in it" (Weisband 41). Another company, Intel Corporation, won a 1999 case against a former employee, restricting the employee from sending anti-Intel e-mail messages to the company. And in 1999, the Microsoft Corporation was found guilty of unfair business practices, in part on the basis of e-mails sent by CEO Bill Gates and other corporate officers.

Each of these court cases deals with ethical issues concerning e-mail: Is e-mail private? Who is responsible for the content of an e-mail message—the sender or the receiver? Who owns an e-mail message—the employee or the employer? For technical professionals, however, a more important question is how to avoid crossing these ethical lines. One step is to recognize the confusion that comes with e-mail. Using a password, for example, may "reinforce the perception that messages are not readily accessible by anyone other than the sender" (Weisband 40). In reality, e-mail messages are accessible to others, even after they are deleted. As well, the easy use of e-mail messages at the workplace encourages employees to send and receive personal messages, obscuring the fact that e-mail hardware and software are company property.

The best advice for using e-mail? "Experts were asked to list the 10 commandments of using e-mail, but they could come up with only two: Don't operate under the assumption that e-mail is private, and don't believe that the delete key actually makes e-mail disappear." ("E-mail")

What are some ways to write e-mails that deal with sensitive issues?

Do you view e-mail as private? Should you be responsible for e-mail you receive? Does a company have the right to read personal employee e-mails?

or e-mail message, think of the workplace environments as well as the specific purposes and audiences. The correspondence is presented in sequence so that you can see the evolving story and recognize that people at Tele-Robics were writing in response to the situation in which they were involved. For example,

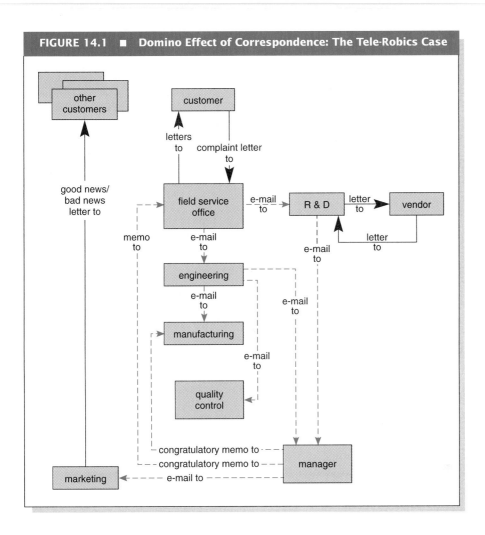

FIGURE 14.1 ■ Domino Effect of Correspondence: The Tele-Robics Case

John Hernandez did not say, "How can I write a response letter to a customer?" Instead, he said, "How can I best respond to James Crocker's concerns?"

As you read the sequence of letters, memos, and e-mail messages, you see that this correspondence produced the reactions that the various professionals involved hoped they would. In other words, the readers seemed to interpret the messages the way the writers intended. Tele-Robics resolved their technical problems, and corporate accounts with customers were maintained. The examples in this series can serve as guidelines as you compose your own correspondence. While correspondence does not have rigid prescriptions, it should follow conventions in format, organization, and tone that are illustrated by the samples. Generally, if your correspondence has the effect you desired on your intended audience, it is effective.

In the Tele-Robics case, the letters and e-mail messages involve a number of people both in the company and outside the company. The case deals with one of Tele-Robics's products, the Lightening IV Illuminator. The chain reaction starts when an important Tele-Robics customer, James W. Crocker at Crocker Computers, Inc., voices a complaint in a letter. The chronology of the correspondence will help you preview the situation.

1. Mr. Crocker writes a letter to John Hernandez, the field service manager for Tele-Robics, expressing disappointment with equipment and service (Figure 14.2).

2. John Hernandez writes a letter to Crocker, acknowledging his complaint, identifying the cause of the problem, and explaining how and when it will be resolved (Figure 14.3).

3. John Hernandez also sends two e-mail messages: one to Sarah Bell, Tele-Robics's manager of research & development, and the other to Tom Watt, manager of engineering, the group that developed the specifications for the illuminator (Figure 14.4 and Figure 14.5).

4. Sarah Bell writes a letter to Chuck Taylor at Optical Coatings, Inc., one of Tele-Robics's prime vendors, and sends an e-mail message to Brian Bartlett, division manager for Tele-Robics (Figure 14.6 and Figure 14.8).

5. Chuck Taylor at Optical Coatings responds to Sarah's inquiry and requests additional information (Figure 14.7).

6. Tom Watt sends two e-mail messages: one accompanying an ECO (engineering change order) to Mike Maxwell in Manufacturing, with a copy to Quality Control; the other to Brian Bartlett, his manager (Figure 14.9 and Figure 14.10).

7. Brian Bartlett writes an e-mail message to Shawna Simons, marketing manager, giving her an update of the problem and asking that the marketing representatives contact customers with the problem equipment (Figure 14.11).

8. Shawna Simons writes to customers who have bought a Lightening IV Illuminator. She sends a blind copy of the letter to Brian Bartlett (Figure 14.12).

9. Brian writes memos to Mike Maxwell and John Hernandez. He thanks them and their co-workers and crews for their quick and appropriate response to the problem (Figure 14.13 and Figure 14.14).

Complaint Letter.   As you can read in Figure 14.2, Mr. Crocker writes to John Hernandez, the field service manager for Tele-Robics. Mr. Crocker expresses disappointment in equipment that his company has purchased from Tele-Robics and with the field service technicians sent to repair the equipment. He makes clear that using the flawed equipment has been costly. He is specific about the steps that have been taken to repair the problem ("your field service office has

FIGURE 14.2 ■ Complaint Letter from Customer

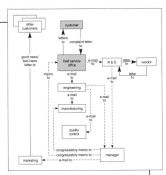

Crocker Computers, Inc.
1932 Sylvan Avenue
Granbury, Texas 78048

January 21, 20—

Mr. John Hernandez
Manager, Field Service
Tele-Robics, Inc.
799 Warren Avenue
Greenville, TX 75933

Dear Mr. Hernandez:

Our recently purchased Lightening IV Illuminator is a disappointment. Instead of increasing our productivity, it has cost Crocker Computers, Inc., thousands of dollars in downtime.

Your field service office has sent three different technicians in the past week to service this new illuminator, with no success. Either your technicians do not know how to repair the Lightening IV Illuminator, or your company cannot manufacture this illuminator to meet our specs.

I expect that you will correct this problem immediately.

Sincerely,

James W. Crocker

James W. Crocker

JWC:cd

FIGURE 14.3 ■ Response Letter to Customer

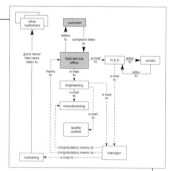

TELE-ROBICS, INC.
799 Warren Avenue Greenville, TX 75933

January 23, 20—

Mr. James W. Crocker
Crocker Computers, Inc.
1932 Sylvan Avenue
Granbury, TX 76048

Dear Mr. Crocker:

Our field service representatives have filed reports detailing the energy failure of the Lightening IV Illuminator reported by your company. Based on this information, I have concluded that your illuminator contains lenses that have defective coatings.

The engineering staff here at Tele-Robics, Inc., assures me that your energy spec can easily be met once the original lenses are replaced. Our manufacturing facility has already sent a new illuminator to you. Your field service representative will contact you to install the replacement this week.

The replacement illuminator will meet your specs, enabling you to increase productivity.

Sincerely,

John Hernandez

John Hernandez
Manager, Field Service

JH:jn

sent three different technicians") and the lack of success they've had. Naturally, he is forthright in asking that the problem be corrected.

Response to Complaint Letter. John Hernandez immediately responds to the customer complaint. In his letter, Figure 14.3, he acknowledges the complaint, identifies the cause of the problem, and explains how and when it will be resolved. Notice that the letter is addressed to "Mr. Crocker," not "Jim."

Internal Memos: Peers. But responding to the customer is not enough. John Hernandez also sends two e-mail messages, thus beginning the domino effect. One memo, Figure 14.4, is sent to Sarah Bell, Tele-Robics's manager of Research & Development. Her group designed the illuminator and is now working on a new, similar version. John informs Sarah about the recent complaints so that she can make appropriate changes in the current project. John Hernandez's second e-mail message, Figure 14.5, is to Tom Watt, manager of Engineering, the group that developed the specifications for the illuminator.

Information Letter. When Sarah Bell receives the e-mail message from John Hernandez, she and her team study how the complaint affects the development of similar products. Once the team reaches a decision, Sarah writes two pieces of correspondence. The first is a letter to Chuck Taylor at Optical Coatings, Inc., one of Tele-Robics's prime vendors. The letter, Figure 14.6, informs Chuck about a design change that affects an order. Even though Sarah is on a first-name basis with Chuck, her letter is clear and precise, not chatty. Sarah

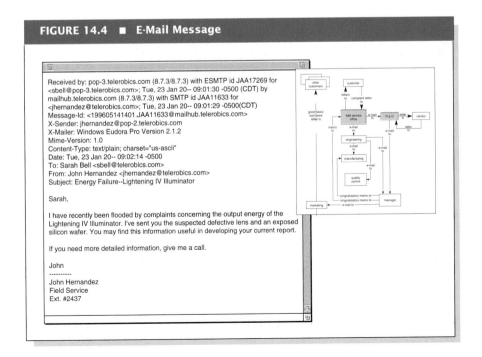

FIGURE 14.4 ■ E-Mail Message

Received by: pop-3.telerobics.com (8.7.3/8.7.3) with ESMTP id JAA17269 for
<sbell@pop-3.telerobics.com>; Tue, 23 Jan 20-- 09:01:30 -0500 (CDT) by
mailhub.telerobics.com (8.7.3/8.7.3) with SMTP id JAA11633 for
<jhernandez@telerobics.com>; Tue, 23 Jan 20-- 09:01:29 -0500(CDT)
Message-Id: <199605141401.JAA11633@mailhub.telerobics.com>
X-Sender: jhernandez@pop-2.telerobics.com
X-Mailer: Windows Eudora Pro Version 2.1.2
Mime-Version: 1.0
Content-Type: text/plain; charset="us-ascii"
Date: Tue, 23 Jan 20-- 09:02:14 -0500
To: Sarah Bell <sbell@telerobics.com>
From: John Hernandez <jhernandez@telerobics.com>
Subject: Energy Failure--Lightening IV Illuminator

Sarah,

I have recently been flooded by complaints concerning the output energy of the Lightening IV Illuminator. I've sent you the suspected defective lens and an exposed silicon wafer. You may find this information useful in developing your current report.

If you need more detailed information, give me a call.

John

John Hernandez
Field Service
Ext. #2437

FIGURE 14.5 ■ E-Mail Message

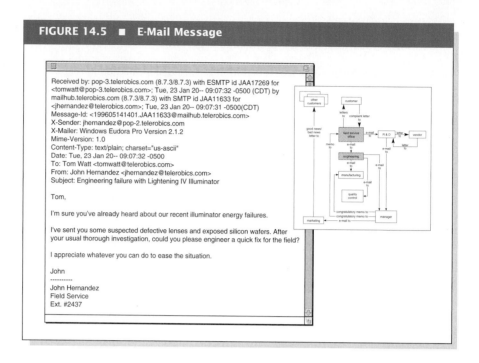

Received by: pop-3.telerobics.com (8.7.3/8.7.3) with ESMTP id JAA17269 for
<tomwatt@pop-3.telerobics.com>; Tue, 23 Jan 20-- 09:07:32 -0500 (CDT) by
mailhub.telerobics.com (8.7.3/8.7.3) with SMTP id JAA11633 for
<jhernandez@telerobics.com>; Tue, 23 Jan 20-- 09:07:31 -0500(CDT)
Message-Id: <199605141401.JAA11633@mailhub.telerobics.com>
X-Sender: jhernandez@pop-2.telerobics.com
X-Mailer: Windows Eudora Pro Version 2.1.2
Mime-Version: 1.0
Content-Type: text/plain; charset="us-ascii"
Date: Tue, 23 Jan 20-- 09:07:32 -0500
To: Tom Watt <tomwatt@telerobics.com>
From: John Hernandez <jhernandez@telerobics.com>
Subject: Engineering failure with Lightening IV Illuminator

Tom,

I'm sure you've already heard about our recent illuminator energy failures.

I've sent you some suspected defective lenses and exposed silicon wafers. After
your usual thorough investigation, could you please engineer a quick fix for the field?

I appreciate whatever you can do to ease the situation.

John

John Hernandez
Field Service
Ext. #2437

provides the necessary technical information and asks a specific question about price and delivery.

Request for Information.   Within a few days, Sarah receives a reply from Chuck Taylor at Optical Coatings (Figure 14.7). He responds to Sarah's inquiry and provides specific information. He also asks her about stripping and recoating 10 lenses already coated to the old specs, maintaining good business relations by not adding any charge for this extra work.

Internal Memos: Managers and Secondary Readers.   The second piece of correspondence Sarah writes is an e-mail message to Brian Bartlett, Division Manager for Tele-Robics (Figure 14.8). She informs him about the work her group is doing to solve the problem of the energy failure, both with the current and the new models of the illuminator.

Now recall that Tom Watt received an e-mail message from John Hernandez (Figure 14.5). This e-mail message prompted Engineering to locate the problem, necessitating that an ECO (engineering change order), accompanied by an e-mail message (Figure 14.9), be sent to Mike Maxwell in Manufacturing. Notice that Tom also sends a copy of the message and ECO to Quality Control so they'll know about the changes in specifications.

Tom Watt also sends an e-mail message to Brian Bartlett (Figure 14.10) to let his manager know the major steps he's taken to resolve the problem. Notice that this is the second e-mail message Brian has received; the department managers believe he should be informed about problems and their solutions to these problems.

FIGURE 14.6 ■ Letter to Vendor

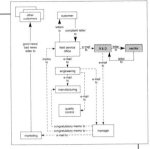

TELE-ROBICS, INC.
799 Warren Avenue Greenville, TX 75933

January 28, 20—

Charles D. Taylor
Optical Coatings, Inc.
536 Stevens Street
Cypress, TX 77429

Dear Chuck:

SUBJECT: Revision of spec for lens coating on Lightening IV Illuminator

The engineering staff at Tele-Robics has informed me that the lens coatings that Optical Coatings did for the Lightening IV Illuminator are not adequate for long life. The coating degenerates with the lens use, allowing longer exposure times because of lowered energy output.

This, of course, affects our work in the Lightening V. As a result, we're changing the specs for the coatings, which should eliminate any problem.

Hold up on coating all Tele-Robics lenses you currently have in-house.

Coat the enclosed lens to the following revised spec:

    narrow band coating 405 nm 1/4   mag fluoride

How does this change affect the price and delivery schedule for the 25 lenses you've already quoted?

Please let me know when you'll have the lens with the new coating ready for testing.

Sincerely,

Sarah Bell

Sarah Bell
Manager, Research and Development

SB:mj

FIGURE 14.7 ■ Response from Vendor

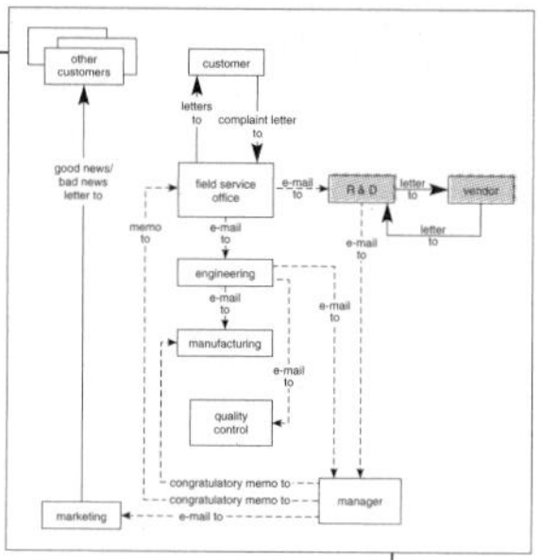

OC
Optical Coating, Inc.

1701 Industrial Park
Titusville, FL 32780

January 30, 20—

Sarah Bell
Manager, Research and Development
TELE-ROBICS, INC.
799 Warren Avenue
Greenville, TX 75933

Dear Sarah:

We will have no problems in coating the lenses to your new specs.

We currently have 10 lenses already coated to the old specs and another 15 lenses that have not yet been coated. Would you like us to strip the coating and recoat the lenses to the new specs? There is no charge in the per piece price for the new coating.

	per piece x	# pieces =	net $
Coat experimental lens:	$33.00	1	$ 33.00
Strip lens coating:	$ 6.00	10	$ 60.00
Coat lens to new spec:	$27.00	15	$405.00

The coating on the one lens you sent will be ready on Tuesday morning. As soon as you contact me, we can begin the new coatings on the other 25 lenses.

Sincerely,

Charles D. Taylor

Charles D. Taylor

CDT:lp

Brian Bartlett examines the information he receives from John in Field Service and from Mike in Manufacturing. Brian gathers some additional information, beyond what John or Mike would be expected to provide in short update memos

FIGURE 14.8 ■ E-Mail Message

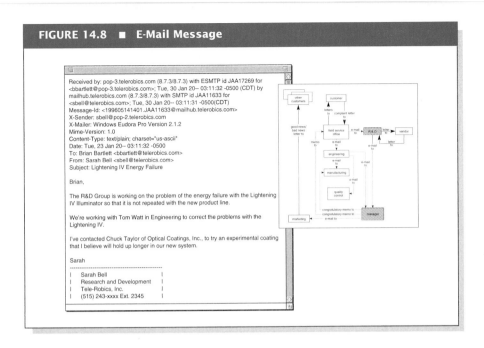

Received by: pop-3.telerobics.com (8.7.3/8.7.3) with ESMTP id JAA17269 for
<bbartlett@pop-3.telerobics.com>; Tue, 30 Jan 20-- 03:11:32 -0500 (CDT) by
mailhub.telerobics.com (8.7.3/8.7.3) with SMTP id JAA11633 for
<sbell@telerobics.com>; Tue, 30 Jan 20-- 03:11:31 -0500(CDT)
Message-Id: <199605141401.JAA11633@mailhub.telerobics.com>
X-Sender: sbell@pop-2.telerobics.com
X-Mailer: Windows Eudora Pro Version 2.1.2
Mime-Version: 1.0
Content-Type: text/plain; charset="us-ascii"
Date: Tue, 23 Jan 20-- 03:11:32 -0500
To: Brian Bartlett <bbartlett@telerobics.com>
From: Sarah Bell <sbell@telerobics.com>
Subject: Lightening IV Energy Failure

Brian,

The R&D Group is working on the problem of the energy failure with the Lightening
IV Illuminator so that it is not repeated with the new product line.

We're working with Tom Watt in Engineering to correct the problems with the
Lightening IV.

I've contacted Chuck Taylor of Optical Coatings, Inc., to try an experimental coating
that I believe will hold up longer in our new system.

Sarah

| Sarah Bell |
| Research and Development |
| Tele-Robics, Inc. |
| (515) 243-xxxx Ext. 2345 |

FIGURE 14.9 ■ E-Mail Message

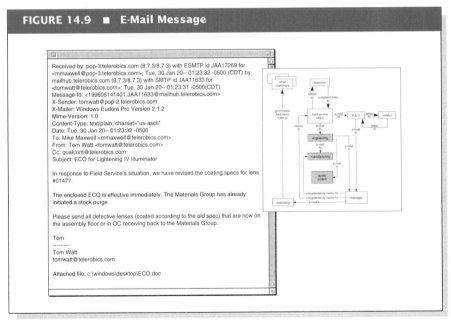

Received by: pop-3.telerobics.com (8.7.3/8.7.3) with ESMTP id JAA17269 for
<mmaxwell@pop-3.telerobics.com>; Tue, 30 Jan 20-- 01:23:32 -0500 (CDT) by
mailhub.telerobics.com (8.7.3/8.7.3) with SMTP id JAA11633 for
<tomwatt@telerobics.com>; Tue, 30 Jan 20-- 01:23:31 -0500(CDT)
Message-Id: <199605141401.JAA11633@mailhub.telerobics.com>
X-Sender: tomwatt@pop-2.telerobics.com
X-Mailer: Windows Eudora Pro Version 2.1.2
Mime-Version: 1.0
Content-Type: text/plain; charset="us-ascii"
Date: Tue, 30 Jan 20-- 01:23:32 -0500
To: Mike Maxwell <mmaxwell@telerobics.com>
From: Tom Watt <tomwatt@telerobics.com>
Cc: qualcont@telerobics.com
Subject: ECO for Lightening IV Illuminator

In response to Field Service's situation, we have revised the coating specs for lens
#01477.

The enclosed ECO is effective immediately. The Materials Group has already
initiated a stock purge.

Please send all defective lenses (coated according to the old spec) that are now on
the assembly floor or in OC receiving back to the Materials Group.

Tom

Tom Watt
tomwatt@telerobics.com

Attached file: c:\windows\desktop\ECO.doc

and then writes an e-mail message to Shawna Simons, marketing manager for Tele-Robics (Figure 14.11). He gives Shawna an update of the problem and asks that the marketing representatives contact customers with the problem equipment, informing them that Tele-Robics will retrofit their illuminator lenses at no charge.

Chapter 14: Correspondence

503

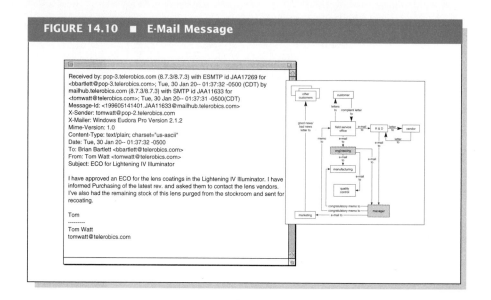

FIGURE 14.10 ■ E-Mail Message

Received by: pop-3.telerobics.com (8.7.3/8.7.3) with ESMTP id JAA17269 for
<bbartlett@pop-3.telerobics.com>; Tue, 30 Jan 20-- 01:37:32 -0500 (CDT) by
mailhub.telerobics.com (8.7.3/8.7.3) with SMTP id JAA11633 for
<tomwatt@telerobics.com>; Tue, 30 Jan 20-- 01:37:31 -0500(CDT)
Message-Id: <199605141401.JAA11633@mailhub.telerobics.com>
X-Sender: tomwatt@pop-2.telerobics.com
X-Mailer: Windows Eudora Pro Version 2.1.2
Mime-Version: 1.0
Content-Type: text/plain; charset="us-ascii"
Date: Tue, 30 Jan 20-- 01:37:32 -0500
To: Brian Bartlett <bbartlett@telerobics.com>
From: Tom Watt <tomwatt@telerobics.com>
Subject: ECO for Lightening IV Illuminator

I have approved an ECO for the lens coatings in the Lightening IV Illuminator. I have
informed Purchasing of the latest rev. and asked them to contact the lens vendors.
I've also had the remaining stock of this lens purged from the stockroom and sent for
recoating.

Tom

Tom Watt
tomwatt@telerobics.com

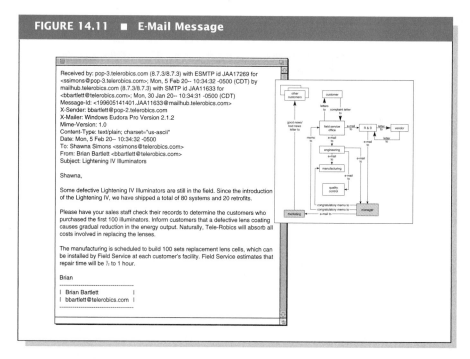

FIGURE 14.11 ■ E-Mail Message

Received by: pop-3.telerobics.com (8.7.3/8.7.3) with ESMTP id JAA17269 for
<ssimons@pop-3.telerobics.com>; Mon, 5 Feb 20-- 10:34:32 -0500 (CDT) by
mailhub.telerobics.com (8.7.3/8.7.3) with SMTP id JAA11633 for
<bbartlett@telerobics.com>; Mon, 30 Jan 20-- 10:34:31 -0500 (CDT)
Message-Id: <199605141401.JAA11633@mailhub.telerobics.com>
X-Sender: bbartlett@pop-2.telerobics.com
X-Mailer: Windows Eudora Pro Version 2.1.2
Mime-Version: 1.0
Content-Type: text/plain; charset="us-ascii"
Date: Mon, 5 Feb 20-- 10:34:32 -0500
To: Shawna Simons <ssimons@telerobics.com>
From: Brian Bartlett <bbartlett@telerobics.com>
Subject: Lightening IV Illuminators

Shawna,

Some defective Lightening IV Illuminators are still in the field. Since the introduction
of the Lightening IV, we have shipped a total of 80 systems and 20 retrofits.

Please have your sales staff check their records to determine the customers who
purchased the first 100 illuminators. Inform customers that a defective lens coating
causes gradual reduction in the energy output. Naturally, Tele-Robics will absorb all
costs involved in replacing the lenses.

The manufacturing is scheduled to build 100 sets replacement lens cells, which can
be installed by Field Service at each customer's facility. Field Service estimates that
repair time will be $\frac{1}{2}$ to 1 hour.

Brian

| Brian Bartlett |
| bbartlett@telerobics.com |

Letters for Good Customer Relations. Figure 14.12 shows the letter
(here addressed to Leigh Ward, a buyer for Omnitech) that Shawna Simons
writes to customers who have bought a Lightening IV Illuminator. Each customer
will receive an individualized letter, signed by the marketing representative who
handles the account. Shawna explains that the retrofit is covered under the

FIGURE 14.12 ■ Letter to Customer

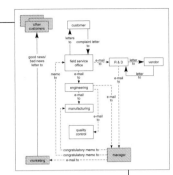

TELE-ROBICS, INC.
799 Warren Avenue Greenville, TX 75933

February 7, 20—

Leigh Ward, Buyer
Omnitech, Inc.
17 Industrial Park
Scranton, PA 18505

Dear Ms. Ward:

SUBJECT: Lightening IV Illuminator Modification

Your Lightening IV Illuminator is designed for continual use. Recently, we became aware of less than 100% operation with some of these systems. Specifically, the original lens coatings—after extended use—gradually permit higher than normal exposure times due to lower energy output.

Your field service representative will contact you this week to arrange a time to replace the original lenses, as part of the equipment's warranty. Down time will not exceed one hour. This short interruption in your production schedule will assure continued operation of your Lightening IV Illuminator.

Sincerely,

Shawna Simons

Shawna Simons
Marketing Manager

SS:rg

equipment warranty and will cause little interruption in the production schedule. Shawna sends a blind copy of the letter to Brian Bartlett (that is, she doesn't include the copy notation on her letter to Ms. Ward that she is sending a copy to Brian Bartlett).

What's your opinion about whether a manager or supervisor should write a letter to an employee expressing thanks or acknowledging excellence for doing something that is part of the employee's regular job?

Letters for Good Employee Relations.   Once Brian is assured that the problem is resolved and that customers will be contacted, he takes the time to write a memo (Figure 14.13) to Mike Maxwell. Brian thanks Mike for his role in resolving the illuminator problem and gives additional thanks to Mike's crew in Manufacturing.

Brian also sends a memo to John Hernandez (Figure 14.14), thanking him and his group for their quick and appropriate response to the problem. Managers who take the time to thank employees for doing a good job generally have smooth-running, productive organizations.

After reading the series of letters and memos in Figures 14.2–14.14, you can see that correspondence creates a complex network. Solving the technical problem with the Lightening IV Illuminator required a chain of correspondence that articulated the problem, asked questions, and explained decisions. The writers not only considered content, purpose, audience, organization, language, and format, but they were also sensitive to interpersonal and political factors.

FIGURE 14.13 ■ Memo

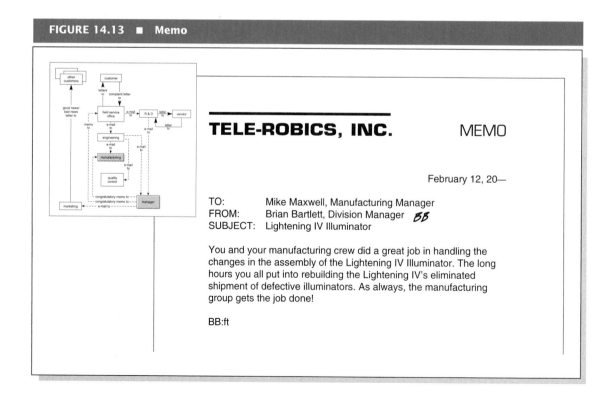

TELE-ROBICS, INC.   MEMO

February 12, 20—

TO: Mike Maxwell, Manufacturing Manager
FROM: Brian Bartlett, Division Manager   *BB*
SUBJECT: Lightening IV Illuminator

You and your manufacturing crew did a great job in handling the changes in the assembly of the Lightening IV Illuminator. The long hours you all put into rebuilding the Lightening IV's eliminated shipment of defective illuminators. As always, the manufacturing group gets the job done!

BB:ft

FIGURE 14.14 ■ Memo

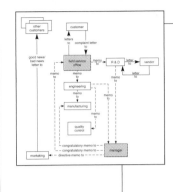

TELE-ROBICS, INC.   MEMO

February 12, 20—

TO: John Hernandez, Field Service
FROM: Brian Bartlett, Division Manager *BB*
SUBJECT: Lightening IV Illuminator Servicing

Congratulations to you and your group on the way you handled the
coating failure on the Lightening IV. Due to your quick response
to a customer, the manufacturing plant was able to avert further
shipment of defective illuminators. Good job!

BB:ft

Composing Letters, Memos, and Electronic Mail Messages

The following guidelines should help you compose effective correspondence:

- Analyze your audience.

- Include a subject line if appropriate.

- State objectives or ask questions initially; follow with explanatory material.

- Organize material in direct (descending) order if you anticipate a neutral or positive response.

- Organize material in indirect (ascending) order if you anticipate a negative response.

- Enumerate items that are clearer if listed.

- Be specific about the action (if any) that you want the reader to take.

- End with a friendly comment.

This section of the chapter identifies several additional guidelines you will find useful and suggests that when composing letters, memos, and electronic mail (e-mail) messages you consider these factors:

- Attitude and tone
- Audience
- Organization of information
- Format
- Visual displays

Attitude and Tone

Agree or disagree with this statement: Readers tend to be much more affected by the tone of a one- or two-page letter or memo than by the tone in a multi-page report.

Some people know you only through your correspondence and form an opinion of your competence from the content and style of your letters, memos, and e-mail messages. Although this may not seem fair, it is realistic. Because people do judge you by your correspondence, use a positive, sincere approach; avoid trite, outdated expressions as well as exclusionary language; and involve the reader by using the you-attitude. This section suggests ways to create a professional image in your correspondence.

Simple, Direct Language.   One way you can create a positive, sincere approach is to use simple, direct language. Your readers are as busy as you are. They don't have time to wade through the formal, pompous phrasing some people employ in a misguided attempt to enhance their image of competence.

Few people begin a telephone conversation or open a business meeting by saying, "This serves as notification of our agreement, as per our conversation of 10 October, that all orders processed on and following 12 October will meet the rev. 2 specifications." Why not just say, "Beginning on October 12, all orders will meet specifications of rev. 2"? To clarify your correspondence, avoid trite phrases such as the following:

Trite Phrases	*Possible Revisions*
attached please find	attached enclosed
in reference to said specification	in reference to the specification
re your claim	regarding your claim about your claim
under separate cover	separately mailed by air freight
each and every one of you	each of you all of you
If I can be of any further service to you, please do not hesitate to let me know.	You can reach me at 555-3941 if you have any questions or comments.

You-Attitude.   Substitute the *you*-attitude for the *I*- or *we*-attitude whenever possible. Focus on and emphasize the readers rather than yourself as the writer:

I- *or* We-*Attitude*	**You-*Attitude***
I appreciate your hard work on this project.	Your hard work on this project has been valuable.
We need your crew to follow the new procedures.	Your crew will benefit from following the new procedures.
Our department is backlogged, so your order will be delayed a week.	Your order will be shipped on March 17, one week later than originally scheduled.

Your writing should be sincere; using the *you*-attitude helps achieve this tone by implying that you recognize readers' perspectives. However, overuse of the you-attitude results in writing that sounds insincere; be aware not only of the language in your writing but also of the image it projects.

Exclusionary Language.   Exclusionary language (for example, assuming dieticians are women or engineers are men) causes several problems. It is simply inaccurate; technical professionals, who are seldom limited to a single gender in any particular field, pride themselves on precise, factual presentations. Moreover, use of exclusionary language reflects badly on you as an individual, reflects a negative corporate image, and has resulted in legal battles because corporate language is often assumed to reflect corporate policies.

Audience

Generally, letters are intended for external readers (those outside an organization), whereas memos and notes communicate to internal readers. E-mail can be for internal or external readers.

A writer should always identify by name or position the specific reader(s) of correspondence. Letters are usually directed to a single person, memos to either persons or specific groups. In some companies, distribution or mailing lists identify groups of readers who should receive memos about particular topics or from particular departments. E-mail messages are often sent to distribution lists (sometimes called d-lists); sending a message to a d-list address automatically forwards the message to everyone on that list—perhaps an entire department or organization.

A writer identifies the recipient of correspondence and tries to judge readers' mind sets and anticipate reactions. More "psychological noise" can be eliminated in correspondence than in such documents as reports and proposals, which are written for broader audiences. (Chapter 3 provides detailed information about analyzing and adjusting to an audience.)

Organization of Information

The content in any correspondence should be organized so that it can be read easily and quickly. This section suggests ways to effectively organize correspondence that fulfills these common functions:

- disseminating information
- making requests or inquiries
- responding to requests or inquiries

The following suggestions are not unbreakable rules but, rather, guidelines that can be modified to suit specific situations.

Disseminating Information.   Information can be disseminated in a variety of documents: directives, policy statements, announcements, and press releases. The standard 5W's plus H formula used in journalism—who? what? when? where? why? how?—forms the basis for organizing information for readers within your own company, other companies, and the public. Internal information is commonly dispensed through memos, often posted on bulletin boards, or delivered via a paper or electronic distribution list. These postings convey information about such diverse subjects as changes in insurance coverage, holiday party plans, and quarterly quotas.

Correspondence with other companies or agencies may be addressed to a particular person or department. For example, a company might announce to customers dates for the summer shutdown or changes in the price structure. Press releases within an industry or for the general public announce such things as new products, research successes, and outstanding employee achievements.

The organization of correspondence that disseminates such information varies depending on the receptivity of the audience:

Receptive or Neutral Audience	*Negative or Neutral Audience*
1. Identify the *who* (including individual and company).	**1.** State the relevant background (such as the problem or situation that necessitates the change).
2. Identify the *what*.	
3. Include details of *when, where, why, how.*	**2.** Identify the *who* and *what*.
4. Explain the impact.	**3.** Include details of *when, where, why, how.*
5. Provide a name and number for people to contact for additional information. (optional)	**4.** Explain the impact.
	5. Provide a name and number for people to contact for additional information.

Making Requests or Inquiries.   Routine requests and inquiries usually seek information; however, they may also ask for actual samples of a product or a specific action. Requests or inquiries usually contain the following elements, with amount of detail dictated by the situation:

1. State the reason for the request.

2. State the request directly.

3. Explain the benefit of the information, sample, or action.

4. Ensure confidentiality, if warranted.

5. Identify when the information, sample, or action is needed.

6. Thank the recipient.

Responding to Requests or Inquiries.   Some routine requests can be handled by sending prepared information, such as a price list, catalog, spec sheet, or brochure. Other routine requests can be handled with a form letter that is personalized by using the inquirer's name and address. One of the many benefits of word processing is that it enables a company to generate original copies of form letters.

When a request or inquiry requires an original response, the letter or memo can be either positive or negative. A positive, nonroutine response not only answers the question(s) but also offers additional information if appropriate and builds good will. Letters that deny a request, claim, or order usually follow a sequence that explains the negative response while maintaining good will:

Positive Responses

1. Acknowledge the request or inquiry.

2. Say "yes."

3. Include the information or identify an accessible source for the information.

4. Offer additional helpful suggestions, if appropriate.

5. Build good will.

6. Conclude in a friendly manner.

Negative Responses

1. Acknowledge the request or inquiry.

2. Explain briefly what makes a refusal necessary.

3. Say "no" directly to avoid misunderstanding.

4. Offer an alternative.

5. Build good will.

6. Conclude in a friendly manner.

Other Types of Correspondence.   Several other types of correspondence are discussed in other chapters of this text:

- Proposals in memo format—Chapter 16

- Memos used for short and informal reports (trip/conference reports, field studies, progress reports, and so on—Chapter 17)

- Cover letters (letters of transmittal—Chapter 17)

- Letters of application (Chapter 20)

When you need to write a memo or letter dealing with a situation not illustrated in this text, refer to that old standby—common sense.

Format

Literally hundreds of minor variations exist in the formats used for correspondence, and with the widespread use of computers, conventions are changing rapidly. You need to be familiar with formats and conventions for two reasons. First, with the widespread use of word processing, many document originators (who traditionally dictated or composed in longhand) are entering their own drafts of correspondence and documents directly into a computer. If you choose to write directly on a computer, you need to be familiar with conventions and formats of correspondence. Second, when you sign a letter or initial a memo, you are acknowledging that it meets your standards of format as well as content.

What circumstances might warrant a blind copy of a letter or memo?

In deciding which format to use, search in your organization's files for examples of previous correspondence that are logically arranged and that meet the approval of your supervisor. Also, many organizations have a corporate style guide that specifies preferred formats. If these avenues are closed to you, consult any good secretarial or business writing handbook. Composing your own letters lends a personal tone that can never be achieved with a form letter. However, if you are rushed or encounter a mental block, you can get ideas from books of form letters designed to meet hundreds of situations you might encounter in business or industry. For your reference, two common letter styles, a common memo style, and a common e-mail style are included here.

- *Standard block style letter*—All lines start at the left margin (see Figure 14.15).

- *Standard modified block style letter*—The date and closing lines are centered and all other lines begin at the left margin. Paragraphs may be indented or flush with the margin (see Figure 14.16). Complimentary closing and signature may be indented as shown in Figure 14.16.

- *Memos*—The "to/from/subject" heading is so widely accepted that many companies have memo forms printed to eliminate having to write the headings (see Figure 14.17).

- *E-mail*—Most e-mail messages are brief, contain a detailed subject line, a list of who else has received the message, and are signed with a "signature block," a brief text containing the writer's address and telephone information (see Figure 14.18).

While memos, letters, and electronic messages have distinct formats, they also have several conventions, as illustrated in Figures 14.15 through 14.18. Figure 14.19 identifies these conventions and explains how they are typically used.

FIGURE 14.15 ■ Block Form for Letters

```
                    xxxxxxxxxxxxxxxxxxxxxxxxx    (printed letterhead)
                      xxxxxxxxxxxxxxxxxxx
                    xxxxxxxxxxxxxxxxxxxxxxxxx    (If a printed
                                                 letterhead is not
                                                 used, type the
xxxxxxxxxxxx   (date)                             return address a
                                                 double space above
                                                 the date line.)
xxxxxxxxxxxxxxxxxxxxxxxxxxx   (inside address)
xxxxxxxxxxxxxxx
xxxxxxxxxxxxxxxxxxxxx

xxxxxxxxxxxxxxxxxxxxxxxxx:   (salutation)

xxxxxxxxxxxxxx:  xxxxxxxxxxxxxxxxxxxxxxxxxxxxxxxxx   (subject line)

xxxxxxxxxxxxxxxxxxxxxxxxxxxxxxxxxxxxxxxxxxxxxxxxxxxxxxxxxxxxxx
xxxxxxxxxxxxxxxxxxxxxxxxxxxxxxxxxxxxxxxxxxxxxxxxxxxxxxxxx
xxxxxxxxxxxxxxxxxxxxxx   (body of message)   xxxxxxxxxxxxxxxxxxxxxxxxx
xxxxxxxxxxxxxxxxxxxxxxxxxxxxxxxxxxxxxxxxxxxxxxxxxxxxxx

xxxxxxxxxxxxxxxxxxxxxxxxxxxxxxxxxxxxxxxxxxxxxxxxxxxxxxxxxxxxxx
xxxxxxxxxxxxxxxxxxxxxxxxxxxxxxxxxxxxxxxxxxxxxxxxxxxxxxxxxxxxxx
xxxxxxxxxxxxxxxxxxxxxxxxxxxxxxxxxxxxxxxxxxxxxxxxxxxx

xxxxxxxxxxxxxxxx,   (complimentary closing)

signature      (signature)

xxxxxxxxxxxxxxx     (name of writer)
M/S xxx-xx         (extension reference/mail stop)

XX:xx              (identifying initials)
enc.               (enclosure notation)
c: xxxxxxxxxxxxxx  (copy notation)
```

FIGURE 14.16 ■ Modified Block Form for Letters

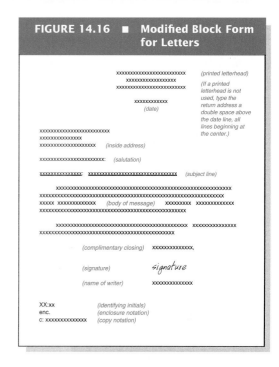

FIGURE 14.17 ■ Memo Format

```
                                          (date) xxxxxxxxxxxxx


TO:       name, title
          xxx-xxxx ext xxx   (extension reference
                             telephone)
FROM:     name, title (initials here or signature line    REB
                       at the end)

SUBJECT:  memo subject


xxxxxxxxxxxxxxxxxxxxxxxxxxxxxxxxxxxxxxxxxxxxxxxxxxxxxxxxxxxxxx
xxxxxxxxxxxxxxxxxxxxxxxxxxxxxxxxxxxxxxxxxxxxxxxxxxxxxxxxx
xxxxxxxxxxxxxxxxxxxx   (body of memo message)   xxxxxxxxx  xxxxx

xxxxxxxxxxxxxxxxxxxxxxxxxxxxxxxxxxxxxxxxxxxxxxxxxxxxxxxxxxxxxx
xxxxxxxxxxxxxxxxxxxxxxxxxxxxxxxxxxxxxxxxxxxxxx

xxxxxxxxxxxxxxxxxxxxxxxxxxxxxxxxxxxxxxxxxxxxxxxxxxxxxxxxxxxxxx
xxxxxxxxxxxxxxxxxxxxxxxxxxxxxxxxxxxxxxxxxxxxxx



XX:xx   (identifying initials)
enc.    (enclosure or attachment notation)
c:      (copy notation)
```

FIGURE 14.18 ■ Format Elements for E-Mail Message

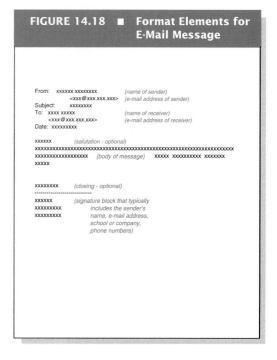

FIGURE 14.19 ■ Format Conventions Used in Correspondence

Convention	Typical Use
Reference Initials	Reference initials identify the document originator (the writer) and the document copier (usually the secretary). These initials appear near the lower left corner of a letter or memo; commonly, the document originator's initials are displayed in capital letters, followed by a colon, and then the document copier's initials in lowercase letters. The notation DC:jm indicates that a person with the initials D. C. wrote the letter, and someone with the initials J. M. typed it.
Signature or Initials	The signature or initials of the document originator indicate the person has *read* and *approved* the correspondence after it was input.
Extension Reference	The extension reference is usually a telephone extension or mail stop that the reader can use to contact the writer to discuss or question information in the correspondence.
Enclosure Notation	The enclosure notation—usually *Enc.* or *Encl.*—indicates that additional sheets beyond the letter or memo itself are included. In electronic mail messages, an "Enclosure" indicator may mean that the user should click on the file to open an attached electronic document.
Copy Notation	The copy notation identifies names of people who have received copies of the correspondence. This notation is courteous as well as practical: ♦ cc: for "correspondent copy" (originally meant "carbon copy," a term seldom used anymore since carbon paper is seldom used) ♦ c: for "copy" (used more frequently and accurately because of photocopying and word processing). If the copy is a "blind copy," the original letter will not have a copy notation, but the copy itself will be clearly marked COPY. This "blind copy" procedure is used when, for whatever reason, it is not diplomatic for the receiver of the correspondence to know that a copy has been sent to someone else.
Subsequent Page Caption	The second and succeeding paper pages of a memo or letter should be clearly marked, usually in the upper right-hand corner with the page number and date.

Visual Displays

Some organizations provide a portfolio of model letters for recurring tasks. What advantages do you see in this procedure? What risks?

Because correspondence is read quickly, readers benefit greatly from visual devices that highlight, outline, or separate sections and identify main points. Any devices that increase comprehension are appropriate. (Chapter 9 discusses and illustrates visual devices in more detail.) Several visual devices that make your correspondence more effective are common to both memos and letters:

- precise subject line
- underlining or italicizing

- bulleting or enumerating
- section headings and subheadings

A *precise subject line* helps orient and prepare your reader for the content of the correspondence, as the differences in two versions of a subject line for the same memo show.

An innovative letter format omits the salutation and complimentary closing and incorporates the addressee's name in the first sentence. Can you find any reasons why an organization (or individual) should adopt or reject this style?

■ EXAMPLE

SUBJECT: Shipping delay

■ REVISION

SUBJECT: Shipment of P.O. #547-0331 delayed 2 weeks

The first subject line does not identify the shipment or the length of the delay; the revision is more effective because it specifies the purchase order number as well as the length of the delay.

You can *underline* or *italicize key terms,* as the following example illustrates, to emphasize the importance of the deadline.

■ EXAMPLE

The proposal must arrive at our offices *no later than* February 15.

You can also effectively emphasize a series if you *bullet* or *enumerate* a list of items.

■ EXAMPLES

Milestones for the program are
- May 2001
- July 2002
- June 2003
- December 2003

The top three energy resources in New England in 1996 were
1. oil—68 percent
2. natural gas—12.3 percent
3. nuclear—11 percent

A lengthy memo or letter benefits from *section headings* that identify the main ideas. As Figures 14.20 and 14.21 show, you have a choice of more than one way to set up the subheadings.

FIGURE 14.20 ■ Letter with Separate Headings

LETTERHEAD
June 4, 20—

791 Balboa Drive
San Diego, CA 92109

Dear Ms. Jackson:

SUBJECT: Analysis of soundproofing for asbestos

Problem:
xxxxxxxxxxxxxxxxxxxxxxxxxxxxxxxxxxxxxxxxxxxxxxxxxxxxxxxxxxxxxxx
xxxxxxxxxxxxxxxxxxxxxxxxxxxxxxxxxxxxxxxxxxxxxxxxxxxxxxxx
xxxxxxxxxxxxxxxxxxxxxxxxxxxxxxxxxxxxxxxxxxxxxxxxxxx

Investigation:
xxxxxxxxxxxxxxxxxxxxxxxxxxxxxxxxxxxxxxxxxxxxxxxxxxxxxxxxxxxxxxx
xxxxxxxxxxxxxxxxxxxxxxxxxxxxxxxxxxxxxxxxxxxxxxxxxxxxxxxxxxx
xxxxxxxxxxxxxxxxxxxxxxxxxxxxxxxxxxxxxxxxxxxxxxxxxxxxxxxxxxx

Recommendation:
xxxxxxxxxxxxxxxxxxxxxxxxxxxxxxxxxxxxxxxxxxxxxxxxxxxxxxxxxxxxxxx
xxxxxxxxxxxxxxxxxxxxxxxxxxxxxxxxxxxxxxxxxxxxxxxxxxxxxxxxxxx
xxxxxxxxxxxxxxxxxxxxxxxxxxxxxxxxxxxxxxxxxxxxxxxxxxx

Sincerely,

William DeAngelis

William DeAngelis

FIGURE 14.21 ■ Letter with Run-in Headings

LETTERHEAD
June 4, 20—

791 Balboa Drive
San Diego, CA 92109

Dear Ms. Jackson:

SUBJECT: Analysis of soundproofing for asbestos

Problem: xxxxxxxxxxxxxxxxxxxxxxxxxxxxxxxxxxxxxxxxxxxxxxxxxxxxxxxxxx
xxxxxxxxxxxxxxxxxxxxxxxxxxxxxxxxxxxxxxxxxxxxxxxxxxxxxxxxxxxxxxx
xxxxxxxxxxxxxxxxxxxxxxxxxxxxxxxxxxxxxxxxxxxxxxxxxxxxxxx

Investigation: xxxxxxxxxxxxxxxxxxxxxxxxxxxxxxxxxxxxxxxxxxxxxxxxxxxxxxx
xxxxxxxxxxxxxxxxxxxxxxxxxxxxxxxxxxxxxxxxxxxxxxxxxxxxxxxxxx
xxxxxxxxxxxxxxxxxxxxxxxxxxxxxxxxxxxxxxxxxxxxxxxxxxxxxxxxxxxxxx

Recommendation: xxxxxxxxxxxxxxxxxxxxxxxxxxxxxxxxxxxxxxxxxxxxxxxxxxxx
xxxxxxxxxxxxxxxxxxxxxxxxxxxxxxxxxxxxxxxxxxxxxxxxxxxxxxxxxxxxxxx
xxxxxxxxxxxxxxxxxxxxxxxxxxxxxxxxxxxxxxxxxxxxxxxxxxxxxxx

Sincerely,

William DeAngelis

William DeAngelis

End-of-Chapter
Recommendations for Technical Communicators

1. Use correspondence to provide a record of transactions.

2. Remember that each piece of correspondence you send can trigger a series of memos and letters, causing a *domino effect*.

3. Generally use direct or descending order for good news; generally use indirect or ascending order for bad news.

4. Convey a positive professional image through the content and style of your correspondence:
   - Use simple, direct language.
   - Use a *you*-attitude whenever possible.
   - Avoid exclusionary language.

5. Address correspondence to particular persons or groups with a defined distribution list.

6. Organize correspondence so that it can be read easily and quickly.

7. Learn the conventional formats for correspondence: block and modified block letters and memos. Correctly use conventional elements of corre-

spondence: reference initials, enclosure notations, copy notations, subsequent page captions.

8. Select visual devices that highlight, outline, or separate sections and identify main points for readers.

9. Use various forms of asynchronous correspondence: e-mail, newsgroups, electronic lists, and chats. Follow the conventions for computer-mediated communication.

Practicum

Weisner Associates Inc

Located in Minneapolis, Minnesota, Weisner Associates Inc. (WAI) provides a full range of on-line information design and development services, including consulting, outsourcing, and training. WAI's 9-member staff includes trainers and technical writers who work with customers from Minnesota and the rest of the country. Customers' requirements range from short-term consulting to long-term projects in need of our writers' full-time efforts, as well as publicly scheduled and onsite training.

To serve our customers, we find solutions to ever-changing technological problems related to new tools and recently-released software. Providing solutions includes training customers' employees and keeping them up to date with the latest developments in on-line information design and development.

Scenario

Working in a small company requires taking on responsibilities that would ordinarily be performed by more than one person (even many people) in a larger company. In a recent case, a WAI employee needed help with health insurance coverage. The insurance company's title of choice for me under these circumstances is "Benefits Administrator," so I signed the letter with that title.

Here are the details: WAI employee Pete Frye moved from Minnesota to Ohio to open a branch office. As a full-time employee, Pete is eligible to receive health benefits, as he did while living in Minnesota. After moving to Ohio, Pete saw a doctor a few times but was shocked when he received the bill for the doctor's services. Based on a phone conversation Pete had with the insurance company before the doctor visits, Pete expected the Ohio doctor visits to be covered under the health insurance plan just as they would have been if Pete had seen a doctor in Minnesota. According to the bill, Pete is now expected to pay. The insurance company doesn't see it that way anymore, or maybe never did.

The solution to Pete's insurance problems has two parts: enrolling him a plan that will cover future doctor visits and getting help with paying the bills he has received. Enrolling Pete in the new plan is simple enough, but getting help to pay for past visits won't be nearly as easy.

It's been weeks since Pete's first visit to the doctor in Ohio. Pete has no record of his conversation with the insurance company to back up his claim that he was told the Ohio doctor visits should be covered under the old insurance plan. Technically, Pete should have to pay the bills, and the insurance company may simply say Pete has to pay. However, a well-written letter may be enough to sway the opinion of the person with the authority to help Pete.

E-mail examples

Figures 1 and 2 show the actual e-mail messages that Kate and Pete exchanged about the problem.

Assignment

Write the letter to Jim Hoiberg, WAI's service representative at the insurance company, to ask that Pete's Ohio doctors' bills be covered. Include the circumstances—Jim already knows them from previous phone conversations: they need to be put in writing in case the formal appeal process is necessary.

In the letter, request that Pete be switched to the CMM Co-pay Plan with a start date that goes back to Pete's first doctor visit in Ohio, which was March 29. (Typically, the start date would be the first of the next month, which would be June 1.) You'll need to reference the following numbers in the letter:

WAI's group#: QI-864-11

Pete's ID#: BAZ 987-65-4321

FIGURE 1 ■ Pete's E-mail to Kate

Kate—

HELP! I just got a stupidly huge bill from my doctor. Insurance isn't covering any part of it. I know I shouldn't have to pay so much because somebody at the insurance company told me that seeing a doctor in Ohio would be the same as seeing a doctor in Minnesota. I called the insurance company BEFORE seeing a doctor here.

Now I find out that I have a $1,000 deductible to pay before any Ohio doctor fees are covered. There's NO way I'd have gone to a doctor in Ohio if I knew it wouldn't be covered. Now I've got the doctor's office after me to pay the bills for visits that I know should have been covered.

And I thought I had high blood pressure at the first appointment for my physical—HA!! It's only getting higher as they keep after me to pay these bills. Honestly, I need to get this resolved sooner rather than later because it's been going on way too long as it is. Please do whatever you can to make this go away.

P.

```
Pete—

I just got off the phone with Jim at BCBS. Here's what's up:

We've found a different plan for you that will cover future doctor
visits in Ohio. There's more paperwork ahead of us to try to get
the old bills resolved.

What I'll do is write a letter to Jim asking that you be switched
to a different plan that will cover your future visits to doctors
in Ohio. I'll ask that the new plan have a start date that goes
back to your first doctor visit in Ohio. Switching to the new plan
won't be any problem, but Jim can't predict, let alone guarantee,
that they'll adjust the start date. But it's worth a try.

Without that earlier start date, you'd still be stuck with the high
deductible, but we'd have one more thing to try. If the earlier
start date doesn't fly, Jim will use the letter I write to start a
formal appeal process with the company's consumer service center,
which might allow the charges from March to go through as if they
were made with you under the new plan. A technicality, I know, but
it'd get the results you want.

Kate
```

Preparing the letter requires enough thought, time, and effort to present the information effectively. You need to structure the information clearly as well as state what you'd like to have happen as a result of the letter. State your case clearly, but in the back of your mind, know that you're asking the person at the insurance company to make an exception for Pete.

Bottom line—There's one guideline for assessing the quality of the letter: whether the person reading it decides Pete gets help paying the doctor bills.

Kate Molitor is Marketing and Operations Manager with Weisner Associates Inc. She says, "The importance of the writing task in this practicum doesn't come from it making or breaking any high-priced deal for the company; yet to Pete, it's very important. In this case, the pricetag to WAI is in the satisfaction of its employee to find the help he needs to get out of a bind."

At WAI, Kate manages everyday operations as well as puts out the fires that inevitably pop up in a small company. Her responsibilities include but are, by far, not limited to marketing, administering personnel/benefits, accounting (payroll; accounts payable and receivable), and acting as an executive advisor.

Kate is a senior member of the Society for Technical Communication and a member of the Minnesota Professional Association for Computer Training.

She earned a B.S. in Mass Communication from Mankato State University and a M.A. in Business and Technical Communication from Iowa State University. Prior to WAI, she worked as a research associate with the Information Design Center of the American Institutes for Research in Washington, D.C. You can e-mail her at <katem@weisner.com> or check the WAI Web site at <www.weisner.com>.

1. **Revise a memo.** Read the following memo and revise it using visual displays to improve the clarity of the message. If any details are missing, invent them.

October 3, 20—

TO: Carole Marcotte, General Manager
FROM: Richard Curtis, Marketing
SUBJECT: Major order for 024BL6 carrier

There is a possibility of our receiving an order for 200,000 nibs for the 024BL6 carrier, but it must be delivered before July 31. Do you think we have the production capability to accept such an order?

Here are some data to help you come to a decision: Last year in January we produced 150,000, in February 155,000, in March 145,000, in April 140,000, in May 143,000, in June 147,000, in July 90,000 (plant closed two weeks for vacations), in August 120,000, in September 160,000, in October 25,000 (strike), in November 120,000, and in December 153,000.

We have been very successful with this product. Some of our largest sales have been to Fortune 500 companies, although last month we shipped to many less well known organizations. Lagassee, Inc., bought 10,000. Demonsthanes bought 16,000, P&C bought 22,000, Clairbridge Brothers bought 17,500, and Harpswell bought 8,250. We must not commit ourselves to one large order to the exclusion of these others.

One of my main concerns about accepting so large an order is the question of material supplies. Before coming to a decision, you might want to contact some of our more reliable vendors. Mr. Edwin Mundale of LaSol Iron Works, at 1125 Industrial Avenue in Tyngsboro, Missouri, is one suggestion. Another is Ms. Ramona Fitzdurwood who is the liaison officer for Abruters, Inc. Their plant is on Liatris Road in Pobgardner, Kansas.

Let me have your advice within two weeks. I hate to turn down such a plum, but I don't want to risk our reputation for reliability, either.

Richard Curtis

---

2. **Write a response to a memo.** Assume the role of Carole Marcotte, General Manager, and compose a response to the memo in Assignment 1. Your memo should be addressed to Richard Curtis, Marketing.

3. **Write two different types of letters or memos.** Incorporate the following facts into two different letters or memos. Use priority order in the first and chronological order in the second. Determine which you prefer and justify your preference in a memo to your instructor.

   - Our production of component Z43X has dropped.
   - A meeting of production supervisors will be held.
   - Two of our best customers have complained about late shipments.
   - Supervisors should bring to the meeting figures on costs, equipment, personnel, and so on.
   - One customer has canceled his standing order and is buying his Z43Xs from our competitor.
   - The meeting will be held on March 4 at 2:30 p.m.
   - Last month four machines had excessive down time.
   - The supervisors are to meet in Conference Room G in the administrative wing.
   - Two months ago our production of component AB22X also plummeted.

4. **Write memos or letters to respond to a situation.** Early this morning you found out that part of an already-delayed order for a major account (Bit-Byte Corporation) will not meet the new deadline and that the customer has serious complaints about some of the delivered portion of the order.

   Specifically, the production schedule for system XY-9 has been set back because of manufacturing backlogs, equipment malfunction, and duplicate scheduling. Your supervisor is busy sorting out another complex problem and asks you to write a detailed memo explaining how you have decided to handle the problems with manufacturing and with the customer.

   Meanwhile, the customer has serious complaints. The equipment that was delivered is missing an I/O board for the CPU, has the wrong character set for the printer, and has broken prongs on the disk-drive plug. Beyond these problems the shipment was five weeks late because it was originally delivered to the wrong customer. Bit-Byte Corporation demands an explanation and a guaranteed solution to the problems.

   Help! You're due in Maynard for an important lunch meeting, but you must write a memo to your supervisor and then a letter to the customer before you leave. Answer the following questions:

   - Can you send both the same information?
   - What should you say to each?
   - What tone should you take?

- How much of an explanation should you include?
- Should you make excuses?
- Should you make promises?
- What should you focus on or emphasize?
- Could you respond to either of these people on e-mail? Why or why not?

5. **Analyze a piece of correspondence.**
   (a) Locate a piece of business correspondence—either something that was addressed to you or that you have access to.
   (b) Using the criteria you learned from this chapter and the existing criteria you have established for effective technical communication, create a rubric to assess the document.
   (c) Write a brief report for your instructor in which you include the original document and your rubric.

Intertext

Handling Customer Service on the Web: The Robots are Here[7]

If you're doing business on the Web, you've got mail. Lots of it. Lots of complaints, questions, and kudos from customers. Electronic mail is fast and direct, and an increasing number of companies encourage its use in an effort to stay close to customers without spending a fortune on toll-free telephone lines. And customers like e-mail because there's no per-minute charge and no holding for a customer service rep. As a consequence, however, companies are bombarded with hundreds of messages per day, each from a valued customer who expects a rapid response.

Now computer technology is trying to solve the problem it helped create. Chances are, the next time you send a note to Corporate.com, the personalized answer you get will come from software that has guessed what you're after—the Internet's equivalent of the form letter. This may or may not result in better service, but one thing's clear: On the Web, the robots aren't coming; they're here.

Robots is the term techies have given to software programs that can scan the text of an incoming e-mail and respond intelligently—without human intervention. Natural language understanding—or the ability of computers to understand and respond appropriately to written sentences of the kind that people use every day—hasn't advanced nearly as far as speech recognition, which is passing into the mainstream. Still, in areas such as electronic commerce and customer service, we're beginning to see some noteworthy progress.

For example, Klone Server, a new customer support program from Big Science of Atlanta, can respond without human assistance to the majority of inquiries on a Web site. The company says that Klone Server will perform even when the questions are entered in conversational language. Similarly, Adante of Carlsbad, California (a subsidiary of Genesys Telecommunications); Egain Communications of Sunnyvale, California; Kana Communications of Palo Alto; and Mustang Software have created e-mail routing programs that scan the text of messages for keywords.

Still deeper analysis of incoming messages is performed by customer response programs from Aptex Software of San Diego (a subsidiary of HNC Software), Brightware of Novato, California, and General Interactive of Cambridge, Massachusetts. Programs developed by Ask Jeeves of Berkeley are designed to generate immediate responses to customer queries on a corporate Website. Inference, which makes artificial-intelligence software used in telephone call centers, recently expanded its programs to handle electronic mail as well. Two additional companies, Neuromedia of San Francisco and Reticular Systems of San Diego, supply tools to create digital impersonators that can respond in a humanlike fashion to e-mail.

At the Web sites of these companies, you can download examples of these latest advances in customer interaction, call-center automation, and message-routing software and test them yourself at no charge. The easiest way to understand the state of the art, however, is to try an online demonstration. While some of the examples are sophomoric, check out Shallow Red (a takeoff on IBM's digital chess master Deep Blue) at www.neuromedia.com. I toyed around with it for a while, and Shallow Red seems pretty good at answering the types of questions that potential customers would ask.

For extra realism, Big Science has added photographs to its demonstration site (www.bigscience.com). Surf there, and you can meet Andrette, a virtual woman who'll tell you all about the company (or even politely decline a request for a date).

My favorite demo site is Ask Jeeves. Point your browser to www.ask.com and type in a query or two. For example, if you enter, "When is the next blue moon?" in the search area of a widely used Internet portal, you'll get long lists of generally unhelpful responses, but at Ask Jeeves, the answer (March 31) is only two mouse clicks away.

Like other software robots on the Web, Jeeves tries to figure out if you're asking a question to which it already knows the answer. It also extracts keywords from your question and runs them through a half-dozen search engines, providing a list of possibly informative links. It's a strategy that often works. But not always. If, for example, you type in "Where is the best surfing in California?" you're asked if what you meant was "How can I find a good neighborhood?" or "How can I find *Money*'s list of the best places to live in the U.S.?" Worse yet, if you type in "What is Technologic Partners?" (that's my company), the computer asks whether your real question is "How can I find my ideal mate?" Such quirkiness is the reason that one young software supplier, Aditi of Bellevue, Washington, avoids Web robots altogether. Instead, Aditi relies on computers to route messages to the people within a company who can provide the right answers.

Still, despite the obvious limitations of natural language understanding, customer service without human intervention is the wave of the future. Jeeves is good enough for Dell Computer to test the technology in its Ask Dudley customer support area <support.dell.com/askdudley/>. Compaq is using a similar approach, developed in-house, called Info-Messenger.

There's opportunity here; every company is looking for ways to reduce the cost of customer support. Electronic mail is the ideal medium for automated response systems. As friendly front ends to databases offering technical specifications, product instructions, or troubleshooting tips, these robotic digital mimics hold great commercial promise. Just don't try asking, "Where are the snows of yesteryear?"

Richard A. Schaffer is founder of Technologic Partners, an information company focused on emerging technology. If you have any comments, please send them to shaffer@technologicp.com.

15

Instructions

This chapter deals with designing a variety of instructional texts, all of which have the same purpose: to enable a reader to complete a task.

Defining and Designing Instructional Texts

Instructional texts generally fall into one of four categories: actions/behavior of personnel, assembly of objects or mechanisms, operation of equipment, and implementation of a process.

When you are planning instructions, you need to conduct two types of analysis: *task analysis* and *audience analysis.* You need to use this information as you consider the design of instructions:

Considering International Audiences. Instructions for international audiences need special attention to ensure effective explanations and appropriate visuals.

Adapting Task to Audience. Chunking, labeling, and using appropriate details helps users.

Organizing Instructions. Although there is no "correct" or "best" structure for manuals, many of them have the following elements:

- title page
- background information
- training section
- step-by-step instructions
- frequent users' guide
- troubleshooting and maintenance

Locating Information. Several devices—including previews and reviews, cross references, and a glossary—help readers keep track of where they are in a document and help them locate information they need.

Constructing Instructional Texts

Effective instructions have critical content elements and visual and design elements.

Content Elements. These include identifying purpose, listing needed components, following proper chronology, using direct wording, ensuring accurate details, providing rationale, giving legal warnings, and using proper grammar.

Visual and Design Elements. These include selecting appropriate visuals, balancing verbal and visual content, supplying accurate visuals accurately labeled, and designing an appealing format.

Document Testing

You have several choices to make in testing your instructions: user assessment, expert assessment, and text assessment.

Examining Sample Instructions

The "illustruction" is a particularly effective approach to creating instructions.

I
nstructions are everywhere—from the arrow painted on the lid of a peanut butter jar that indicates the way the lid twists off to multivolume manuals detailing every step in the operation of field artillery. This chapter deals with designing instructional texts, all of which have the same purpose: to enable a reader to complete a task. However, manuals often present a greater challenge, partly because readers not only need information but also need to know how to find that information in a manual. In this chapter, you'll read about defining, designing, and constructing instructional texts.

Defining and Designing Instructional Texts

Instructional texts are documents designed to help a reader complete a task. Regardless of their length or format, instructions are extraordinarily important, accounting for a major portion of documents in business, industry, and government. These instructions generally fall into four categories:

- actions/behavior of personnel
- assembly of objects or mechanisms
- operation of equipment
- implementation of a process

The design of instructional texts, whether single sheets of directions or lengthy manuals, should be driven by the task and assumptions about the users' experience with and resistance to the task. Therefore, when you are planning instructions, you need to conduct two types of analysis: *Task analysis* focuses on the purpose of the instructions; *audience analysis* focuses on the user who completes the task.

In what ways might the accuracy, appropriateness, appeal, and accessibility of the documentation—the manuals, tutorials and training information, online help—that comes with a product influence the purchase of that product?

Task Analysis

One of your first steps in planning instructions is *task analysis*. The goal of instructions is to accomplish a task, regardless of who is following the instructions. Of course, when you prepare instructions, you need to make some concessions that respond to the user's needs, but this should not be done in violation of the task.

The task doesn't change even if the users do. When you are planning instructions, you can analyze the task by asking yourself the series of questions shown in the first segment of Figure 15.1. Your responses to these questions should guide the way you represent the task, not only determining the steps of the instructions but also influencing the kind and amount of detail you include. Clearly, you need to specify the steps necessary to complete the task. List them chronologically, distinguishing the key part of each step from the details and explanations that help users complete it. You also need to ask yourself about the constraints that will affect completing the task, as listed in the second segment of Figure 15.1.

Part of your responsibility is to restrict the instructions to qualified users by incorporating guidelines that caution users about the knowledge or experience they need in order to complete the task. For example, you can caution users with sentences such as this: "Before you begin the next phase, make sure you have the available equipment listed below." The questions shown in the third segment of Figure 15.1 should help you begin to relate task and audience.

FIGURE 15.1 ■ Questions for Task Analysis

Representing the Task

◆ What task has come before?

◆ What knowledge or skill is necessary to complete the task?

◆ What is the situation or environment?

◆ What steps are involved in the process?

◆ What will the final product be?

Identifying Constraints on Task Completion

◆ What safety precautions must be observed?

◆ How long should the task take?

◆ What might influence the length of time needed to complete the task?

◆ What complications might arise during performance of the task?

◆ What cost factors are involved?

◆ What might make completion of the task more or less expensive?

Relating Task and Audience

◆ What level of understanding do users need to complete the task?

◆ What preliminary or preparatory work must be completed by the users?

◆ What resources (materials, tools, and equipment) do users need?

◆ What level of skill do users need to operate the tools and equipment?

The task and the environment should influence your design decisions. For example, the quality of paper should suit the frequency of use. Instructions that will probably be used only once—perhaps for the installation of an air conditioner or the assembly of a rototiller—can be printed on inexpensive paper. However, instructions that will be used repeatedly should be on high-quality paper that can withstand frequent handling. Similarly, the task should influence the binding of multipage instructions. If users need to refer to the instructions while working on the task, the instructions should lie flat. Instructions that are likely to be updated from time to time can be placed in a loose-leaf binder so that revisions can be inserted. If revisions are relegated to a separate binder, they might be overlooked. The task analysis section of the worksheet in Figure 15.2 summarizes the critical task information that should be considered when preparing instructions.

Analyzing and Adapting to Audiences

Because instructions address users who actually do something—complete a task—they need to address audience needs and experience. (Refer to Chapter 3 to review audience analysis.) Effective instructions pay attention to the tone appropriate for the audience and uses consistent design features.

How many ways can you think of to test whether the directions you write are appropriate for the intended audience? What are the benefits and drawbacks of various kinds of testing?

The tone in most instructions is conversational. The term *user-friendly* implies that writers take a personal interest in the users. To a greater extent than any other type of technical writing (excluding correspondence), instructions attempt to establish a direct relationship between a writer and the readers.

Most manuals are written in second person (using "you"), suggesting a link between the manual writer and users. The imperative mood of verbs (e.g., "*Turn* the knob." "*Adjust* the fluid level.") is for the commands in individual steps. However, within these imperative steps, the vocabulary and level of detail can be adapted to the individual audience. For example, the instructions in the user reference manual that came with the word-processing software used to type sections of the original manuscript for this textbook approach the novice user in a direct, friendly manner:

■ EXAMPLE

To enter text, just start typing. Each non-control character typed is entered into the text of your document. If you type beyond the right margin, notice that WordStar moves the word that wouldn't fit inside the margin to the next line, positioning the cursor after the word to allow you to continue typing. This is word wrap.[1]

The installation manual for the same software, although dealing with far more complex content, also speaks directly to the technician:

■ EXAMPLE

Patch "RUBFXF" below to non-zero. The contents of "RFIXER" will then be output immediately after a "DELETE" is input; this character, rather than the next cursor

FIGURE 15.2 ■ Worksheet for Instructions

Title of instructions: _____

Task Analysis

Purpose of task (product created; behavior changed): _____
_____

Environment where task is completed: _____

Resources needed (materials, tools, equipment): _____
_____

Steps to complete task: _____
_____

Constraints to completing task (safety, time, resources, cost, etc.): _____
_____

Other important task considerations: _____
_____

Audience Analysis

User (organizational position/role): _____

User needs: _____

Attitude: *enthusiastic* ■----------■----------■----------■ *resistant*

Sources of resistance: _____

Other user characteristics: _____

Education/experience needed to complete task: _____

User's education/experience with task: _____

Other important audience considerations: _____
_____

Testing

Specify types and dates of document testing:

	User-based testing	Expert-based testing	Text-based testing
In-process dates			
Testing methods			
Final date			

positioning string, should thus be replaced with backspace-space-backspace, reducing the consequences of your system's machinations. Try null (zero) in RFIXER first; if this doesn't work, try backspace (08) or space.[2]

Responses to the audience analysis questions in the worksheet in Figure 15.2 help you construct and present effective instructions. The following list identifies specific benefits of the audience analysis section of the worksheet.

Analysis Factor	*Impact on Instructions*
user attitude	■ need to justify individual steps or entire instructions
	■ use of attention-getting devices
user education	■ level of vocabulary
	■ definition of terms
	■ types of visuals
user experience	■ expectations of prior knowledge
	■ amount and type of detail to use

In analyzing and adapting instructional information to audiences, you need to consider whether the readers will use the text in print or online. Some companies provide users with both print and online documentation. More and more companies, however, provide only online documentation that includes an electronic help system accessed through the pull-down help menu. The help system files contain hypertext links, popup topics, and a keyword search capability.

Software programs like RoboHelp, ForeHelp, DoctoHelp, and WinHelp automate the creation of help systems that aid readers in several ways:

■ They use hypertext links to make information more accessible.

■ They provide a searchable index of key words.

■ They provide more than one path to information.

Considering International Audiences

As the global economy makes products available to more and more people around the world, manuals need to be accessible to a broad range of users who come from very different cultures and have varying degrees of literacy. Some companies have the resources to produce manuals in multiple languages; for example, Sony's Document Design Development Center in Tokyo produces manuals in more than 20 languages, ranging from Japanese, English, and most European languages to Arabic, Korean, and Russian. Most companies, however, have limited resources and produce documents in only a few languages. The more a company's manuals for the same (or similar) products have in common in both content and design, the less expensive they are to produce and the greater the chances that the information will be accurate.

Instructions accompanying foreign-made products are sometimes written in stilted, nonidiomatic English. How do you react to this? Is your confidence in either the product or the accuracy of the instructions affected? If a product made by your company were intended for export, how would you avoid such problems in translation?

FIGURE 15.3 ■ Excerpt from Effective Japanese Manual[3]

コピー後のドラムに残ったトナーは、かき集められてトナー回収ボトルにたまります。
トナー回収ボトルがトナーで一杯になると、「トナー回収ボトルを交換してください」とメッセージが表示されます。
メッセージの表示後、約300枚のコピーで機械は停止します。コピー枚数は原稿によって異なります。新しい空の
ボトルと交換してください。

 注意
・トナー回収ボトルを火中に投じると危険ですので、絶対に焼却しないでください。
・使用済みのトナー回収ボトルは、弊社または販売店にお渡しください。
・トナー回収ボトルに回収されたトナーは使用しないでください。

操作手順 **1** 前面カバーと前面右下のカバーを開けます。
回収されたトナーが落ちる可能性もありますので、機械
の下に新聞紙などを敷いておくと床が汚れません。

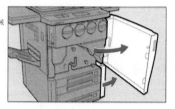

2 トナー回収ボトルを止まるまで手前に引き出し
します。

3 トナー回収ボトルを右下に引き、機械から
トナー回収ボトルの入口をはずします。

Cautions are signaled with a △, a widely recognized international icon. The seven steps in the task are clearly numbered.

The arrows show the direction in which parts move.

The hand shows what the operator should do at each step.

Sometimes manuals in the international market are so well done that the visuals carry the meaning, regardless of the language. For example, Figure 15.3 is an excerpt explaining how to replace a waste toner bottle in a photocopier, taken from a Japanese-language manual produced by Fuji-Xerox. Although there is text (accessible to readers of Japanese), the conventions in the illustrations make the steps in the process easy to understand—for example, international icons, numbered steps, human involvement, close-ups.

However, not all procedures are so easy to explain. When writing manuals for an intercultural market, writers should consider several suggestions:

- Provide an easy-to-use table of contents as well as introductory visual maps that help readers understand how to use the manual.

FIGURE 15.3 ■ *Continued*

4 機械から取り出したトナー回収ボトルの口に
キャップをしてビニール袋へ入れます。
次にトナー回収ボトルを箱に入れ、箱には
「U」シールを貼ってください。
キャップはトナー回収ボトルの下に付いています。

使用済みのトナー回収ボトルは、弊社または販売店へ
お渡しください。

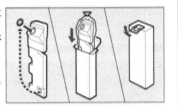

*A series of visuals
shows details for
sealing and storing
the used toner for
safe disposal.*

5 新しいトナー回収ボトルの入口を機械のトナー
の出口へ差し込みます。

注意 トナーの出口とボトルの入口は、確実に差し込
んでください。少しでもずれているとトナーの
こぼれる原因となります。

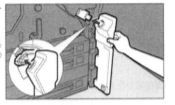

*A close-up visual
shows how the
new toner bottle is
attached.*

6 トナー回収ボトルを奥へ押し込みます。
トナー回収ボトルを奥へ押し込んだとき、オレンジ色の
板が突出している場合は、操作手順5に戻って再度トナー
の出口とボトルの入口を差し込んでください。

オレンジ色の板

*The operator's hand
shows how the toner
bottle slides back into
the photocopier.*

7 前面の右下カバーと、前面カバーを閉めます。

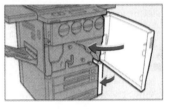

- Be consistent in the way words and visuals are used.

- If words or visuals will work equally well to convey information, choose the visuals. Whenever possible, illustrate verbal information with visuals.

- Use visual cues to help readers understand sequence and direction—for example, numbers to label the sequence of steps, arrows to indicate the direction knobs should be turned, and shading to highlight a key.

- Visually distinguish main steps from details and explanations, perhaps by font size, type, or style (for example, details can be in a smaller font, a sans serif font, or in italics).

- Make sure that colors and icons do not carry meanings that may be inappropriate or offensive to particular cultures.

- Have a native reader and writer carefully edit the document to make sure all usage is idiomatic.

Adapting Task to Audience

Because instructional documents expect readers to *do* something, certain conventions are important. Three are particularly important: chunking, labeling, and using parallel structure. Using these conventions makes instructional documents easier to read because the information is logically sequenced and presented. If readers don't understand the logic of your instructions, they may become confused about what they're supposed to do, whether completing a form or adjusting a piece of equipment. In any case, completion of the task is probably derailed.

When chunking and labeling (see Chapter 8) are ignored in instructional documents, readers have difficulty differentiating the background information from the task to be completed and may not be sure what they're actually supposed to do. Take, for example, the manager of the Quality Control Department in a company that specialized in cleaning up hazardous waste sites. He was reviewing a set of instructions in preparation for an on-site inspection by a potential customer. During this preliminary review, he noticed a problem. In several sets of instructions used by technicians, such as the example in Figure 15.4a, the steps were preceded by a dense block of text that contained important safety information. Not only were general labels missing (e.g., task or equipment), but labels to signal warnings and safety precautions were missing, which could be a serious liability problem.

The manager recognized that technicians were likely to resist reading the dense blocks of information in Figure 15.4a, even though the warnings were

FIGURE 15.4a ■ Original Version of Instructional Information, Unchunked and Unlabeled

Because this information is not chunked and labeled, readers cannot easily differentiate what they need in order to perform the task safely and accurately.

The technicians who need to understand and act on this important safety information are likely to resist reading undifferentiated blocks of text.

The post assembly optical alignment of the SSL100 Nd:YAG laser head is performed by a laser technician after the laser head is assembled but prior to its installation in the system. Dangerous levels of laser radiation are emitted from the laser during the test. All windows must be covered so that the laser light will not exit. Doors must be lockable from the inside. The laser technician should not be disturbed or distracted while performing this procedure. The laser technician should be the only person in the room during the test. Laser safety glasses must be worn while the laser is on. The test station consists of an electrical power supply, a D.I. water recirculation system, a cooling system, and power and temperature controls. In addition to the test station, the following equipment is required: a HeNe laser and power supply, a laser power meter, an optics cleaning kit, and an I.R. source detector.

important. He recommended that this preliminary information be redesigned so that employees would be likely to read and act on it. The revised version in Figure 15.4b shows how chunking and labeling the warnings and safety precautions increase the likelihood that users will better understand not only what they have to do but also how to do it safely.

Organizing Instructions

No "correct" or "best" structure exists for instructions, whether they are designed as short directions or manuals. Manuals are simply very long instructions with sections added to provide background and to answer anticipated questions from users. Most manuals—whether they are user's manuals, repair manuals, operation manuals, or procedure manuals—have a similar sequence of sections, shown in Figure 15.5. You can decide which introductory, instructional, and support

---

FIGURE 15.4b ■ **Revised Version of Instructional Information, Chunked and Labeled**

Task	The post assembly optical alignment of the SSL100 Nd:YAG laser head is performed by a laser technician after the laser head is assembled but prior to its installation in the system.	*Chunking and labeling the task increases the likelihood that the technicians will read this information.*
Warnings	△ Take precautions. Dangerous levels of laser radiation are emitted from the laser during the test. △ Cover all windows so that the laser light will not exit. △ Before the test, lock all doors from the inside.	
Safety Precautions	• The laser technician should not be disturbed or distracted while performing this procedure. • The laser technician should be the only person in the room during the test. • The technician must wear laser safety glasses while the laser is on.	*Labeling the warnings and safety precautions increases the likelihood that the technicians will perform the task without injury to themselves or damage to equipment.*
Test Station	The test station has four components: • electrical power supply • D.I. water recirculation system • cooling system • power and temperature controls	
Required Equipment	The post assembly optical alignment of the SSL100 Nd:YAG laser head requires four pieces of equipment: • HeNe laser and power supply • laser power meter • optics cleaning kit • I.R. source detector	

FIGURE 15.5 ■ Standard Components of Manuals

Introduction

Background	Consider one or more of these subsections:
	◆ Identify intended users (for example, "These instructions are designed for technicians who will be working with customers . . .").
	◆ Include information about how to use the manual.
	◆ Provide overview, including a general definition, description, and functions of the equipment or process.
	◆ Include the theory of operation for users who might want to know the *why* of things, not just the *what*.
	◆ Include general background such as project history.
Training Section	Consider a training section that takes first-time users through an illustrated introductory lesson, including basic operations, terminology, and sample applications.

Instructions

Step-by-Step Instructions	Include illustrated instructions for the user. This critical section needs careful user testing.

Support

Frequent Users' Guide (Summary of Steps)	Consider a list that summarizes the steps (with cross references to the step-by-step instructions). This section is usually placed after the step-by-step instructions so that new users aren't tempted to follow these abbreviated instructions when they need the detailed ones. Some companies print frequent-user summaries on plastic or cardboard that users can place near the equipment for easy reference.
Troubleshooting and Maintenance	Consider a troubleshooting section and a maintenance section. The troubleshooting section says, "If this happens, this is what might be wrong and what you should do." Troubleshooting sections often begin with a matrix that lists problems, probable causes, and possible solutions. The maintenance section recommends basic upkeep. Both of these sections often save unnecessary service calls and give users more control.

sections to include by asking yourself what your readers would be willing to read and what they'll find most useful. You can also modify or rearrange these sections to meet your readers' needs.

Locating Information in Manuals

A critical distinction between manuals and shorter directions is the amount of information—and the need to provide several ways for readers to access that

FIGURE 15.6 ■ Devices for Locating Information in Manuals

Title Page	Identify the Task and the Users
Table of Contents	Identify main sections and subsections. A variety of techniques—numbering, boldfacing, capitalizing, and indenting—can signal the relationship between main and subordinate sections.
Pagination	Number the pages. In a dual-numbering system, page 6.7 refers to page 7 in section 6. (The specific form varies: 6.7 or 6/7 or 6•7 or 6-7.) For revisions, only the page numbers in the affected section require changing, which saves time and money.
Previews and Reviews	Provide previews—brief paragraphs or numbered or bulleted lists—at the beginning of sections to let users know what's covered in that section. Provide reviews at the end of sections to summarize the key points that have been covered. Sometimes these reviews take the form of "Now you should be able to . . ." or "At this point you should have. . . ."
Cross References	Use cross references—both in the text itself and in the index—to direct users to other relevant sections. For example, the section of a manual listing steps for calibrating a piece of test equipment might refer users to another section that discusses the theory for establishing the calibration levels. Or the summary of steps for frequent users might refer readers to the more detailed version of the same process.
Glossary	Use a glossary—a mini-dictionary defining key terms that appear in the manual—as one of the early sections or as an appendix. Entries may contain definitions, examples, and explanations. A carefully prepared glossary boldfaces or italicizes terms defined elsewhere in the glossary; entries may also include a "See . . ." reference.
Index	Use an index to alphabetically list and provide page numbers for all the important concepts, terms, and processes in the document. If users can't locate a term in the index, they're not likely to use that section of the manual—unless they come across the information accidentally when flipping through pages.

information. For example, a person using a word-processing manual should be able to locate information about suppressing page numbers or creating headers by looking at the table of contents, the appropriate section preview, the glossary, the index, and maybe a quick-reference card. Figure 15.6 summarizes important devices that help readers locate information in manuals.

Constructing Instructional Texts

For many people, instructions have a tarnished reputation. How many times have you heard the adage, "When all else fails, check the directions"? In spite of this sentiment, well-constructed instructions inspire confidence in users. The following *content elements* and *visual and design elements* were compiled by business and industry professionals during a technical communication seminar; checking your instructions against this list may help you produce documents that users refer to *before* problems occur.

Content Elements

- Identify purpose with a title and goal statement or objective.
- Include necessary components: parts list, equipment list, materials list.
- Use accurate chronology, with time factors.
- Choose clear, direct wording and consistent terminology.
- Select accurate, relevant details.
- Provide rationale.
- Include necessary warnings and cautions.
- Adhere to stylistic and grammatical conventions.

Visual and Design Elements

- Select appropriate visuals, especially for key parts and processes.
- Balance visual and verbal content.
- Select accurate visuals that are easily understood.
- Juxtapose labeled visuals with relevant text.
- Design an appealing, usable format.

Using content elements and visual and design elements correctly is crucial to constructing effective instructions. The following sections examine these elements in more detail and provide suggestions for implementing them.

Content Elements

Select some of the poorest instructions you have used. What features on the list of criteria for effective instructions are omitted? How could the instructions have been improved?

The content elements of instructions include the title, essential components such as parts and materials, logically ordered steps, and legal warnings and cautions.

Purpose. Instructions need a precise title and a clear identification of purpose, goal, or objective. This identification can be achieved in a variety of ways, applied separately or in combination:

- Title may imply or state purpose:
  Operation Manual for Garden Tractor
- Title may be accompanied by visual that illustrates final objective.
- Title may be supplemented by separately stated objective:
  Objective: To use mail-merge with word-processing software.

Necessary Components. Technical instructions benefit by listing parts, materials, equipment, and definitions. For example, kits (for hobbyists who build model rockets or industrial assemblers who build electronic monitors) should come with both a list of the parts and a list of tools or equipment needed to complete the assembly.

A *parts list* identifies parts by name and part number (if needed for verifying or reordering) as well as the quantity provided or needed. In addition, parts may need to be identified by a description or diagram if several are very similar or if the user may be unfamiliar with part names. For example, a parts list that identifies "washers" and "lock washers" may need a diagram to differentiate the types; a list that identifies several capacitors may need labeled diagrams to distinguish them. Even on parts lists that have no similar parts, diagrams benefit inexperienced users.

A *materials and/or equipment list* specifies what users require to complete the task. Such a list is helpful because users can order special tooling or materials and organize the work area.

Most novice users appreciate *definitions* of unfamiliar parts and processes. Definitions can be presented in several ways—as parenthetical definitions directly in the steps, as visuals, in a glossary in a preliminary section, or as an appendix. (For a more detailed discussion of definitions, refer to Chapter 10.)

Chronological Order.   Instructions should be presented in chronological order. Steps are easiest to follow if they are enumerated and separated. Not only should the overall sequence of steps in instructions be chronological, but each individual step should be in order, as the following examples show.

Inadequate—Not Chronological	*Improved—Chronological*
Anodize the aluminum housing after the surfaces have been deburred.	After the surfaces have been deburred, anodize the aluminum housing.

The second version is logical because the steps are identified in the order in which they are done.

Effective instructions also specify details dealing with time. The following example illustrates the benefit of including chronological details:

Inadequate—Without Chronological Details	*Improved—With Chronological Details*
Pump the lever to prime the lantern.	Pump the lever for 15–20 seconds to prime the lantern.

Appropriate Diction.   Instructions are useful only if the user can read them. As a general guideline, select the simplest term that accurately conveys the information. One way to make instructions more direct is to use the verb form of a word, as the following list shows:

What are some of the predictable results of using directions with careless diction?

Noun Form	*Verb Form*
Determine the calculation	Calculate
Make an estimation	Estimate
Begin the removal	Remove
Take a measurement	Measure

Another way to make writing clearer is to use a word consistently as the same part of speech, even though some words can easily be used as two or three parts of speech.

■ **EXAMPLES**

Filter the solvent. (*verb*)	Base the design on current cost. (*verb*)
Wash the filter. (*noun*)	Adjust the base. (*noun*)
Order a filter frame. (*adjective*)	Seal with a base coat. (*adjective*)

In such cases, appropriate usage is not a matter of being right or wrong but of being consistent. Conscientious writers try to employ the same word or phrase the same way within one set of instructions.

Writers also need to be consistent with terminology. Do not refer to a part as the "5-mm tubing connector" in one place and the "Y connector" later in the same document. Once the term for a part or a step is established, use it throughout.

Appropriate Details.   Generally, the instructions you construct should be as simple as possible without sacrificing accuracy. Those that are overly detailed show little sense of audience needs and are as difficult to use as those that skimp on information and leave users unable to complete the task.

Rationale for Steps.   Should instructions only specify the required action, or should the action be explained or justified? The amount of detail you include depends on both the task and the audience. Explanations are essential in situations in which personal injury, equipment damage, or procedure malfunction might otherwise occur, but they are probably unnecessary if the audience is predisposed to comply with instructions. To determine whether justifications are necessary, ask yourself several questions:

1. Is the user/operator more likely to complete the step if a justification is included?

2. Does the inclusion of a justification influence the user's precision or accuracy?

3. Will the justification delay or interfere with the user's immediate understanding and implementation of the step?

The responses to these questions should guide your decision to include or omit justifications as part of the steps. If the user is more likely to complete the step, and with greater accuracy, then the justification will be beneficial. If the justification interferes with the user's understanding or implementation of the step, then it should be omitted. Figure 15.7, from "Thermal Measurements of Building Envelope Components in the Field," specifies the first three steps for determining building component R values. Each step includes an explanation

FIGURE 15.7 ■ Directions with Rationale Included in Steps[4]

DETERMINING BUILDING COMPONENT R VALUES

Step 1 *Establish the type of building component to be analyzed.*
This determines the length of the testing and a choice of environmental conditions. A southerly wall may require testing early in the morning, after a cloudy day, or after several days of recording. A window sash may require only a few hours to determine its R value.

Explanation of ways choices influence time and duration of test.

Step 2 *Estimate the time constant of the component to be analyzed.*
This gives some guidance on test duration based on expected capacitive effects of the component. Quick time-constant calculations can be accomplished as shown in Eq. 2. A finite-difference numerical analysis can also be used for complex systems that may involve phase changes.

Explanation of how to approach calculations.

Step 3 *Choose the appropriate weather conditions for the test, and be prepared to test as soon as these conditions appear imminent.*
On the West Coast and in the Southwest, periodic temperature excursions may exceed 40°F (22°C). These conditions require testing over several diurnal cycles to isolate the capacitive effects. In the Midwest, there may be several days during the winter when ambient temperature variations are less than 10°F (6°C) for several days with no solar radiation. In this case, a highly heat-capacitive wall may be analyzed in a relatively short period of time.

Explanation of geographic differences.

that enables the engineer to perform the evaluation with greater understanding and accuracy.

Necessary Warnings and Cautions. Products liability laws provide compensation for harm—personal injury, death, property damage, or financial loss—caused by a defective product. A manufacturer can be held responsible for any number of causes: faulty design, manufacture, installation, preparation, assembly, testing, or packaging. Or the defect may come from failure to provide either adequate directions or adequate cautions or warnings. Companies should protect their employees by providing accessible information about safety, protect their clients and customers by increasing the chances that work will be performed appropriately, and protect their own corporate interests by reducing any risk of litigation resulting from inadequate instructional documents.

What is your ethical responsibility in preparing accurate, usable instructions? What is your legal responsibility?

Because of the inherent risks associated with some instructions, writers have an obligation to provide users with sufficient notices about cautions, warnings, and dangers. *Cautions* usually indicate potential hazards that, if not avoided, might cause damage or injury. *Warnings* usually indicate potential hazards that,

Warning Labels and Cartoons: Ethics in Instructional Texts

"If a technical writer's prose on a prescription drug data sheet is unclear, and a patient blows his brains out in a medicinally caused fit of depression, is the pharmaceutical company liable?"[5]

Researcher John Caher poses this question in his review of a 1993 court case relevant to technical professionals. The answer provided by the court in this case is that technical professionals and their companies are responsible for the documents they produce. The 1993 case argued that a retired state trooper committed suicide after taking several different drugs because the warnings included with one of the drugs were insufficient. After a thorough review of the usage and warnings sections of the documents included with the drug, the court ruled that the instructions and warnings were legally sufficient to warn of potential problems. The court case, according to Caher, indicates both the ethical and legal requirements that technical professionals must recognize when including warning sections in instructional and informational texts.[6]

Warning labels are not the only element of instructional texts that technical professionals must write with caution. Cartoons or cartoon-like drawings are another feature found in many instructional texts. Such drawings have multiple benefits: They allow readers to visualize difficult steps; they emphasize dangerous procedures; and they can help overcome language and cultural differences for international audiences. These differences, however, can create ethical problems as well. These ethical problems, researcher Philip Rubens argues, arise because "certain cultural elements must be evoked to inform the viewer's interpretation of the [cartoon]."[7] If an audience does not have the right cultural elements to understand a cartoon, then confusion can occur. This confusion can be especially problematic when groups have similar images that have different meanings. For example, wavy lines can denote water as well as an electrical component. Confusing the difference in meaning of the wavy line would be potentially dangerous in an instructional text.

To create ethical instructional texts, technical professionals must recognize how the audience may interact with the document. Warning labels and cartoons provide avenues for communicating important information to the audience, but technical professionals must be aware of the impact of these forms on the audience. As Caher indicates in his review of warning labels, "When a technical writer's work is unclear, and an operator inadvertently reformats a hard drive, that's unfortunate. But if a technical writer's inaccuracy or imprecision claims a life, that's another matter altogether."[8]

How would you avoid sending mixed cultural messages in cartoons?

Have you ever found a warning label in an instructional text unclear? How do you make sure cartoons in an instructional text clearly communicate with your audience?

if not avoided, might cause injury or death. *Dangers* usually indicate an immediate hazard that, if encountered, will cause serious injury or death. The △ symbol is commonly used to signal cautions, warnings, and dangers; users can expect that whenever it appears they should pay close attention to reduce the likelihood of accidents or injuries. Adequate cautions, warnings, and dangers are usually expected to meet these needs:

- Identify the seriousness of the risk involved.

- Describe the risk clearly and in terms the user can understand.

- Provide instructions about how to avoid the risk.

Notices of cautions, warnings, and dangers should be clearly labeled and separated from the rest of the text. Some companies place all cautions, warnings, and dangers in a separate section at the beginning of the document. This may satisfy a legal requirement and create an overall impression about the importance of careful operation, but it is also very important to place cautions, warnings, and dangers in the text—in the actual place where the users will need this information.

Although writers have a number of choices about how they present cautions, warnings, and dangers, they need to know that providing inadequate safety information is a liability issue. The ethics sidebar on the previous page addresses questions about who is responsible, who is liable when something goes wrong.

When you prepare instructions, you need to be sure that they satisfy the "legal requirements for adequacy."[9] In general, if you assure that your instructions are accurate, appropriate, appealing, and accessible, as described in Figure 15.8 on the next page, you will be on your way to meeting the legal requirements for adequacy.

The user's manual that accompanies the AC Powered Ionization Smoke Detector manufactured by BRK Electronics provides an example of a document that appears to meet these criteria for adequacy. The excerpts in Figure 15.9 on pages 548–549, from the user's manual, are annotated to illustrate the way the BRK writers address product liability concerns in clear, easy-to-understand language with helpful visuals.

Grammatical and Stylistic Conventions.   The individual steps in instructions are written in *parallel structure*, with each statement using the same grammatical structure. The instructions in the following examples show how confusing nonparallel directions can be:

■ EXAMPLE

Nonparallel Structure	**Parallel Structure**
Always Observe Safety Rules	*Always Observe Safety Rules*
1. Wearing of safety glasses	1. Wear safety glasses.
2. Proper tool for the job	2. Select proper tool for the job.
3. Use only tools that are functioning.	3. Use only properly functioning tools.
4. Maintain a clean, organized work area.	4. Maintain a clean, organized work area.
5. Questions relating to procedures or the proper handling of tools should be presented to your group leader.	5. Ask your group leader questions about procedures and tool handling.

FIGURE 15.8 ■ Adequacy of Instructional Documents

Accurate: Are the instructions accurate?

- *Understand the product and its likely users.* You need to know such things as the product's purpose and operation as well as users' probable experiences and capabilities.

- *Describe the product's functions and limitations.* You need to know what the product can be expected to do and not do.

- *Fully instruct on all aspects of product ownership.* You need to deal with factors such as assembly, installation, use and storage, testing, maintenance, and emergencies.

- *Contain clear, correct, and tested instructions.* You need to check the instructions using a variety of text-based, expert-based, and user-based testing.

Appropriate: Are the instructions appropriate?

- *Use words and graphics that suit the intended audience.* You need to make sure that all the verbal and visual information can be understood by intended users.

- *Appropriately warn of product hazards.* You need to identify the nature of dangers, normal misuses that can cause danger, and the extent of harm that can result from misuse.

- *Meet government, industry, and company standards.* You may need to cite specific state and/or federal standards that the product meets.

Appealing: Are the instructions appealing?

- *Reach product users.* You need to consider the most effective way to get the instructions to the user: Package insert? Separate manual? Printed in the packaging? Web site? Online help?

- *Offset claims of product safety in advertising or other materials without intense warnings.* If the advertising downplays dangers, you must be especially careful to include warnings to counter these promotional claims.

Accessible: Are the instructions accessible?

- *Present important directions or warnings so users spot and follow them.* You need to make the warnings, cautions, and dangers conspicuous by using design factors such as placement, type size, type style, leading, line length, and cueing devices (such as indentation, icons, and boxes).

- *Inform users in a timely manner of defects discovered after marketing.* After the instructions are complete and the product is marketed, you should continue to determine the product's safety and effectiveness and have a plan for informing users if you discover problems.

Instructions use the *imperative mood* because individual steps are commands to the users, not statements about the process. The next example illustrates the difference between imperative mood and indicative mood.

Imperative Mood	Clamp the specimen onto the flat plate.
Indicative Mood	The specimen is clamped onto the flat plate.

Instructions that employ *second person*, referring to the user as *you*, are the most concise and effective. Sometimes the *you* is not stated, but the users—whether readers or listeners—understand that they are being directly addressed:

Use only properly functioning tools.

Second Person

Make sure you don't type anything after the target drive name, not even a space.

Instructions written in *active voice* have the stated or implicit subject of the sentence as the doer of the action:

[You] Wear safety glasses.

Active Voice, Second Person

Additional elements of grammar and style are discussed in the Usage Handbook.

Visual and Design Elements

This section of the chapter discusses selecting and incorporating visuals into instructions. Users should be able to expect that the same design feature means the same thing every time they encounter it. Thus, headings and subheadings; typeface, size, and style; placement of illustrations; sequence of information; and so on should be consistent throughout a manual or series of manuals.

Appropriate Visuals. Visuals play an important role in many kinds of instructions. The combination of verbal and visual components conveys information in a particularly accurate manner. Visuals can be used to illustrate a variety of elements:

- parts, tooling, equipment

- sequence of steps

- positioning of the operator and/or equipment

- development or change of object or equipment

A diagram often identifies a part or tool more accurately than does a verbal description. For example, sketches of different kinds of screws for assembling a cabinet help the assembler. A series of illustrations can effectively trace the movements in a sequence. In directions for knitting, the most efficient way to demonstrate hand or body position is through illustrations. Changes that occur as a result of following the instructions are often more clearly illustrated visually than explained verbally.

Making the decision about whether to include visuals must be balanced by space requirements and production costs. The following checklist can help you determine whether visuals are appropriate for a particular set of instructions. A "yes" answer to any of these questions indicates that visuals should be integrated:

- Will a flowchart or series of visuals clarify the overall process for the user?

- Will visuals enable the user to clearly understand the end result?

AC POWERED IONIZATION SMOKE DETECTOR
WITH BATTERY BACK-UP
INPUT: 120 VAC, 60 Hz, .045A

USER'S MANUAL

BASIC INFORMATION ABOUT YOUR SMOKE DETECTOR

* **Put detectors inside and outside of every bedroom area and on every floor of your home.**
* **Put detectors close to the center of the ceiling when ceiling mounted.**
* The detector may beep when you put the battery in it.
* If the **indicator light** on the detector **is on, the detector is receiving AC power.** This does not ensure that the detector is working properly.
* **Test the detector weekly by holding the test switch button in for about 10 seconds until the alarm sounds.** The alarm may not sound immediately when you press the button. This checks all detector functions.
* If the detector **beeps once a minute, it needs a new battery.**

Bulleted list indicates awareness of information needs of consumers using the product.

WARNING
GENERAL LIMITATIONS OF SMOKE DETECTORS: WHAT SMOKE DETECTORS CANNOT DO

Smoke detectors have played a key role in reducing home fire deaths in the United States. However, according to the Federal Emergency Management Agency (an agency of the U.S. Government), they may not go off or give early enough warning in as many as 35% of all fires. What are some reasons smoke detectors may not work?

Smoke detectors will not work without power. Battery operated smoke detectors will not work without batteries, if the batteries are dead, if the wrong kind of batteries are used, or if the batteries are put in wrong. AC powered smoke detectors will not work if the power supply is cut off for any reason. Some examples are a power failure at the power station, a failure along a power line, a failure of electrical switching devices in the home, an open fuse or circuit breaker, an electrical fire, or any other kind of fire that reaches the electrical system and burns the wires. If you are concerned abo⌐ ⌐ limitations of ⌐ither batteries or ^C power for you⌐ ⌐noke detec-'⌐rs, ins⌐ ⌐nes o⌐ ⌐detectors ⌐ securi⌐

Limitations of performance are identified.

The manual uses clear, easy-to-understand vocabulary.

WHAT THIS SMOKE DETECTOR CAN DO

This smoke detector is designed to sense smoke that comes into its sensing chamber. It does not sense gas, heat, or flame.

This smoke detector is designed to give early warning of developing fires at a **reasonable cost.** This detector monitors the air. When it senses smoke, it sounds its built-in alarm horn. It can provide precious time for you and your family to escape before a fire spreads. Such **early warning is only possible,** however, **if the detector is located, installed, and maintained as described in this User's Manual.**

⚠WARNING This smoke detector is designed for use in a **single residential living unit only.** In other words, it should be used **inside** a single-family home or apartment. It is not meant to be used in lobbies, hallways, basements, or another apartment in multi-family buildings, **unless there are already working detectors in each family unit.** Smoke detectors placed in common areas outside of the individual living unit (such as on porches or in ⌐allways) may not ⌐rovide early warning to residents ⌐n multi-f ⌐ ⌐dings. e⌐ ⌐ing unit sh⌐ ⌐ave its o⌐ ⌐ors.

Clear, easy-to-read headings signal each section of the instructions.

Icons and boxes flag critical information.

The product's expected performance is clearly stated.

WHERE SMOKE DETECTORS SHOULD NOT BE PUT

Nuisance alarms occur when smoke detectors are put up where they will not work properly. **To avoid nuisance alarms, do not place detectors:**

* **In or near areas where combustion particles are present.** (Combustion particles are the by-products of something that is burning.) **Areas to avoid include kitchens with few windows or poor ventilation, garages** where there may be vehicle exhaust, **near furnaces, hot water heaters, and space heaters.**
* **Put up smoke detectors at least 20 feet (6 meters) away from places where combustion particles are normally present, like kitchens.** If a 20-foot distance is not possible, put the detector as far away from the combustion particles as possible, preferably on the wall. To prevent nuisance alarms, provide good ventilation.
* **If smoke detectors are to be located in halls or rooms near or adjacent to kitchens where there is no wall above the doorway between rooms, mount detectors on an inside wall closest to the bedroom area and furthest from the kitchen.**

IMPORTANT: In mobile homes where a 20-foot distance is not possible, put smoke detectors as far away from combustion particles as possible. Provide good ventilation. **Do not, for any reason, disable the detector to avoid nuisance alarms.**

* **In air streams passing by kitchens.** Figure 6 shows how a detector can sense combustion products in normal air-flow paths. The picture shows how to correct this problem.

Typographic cues such as boldfacing signal especially important information.

Definitions or explanations of unfamiliar terms are provided.

Figures present information that would be difficult to explain in words.

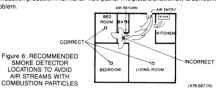

Figure 6: RECOMMENDED SMOKE DETECTOR LOCATIONS TO AVOID AIR STREAMS WITH COMBUSTION PARTICLES

(A78-667-05)

Figure labels give users critical information from the captions.

Incorporated figures illustrate information in the text.

FIGURE 15.9 ■ *Continued*

Terminology about wiring is specialized since directions clearly state wiring should be performed only by a licensed electrician.

Visuals show how user interacts with the product.

Information about proper operation is easily accessible.

Information about regular maintenance and testing is provided.

Harm that could result from misuse is clearly specified.

Normal misuses that could cause danger are presented.

HOW THIS DETECTOR SHOULD BE PUT UP

This detector is made to be mounted on any standard 4-inch octagonal junction box.

Model 86RAC is made to be mounted on the ceiling, or on the wall if necessary. Model 86RAC can serve as a single-station stand-alone unit **or** be interconnected with other 86RAC units.

⚠WARNING Detector installation must conform to the electrical codes in your area and to Article 760 of the U.S. National Electrical Code. Wiring should be performed only by a licensed electrician.

⚠WARNING The circuit used to power the detector must be a 24-hour 120 VAC 60Hz circuit. Be sure the circuit cannot be turned off by a switch, ground fault ▪▪▪▪.

7. Grasp the tab on the battery drawer and pull it straight out as shown in Figure 8.

⚠WARNING The battery is positioned WRONG in the factory to keep it fresh until installation. It must be re-positioned to provide DC back-up power.

8. Remove the battery and re-position it properly, as shown on the label in the drawer. Push the drawer straight in until it is flush with the housing.

⚠CAUTION This smoke detector comes with a "missing battery" indicator that will prevent the battery drawer from closing if a battery is not installed. This is to warn you that the smoke detector will not work under DC power until a new battery is installed.

(A78-1130-00)

Figure 8: BATTERY DRAWER BEING PULLED OUT

HOW TO TELL IF THE DETECTOR IS WORKING PROPERLY

When the indicator light (seen through the clear push button of the test switch) glows continuously, the detector is receiving AC power.

NOTE: For interconnected Model 86RAC Detectors:

When an interconnected system of Model 86RAC detectors goes into alarm under AC power, the indicator light will be OFF on the detector(s) sensing smoke, and will be ON all other detectors. When under DC power, no indication is provided.

Test the detector weekly by pushing firmly on the test button until the horn sounds. This should take TEN seconds. If the alarm horn makes a continuous loud sound, the detector is working properly. **THIS IS THE ONLY WAY TO BE SURE THAT THE DETECTOR IS WORKING. TEST THE DETECTOR WEEKLY. IF THE DETECTOR FAILS TO TEST PROPERLY, HAVE IT REPAIRED OR REPLACED IMMEDIATELY.**

⚠WARNING Never use an open flame to test your detector. You may set fire to and damage the detector, as well as your home. Also, do not use "aerosol" spray smoke detector testers. Build up of chemicals used in the spray can change detector sensitivity, or in some worst cases, impair detector functioning. The built-in test switch accurately tests all detector functions, as required by Underwriters' Laboratories.

⚠DANGER If the alarm horn sounds a loud continuous sound and you have NOT pushed the test button, the detector has sensed smoke or combustion particles in the air. THE ALARM HORN IS A WARNING OF A POSSIBLY SERIOUS SITUATION. IT REQUIRES YOUR IMMEDIATE ATTENTION.

The alarm could be caused by a nuisance situation. Cooking smoke or a dusty furnace, sometimes called "friendly fires," can cause the alarm to sound. If this happens, open a window or fan the air to remove the smoke or dust. The alarm will turn itself off as soon as the air completely clears. **DO NOT DISCONNECT THE POWER. THIS WILL REMOVE YOUR PROTECTION.**

HOW TO TAKE CARE OF AND TEST THIS DETECTOR

Your smoke detector has been designed to be as maintenance-free as possible. To keep your detector in good working order, you must;

• **Test the detector weekly.** (See section "How to Tell if the Detector Is Working Properly."

• **Replace the battery once a year or immediately when the low battery "beep" signal sounds once a minute.** The low battery "beep" should last at least 30 days.

NOTE: For best performance, we recommend that you only use alkaline batteries (First Alert, Model FB2) as replacement batteries in this smoke detector. (Carbon zinc batteries are acceptable, but do not last as long.) First Alert batteries can be purchased at any retail store that sells batteries.

(If you cannot obtain a First Alert battery, the following batteries are also acceptable for proper smoke detector operation: Eveready #522, #1222, #216; Duracell #MN1604; or Gold Peak #1604P, #1604S.)

Directions for assembly and installation are provided.

Multiple cueing devices signal warnings, cautions, and dangers.

Information is presented in a logical, step-by-step sequence.

The manual warns against misuse.

Information about what to do in emergencies helps users.

- Will visuals help the user correctly identify parts?

- Will visuals help the user understand and implement individual verbal steps?

- Will including visuals emphasize safety and decrease risk?

Visuals are often essential in illustrating and clarifying a sequence. Imagine trying to follow instructions for electronic troubleshooting, botanical identification, or celestial navigation without visual support. The visuals eliminate ambiguity by providing diagrams or maps where appropriate in the text. Figure 15.10 illustrates a series of steps and accompanying flowchart from a *Dell Diagnostics and Troubleshooting Guide.* This process for troubleshooting a parallel printer is accompanied (as are virtually all of the processes in this Dell guide) by a Help Map that gives users a choice—step-by-step instructions or flowchart instructions, which some users will find faster and easier.

The writer who wants to incorporate visuals has to make a decision about the kind of visuals to employ. (Chapter 9 discusses types of visuals in detail.) Generally, keep the visuals as simple as possible. For this reason, drawings are often preferred over photographs, which can present unnecessary and distracting detail.

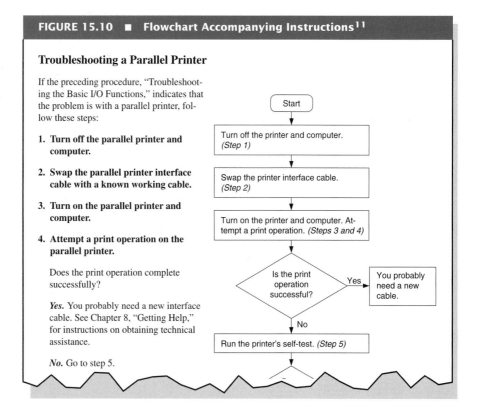

Do you believe that the extra time, effort, and ink of creating a flowchart to accompany the steps is worthwhile? What are some benefits?

FIGURE 15.10 ■ Flowchart Accompanying Instructions[11]

Troubleshooting a Parallel Printer

If the preceding procedure, "Troubleshooting the Basic I/O Functions," indicates that the problem is with a parallel printer, follow these steps:

1. **Turn off the parallel printer and computer.**

2. **Swap the parallel printer interface cable with a known working cable.**

3. **Turn on the parallel printer and computer.**

4. **Attempt a print operation on the parallel printer.**

   Does the print operation complete successfully?

   Yes. You probably need a new interface cable. See Chapter 8, "Getting Help," for instructions on obtaining technical assistance.

   No. Go to step 5.

Start

Turn off the printer and computer. *(Step 1)*

Swap the printer interface cable. *(Step 2)*

Turn on the printer and computer. Attempt a print operation. *(Steps 3 and 4)*

Is the print operation successful? — Yes → You probably need a new cable.

No

Run the printer's self-test. *(Step 5)*

Visual and Verbal Balance.   Some processes are more easily understood through a visual presentation than a verbal one. For example, suppose that you are eating in a restaurant when you choke on a piece of chicken. You give the international sign of choking—hands to your throat. Your friends have put off learning the Heimlich maneuver, but they see a "Choke Saver" poster on the restaurant wall. Which version of the poster would you want them to check?

1. *Entirely verbal* well-organized chronological paragraphs include causal elements, clear topic sentences, and good chronological transitions.

2. *Verbal and visual* sequence of captioned photographs shows a choking victim being saved by a trained person.

3. *Verbal and visual* sequence of clear, captioned sketches shows a choking victim being saved by a trained person.

4. *Entirely visual* sequence of clear sketches shows a choking victim being saved by a trained person, with arrows and inserted enlargements of critical positioning.

No doubt you would select version 3 or 4, and probably version 4. Version 1 would take too long to read, and without the sketches the saver would not be sure of correctly positioning hands on the victim's body. Version 2 would be an improvement, but photographs frequently show too much detail; also, people's clothing would obscure correct positioning. Version 3 would be a good choice, as long as the saver took the time to read necessary information in the captions. But, assuming the sketches and enlargements are accurate, version 4 would ensure the fastest and most accurate response.

Most instructions require a balance of verbal steps and visual support. Visuals should be included when they help the user complete the task more quickly or accurately and with less anxiety.

Accurate Visuals.   Accuracy is of the utmost importance in any type of visuals in instructions. Visuals that cannot be easily understood—whether drawings, diagrams, photographs, or maps—are not much help to the user. Many problems can be eliminated if writer and artist consider visuals as an integral part of the direction, not just a decorative addition.

The accuracy and appropriate use of each visual must be double-checked by both the artist and the writer. How helpful is a wiring diagram that omits some of the circuits? How can a user confidently follow a step that reads, "Add two drops of oil in all set-screw holes, locations shown in the diagram," when the diagram does not label the set screws? How can a user be expected to follow directions that say, "Calibrate by turning the middle knob to zero," with a diagram that shows only two knobs? Accuracy means completeness of the visual itself, inclusion of accompanying labels, and visuals and text that are related.

Figure 15.11 illustrates a simple mechanical process—changing the air filter on a lawn mower. This simple maintenance task is easier to understand and

FIGURE 15.11 ■ Visuals to Illustrate Parts and Process[12]

AIR FILTER

Your engine will not run properly and may be damaged by using a dirty air filter.

Replace the air filter every year, more often if you mow in very dusty, dirty conditions. Do not wash air filter.

TO CHANGE AIR FILTER (See Fig. 10)

• Remove the air filter by turning counterclockwise to the stop and pull away from collar.
• Remove filter from inside of cover.
• Clean the inside of the cover and the collar to remove any dirt accumulation.
• Insert new filter into cover.
• Put air filter cover and filter into collar aligning the tab with the slot.
• Push in on cover and turn clockwise to tighten.

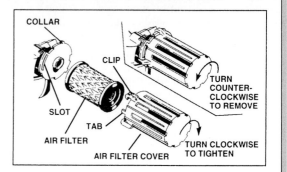

FIG. 10

complete because the text is accompanied by a drawing that shows the assembled and unassembled air filter and labels each of the parts.

The size of visuals can affect users' ability to interpret these visuals accurately. If a drawing is too small, users won't be able to identify the important parts of the subject. Occasionally, a full-view drawing or photograph is accompanied by an enlargement of a crucial part. A drawing or photograph may have small parts identified by arrows, circles or boxes, or highlighted portions. Visuals should always be labeled with an indication of the scale (actual size, 1/2 scale, 1/5 scale, 1 inch = 1 foot, 1 inch = 10 miles, and so on).

Placement of Visuals. Visuals in technical communications are usually placed as close as possible following or next to the text reference. Unless there is no possibility of confusion or ambiguity, visuals should always be referred to in the text, by figure number or title, so that users are led to look at the correct visual for each step.

Figure 15.12 illustrates effective visuals that are well-integrated with the text. The placement of the disk in step 1 lets users quickly locate the locking tab. Without the visual, an inexperienced person might read only the boldface text in step 1 and mistakenly move the metal shutter (which can damage the surface of the disk). The enlargements that accompany steps 2 and 3 show how to move the tab to lock or unlock the disk.

Appealing, Usable Format. In designing the physical layout of instructions, you need to make sure that the steps and visuals are clear and easy to read. The layout should not discourage users with small print, haphazard page design, or insufficient differentiation of steps, explanations, and examples.

The white space should enhance the readability of instructions—text and visuals should not be crowded or bunched together. Steps should be enumer-

FIGURE 15.12 ■ **Visuals Integrated into Instructional Steps**[13]

Locking a disk
to protect its contents

When a disk is locked, you can read the information on it but you can't add, change, or delete information. You might want to lock a disk to prevent someone else (or yourself) from accidentally making changes to it.

1. **Find the locking tab on the disk you just ejected from the disk drive.**

If you hold the disk with its back side facing up and the metal end away from you, the locking tab is in the lower-right corner.

2. **To lock the disk, slide the tab toward the outer edge of the disk.**

It's often easiest to do this with your fingernail.

Locking the disk reveals a small hole.

3. **To unlock the disk, slide the tab to its previous position (covering the hole).**

You can lock and unlock any floppy disk in this way.

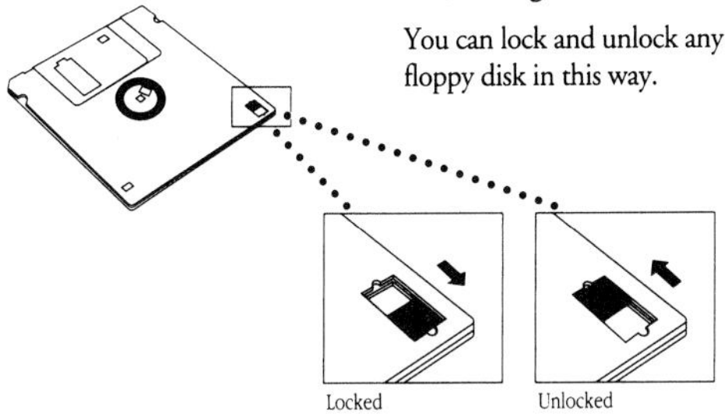

Locked   Unlocked

ated, with white space between each entry. Explanations or justifications that follow the steps should be physically set off, so that the steps clearly stand out and the explanations are seen as subordinate. Particularly in instructions that will be used frequently, the page layout should leave enough white space, perhaps even a column, for personal notes by the user.

Visual devices are valuable in instructions. For example, boldfaced or boxed information alerts users to cautions and warnings. Bullets or type variations such as italics identify justifications that are not part of the actual step. Shading signals major sections in a process, with steps to complete that process listed below.

Total Visuals.   In response to the problems raised by international and multinational users as well as American users who find visual steps faster or easier, several companies have experimented with totally visual instructions.

Creating totally visual instructions is not easy because pictures, signs, and symbols do not all have universal meanings. For example, could the up-arrow sign on shipping cartons be misinterpreted? Should the carton be placed with the arrow pointing up to indicate the top of the carton? Or should the carton be placed with the arrow pointing down, indicating the carton's most stable position? The answer depends on a person's perception.

In the development of nonverbal instructions, color coding can be very important. Coloring parts of drawings often effectively replaces verbal emphasis and is also valuable for differentiating similar elements in a drawing. Problems arise, however, if instructions are to be reproduced (perhaps photocopied) in a manner that ignores the color. For this reason, color coding is often combined with a variety of design patterns. (See Chapter 9 for a more detailed discussion of color.)

Document Testing

The best way to determine whether all of the elements of your instructions—content elements as well as visual and design elements—are effective for the intended audience is to test them, both during their development and upon completion. You have several choices to make in testing your instructions. (Refer to Chapter 13 to review the types and categories of testing.) First, you need to decide about the type of document testing:

- user-based testing

- expert-based testing

- text-based testing

A combination of these types of testing gives you the most helpful information for revising your instructions. Each provides valuable information the others do not.

You need to know several things. Do the instructions actually work? Users can give you feedback about whether they work in several ways: performance tests, think-aloud protocols, and retrospective comments. Are the instructions accurate and consistent? Experts can provide reviews for technical accuracy and conduct several levels of edit. (Review the levels of edit discussed in Chapter 13.) Is the text itself clear and correct? You can assess the text by applying various checklists and guidelines and evaluating it on a computer for readability and style.

Explain whether you believe equipment operators need to understand why each step in a set of directions is included and needs to be followed. Does this understanding ensure that the instructions will be more carefully followed?

Although all types of testing are invaluable, you shouldn't underestimate the importance of user testing. One example clearly shows the problems that result if instructions are not properly tested. Recently, a nationally known high-tech company that manufactures circuit boards in one of its facilities had a serious problem with assembly workers who were not following new inspection procedures at each work station. The detailed instructions, written and tested by engineers who supervised the production assembly, were intended for assembly-line workers, many of whom had not finished high school and whose only training was received on the job. The communications consultant called in to analyze the situation identified the problem: The line workers couldn't understand the instructions because users' knowledge was miscalculated, multiple operations were presented as single steps, and vocabulary level and sentence structure were too difficult. These problems (as well as the frustration and expense) could have been prevented if the engineers had initially tested the instructions with representative users.

After you have decided what types of testing to use, you need to schedule the testing. Ideally, you will have both in-process testing and final testing. This, however, requires careful planning so that you can test the instructions section by section as they're developed and then have time to revise them before the final testing of the entire document. The testing section of Figure 15.2 provides a convenient matrix you can use.

Once instructions are written and tested, they still need to be monitored for updating, both in projects with long-range development cycles and for products that are released (published). A company that uses long-range planning coordinates research and development, manufacturing, and publication cycles for the same product. Such coordination ensures that the instructions reflect the most recent version of the product. Instructions are updated when the product is modified during development, when new versions of the product are released, and when errors or omissions in the instructions themselves are noted.

Do reasons and explanations take up too much space, thus making the instructions too long and cumbersome?

Examining Sample Instructions

More varieties of instructions exist than could ever be presented in this chapter; however, one approach developed by Deere & Company is particularly effective and can be adapted to many situations. Deere & Company created what they call "illustruction," which is a contraction of "illustration" and "instruction." The premise underlying the approach is that visuals carry more of the instructional message than text. Because many agriculture workers who use Deere equipment have limited literacy (especially foreign workers and recent immigrants), the instructions must use simple language, depend more on visuals, and be designed so that each step is accessible and appealing.

Deere illustructions begin with safety messages. Because agriculture work is among the most dangerous in the country, Deere presents safety hazards in every owner/operator manual. Figure 15.13 illustrates two of the safety modules that are included in the owner/operator manual for a small tractor.

The basic grid for each page in a Deere manual is horizontal quarters; however, this layout is very flexible so that writers can use four modules on a page—or three, two, or one, depending on the amount of explanation and illustration that's necessary and the number of cautions and warnings that are needed.

Illustructions appear to have positive customer feedback and stand up successfully in product liability litigation. Moreover, though the illustruction manuals are longer (by about 20 percent) than conventional manuals, the overall cost is less because they use simple drawings and Polaroid photography, and the modules for common systems (e.g., engines, transmissions) can be used for several products.[15] The highly visual, modular approach could be adapted and used successfully in a number of other situations.

PROTECT CHILDREN

Keep children and others away when you operate machine.

BEFORE YOU BACK UP:
—Stop the PTO.
—Look behind tractor for children.

Do not let children operate tractor.

Do not let children ride on tractor or any implement.

AVOID TIPPING

Do not drive where machine could slip or tip.

Stay alert for holes, rocks, and roots in the terrain, and other hidden hazards. Keep away from drop-offs.

Slow down before you make a sharp turn.

Driving forward out of a ditch or mired condition or up a steep slope could cause tractor to tip over backward. Back out of these situations if possible.

Use care when pulling loads or using heavy equipment. Use counterweights or wheel weights suggested in this operator's manual.

End-of-Chapter
Recommendations for Technical Communicators

1. Identify the kind of instructions you need to prepare: actions/behavior of personnel, assembly of objects or mechanisms, operation of equipment, and implementation of a process.

2. Carefully analyze the task by asking a series of questions, which include (but aren't limited to) these:

- What task has come before?
- What knowledge or skill is necessary to complete the task?
- What is the situation or environment?
- What steps are involved in the process?
- What will the final product be?

3. Carefully analyze the audience to help avoid problems that often plague instructions, such as inappropriate vocabulary and visuals and overly complex or simple explanations.

4. Consider the special needs of international audiences.

5. Decide what sections to include and how to organize them by asking yourself what readers would find most useful.

6. Design a manual that gives users easy access to carefully organized information by using devices—including previews and reviews, cross references, and a glossary—that help readers keep track of where they are and locate information that they need.

7. Assure that the necessary content elements are present: title, essential components such as parts and materials, logically ordered steps, and necessary warnings and cautions.

8. Assure that visuals have been appropriately selected and incorporated into the instructions.

9. Assure that the overall design of the document is usable and appealing.

10. Establish a document testing plan that appropriately incorporates
    - user assessment
    - expert assessment
    - text assessment

Practicum

Vidiom: The Case of the Multiple Versions

The digital broadcast industry is very new. It currently includes all satellite delivery and some cable. Most cable is analog. Digital cable is being introduced at premium prices to select markets. Some of the touted features of digital broadcast include the hundreds of channels, interactive programming, video on demand, and active Internet browsing.

Vidiom is a small consulting company that actively works in the interactive television and digital broadcast market. We are located in Boulder, Colorado. Currently, we consist of 13 employees: 9 writers, 2 engineers, a trainer, and an office manager. The core of Vidiom consists of ex-Philips employees who worked in the Compact Disc-interactive (CD-i) industry. Our experience in television-based applications in CD-i provided a solid base for us to approach the television industry. Now, Vidiom provides engineering architecture and technical writing services to the digital broadcast (cable/satellite television) industry. Our clients are centered in two main locations: Denver and Silicon Valley. Among our clients are CableLabs, Time-Warner, Canal+, and OpenTV.

The digital broadcast market has a special need for consultants because historically television networks did not have software departments. As television broadcasting has become digitized, the networks have begun building software departments. This industry has an even greater need for technical writers who can write manuals for these new engineering departments.

Scenario

A set-top box is the cable/satellite box that typically sits on top of the television and controls channel-changing, pay-per-view ordering, etc. The set-top box acts as a small computer to run interactive applications in a digital broadcast system. The television acts as the monitor.

One client in particular provides a telling example of the needs and problems in this market. Five years ago, XYZ was a start-up software company providing operating systems in set-top boxes for satellite TV. Vidiom knew the main players in XYZ through our work at Philips. XYZ approached us to write an authoring tool to create interactive applications that would run on the set-top boxes. Through the course of the contract for the authoring tool, XYZ's documentation department asked Vidiom for more and more help, until Vidiom was handling over half of the company's documentation needs.

Vidiom has been given the task of handling all of the documentation for XYZ, a staggering 11,000 pages that are updated two or three times a year. Because XYZ is located in California, all Vidiom work is done through telecommuting: e-mail, phone calls, and data transfer over the Internet. Vidiom writers visit XYZ once a year, usually after a major project release.

To make this type of relationship work, XYZ has a technical documentation department that now solely consists of a manager. The manager, Bill, is the Vidiom contact. Bill negotiates Vidiom's contracts, manages the documentation projects, attends all project meetings requiring a documentation presence, and handles the printing of the documentation. Historically, XYZ has cycled through documentation managers and staff yearly. The only continuity existing in the documentation is that it is supplied by Vidiom.

On the Vidiom side, each project has a lead writer and a supporting writer. For example, Walden is the manager of documentation, the lead writer on the authoring tool project, and a support writer on the Software Development Kit (SDK) project. Chris is the lead writer for the SDK, Ellen is the lead writer for the Hardware Porting Kit (HPK), and Jennifer is the support writer for the HPK. Because of the past instability of XYZ's technical documentation department, Vidiom has created and maintained its own contacts into XYZ's engineering and marketing department. Vidiom has relied heavily on these contacts to provide realistic information concerning project scope and the probability of meeting current deadlines.

Bill, the XYZ documentation manager, has little to do because of the effectiveness of Vidiom's staff. He has no experience managing documentation but has a great deal of experience in training and developing training materials. As a side note, Bill loves online documentation and does not believe in the future of hard-copy documents. Bill loves wildly colorful online docs that use multiple-color schemes to differentiate tasks, links, etc. Initially, Vidiom was thrilled to find someone with Bill's talents, but after some non-disclosed research (examining training modules from Bill's prior company), Vidiom has determined that he has little design sense (i.e., the training modules look like patchwork quilts). Despite Bill's lack of documentation experience and the occupational problems that follow from the inexperience, all Vidiom staff like Bill personally.

How do you approach a manager whom you have little professional respect for in your field but consider a friend?

Although Bill was not told, Vidiom has also found out that Bill was hired into the documentation manager slot only to "get him into the company." Bill is to be moved into the training management slot as soon as it is vacant. The vice president of engineering believes the current training manager is ineffective and hired Bill, hoping to quickly move him to training.

Does the fact that Bill will not be the manager of technical documentation for long affect how you deal with him?

To complicate the issue even further, XYZ's product line is very reactive to the changing world markets. Consequently, the company offers different set-top operating systems for different television networks. Each set-top box essentially supports a different set of features, depending on the underlying operating system. Examples of these varying features are support for modems, advanced MPEG and JPEG graphics, and set-top based picture-in-picture technology. Future features will support hard drives that record television programs, giving viewers the ability to pause television programs and then fast-forward to "catch up."

The Software Development Kit (SDK) is a product that provides the instructions, tools, and source code for programmers to write interactive television software to be run on an XYZ set-top. Because of the many supported operating systems, the SDK programmer could write a program that would either run on one system or run on multiple systems. The documentation page count for the SDK is currently 2,100 pages. To create a different documentation set for each operating system would mean writing and maintaining a 2,100-page document set for all four major operating systems. This plan would require increasing the documentation staff by 4–6 people.

This solution is not acceptable to XYZ. Instead, all variations of the SDK will be combined into a single product that differentiates the programming functions that are supported by each operating system. Vidiom's plan is to combine all the documentation information into a single document and to differentiate the specifics of each operating system using some sort of graphical or in-text documentation scheme.

What percentage of the population is color-blind? What color combinations cause problems in perception? XYZ is an international company. Are there cultural interpretations of color that should inform your color choices?

To complicate the problem, the documentation will be released in PDF (online) format as well as hard copy. The source for both releases must be the same. The hard copy will not be produced with any color other than gray-scale/black. Consequently, any color used in the manual must reproduce well online as well as in gray-scale hard copy. There is no style guide that handles the use of color in manuals at this time. Bill looks forward to moving the docs into a color format. All decisions concerning the new style must be approved by Bill.

FIGURE 1 ■ C Feature Differentiation

ChangeStream

changes the current channel to a specified channel

Prototype
```
int ChangeStream( handle tstream,
            handle old,
            handle new )
```

Argument(s)
tstream	is a handle for the current transport stream.
old	is a handle for the current channel.
new	is a handle for the new channel.

Return Value ChangeStream returns SUCCESS if the channel is changed to new; otherwise an error code is returned.

Description This function is supported only by ITV-B. . . .

SetTopInit

initializes the set-top box during a cold boot

Prototype
```
int SetTopInit( void )
```

Argument(s) None.

Return Value SetTopInit returns SUCCESS if the set-top box is successfully initialized; otherwise an error code is returned.

Description This function is supported only by ITV-B+ and ITV1.2. . . .

Examples

The examples in Figures 1 and 2 are typical of the types of material you must differentiate for your audience.

- Figure 1 shows two typical C function descriptions. Programmers need to quickly be able to see which operating system supports the function. In this example, that information is buried in the description.

- Figure 2 shows explanatory text that is provided by XYZ's engineers. This is an overview to a lengthy description of set-top box display and the display planes. Notice that each operating system supports different planes. This type of feature differentiation is found throughout the SDK.

FIGURE 2 ■ Feature Differentiation

Display Planes

The television display is a composite of multiple display planes. The number and type of supported planes is determined by the set-top's operating system.

- The cursor plane (supported by all set-top boxes) allows the application to display cursors and sprites "on top of" the application.
- The graphic plane (supported by all set-top boxes) allows the application to display bitmap graphics of type BMP, GIF, TIF, and PIXMAP. ITV1.2 supports two graphic planes.
- The MPEG plane (supported by all set-top boxes) displays the decoded television video stream as well as any MPEG still images used by the application.
- The JPEG plane (supported by ITV-B, ITV-B+, and ITV1.2) displays decoded MPEG still images or decoded JPEG still images. ITV1.2 supports two JPEG planes.

All regions of a plane that do not contain graphic information are transparent to the planes behind it. The order of planes is set-top box specific as follows (plane order is given from front to back):

ITV-A: cursor, graphic, mpeg

ITV-B: cursor, graphic, mpeg, jpeg

ITV-B+:   cursor, graphic, mpeg, jpeg

ITV1.2:   cursor, graphic, graphic, jpeg, mpeg, jpeg

Assignment

As part of the three-person team to develop the *Software Development Kit (SDK) Reference Manual,* you will propose a design for the new manual that includes a graphical and in-text scheme that can easily differentiate which features will be supported by which operating systems. The previous examples provide a starting point for your page layout design. Further background information you will find necessary to use in your solution follows:

These operating systems are currently supported:

- **ITV-A** ITV-A is the basic core operating system. All ITV-A features are included in all other ITV operating systems.

- **ITV-B** ITV-B is the second generation ITV operating system. It contains enhancements to ITV-A.

- **ITV1.2** ITV1.2 is a custom version of ITV-B. ITV1.2 and ITV-B share some enhancements, but ITV1.2 contains many more unique features. ITV1.2 is not a complete superset of ITV-B. ITV-B has some features not contained in ITV1.2.

- **ITV-B+** ITV-B+ is an enhanced version of ITV-B. The new features in ITV-B+ are all optional to set-top box manufacturers. Consequently, ITV-B+ is not a set definition, but a set of potential features added to ITV-B.

Your solution must handle the following scenarios:

- Instances in which a paragraph/section/chapter complies with all versions

- Instances in which a paragraph/section/chapter complies with only one version

- Instances in which a paragraph/section/chapter complies with more than one, but not all versions

Finally, the *SDK Reference Manual* places one C language function per page (Figure 1 provides two such functions). Each function fits into the following categories:

- Supported by all versions

- Supported by one version

- Supported by more than one, but not all versions

Given different updating strategies (such as replacing only the changed pages or updating online versions, but not hardcopy), does this change the way you approach your solution?

Whatever solution you propose should take into consideration that XYZ's reaction to market changes will not slow down. Future versions of the SDK will support more operating systems; however, the core of each operating system remains the same for each version.

The proposal about the new manual should include an explanation of the ways your solution handles the above scenarios as well as examples of pages that demonstrate your solution. Your proposal should include references to the examples. You should also include an explanation of any shortcomings contained in your solution.

Remember, there is no single right answer. You may identify many solutions.

Walden Miller is the Manager, Technical Documentation for Vidiom Systems in Boulder, Colorado. He has managed technical documentation departments in high tech companies for 15 years, including Microware Systems, Philips Media/OptImage, and Xaos Tools. Walden is responsible for managing all Vidiom writers as well as managing all Vidiom writing clients. He acts as a mentor for junior-level writers and as a consultant to senior writers. Walden explains that, "The type of problem in this practicum is typical of documentation issues raised in engineering writing situations. Elegant handling of these issues not only ensures future contracts but provides writers with a portfolio of solutions to problems, not just writing samples." You can reach Walden at wmiller@vidiom.com.

Hint: *Because you do not have access to the complete manual, you must generate sample text. Consequently, when creating your example pages, the actual text is somewhat immaterial. The form of the paragraphs should be considered, however. Does your solution work with headings, bulleted lists, lengthy paragraphs, etc.*

1. **Identify appropriate audiences.** Examine the variations in wording of a single step in the following three sets of instructions. Identify audiences appropriate for each version. Explain which version you think is the most effective.

   Set I

   Version A   Close the valve completely by turning the knob until the arrow points to the red dot.

   Version B   Close the valve completely by turning the knob until the arrow points to the red dot. Failure to close the valve completely will result in pressure loss, decreasing the efficiency of the system.

   Version C   So the system does not lose pressure, close the valve completely by turning the knob until the arrow points to the red dot.

   Set II

   Version D   Lower the safety bar before turning on the machine. If you operate the machine without the safety bar in place, you might severely injure your hand.

   Version E   Lower the safety bar before turning on the machine to avoid personal injury.

   Version F   Lower the safety bar before turning on the machine.

   Set III

   Version G   If the patient's pain persists, turn her on her side.

   Version H   If the patient's pain persists, turn her on her side in order to alleviate the pressure.

   Version I   If the patient's pain persists, turn her on her side. This change in position alleviates the pressure on the spine.

2. **Write verbal instructions for effective visuals.** In a small group, look at the instructions for changing the waste toner bottle in a photocopier (Figure 15.3). Write the steps (in English) for each of the seven illustrated steps.

3. **Revise an instructional document.** The following figure is taken from the draft of a project report submitted to the U.S. Department of Energy by an organization proposing a more efficient method of identifying the characteristics of substances at hazardous waste sites. The organization wanted both to convey its awareness of federal safety regulations for working at hazardous waste sites and to reinforce the idea that its employees had been given these guidelines that were treated as instructions for head-to-foot protection.

Unfortunately, information was not formatted as instructions, and the lack of parallelism made reading difficult. Most readers would expect the two bulleted lists to order items the same way—from the head to foot (or vice versa). However, the order of the items in the two lists is different. The list for 6.5.1 begins with disposable coveralls, while the list for 6.5.2 begins with a respirator.

Revise this excerpt so that the information is likely to be perceived as instructions, the sequence of information is logical and parallel, and the wording conveys the necessity of following the guidelines.

6.5.1 PPE Level D: Level D is the minimum PPE level. No respiratory protection is required; limited skin protection is required. Recommended equipment for Level D includes

- disposable coveralls over work clothes
- work gloves
- hard hat
- safety glasses or goggles
- chemical resistant boots or shoes

6.5.2 PPE Level C: Level C requires limited respiratory protection and skin protection from airborne hazards. Recommended equipment for Level C includes

- full-face purifying respirator
- chemical resistant clothing: overalls and long sleeve jacket; hooded, one or two piece chemical splash suit or limited use chemical resistant one piece suit
- hard hat
- chemical resistant boots
- inner and outer chemical resistant gloves

---

4. **Rewrite poor or outdated instructions.** Individually or in a small group, select a set of poor instructions or outdated instructions (or, if you are particularly ambitious, select a procedure or activity that needs a set of effective instructions). Rewrite (or write) them so that they are accurate, appropriate, appealing, and accessible for the identified audience.

5. **Evaluate a manual.**
   (a) Locate a manual that is used by people in your field of study. In small groups (preferably with people who share your field of study or a similar one), establish criteria for evaluating manuals.
   (b) Create a rubric in which you list these criteria and evaluate the manual you have selected accordingly.
   (c) Prepare a short report that identifies the manual's strengths and recommends specific changes to eliminate weaknesses. Include discussion

about how various kinds of document testing could have eliminated many of the problems.

6. **Evaluate an online manual.** Many companies include electronic documentation (CD-ROMs) with their products or have instruction manuals available on the Web for users of their products.
   (a) Use (and modify) the rubric you created in Assignment 5 and evaluate an electronic manual.
   (b) Present your findings to your classmates and discuss some of the advantages and disadvantages of electronic instructions.

Intertext

Design Learner-Friendly Training Manuals[16]

No training department would send a presenter dressed in blue jeans and a T-shirt to conduct a class. Why? Because it's just not professional. And it wouldn't issue a black-and-white handout with pages and pages of block text either, right?

The appearance of presentation materials is just as important as the appearance of the presenter. The advent of computers, color monitors, and high-quality laser printers is raising document standards. "Plain Jane" documents that were considered acceptable several years ago are the unprofessional blue jeans and T-shirt look of today.

Here are some ways training professionals can enhance the look of their handouts and their own image at the same time.

- *Reproduce visuals, and provide space to take notes.* It's difficult for participants to copy a visual and absorb key messages at the same time. By reproducing the visual image on paper, trainees can spend more time listening to the presenter and take notes on information that will help them retain the content.
- *Use charts and graphs to reinforce key messages.* Graphics improve the comprehension of underlying principles and maintain a viewer's interest. Modern word-processing programs support most common business graphics, such as bar and pie charts.

More detailed line drawings and even photographic images can be imported into a file if the subject warrants. Service and operations manuals are just one example where top-quality graphics are a necessity.

- *Design training materials to be convenient reference tools.* Most training materials will be used not only during the course, but also for subsequent reference. It's important that the manual's organization and indexing method make it easy to look up specific subjects.

NovaCare, a national provider of specialty health services, uses several indexing techniques to speed retrieval. In addition to a table of contents at the front of the book, each tab page contains a more detailed table of contents.

"Those manuals are designed so that a reader can open the book, select the appropriate subject matter based on the tab or introductory index, and then find the specific page number based on the second contents listing that includes all subcategories," says Paige Marks, NovaCare's training center supervisor.

"Workers don't have time to scan an entire chapter to find the desired topic, and it's inconvenient to flip back and forth to the table of contents in a two-inch manual. Many participants report that it's much faster and easier to find answers to their questions with that additional indexing feature," she says.

Home Depot has designed some of its product training materials to fit in aprons worn by associates on the floor. Additional reference materials, such as measurement guides and dictionaries, are included at the back of each book, explains Diane Linke, manager of training support services.

- *Use color to accelerate learning.* Color is the ideal companion to all training materials, from overhead transparencies to handouts. Market research indicates that color can increase learning and retention by up to 78 percent. Because color makes documents more attractive, it also increases readership by 40 percent.

  When we talk about color, we're also talking about cost. Color reproduction is undeniably more expensive than black-and-white, but it's not necessary to produce full-color images on every page of a document. Judicious use of color can achieve all benefits at an affordable, incremental cost. Consider, for example, printing chapter headings in a color. Or highlight key sentences in a single color so viewers can easily find the key points.

  To be understood, many graphics demand color. You can ask your printer to produce pages with full-color images or graphs on a color laser printer and collate those pages into the document before it's bound. That method will give you color images at an affordable price.

- *Customize content as much as possible.* Each training manual should contain materials specific to the topic or employees' responsibilities. Modem network printing options make it possible to generate high-quality materials in extremely small quantities. Desktop computers make it fast and easy to cut and paste content electronically. There's no reason to issue a 150-page manual when only 50 pages pertain to the subject. Any additional cost from customization can be at least partially offset by reducing the total volume. In the case of training materials, bigger is not better.

- *Put the recipient's name on the cover.* Nothing impresses an attendee more than seeing his or her name on the cover of a manual or booklet. That simple action almost guarantees that a participant will value and use the manual. It also conveys the message that the training department or company views each participant as an individual. A personalized approach is especially important for middle- and upper-level managers.

  Creative cover designs make personalization an affordable option. Full-color covers can be printed on stock with a die-cut window in the upper center. The names of the individual and company are printed on plain paper so that they show through the window.

- *Develop a guide for presenters.* Creating a separate guide for facilitators provides helpful prompts and ensures that all presenters use a consistent approach. The training department at NovaCare has designed a workbook template for participants and leaders. In the facilitator guide, visuals occupy two-thirds of the page; the remaining third lists prompts and key messages to accompany each visual. The participant workbook is created from the facilitator guide by eliminating the prompts to allow space for participants to record their notes.

- *Make manual covers distinctive.* Many employees have several manuals on their desk. The cover and spine marking should quickly distinguish the content of each manual. At Home Depot, cover designs and color-coded spine markings distinguish one type of manual from another.

- *Choose a binding method that's durable and convenient.* Many companies are switching from three-ring binders to spiral binding for smaller booklets. Participants say that the spiral-bound books are lighter and easier to use. For large manuals, binders remain the favorite choice because they are long-lasting.

- *Make sure your supplier can accommodate last-minute changes.* Digital printing systems let presenters make changes to materials up to a day or hours before a class is held. Allowing a week for production is no longer necessary. In general, suppliers should be able to support one- or two-day turnaround on routine jobs.

Successful trainers use the capabilities of modern digital printing systems to improve the content and appearance of training materials. Professional manuals and handouts create an upscale image for the training company, and earn the respect of internal and external customers. Isn't that worth a few pennies a page?

Karen Kelty is director of marketing at XYAN, a printing and imaging center in King of Prussia, Pennsylvania. Karen Kelty credits her brain as her most valuable work tool and predicts that e-commerce will be the norm in one to three years.

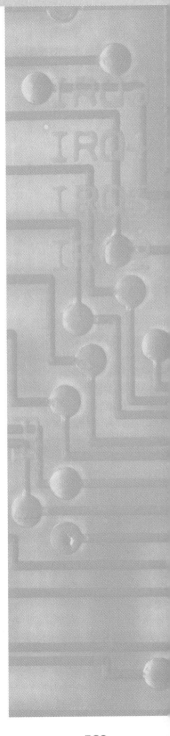

16

Proposals

CHAPTER 16 IN BRIEF

Characterizing Proposals

Proposals attempt to convince an audience that a proposed plan fulfills a need while being workable, manageable, logically organized, and cost efficient. Sometimes proposals offer a range of possibilities, each evaluated according to the same criteria.

Proposals can have one of several purposes: to solve a problem, to investigate a subject, or to sell a product or service.

Types of Proposals. Solicited proposals are written in response to an RFP (a request for proposal). Unsolicited proposals are written in response to a perceived need rather than to an RFP.

Sources of RFPs. RFPs are issued by several organizations: research and nonprofit foundations, educational institutions, government agencies, and private business and industry.

Using Persuasion in Proposals

Your analysis and response to audience needs, awareness of your own credibility, and attention to logic go a long way in building a case that wins approval.

Preparing Proposals

Like any writing task, preparing a proposal benefits from your awareness of the writing process—managing, planning, drafting, evaluating, and revising.

Organizing Proposals

Proposals can be presented in a variety of formats, ranging from an informal, one-page memo to a business letter to an extensive formal document of perhaps several hundred pages. The following sections usually occur in this sequence:

- The introduction defines and substantiates the problem and provides an overview of the solution or plan.
- The background section situates the problem.
- The technical solution gives readers the details of the plan.
- The management section explains how the plan will be implemented.
- The budget provides specific information about all costs.
- The schedule identifies when things are going to happen.
- The evaluation section provides details about how progress will be monitored and how success will be determined.
- The final section is often a boilerplate presentation of the structure and capabilities of the proposing organization and the resumes of key personnel to implement the proposal.

Examining a Sample Proposal

A sample proposal illustrates many of the points in this chapter.

P roposals occur in a variety of situations, as the following list suggests:

- The U.S. Department of Energy is willing to fund plans for research that investigates the practicality of biomass as an energy source.

- The Kellogg Foundation is willing to fund plans for research that proposes nontraditional approaches to agriculture.

- Media Designs' warehouse for storing damaged and returned goods is overflowing. The manager, Judith Greene, meets with a business consultant, Donald Ayers, to discuss the problem and identify the goal that she has in mind.

- Mark Garcia, a drafter for Richardson Technology, Inc., believes that a CAD (computer-assisted design) system would increase the productivity of the drafting department. The department manager, Warren DeSola, is willing to hear what Mark has to say.

All of these cases result in the development and submission of proposals. The U.S. Department of Energy and the Kellogg Foundation solicit input through a published *request for proposal* (RFP). Donald Ayers submits to Media Designs a proposal to develop a plan for managing its warehouse full of damaged and returned goods. At Richardson Technology, Inc., Mark Garcia writes an unsolicited proposal to assess the potential benefits of using CAD equipment.

In each situation, the readers—the decision makers—have certain expectations about the proposal they read. Typically they expect some or all of the following information to be included:

- ***Situation.*** Provide a definition of the *need* or *problem*, including information that situates the problem in the organization.

- ***Plan.*** Present a plan for addressing the need or resolving the problem.

- ***Benefits.*** Explain probable benefits that will result from adopting the plan.

- ***Approach.*** Outline methods for implementing the plan, including management plans, schedule, and costs.

- ***Evaluation.*** Identify evaluation strategy for determining whether the proposed plan works.

- ***Qualifications.*** Establish your qualifications for submitting the proposal and implementing the plan.

Sometimes this information is presented in sections that correspond to the six categories; other times, the information is combined into fewer sections. The selection and focus of the information depend on the purpose and audience for the proposal.

In this chapter, you'll learn about preparing and organizing proposals, which differ in important ways from reports (which you will read about in Chapter 17). Reports are about information the writer already knows and things that have already happened; reports present an "answer." Proposals are about things that the writer wants to happen and offer ways to do those things; proposals suggest approaches to discover an "answer."[1]

Characterizing Proposals

As a form of persuasive writing, *proposals* attempt to convince an audience that a proposed plan or set of objectives addresses a problem or fulfills a need while being workable, manageable, logically organized, and cost efficient. As the list at the beginning of this chapter indicates, proposals range from responses to formal requests for proposals (RFPs) to unsolicited proposals to solve perceived problems. Proposals can have one of several purposes:

- ***Solve a problem***—The problems that proposals try to solve vary, from designing or manufacturing a mechanism to modifying a process or establishing a new business procedure.

- ***Investigate a subject***—An important part of technical communication in business and industry as well as in government and research institutions is generating investigative proposals for a variety of projects.

- ***Sell a product or service***—Sales proposals offer a service or product, providing the potential customer with information needed to make a decision.

Which kind of proposals are you likely to need to write or contribute to in your professional work?

In this section, you'll read about differences between solicited and unsolicited proposals as well as about sources of RFPs (requests for proposals).

Types of Proposals

A *solicited proposal* is written in response to an RFP. When an organization turns to an outside source to address a problem, it issues an RFP that identifies all of the specifications the proposal must fulfill in order to be accepted. The requirements and restrictions in RFPs vary according to the needs of the issuing organization. Since an RFP provides the specifications for the proposal, a successful proposal writer adheres to the RFP. Some RFPs even indicate a point value assigned to each section, so a proposal writer can emphasize those sections most important to the organization that issued the RFP.

When the need that stimulated the RFP is actually a product or service, the solicited proposal may also be called an invitation to bid, a bid request, a purchase request, an invitation for proposal, or a request for quotation (RFQ). RFPs, RFQs, and similar requests are usually external documents, directed to and responded to by people outside an organization.

Sometimes a problem exists but no one issues an RFP. A person who identifies the problem and has the skill or experience to solve it may submit an *unsolicited proposal*. Thus, an unsolicited proposal is written in response not to an RFP but to a perceived need. Unsolicited proposals are often internal documents, responses to a perceived need by someone in an organization.

Under what circumstances would you submit an unsolicited proposal? Would you be inclined to discuss your plans with your supervisor before you submitted it?

Sources of RFPs

RFPs are not always sent to every organization or company that might want to respond, so an interested person might be unaware of a particular RFP. However, because approved proposals are a potential source of income for business and funding for human services organizations, an enterprising individual should seek RFPs pertinent to corporate or organizational objectives. The acceptance of a proposal means the award of a contract or a financial grant.

RFPs are regularly issued by several organizations:

- research and nonprofit foundations
- educational institutions
- government agencies
- private business and industry

You can locate funding agencies and RFPs from a variety of sources, including university grant offices, which list available RFPs as well as assist in preparing the proposals.

Public, university, and corporate libraries usually have reference volumes that can assist you. For example, the *Annual Register of Grant Support* provides listings of grant programs and requirements for applications. The *Foundation Directory* lists more than 2,500 foundations that fund research. Another useful reference is the *Foundation Grants Index*.

The Grantsmanship Center publishes *The Whole Nonprofit Catalogue* three to four times a year. This catalog includes sources of funding for nonprofit organizations, a schedule of the Grantsmanship Center's training programs for grant writing, and a list of publications on proposal writing.

Other excellent resources that identify specific grant and contract announcements include these publications, available in libraries or university grant offices:

- *Catalog of Federal Domestic Assistance*
- *Commerce Business Daily*
- *Federal Grants and Contracts Weekly*

- *Federal Register*

- *Research Monitor News*

- *Research Monitor Profiles*

Figure 16.1 reproduces excerpts of grant and contract announcements that are in *Commerce Business Daily* that publishes, for federal agencies, synopses of proposed contract actions that exceed $25,000. Just these few announcements selected from various categories illustrate the tremendous number of possibilities:

- Develop and implement "a biennial system of gathering, analyzing and publishing information needed for the Special Supplemental Food Program for Women, Infants, and Children (WIC)" (Special Studies and Analyses—Not R&D)

- "Provide . . . information on reptiles and amphibians considered sensitive by USFWS or California Department of Fish and Game . . ." (Natural Resources and Conservation Services)

- "Provide labor, equipment, materials and transportation required to furnish fugitive emission inspection services . . ." (Quality Control, Testing, and Inspection Services)

FIGURE 16.1 ■ Excerpts from *Commerce Business Daily*[2]

A Research and Development—Potential Sources Sought

National Renewable Energy Laboratory, Subcontracts Section, M/S 6320-17/2, 1617 Cole Boulevard, Golden, CO 80401-3393
A—RESEARCH AND DEVELOPMENT SOURCES SOUGHT—ECONOMIC DEVELOPMENT THROUGH BIOMASS SYSTEMS INTEGRATION Synopsis No. 3-230. Contact Doug Mourning, Staff Subcontract Administrator (303)231-7055, George Honold, Contracting Officer/Manager, Subcontracts Section (303)231-1290. The National Renewable Energy Laboratory (NREL) anticipates issuing a Letter of Interest (LOI) for feasibility studies to determine the technical, environmental and economic viability of integrated biomass production and conversion systems. The project, entitled "Economic Development through Biomass Systems Integration" will have two components (A) liquid fuels, and (B) electricity production. Respondents to this synopsis will receive a Letter of Interest which provides a general statement of work addressing both components of the project. Multiple awards, on a cost-sharing basis, are anticipated as a result of the LOI. The goal of the project will be to evaluate proposed combinations of Dedicated Feedstock Supply Systems (DFSS) with conversion technologies producing either electricity, liquid fuels, or combinations there[...] and to prep[...] project/busi[...] outlining[...]ry d[...]

B Special Studies and Analyses—Not R&D

USDA, Food and Nutrition Service, Contracts Management Branch, 3101 Park Center Drive, Room 914, Alexandria, VA 22302
B—STUDY OF WIC PARTICIPANT AND PROGRAM CHARACTERISTICS—PC94-PC96 SOL FNS 93-026LY DUE 080593 POC LINDA YOUNG, CONTRACT SPECIALIST (703) 305-2250, ELAINE S. LYNN, CONTRACTING OFFICER (703) 305-2250. The U.S. Department of Agriculture, Food and Nutrition Service (FNS) plans to award a contract to further develop and implement a biennial system of gathering, analyzing and publishing information needed for the Special Supplemental Food Program for Women, Infants, and Children (WIC). Public Laws 99-500 and 99-591 enacted in 1986 require FNS to submit a biennial report on WIC participant and program characteristics to Congress. The legislation specifies that this report include: (1) the income and nutritional risk characteristics of participants in the program; (2) participation in the program by members of families of migrant farm workers; and (3) such other matters relating to participation in the program as the Secretary (of Agriculture) considers appropriate. The study for 1994 and the option for study in 1996 will build upon the WIC minimum data set which is collected through ongoing manag[...] in[...]of WIC state agen[...]

D Automatic Data Processing and Telecommunication Services

Naval Undersea Warfare Center Division, Newport Commercial Acquisition Department, Code 09, Building 11, Newport, RI 02841-1708
D—SERVICES SOL N66604-93-R-C136 DUE 071993 POC Contact H. Marsocci, Contracting Officer, at 401/841-2442 X274. The Naval Undersea Warfare Center Division, Newport RI requires a dedicated, turnkey, gateway system to connect NUWCnet (Internet network 129.190) to the Internet regional network, National Science Foundation Network (NSFnet), via a T! communications line. Provide network support services, as well as, an Internet protocol router and its required interfaces to serve as a gateway between the local network (NUWCnet) and the T! communications line. The period of performance shall be for one year, anticipated to begin 01 Oct 93, with four additional option years.—All responsible sources may submit an offer which will be considered. Requests must be made in writing, specifying solicitation number; telephone requests will not be honored. (0155)

You can also identify possible sources of funding through computerized databases that use a keyword system to help you locate grant announcements for research in specific areas. Most university grant offices offer assistance in computerized searches.

Using Persuasion in Proposals

To write effective proposals, you need to understand persuasive techniques. Effective use of such techniques helps convince the nonprofit foundation, educational institution, government agency, or private business to approve or accept your proposal. Essentially you're establishing agreement about the situation—that is, the *problems* that need to be addressed—and you're posing a *plan* to address the problems and identifying *benefits* that will accrue if your plan is adopted. The process of preparing a proposal is like a refined debate, with you imagining, anticipating, and responding to opposing arguments.

Traditionally, persuasion has been identified with emotion and, therefore, has sometimes been viewed as inappropriate for technical communication. The actual practice of technical communication is quite different from this "unemotional" model: There is always a persuasive element. Persuasion does not connote manipulation; rather, it applies credible, logical argument to convince readers that the writer's view is appropriate. Readers who develop positive attitudes toward the subject of a proposal are more likely to accept that proposal.

Technical communicators have a responsibility to produce proposals that are credible, logical, and ethical. Three factors influence the success of persuasion:[3]

- the needs of readers

- the credibility of the persuader

- the logic of the message

What are the ethics of using what are popularly called propaganda techniques *(fallacious appeal to authority, appeal to pity, appeal to emotion, question begging, slanting, etc.) in preparing a proposal?*

Clearly proposals have strong persuasive elements. In what ways are other kinds of technical documents also persuasive?

Readers' Needs

The readers must have some sense of need in order to agree with the changes advanced by a proposal. Part of your job as a proposal writer is to identify this need for readers. You can identify the readers' needs by conducting a careful audience analysis, assessing receptivity and resistance. (Refer to Chapter 3 to review the elements of audience analysis.) Once their needs have been determined, you can take time to think about how you will meet those needs.

The more sweeping the changes you advocate, the greater the readers' need must be and the more completely the proposal must establish the need and then substantiate the validity of the changes. This is one of the single most important aspects of preparing a proposal: Establish that the need or problem exists and then clearly show how your plan eliminates the problem.

Understanding why readers react the way they do to new material in a proposal may help you write more persuasively. Theorists in psychology and communication believe that people reject or at least devalue information that conflicts with their current beliefs. As a writer, you will find that this principle— called *cognitive dissonance*—has important, practical applications. The more readers adhere to existing beliefs, the less likely they are to accept proposed changes.

In your proposal, you can negate the effects of cognitive dissonance by suggesting to your readers why the change will be beneficial. After you identify elements that may cause anxiety in readers, offer a solution that dissipates the anxiety. Explain how the solution meets the readers' needs and thus results in a decision that benefits the organization as well as the decision maker.

Persuaders' Credibility

After you have established the need or problem, you must develop your credibility. If readers believe that you are trustworthy and competent, then you have *credibility*. You gain credibility through a variety of qualities: technical expertise, favorable reputation, corporate status, values similar to those of the readers, and characteristics in your writing that show you to be understanding, well informed, carefully organized, articulate, and fair minded.

The importance of credibility has been substantiated in research, clearly demonstrating that in many situations credibility is the single most important factor in awarding contracts. For example, some firms choose a vendor on the basis of reliability for delivery and reputation for integrity—before they consider cost. Similarly, your credibility may be the deciding factor in the approval of your proposal.

The more far-reaching or expensive the changes that you have proposed, the more credibility you must have if the proposal is to be seriously considered. In fact, credibility is so important that gaining the support of a person with higher credibility than yours increases the likelihood that a proposal will be accepted. Although this is a political issue, you should be aware that it can affect the acceptance or rejection of your ideas.

Additional aspects of a writer's credibility are addressed in the ethics sidebar on the next page. The Food and Drug Administration has had so many difficulties with authorship that this federal agency has proposed a rule that restricts authorship of proposals submitted to the FDA to scientists. See if you agree.

Logic of Message

After readers' needs and your credibility are established, you should make sure a proposal is logical. First, your document must be based on sound assumptions. Then you should build a reasonable case that explains and relates audience needs to your proposed plan, supporting each point with valid, reliable evidence. In addition to presenting a logical case, you also need to acknowledge and

"The odor of mendacity": Ethics and Skillful Writing

In 1992, the Food and Drug Administration proposed the following rule:

> Independent scientific and educational articles about a company's drug or directly competing drugs should not be written by medical writers employed by the firm, including freelance writers hired by the firm for specific projects. In addition, medical writers employed by the firm should not ghostwrite, edit, or otherwise influence the content of articles, purporting to be independent, on the company's drugs or directly competing products written by others.[4]

Researcher Edmond Weiss argues that the goal of this proposed rule is to have scientists, not professional writers, compose certain drug documents. This rule, Weiss argues, comes from the suspicion that professional medical writers cannot be trusted to write objectively: medical writers "overstate the virtues of their employer's products in a way that could not happen if scientists wrote the documents alone."[5] Why would professional medical writers be under this suspicion? Weiss believes this suspicion is founded on a cultural belief that "rhetoric is, to a considerable extent, the art of deception."[6] This suspicion can be traced to ancient texts on rhetoric; the philosopher Plato was particularly critical of rhetoric, labeling it as the art of flattery and deception. Since then, the implication has lingered that skillful, persuasive writing is untrustworthy.

Weiss believes that some corporate writing has unfortunately reinforced this belief. He refers to it as corporate mendacity—professional communication that is characterized by deception. He identifies three precepts that sustain corporate mendacity:

- The impulse to put things in the most favorable light
- The use of vague language to avoid acknowledging responsibility
- The belief in consistency and persistence over truth

Weiss acknowledges the strong social and cultural pressures on writing that can produce these ethical problems. He believes, however, that good ethical writing is possible if we focus on being just and fair: "We can insist that all writing be fair to the parties it affects."[7]

How can technical professionals avoid the problems Weiss identifies, such as when writing a persuasive proposal? Researchers Lori Allen and Dan Voss propose a checklist that technical professionals can use to focus on writing quality documents:[8]

1. *Accuracy.* Is it right?
2. *Balance.* Is it fair?
3. *Completeness.* Is it thorough?
4. *Correctness.* Is it mechanically sound?
5. *Consistency.* Is it stylistically uniform?
6. *Clarity.* Is it simple and easy to understand?
7. *Conciseness.* Is it brief and to the point?
8. *Coherence.* Is it easy to follow?
9. *Creativity.* Is it memorable?

Using these guidelines, Allen and Voss believe that technical professionals can help promote an image of writing as ethical and trustworthy.

How could you write a persuasive proposal without appearing to be manipulative?

Is the suspicion of skillful writing fair? How do you write an effective proposal to an audience that may feel this mistrust?

respond to opposing views. (Chapter 2 identifies other aspects of logic—fallacies that are likely to infiltrate a technical document.)

You can develop a sound argument and organize your ideas by reasoning, either inductively or deductively. *Induction* is reasoning from the particular to the general. You reach a conclusion about all of the members of a group after examining representative examples (as in the Gallup poll or the Neilsen ratings). *Deduction* is reasoning from the general to the specific. Traditionally, this reasoning takes the form of a syllogism: a major premise, a minor premise, and a logical conclusion.

Developing a strong proposal that persuades readers is easier if they believe you have advanced a strong plan to meet identified needs. Your analysis and response to audience needs, awareness of your own credibility, and attention to logic go a long way in building a case that wins approval.

Preparing Proposals

Preparing a good proposal is easier if you know why so many are turned down or rejected. The National Institutes of Health, a federal organization that funds a great deal of research, has published a list of the ten most common reasons that proposals submitted to them are disapproved. The reasons can be easily adapted to other kinds of proposals.[9]

- Lack of new or original ideas
- Diffuse, superficial, or unfocused research plan
- Lack of knowledge of published relevant work
- Lack of experience in the essential methodology
- Uncertainty concerning the future directions
- Questionable reasoning in the experimental approach
- Absence of an acceptable scientific rationale
- Unrealistically large amount of work
- Insufficient experimental detail
- Uncritical approach

Referring to these reasons and making sure none apply to your proposals may increase the chances that your document will be approved.

Preparing a proposal is also easier if you are familiar with the preparation process and know some of the guidelines that professionals find especially helpful. Like any writing task, preparing a proposal benefits from your awareness of the writing process—managing, planning, drafting, evaluating, and revising.

Although the steps are listed as if the process is linear, the process is in fact recursive—you repeat some steps several times as various stages of the process.

Of the five steps described for preparing a proposal, which ones are you skillful at doing? Which ones do you need to strengthen?

Managing

Preparing proposals will generally go more smoothly if you manage the project. The following guidelines should help:

- Be aware of deadlines. If possible, submit the proposal early.

- Establish an achievable schedule for completing the proposal.

- Know the review and evaluation procedure that will be used to assess the document.

- Analyze the background knowledge and experience of the intended readers/decision makers.

No matter how good the proposal you prepare, if it misses the deadline, it won't be considered. Many proposals for external funding have absolute deadlines: If a proposal is submitted after a certain time on a particular date, it won't be considered. Internal proposals usually don't have deadlines that are quite as rigid, but still need to be completed on time.

You also need to know the procedure that will be used for reviewing your proposal. Will the decision makers be experts about the subject? Will the reviewers have a very limited amount of time to evaluate the proposals? You can adjust things such as the amount and kind of details you choose to include in the document or its structure and design once you know the evaluators' background and the circumstances in which they'll be reading your document.

Planning

Once you have the project schedule established, you need to do a detailed review of what's expected by studying the RFP very carefully. The following guidelines should help your preliminary planning:

- Read and reread the RFP.

- Identify and substantiate the problem you are addressing.

- If at all possible, meet with the key people involved to discuss the need or problem.

- Propose a plan that addresses the need or responds to the problem.

- Organize the plan in an outline or a flowchart to help you create time schedules and budgets.

- Know the evaluation criteria that will be used to determine acceptance or rejection.

- Analyze probable competition.

- Consult with colleagues to receive feedback about the plan.

- Create a manageable budget for implementing the proposal.

Note the specifications that are identified in the RFP, paying special attention to the proposal structure that is expected and the evaluation criteria that will be used. Keep track of the names and numbers of people to contact to discuss your plan—and call them. They very often have extremely useful information that will help you shape the proposal.

You may need to spend time documenting the need or problem. Even if you *know* the need or problem exists, you should take the time to find supporting evidence. After you have defined and substantiated the problem, you can start to rough out a plan that resolves the problem. As you develop this plan, make sure that it fits the evaluation criteria established in the RFP. For example, is low cost a prime consideration, or is ease of implementation more important? When your plan is on paper, you should take a little time to imagine what competitive proposals may suggest. How is your plan better?

Budgets are another critical consideration. You may have developed a wonderful plan, but have you considered how much it will cost to implement? Costs include obvious things such as facilities, personnel, and equipment, but they also include less obvious things such as utility expenses and support services. Many organizations have experts whose primary job is to help develop budgets for projects.

Drafting

When you're ready to begin drafting the proposal, you need to turn again to the RFP. Follow the recommended structure or sequence of information. In general, these guidelines may help you during drafting:

- If an RFP exists, follow it exactly. If no recommended format exists, use the generic one presented in this chapter.

- Establish a clear link between the problem you have identified and substantiated and the plan that you are proposing to solve the problem.

- Provide information about the implementation of your plan: Who? When? How? Where? How much?

- Anticipate and address potential objections.

- Support your generalizations with specific details and examples. Cite your sources.

- Use a "you-attitude" when possible and appropriate (see the following paragraphs).

While many RFPs mandate a specific format, others do not. If no structure is recommended, first inquire if one is typically used in that particular business or organization or discipline. If no standard exists, then you can use the generic structure for a proposal that is presented in this chapter.

You can't assume that what you see as an obvious relationship between the problem and your proposed solution is obvious to everyone else. You need to make the connections clear. You also need to explain how your plan will be implemented: Who is involved? What is the schedule? What facilities will be needed? How much will the plan cost?

You can help readers accept your plan by anticipating their objections. What will they find confusing? What will they criticize? If you address potential objections and support your explanations with specific details and examples, you are more likely to convince readers. Another way you can help your cause is to adopt a "you-attitude," which emphasizes the attitudes and interests of readers. The emphasis moves from "I" to "you." Such an attitude requires that you identify with readers and understand their perspectives.

Evaluating

Once the draft is done, you need to evaluate it, trying to view it the same way as the intended audience. The following guidelines may be useful at this stage:

- Determine if RFP/RFQ directions have been followed.
- Determine if the draft meets or exceeds the criteria for evaluation.
- Examine accuracy of technical content.
- Study feasibility of the plan.
- Review acceptability of cost.
- Solicit reviews of the draft from colleagues.

This evaluation is the document-testing phase. One of the most difficult things will be building time enough into the process to actually review and evaluate your proposal. This is also a time to assess whether your document is persuasive. As the previous section of this chapter urged, ask whether you have responded to the readers' needs, established your own credibility, and built a logical case.

Revising

Your own careful evaluation of the draft as well as feedback from other reviewers will give you ideas for revising the proposal. As you make this close-to-final pass through the document, check the following elements:

- Add, modify, or delete information to meet evaluation criteria.
- Make sure the sequence of points is parallel throughout the document.
- Check that the document is visually appealing.

The revision will give you another chance to check that the relationship between the problem and the plan is clearly established and that you have responded to the evaluation criteria in the RFP. You also need to check the various levels of edit (see Chapter 13) to catch any errors and inconsistencies that have eluded you and other reviewers. One easy place to slip up is having inconsistent wording or order in the table of contents, the summary or abstract, and the text of the document itself. Finally, you need to ensure that the design of the document makes all the information accessible.

Organizing Proposals

Proposals can be organized in a variety of ways and presented in a variety of formats, ranging from an informal, one-page memo to a business letter to an extensive formal document of perhaps several hundred pages. If you are not required to present your proposal in a specific sequence, the following one works in virtually all situations.

- The **introduction** describes the situation by defining and substantiating the need or problem. Unless the need or problem is clearly established, the plan will have no context; readers won't be able to assess whether the plan is appropriate if they don't know what it's intended to resolve. This section gives the background of the need or problem, often summarizing previous attempts to deal with the problem and reviewing current work that would make the plan acceptable.

- The **plan** gives readers the details about the specific ways in which the problem will be addressed—that is, it identifies objectives to be met.

- The **benefits** section explains probable benefits that should result from adopting the plan.

- The **approach** explains the *methodology* that will be used to implement the plan, the *management* of the plan, the *budget* (including specific information about all direct and indirect costs), and the *schedule*, which identifies when things will happen (the implementation, the milestones, the evaluation). Sometimes these are separate sections.

- The **evaluation** of the plan identifies ways to determine whether the proposed plan accomplished its objectives.

- The **qualifications** of the organization usually describes the proposers' capabilities and the structure of the proposers' organization, if any. It may include resumes of key personnel who will implement the plan. The qualifications section is often boilerplate—"canned," prewritten material that is used to save time when preparing this standard section of a proposal.

Figure 16.2 identifies components that are normally found in proposals. However, only the most formal proposals contain all of them; less formal proposals

FIGURE 16.2 ■ Components for Formal, Less Formal, and Informal Proposals

	Formal	Less Formal	Informal
Front Matter			
Title Page	•	•	
Table of Contents	•		
Abstract/Executive Summary	•		
Introduction			
Establish current situation	•	•	•
Define the problem	•	•	•
Provide evidence to substantiate problem	•	•	
Provide relevant background	•		
Plan			
Define proposed plan	•	•	•
Present objective of the plan	•	•	•
Discuss plan in relation to established criteria, standards, or specifications	•	•	
Benefits			
Explain probable benefits accruing from plan	•	•	•
Approach (may be separate sections)			
Methodology: Relate the plan's objective to specific tasks for achieving it	•	•	•
Schedule: Identify time for planning, implementation, and evaluation	•	•	•
Costs/Budget: Present direct and indirect costs for personnel, materials and supplies, and support services	•	•	
Management: Explain the administration, including organization and personnel	•		
Evaluation			
Assess progress in meeting plan objective	•		
Qualifications			
Consider capabilities of personnel and appropriateness of organization's experience, facilities, resources	•	•	
End Matter			
Appendix: Include supporting information useful to readers that would interrupt flow of the proposal's persuasive argument	•		
Sources Cited: Include references	•		

eliminate several components; informal ones eliminate even more. Also, a formal proposal contains more front matter, and it usually presents background information, organizational capabilities, and a summary, which are seldom included in less formal proposals. In contrast to the complexity of a formal proposal, informal proposals contain only essential material: an introductory statement, the technical solution, and a schedule. In most proposals, these components are easily identifiable, but they are often combined and reordered to meet the perceived needs of the audience.

The three general types of proposals mentioned earlier in the chapter—solving a problem, investigating a subject, and selling a product or service—have similar components, but their content varies in the introduction and the technical solution. Other sections, such as management, budget, and schedule, are less influenced by the type of proposal.

This section of the chapter provides examples of sections of a proposal so that you can see some of the ways one might be developed. All of these examples are taken from a student proposal. The student, Sherry McGough, created a fictional company (Connections Stationery Recyclers) that had a realistic problem and a fictional consulting company (Capstone Consulting) to address the problem.

The section of Sherry's proposal that presents the *situation* provides background and defines the problem, including information that situates the problem in the organization. Sherry writes about her understanding of the current situation with Connections Stationery Recyclers so that Hannah Frantz, the manager, will know that Sherry and her colleagues understand the problem they're dealing with.

■ **EXAMPLE**

The situation stimulating the proposal is clearly explained.

Over the past five years, the market for recycled paper products has steadily expanded with growing consumer concern for the environment. In response to this movement, Connections Stationery Recyclers has successfully met the marketplace's demands with its new lines of office paper products to complement its personal stationery line. The move in the last two years into professional papers, combined with dedication to excellence, has positioned Connections Stationery Recyclers to successfully enter the markets of its competitors: Hallmark, Office Depot, and Office Max. Like the competition, Connections has benefited from the changing attitudes about recycling. . . .

In spite of the optimistic outlook for Connections' financial future, profits in 2000 and 2001 reflect a decline from the late 1990s. Connections' growth has forced rapid expansion of the professional staff. Of necessity, Connections has recently hired directors of marketing and operations and a new vice president of sales, Sarah White, who doubled the marketing staff. The effectiveness of the professional staff is hindered, however, by a severe shortage of support personnel and office equipment.

As a result, Connections reports that deadlines are frequently missed, some support personnel stand idle while waiting for computer access, mass copying is being hired out of house, mistakes are being made, and customers are increasingly disappointed. The end product of this inefficiency is that sales are stagnant, employee morale is slumping, and the company is suffering a marked—though assumed temporary—financial downturn.

Sherry is proposing to develop a *plan* for Connections Stationery Recyclers (rather than proposing a finished plan for the company to consider). In the next section of her proposal, she raises questions that identify what will be addressed in the plan she and her colleagues hope to develop. These questions show a clear understanding of the situation and the problems that need to be addressed.

■ **EXAMPLE**

Connections Stationery Recyclers needs a plan to increase efficiency by enabling the support staff to better serve the needs of the professional staff. The plan developed by Capstone Consulting will answer key questions like these:

- Should Connections purchase new computer hardware and copiers or lease this equipment?

- Would it be better to hire temporary employees, or should Connections hire more permanent support staff members?

- Is flex-time an alternative that the Connections' support staff would embrace?

- Is the best solution some combination of these options?

Questions that will shape the plan that will be completed if the proposal is accepted are listed.

In this next section of her proposal, Sherry focused on the approach she and her colleagues at Capstone will use as they develop a plan to address the problems at Connections Stationery Recyclers. (In other parts of the proposal, Sherry and her colleagues also deal with the schedule and budget.)

■ **EXAMPLE**

Connections needs a plan that will answer the key questions, thereby enabling management to select the best plan to increase the support staff's efficiency in meeting the needs of the professional staff. To develop an effective plan, we propose the following eight tasks:

- *Confirm Connections' long-term financial forecast.* We will confirm Connections' market-share projections.

- *Confirm the current staffing.* We will specify the number of professional and support personnel and their responsibilities, salaries, and needs.

- *Define current equipment situation.* We will complete an equipment inventory of computers and copiers and track use during the workday. (This will let us identify a number of problems including maintenance, outdated software, malfunctions.) . . . (*The proposal itself included all eight tasks.*)

Tasks that will be completed if the proposal is accepted are defined.

Sherry includes a section in the proposal that presents the *qualifications* of Capstone Consulting as an organization and of the individuals on the consulting team that would work with Connections Stationery Recyclers if they accept the proposal.

■ EXAMPLE

Qualifications of the organization and individuals involved are presented.

Connections Stationery Recyclers faces a challenge as it continues to expand its market while working to solve problems with support staff and equipment shortages. Capstone Consulting is prepared to quickly complete our study and provide Connections with meaningful, money-saving, and efficiency-producing recommendations.

Since 1981, Capstone Consulting has built a client base of more than 75 manufacturing firms in the Midwest. In 2001, our company plans to complete 22 consulting projects; two of those involved businesses with staffing dilemmas similar to yours.

Upon winning the consulting contract with Connections Stationery Recyclers, Capstone Consulting will immediately schedule a team of specialists to work with you and your vice presidents, Bob Sturm and Sarah White. Together we will develop a plan to increase the efficiency of Connections. Our experienced team will include Susan Booker, Lee-Ann Kastman, and myself.

Susan was part of the consulting team that worked last year with a business hampered by a staffing problem. A former director of sales for a national office-supply chain, Susan has excellent insight into the forces at work within an expanding professional staff like yours and a keen awareness of budget restrictions.

Lee-Ann is one of the original partners in our firm, bringing 15 years of experience to investigating and interpreting complex situations like the one Connections now faces. . . . (*The proposal itself presented information about each team member.*)

Sherry decides to conclude her proposal with a section presenting the *benefits* that will probably accrue if Connections Stationery Recyclers accepts the proposal from Capstone Consulting. She believes that ending with benefits will leave a positive image in the mind of Hannah and other readers at Connections.

■ EXAMPLE

Benefits resulting from accepting the proposal are enumerated.

The collaboration of Connections Stationery Recyclers and Capstone Consulting will create a powerful and winning team that will enable Connections to solve the problems that stand in the way of reaching 2002 revenue goals. . . .

Part of our study will involve surveying your support staff. The outcome of this process will be a clear sense of their perception of problems. Equally important, your staff will have the opportunity to express their opinions. Studies show that employees who are allowed input into the future of an organization respond with a sense of teamwork and ownership that renews interest, enthusiasm, and energy for their jobs. Better employee attitudes and work habits translate to fewer errors and higher productivity.

Once the study has been conducted, we will generate a report that will contain these elements:

- A market forecast for Connections in relation to the recycled-paper industry

- An account of the factors affecting the support staff and equipment use

- Specific comparisons of costs and benefits of the options open to Connections

- An implementation plan that specifies tasks, resources, evaluation criteria, and scheduling.

We are certain that once you implement our plan, the situation at Connections will improve. Improved employee morale and working conditions will result in increased production and more professional performance.

Examining a Sample Proposal

Proposals are usually intended for management personnel or external readers and may range from four or five to several hundred pages. Figure 16.3 is an unsolicited internal proposal that offers a plan to merge two departments in a company. As you read this proposal, you should consider ways in which it could be improved.

FIGURE 16.3 ■ Internal Unsolicited Proposal

PROPOSED MERGER:
MECHANICAL ASSEMBLY WITH FINAL ASSEMBLY[10]

Submitted to
Brian Donnelly
Manager, Production
Cybertronics, Inc.

Prepared by
Craig Wilder
Supervisor, Mechanical Assembly
Cybertronics, Inc.
October 27, 20—

PROPOSAL ABSTRACT

The cost and inconvenience of moving an entire department must always be weighed against the long-term benefits to be derived from such a move. Both the company and the employee could benefit from moving the Mechanical Assembly line from its current building into the Final Assembly area. Valuable work space would be better utilized, opening up the much needed space for new products scheduled for production. The move would also reduce handling and shipping costs, cross-train employees, and reduce overhead by 50 percent.

FIGURE 16.3 ■ *Continued*

PROPOSED MERGER:
MECHANICAL ASSEMBLY WITH FINAL ASSEMBLY

THE SITUATION AT CYBERTRONICS

Understanding the proposed merger requires a review of recent sales history at Cybertronics, a clear statement of the space problem, and an explanation of the differences between the Mechanical Assembly and Final Assembly areas.

History

For the past seven years, Cybertronics has been a leader in the ink jet printer industry. This success is largely because of the company's model 800 series printers. This product line has been the heart of the company's revenue growth and rapid expansion. Five years ago Cybertronics was shipping 300 units per day of 800 series products alone. Today, however, Cybertronics is shipping only 75 series 800 printers per day. The forecast ramps down to 50 per day in three months, and the backlog for sales is soft for the next fiscal quarter. Cybertronics is shifting away from the series 800 products and emphasizing the new product lines.

How effective is the writer in describing the situation, including defining and substantiating that problem?

Statement of Problem

Two new products going into production need the space, tools, and equipment now used for older products. Specifically, the Mechanical Assembly and Final Assembly areas need more space.

The current locations of the Mechanical Assembly and Final Assembly areas do not make efficient use of space. Space is being wasted in both areas, as Table 1 shows. Combining the Mechanical Assembly area and the Final Assembly area would free approximately 14,500 square feet.

TABLE 1
Allocation of Space in Mechanical Assembly and Final Assembly

AREA	SPACE		
	Available	Used	Unused
Mechanical Assembly	14,500 sq ft	8,000 sq ft	6,500 sq ft
Final Assembly	13,000 sq ft	7,000 sq ft	6,000 sq ft

Displaying square footage in a table emphasizes the inefficient use of space in both assembly areas.

FIGURE 16.3 ■ *Continued*

Background

At present, the two assembly areas are operated in different ways. The Mechanical Assembly area has a conveyor that is automatically timed to advance one unit every $3^1/_2$ minutes. The assembly line has nine different positions, each with a certain job on mechanisms as they pass through that station. After a mechanism reaches the end of the line, it is a finished unit. This "progressive assembly line"—one mechanism every $3^1/_2$ minutes—is a steady flow that is easily controlled and very predictable. It is efficient for two reasons:

1. The mechanism moves to the worker rather than the other way around.
2. Each worker becomes specialized by repeating the same job.

Workers are rotated from job to job on a weekly basis to avoid boredom and excessive repetition.

In Final Assembly, on the other hand, mechanisms are unpackaged and put on a long conveyor line, about 20 at a time. When workers select (or are assigned) a task, they take the necessary tools, parts, and hardware and walk up and down the line doing their job. Each worker goes along at an individual rate; when all the jobs are done, the line is emptied and the process begins again. The process offers no incentive to work quickly because the mechanisms will stay on the line until everyone is done. A lot of time is wasted; a lot of effort is spent walking around and looking for tools and parts. The units are not finished one at a time but rather in batches of 20. This uneven flow makes predicting production speed nearly impossible; management has little control over the speed of production in the assembly area.

PROPOSED PLAN TO MERGE MECHANICAL ASSEMBLY AND FINAL ASSEMBLY

The proposed plan has specific goals and a clear way to reallocate available space.

Goals

The proposed plan has two goals:

1. Make more efficient use of space in manufacturing.
2. Provide space for the new products going into production.

Using numbered lists to present reasons for progressive assembly (here) and plan goals (below) helps readers understand and remember these critical parts of the proposal.

After reading about the situation at Cybertronics, what questions come to mind that you hope the writer considered in shaping a plan?

2-

FIGURE 16.3 ■ *Continued*

Reallocation of Space

Both the Mechanical Assembly and Final Assembly areas could fit into 13,000 square feet because some of the area now needed would not have to be used if the departments were combined. Most of this space saving comes from two areas:

1. Packing and shipping in Mechanical Assembly would be combined with receiving and unpackaging in Final Assembly.
2. Final Assembly could eliminate their entire storage location that is now being used to hold spare parts to fix defective mechanisms.

IMPLEMENTING THE PLAN

The 13,000 square feet could be saved by implementing the three following space-saving measures.

Space Saving Measure 1

The packing area could be nearly eliminated. At present we use about 1,500 square feet for packing mechanisms, holding them in a loading area while waiting for pickup. Final Assembly uses more than 500 square feet to receive and unpack mechanisms received from stock. Nearly all of the 2,000 square feet now allocated to packing, shipping, and receiving would be eliminated. A small area—less than 500 square feet—would still be needed for packing and shipping overseas and for occasional excess being moved into stock. In addition to the space savings, the overhead would be reduced.

Space Saving Measure 2

The storage space in Final Assembly that is now used to store spare parts to repair defective mechanisms would be totally eliminated. If there were one department containing both the mechanism build and the final build, then all the mechanism parts would already be in the department.

Space Saving Measure 3

To further reduce the materials handling requirements and inefficient use of space, we could join the two assembly-line conveyors and make them into one continuous flow of production.

What additional information would you need to know in order to accept this proposal?

The writer could increase the readers' retention of the information by creating new subtitles that identify each actual space-saving measure— for example, "Reducing the Packing Area" rather than "Space Saving Measure 1."

-3-

FIGURE 16.3 ■ *Continued*

Do these benefits seem convincing? Can you recommend any strategies to strengthen the benefits section?

BENEFITS OF IMPLEMENTING THE PROPOSED PLAN

Implementing the proposed plan would result in a number of benefits for Cybertronics.

Reduction in Supervision

If the two areas were combined, supervision overhead would be cut in half because there would be only one line and a smaller total work force; one supervisor could do an effective job.

Cross-Training

Cross-training requirements would also be an advantage. According to a manual, *Modern Supervisory Techniques,* when people become bored with their jobs, they are unmotivated. However, cross-training on new jobs sparks interest and, therefore, increases motivation. Additionally, the National Foreman's Institute's manual, the *NFI Standard Manual for Supervisors,* says that when employees understand the "big picture" of how their jobs affect the product and the company, they will have more pride in their work, improve the quality of their work, and increase their motivation. Combining the two assembly areas would provide many opportunities for cross-training, so employees could understand the entire assembly operation.

The writer needs to revise the entire benefits section so that the discussion of the benefits (above) corresponds exactly with the summary presented here.

Summary of Benefits

The combination of Mechanical Assembly and Final Assembly into a single area that uses progressive assembly has distinct benefits:

1. It frees space for new product line.
2. It increases productivity in Mechanical and Final Assembly.
3. It increases employee motivation.
4. It increases management control of production.
5. It lowers overhead and management costs.

-4-

End-of-Chapter
Recommendations for Technical Communicators

1. Locate funding agencies and RFPs from a variety of sources, including libraries and university grant offices.

2. Help readers understand the need or problem you have identified. The more sweeping the changes you advocate, the greater the readers' need must be and the more completely the proposal must establish the need and then substantiate the validity of the changes.

3. Develop your own credibility. The more far-reaching or expensive the changes that you have proposed, the more credibility you must have if the proposal is to be seriously considered.

4. Make sure your proposal is logically organized and supported.

5. As you prepare your proposal, take time to manage, plan, draft, evaluate, and revise.

6. Learn a generic form for proposals so that you can easily modify the format when you need to for specific situations.

   - Define and substantiate the problem and provide an overview of the solution or plan.
   - Situate the problem, summarizing previous attempts to deal with the problem.
   - Present a technical solution, including details of the plan.
   - Explain how the plan will be implemented.
   - Provide specific cost information.
   - Schedule the implementation, the milestones, the evaluation.
   - Evaluate how progress will be monitored and how success will be determined.
   - Describe your organization's capabilities and those of the key personnel who will implement the proposal.

Individual and Collaborative Assignments

1. **Identify a problem and propose a solution.** Work with a group or class-mates who are in the same academic field or department.
   (a) Identify a problem that you all agree with. Record the process or steps your group uses to identify the problem.
   (b) Propose a solution that you all agree upon. Record the process or steps the group uses to evaluate the proposed solution.

2. **Outline a proposal.** You need to persuade an engineering committee in your company to support and fund leaves of absence for employees to teach technical courses at City College. These four-month leaves enable the college to offer courses in state-of-the-art technology. Outline the proposal you could present to have the plan approved.

3. **Prepare an RFP.** Assume you represent a private foundation whose concern is to increase scholarship in and public support for foreign language capability (particularly for technical experts working for multinational companies). Prepare an RFP and decide to whom you will send it.

4. **Write a proposal.** In a small group, identify a need or problem in your school, community, or workplace. Develop a proposal that addresses the problem. Be sure that you speak with the people directly involved to learn more about the history of the problem, the solutions that have already been attempted, the restraints that must be considered, and so on. Direct your proposal to the decision maker(s) involved.

5. **Analyze resources for proposal writers.** Visit the following Web site: <http://www.kn.pacbell.com/wired/grants/>
   What kind of information does this site provide for writers of proposals? Analyze the rhetorical situation (audience, purpose, context) of this site, and determine whether you think it is effectively designed in terms of the rhetorical situation. For whom would this site be particularly useful? Search the Web on your own to discover other sites that might be useful to proposal writers.

Intertext

Goof-Proofing Your RFPs[11]

B̲e clear. Be concise. Ask the right questions. These are the requirements for requests for proposals (RFP) that hit the mark. Consider these tips, and get your next RFP on target.

The key to developing the right solutions is asking the right questions. Nowhere is that more true than in the request for proposals process. But asking the right questions is harder than it sounds, because doing so often requires knowledge and insight you may not have in-house—that's why you're seeking help from an outside specialist, right?

Therein lies the conundrum of the RFP. You have an idea of what the association needs to have accomplished by a vendor, but it usually takes the perspective of a professional to help refine your vision. So, how do you select that specialist via an RFP when your vision's a little cloudy?

Study Up
Consult internal sources to help zero in on the organizational outcome you want to achieve through hiring a vendor. Also, allow as many staff members as possible—even those individuals whose functions do not directly relate to the area in which you will be soliciting proposals— to suggest, critique, and help refine the process.

While developing RFPs, the American Association of Orthodontists, St. Louis, "gathers the entire management team and seeks input about what to include in the document and how to design the process," says John J. Terranova, director of finance and administration. By doing this, "we've found that we take advantage of the specific expertise of each member of the management team, and the process gives others in the organization a chance to play devil's advocate. I think that's always good."

Feel Free to Share
To get helpful proposals back from vendors, it is vital that you provide as much background information as possible about the organization in your RFP.

"Not providing enough information is one of the most common mistakes I see in RFPs," says Monica Dignam, president of Milwaukee-based Monalco, Inc., a market research firm that responds to many RFPs. Dignam sometimes helps her clients develop requests for proposals and says that the standard three- or four-sentence organizational overview many associations provide just doesn't do the job.

"The more detailed information the vendor receives about the [association], the more accurately the response can be customized to the needs of that organization," she points out. Conversely, if the association provides minimal, general data, it's more likely that the organization will get boilerplate responses that are poorly suited to its needs.

Providing this information is easier if you are submitting an electronic RFP.

597

Take advantage of technology and pull information about your association from existing documents. Use file attachments or Web hyperlinks to include the data in the proposal.

Give Vendors Some Power

Clearly conveying the product or service you need is one of the most challenging aspects of writing the goof-proof RFP. But too many limitations in your specifications can create problems. Why? Because you may be depriving yourself of better solutions of which you—not being a specialist—are unaware. And because you may find, once you get what you said you wanted, that it doesn't solve the association's real problem at all.

Holly Townsend, president and chief executive officer of Association Publishers, Inc., Bethesda, Maryland, an association publication research firm, was once asked to conduct an editorial research study for a large health care association. "When we initially bid on the project, it was described in the RFP as a standard, four-page readership study aimed at providing data for a graphic redesign of their magazine," Townsend explains. In the process of creating the survey instrument, she met with several of the publication's staff members. During these conversations, "staff made it clear that their larger concerns had to do with editorial content rather than design. They felt certain that their take on what the magazine should be differed from what others in the organization wanted.

"As they aired these concerns, it became obvious that their real need was for a comprehensive publications audit," she recalls. "This required a series of studies that included focus groups and mailed studies, as well as several meetings with staff and leadership to address a wide range of concerns that went well beyond a visual face-lift."

What Townsend had expected to be a $10,000 study ended up as a vastly more complex and expensive project, with a price tag exceeding $30,000. "Luckily, our client realized that they had underestimated their needs just about the time that we did; they were willing to revisit the RFP and fund the larger project." But the situation could have been a disaster. Had Townsend delivered exactly what the association initially asked for, and no more, the group's needs would not have been met. At $10,000, that's an expensive lesson.

"That experience taught me how important it is for us to thoroughly interview prospective clients about their research goals prior to responding to RFPs. [By doing so], we can determine exactly what problems we are being hired to address. It doesn't hurt to understand who at the association is behind the decision to do the research, what their goals are, and how they intend to use the data. In most cases, many people within the organization use research studies; each may have slightly different goals. The challenge is to be sure that everyone's needs are being met."

The American Association of Orthodontists' Terranova avoids such problems by expressing his expectations of vendors in a flexible way. "Rather than say, 'Here's my problem and here's what I want to solve it,' I prefer to say, 'Here's my problem. Here's my goal. How would you achieve it?'" he explains. "We provide expectations for what we want to see addressed in the proposal so that there is some uniform basis for rating the

RFPs, but we want to give vendors a way to be creative and ourselves a way to draw on their expertise."

That kind of flexibility also allows associations to identify which vendors simply spew out standard language and which ones take the time to customize their responses. "We value customization," Terranova says. "It tells us that rather than just going through the motions, the vendor is making a serious effort to respond to our needs."

Be Cautiously Open-ended

"My biggest past mistake was not being sufficiently detailed in what I expected from the vendors," says Dave Dancy, marketing director, American Public Works Association, Kansas City, Missouri. "When I got all the responses back, they didn't really tell me anything because I couldn't compare apples to apples." Thus, he ended up creating extra work for himself because he had to call the vendors, re-explain his needs, and pull additional information from them.

"When you're relying on vendor expertise about process or product, tell them in the RFP that you're giving them such latitude and expecting them to make and support recommendations," he notes. "But if you're only expecting quotations on a mail survey, for example, then say so: If you're asking for their recommendations and costs for other membership survey approaches, say that, too."

The bottom line, Dancy says, is to make sure you provide enough information so that you will receive consistent responses from vendors—at least in core areas. Without that consistency, comparisons are virtually impossible. Such details include:

- A specific statement of the vendor's responsibility
- Whether travel will be required—if so, to where and how often
- Whether a board presentation is expected
- How you want the proposals organized
- What kinds of "collaterals" you're expecting (report, slide presentation, staff briefing, etc.)
- Details about every product and service you want priced

Take Two Steps

The RFP process doesn't have to be long and drawn out. A two-phase process can save you time and increase your understanding of what the association needs by involving vendors early.

Phase one of the process is a formal or informal screening of potential vendors based on their

- qualifications and credentials
- capabilities of staff including longevity and turnover—and equipment
- availability and scheduling needs
- products and services
- experience with other organizations of similar size and scope
- recommendations from other association executives

Winnowing the broad vendor field through this type of screening and reference check yields a more workable-sized group to which the RFPs will be sent. It also saves you time by limiting in-depth RFP evaluations to a small group of top contenders.

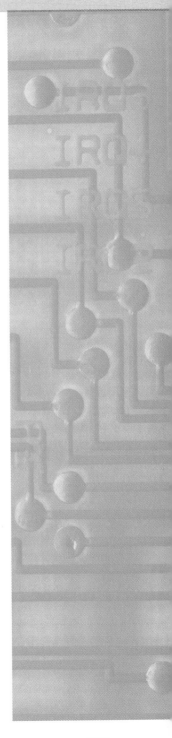

Though not appropriate in all cases, some associations take the intermediate step of inviting the selected group of vendors to a bidder's conference, which serves several purposes.

1. It allows the association to present its needs to all potential vendors at once.

2. It gives each bidder a chance to clarify his or her understanding of the association's needs by asking questions.

3. It lets the group know who their competitors are and how many people they're competing against.

4. By their participation in the conference—or lack thereof—it helps you determine which vendors are already focusing on the association's needs.

5. Via vendor questions and comments, it helps surface information you can use in drafting a more effective RFP.

Kathleen Berry, CAE, vice president, finance and administration, of Associated Builders and Contractors, Rosslyn, Virginia, likes the idea of a bidder's conference. "It allows you a tremendous amount of give and take before you issue the RFP," she notes. "And whatever information you can get up front is always a good idea."

Phase one's focus on vendor track records and capabilities also gets at what Berry has found to be one of the worst mistakes she's seen associations make during the RFP process—not asking for enough information on the vendor's background. "You need to get references from both current and past clients. Get a complete client list if you can, and ask the vendor if you can check with anyone you want on that list. Then do it," she advises. "Otherwise, you'll get a sales job, which may not accurately depict the vendor's performance."

Issuing the RFP to the selected group starts *phase two* of the process— evaluation. If you've thoroughly checked references and held a bidder's conference, then this step should go smoothly. Terranova recommends that the entire management team comes together, once again, to independently score the proposals received based on the association's established criteria. "After the independent scoring, we have a give-and-take discussion about each proposal," he says. "This helps eliminate unintended biases."

However you decide to evaluate the proposals—with a single person, a management team, or a blended team of board and management members, following the suggestions in this article will ensure that you assess proposals on the same, consistent bases. Your RFP process will be efficient, professionally applied, and fair to all. And you will have given yourself the best chance to meet the association's true needs—and have quality vendors clamoring to participate in your next call for proposals.

RFP Musts and Mustn'ts

Creating a request for proposals can be a daunting process. Heed these tips to get you through it unscathed.

- Appoint an RFP coordinator to act as the point person for vendors and to keep the process on track.

- Disclose details about the RFP evaluation process, including the timetable, confidentiality expectations, judging criteria, and so forth.

- Return all telephone calls related to the RFP process and promptly notify all vendors, in writing, of your selection. Keep in mind that even if you didn't pick a particular vendor this time out, you may need him or her in the future.

- Give vendors enough time to prepare a proposal that will meet your needs.

- For the most straightforward proposals allow at least two weeks. The more complex the proposal, the more time vendors will need.

- Don't give one vendor unintended advantages over another vendor. If you meet with one prospect, meet with them all. If you answer a question with additional or clarifying information for one person, share the information with everyone. For instance, if you get a question from a vendor by e-mail, use the carbon copy function to send the question and your answer to all vendors. Also, consider creating a frequently asked questions document.

- Don't harm your relationship with vendors by using the RFP process to test the market if you have no intention of awarding a contract. Vendors may not take you seriously the next time around.

RFP Resources

For proposal samples and tips, check out these Web sites:

- <www.doas.state.ga.us/Department/ AUDIT/index/dept/med/rfpguide.htm>

- <www.enginered.com/writing_an_ rfp.html>

- <www.asaenet.org/Sections/ technology/rfp_aan_computer_ online.htm>

- <www.acs.utah.edu/purchasing/ genrfp.htm>

- <www.cybercow.com/html/how-to_ rfp.html>

- <www.nctweb.com/columns/ writerfp.html>

- <www.maine.edu/admin/stsys/ isisuser/sisrfp/sisrfp.all.htm>

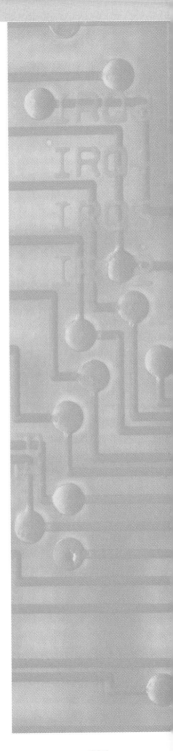

17

Reports

CHAPTER 17 IN BRIEF

Preparing reports will make up a major portion of the writing you do.

Differentiating Informal and Formal Reports

Informal report are usually for readers with whom you're in regular contact; formal reports are usually for readers with whom you have less contact.

Purposes and Characteristics of Reports

Reports typically have three main purposes: to report information, to analyze information, to persuade readers. Many kinds of reports follow the same sequence, modified for each report: overview, background, recommendations, evidence, discussion.

Planning a Report

Identify Audiences. Knowing about the readers helps you determine a report's purpose and organization.

State Purpose. Writing a purpose statement gives you a clear focus for a report and provides a way for you to control content, format, and organization.

Organizing Informal Reports

Informal reports generally fall into these categories:

- task reports
- periodic activity reports
- progress reports
- meeting minutes

- trip and conference reports
- "to file" documents

Formats of Reports

Reports can be presented as prepared forms, memos, letters, and formal reports.

Organizing Formal Reports

Deductively organized reports usually use a two-tiered approach:

1. Give an overview and then summarize the preferred solution.

2. Cite evidence or support for the solution in descending order of significance, dealing with both positive and negative points.

You'll need to modify the generic report format (front matter, body, end matter) as well as the format elements (headings, pagination, and visuals) presented in this chapter to suit the needs of specific situations.

Examining a Sample Report

A technical report illustrates features of effective reports.

R eports account for a substantial amount of writing in business, industry, government, and nonprofit organizations. In fact, unless writing is your primary job, preparing reports and correspondence (discussed in Chapter 14) will make up most of the writing you do. This chapter differentiates informal and formal reports, examines the purposes and characteristics of reports, suggests ways to plan and design them, and then discusses specific types and formats of informal and formal reports.

Differentiating Informal and Formal Reports

Reports can be described on a continuum from informal to formal. The primary differences have to do with the writer's familiarity with the audience, the amount of documentation in the report, and the tone.

Generally, if the organizational roles of the writer and reader(s) are close, an informal report is often more appropriate than a formal report. Usually you write an informal report if you have regular contact with your readers because it's likely that they already know the background. As a result, the need for intensive documentation and detail is sidestepped. This regular contact also means that your tone can be informal; however, informal doesn't mean chatty and personal. Informal reports can be written as memos, letters, or short reports (without front matter or end matter).

In contrast, writers of formal reports probably don't have regular contact with their readers. Because the readers may not be familiar with the background, it needs to be included in formal reports, usually making the reports longer and more detailed. These reports need more documentation because the readers may not know the history or sources. Formal reports generally adhere closely to strict conventions of language. Most formal reports also have a number of standard sections: front matter such as an abstract and table of contents, end matter such as references and appendices.

Because of the extensive front matter in a formal report, it tends to repeat content, something that seldom occurs in an informal report. However, this is usually an advantage rather than a disadvantage because the multiple audiences for formal reports read various sections for different purposes. For example, managers focus on conclusions and recommendations so they can make informed decisions. Technical professionals focus on the accuracy and feasibility of the technical details. Individual readers seldom go through an entire formal report from beginning to end; rather, they read the sections relevant to their jobs.

Deciding whether a report should be informal or formal has less to do with the subject of the report than with your relationship with the readers and your assessment of their information needs. After you decide who your readers are and what they need to know, you can decide whether to write an informal or a formal report. For example, imagine you are writing a progress report about your investigation of several varieties of high-yield, disease-resistant wheat. You would probably write an informal report for the members of your research team. However, you would write a formal report to be submitted to the funding agency, the U.S. Department of Agriculture.

Purposes and Characteristics of Reports

Reports record, and sometimes influence, current operations and also information that may be needed in the future. How could you buy a computer printer without a report on comparative models? Why would you finance a business trip or conference attendance if you never expected to be told what was accomplished? How could you plan a production schedule if you didn't know the current status—how much was finished, how much was yet to be completed, what supplies were on hand, what personnel were available? Reports generally have one of three sometimes overlapping purposes:

Regardless of the purpose of a report, can one be written that has no argument? No persuasive element? No position?

- to report information, including key aspects of daily activities, meetings, trips, and conferences; to report progress on projects

- to analyze information, including data for decision making and data from laboratory studies or field studies

- to persuade readers to consider the analysis and accept any recommendations

Regardless of the type of report you are preparing, always consider *why* it is needed: Someone needs information to stay informed, make a decision, or justify an action. The content, style, and format of your reports should simplify the readers' work.

Readers are generally neutral or positive because most are willing to form opinions based on currently available information rather than on previously held beliefs. Generally, the information in any report follows the same sequence.

1. *Overview:* This section states the purpose and/or problem that necessitates a report. (On a prepared form, the title and column heads may provide this information.) Sufficient information is provided for readers to understand the context of the report.

2. *Background:* This optional section presents information dealing with methods of investigation as well as materials and equipment used.

3. *Recommendations:* This section identifies any conclusions and/or recommendations (usually in priority order). Sometimes a summary of the recommendations is placed near the beginning to save busy readers time, and then a more detailed discussion comes later in the report. Some informal reports do not need a separate section for recommendations.

4. *Evidence:* This section presents the results. Sometimes the results are summarized before being presented in detail. On a prepared form, this summary might be a final column showing net gain or good/fair/poor evaluation.

5. *Discussion:* This section explains or justifies the conclusions or recommendations on the basis of the supporting results. If the report does not contain recommendations, this section can review or summarize the major points. In an informal report, this section is often omitted.

As discussed in Chapter 7, you organize a document according to your understanding of your readers' attitudes. If they are generally receptive and positive, or at least neutral, your material should be organized with the most important information (problem statement and recommendations) first, followed by discussion and supporting details. If the readers have negative attitudes toward the subject of the document or might be opposed to its recommendations, the material should be organized with the recommendations at the end, to enable them to follow your reasoning.

To organize information for any kind of report, you will find the patterns introduced in Chapter 7 particularly useful for responding to various situations and audiences. For some situations and audiences, only a straight *chronological* listing of actions or activities is required. For example, a report describing a new accounting procedure could easily list the revised steps. Occasionally, *spatial order* will help you describe physical characteristics of objects, mechanisms, organisms, or locations. *Cause and effect* is valuable for projections and estimates; *comparison and contrast* is useful for reports surveying the similarities and differences between various equipment or services. In every case, the organization you use should be determined by your purpose and your readers' task.

Planning a Report

When you begin to plan a report, you need to ask yourself a series of questions to identify the audience for and the context, purpose, and organization of the report:

- Who will read this report? What do they want to know? What is their task?

- What is the context or situation in which the report will be written? Read?

- What is the overall purpose of this report? What is my goal as writer?

- What should be the scope of the report?

- What should be the balance of technical and nontechnical material?

- Which information should be presented visually and which verbally?

- How should the report be organized? How should information be designed?

Identify Audiences

Knowledge about your report's audiences helps you clarify its purpose and organization. One of the most difficult aspects of preparing reports is tailoring your material for readers with a variety of backgrounds and needs.

When you begin planning a report, the information in Chapter 3 about audience analysis will help you to identify the organizational relationship between you and your readers. Are your readers on a different organizational level from you, or on the same organizational level but with a different technical specialization? Or are they in a different organization?

Once you have answered these questions, concentrate on how the readers will use the report. *Primary readers* fall into one of two categories: those who will use the recommendations for decision making and those who will be interested in the technical details, particularly the accuracy of data and the feasibility of the conclusions and recommendations, as they affect their work. *Secondary readers* are indirectly affected by the conclusions and recommendations of a document. For example, a report recommending reroofing and insulating a manufacturing plant would have the facilities manager as one of the primary readers. Department supervisors, whose work might be disrupted by the construction, would be secondary readers.

State Purpose

After you have identified the audiences for a report, focusing on the purpose is easier. In addition to having mixed audiences, reports also frequently have multiple purposes—to inform, to analyze, or to persuade; you need to specify the purpose(s) of your report, both for yourself and for the readers. Writing a purpose statement gives you a clear focus for a report and provides a way for you to control content, format, and organization. The readers benefit from a purpose statement that focuses on the intent of a report and explains how it fulfills their need(s) for certain information.

The purpose, placed at the beginning of a report, should follow a specific pattern: State the problem, identify questions and activities related to the problem, and explain how the report responds to the problem and to related questions and activities.

Preparing a report often seems fairly straightforward—state the problem, present the information about it . . . and that's it. But the writers of reports often find themselves entangled in complex situations that require them to take a stand. The ethics sidebar on the next page suggests some of the issues that workplace professionals need to consider.

"They cannot speak for themselves": Ethics and the Environment

Imagine this scenario:

You are working on an internal recommendation report at a company that manufactures plastics. The report recommends a new mixing process that will solve a product strength problem. In the process of writing the report, you discover that post-mix waste is being discarded into a local water basin. Although tests reveal that the current level of contaminants in the water basin is safe, you are concerned that accumulation over decades could have negative effects on the water's potability. The report, though, has no section designed to deal with waste products; the report was commissioned to deal with a single technical problem, strength.

Do you include a section in the report about waste? Are you responsible for looking at long-term environmental effects? Yes, you are, according to researcher Laurel Grove. Grove believes that professional communicators have a responsibility to "represent things that cannot speak for themselves," namely, the environment.[1] Environmental ethics "stipulates limits on what society can do to ensure that resources are preserved for the longer term."[2] Because we live in a global society, we can no longer look only at the effects of our activities on local communities. Our increased connections with other parts of the world require us to recognize our dependence on shared resources like water and air. Environmental ethics requires us to look at how we affect those resources for ourselves and for others.

Grove believes professional communicators "are uniquely positioned to do good in the cause of environmental ethics."[3] Why are professional communicators so "uniquely positioned"? Because professional communicators have the ability to look at an issue from a global perspective and see both specific and overall consequences:

Our advantage is that we are accustomed to sorting through issues, separating rhetorical wheat from hyperbolic chaff, and making information clear. It is often a major part of the communicator's job to bring out issues completely, a task at which other specialists may fail . . . . Professional communicators, who speak both the language of technology and that of the lay person, can translate the concerns of both sides to help them understand each other, instead of talking at cross purposes.[4]

Professional communicators are certainly not alone in their responsibilities for looking at how we affect the environment—"We are all responsible for one another and for the environment around us."[5] However, as professional communicators, we are often able to see what others do not.

Would you include a section on waste disposal in the report described above? What are the potential consequences if you do? If you don't? What factors will influence your decision about including report sections that are not required (and may even place the organization in a bad light)?

How would you integrate negative environmental effects into a report?

Organizing Informal Reports

This section discusses the function and organization of the most frequently used informal reports:

- task reports (recommendation, justification, inspection, information, investigation)

- periodic activity reports (daily, weekly, monthly, quarterly)

- progress (interim, status) reports

- meeting minutes

- trip and conference reports

- "to file" (archive) documents

Task Reports

Technical professionals deal with many tasks that result in reports. Most common are recommendation or justification reports, inspection or examination reports, and information or investigation reports.

A *recommendation report* or *justification report* primarily presents or defends a specific suggestion or solution for a particular situation. Such a report might recommend purchasing particular equipment or justify changes in procedures, personnel, or policies. For example, when a department manager wanted approval for changes in his department's procedures for storing solvents, he prepared a memo to his manager in which he explained the problems with the current procedures, recommended specific changes, and summarized reasons why the new procedures would be safer and encourage better record keeping.

An *inspection report* or *examination report* focuses on recording observable details, sometimes followed with recommendations. In some cases, an inspection report is completed on a prepared form, for example, when the task involves the inspection of mechanical parts. In other cases, a report follows the sequence presented earlier in this chapter: overview, background, recommendations, evidence, and discussion. For example, imagine that a civil engineer needed to file a report with her supervisor, the director of public health, following her visit to the community's waste treatment plant. She gave an overview of the reason for her visit (to see if new regulations had been implemented), focusing on her observations of how well the workers were able to follow the new regulations using current equipment. As a result of her observations, she recommended equipment modifications (to allow the new regulations to be more easily followed) and offered evidence that her recommendations would not only improve plant efficiency but also would be more cost effective. She concluded with a discussion about the overall benefits that implementation of the new regulations would have.

An investigation results in an *information* or *investigation report* that collects and evaluates information about some existing situation, but the writer need not always include a recommendation. For example, after a manufacturing engineer noticed a pattern of equipment malfunction following certain production runs, he reviewed the maintenance records for the quarter and compiled a report for his manager that identified the problem, provided a summary of the malfunctions, and suggested probable causes. However, he stopped short of making recommendations because his primary purpose was to provide his manager with information.

Although the audience, purpose, and content of each report determine its organization, the general guidelines presented at the beginning of this chapter apply to all types of task reports.

Should the recommendation come near the beginning of a report or near the end? It depends on the audience's attitude toward the recommendation. In general, if the audience will be receptive, it can be presented and discussed near the beginning; if the audience is likely to be resistant, the evidence and discussion should be presented before the recommendation.

The report in Figure 17.1, opposing the use of foam-in-place packaging, is written as a memo for a manager who has expressed some enthusiasm for this packaging system. Because of his expressed support for FIP packaging, the manager is not likely to be initially receptive to the report's negative conclusion; therefore, the writer places his recommendation at the end of the report rather than its more typical place near the beginning. The writer hopes that by the time the manager has read the points opposing FIP packaging, the argument will have been strongly made. Once the manager understands the problems with FIP packaging, he may be receptive to the negative recommendation.

Periodic Activity Reports

Efficient organizations have developed reporting methods to keep track of ongoing activities within the organization. These reports, filed daily, weekly, monthly, or quarterly, are compiled by supervisors and managers to describe the work completed by their section or group. Typically, each engineer compiles weekly reports, which an engineering manager uses for a monthly report; a section manager turns the monthly reports into a quarterly report. Sometimes information from these reports is used as the basis for projections that anticipate changes in project design, scheduling, or budgeting.

When the work is routine, daily or weekly periodic activity reports can be recorded on prepared forms. However, nonroutine activity reports require more than merely filling in the blanks. These reports, whether routine or not, should be factual and honest; exaggerating to make a particular time period look better than it really is is simply bad policy. When you are determining the content and format of a report, be particularly careful to include necessary information; omit information that is interesting but not critical. Organizations usually list information they expect in a periodic activity report:

1. *Overview:* Identify projects.

2. *Activities:* Specify project activities that are completed, in process, and planned.

3. *Recommendations:* Establish needed changes in scheduling, personnel, and budget.

FIGURE 17.1 ■ Recommendation Report to Nonreceptive Reader[6]

Meredith Manufacturing Memo

TO	Lan Wu	DATE	08 April 20—
		FROM	George Buchanan
		DEPT	Quality Assurance
		EXT	555-5597
		LOC/MAIL STOP	NQ/509

SUBJECT   Recommendation about using foam-in-place (FIP) packaging

We have been considering foam-in-place (FIP) packaging as an alternative that may resolve our packaging problems. Since a number of companies in the area have implemented FIP systems, we can benefit from their experiences. Many have found that FIP creates as many problems as it solves and have since turned to other packaging.

While investigating FIP, I have read FIP promotional material and discussed the product with representatives from three local FIP distributors. I have also spoken with quality assurance managers and packaging engineers at five local companies that have tried FIP.

FIP has many pitfalls that affect its use. This memo highlights information about material density, shipping, drop tests, costs, operator protection and health, and chemical disposal.

1. **Material Density.** Material density is very important in determining the "G" level or shock transmitted to a packaged product. The density of the foam in FIP is not uniform. Regardless of what the FIP suppliers advertise, the density varies from operator to operator.

2. **Shipping.** The effective static stress of FIP is from 0.04 to 0.2 pound per square inch (psi), which means a large contact surface area is required to cushion a dense product properly. Other cushioning materials such as polyethylene have an effective static stress range of 0.3 to 1.0 psi, which means less surface area is required. In general, a FIP package is larger than the equivalent expanded polystyrene or polyethylene package, based on the same fragility level. This means that shipping charges are greater for FIP packages.

3. **Drop Tests.** FIP obtains its cushioning ability from its foam structure. FIP suppliers in our area show cushioning curves for only the first drop test. Second and third drops are less favorable because the cell structure breaks down during the first drop. Other cushioning materials such as polyethylene do not break down and are much more consistent according to ASTM's standard 10-drop test. The probability that a packaged product will be dropped more than once during transportation is very high.

4. **Costs.** FIP has many hidden costs.
   a. Additional costs include continued maintenance and spare parts, gun cleaning solvents, nitrogen, protective clothing, and utilities.

---

*Because this is an informal report, the identifying information can be in the **heading**.*

*A **subject line** helps the reader focus, but because the reader has been judged as nonreceptive, the subject line doesn't establish a position as it would for a receptive reader.*

*The **overview** in the opening paragraph introduces the circumstances necessitating the report.*

*The brief **background** section establishes the sources the writer checked and the criteria he used.*

*The **recommendation** itself is deferred until the end of the report when, the writer hopes, the reader will have been persuaded by the weight of the evidence.*

*The **evidence** and **discussion** are combined in a seven-item list that establishes the reasons that FIP packaging is not the option that Meredith Manufacturing should choose.*

FIGURE 17.1 ■ *Continued*

   b. If the foam touches any part of a product, the product is damaged and must be reworked. Once the foam adheres to a surface, no chemical will remove it. If the person operating the FIP system is careful, most rework expenses can be avoided. However, many people working on the packaging line are the least skilled hourly workers; often they are not careful.

   c. On an annual basis, the cost is substantial for plastic film to cover the product before the foam is molded around the product.

   d. FIP chemicals are typically sold by weight. However, in every canister, some of that weight is not converted into foam. Chemicals that cannot be extracted are left in the bottom of the canisters. Additionally, a 15 to 20% weight loss occurs because of gasses that escape during chemical mixing.

   e. The largest initial cost is the FIP equipment. The cost of providing ventilation equipment must also be included.

5. **Operator Protection.** Most FIP systems use an MDI form of isocyanate, which is an irritant to the human body. This means that FIP work areas must be well ventilated, operators must wear special clothing to protect their garments, and goggles are mandatory to prevent eye injuries.

6. **Operator Health.** Regardless of which FIP system—with operator safeguards—is installed, the health of the operators is still a concern. All FIP systems use urea formaldehyde isocyanate chemicals, which according to medical experts can cause cancer. OSHA regulations clearly specify that overexposure to the chemicals results in irritation to the respiratory tract. (See attached OSHA regulations.)

7. **Chemical Disposal.** The biggest deterrent to using an FIP system is the fact that EPA regulations classify urea formaldehyde isocyanate as hazardous waste; any residual chemicals must be disposed of in accordance with local, state, and federal guidelines.

Because of the engineering, health, and environmental limitations of FIP systems, I recommend that we no longer consider installing such a system. Instead, we should investigate other alternatives for packaging our product.

George Buchanan
_____
George Buchanan

GB/ml
Attachments

Although the cost information could be written in a single paragraph, it is easier for the readers to comprehend when the separate points are enumerated in a list.

*The **recommendation** is at the end of the report because the reader is likely to be nonreceptive earlier.*

page 2

Organizations also often have a required format (even if they don't have prepared forms) so that you usually won't have to spend much time selecting the information to include or organizing it. In some situations, though, you may be given the criteria for the reports and then left on your own to organize and present the information in the activities section. Basically, you organize in one of two ways, depending on your readers' expectations and needs.

- *Chronological order* is appropriate if readers expect a straightforward listing of the activities, with no comment or evaluation.

- *Descending priority order* is appropriate if readers need the report to rank order the completed and in-process work by importance.

For example, in preparing a monthly report, the head of a software development department might use descending priority order, writing in great detail about the significant activities of the month and giving routine matters only cursory attention. But a hotel banquet manager could logically use chronological order for periodic activity reports because those reports must identify the daily use of the banquet facilities.

The recommendation section in a periodic activity report is used only if you need to suggest changes based on the activities. Evidence and discussion sections seldom appear in periodic activity reports.

Progress Reports

Unlike periodic activity reports that are prepared on a regular schedule regardless of current projects, progress reports summarize the progress, status, and projections related to a particular project. Progress reports (sometimes called status reports or interim reports) are part of almost all long-range projects and may also be expected in short-term projects.

Information about the *progress* of an activity answers a variety of reader questions:

- How is the project going?

- What has been accomplished during this phase of the project?

- How much time or effort, money, and so on did these tasks take?

Information about *status* answers additional reader questions:

- Where are we now?

- How do current activities relate to the overall project?

- How does this work affect other phases of the project?

Information about *projections* answers even more reader questions:

- Are we on schedule to meet our completion date?

- What plans need to be changed or altered?

- What will we do in the future?

A progress report generally follows this sequence of information:

1. *Overview:* Introduce the project.

2. *Progress:* Summarize the progress to date.

3. *Recommendation:* Identify major recommended schedule changes.

4. *Evidence:* Provide reasons for changes.

5. *Discussion:* Discuss the impact of the changes.

The overview of a progress report orients readers to the project, identifying the purposes of both the project and the report. Additionally, the overview surveys the project and specifies the dates covered in the report. This section of the report is crucial, dealing with both specific times and number of tasks, but one or the other can be emphasized, depending on the desired focus. Some progress reports recommend changes necessitated by the progress—or lack of progress. Less frequently, additional reports establish and discuss reasons for these changes.

Like periodic activity reports, progress reports can be organized in either chronological or priority order. A chronologically ordered progress report emphasizes the time period, listing dates and then specifying the tasks that were completed during that period. If you prefer to emphasize the tasks, place them before the time period in your report; these tasks can be arranged in chronological or priority order, depending on the readers' needs. The data should be clearly organized and presented in tables, graphs, and charts—a more effective method than placing the data in conventional paragraphs.

A progress report is particularly easy to prepare if the schedule with the original project proposal is structured so that the progress on each task can be monitored. Figure 17.2 shows a progress summary prepared at the end of the second week of the project: Task 1 is completed, task 2 is on schedule, task 3 is slightly ahead, and task 4 is behind.

The chart in Figure 17.2 would be accompanied by a narrative section in the report giving further details about the project, as shown in the following example. (In fact, in most documents, a text discussion of every figure and table is expected.)

■ EXAMPLE

Task 1 (foundation pouring) progressed right on schedule and is now completed. Fortunately, the weather was in our favor, and we were able to beat our target date for *task 2;* the floor was almost finished by the beginning of week 3. By using two trucks from the maintenance department, we were able to get *task 3,* the erection of the first-floor girders, started ahead of schedule. We should complete that phase in the next day or two. Unfortunately, shipping delays have caused us to fall behind schedule on the first-floor walls. . . .

Meeting Minutes

The record of the proceedings of any deliberative group is usually called the *minutes,* or sometimes—particularly in legislative bodies—the *journal.* Minutes provide a record of the discussion and decisions that occur at meetings, serving as official (sometimes even legal) records. Beyond their function of official documentation, minutes provide a convenient review of the meeting for people who attended as well as for those who didn't.

Preparing the minutes for a meeting requires both organization and attention to long-established conventions. The agenda for a meeting can provide you with a basis from which you can organize the information. If the meeting was recorded, you can use the tape to fill in details you may have missed while taking notes. Figure 17.3 provides an excerpt from *Robert's Rules of Order* that recommends the traditional format and sequence of information for meeting minutes.

What are possible reasons for making minutes a record of actions at a meeting rather than a record of opinions that were voiced?

Ordinarily, unless the minutes are to be published, they should contain mainly a record of what was *done* at the meeting, not what was *said* by the members. The minutes should never reflect the secretary's opinion, favorable or otherwise, on anything said or done.

Trip and Conference Reports

Trip and conference reports are important for several reasons. They force the traveler to review and evaluate the activities of the trip or conference and distinguish the major accomplishments from those less important. Such reports also enable the traveler to share activities and information with people who

FIGURE 17.3 ■ *Robert's Rules of Order—Guidelines for Meeting Minutes*[7]

CONTENT OF THE MINUTES. The *first paragraph* of the minutes should contain the following information (which need not, however, be divided into numbered or separated items directly corresponding to those below):

1. the kind of meeting: regular, special, adjourned regular, or adjourned special;
2. the name of the society or assembly;
3. the date and time of the meeting, and the place, if it is not always the same;
4. the fact that the regular chairman and secretary were present or, in their absence, the names of the persons who substituted for them; and
5. whether the minutes of the previous meeting were read and approved—as read, or as corrected—the date of that meeting being given if it was other than a regular business meeting.

The body of the minutes should contain a *separate paragraph for each subject matter,* and should show:

6. all main motions or motions to bring a main question again before the assembly—except any that were withdrawn—giving:
   a. the wording in which each motion was adopted or otherwise disposed of (with the facts as to how the motion may have been debated or amended before disposition being mentioned only parenthetically);
   b. the disposition of the motion, including—if it was *temporarily* disposed of—any primary and secondary amendment and all adhering secondary motions that were then pending; and
   c. usually, in the case of all important motions, the name of the mover;
7. all notices of motions, and
8. all points of order and appeals, whether sustained or lost, together with the reasons given by the chair for his [or her] ruling.

The *last paragraph* should state:

9. the hour of adjournment.

Additional rules and practices relating to the content of the minutes are the following:

- The name of the seconder of a motion should not be entered in the minutes unless ordered by the assembly.
- When a count has been ordered or the vote is by ballot, the number of votes on each side should be entered; and when the voting is by roll call, the names of those voting on each side and those answering "Present" should be entered. If members fail to respond on a roll call vote, enough of their names should be recorded as present to reflect that a quorum was present at the time of the vote.
- The proceedings of a committee of the whole, or a quasi committee of the whole, should not be entered in the minutes, but the fact that the assembly went into committee of the whole (or into quasi committee) and the committee report should be recorded.
- When a question is considered informally, the same information should be recorded as under the regular rules, since the only informality in the proceedings is in the debate.
- When a committee report is of great importance or should be recorded to show the legislative history of a measure, the assembly can order it "to be entered in the minutes," in which case the secretary copies it in full in the minutes.
- The name and subject of a guest speaker can be given, but no effort should be made to summarize his [or her] remarks.

THE SIGNATURE. Minutes should be signed by the secretary and can also be signed, if the assembly wishes, by the president. The words *Respectfully submitted*—although occasionally used—represent an older practice that is not essential in signing the minutes.

didn't make the trip or attend the conference. Of course, the report also justifies the time and expense of the trip or conference (it can even be used to verify business trips for IRS inquiries and audits).

A trip or conference report is seldom completed on a prepared form. Instead, the information listed below is incorporated into a logically organized, clearly stated report:

Trip	*Conference*
purpose and date of trip	purpose and date of conference
primary task(s)	primary task(s)
personal role	personal role
people contacted	sessions attended
question(s) raised or resolved	information gained
conclusions	conclusions

FIGURE 17.4 Trip Report

Memorandum
May 13, 20—

TO: Amanda Boyd
FROM: Scott Thompson
SUBJECT: Report on Marketing Seminar Trip, May 8–10

The National Management Association's seminar entitled "Making Market Research Work for Your Organization" turned out to be an efficient way to learn about market research and about strategies that will help us build empirical models based on survey data sets. I attended the seminar from May 8–10. The course was separated into six areas that will be useful to our program:

- **Market Research: Its Value and Design**
  This section defined the critical success factors for useful market research, outlined product life-cycles, and discussed research design.
- **Research Methodology**
  This section defined qualitative and quantitative research. It also discussed setting research parameters, sampling, and reliability and validity of data.
- **Survey Instrument Design**
  This section covered the survey development process, elements of a good survey, and evaluating the effectiveness of surveys.
- **Data Analysis**
  This section covered editing, coding, and checking raw data, as well as using different methods to analyze data including cross-tab tables and regression analysis.

To present the potential benefits of the seminar for the company, Scott focused the trip report on what he learned and would be able to do with that knowledge.

After reminding Amanda about the trip and its purpose, he outlined the concepts he learned by presenting them in a bulleted list with supporting explanations.

As you can see, the information presented in trip and conference reports is very similar. Unlike periodic activity reports and progress reports, which frequently use chronological order, effective trip and conference reports employ priority order: You rank the tasks and information according to their value to your organization.

Figure 17.4 shows a trip report written by Scott Thompson, a project specialist in an environmental technology consulting firm. Sensing a need for the company to enlarge its customer base, Scott suggested during his last performance review that he would like to begin working on a marketing plan. His proposal was accepted; he was asked to identify professional development seminars he could attend to gain the necessary knowledge. The seminar he attended was his first choice, so he wanted his supervisor, Amanda Boyd, to see the benefits of this expensive training she approved.

FIGURE 17.4 *Continued*

- **Reporting Research Results**
  Reference materials were provided pertaining to this topic, but it was not discussed during the seminar.
- **Working with Suppliers**
  This section covered firms and individuals that offer market research services, procurement models for picking a supplier, writing RFPs, evaluating proposals, and developing working relationships with suppliers.

The scope of the seminar was broad. Perhaps most valuable was the information that will help me to define a research problem, establish research objectives, and design a survey questionnaire to meet them.

Overall, what I learned about market research will serve as a strong foundation for investigating the needs of technology users across our organization. In addition, the acquaintances I made among other attendees who use market research on a regular basis and with the instructor, a vice president of the Kastman & Booker Corporation, are potentially valuable resources to draw on when we are seeking specific information.

On a side note, although I found the course useful, several high-level marketing managers who attended felt that the course did not entirely correspond to its advertisement in the registration brochure. Because of that, NMA has offered to waive the tuition of a follow-up seminar for all participants. I have attached the outline for a course they have suggested on writing superior surveys (St. Louis, late August). Please let me know if you would like me to attend. While a follow-up to the first seminar would be very beneficial, I am also in a good position to study this area independently, beginning with the recommended reading list in the course materials.

- 2 -

The bulleted list is followed by a discussion about how that information could benefit the organization.

Amanda was enthusiastic about Scott's plan to develop a strategic marketing program for the organization's environmental technologies. However, several people in the organization were skeptical about the plan. She was anxious to see what benefits this professional seminar would allow Scott to bring to the organization. Scott's trip report allowed her to quickly see what he learned and why that information is valuable.

"To File" Reports

In what circumstances might you write a "to file" report?

"To file" reports are prepared for the express purpose of documenting an idea or action. These reports, available for reference if questions ever arise about some aspect of a project, form an archival history of a project.

Frequently, such reports simply record oral conversations, discussions, directives, or decisions in a concise, permanent document. If appropriate, the name and title of any person(s) responsible for (or having authority to sponsor) actions that develop from the "to file" report are included. A copy of the report is sent to that person so the information in it can be verified or amended before it reaches the file. Because people occasionally retract, change, or forget positions they've taken, you can avert confusion by carefully and consistently documenting discussions and commitments.

The problem with "to file" reports is that people sometimes spend an excessive amount of time documenting activities as a political protection. Accurate archival records are important, but they should not take an inordinate amount of time, effort, or attention.

Formats of Reports

Reports vary not only in purpose but in format as well: They can be prepared forms, memos, letters, or formal reports. The choice of format generally depends on a combination of factors: whether the document is routine or not, whether the audience is internal or external, and whether the tone should be informal or formal. Figure 17.5 identifies the most likely format for various reports.

FIGURE 17.5 ■ Formats for Reports

	Task		Audience		Tone and Format	
	Routine	Nonroutine	Internal	External	Formal	Informal
Prepared Forms	■		■	■		■
Memos	■	■	■			■
Letters		■		■	■	■
Formal Reports		■	■	■	■	

Prepared Forms

An appropriate method for routine, informal communication for both internal and external readers is *prepared forms.* Accounts of day-to-day operations most frequently use prepared forms and memos, seldom formal reports. For example, inspection and evaluation reports are often done on prepared forms, whether the subject is a precision machined part or a patient admitted to a pediatric unit.

Forms can be a tremendous timesaver for both writers and readers. Forms assist writers by reminding them to include every essential item. And they assist readers by ordering information in the same sequence in each report of a series, so the readers can quickly locate whatever information they need.

Unfortunately, forms are often poorly designed or outdated. As part of your work, you may need to design or redesign forms. Four areas of design are important to consider: content, layout, visual elements, and paper stock. The more carefully you adapt these four elements, which are detailed in Figure 17.6, to the form's purpose and audience, the easier the form will be to complete and the more likely to provide you with useful information.

In what circumstances would you prefer to submit reports on a prepared form?

Memos and Letters

Routine information can be easily presented in *memos* and *letters,* accounting for the widespread use of form memos and letters, which were popular long before word processing made individualization possible. Often, though, memos and letters deal with nonroutine information, with memos going to internal readers (either an individual or a group) and letters going to external readers (a single individual, though copies may be sent to others). Both memos and letters range from informal to fairly formal. (Chapter 14 presents a detailed discussion of correspondence.)

Reports

Communication that does not fit neatly on a prepared form and requires a more formal tone and format than a memo or letter is placed in a *report.* Reports can be intended for internal or external readers. Regardless of purpose, audience, or degree of formality, a report should be easy to read and visually appealing. Even in an informal report, headings and subheadings can ease reading. Data should be presented clearly and directly; often tables, charts, and graphs are used.

Organizing Formal Reports

A formal report's audience and purpose influence not only its content but also its organization. Writing for a mixed audience requires you to organize the material so that it serves all categories of readers, whatever their different needs.

One approach to writing a report for a mixed audience is to imagine the reader as a composite of decision makers and technical professionals. However,

FIGURE 17.6 ■ Guidelines for Effective Form Design

Content

- The purpose of the form is clearly identified by number and an accurate, descriptive title.
- Content of the form is consistent with its stated purpose.
- The instructions and labels are easy to understand.
- No unnecessary information is requested.
- The routing sequence is clearly identified.
- Filing information is clearly labeled.
- The necessary number of copies is provided and clearly named and numbered in the order each copy can be removed.

Visual Elements

- The printing on the form is easy to read.
- Visual devices (boldface, type variation, shading, color variation, enumerated items) assist the user in completing and routing the form.
- Thick (or double) rule lines set off the major sections of the form.
- Check-off boxes are used to minimize filling in information.
- Boxes identify areas for recording brief answers.
- Lines (rather than boxed areas) or blocks of blank space provide areas for longer answers.

Layout

- The form sections are not crowded.
- The margins have sufficient space for binding.
- The instructions are in a logical location, clearly labeled, and enumerated.
- The horizontal spacing is appropriate for a typewriter or computer printer (for example, the need for tab stops is minimized).
- The vertical spacing is appropriate for a typewriter or computer printer.
- Signatures and conditions for the form's validity are at the bottom of the form.
- The address box is appropriately placed for a window envelope if the form is mailed.

Stock

- The paper stock is appropriate (weight, color) for the purpose of the form.
- Multiple-copy forms use NCR (no carbon required) paper or inserted, easy-to-remove carbon.
- Judicious placement of carbon and blanking out of areas for some information allows data to be omitted on some copies.
- The form fits in standard envelopes, binders, and file folders.

Complex reports are often prepared collaboratively. What can people do to ensure that the report is a coherent team document (rather than a cobbled-together effort by individuals)?

such a compromise does not fully address the needs of any group of readers. A second possibility is to write completely different reports for different audiences. However, separate reports not only require additional writing time, but also eliminate the natural and necessary interaction between decision makers and technical professionals. The most realistic approach, then, is a single report responsive to the needs of both groups.

Knowledge of the audience plays an important role in choosing the overall structure of a report. Recall that inductive reasoning moves from specific to general and deductive reasoning from general to specific. Receptive readers generally appreciate reports that are organized deductively, giving the conclusions first and then providing the substantiating details; most reports are arranged this way. Sometimes, however, a report might be better received if arranged inductively, giving specifics first and letting them lead to general conclusions and recommendations.

Most reports first state a position and then establish its validity. Thus, a deductively organized report usually uses a two-tiered approach:

1. Give an overview and then summarize the preferred solution.

2. Cite evidence or support for the solution in descending order of significance, dealing with both positive and negative points.

You might assume that formal reports have a specific format that everyone follows. However, few professionals agree as to what constitutes the best format, nor is there any definitive list of what must be included. This lack of consistency shows up in the dozens of style guides published by individual companies and professional associations. Further evidence for the disparity of report formats comes from NASA: "The preliminary findings of a NASA study revealed that (1) nearly one hundred components were used [in different technical reports], (2) there was an apparent lack of consistency in the terms used for the components, and (3) there was an apparent lack of consistency in the location of the components."[8]

This text employs a generic report format that incorporates the standard elements of most reports; if your company prescribes its own format, use that instead. The components are first defined and then illustrated in sample formal reports reproduced at the end of the chapter.

Front Matter of a Report

The front matter in a report consists of the sections that come before the body of the document. The sections that are identified in Figure 17.7 are those often used in reports. Front matter is common in formal reports—though not every report includes every item. The less formal the report, the less likely it is to include front matter.

Some elements of front matter require more discussion than the summary provided in Figure 17.7. Specifically, this section discusses issues you need to consider when you write a letter of transmittal and a table of contents for a report.

Whether to include a *letter of transmittal* depends on company policy. The author of the report can use a letter of transmittal to introduce the primary reader to the document. Using a standard letter format (illustrated in Chapter 14), a letter of transmittal generally has three paragraphs. The first introduces the document's subject and purpose. The second usually focuses on one or two key points dealing with the document's preparation or content: problems, resources, additional work, conclusions, recommendations. The third paragraph is a courtesy that encourages the reader to contact the writer with any questions.

An effective *table of contents* uses subject headings, not section labels, to identify major sections and subsections of a report.

FIGURE 17.7 ■ **Purposes and Practices of Front Matter**

Letter of Transmittal	
Purpose:	◆ Introduce the primary reader to the document.
Practice:	◆ Introduce the document's subject and purpose (¶1).*
	◆ Focus on one or two key points dealing with the document's preparation or content: problems, resources, additional work, conclusions, recommendations (¶2).
	◆ Encourage reader to contact the writer with any questions (¶3).
	◆ See Figure 17.11a for a typical letter of transmittal.
Cover	
Purpose:	◆ Secure the pages of the report.
	◆ Create a professional image.
Practice:	◆ Match weight of cover to length of report (a brief report needs only a lightweight cover; a lengthy report requires a sturdy cover).
	◆ Select cover that stays flat when report is open.
Title Page	
Purpose:	◆ Identify title/subtitle, author(s) and organization, person and organization for whom report was prepared, date.
Practice:	◆ Sometimes include project identification and report numbers.
	◆ See Figure 17.11b for a typical title page.

■ EXAMPLES

Too vague   1.0 Introduction

Specific   1.0 Problems in Treating Postoperative Lung Congestion

The various sections can be differentiated both typographically and spatially. These are some of the common ways to differentiate levels of a document:

- ***Indentation:*** The more indented the heading, the more subordinate it is.

- ***Type size:*** The smaller the heading, the more subordinate it is.

- ***Type style:*** More aggressive type styles are used for titles and level-1 headings, less aggressive styles for level-2 and -3 headings.

Figure 17.8 illustrates a numeric outline, a format often used by government agencies, companies that have government contracts, and some scientific organizations; the levels are indicated in three ways: numbers to signal the sections

FIGURE 17.7 ■ *Continued*

Table of Contents

Purpose:	◆ Identify major sections and subsections of the report.
Practice:	◆ Differentiate sections both typographically and spatially.
	◆ See Figure 17.11c for a typical table of contents.

List of Tables and Figures

Purpose:	◆ Use as a table of contents for visuals in a report.
Practice:	◆ Omit if there are fewer than five tables or figures.

List of Appendixes

Purpose:	◆ Use as a table of contents for appendixes.
Practice:	◆ Omit if the report has only one or two appendixes; listing can be included as a major section in the table of contents.

Abstract or Executive Summary

Purpose:	◆ Summarize major points, findings, or recommendations of the report.
Practice:	◆ Do *not* use as introduction to the report but as independent, entirely condensed version—the report in miniature.
	◆ See Figures 17.11d and 17.11e for a typical executive summary.
	*Symbolizes *paragraph*.

(as in the body of the report), typographic variation (the use of **Bold Small Caps** for level-1 heading), and indentation for each succeeding level of heading.

Figure 17.9 shows a more conventional table of contents. The levels are indicated in three ways: **BOLD ALL CAPS** for major headings, indentation to indicate level-3 subsections, and type style changes (***bold italics***).

Body of a Report

The selection and sequence of elements in the body of a formal report depend on audience and purpose. Usually some or most of the following elements are included:

Part I

- statement of purpose or problem
- summary of findings
- summary of recommendations

FIGURE 17.8 ■
Numeric Table of Contents

TABLE OF CONTENTS

1.0 FIRST LEVEL-1 HEADING
    1.1   Level-2 Heading
        1.1.1   Level-3 Heading
        1.1.2   Level-3 Heading
    1.2   Level-2 Heading

2.0 SECOND LEVEL-1 HEADING
    2.1   Level-2 Heading
    2.2   Level-2 Heading
    2.3   Level-2 Heading

3.0 THIRD LEVEL-1 HEADING

and so on

FIGURE 17.9 ■
Conventional Table of Contents

Table of Contents

FIRST-1 HEADING
Level-2 Heading
   Level-3 Heading.
   Level-3 Heading.
Level-2 Heading

SECOND LEVEL-1 HEADING
Level-2 Heading
Level-2 Heading
Level-2 Heading

THIRD LEVEL-1 HEADING

and so on

Part II

- background to problem

- literature search of information relevant to problem

- approach, method, and materials (for reports of experiments, surveys)

- available options (solutions)

- results: collected data or findings

- discussion

- interpretation(s)

- conclusion(s)

- recommendation(s)

Separating the body into two major segments responds to the needs of the two very different kinds of primary readers—decision makers and technical professionals. Part I of the body states the purpose or problem and then summarizes the findings and recommendations, immediately giving decision makers the information they need without making them sort through myriad technical details. Part II of the body provides details for technical professionals. The organizational patterns presented in Chapter 7 provide a variety of structures whose application depends on both purpose and content. The following list reviews these patterns and suggests appropriate uses:

- *Chronological order*—Chronology is used for explaining processes, such as setting up a new production line.

- *Spatial order*—Descriptions of objects or locations are best arranged spatially; that is, in the same sequence in which an operator or observer encounters the subjects described. For example, such an organizational pattern would work in describing the physical facilities in a remodeled plant.

- *Cause and effect*—Problem-solving situations are easily explained this way, often arranged in descending order of importance. For example, suggestions of ways to increase the acceptance ratio of items passing through quality control could be explained using cause and effect.

- *Comparison and/or contrast*—Focusing on the similarities and differences, also often arranged in descending order, provides a reader with the basis for decision making. A report using comparison and contrast might advocate the lease/purchase of new equipment or recommend a change in vendors.

End Matter of a Report

The end matter of a report comes after the body. It can be made up of any of the elements in Figure 17.10. The formality of the report and the needs of the

FIGURE 17.10 ■ Purposes and Practices of End Matter

Appendixes

Purpose:	◆ Present useful information that might otherwise interrupt the flow of the report.
Practice:	◆ Include or omit items depending on purpose, audience, and situation:
	◇ formulas used in calculations
	◇ complex calculations of which only the results are used in report itself
	◇ survey forms
	◇ interview questions
	◇ transcripts
	◇ correspondence related to the document subject
	◇ detailed figures from which selected information is taken for report
	◇ references for further reading

Glossary, List of Symbols, List of Abbreviations

Purpose:	◆ Define terms unfamiliar to the readers.
Practice:	◆ Signal defined terms in some consistent way (italics, asterisk).

Footnotes, Sources Cited, Works Cited, or References

Purpose:	◆ Document the sources of all cited information.
Practice:	◆ Select format appropriate for discipline and profession.
	◆ Provide internal (in-text) citations or footnotes for (1) direct quotations, (2) paraphrased information that's not common knowledge for the intended audience, (3) statistical and other factual information, and (4) visuals.
	◆ List all sources referred to in the document in a sources cited, works cited, or references section.

audience influence what is included. Very formal reports typically include a great deal of end matter; very informal reports usually include none.

Appendixes present supplementary information to increase readers' knowledge or understanding. What to include depends on the purpose and audience of the document (Figure 17.10). For example, primary readers who have a technical background benefit from detailed technical data in the body of the document far more than do readers who rely on the writer's technical expertise to summarize pertinent information. For primary readers with backgrounds in business rather than a technical field, detailed data are appropriately placed in an appendix.

A *glossary* defines terms unfamiliar to readers (boldface the first occurrence of each term defined in the glossary). It is an optional section; you decide whether to include one according to the expertise of the audience and the complexity of the content. Sometimes the glossary is placed with front matter if the primary reader is not likely to know the terms. If the report has only a few unfamiliar terms or concepts to define, information notes can be used instead of a glossary.

Information notes (usually numbered) are most convenient if placed at the bottom of the page on which the reference appears; occasionally, however, these notes are combined with the end notes.

The list of *sources cited* or source notes is the final section of the end matter. Complete citation information enables readers both to check where you obtained your information and to locate sources if they need to follow up a particular lead. See the Documentation section of the Usage Handbook for standard formats for citations.

Format Elements

A writer of a formal report needs to be attentive to several aspects of format:

- headings and subheadings
- pagination
- figures and tables

Headings and subheadings should match those listed in the table of contents—in typography, placement on page, and wording. These headings and subheadings do more than provide visual breaks for the reader; they also act as cohesive devices, identifying the movement from one topic to the next.

By convention, most reports identify the first page of the body as page 1 of the report, continuing sequentially until the final page of the end matter. The front matter of the report is usually numbered with lowercase roman numerals (i, ii, iii, iv, v, vi, and so on).

Visual material (figures, tables, and so on) should generally be incorporated into the report, closely following textual reference. Incorporating visuals makes more work for the writer in designing the layout of each page but benefits the reader who can immediately refer to the appropriate figure or table without turning to an appendix.

Examining a Sample Report

This final section of the chapter presents a technical report written by an eight-member team of engineering students. You'll notice that it's not very long. Workplace professionals are sometimes expected to produce very detailed and

Multidisciplinary Engineering Design
239 Zachry Engineering Hall
Iowa State University
Ames, IA 50011-1201

October 11, 20—

Ms. Danielle Conner
Cottrell Technologies, Inc.
1401 Highland Heights
Cedar Rapids, IA 52046

Dear Ms. Conner:

The multidisciplinary engineering design team at ISU is hard at work on the digital controller project we discussed at the beginning of the term. Before we may proceed much further, however, a decision must be made. We are considering two alternative input interfaces for the controller unit: a bar code scanner and a telephone-style keypad.

This report analyzes the two alternatives according to three criteria that you have suggested are important to Cottrell Technologies: compatibility with the existing Techni-Veyor, cost, and relative ease of operation. The input alternatives are described, analyzed, and compared based on these criteria; one is recommended for your approval.

Should you have any questions, please contact me. I look forward to hearing your opinion about our team's recommendation, so we may move forward with the next phase of the project.

Sincerely,

Nancy F. Hitch

Nancy F. Hitch
Multidisciplinary Engineering Design
515-555-3728
nhitch@iastate.edu

The student team created a professional letterhead for correspondence with their client.

Nancy Hitch, as the team's liaison with Midwest Technologies, sends the correspondence.

Nancy briefly reviews the status of the project and then states the purpose for her letter and the accompanying report.

Nancy previews the content and structure of the report.

In her closing paragraph, Nancy invites questions and makes it clear that she and the team need a response.

Nancy includes her telephone number and e-mail address so that Danielle Conner can easily contact her.

FIGURE 17.11b ■ Final Version of Title Page for Recommendation Report

Analysis of Input Interfaces
for the
Cottrell Technologies, Inc.
Techni-Veyor Controller

Submitted to

Danielle Conner
Cottrell Technologies, Inc.
1401 Highland Heights
Cedar Rapids, Iowa 52046

Prepared by

Multidisciplinary Engineering Design Team
Iowa State University
Ames, IA 50011-1201

October 11, 20—

lengthy reports (the excerpt from the battery site report in Chapter 1 is an example from a series of reports that typically ran more than 30 pages). More frequently, however, you'll be expected to write relatively short, well-organized reports for experts who will be interested in the information you present.

Figures 17.11a–n present a collaborative recommendation report written by a student team in the multidisciplinary design class (College of Engineering at

FIGURE 17.11c ■ Final Version of Table of Contents for Recommendation Report

TABLE OF CONTENTS

EXECUTIVE SUMMARY ii

OVERVIEW OF ALTERNATIVES 2
Bar Code Interface 2
Keypad Interface 2

ANALYSIS OF ALTERNATIVES 2
Compatibility 3
Cost 4
Ease of Operation 4

DISCUSSION 5

RECOMMENDATION 5

The font of the sections in the table of contents should match the font used for those same sections in the document.

The page numbers should be right justified.

Iowa State University). The class worked on a term-long project to develop a digital controller for Cottrell Technologies, Inc. During the project, the class and the company communicated frequently to ensure that the recommendations in the final report met the company's design, financial, and quality requirements.

Cottrell Technologies is a mid-sized production company that manufactures hardware for retail and industrial organizations. For example, they manufacture

FIGURE 17.11d ■ Draft of Executive Summary of Recommendation Report

The report should use conventions for capitalization.

Abbreviations should be spelled out the first time they're used.

Readers will expect the general (the company) to precede the specific (the product).

The reasoning isn't logical. The "Because . . ." isn't the reason one interface or the other must be chosen.

Using active voice ("We recommend . . ." rather than ". . . is recommended") lets the decision makers take credit for their recommendation.

Rather than just saying two options exist, the writer needs to identify and characterize them— in the same order that they're presented in the text.

Direct language is more effective.

Using consistent terminology makes it easier for readers to follow the ideas in a paper.

Most workplace documents paginate front matter with lower-case Roman numerals and label the first page of substantive text as page 1.

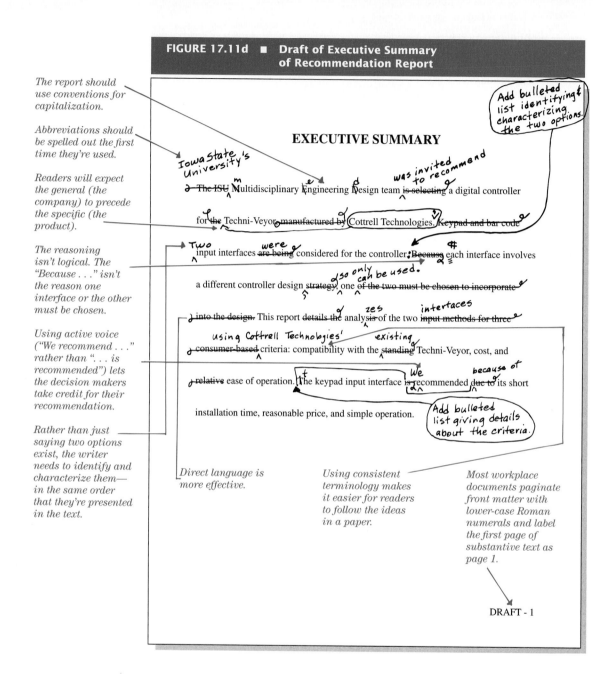

garment storage racks and conveyor systems for retail dry cleaners. The conveyor systems they have sold during the last two decades have failed to attract new customers. To become competitive in this market again, the company decided to manufacture a new conveyor system that includes state-of-the-art technology. After making arrangements with the university, they turned the project over

EXECUTIVE SUMMARY

Iowa State University's multidisciplinary engineering design team was invited to recommend a digital controller for Cottrell Technologies' Techni-Veyor. Two input interfaces were considered for the controller:

- The **bar code interface** is similar to scanners used in video rental stores, automatically recording item when the scanning bar is passed over the appropriate code.
- The **keypad** interface also records the type of item, but its memory functions are performed manually rather than automatically with a scanner.

Each input interface involves a different controller design, so only one can be used. This report analyzes the two interfaces using Cottrell Technologies' criteria: compatibility with the existing Techni-Veyor systems, cost, and ease of operation.

- **Compatibility.** The bar code interface is not compatible with the systems currently used by Cottrell Technologies. The bar code interface could be installed only after modifying current systems—a process that could take several hours. The keypad interface is more readily compatible with the existing systems; installation would take less than an hour.
- **Cost.** Both bar code and keypad interfaces are widely available; however, bar code interfaces typically cost at least five times more than keypad interfaces.
- **Operation.** Either controller is an improvement over the current method for retrieving garments. Neither system would require lengthy training of operators. The bar code scanner has a slight input time advantage and reduces the possibility of operator error.

We recommend the keypad interface because of its short installation time, reasonable price, and simple operation.

page ii

The revised executive summary is easier to read because the two options are emphasized in several ways:
- *using bullets to signal each interface*
- *boldfacing the key terms*
- *indenting the short list*

Identifying the three criteria in a bulleted list helps readers anticipate both the organization of the report and the major point that will be made.

to the multidisciplinary engineering design class and challenged the team of students to design a new system. The new system would be sold to new customers and marketed to past customers as a system upgrade.

The design team elected an electrical engineering major, Nancy F. Hitch, to serve as the liaison with Cottrell Technologies. In this role, she was to present

FIGURE 17.11f ■ Draft of Recommendation Report

The use of **BOLD ALL CAPS** makes the long title and level-1 headings difficult to read. **BOLD SMALL CAPS** would be more effective.

Readers can be distracted or misled by dangling modifiers.

Active voice is generally more effective unless the writer has a specific reason to use passive voice.

A preview paragraph here would help readers anticipate what's coming.

Readers are less confused if you use the same term consistently to refer to the same object ("interface" throughout rather than "system," "method," or "unit.")

An additional level-2 heading would help readers.

Agreement errors can distract or confuse readers: "patron" is singular; "their" is plural.

ANALYSIS OF INPUT INTERFACES FOR THE COTTRELL TECHNOLOGIES, INC. TECHNI-VEYOR CONTROLLER

Iowa State University

The ISU Multidisciplinary Engineering Design team has recommended a digital controller for Cottrell Technologies. The controller will be installed to work with Techni-Veyor, a dry cleaning conveyor system manufactured by Cottrell Technologies and used by cleaning companies nationwide. As part of the controller selection process, two popular input interfaces are being considered: a bar code method and a digital keypad method. This report analyzes both input methods and recommends one for your approval.

Our team used 1 2 3

The two input interfaces are analyzed for three different criteria: compatibility with the current conveyor, cost, and relative ease of operation. Data is drawn from the most recent *Thomas Register* and from interviews with both Danielle Conner and a customer currently using the Techni-Veyor system.

Add a preview of the report.

Add level-2 heading: Bar Code Interface

ALTERNATIVES OVERVIEW of

The two input interfaces in consideration are a bar code scanner and a telephone-style keypad. The bar code scanner is similar to those in many video rental stores. When a garment is brought in, it is assigned a bar code identification tag. The bar code is scanned into the computer's memory and assigned a patron's name. After the garment is cleaned, its bar code is scanned into the computer along with its position on the conveyor. Just as a video tape is assigned to a patron, each garment and respective location is assigned to a specific patron. For every patron, the computer retains their garment bar code and coded position on the conveyor. When the patron returns, their name is entered into the computer and their garment is automatically retrieved by the digital controller.

DRAFT - 2

---

the team's recommendation for an input interface to be used with the controller system. The analytical report she coordinated was based on the class's investigation and comparison of input interface devices.

The design team members completed their preliminary design for the basic conveyor system and started work on the subsystems. Nancy took the lead during the input interface phase of the project, researching available technolo-

FIGURE 17.11g ■ Final Version of Recommendation Report

ANALYSIS OF INPUT INTERFACES FOR THE COTTRELL TECHNOLOGIES, INC. TECHNI-VEYOR CONTROLLER

The Iowa State University multidisciplinary engineering design team has recommended a digital controller for Cottrell Technologies. The controller will be installed to work with Techni-Veyor, a dry cleaning conveyor system manufactured by Cottrell Technologies and used by dry cleaning companies nationwide. As part of the controller selection process, our team considered two popular input interfaces: a bar code interface and a digital keypad interface. We analyzed both input interfaces and recommend one for your approval.

Using first person ("our team," "we") emphasizes the team's analysis and decision making. The people who made the recommendations are acknowledged. In addition, the audience of the report is identified.

Our team used three criteria to analyze the two input interfaces: compatibility with the current conveyor, cost, and relative ease of operation. We took our data from the most recent *Thomas Register* and from interviews with both Danielle Conner and a Cottrell Technologies customer currently using the Techni-Veyor system.

Readers need information that identifies criteria and sources of data.

This report presents the following information:

- an overview of the two alternatives: bar code interface and keypad interface
- an analysis of alternatives according to three criteria: compatibility, cost, and operation
- conclusions: cost and down time are critical in selecting appropriate option
- recommendation: keypad interface is better option

Foregrounding the sequence of sections in a preview paragraph lets readers know what's coming in the report.

page 1

gies and analyzing them with her teammates. The team identified two interface devices that would work with the conveyor system.

The team was most impressed with the bar code scanning interface but noticed that it would be more expensive than the keypad units they were also considering. Unsure whether the price difference was an important factor for Cottrell Technologies, the team presented its findings in a recommendation report to the company.

FIGURE 17.11h ■ Draft of Recommendation Report

An additional level-2 heading *would* help readers.

Agreement errors can distract or confuse readers: "patron" is singular; "their" is plural.

The spacing between the headings and the text must be adjusted. Here the spacing above and below each heading is the same, so the headings look as if they're floating equi-distant between the chunks of text. The headings should be chunked with the appropriate text by putting more space above than below the heading.

A preview paragraph in the Comparability section will convey the importance of this criterion.

Adding Manfield's title clarifies her position and contributes to the authority of her opinion.

"Therefore" is unnec-essary because a cause–effect relation-ship doesn't exist.

Add level 2 heading **Keypad Interface**

activating *is*
The keypad interface works like the bar code scanner, except its memory functions are performed manually with a card file. When a garment is brought in, it is assigned a four-digit number that is recorded by hand with the patron's name in a card file. After the garment is cleaned, its position number on the conveyor is written on the appropriate patron's card and once again filed. When the customer returns, their card is taken from the file and their garment location number entered into the computer with a telephone-style keypad. The digital controller then turns the conveyor and retrieves the patron's garment.

ANALYSIS *of ALTERNATIVES*

The alternatives were analyzed for three criteria considered essential by Cottrell Technologies: the compatibility of the controller with the existing Techni-Veyor system, the cost of the unit and system modifications, and the relative ease of operation. | *Present in a bulleted list.*

Compatibility

Add ¶ about importance of compatibility.

Add a reason

Bar Code Input
The compatibility of the bar code system involves a lengthy installation period. The Techni-Veyor rack is labeled with four-digit numbers above each slot. Installation of the bar code system requires labeling the entire rack with bar code decals. Depending on the size of the rack, this takes from a couple of hours to a day.

general manager
Charlotte Manfield of Fairfield Cleaners in Ames, said a downtime could cost her consid-erable business. Ms. Manfield emphasized the importance of maintaining an efficient garment-retrieval system of some sort in the event of a mechanical problem, break-down, or system upgrade. ~~Therefore,~~ some advance planning would help Ms. Manfield to avoid delays and customer dissatisfaction due to the installation of a bar code con-troller system.

time delays caused by

(and other customers with similar large dry cleaning businesses.)

DRAFT - 3

Nancy coordinated both the draft and final versions of the report. Other team members contributed information for the analysis and reviewed the document. Several people on the team—including Nancy—were enrolled in a technical communication course at the same time that they were working on this project for Cottrell Technologies. As a team, they agreed that their report should reflect the high standards that their client would expect from workplace professionals.

FIGURE 17.11i ■ **Final Version of Recommendation Report**

OVERVIEW OF ALTERNATIVES ◄─────────────────────────────────

The two input interfaces our team considered were a bar code scanner and a telephone-style keypad.

Bar Code Interface ◄

The bar code scanner for use with the Techni-Veyor is similar to those used to control inventory in many video rental stores. When a garment is brought into a dry cleaners, it ◄ is assigned a bar code identification tag. The bar code is scanned into the computer's memory and assigned the patron's name. After the garment is cleaned, its bar code is scanned into the computer along with its numbered position on the conveyor. Just as a videotape is assigned to a patron, each garment and respective location is assigned to a specific patron. For every patron, the computer retains the garment bar code and coded position on the conveyor. When the patron returns, the name is entered into the computer, and the garment is automatically retrieved using the digital controller.

Keypad Interface

The keypad interface works like the bar code scanner, except activating its memory functions is performed manually with a card file. When a garment is brought in, it is assigned a four-digit number that is recorded by hand with the patron's name in a card file. After the garment is cleaned, its position number on the conveyor is written on the appropriate patron's card and once again filed. When the customer returns, the card is taken from the file and the garment location number entered into the computer with a telephone-style keypad. The digital controller then turns the conveyor and retrieves the patron's garment.

ANALYSIS OF ALTERNATIVES

The alternatives were analyzed for three criteria considered essential by Cottrell Technologies:

- the compatibility of the controller with the existing Techni-Veyor system,
- the cost of the unit and system modifications, and
- the relative ease of operation.

page 2

Headings and subheadings help readers preview and review the major chunks of information.

The reference to video stores reminds readers that they are probably already familiar with bar code scanners.

The operation of two different interfaces (the bar code scanner and keypad) is presented in similar ways so readers give the interfaces equal consideration.

The foregrounding of the analysis section of the report lets readers know what to anticipate.

The penultimate (next-to-final) drafts of the executive summary (Figure 17.11d) and the body of the report (Figures 17.11f, h, k, m) have been edited by Nancy. In these penultimate drafts, Nancy not only makes minor grammatical and mechanical corrections (and runs the spell checker), but she also sees places that need foregrounding (previewing), that need additional clarifying information, and that need some reordering of information.

FIGURE 17.11j ■ **Final Version of Recommendation Report**

Readers need to know why each criterion is important.

Compatibility

Because many customers already have a Techni-Veyor system in place, compatibility between the existing system and the new input controller is an important consideration. The new controller should be easily adaptable to customers' existing hardware. The bar code and keypad controllers differ in their compatibility with Techni-Veyor hardware.

The two alternatives should be discussed in the same order—first the bar code interface and then the keypad interface—for each criterion.

Bar code interface. The bar code interface involves a lengthy installation period because of problems with compatibility. The Techni-Veyor rack is labeled with four-digit numbers above each garment slot. Installation of the bar code system requires labeling the entire rack with bar code decals. Depending on the size of the rack, this takes from a couple of hours to a day.

Charlotte Manfield, general manager of Fairfield Cleaners in Ames, said that the installation downtime could cost her considerable business. Ms. Manfield emphasized the importance of maintaining an efficient garment-retrieval system of some sort in the event of a mechanical problem, breakdown, or system upgrade. Some advance planning would help Ms. Manfield (and other customers with similar large dry cleaning businesses) to avoid delays and customer dissatisfaction due to time delays caused by the installation of a bar code controller system.

Keypad interface. The compatibility of the keypad interface with an existing Techni-Veyor is very good. The only installation time involves plugging the controller into the conveyor and calibrating it for the size of the rack. Installation time is no more than an hour, including learning to use the controller in the process of setting it up. The Techni-Veyor rack is already numbered for use with the keypad interface and requires only the patience of the operator in becoming familiar with the digital controller.

page 3

The final report begins with a letter of transmittal (Figure 17.11a) followed by a title page (Figure 17.11b), a table of contents (Figure 17.11c), an executive summary (Figure 17.11e), and the body of the report (Figure 17.11g, i, j, l, n).

As the liaison between the team and the company, Nancy must make a formal presentation of the report's recommendations to Cottrell Technologies. (Also see Chapter 18, Figure 18.3 and Figure 18.6 to review the team's outline and overhead transparencies accompanying the presentation to Cottrell Technologies about the team's recommendations.)

In comparing the draft and final versions of this report for Cottrell Technologies, you can see a number of revisions. The ability to assess the qualitative differences in these revisions helps distinguish skillful communicators from those less skillful. At this point, you might benefit from reviewing the guidelines presented in Chapter 1 (see Figure 1.1) to help analyze and assess technical documents. The following bulleted list uses these guidelines to identify some of the changes up to this point in the report for Cottrell Technologies.

- **_Identify the content and context._** In preparing the final version of the report, the writers provide readers with more information right from the beginning. For example, they revise the executive summary to more accurately reflect the content and organization of the report.

- **_Anticipate reader's needs._** In preparing the final version, the writers anticipate readers' needs in a number of ways. For example, they present general information first, followed by specific information; they make sure to use terminology consistently; and they discuss the two alternatives in the same order—first the bar code interface and then the keypad interface—for each criterion so that readers make comparisons more easily.

- **_Establish connections._** In preparing the final version, the writers create clear links between ideas; thus, the information is more understandable. For example, they help readers by presenting parallel amounts of information about different interfaces in similar ways, so readers give these points similar consideration.

- **_Use effective design and visuals._** In preparing the final version, the writers improve the design. For example, they more clearly chunk information, emphasize key points with design elements, use type choices and spacing consistently, and make information easier to locate by using elements such as headings and bullets.

- **_Make the text accessible._** In preparing the final version, the writers make the information more accessible by adding introductory paragraphs that preview upcoming information. For example, they add a preview paragraph in the Comparability section to explain the importance of the criterion.

- **_Reflect professional standards._** In preparing the final version, the writers conform to conventions for style and usage. For example, they generally use active voice, select appropriate diction; adhere to conventions for capitalization and abbreviations, and eliminate problems with dangling modifiers and agreement.

When you finish reading the draft and final versions of the report for Cottrell Technologies, you can use these guidelines to compare changes made in the final pages. You need experience in applying these guidelines, both to become more skillful in revising your own documents as well as to become a more constructive colleague when co-workers ask you to review their documents.

FIGURE 17.11k ■ Draft of Recommendation Report

"Solicit" is simply the wrong word to use here.

An introductory paragraph in the Cost section would help readers understand the variability of cost.

The table needs to be
a. referred to in the text by a table number;
b. given a clear, descriptive title;
c. redesigned so information is easier to read quickly.

Someone should have double-checked the arithmetic.

Keypad Interface

The compatibility of the keypad system with an existing Techni-Veyor is very good. The only installation time involves plugging the controller into the conveyor and calibrating it for the size of the rack. Including learning to use the controller in the process of setting it up, installation time is no more than an hour. The Techni-Veyor rack is already numbered for use with the keypad interface and solicits *requires* only the patience of the operator in becoming familiar with the digital controller.

Cost *Add ¶ introducing cost issues.*

Bar code and keypad interface units are sold by many different manufacturing companies. Five different companies were researched through the *Thomas Register* and quoted for prices on appropriate bar code and keypad units. A summary of the findings are shown below. *Table 1 presents*

Table 1

	Bar Code	Keypad
Cutler-Hammer Eaton	$879	$149
North Brook Electric	$799	$139
KB Electronics, Inc.	$820	$180
Cableform, Inc.	$699	$169
Hybrid Microelectronics	$850	$150
Average Cost	$819	$157

less expensive *interface*

Add $ to table

Clearly, investing in a keypad interface is far cheaper than purchasing a bar code unit. The cost of the remaining digital controller package is not detailed here because it is approximately $100 for either input interface. Therefore, the cost of the bar code controller package is roughly $920 versus the keypad controller package at around $250.
averages $909 *With the additional expense, which averages $257*

DRAFT - 4

FIGURE 17.11I ■ **Final Version of Recommendation Report**

Cost

Both bar code and keypad interface units are widely available, but they differ considerably in cost. To continue building a competitively priced system, Cottrell Technologies should choose a cost-effective input unit that satisfies customers without incurring excessive hardware costs.

Bar code and keypad interface units are sold by many different manufacturers. Five different companies were researched through *Thomas Register*. Table 1 presents a summary of the prices on appropriate bar code and keypad units.

Table 1. Comparative Costs of Bar Code and Keypad Interfaces

Vendors	Bar Code Interface	Keypad Interface
Cutler-Hammer Eaton	$879	$149
North Brook Electric	$799	$139
KB Electronics, Inc.	$820	$180
Cableform, Inc.	$699	$169
Hybrid Microelectronics	$850	$150
Average Interface Cost	**$809**	**$157**
Additional Costs	$100	$100
Average Total Cost	**$909**	**$257**

Investing in a keypad interface is far less expensive than purchasing a bar code interface. The costs of the remaining digital controller package are not detailed here because these expenses are approximately $100 for either input interface. With the additional expenses, the cost of the bar code controller package averages $909 versus the keypad controller package which averages $257.

Ease of Operation

Entering data with either input interface is simple. Both devices are widely used as input devices and require little training.

page 4

The most efficient way to present cost comparisons is to create an easy-to-read table. The table title clearly describes information readers will find.

This revised table uses horizontal and vertical rules and adds some white space to separate the five vendors and the two kinds of interfaces.

Boldface column heads and averages highlight this information.

Writers and editors always need to double-check numbers. The simple arithmetic errors in the draft have been corrected.

An introductory paragraph to the next section orients readers before they turn the page.

FIGURE 17.11m ■ Draft of Recommendation Report

Ease of Operation

[handwritten: Expand overview +]

Entering data with either input interface is a simple task. Typing the four-digit garment location number on a telephone-style keypad is as easy as entering a telephone number. Efficiency at keypad data entry requires dexterity as well as practice. Scanning a bar code also demands little effort. ~~The act of~~ placing the scan wand on the bar code decal or identification tag requires little or no practice and is slightly faster in the long run than typing in a number.

[handwritten left margin: Add ① disadvan ② contrast w/ scanner ^]

DISCUSSION

[handwritten: Add intro. sentence ←]

In review, the bar code interface requires more installation time, is more expensive, and is the easier of the two methods to operate. The keypad interface requires minimal installation time, is considerably cheaper, and takes slightly longer to operate than the bar code system. From the consumers' point of view, the keypad interface is more user-friendly in terms of set-up time and is more cost-effective. The bar code system takes less practice to operate, but requires virtually the same time to enter data as does a keypad.

[handwritten right margin: Turn into 2-col. list to compare.]

Large dry cleaning companies may be less concerned with the cost of the ~~controller,~~ *[handwritten: interface]* but may object to shutting down their conveyor for more than an hour. Small dry cleaning outfits may not be worried about installation time and also unable to afford an upgrade over a few hundred dollars.

RECOMMENDATION

~~In light of the analysis criteria as a whole,~~ we recommend ~~investing in~~ a digital controller with a keypad input interface. The keypad input method is quick and easy to install onto an existing Techni-Veyor, is relatively inexpensive, and is nearly as fast as scanning a bar code. It saves the owner from losing much business during installation, and does not exclude the small-~~time~~ dry cleaning company from investing in a system upgrade. ~~All things considered,~~ the keypad input controller is a cost-effective upgrade for dry cleaning businesses of all sizes.

DRAFT - 5

Adding a sentence provides an overview of the Ease of Operation section.

The interfaces should be discussed in the same order as in the previous two sections—bar code scanner first, keypad second.

Chunking related information into separate paragraphs makes it easier for readers to understand.

Adding a sentence to compare the operation of the two interfaces makes it easier for readers to understand the team's recommendation.

The difference between "small companies" and "small-time companies is noted."

FIGURE 17.11n ■ **Final Version of Recommendation Report**

Bar Code Interface. Scanning a bar code requires almost no effort. Placing the scan wand on the bar code decal or identification tag requires little or no practice and is slightly faster than typing in a four-digit number on a keypad.

Keypad Interface. Typing the four-digit garment location number on a telephone-style keypad is as easy as entering a telephone number. Speed and accuracy at keypad data entry require dexterity as well as practice. Keypad entry is susceptible to operator error though such mistakes are easily corrected. The time difference between scanning a bar code and typing the four-digit number on a keypad is insignificant for this application.

Changing the order to discuss bar code scanners before keypads makes the sequence consistent in each criterion. (In the draft, keypad operation was discussed first.)

DISCUSSION

Our team has identified the following differences between bar code interfaces and keypad interfaces:

Chunking information into separate paragraphs helps readers comprehend and recall that information.

bar code interface	keypad interface
• compatibility: adjustments	• compatibility: immediate
• installation: 2–10 hours	• installation: 1–2 hours
• cost: average $909	• cost: average $257
• training: minimal	• training: minimal
• operation: very easy	• operation: easy

The discussion summarizes the findings about the differences between the bar code interface and the keypad interface. Information in a two-column list is easier to compare than information in a paragraph.

Large dry cleaning companies may be less concerned with the cost of the interface but may object to shutting down their conveyor for more than an hour. Small dry cleaning companies may be worried about installation time and also unable to afford an upgrade over a few hundred dollars.

RECOMMENDATION

Based on our analysis, we recommend a digital controller with a keypad input interface. The keypad input interface is quick and easy to install onto an existing Techni-Veyor, is relatively inexpensive, and is nearly as fast as scanning a bar code. A keypad interface saves the owner from losing much business during installation and does not exclude small dry cleaning companies from investing in a system upgrade. The keypad input controller is a cost-effective upgrade for dry cleaning businesses of all sizes.

The recommendation is based on the concluding summary and the team's knowledge about the preferences of managers of dry cleaning companies.

page 5

End-of-Chapter
Recommendations for Technical Communicators

1. Decide whether you want a report to present or to analyze information.

2. Learn a generic sequence for reporting information, a sequence that you can modify depending on the specific purpose and audience:
   a. Overview
   b. Background
   c. Recommendations
   d. Evidence
   e. Discussion

3. Identify the audience and purpose of the report.

4. Learn the basic functions and forms of these frequently used informal reports:
   - task reports
   - periodic activity reports
   - progress reports
   - meeting minutes
   - trip and conference reports
   - "to file" documents

5. Select the form of a report that is most appropriate for the purpose and audience. Choose from prepared forms, memos, letters, or formal reports.

6. Use a two-tier approach for most reports:
   a. Give an overview and then summarize the preferred solution.
   b. Cite evidence or support for the solution in descending order of significance, dealing with both positive and negative points.

7. Learn a generic formal report format that incorporates the standard elements of the front matter, body, and end matter of most reports. Be familiar enough with the format that you can modify it to meet the needs of specific situations.

8. Use design elements to make reports more appealing and accessible: headings and subheadings, pagination, figures and tables.

Practicum

Responding to Change

Wellmark, Inc., which is located in Des Moines, Iowa, is a Medicare contractor for HCFA (Health Care Financing Administration). As a contractor, Wellmark processes Medicare claims for health care providers located across the United States. Wellmark serves health care providers in every state except Maine.

A bit of history: Wellmark has an entire division consisting of 426 employees dedicated to the Medicare contract and has been a HCFA contractor since the inception of the Medicare program in 1966. In 1998, Wellmark served 4,063 health care providers and processed 6,228,020 claims.

In addition to the Medicare contract, Wellmark operates six subsidiaries and two charitable foundations:

Subsidiaries

- Wellmark Blue Cross and Blue Shield of South Dakota, the first health insurer in South Dakota

- Wellmark Administrators, Inc., a nationwide third-party administrator (TPA) headquartered in Des Moines

- Wellmark Administrators of South Dakota, Inc., a third-party administrator located in Sioux Falls

- Wellmark Community Insurance, Inc., a life and health insurance company licensed in 30 states and offering health insurance in Wisconsin, Illinois and Nebraska

- Wellmark HealthNetwork, Inc., one of the largest preferred provider organizations (PPOs) in the Midwest

- Wellmark Benefit Consultants, Inc., an insurance agency

Foundations

- The Wellmark Foundation, a private foundation that supports public health improvement in Wellmark communities

- The Caring Foundation, a public charity that provides free health care coverage to uninsured children in Iowa and South Dakota

Scenario

One of the challenges faced by the Wellmark Medicare division is communicating information to its geographically diverse health care provider audience. The primary method of communication is a monthly newsletter called the *Medicare A Newsline*, which is mailed to every provider.

The *Newsline* provides short reports and news articles that inform providers about changes in Medicare coverage, educate providers about billing information, and respond to specific provider questions in its Forum section. Providers rely on the *Newsline* for Medicare information, especially since Medicare coverage and billing requirements can change rapidly. For example, last summer, our home health care providers were mandated by HCFA to bill all of their health care claims sequentially. This meant that a home health agency had to submit June's claim and receive payment for it before the July claim could be billed.

This new requirement was controversial for home health care providers because billing sequentially meant delayed payments and closer tracking of their claims, which required additional staff time. Providers were very frustrated with this process, and while we understood their frustration, we could not reverse HCFA's decision to require this billing process.

Example

Teaching providers about the sequential billing process fell to the department in which I work, Medicare Education and Outreach; thus, throughout the Summer and Fall of 1998, we provided extensive education to providers. During the course of providing this education, we saw how the change in the billing process was negatively impacting providers. Specifically, payments were delayed, claims were not being processed in the electronic billing system correctly, etc.

Fortunately, after much input from the provider community and from Wellmark and other HCFA contractors, HCFA decided to remove the sequential billing requirement. This is what was published in the July 1, 1999 *Newsline* to inform providers of the removal of sequential billing:

Removal of Sequential Edits for Home Health Claims

Effective July 1, 1999, claims for home health services under a plan of care (bill types 32X and 33X) are no longer required to be submitted in sequence.

The shift of payment for home health visits from the Part A to Part B trust fund after one hundred visits, as mandated by §4611 of the Balanced Budget Act of 1997, remains in effect. **The first one hundred visits will be counted in the order in which they are processed;** therefore, we suggest that you continue to submit your claims in sequence in order to prevent the need for later adjustments.

The sequential billing for other claims, such as hospice claims is still required. The Florida Shared System (FSS) sequential edits for home health claims (32X and 33X) will be removed as of July 1, 1999. Any backlog of claims that you may be holding due to sequential billing requirements may be submitted on or after July 1, 1999.

Assignment

1. Given the scenario described above about provider frustration with the sequential billing process, consider the following issues and questions:

   - Do you think the explanation published above was appropriate? Accomplished its purpose? Pay special attention to the highlighted areas of the explanation.

   - If you were a provider, how would you feel about this response to a problem you have been struggling with for the past 12 months?

   - Is this an example of good customer service?

   - No explanation is given about why the billing requirement was removed. Speculate about why. Do you think this was an appropriate decision?

   - What questions might providers have after reading this explanation?

   - What tone does the explanation convey?

   - If you were going to re-write this explanation, what would you need to consider? How would you begin the explanation? How would you end it?

   - Imagine that this explanation is also part of a report. What else should be included in the report?

2. Now that you've considered some of the primary issues and questions involved, rewrite the explanation so that it is more responsive to needs that you imagine providers have. Additionally, include a memo to your instructor that explains the rationale for your revision decisions. Remember to consider the following points as you rewrite the explanation:

   - Wellmark enjoys a close, productive working relationship with its providers and encourages an environment of open communication between itself and its customers.

   - Many providers were adversely affected by the sequential billing requirements and encountered grave financial difficulties because of the requirement.

   - This explanation is the first and only communication about the removal of sequential billing.

Elizabeth M. Herman is the Senior Technical Coordinator and Webmaster in the Medicare Education and Outreach department at Wellmark, Inc. Her major job responsibilities include designing and conducting computer-based training classes, writing and editing education materials, and managing the Medicare Web site. Prior to joining the Medicare Education and Outreach department at Wellmark, Inc., she worked as a technical writer for a higher education consulting firm. She completed a B.A. in journalism at the University of Iowa and M.A. in rhetoric, composition, and professional communication at Iowa State University.

Individual and Collaborative Assignments

1. **Evaluate two reports.** Locate a report that has been approved and one that has been disapproved. Using what you have learned in this chapter and your own experience, develop a rubric to evaluate the effectiveness of reports. Review both reports and fill the rubric in accordingly. Discuss why you think one was approved and the other not.

2. **Write a series of reports.** Imagine that you would like your company to fund your travel to a professional conference in your field of study. Write the appropriate reports generated by such a trip: request for authorization to go, request for expense money, report of the trip, expense report, and a recommendation that your company adopt a procedure or product that you learned about.

3. **Conduct research for a report.** The local office of OSHA (the federal Occupational Safety and Health Agency) has requested a report of your plant's accommodations—or lack of them—for disabled workers. What reports would you need to obtain, and what would you need to write? (You are not preparing the actual documents; rather, you are explaining the probable source, type, audience, and context).

4. **Revise a report.** Work with a small group to complete the following tasks based on excerpts from an analytical report on page 650.
   (a) Read through the paragraphs and, with your group, decide a possible purpose and audience for the report from which these paragraphs are taken.
   (b) Decide the sequence of the paragraphs so that they form a logical, coherent discussion. Have reasons for your decisions.
   (c) Create headings and subheadings for this section of the report so that readers can easily follow the discussion. Have reasons for your decisions.
   (d) Compare and discuss your group's decisions and reasons with those of other groups in the class.[9]

5. **Write a formal report.** Identify a problem that needs to be solved and prepare a formal report that supports the most appropriate solution. Subjects come from your personal or community life, your academic work, or your professional work. The list of verbs in the left-hand column may help you decide how to approach a report. Some possible topics are listed in the right-hand column. Try matching the verbs with several of the topics to see how changing the action may change how you think about approaching the report.

Actions to Consider	*Topics for Inquiry*
analyze	agriculture on marginal lands
approve	artificial insemination
change	cable television
compare	capital expenditure for equipment
eliminate	corporate daycare facility
establish	corporate physical fitness program
initiate	drainage problem
install	energy alternatives
institute	food co-op
investigate	insulation alternatives
justify	machine or program X versus machine or program Y
organize	management system for department, warehouse
recommend	manufacturing, testing, marketing procedure
reorganize	over-the-counter cold remedies
synthesize	program to eliminate electrostatic discharge
verify	solar hot-water heater
	telemarketing program
	test and immunization program
	toxic waste dump in your community
	water quality in local lake, river, reservoir
	wetlands disruption

1. Perhaps the most appealing aspect of developing this site is the availability of existing infrastructure. All major utilities are immediately available: electric, gas, water, sanitary sewer, storm sewer, telephone, and fire hydrant lines. All of these services are currently available on the site or are on the border of the site. All road surfaces are in moderately good-to-excellent shape, and Mortensen Road is being newly paved westbound from State Avenue. Mortensen Road, eastbound from the site, is already a 4-lane roadway leading to an exit ramp for Highway 30.

2. As noted in Perceptual Characteristics of the Site Analysis, the site is generally flat. More visual diversity would aid in the creation of a development concept and general excitement for what could be created. All other unique features are human-made structures that are intended to be torn down or relocated.

3. This site is located at the intersection of two major arterials, State Avenue and Mortensen Road. Additionally, reasonable and ready access is available to Highway 30 and Lincoln Way via Mortensen Road and State Avenue. With these three arterial roadways and access to Interstate 35, access to the site and the area is excellent. Appendix 5 shows an area map and traffic counts to give a feel for the area.

4. The close proximity to infrastructure is arguably the most compelling reason for development of this site. All current University facilities are easily relocated. The negative aspects of site development are readily overcome. Another compelling reason to develop is the need for affordable housing. With a proper combination of housing types, a site of this size and location could produce hundreds of safe, inexpensive, easily accessible, and well-planned homes.

5. This site has three major negative aspects of development. The first is its lack of visual diversity. Second, ownership of this property and the current lease status could create significant problems in terms of delays and stoppages. Finally, the existence of pollutants could cause limited but significant problems.

6. The residue of agricultural chemicals may or may not cause short-term problems. The primary concerns for ongoing pollution problems are the compost facility run by the university and noise pollution from the college dormitories and Highway 30.

7. This site is buildable for more than its physical characteristics. On the physical side, the topography is generally flat, and soils are favorable for or adequate for development. But other benefits immediately present themselves. It is a negative that there is a lack of visual diversity, but that also means there is less to do to prepare the site for construction. The vegetation is light to non-existent, wildlife is no factor, and other animals will relocate with the movement of the existing facilities. Existing facilities have already discussed moving or have made plans to relocate. The site is high above the flood way and has moderate-to-excellent drainage. Overall neighboring and existing land use is not an encumbrance to most if not all development plans.

8. This site has three major positive aspects of development. First is its excellent transportation access. Second is its favorable developmental characteristics. And third is its excellent access to existing infrastructure.

9. The University is the current owner of the site. Aside from the lengthy approval process for any sale involving a government agency of this type, there is also a 99-year lease that is currently only 17 years old. This lease is with the USDA. Potential delays should be anticipated when dealing with these agencies.

Intertext

Clearing the Air: Some Thoughts on Gender-Neutral Writing[10]

A technical writer friend described a disagreement he'd had with his editor over gender-specific pronouns. In describing the use of the cockpit equipment in a fighter plane, the writer had used *he* to refer to the pilot—not because he favors generic *he,* but because the choice seemed natural. After all, he said, "there are no women fighter pilots, not even in Israel." But later, he told me, his editor had changed every *he* to a *he or she.* The writer's reaction: "I turned the air blue."

I sighed, but I sympathized with both of them because I face the same issues frequently in my work with drafting statutes. I believe my friend is a person of good will, and he says he accepts the arguments for gender-free, or gender-fair, writing. I don't know my friend's editor, but I know the editorial predicament. The editor is someone who knows that a writer's *he* can easily be read as a deliberate exclusion, who has heard plenty about the issue of sexism in writing, and who wants to avoid giving offense, for the sake of the company or the publication. The editor is also pressed for time and careful enough of the writer's ego to hesitate to do wholesale rewriting. To a person in this situation, *he or she,* even when used repeatedly, might seem like a harmless solution.

To my friend, it was anything but harmless. His editor's changes seemed to accuse him of sexism; they implied that he had forgotten or ignored women's role in his subject when in fact he had considered it carefully. At the same time, the changes seemed to him to introduce awkwardness and inaccuracy—awkwardness because they produced more repetition than English sentences can comfortably handle, and inaccuracy because a female fighter pilot is a being who doesn't yet exist.

This disagreement is a good example of the challenges we face when we try for gender-neutral writing. Unquestionably, it can make us angry. On the small scale of daily work, it can be a grind to try to reshape one's usual feel for pronouns.

In technical writing especially, feelings about gender-neutral writing run high because, even now, few women enter technical fields and the ones who do sometimes feel embattled. The men feel embattled, too; it's not pleasant to be accused of sexism. But disagreements about pronouns happen for other reasons apart from the issue of sex discrimination. The purpose of this article is to explore the reasons for the irritation we sometimes feel about gender-neutral writing and to suggest ways to avoid it.

Practical Writing and Pronoun Fatigue

In humanistic writing, depicting women and men as equals is a many-faceted problem, even an interesting one (*1*). It can be a test of one's ear, a challenge to one's sense of metaphor: Which word for "people in general" should I use here? Am I being offensive if I call someone an Amazon? But in "practical" writing the writer is rarely called on to talk about humanity. Questions about the correct use of sex-linked images and metaphors do not arise for someone writing a regulation, a user's manual, or a product insert. Rather, the practical writer's focus is on do's and don'ts—on equipment and the equipment operator, or on the rights and obligations of each member of a certain class. The goal is usually to describe, or prescribe, the actions of one person following a procedure or interacting with an apparatus. In this context, the only questions are about pronouns. Do I use *he/she, he or she,* or do I look for another solution? The questions are a distraction from the writer's subject and they arise repeatedly, monotonously.

The solution to a monotonous problem lies, in part, in avoiding a single, monotonous solution. Editors who are anxious to promote gender-neutral writing assure us that any problem can be handled with the right attitude and a few simple rules. In fact, any prepackaged answer to the pronoun problem will have its own problems, especially in technical or legal writing.

Sometimes the question "What pronoun should I use?" has a simple answer: Don't use any third-person singular pronouns. Use the imperative; that is, use commands or directions: "Simmer 5 minutes over low heat" or "Insert tab A into slot B." Or use *you:* "You agree not to keep pets in the apartment unless you have my written permission." Or use the plural: "Users of model d38 should turn to chapter 12." Or repeat the noun.

These are familiar solutions by now, and valuable ones. Those of us who do legal writing owe a debt of gratitude to technical writers for devising these solutions. It is a boon to writers as well as readers that *you* and the imperative can be used now in types of writing where they would have been unacceptable 15 years ago: consumer contracts, insurance policies, and some administrative regulations (2). But these familiar solutions are not appropriate in every case.

For example, if I am describing a problem with a piece of equipment, the mode of discourse I want to use is description, not directions. Consider the following problem report about some in-house indexing software:

"The online instructions for routine 5 (combining index working documents) are unclear. The prompt 'Enter new COMBINED document id' doesn't tell the indexer that she must create a completely new, empty document."

The people in this sentence and the balance of this report—the indexers—need to be discussed in the third person, not addressed in the second. They, and their reactions to the software, are the subject of the piece, not its audience. In such a situation, using the third person—nouns supplemented by *he, she, it,* and *they*—is still the only acceptable choice.

The plural isn't always a solution either. Most commonly, the plural fails to satisfy when the writer's focus is on a single person, not a class of persons. For example, there is only one commissioner of agriculture in a state at any one time, so it feels unnatural to draft a law that assigns a duty to "them." And in cases where the plural does sound natural, it must be used with care to avoid legal problems. Suppose a drafter writes "A person convicted of a crime under sections 609.33 to 609.35 is eligible for supervised release if he . . ." An editor bent on avoiding *he* might change this to read "Persons convicted of crimes . . . are eligible . . . if they . . ." But this creates an ambiguity:

does the eligibility apply only to those convicted of multiple offenses? This sort of ambiguity can be cured if the editor is alert to it, but the usual advice in legal drafting manuals is to draft in the singular, always.

So, despite the standard solutions, we still have a problem: Sometimes, what we really want to do is refer, over and over again, to an individual in action. To do that, we can use the noun over and over, or we can use pronouns. Because either a noun or a pronoun repeated too often can sound unnatural, we need a variety of techniques to help us reduce the number of instances of the noun or pronoun chosen. The drafters in my office used every technique available in English to make Minnesota statutes gender-neutral. Here are a few of them:

- Many instances of *his* can be removed or replaced with *a, an,* or *the.*
- Sometimes *his* can be avoided by changing a nominal to a verbal expression:

  A person who imports or [has in his possession] possesses untaxed intoxicating liquor is guilty of a misdemeanor.
- *If . . . then he* clauses can often be changed to *who* (or *which* or *that*) clauses:

  [If] An applicant who has been licensed in another state [he] shall submit verification of licensure and the required fee.
- *When* clauses can be changed to *on* or *upon* phrases, or modifiers without expressed subjects:

  [If the commissioner finds] Upon finding that the sampling frequency can be safely reduced, [he] the

commissioner may order it reduced as specified in clause (2).

- Changing *himself* is tricky because *himself* or *herself* is more obtrusive than *he* or *she.* One solution is to omit or replace the reflexive pronoun rather than substituting *himself* or *herself.*

All these methods are useful for cutting down the number of nouns and pronouns, but all have their limitations. And some methods are positively dangerous.

The Dangers of Pronoun-Dodging

One standard solution, the passive voice, is tempting for technical and scientific editors. Technical writing has, after all, a much higher tolerance for the passive than do most other kinds of writing. But a writer runs two big risks in making active sentences passive in order to avoid pronouns. The first is the risk that the sentences will be squeezed into an unnatural shape, so that the emphasis falls in the wrong place and misleads the reader. As George Gopen and Joseph Williams have pointed out, "readers tend to expect that the material the writer intends to emphasize will appear at the end of the sentence" (3). They also point out that "readers expect a unit of discourse to be about whoever shows up first." If a sentence is composed in the active voice, and an editor makes it passive, chances are the reader will get a slightly different sense of what the sentence is about and what the writer wanted to emphasize. (The same holds, of course, for the sentence changed from passive to active by an editor with more training in writing than in technical fields.)

The second risk of the passive is the legal risk that the sentence will say what

should be done without explaining who is supposed to do it. If "all improvements of the patented invention which are made hereafter shall be promptly disclosed," we have no idea who must disclose them, or to whom (*4*).

Trying to do without pronouns is tricky. And we need to avoid the feeling that we must run from every pronoun. Unless we shake that feeling, we will start writing sentences like "Failure to file an objection shall be deemed an assent," sentences from which the people have disappeared. In the end we have to decide about pronouns: masculine or feminine, or both?

He: What Does It Mean?

We are in the middle of a linguistic change that is a big part of our pronoun problem. The word *he* actually means different things to different speakers.

The English pronoun system has undergone this kind of change before. Early in the history of English, *his* could mean "of it" as well as "of him" (*5*). But in the late Middle English period, the meaning began to change. With the development of the possessive case rule for most nouns (the rule that says "add an s-sound to a word to make it possessive") people began to take the pronoun *it* and add -s to it, producing *its*. There were then two words that could mean "of it" and a deep disagreement over the meaning of *his*. Did it mean "of it" and "of him" or only "of him"? Writers nervous about the choice of *his* or *its* avoided both words and used *thereof,* and so we see phrases like "The earth is the Lord's and the fullness thereof" in early English translations of the Bible.

Our tension suggests that a real meaning change is going on. We are doing ex-actly as our forebears did, and as speakers have often done when a rule of the language is changing: We are avoiding *he* because we know we do not agree about what it means. Now, as in the 16th century, there are three camps of pronoun users in English, two in opposition and a third shifting between them.

In one group are the people who sincerely believe that *he* includes both sexes if used in a context where sex is not relevant. For them, *he* is not sexist when they write it; it depicts a person of unspecified gender, or even a genderless entity like a corporation. These writers find it very hard to believe that anyone really reads generic *he* as exclusive. They find the phrase *he or she* needless and intrusive because it introduces the idea of an actor's sex where it doesn't belong. Reed Dickerson, the country's foremost authority on legal drafting, makes a complaint that is typical of this group: "The sexism, if any [in generic *he*] consists of residual overtones of maleness significant mainly to persons hypersensitized by a preoccupation with feminist concerns" (*6*).

In the second group are the people for whom *he* is truly exclusive; it means male persons only. Some people in this group resent the language they see as exclusive; others gloss over *he* without notice because it agrees with their mental image. The members of this group doubt that anyone really reads the generic *he* as inclusive. They have produced a significant body of research in support of the thesis that readers do not understand *he* as a true generic, but none that takes seriously the users of generic *he* (*7*). This difference is the second major source of our anger over gender-neutral writing. Each group disbelieves the other's statements about what *he* means and accuses the other of ill will.

In the third group are the readers who can genuinely shift between meanings of *he*. They may be able to understand *he* as inclusive or not, as needed. They may not recognize their own shifts. Most important, though, they recognize that other people will read *he* in different ways. That recognition is important in preserving the peace about gender-neutral writing. Writers and editors benefit from seeing their problems as rooted in linguistic change and not in politics or stubbornness.

Working with Our Differences

In a linguistically divided world, is there any advice that will hold for all writers and editors of technical material, no matter how they read *he*? I think so, and I will offer some. My advice, though, can only make sense to readers who accept my arguments about the changing meaning of *he* and who will grant that speakers of English can understand *he* in different ways.

First, writers and editors must be conscious of the mental images they form. A writer who can use *he* as a true generic may be able to write *he* while holding in mind the image of a woman, or no image at all. But such a writer must remember that some readers will form a different mental image: to those readers, *he* can only depict a man. Similarly, a writer who uses *he* exclusively must remember that some readers will see it as generic, the kind of *he* that is supposed to refer to both sexes. (In other words, a writer can deliberately choose *he* to talk about a situation that applies to men only, yet end up being scolded because readers believe the *he* means *he or she* and should have been written so.)

Both writers and editors need to remember that the mental image called up by *he* depends on the reader's understanding—unless the writer takes extra steps to control that mental image. To do so, a writer can try the technique of forewarning readers about the mental image they are expected to make. A very short sentence like "Assume for the moment a male technician" will do. Many good examples of this technique appear in Benjamin Spock's *Baby and Child Care (8)*. This type of forewarning puts readers on notice that the writer's choice of pronoun is considered and not thoughtless. Some writers may feel that the notice is unnecessary when the mental image is of a woman, but in a female-dominated technical field, such as nursing, it can be useful to remind the reader that the person in an example could have been male. The reminder should be brief and understated.

Both writers and editors need to create a consistent image. Although some editors advise writers to alternate male and female examples in order to write gender-neutrally, no one seriously advocates alternating pronouns within the frame of a single example. Alternation of that type is either funny or incomprehensible, like the following hypothetical version of state extradition law:

"A person arrested under an extradition warrant must not be delivered over to the agent whom the executive authority demanding him has appointed to receive her until he has been taken before a judge, who must inform her of the demand made for his surrender and of the crime with which she is charged."

Clearly, the person in an example can only have one sex at a time. If the writer is truly asking a reader to focus on one individual, that individual must be male or female. Therefore, editors should beware of reading every *he* as a deliberate exclusion of women. It is not wrong for a writer to use *he* to direct a reader to call up the mental image of a man.

It is insensitive, though, to refuse to acknowledge the presence of women or to refuse to envision them in jobs they do not commonly hold. Therefore, both writers and editors need to expand their mental images. Both should be willing to use *she*. This is easier now than it used to be; feminine pronouns are now appearing in all sorts of practical writing. A blister pack of diaper pins carries the warning: "To protect your baby when diapering, always place your fingers between her and the diaper." A text on legal writing notes that "[w]hen . . . a lawyer acts as the editor of another lawyer's writing, she must summon a variety of skills. . . ." (*9*). I have never seen a serious argument that this usage denies the existence of male babies or male lawyers.

Both writers and editors need to avoid mechanical solutions. In general, this means reserving *he or she* for times when we want the reader to call up two separate mental images. This might happen, for example, when there is a real sex difference to acknowledge, some evidence that men and women will really use a piece of equipment in different ways. At all costs, writers and editors need to avoid plugging in a uniform pronoun substitute throughout a passage without paying attention to sentence position and context.

It should be some consolation to know that writers before us have survived linguistic disagreements. As long as we acknowledge that no technique is a panacea, and that there are real differences among speakers of English regarding *he,* we can produce good practical writing that is gender-neutral. No one will have to alienate a portion of the intended audience, or write badly, in the name of gender equity. And no one will feel like turning the air blue.

References

(1) For a complete and current look at the range of these problems, and useful solutions, see Maggio, R. *The Nonsexist Word Finder: A Dictionary of Gender-Free Usage;* Oryx Press: Phoenix, 1987.

(2) For examples, see *Drafting Documents in Plain Language;* Practicing Law Institute Course Handbook Series Number 254, Practicing Law Institute: New York, 1981.

(3) Gopen, G.; Williams, J. *U. of Chicago Law Rev.* 1987, 54.

(4) Wydick, R. *Plain English for Lawyers;* 2nd ed. Carolina Academic Press: Durham, N.C., 1985, p. 28.

(5) The evidence for this meaning is collected in the *Oxford English Dictionary*'s entry for *his.*

(6) Dickerson, R. *Fundamentals of Legal Drafting;* 2nd ed. Little, Brown: Boston, p. 229.

(7) Thorne, B. et al. *Language, Gender, and Society: Annotated Bibliography;* Newbury House: New York, 1988, p. 166.

(8) Spock, B. *Baby and Child Care;* Simon & Schuster: New York, 1977.

(9) Weisberg, R. H. *When Lawyers Write;* Little, Brown: Boston, 1987.

Maryann Z. Corbett is Assistant for Writing Standards in the Office of the Revisor of Statutes, a service office of the Minnesota Legislature.

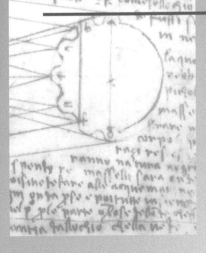

PART V

Creating a
Professional Image

18

Oral Presentations

Managers rated "the ability to communicate ideas and plans effectively in front of an audience" as the most important career skill.

Types of Presentations

Throughout your career, you will give presentations, from informal to formal.

Preparing a Professional Presentation

Once you have identified your audience, you can focus on the purposes for your presentation and determine the kind of research to conduct.

Organizing a Professional Presentation

You can make your presentation more professional by engaging the listeners, by organizing information in various ways, and by using notes or outlines to help you keep track of what you're doing.

Preparing Materials for a Professional Presentation

You can design appropriate visuals and handouts to accompany your presentation. Or you can prepare an entire poster session.

Presenting Yourself

Your professional image depends in part on your appearance and demeanor during the presentation, your vocal characteristics, and the way you handle questions from the audience.

Evaluating Presentations

To be a good critic, you have to be a good listener, an active listener. You also need to know what to look for—and listen to—in the presentations you are asked to evaluate.

O ral presentations play an important part in professional communications. A recent survey of more than 700 managers rated "the ability to communicate ideas and plans effectively in front of an audience" as the most important career skill.[1] Twenty-five percent of these managers said they give presentations at least once a week. Their views confirm that professional reputations (as well as promotions and raises) are positively related to effectiveness in making oral presentations.

This chapter will help you develop oral presentation skills. You first learn about different types of presentations. Then you review the importance of identifying your audience and purpose. Next you learn how to organize your presentation, with particular emphasis on the needs of the audience. Then you deal with the actual presentation—your appearance and your voice. Finally, you review criteria for evaluating presentations in the way that listeners do.

Types of Presentations

Throughout your career, you will give presentations in a variety of settings: meetings, seminars, academic and industrial classes, community meetings, and professional conferences. These settings affect audience expectations and thus your approach. Think of presentations as existing on a continuum from informal to formal, with class presentations as a unique variation.

Often, people speak on the same subject to different audiences in different settings. For example, Lorraine Higgins, a member of a county extension agricultural research group, is investigating the impact of daminozide (commonly known as alar), which is used on some of the apple crop in the United States. Lorraine has sorted out the fiction from the facts of the daminozide controversy in an effort to inform interested people. In disseminating her information, Lorraine will speak to a number of groups: her co-workers, farmers, nutritionists and WIC (Women, Infants, and Children) counselors, parents, newspaper food editors, and EPA officials. Some of her presentations will be informal; others will be formal.

Informal Presentations

One kind of audience for an informal presentation consists of your professional peers or your immediate subordinates or supervisors. You can be informal with this audience because these people are probably familiar with you and your work. Informal presentations often take place in weekly departmental meetings, when you are asked, for example, to describe how you're solving an inventory control problem or to explain progress you've made designing a circuit board for a customer. Informal meetings, which generally include discussion, are often an extension of day-to-day professional activities and conversations.

Another type of informal presentation occurs when a group of people wants to learn new information (which you provide), and your presentation is followed by extensive discussion. Your presentation is a springboard for exploring an idea or issue. Such informal presentations might be given to community groups or special-interest groups.

Whether your informal presentation is for an internal or an external audience, do not think of it as an impromptu presentation that doesn't require preparation. Informal simply means that the people know you, and you already have a working relationship with them. Or it means that the information you're providing will act as the stimulus for a discussion. Even though the presentation is informal, you still need to prepare so that your information is logically organized and your explanations are clear. You may decide to use visuals or handouts. Planning ahead is a good idea so that you present information efficiently.

What types of informal presentations are you likely to give as part of your professional work?

When Lorraine Higgins talks to her co-workers about daminozide, she'll be informal, summarizing her reexamination of the available data. Lorraine will also be informal when she talks to members of the local parents' association, knowing that they not only want facts, but they also want to discuss possible ways daminozide might affect their children. For example, she can tell them that daminozide does penetrate the skin of apples so peeling does no good, but she can also tell them that it's used on less than 5 percent of the apple crops and that less than 1 percent of baby apple juice has shown signs of daminozide. She also speaks informally to a group of food editors from regional newspapers who invite her to a roundtable discussion.

Formal Presentations

The audience for a formal presentation may not be familiar with either you or your work. As a result, formal presentations usually take more time and effort to prepare because you need to provide more background information and adjust the material to the audience's needs. For example, in a formal presentation you might justify departmental reorganization to corporate executives, introduce your company's manufacturing and inspection capabilities to international customers, or explain research findings at a professional society conference.

Sometimes the distinctions between informal and formal presentations are blurred. A project progress report about the development of a new aircraft engine might be submitted informally to other project managers in the same group; however, when the report is given to the customers who are officials from a foreign government, the presentation will certainly be formal.

Both informal and formal presentations may be effectively used in lengthy sessions. For example, a day-long seminar for independent farmers interested in the uses of marginal land might begin with a formal presentation about techniques to extend land use that includes research by the local university and results from experimental farms. This session could be followed by an informal brainstorming session to exchange ideas about ways to practically and profitably use marginal lands. Other formal sessions could deal with financial implications, ecological impact, and government support. Informal sessions would give participants a chance to express their own views and talk with other farmers who have similar concerns and problems.

What types of formal presentations are you likely to give as part of your professional work?

Lorraine Higgins needs to prepare formal presentations for three very different audiences. When she is asked to appear on a panel with two other experts at the fall conference for the region's nutritionists and WIC counselors, she prepares a 15-minute talk that is reinforced with transparencies (vu-graphs). She leaves plenty of time for questions and also hands out information sheets that the audience can pass on to their clients. When Lorraine is invited to address the annual meeting of Eastern Apple Growers, she prepares a formal 25-minute presentation, with transparencies to reinforce her points and handouts for later reference. When she prepares to testify at an EPA hearing, she writes a formal statement and also prepares responses to questions that she expects to be asked.

Class Presentations

Class presentations represent a valuable opportunity to strengthen your oral presentation skills. The class audience provides reactions from a variety of academic and professional interests. In some situations the class can role-play a particular audience. For example, you might have developed an information session for summer interns in mechanical engineering. You could ask the class audience to imagine they are third-year mechanical engineering majors; their role-playing will give you a sense of how the presentation would be received by the actual intended audience.

Class presentations have another benefit that you seldom receive in the professional world. Members of the audience can give you honest, helpful criticism as well as identify areas in which you are particularly effective. Such feedback gives you the chance to maintain and develop your strengths while improving weak areas.

Preparing a Professional Presentation

To give an effective presentation, you must prepare carefully. This section of the chapter discusses steps in preparation, beginning with identifying the audience, followed by focusing on the purpose for your presentation and determining the kind of research you need to conduct.

Audience

The more you know about the listeners you're speaking to, the more likely you are to tailor the presentation to their needs and interests and focus on information that is relevant to them. You must make adjustments for specific audiences in complexity of content, vocabulary, and amount of detail.

Who are you likely to speak with as part of your professional work?

The four audiences in Figure 18.1—professional peers, professional nonexperts, international audiences, and general audiences—are ones you can expect to address at various points in your career. *Professional peers* understand your field's jargon and can draw on relevant background knowledge to understand your points and follow complex ideas. Your presentations to them should be carefully organized, thoroughly documented, and supported by evidence. *Nonexpert professionals* have expectations similar to those of professional peers but are less comfortable with technical jargon and less familiar with current theory and practice. They understand conclusions and recommendations more easily if you precisely define terms, clearly identify benefits as well as problems, employ visuals to stress key information, and provide a logical, easy-to-follow sequence of points. Addressing *international audiences* should require that you be familiar with the customs of those you are addressing, for both courtesy and effective-

---

FIGURE 18.1 ■ Characteristics of Audiences

Possible Audiences	Characteristics
Professional Peers	◆ Assume a high degree of technical expertise
	◆ Expect support that substantiates points
	◆ Typically ask more difficult questions than any other audience
Nonexpert Professionals	◆ Include people in decision-making positions who may have limited technical experience—corporate officers, government officials, military leaders, and the like
	◆ Want technical information but do not need abundant peripheral technical details
	◆ Listen especially carefully to conclusions and recommendations
International Audiences	◆ Appreciate presenter's awareness of and respect for their culture
	◆ May interpret verbal and nonverbal parts of the presentation differently than the presenter intends
	◆ Appreciate well-designed visuals to help define terms and clarify the sequence of processes
General Audiences	◆ May have multiple agendas, but typically come together for a common purpose
	◆ Appreciate a clear statement of purpose, defined terms, useful analogies, interesting examples, effective visuals, and clear transitions
	◆ Respond well to becoming involved

ness. *General audiences* have wide-ranging needs and interests. Such audiences might include a community group with people of varying backgrounds: auto mechanics, supermarket managers, Ph.D. biologists, kindergarten teachers, civil engineers, hair stylists, secretaries, dentists, highway department workers, and so on. (Refer back to Chapter 3 for more discussion about audience.)

Purposes of Presentations

As with so many types of technical communication, once you identify the audience, you can establish the purpose. Knowing the purposes of oral presentations helps you define primary and secondary goals for your own presentations. The nature of a presentation—informal or formal—influences the tone you establish and your audience's expectations.

Oral presentations in business and industry have several purposes that may occur separately or in combination.

- *Informative presentations* give your audience verifiable information, usually for decision making or background. For example, a project supervisor could present a status update report to other project supervisors in the same division of the company.

- *Persuasive presentations* attempt to convince your audience about the advantages of accepting a particular proposal or position. You establish common ground between your own ideas and the ideas of the audience. For example, an engineer could present an oral proposal to the division manager suggesting the restructuring of incoming inspection procedures.

- *Demonstrations* show your audience how something is done, defining and describing a process as it happens, educating the audience without drawing attention to yourself. For example, a company safety officer could demonstrate to summer interns how each piece of equipment in the department operates.

- *Training sessions* teach your audience how to do something, giving them the opportunity for hands-on experience and practice. As a trainer, you have a double task: to teach concepts and techniques to the entire group and also to provide individual assistance. For example, a lab manager could train operators and technicians to follow procedures for safeguarding against contamination of samples.

What persuasive element is part of each of the following presentations?
a. Training to use software to monitor inventory
b. Decision to change production procedures
c. Explanation of control panel on ovens used to heat-treat metal parts
d. Demonstration of CNC (computer numerical control) machines

To accomplish your stated purpose in a presentation, you need specific information; obtaining it may require research or at least the coordination of information you already have. Generally, the research falls into two categories: information you need in order to make the presentation and additional information the audience might ask about. The same primary and secondary research you do for a written report is useful for an oral presentation. (Refer to Chapter 6 for detailed discussion about locating and assessing information.)

Organizing a Professional Presentation

This section of the chapter suggests ways to make your presentation more professional by engaging the listeners, by organizing information in various ways, and by using notes or outlines to help you keep track of what you're doing.

Engaging the Listeners

Your listeners need a reason to pay attention. Some members of your audience—maybe as many as 30 percent—will probably be receptive because they already know that they're interested in the information you have to present. However, another 30 percent aren't sure you have anything important for them; you'll need a little entertainment value to get them to listen. Another 30 percent don't even really want to be there; they'll need to be motivated to even pay attention. (And probably 10 percent of your audience aren't ever going to be engaged with you.)

So what can you do to engage your audience—to inform, entertain, and motivate the individuals listening to your presentation?[2] You have several options for increasing audience engagement. These four clusters of strategies won't ensure a perfect presentation, but they will help you get a good start.

Strategy Cluster 1: Create an audience-centered atmosphere.

- If you're making a presentation to a group outside your own organization, find out something about the audience beforehand so that you can relate your opening comments to the group.

- Act like you're glad to be giving the presentation and interested in the audience as well as the topic.

- Use questions creatively:
  - ◇ Imagine the questions that the audience will ask and incorporate responses into your presentation.
  - ◇ Build in rhetorical questions that members of the audience can answer in their minds and relate to your presentation.
  - ◇ Provide the audience with a list of intriguing, problem-oriented questions that extend the ideas in your presentation.

Strategy Cluster 2: Encourage active involvement.

- Involve everyone in an activity—solving a problem related to your topic, coming up with ways to approach an ethical dilemma, or viewing a videotape and monitoring events on it, for example.

- Get audience volunteers to help with a demonstration.

- Encourage audience members to answer specific questions you ask during the presentation, and then adjust your presentation to consider those responses.

What are some of the best things you have seen people do in oral presentations to keep your interest and ensure your understanding?

Strategy Cluster 3: Make what you say easy to listen to (and remember).

- Make some of your points with brief stories . . . no, not rambling stories with only the most tenuous relevance but, instead, tightly crafted anecdotes (what *Time* magazine writers call "nuggets"). People tend to remember information presented as part of a narrative long after they have forgotten separate pieces of information.

- Remember the limits of short-term memory; that is, the number of chunks of information we can hold in our mind at the same time. Typically, short-term memory holds a maximum of five to seven chunks of information, a number that decreases rapidly as the complexity of the information increases. It's also a number that decreases when information is presented orally. You're better off saying

    "Let me illustrate the three main stages in this complex process, each of which has five steps."

    (which is well within short-term memory limits), than saying

    "Let me move through the fifteen steps of this complex process."

Strategy Cluster 4: Vary the pacing and structure of your presentation.

- Avoid cramming too much information into the time allotted for your presentation. Your audience will understand and recall what you've said far better if you avoid being cryptic or verbally dense.

- Intersperse difficult material with easy material.

- Schedule lengthy presentations in facilities that allow you to use a variety of activities to change the pace and encourage audience participation. For example, in a multihour session, follow your formal presentation with a break-out session—perhaps using a case situation or simulation activity that encourages members of the audience to work together in small groups to develop creative solutions related to the issues identified in your formal presentation.

Organizing for the Listeners

The way you organize your presentation determines its success. Your listeners must be able to follow your ideas easily. The same patterns that you use in writing—chronological, spatial, priority, comparison and contrast, and cause–effect—can and should help you organize oral presentations. For example, if you are giving a status update, chronological order summarizes the weekly or monthly progress and descending order identifies the most significant gains or losses. A marketing presentation applies descending order to identify the features of your product and applies contrast to identify significant differences between your product and your competitor's.

Beyond the standard patterns, additional conventions of organization can make your presentation more appealing and understandable. Far more than in

FIGURE 18.2 ■ Ways to Organize Information

Strategy	Suggestions and Examples
Use Purpose/ Audience Statements	Draft a one-sentence purpose/audience statement to use in the introduction of your presentation. ■ **EXAMPLE** This presentation introduces computer-assisted design (CAD) to apprentice drafters by demonstrating the CAD software and beginning the training with a simulation program.
Establish Organization	Use an appropriate organization and tell the audience how you're organizing the information. Help listeners differentiate main points and subordinate points. ■ **EXAMPLE** I will give a time line of the steps to eliminate the asbestos problem.
Preview Information	Preview what the presentation covers. ■ **EXAMPLE** First I'll summarize design changes in this component. Then I will identify problems these changes have caused and explain the steps we've taken to eliminate them.
Use Transitions	Include clear transitions to mark movement from one topic to the next or to indicate a shift in perspective. ■ **EXAMPLE** Now that I've identified the few disadvantages of the continuous assembly line, I will discuss the significant benefits this change in the procedure could bring.

written documents, which audiences can reread, oral presentations need strong, obvious guideposts and transitions to indicate the organization of and movement through the presentation. Figure 18.2 summarizes structural and organizational strategies that make presentations easier for listeners to comprehend.

Using Note Cards or Outlines

Unless you are a very lucky, gifted, or experienced speaker, you will not be able to give an effective presentation without referring to notes or an outline. These notes, written on index cards or sheets of paper, should contain the main points of the presentation and specific facts, details, or statistics that you can refer to during your presentation. An outline is far more useful to you than a complete text of your presentation.

If you write out the entire presentation, you might be tempted to memorize the material and then recite it as if giving a speech. Remember, an audience is interested in hearing you talk to them and with them—not read to them. Even if

FIGURE 18.2 ■ *Continued*

Strategy	Suggestions and Examples
Include Summaries	Periodically summarize what you've covered so far.
	■ **EXAMPLE**
	So far I've explained three common methods to eliminate exposed asbestos areas in your facility.
Embed Verbal Signals	Signal particularly important points. Follow up with an example for each point.
	■ **EXAMPLE**
	The most severe health problems occur in two high-risk groups: infants and elderly. Let me compare infant mortality in this country with infant mortality in other industrialized nations. [specific example] . . . Now let me show that our country doesn't fare any better when we compare our geriatric care with that in other industrialized nations.
Draw a Conclusion	Provide a conclusion that reviews the major points and indicates preferred action of the audience.
	■ **EXAMPLE**
	As you can see on the transparency, we have covered five key points dealing with possible contamination of local wells. With this information, you should be able to justify your request for more frequent state inspection.

you prepare the complete text of the speech (perhaps for publication in an in-house newsletter or in conference proceedings), your presentation is far more appealing if you do not read the paper.

An outline or note cards should also include key quotations and statistical information you'll need during a presentation. Even an informal presentation is strengthened by specific facts; you'll find them easier to remember and locate if you put them in your notes.

A topic outline is one of the most useful ways to organize main and subordinate ideas. Figure 18.3 shows the topic outline that Nancy and her teammates put together for the presentation to Cottrell Technologies. Nancy was the liaison between her multidisciplinary engineering design team at Iowa State University and Danielle Conner, a project manager at Cottrell Technologies, who had asked the senior multidisciplinary engineering design class to design a digital controller system.

The design team had completed most of its work on the system, but as they were considering input interface devices, they discovered two options and could

FIGURE 18.3 ■ Outline for Oral Presentation

Analysis of Input Interfaces for the Techni-Veyor Controller

Beginning each part of the outline with a verb helps Nancy remember that she is engaged in a series of actions.

1.0 Introduce the project
    1.1 The goals and objectives involve company and customer needs.
    1.2 Today's situation involves the need for a controller.

2.0 Identify the available options
    2.1 A bar code interface is easy to operate.
    2.2 A telephone-style keypad interface is inexpensive.

Using a numbering system helps organize main and subordinate points.

3.0 Specify the selection criteria
    3.1 The controller must be **compatible** with the existing system.
    3.2 The **cost** of the interface and system modifications is critical.
    3.3 The relative **ease of operation** is also important.

4.0 Present unit cost

Boldfacing key terms helps Nancy remember to stress these points.

5.0 Summarize conclusion
    5.1 Both systems are compatible though the bar code system is faster to install.
    5.2 The keypad is much less expensive.
    5.3 Both interfaces are easy to operate.

6.0 Make recommendation

not decide which one Cottrell Technologies would prefer. Nancy had overseen the analysis of the two input interface devices. To explain the team's recommendation, Nancy drew on the technical and communication skills of her classmates. Although she was identified as the principal author of the team's report and would present the team's recommendation, the work represented a collaborative effort.

Nancy scheduled an hour-long meeting with Danielle Conner. Her presentation would take nearly 35 minutes, leaving her enough time to answer questions from the audience. Danielle Conner approved all major decisions in the project, though she worked with a group of technical experts who took responsibility for specific problems. All of these technical experts planned to attend Nancy's presentation. (See the complete report on which this presentation is based in Chapter 17, Figure 17.11.)

Preparing Materials for a Professional Presentation

As you organize a presentation you also need to think about the visuals and handouts that will support and clarify the presentation.

Visuals

Visuals are extremely valuable during an oral presentation. Because most people's visual memories are much stronger than their auditory (hearing) memories, visual aids are particularly useful for presenting facts and statistics. In fact, visuals that illustrate or reinforce your information can increase most people's retention by some 20 percent. Show rather than just tell whenever possible.

You can use visuals to provide support for complex information as well as to preview and review key points. For example, if your presentation contains a great deal of numeric data, your audience members will understand and remember the information better by seeing as well as hearing (reinforcing their short-term memory). Also, most people retain only half of what they hear immediately after hearing it, so again, visuals can reinforce the speaker's points.

When you are deciding what types of visuals to select or design, remember that they are separated into these categories: charts, diagrams, schematics, graphs, tables, maps, drawings, photographs. (Refer to Chapter 9 for a detailed discussion about visuals.) You can use any of these visuals for the following purposes:

Organize Information for Listeners
- Preview and review main points.

- Differentiate main and subordinate points.

Support the Development of Information
- Illustrate or exemplify points.

- Display complex data or information.

Encourage Attention and Engagement
- Provide sensory variety to stimulate interest.

- Vary the pace of the presentation.

- Provide humor.

Keep your visuals simple. If you try to squeeze too much onto one transparency or slide, it loses its effectiveness. But simple doesn't mean that your visuals can't have a strong and appealing visual identity. Maintaining this identity will be easier if you establish consistent specifications for all your visuals (e.g., consistent font style and size, consistent use of color, consistent spacing, and so on).

In most cases, each visual in a presentation should support only one or two of your ideas. For example, the graph in Figure 18.4 would be difficult for an audience to read. Instead, the presenter could prepare four separate graphs, as in Figure 18.5, each clearly showing the changes. If direct comparison is necessary, the presenter could follow the separate graphs with a composite graph. Consider the limits of short-term memory (the ability to hold five to seven chunks of information in your mind at the same time) when you're designing visuals.

Visual information can be presented in many formats, depending on the audience, purpose of the visuals, art or graphic design facilities (your own talent or company artists), finances, physical limitations of presentation room, time

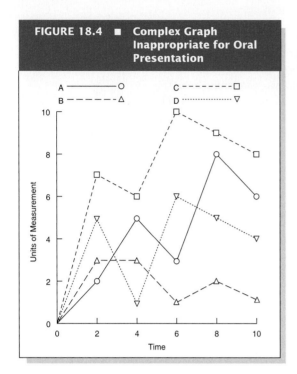

FIGURE 18.4 ■ Complex Graph Inappropriate for Oral Presentation

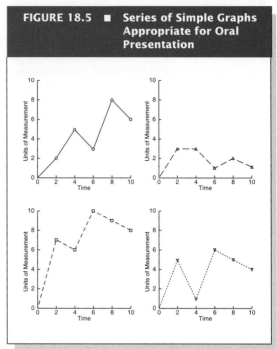

FIGURE 18.5 ■ Series of Simple Graphs Appropriate for Oral Presentation

available, equipment available, your familiarity with each format, and so on. Each type of visual presents both benefits and problems:

- chalkboards or white boards

- flip charts (large pads of newsprint for writing or drawing)

- prepared posters, charts, tables, diagrams, maps, or photos

- slides (35 mm transparencies)

- presentation software slides (e.g., PowerPoint)

- transparencies (vu-graphs)

- videotapes, laser disks, DVM, films

- physical models

- demonstrations

All take time to prepare, from a few minutes for arranging for delivery of a flip chart to several months for filming, developing, and editing a 16 mm production. All involve expenses, from pennies for a piece of chalk or felt-tip marker to thousands of dollars for elaborate models or videos. Ease of use varies also, from simple overhead transparencies to complicated demonstrations. Audience size can influence choice of visuals. Charts work well with small audiences; transparencies and demonstrations are fine for average audiences; presentation software slides and films work well for large audiences. For some audiences, distribute copies of your visuals, which should have plenty of white space for notes.

The size of visuals is important. Few things are more frustrating and annoying to an audience than visuals they cannot see. A good rule of thumb for using flip charts and posters displayed on easels allows a minimum of 1 inch of letter height for every 10 feet of audience. So if there are 30 feet between the flip chart and the last row of the audience, lettering should be no less than some 3 inches high. Clearly, this guideline becomes impractical in a large room, where a presenter should switch from charts to overhead transparencies (vu-graphs) and 35 mm slides, which can be projected even in an auditorium.

Not only are complexity, format, and size important in presentation visuals, but you also need to consider color. Graphic designer Jan White has developed a series of suggestions about ways to use color effectively.[3]

1. Match your use of color in slides or transparencies to the physical environment.

   - In a dark room, use slides or transparencies with a dark background and light, bright drawings and text.
   - In a light room, use slides or transparencies with a light background and dark drawings and text.

2. Use color to emphasize an important point. You can highlight segments of a pie graph, one bar on a graph, or one row of figures on a table.

3. Use color to establish the relative importance of a series of points, for example, putting the most important information in the brightest color.

4. Use color to establish a pattern that the audience will recognize—for example, using a particular color to signal new information or information of a particular type (such as estimates for the upcoming fiscal year).

   given information given information
   given information given information
   new information given information
   given information new information
   new information given information
   given information given information

5. Use color to show a progression through a series of slides or transparencies, moving from dark to light or from dull to bright, so that the audience can see that the movement of your ideas corresponds to the changes in color.

Visuals Accompanying the Presentation to Cottrell Technologies.

Nancy Hitch planned to offer the recommendation made by the multidisciplinary engineering design team during her presentation at Cottrell Technologies. She requested a large conference room with an overhead projector and screen. She asked Danielle Conner how many people would attend the meeting and prepared enough handouts (with extra copies) for all the participants. She also had a

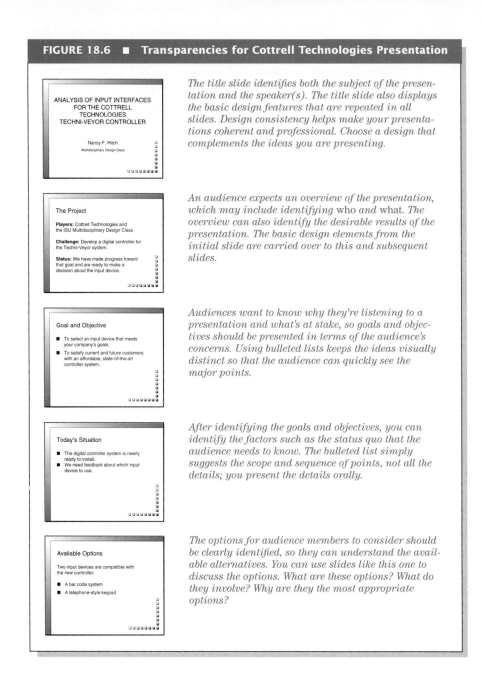

FIGURE 18.6 ■ Transparencies for Cottrell Technologies Presentation

ANALYSIS OF INPUT INTERFACES
FOR THE COTTRELL
TECHNOLOGIES
TECHNI-VEYOR CONTROLLER

Nancy F. Hitch
Multidisciplinary Design Class

The title slide identifies both the subject of the presentation and the speaker(s). The title slide also displays the basic design features that are repeated in all slides. Design consistency helps make your presentations coherent and professional. Choose a design that complements the ideas you are presenting.

The Project

Players: Cottrell Technologies and the ISU Multidisciplinary Design Class

Challenge: Develop a digital controller for the Techni-Veyor system.

Status: We have made progress toward that goal and are ready to make a decision about the input device.

An audience expects an overview of the presentation, which may include identifying who and what. The overview can also identify the desirable results of the presentation. The basic design elements from the initial slide are carried over to this and subsequent slides.

Goal and Objective

■ To select an input device that meets your company's goals.

■ To satisfy current and future customers with an affordable, state-of-the-art controller system.

Audiences want to know why they're listening to a presentation and what's at stake, so goals and objectives should be presented in terms of the audience's concerns. Using bulleted lists keeps the ideas visually distinct so that the audience can quickly see the major points.

Today's Situation

■ The digital controller system is nearly ready to install.
■ We need feedback about which input device to use.

After identifying the goals and objectives, you can identify the factors such as the status quo that the audience needs to know. The bulleted list simply suggests the scope and sequence of points, not all the details; you present the details orally.

Available Options

Two input devices are compatible with the new controller:

■ A bar code system
■ A telephone-style keypad

The options for audience members to consider should be clearly identified, so they can understand the available alternatives. You can use slides like this one to discuss the options. What are these options? What do they involve? Why are they the most appropriate options?

copy of the recommendation report printed on high-quality paper to leave with Danielle at the end of the presentation.

Nancy worked with her teammates to prepare the visuals to support her presentation. She wanted these transparencies to reflect the content and structure of the written report though not contain the same amount of detail. Nancy

FIGURE 18.6 ■ *Continued*

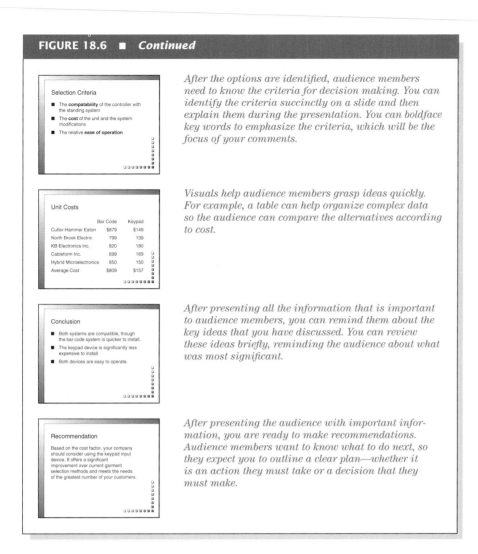

After the options are identified, audience members need to know the criteria for decision making. You can identify the criteria succinctly on a slide and then explain them during the presentation. You can boldface key words to emphasize the criteria, which will be the focus of your comments.

Visuals help audience members grasp ideas quickly. For example, a table can help organize complex data so the audience can compare the alternatives according to cost.

After presenting all the information that is important to audience members, you can remind them about the key ideas that you have discussed. You can review these ideas briefly, reminding the audience about what was most significant.

After presenting the audience with important information, you are ready to make recommendations. Audience members want to know what to do next, so they expect you to outline a clear plan—whether it is an action they must take or a decision that they must make.

rehearsed the details she planned to share with the audience for each overhead transparency. She did not plan to discuss every detail in the report during her presentation though she was familiar with those details should she need to use them during the question-and-answer session after the presentation.

The team decided that in addition to the overheads, Nancy would show the actual input interfaces being considered. As she described the devices, she would indicate the features on actual models.

Figure 18.6 shows the nine transparencies that Nancy and her teammates designed using PowerPoint, one of several presentation programs widely available for both Macintosh and IBM (or clone) computers. They selected a template that is simple, engaging, and professional; this template formed the background for all nine transparencies. If you want to see an actual presentation, go to http://www.osti.gov/govtec.html, a site that includes the 12 slides and text of a presentation about the Digital National Library of Energy Science and Technology.

Handouts

Handouts can be a valuable asset for your presentation:

- They give the audience something to refer to after the presentation.
- They list primary visuals for future reference.
- They explain complex terminology.
- They provide reading lists or bibliography references.
- They summarize key points.

In considering whether to utilize handouts, you must resolve certain questions.

How Should Handouts Be Packaged? Handout material should be collated and bound, if only with a single staple. Loose pages create the impression of inadequate preparation and cause confusion; someone is always missing page 4 while someone else needs page 7. The packet should also have a cover page that gives the title of your presentation, your name and organization, the meeting, the date, and the location. Sometimes you may also include an address, mail stop, and telephone number. This cover information enables the packet to be filed and also provides a way to contact you later for questions or discussion. If you are making an important presentation, consider putting the packet in a folder with the organization's logo.

How do you prefer to use handouts during a presentation—as a place to take notes and confirm details or simply as a post-presentation reference?

When Should You Distribute Handouts? Depending on their purpose, handout packets can be distributed at the beginning or end of a presentation. If the packet is needed for reference or notetaking during the presentation, then the packet should be distributed at the beginning of the session. You generally can keep people from riffling through the pages by saying, "Periodically during my presentation I'll refer to specific sections of your packet. I'll tell you what pages you need to refer to as they come up." If the packet contains sections that "give away" your presentation, or if it is simply a review of the oral and visual information, tell people that a summary will be available after the presentation for those who need it for reference. If you do not plan to refer to the packet during the presentation, certainly it is not necessary to distribute it at the beginning.

How Much Detail Should Handouts Include? Handouts usually do more than duplicate the presentation; they highlight or outline key points and provide details of factual or statistical information that might be difficult to remember. Handout material is similar to visual material in that it supports the presentation. Particularly when the packet is distributed at the beginning of the presentation, the handout material referred to should illustrate the points in the presentation.

Visual material (e.g., copies of transparencies or flip charts) may be reproduced so that the audience can refer to them quickly. Reproducing visuals also safeguards against breakdowns of audiovisual equipment and eliminates problems caused by audience members with poor eyesight.

A handout should exactly reproduce the presentation only for formal conferences where someone presents a prepared paper; copies of the paper are usually available after the presentation and are often published in a collection of conference papers.

How Should You Refer to Handouts During the Presentation?

If you distribute the packet at the beginning of the presentation, tell your audience that you will refer to the appropriate pages as you go along. Each page should have a heading and a page number for easy reference. In a long packet with several sections, you will find references faster if you insert a sheet of colored paper between each section. Then you can say, "Turn to the page immediately after the blue page divider." Audiences seem to find this much easier than turning to page 9.

After you refer to a page in the packet, give the audience a few moments to locate the proper place. This slight pause eliminates most of the paper rustling.

Carefully assess what you want the audience to do during and after the presentation. Having them engaged in reading and note taking may encourage attention—if the activities are necessary and enhance your presentation.

What Is the Real Value of Your Handouts?

Take the time and effort to prepare a packet only if you refer to it directly during the presentation or if people in the audience would need to refer to it afterward. If the packet is never going to be used, spend your time elsewhere to ensure the presentation's success. If the packet will be used, make the information accessible and put it in a clear context. For example, a list of key words and phrases might be meaningful during or immediately after a presentation, but a week or two later, most people will have forgotten the context. A context defines the terms, identifies the situation to which they apply, or explains how they were interpreted in your presentation.

Handouts Accompanying the Presentation to Cottrell Technologies.

Nancy Hitch worked with her teammates to prepare the handouts to support the presentation. They decided to use a feature of the PowerPoint software that enabled them to print miniature versions of their transparencies. They wanted the handout to include the transparencies Nancy showed along with space for notes so audience members could record their ideas and questions during the presentation. Once Nancy and her teammates printed enough copies of the handout sheets, they stapled them into packets to distribute at the beginning of the presentation, so people could take notes.

Poster Displays

Scientists, engineers, and other technical professionals in a variety of fields—from agriculture to zoology—use poster displays to present and share preliminary research findings and to communicate new ideas about technology to their colleagues. You may prepare poster displays for different types of professional conferences or seminars—any gathering that attracts colleagues from your field and asks them to present and share ideas.

Although the type of conference at which a poster is displayed dictates many of its characteristics, nearly all posters strive to accomplish these goals:

- Present information using text and images.

- Convey complicated information—for example, preliminary research results or information about a new product or a new service—in clear, accurate, and aesthetically pleasing ways.

- Abide by design restrictions—that is, the amount of information presented and the poster's design are affected by poster dimension restrictions (typical poster sizes are 2 to 3 feet wide and 3 to 6 feet long).

- Enable poster presenters and many conference participants—oftentimes hundreds—to interact and share ideas.

As you create your poster display, review the following questions that can guide your poster preparation—concerns about available space for display, poster design, transportation, presentation, and time.

Space

- What are the poster dimensions specified by the conference organizers?

- Will a poster mounting surface—such as a wall, or a plastic- or felt-backed panel—be provided?

- Will table space be available to display handouts or your business cards?

Design

- Do the size, shape, texture, and color of the verbal and visual elements attract favorable attention?

- Does the poster present a main message that can be absorbed in 30 seconds?

- Is the print large enough to read at a distance (1 inch height per 10 feet of distance)?

- Are the sections (for example, *title, author, objective, introduction, summary*) (a) easy to identify, (b) short enough to read quickly, (c) interesting enough to hold attention, and (d) substantive enough to be useful?

- Does the overall design enable readers to discern the logical flow of the information?

Transportation

- How will you convey your finished poster to the conference site? Will you roll it? Cut it into sections? Fold or hinge it?

- Whether traveling by car or plane, what materials—heavy cardstock, light-weight poster paper, laminated paper—will make poster transport easier?

- How will you protect your poster *during* transportation? Will you carry it in a mailing tube or a mailing box? Will you use packing material or sheets of cardboard to minimize damage?

Presentation

- What budget for materials—poster paper or card stock, photograph, enlargements, laser printing—is available?

- What supplies—Velcro, pins, tacks, tape—will you need to set up your poster? Will conference organizers provide any of these supplies?

- If your poster is in segments, have you brought a sketch or photograph of your completed poster to use as a guide during set up? Have you brought a measuring tape or straight edge to position segments accurately?

Time

- How much time can you commit to preparing your poster? That is, will you have time to consult with others about its design? Enlist assistance from colleagues or design professionals?

- Have you allotted enough time—10 minutes? 30 minutes?—to properly set up before the poster session begins?

- Will you need to be present at an assigned time during the poster session to briefly present your poster or to answer questions from colleagues?

Presenting Yourself

Making an interesting, informative, well-organized presentation in a confident, appealing manner does not happen automatically. It takes the careful preparation just discussed as well as control of your body and voice, the ability to respond effectively to questions—and lots of practice.

What aspects of making an oral presentation make you the most anxious? The most excited?

Part of the manner in which you present yourself is based on the *ethos* you present to the audience—that is, the image of your personality and character. The ethics sidebar on the next page explores the historical origins of ethos and its contemporary importance in oral presentations.

Professional Appearance

Your professional image depends in part on your demeanor during the presentation. Your material can be accurate and interesting, and your voice can project

Speaking Well: Ethics in Oral Presentations

Classical Greek and Roman texts about rhetoric were primarily concerned with oral communication; more than 2,000 years ago, in the days of scholars such as Plato, Aristotle, and Cicero, communicators were highly valued for their ability to present and defend arguments orally, both in law courts and in public, political meetings. Education for these ancient orators centered primarily on developing the orator's ability to persuade an audience.

This training had at its foundation a recognition of the value of the orator's personal integrity and character in influencing the audience. These characteristics of personality and character, referred to as *ethos,* were important components in building an audience's trust and respect for the orator. Quintilian, a classical Roman scholar, stated the connection between ethos and oration succinctly (despite being sexist): an orator is a "good man skilled in speaking."

Contemporary discussions about ethics and professional communication often focus on the importance of ethos. Researcher Stuart Brown, for example, claims that establishing a respectable ethos is the best way for technical professionals to produce ethical communication. Instead of viewing ethics as rules that you apply, much like applying spell checkers in word processing programs to catch spelling rule violations, you can view ethics as a reflection of a writer's personal integrity—that is, a reflection of the person's ethos.[4]

The connection between ethics and ethos is especially important for presenters—as the classical scholars recognized—because spoken words are so closely linked to the speaker. Researcher Laura Gurak, a specialist in technical presentations, considers the ethos of the presenter important because the presenter is in a position of "power, authority, and responsibility" (p. 30) to the audience. Historical examples, such as Adolf Hitler, clearly demonstrate the extreme consequences of speakers using their position to advocate unethical causes. Because a presenter can be so influential, distinguishing between a projection of ethos (what the audience thinks the speaker is like) and a speaker's true ethos (what the speaker is actually like) is very important. Matching our public and private ethos allows us to speak with more sincerity and make more believable speeches. When public and private ethos differ, however, deception and insincerity are more likely and our speeches are less believable. "As a presenter," Gurak explains, "you are responsible for not only structuring the most effective presentation, but you are also charged with the job of knowing how you feel about the topic and of being the most honest and sincere presenter that you can be." (p. 29)[5]

What are some ways to avoid presenting deceptive information?

Why do we expect presentations to be a reflection of a speaker's ethics? Are you willing to publicly present your beliefs and ideas? Would you state ideas during a public presentation that you don't actually believe? If you were asked to present a position on an issue that you disagree with, how would you respond?

to the back of the room, but if your behavior or appearance detracts from the presentation, its effectiveness is diminished. Some people do strange things when they are in front of a group, partly from nervousness, partly because they do not consider how the audience will react.

What is especially distracting to you when listening to an oral presentation?

Most distracting behaviors disappear when a speaker relaxes in front of an audience. To discover whether you have any of these habits, arrange for a presentation to be videotaped. View the tape and note the areas that you need to improve, then practice to eliminate the problems. Work with groups such as

Toastmasters, a professional organization with chapters throughout the country, for improving workplace presentations. Such a group often helps because you get immediate, constructive feedback from other people who also make professional presentations. Also consider using your company's Training and Development Department staff. These people often are willing to arrange for practice sessions for an important presentation you have to give and may provide a staff member to help polish your delivery. Figure 18.7 identifies some suggestions that will help you give a professional presentation.

Vocal Characteristics

Your "voice print" represents a unique combination of vocal characteristics: volume, articulation and pronunciation, rate, and pitch. Everyone has a distinctive voice that can be used effectively in an oral presentation. Vocal characteristics are so closely intertwined that the improvement of one nearly always improves the others.

A speaker has to be heard. The speaker's voice needs sufficient volume to project throughout the entire room. If possible, practice your presentation in a room the same size as the one you'll make the presentation in. Speak in a voice that can be clearly heard by a person sitting in the back of the room. If you are speaking in a very large room, arrange to have a microphone available and practice with it before you speak.

Your audience will react more positively if you clearly articulate each word: Pronounce every part of each word, without dropping, adding, or slurring letters or syllables. Your presentation will go more smoothly if you are confident of the pronunciation of every word in your presentation; mispronouncing or stumbling over words makes you uncomfortable and lowers your credibility with the audience.

The rate at which you speak affects how the audience reacts and how well they can listen. The average speaking speed is approximately 150 words per minute. Variations in your rate of speech—your pacing—give you some control over the audience's attention. Rapid delivery demands the audience's full attention, and slow delivery allows carefully placed emphasis. Occasional pauses do not detract from a presentation but rather permit the audience (and you) time to collect thoughts.

Use your voice as a tool. Its pitch or tone, its highness or lowness, helps determine your credibility and appeal. Pitch is controlled by muscle tension, so relaxing helps your voice sound natural (and usually prevents the nervous squeak caused by tense muscles). An unvarying pitch creates a monotone, which is boring and difficult to listen to for very long. Your control of pitch allows you to inflect or emphasize important words and thus your speech.

What are your strongest vocal characteristics? Those that need improvement?

Handling Questions

Members of your audience almost always ask questions, so you need to plan not only how but when to respond. Whether you permit questions during the

FIGURE 18.7 ■ Suggestions for Professional Appearance During a Presentation

Goal	Suggestions to Eliminate Potential Problems
Wear Appropriate Clothing	◆ Wear clothes that make you feel good and that you don't have to adjust. ◆ Avoid clothes and jewelry that detract from the presentation. ◆ Check and adjust your clothing and hair *before* getting up to speak.
Handle Notes Comfortably	◆ Number the cards or pages; this is particularly useful if you should accidentally drop them. ◆ If there is no podium, have a firm backing for your notes so that the sheets don't bend and shake.
Make Eye Contact	◆ Look directly at North American audiences to establish a rapport and also give you the appearance of confidence. People are unlikely to let their attention wander if you look, even briefly, directly at them. ◆ Don't stare over the heads of the audience; it makes them uncomfortable and gives them cause to question your credibility.
Handle Mistakes Smoothly	◆ If you make a noticeable error, simply apologize and continue with the presentation. ◆ Don't scrunch your lips, move your tongue inside your cheek, squint your eyes, or giggle.
Relax Your Hands	◆ Use your hands to hold your notes. ◆ Rest your hands on the podium or lectern. ◆ Try one hand casually in your trouser or skirt pocket. ◆ Relax your hands by your side. ◆ Gesture naturally, as you normally would in a discussion. Hold the pointer for the flip chart or overhead projector. ◆ Don't shove both hands in your pockets, clutch the podium, or gesture wildly— all are a distraction during a presentation.
Relax Your Feet	◆ Stand on both feet during your presentation. ◆ Wear shoes that are comfortable (and keep them on your feet). ◆ Don't rock back and forth.
Move Naturally	◆ Do a few relaxation moves before you get up to speak. ◆ While you're speaking, avoid nervous actions such as knuckle cracking, shoulder shrugs, stretches, knee bends. ◆ Avoid standing ramrod straight without moving. ◆ Try to move naturally and comfortably by focusing on what you are saying, not on how you look.
Use the Podium Comfortably	◆ Don't lean on the podium. Don't clutch the podium. ◆ If you're tall, don't lounge on the podium. ◆ If you're short, arrange to have a riser to stand on—or just move to the side of the podium and not use it at all.

presentation or after depends on the nature of the presentation, your reaction to being interrupted, and the size of the audience. If you prefer not to be interrupted, ask people to hold their questions until the question-and-answer session at the end. Questions are usually held until the end in formal presentations, particularly with large audiences. However, if the session is small and informal and you do not mind interruptions (and can easily get back on track), tell the audience you will respond to questions as they arise.

You need to consider problems that might result from questions. For example, if you don't know the answer to a question, don't panic. A presenter is not expected to know everything. An experienced, confident presenter will say, without embarrassment, "I'm sorry, I don't know, but if you'd like me to find out, contact me after the presentation."

A person may disagree with you, in which case you will at least know people are listening. In some cases, you may simply acknowledge the specific area of disagreement, noting that multiple views or interpretations are possible. In other situations, you may want to focus on the likely cause of the disagreement or restate your case, including a response to the person's disagreement.

■ EXAMPLE

I understand your reluctance to commit to the expense of retooling an entire production line, but the market research shows first-quarter sales of this product cover all equipment and tooling.

If one person monopolizes the questioning, you can ask if other people have questions, and then call on another person. If no one except the monopolizer has a question, suggest that the person meet you after the presentation to continue the discussion—and end the presentation.

Occasionally, someone will ask a seemingly stupid question or perhaps a question about something you have carefully explained. Act as if the question is legitimate. You can't tell what provoked the person to ask the question. Keep a straight face and give a straight answer.

Other times a person makes a statement rather than asking a question. In such situations, you can express interest in the person's view and then ask if the person has a question (just as radio talk show hosts do when a caller tries to dominate).

If you or the audience can't hear the question, tell the questioner, and ask him to repeat it. If parts of the audience can't hear a question, you should repeat it so that everyone can hear. Repeating the question has the additional benefit of affirming that you understand what was asked.

When a question is asked that has nothing to do with the topic or that you don't understand, you can ask the questioner to rephrase the question; it may just be poorly worded. If you ask the person to repeat the question, you might get a repetition of the very same one you didn't understand. If the rephrasing doesn't help, you might not be able to provide an answer. Finally, if there are no questions, thank the audience for their attention and conclude the presentation.

Evaluating Presentations

To be a good critic, you have to be a good listener, an active listener. You also need to know what to look for—and listen to—in the presentations you are asked to evaluate.

Active Listening

You can't accurately or fairly evaluate any presentation that you haven't listened to closely. Most good listeners have developed specific techniques that help them listen more effectively—staying attentive, following the speaker's presentation, understanding the content—by engaging internally in a number of activities that increase their listening comprehension. As you listen to a presentation, try to practice the behaviors identified in Figure 18.8, which focus on determining purpose, identifying organization, distinguishing critical elements, monitoring reactions, and making connections.

How can you try to engage an audience that is not paying attention?

As a speaker, you must encourage the audience to listen to your speech so that members recognize the purpose of your presentation, recall significant points, and critically evaluate the content. If research done on the listening patterns of college students is any indication, you have a challenging job. One recent study reported that at any given time only 20 percent of a college audience at a lecture is paying attention, and as little as 12 percent is actively listening. If you develop good listening techniques, you should be able to use this knowledge to improve your skill as a presenter.

Assessing Presentation Skills

Oral presentations are a regular part of academic and professional life. Most of the time you attend a presentation to acquire information. Sometimes, however, a classmate or colleague asks you to assess the presentation he or she has given. The questions in Figure 18.9, though not exhaustive, will help you with such an evaluation.

What are your presentation strengths? What areas need improvement?

You can also use these evaluation questions to assess your final rehearsal of a presentation you're going to give. Have a friend or colleague listen to you practice, or make an audiotape or a videotape of your presentation. You can then evaluate this final rehearsal. Listen to or watch the tape critically, and note the places where you can strengthen the presentation. Play the rehearsal tape at least twice because you'll pick up different things each time. Once you have a list of things to change, you will probably need to rework the presentation. People who give important professional presentations often go through two or three tape-and-review cycles before they are satisfied with their presentation.

FIGURE 18.8 ■ Strategies to Promote Active Listening[6]

Strategies	Activities
Determine Purpose	◆ Determine your own purpose for listening.
	◆ Identify the speaker's purpose.
Identify Organization	◆ Identify and follow the speaker's plan of organization.
	◆ Accurately identify the speaker's main points and ideas.
	◆ Keep track of main points by note taking, use of outline in handout, or mental recapitulation.
	◆ Accurately note the speaker's supporting details and examples.
	◆ Note transitional words and phrases.
Distinguish Critical Elements	◆ Distinguish between old and new material.
	◆ Distinguish between relevant and irrelevant material.
	◆ Distinguish between facts and opinions.
Monitor Your Own Reactions	◆ Note possible speaker bias and emotional appeals.
	◆ Note your own bias and reaction to appeals.
	◆ Recognize speaker inferences.
	◆ Delay criticism until the speaker is finished.
	◆ Ask questions (mentally or on paper) as the talk proceeds.
Make Connections	◆ Predict outcome of presentation.
	◆ Summarize and paraphrase the speaker's main points (mentally or on paper) after the presentation.
	◆ Anticipate possible impact of speaker's remarks.
	◆ Draw conclusions from the presentation.
	◆ Relate the speaker's ideas to your own.

End-of-Chapter
Recommendations for Technical Communicators

1. Decide whether your presentation will be informal or formal—whether in the workplace or in a class.

2. Tailor your presentation to the needs and interests of your audience and focus on information that is relevant to them. Adjust complexity of content, vocabulary, and amount of detail to your audience.

3. Determine the purpose(s) of your presentation: to inform, persuade, demonstrate, or train.

FIGURE 18.9 ■ Questions to Guide Evaluation

Photocopy this figure to use in evaluating presentations.

Categories	Critical Questions	Yes	No
Physical Environment	◆ Is the presentation area set up before the presenter begins?	☐	☐
	◆ Is the presentation area arranged so that everyone in the audience has a clear view?	☐	☐
Content	◆ Is the information accurate and verifiable?	☐	☐
	◆ Is the information adapted to the audience?	☐	☐
	◆ Are the details and examples relevant and appropriate?	☐	☐
Professional Demeanor	◆ Does the presenter appear well-prepared?	☐	☐
	◆ Does the presenter appear poised and confident?	☐	☐
	◆ Does the presenter handle notes unobtrusively?	☐	☐
	◆ Does the presenter adhere to the time limits?	☐	☐
	◆ Does the presenter provide helpful handout material?	☐	☐
	◆ Is the presenter dressed appropriately?	☐	☐
Organization for the Audience	◆ Does the presenter identify the presentation's purpose?	☐	☐
	◆ Does the presenter make the opening interesting?	☐	☐
	◆ Does the presenter preview and review periodically?	☐	☐
	◆ Are the main points in the presentation clearly identified?	☐	☐
	◆ Is the information logically organized?	☐	☐
	◆ Does the presenter provide transitions between ideas?	☐	☐
	◆ Does the presenter use effective examples?	☐	☐
	◆ Does the presenter provide an appropriate conclusion?	☐	☐
Visual Support	◆ Are the visuals used in the presentation large enough to be seen by everyone in the audience?	☐	☐
	◆ Are the visuals appropriate in type/style and professional in appearance?	☐	☐
	◆ In a demonstration, does the presenter complete the actions and speak simultaneously?	☐	☐
Presentation Style	◆ Is the presenter's voice pleasant and professional?	☐	☐
	◆ Is the presenter's body language appropriate?	☐	☐
	◆ Is the presenter's voice loud enough for the size of the room?	☐	☐
	◆ Is the presenter's inflection varied? pronunciation correct? pacing appropriate?	☐	☐
	◆ Does the presenter make eye contact with the audience?	☐	☐
	◆ Does the presenter respond directly to audience questions?	☐	☐

4. Collect information for the presentation itself and for the questions the audience might ask.

5. Engage the listeners by creating an audience-centered atmosphere, encouraging active involvement, making what you say easy to listen to (and remember), and varying the pacing and structure of your presentation.

6. Organize your presentation for the listeners by providing strong, obvious guideposts and transitions to indicate the organization of and movement through the presentation.

7. Use notecards or an outline to summarize the main points of your presentation and specific facts, details, statistics, or quotations that you will need to refer to.

8. Use visuals to help organize information for listeners, support the development of information, and engage their attention.

9. Use handouts to give the audience something to refer to after the presentation, copy primary visuals for future reference, explain complex terminology, provide reading lists or bibliography references, and/or summarize key points.

10. Create a professional image—both in what you say and how you conduct yourself.

11. Develop vocal characteristics—volume, articulation and pronunciation, rate, and pitch—that are appropriate for professional presentations.

12. Respond to questions directly.

13. Evaluate presentations—your own and others'—by engaging in active listening and assessing a range of presentation skills.

Individual and Collaborative Assignments

1. **Design a plan for an effective oral presentation.** Thelma Michelson is a staff chemist doing successful R&D work a year after her graduation. She has returned to college to take an evening course in technical communication to upgrade her professional skills. The only assignment she is apprehensive about is an oral presentation near the end of the term. Throughout the semester, she has used various aspects of her research at work for class assignments. She has often been able to use completed class assignments for writing she is required to do as part of her job.

   One paper describing an innovative analytical process is particularly important to her because when she showed it to the project manager, he added the names of the other project members and submitted it for presentation at the upcoming ACS (American Chemical Society) conference. Thelma was ecstatic when the paper was accepted for presentation at the conference and publication in the conference proceedings. Now she is panic-stricken—her project manager has suggested that she present the findings because she was instrumental in the process development.

   Thelma has a list of reasons why she is the wrong person to represent her company: She'd turn red, her voice would crack or disappear, she'd forget her material, she'd forget to move to the next screen on the computer projection system, she'd forget to refer to the handouts, she'd be unable to answer questions. She is very anxious that her nervousness about talking in front of a group and her inexperience as a presenter will detract from her credibility as a chemist. Her manager has insisted: Thelma will make the presentation.

   She has five weeks to prepare for a full dress rehearsal of her presentation for the upper management of her company. She believes if she can do well in this rehearsal, she will do well in the actual presentation. How should she prepare? Design a practical and effective plan for Thelma to follow. Be very specific. She will need a plan that identifies what she should do and when she should do it. Build in ways that will give her constructive feedback as well as increase her confidence.

2. **Prepare an informative presentation.** Educate your audience about a product or a procedure. Consider these topics:
   - Start-up of a new manufacturing facility
   - Alternatives to traditional burial
   - Career options for social workers
   - Polymer film used to cover food products
   - Building of a microchip

3. **Prepare a presentation to demonstrate how to use equipment or complete a process.** Choose a process or equipment with which most of your audience is unfamiliar. Consider these topics:

- Mountaineering equipment
- SIDS (sudden infant death syndrome) monitor
- Film or tape splicing
- Quilting
- Restringing a tennis racquet

4. **Prepare a persuasive presentation.** Try to persuade your listeners to accept your position. Consider these topics:
    - Tool crib versus individual tool boxes
    - Lowering industrial emissions standards
    - Hospices provide valuable medical care
    - Censorship of the Internet

5. **Prepare a training session that teaches your audience to complete a task.** Consider these topics:
    - Polishing an optical surface
    - Caning a chair
    - Air layering a plant
    - Inspecting a machined part
    - Creating a Website

6. **Utilize visuals effectively in a presentation.** Revise one of the presentations in Assignments 2–5 to utilize PowerPoint or another visually based presentation system.

Intertext

Using Copyrighted Works for Meetings, Seminars, and Conferences[7]

Information technology has given professional meetings and seminars a new look. Speakers now routinely use laptop computers to project visual aids and incorporate into their presentations large portions of material located on the Internet or digitized by optical scanners. Accompanying materials may be distributed in paper, in microform, on CD-ROM, or placed on the Web. As the use of these materials in presentations becomes more widespread, the speakers and the sponsoring associations must consider the copyright implications of such acts.

There are two primary uses made of copyrighted works to support and enhance professional development programs: (1) reproduction of copyrighted articles, chapters, graphs, and other materials distributed as handouts or posted on the Web and (2) display and performance of copyrighted works in the course of a meeting or seminar. Each of these is grounded in section 106 of the Copyright Act.

Reproduction of copyrighted materials

The reproduction of copyrighted materials as handouts and supporting materials for conferences is covered by section 106, subsection (1) and (3). The rights of reproduction and distribution are among the exclusive rights of the copyright holder. There are limitations on these exclusive rights, but none that absolutely exempts the reproduction of materials for conferences and seminars. There are guidelines for reproducing multiple copies of materials in nonprofit educational institutions, but these do not apply. Even though the conference may be sponsored by a nonprofit agency or association, the multiple copying guidelines are available only to schools. The only exemption that could offer some help is fair use. Fair use excuses uses of copyrighted works if certain factors exist. These factors are (1) purpose and character of the use, (2) nature of the copyrighted work, (3) amount and substantiality used, and (4) market effect.

While the purpose of the use is educational, courts have made it clear that educational purpose is not enough. Even uses by nonprofit educational institutions may not qualify as fair use. On the other hand, nonprofit uses are favored over commercial ones. The works reproduced by associations for seminars and meetings are likely to be scholarly articles, book chapters, scientific graphs, charts, and the like. While fair use certainly applies to these works, the third factor may be a problem. As the Texaco opinion indicated, reproduction of a scientific article means that 100 percent of a work is copied, and not a small portion. The same is true for a chart or graph. For market effect, since multiple copies are involved, a court likely would consider the existence of licensing mechanisms such as the Copyright Clearance Center, the availability of publishers' reprints, etc., in judging this factor.

On balance, a court likely would find that permission should be sought and royalties paid for the reproduction of multiple copies to distribute at professional seminars and meetings.

Performance and display at professional meetings

The second issue, performance and display at professional meetings and training sessions, is covered by section 106, subsections (4) and (5), which provide that copyright owners generally may control the public performance and public display of their works. A seminar speaker using a protected work without permission in a setting that qualifies as a public performance or public display would infringe copyright unless the use is excused by a defense, such as fair use.

The initial step in analyzing these situations is to determine whether a particular performance or display is "public" under the Copyright Act since only public performances and displays are subject to copyright protection. So, the threshold question is whether a particular performance or display qualifies as "public" under the statute.

A performance or display is "public" if it satisfies one of three criteria. First, performances and displays occurring in places open to the public qualify, regardless of whether an admission fee is charged or whether the sponsoring association is a nonprofit entity. Second, a performance or display qualifies as "public" if it oc-

curs at any place where a substantial number of persons beyond a normal circle of family and social acquaintances are gathered. Third, any performance or display meets the definition of public if it is transmitted to another location.

Works used in many, if not most, seminar and professional programs will qualify as public performances or displays under these criteria. Even if a performance of a work occurs in a place not open to the public, such as a corporate conference room, it will be "public" if enough people are present. No bright line rule exists concerning the number of people present, although some courts and attorneys general have suggested a 20-person threshold for such performances.

Some performances will be public under the statute by virtue of being transmitted to other locations. A performance of a work that is transmitted to several branch offices of a business, for example, falls within the statutory definition regardless of the number of people viewing or where they are located.

A public performance not authorized by the copyright owner is infringement unless a defense allows it. The defense that might apply to conferences and seminars is fair use. Among the fair use factors, the amount and substantiality of the portion used in relation to the whole work, is probably the most relevant for performances and displays. The more quantitatively and the more qualitatively that one takes, the less likely that the use qualifies as a fair use. Further, if the seminar speaker uses the portion of the work in several presentations, the less likely the use will qualify. Displaying a cartoon or other graphic involves using an entire work and may fail the quantitative portion of this test. Thus, in many instances the performance or display of a protected work in a program will infringe the copyright. Further, the market effect factor may be problematic because public performances often are licensed.

Asking permission to perform or display works is one simple way to avoid these problems. Many copyright owners give permission for uses in nonprofit seminars for little or no cost. It is often better to ask permission before using a work.

Courts have held that using a work within the bounds of fair use even if the copyright owner has refused permission does not indicate bad faith. To the contrary, asking for permission demonstrates one's good faith in respecting copyright.

J. Wesley Cochran is professor of law, Texas Tech University. For more information on Copyright Corner, contact Laura Gasaway <lauragasaway@unc.edu>.

19

Addressing Career Concerns

CHAPTER 19 IN BRIEF

Learning About Jobs

One of the most successful job-hunting techniques is networking, which involves contacting people you know and people they know to gather leads for jobs.

You'll write a better letter of application and do better in interviews if you know something about the companies you'd like to work for. Read publications by Dun and Bradstreet, Moody, and Standard and Poor in the library reference section; use the *Wall Street Journal Index*, *New York Times Index*, and *Business Periodicals Index* to locate articles about the company. Read articles in such periodicals as *Fortune*, *Forbes*, *Business Week*, *Inc.*, and *Electronic Business*. Read the company's annual report. Request promotional literature about one of the company's major products. Talk with people who work for the company.

Preparing Application Letters

Your application letter should be sincere and informative.

1. Opening: Identify yourself.

2. Body: Match your background to the job.

3. Closing: Indicate your availability.

Designing a Résumé

A primary purpose of any résumé is to obtain an interview so that, in person, you can persuade an organization to hire you. Your résumé begins with identifying information: your name, address, telephone number, e-mail address, and Web site. The bulk of your résumé is a summary of your education and work experience, organized in a way—chronological, organizational, or functional—to highlight your strengths. Your résumé may also include other information, generally whatever will influence the reader to invite you for a job interview.

Preparing a Portfolio

A portfolio will demonstrate your communication skills by providing potential employers with samples and analyses of your best work.

Interviewing

Informational interviews are conducted when you are collecting information about a company but do not necessarily want a job with the company. *Job interviews* are conducted when you're seeking employment.

When you decide to look for a new job, you can benefit from reviewing ways of approaching the search. Blanketing the job market with dozens (or even hundreds) of identical letters and résumés seldom results in a job. The traditional grapevine often works, but you have many other ways to learn about jobs.

Learning About Jobs

One of the most successful job search techniques is networking, a modification of the grapevine. Networking involves contacting people you know—as well as people they know—to gather leads for jobs. Networking produces useful information that you might not otherwise learn. For example, imagine that your next-door neighbor is an engineer in a company for which you might be interested in working. She's not in a position to hire you; in fact, her department has a six-month moratorium on hiring. However, she can suggest people you can talk with in another division to learn more about the company—with the understanding that you are not looking for a job, but merely collecting information.

Such networking opportunities exist all around you because you know people in a wide variety of settings:

- classes (classmates, instructors)
- current jobs (full-/part-time; paid; volunteer)
- previous jobs
- professional organizations
- civic and political organizations
- neighborhoods
- social activities
- family gatherings
- religious organizations
- daily activities

Who is in your own network?

People in any one of these settings might provide a lead to a possible job, but you have to let them know of your interest in other jobs.

Whether you know exactly the type of position you're looking for or are simply exploring a range of possibilities, networking can be effective, though it requires effort. You need to talk with people, share your interests and experiences with them, and get to know them so that they, in turn, know you. They may be comfortable offering you employment suggestions, and you should feel comfortable asking for their recommendations and even for introductions to other people.

No single approach to getting a job necessarily works best, so be receptive to a combination of approaches. Apart from networking, you can learn about possible jobs in some of the following ways:

How would you rank order these approaches for doing your own job search?

- Work with your university placement office.

- Attend job fairs.

- Read online job lists.

- Conduct Web searches.

- Attend company open houses.

- Respond to ads in professional journals.

- Sign with an employment agency.

- Register with and attend the employment clearinghouse at professional conferences.

- Mail letters of inquiry and résumés to organizations that might have appropriate jobs.

- Contact a job clearinghouse. Read such publications as *National Business Employment Weekly* (published by the *Wall Street Journal*).

- Read job lists at your state's division of employment.

- Respond to newspaper ads.

- Place newspaper ads.

Although some approaches—such as placing and answering newspaper ads—are notoriously ineffective ways of getting a job, you should be reluctant to eliminate any approach.

Conducting an online search can be a particularly productive way to learn what's available locally and in other parts of the country and world. Figure 19.1 lists some of the many online options available to you. In general, each online site offers some or all of these services: provides information about jobs only (searchable databases); offers sample résumés and job-searching advice, and provides a place to let your résumé be accessed by potential employers (résumé banks). However, some caution is in order when using Web sites for job searches:

- Be cautious about sites that seem to be primarily promotional—that is, they seem more interested in selling their books or services than in helping you get a job.

- Be cautious about sites that charge you a fee for posting your résumé or helping you find a job. Make sure they're legitimate.

- Be cautious about the longevity of the site. Web sites come and go, so be wary about sites that have a short and unproven history.

- Be cautious about sites that seem too good to be true—sites that promise you a job, that promise you high salaries and extraordinary benefit packages.

Once you have identified a job you think you'd like, you need to determine whether your initial impressions are correct, not only regarding the position you're interested in but also the company as a whole. Indeed, you should begin

FIGURE 19.1 ■ Options for Beginning Online Job Searches

Many of the major search engines (for example, Lycos, Excite, MSN, Yahoo) have a career guide or links to job information. These are ten useful sites; many, many more are available:

◆ **4 Work:** <http://4work.com/>
Provides links to job opportunities and articles and advice about job hunting. Job seekers can search for positions by state, job title, or business type; employers can post job opportunities.

◆ **America's Job Bank:** <http://www.ajb.dni.us>
Acts as a national clearinghouse for the public employment service. The site has a searchable database of available positions and is divided into sections for employers and job seekers. There is also a section on trends in the U.S. job market.

◆ **Career Mosaic:** <http://www.careermosaic.com>
Has a searchable database of thousands of job listings. Users can also post their résumés to the site or access company profiles from hundreds of employers. The site also includes job-hunting advice and a schedule of upcoming job fairs.

◆ **Career Path:** <http://new.careerpath.com/>
Includes newspaper postings, employer links, résumé posting, and company profiles. It also lists job fairs.

◆ **Duke:** <http://cdc.stuaff.duke.edu/stualum/employment/JobResources/jregion.html>
Allows job seekers to look for jobs by region. It also lists national classifieds, career help, and summer, postgraduate, and internship positions.

◆ **Government Jobs:** <http://www.govtjobs.com/>
Lists openings for government jobs in city, county, and local governments. It also includes a directory of executive search firms.

◆ **Monster Board:** <http://www.monster.com>
Posts more than 25,000 openings and more than 300,000 résumés.

◆ **Overseas Jobs:** <http://www.overseasjobs.com>
Deals with international jobs. It includes an international job openings search engine, a job search resource guide, and related news.

◆ **Petersons:** <http://www.petersons.com/career/>
Provides a searchable database (of 5,000 employers throughout the United States), including summer jobs. The site also provides access to articles about job-hunting and career management.

◆ **State Jobs:** <http://www.statejobs.com/>
Provides a database where job seekers can search for job listings by state, keyword, or company name. The site also provides links to Fortune 500, state, and federal listings.

your research into such questions before you send a letter and résumé. This information should give you a good idea whether you want to pursue a job in this company. Your investigation might include some of these lines of inquiry:

- Use the company's own Web site to learn things such as their mission statement, organizational structure, clients or customers, products and services, employee resources, and so on.

- Use publications by Dun and Bradstreet, Moody, and Standard and Poor in the library reference section to look up the company's vital statistics—corporate officials, size, services or products, financial position.

- Use the *Wall Street Journal Index, New York Times Index*, and *Business Periodicals Index* to locate articles about the company's people or products. Read articles in such periodicals as *Fortune, Forbes, Business Week, Inc.*, and *Electronic Business*.

- Read the company's annual report, which can be obtained from stockbrokers or the company itself.

- Call the company to request promotional literature about one of their major products.

- Talk with people who work for the company and listen to their impressions.

Preparing an employment package about yourself requires scrupulous honesty. Your integrity may make the difference between getting a job and being discredited. Listen to what can happen if you try to misrepresent your experience. Salette Latas, a technical communicator often responsible for hiring, tells the story of an applicant she interviewed for a professional position:

> A candidate for a contractor position sent us a link to a Web site where he had some samples posted. (I like that kind of portfolio.) Two of the samples were business memos, and one was an elaborate HTML manual. Maybe it was the way that the samples didn't look like they were written by the same person. Maybe it was the way that this candidate's résumé didn't seem to include the skills or experience necessary to produce the HTML manual. Maybe it was the way the HTML manual looked like it needed a table of contents that it didn't have. Something about that manual made me suspicious.
>
> Anyway, I copied a sentence from the middle of the document and pasted the sentence into a search engine. I found the exact same manual, word for word, graphic for graphic. The manual I found had a table of contents, a copyright, and an acknowledgment page that thanked everyone who got near this project, including the administrative assistant. But there was no mention of our candidate.
>
> Needless to say, this candidate not only discredited himself, but his agency as well.[1]

What advice would you give to friends or classmates who indicated they were including materials in their portfolio that they easily could have written, but they didn't?

Preparing Application Letters

Your first contact with a prospective employer is usually the cover letter that accompanies your résumé, so it is important. The letter should be sincere and informative, addressing the reader in the second person (the "you-attitude"), the style of most effective business letters. Kendra King applied the following general guidelines for a letter of application in her response to the newspaper ad in Figure 19.2 for a design engineer:

1. **Opening:** Identify yourself.
   - State your overall qualification.
   - Identify the position applied for.
   - Identify source of information about job.

FIGURE 19.2 ■ **Newspaper Ad for Engineer**

ENGINEERS
DESIGN OPPORTUNITIES

The Product Engineering Center of John Deere Waterloo Works, Waterloo, IA, offers exciting, rewarding opportunities to those professionals whose talents and experience match our requirements. These individuals will join our dynamic Product Design team and realize the benefits of being part of one of *The 100 Best Companies to Work for in America*. As the world's leading producer of agricultural equipment and a top producer of industrial and lawn and grounds care equipment, we can provide an environment in which you can advance and achieve. We seek the following:

- BS, MS, or PhD in Mechanical, Agricultural or Electrical Engineering
- 2-5 years design/development experience in one of the following areas:
  - agricultural tractor/off-highway vehicles
  - power train components
- CAD skills and experience
- Ability to design complex mechanical systems that operate under a wide range of conditions
- Team player who can interface with diverse individuals, both within and outside the company
- Effective oral and written communications skills
- Knowledge of a foreign language desired
- Material and heat treat knowledge

Selected candidates will work on a variety of design applications for existing as well as new products. As an Equal Opportunity Employer, the company offers competitive salary, comprehensive benefits and excellent relocation assistance. We regret that we can respond only to those applicants who possess the qualifications required and in whom we have an initial interest. Please send resume, including salary history and requirements to:

Manager, Recruiting, Dept. # ME-499
Deere & Company
John Deere Road, Moline, Illinois 61265

FIGURE 19.3 ■ **Letter of Application to Accompany a Résumé**

176 Stevens Avenue
Nashua, NH 03060
July 22, 20—

Mr. Donald Grayson
Manager, Recruiting, Dept. # ME-499
Deere and Company
John Deere Road
Moline, IL 61265

Dear Mr. Grayson:

Kendra identifies the position she's applying for and summarizes her qualifications.

I am enclosing my résumé in response to your advertisement for a design engineer. The position matches both my academic background and experience: a B.A. in Mechanical Engineering with a minor in design and extensive experience in designing with a number of CAD packages.

She highlights details about her work experience that match requirements in the ad.

She refers to examples and gives her Web site address where some of her work can be seen.

As a co-op student at Iowa State University, I have had more than two years of experience working for General Motors and for Engineering Animation in Ames, Iowa. At General Motors, I worked in the Testing Department as part of a team in charge of constructing three-dimensional computer simulations of power train failures, which we then presented at several area meetings. At Engineering Animation, I worked with CAD models of crime scenes for several court cases. Slides of some of my work are available in my portfolio, and there are Quicktime movies of some of my team's work for General Motors attached to my World Wide Web site (at http://www.engr.iastate.edu/~king).

She explains how her academic and co-op experiences make her well suited for the position.

My engineering degree gives me the background in physics and mechanics to understand the complicated mechanics of agricultural tractors, and my design minor has given me the theoretical and working knowledge of design principles necessary to understand good modeling and testing principles. Because of my co-op positions, I am comfortable working with engineers and enjoy a fast-paced, technical environment.

Kendra indicates she is available for an interview and tells how to reach her.

I look forward to meeting with you for an interview. I can be reached at my home address or by telephone any day after 3:00 p.m. at 603-555-8140.

Sincerely,

Kendra King

Kendra King
encl: résumé

2. **Body:** Match your background to the job.
   - Determine priority of academic or professional experience.
   - Summarize key qualifications, without repeating résumé.
   - Include specific examples rather than generalizations.
   - Include relevant supplemental information.
   - Refer to résumé, if you've enclosed one.
3. **Closing:** Indicate your availability.
   - Express interest in an interview.
   - Indicate special considerations.

Kendra's background does not exactly match the criteria in the ad, but she believes she has closely equivalent qualifications. Notice that in Figure 19.3, her letter specifically identifies projects she has worked on.

In the job search process, you will also need to write other types of letters. After an interview, you should write a thank-you letter, expressing your appreciation for the time given to you and restating your interest in the position. Sometimes after an interview, you won't hear from a company; if more than two weeks pass, you can call or write to inquire about the status of the selection process. If you receive a rejection, you should respond, thanking them for considering you; this courtesy could keep the door open for a job in the future. Finally, if you receive a job offer, you should respond in writing, indicating whether you accept or refuse.

Designing a Résumé

The primary purpose of any résumé is to obtain an interview for yourself so that, in person, you can persuade an organization to hire you. Unlike a job application form that has questions the employer wants answered, your résumé is designed to highlight your skills and experience.

A résumé reflects your experience as you want others to perceive it, so you might have more than one résumé in order to emphasize different aspects of your background. Because a résumé not only records your experience but also reflects your character, you should be scrupulously honest in selecting and describing your experience. An inflated or "enhanced" résumé misrepresents your background and abilities—and also says something negative about your self-image and integrity. For example, if your job title is "receptionist," do not put "public relations liaison" on your résumé.

Misrepresentation on résumés can be a legal problem as well as an ethical problem. The ethics sidebar on the next page explores some of the ways you can avoid unintentional misrepresentation of your credentials. Your goal is to create a strong, honest representation of your education and experience.

Falsified Credentials: Ethics and Résumés

How would you feel if you found out the chairman of your department falsified his credentials? In the early 1990s, one university found itself faced with this exact problem. A standard review of faculty credentials revealed that a recently hired chairman of the Department of Management lied about his doctorate degree. Instead of having a doctorate in management—as he had listed on his credentials—he actually had a doctorate in communication and speech. The faculty questioned his competency to teach management courses as well as to lead the department. The scandal raised by the falsified credentials led to the chairman's resignation and the creation of a university-wide ethics committee.[2]

Unfortunately, this case is not an isolated one. In academics as well as in the corporate workplace, misleading, distorted, and padded résumés occur. According to researcher Debra Parrish, a recent estimate indicated that approximately 25 percent of the résumés listing an MBA were false.[3] A task force set up by the National Council Against Health Fraud to investigate fraud among nutrition professionals found 70 percent of applicants claiming a doctorate in health care either did not actually have the degree or provide incorrect information about their credentials. And a review of applicants for one gastroenterology fellowship program found that 30 percent who listed publications on their résumés falsified those credentials.

As these studies indicate, professionals are sometimes tempted to pad their résumés. A padded résumé can range from simple exaggeration to outright falsification—and everything between. Repercussions can include reprimands, loss of pay, termination, and sanctions by professional organizations and licensing boards. Parrish also indicates that researchers who falsify credentials can be sued for fraud and prosecuted for embezzlement or theft by deception.

So, how can technical professionals avoid these ethical problems? Obviously, the first step is not falsifying credentials intentionally. To avoid unintentional problems, ensure your résumé is accurate and reflects your current credentials.

- List only those experiences in which you had substantive involvement; don't take credit for something in which you didn't participate or in which you had minimal or marginal involvement.
- Don't exaggerate your job title or position.
- Don't exaggerate your job responsibilities.
- Don't exaggerate your skills.
- Only include citations to publications that have been published or are in post-production—don't include publications in review or draft.
- Divide experience into separate categories—like "Relevant Professional Experience" and "Other Work Experience"—to clearly indicate the difference between an internship related to your career and a summer job.

In a competitive job market, the temptation to pad a résumé can be strong. Remember when employers hire, they want employees they can trust. Your résumé is the first step in establishing that trust.

What are some ways you can avoid exaggeration in your résumé? How would you feel if you lost a job to someone who exaggerated or falsified information on a résumé? Should employers check résumés for false claims? Should padded résumés be liable for legal sanctions?

Employers look for a good match between their needs and your qualifications. If your résumé shows no clear match, it will be rejected. Your résumé can also be rejected for any number of reasons: lack of appropriate training, insufficient experience, inconsistent work history, confusing layout, messy appearance, or typographical, spelling, or grammatical errors. Your goal is to minimize the factors that will get your résumé rejected while remaining scrupulously honest in what you present.

How do you know what information is essential, desirable, optional, unnecessary, or inappropriate? Styles of résumés change; what is appropriate in content and format? For example, years ago people regularly included their physical description; such information is expected today only in career areas where physical attributes are part of the job such as modeling and acting. Résumés for certain careers—for example, graphic design, acting, music—typically follow career-specific variations somewhat different from those described in the following sections. Figure 19.4 separates your choices into essential, optional, and generally unnecessary items.

Essential Elements

A résumé begins with identifying information: your name, address, and telephone number, often followed by a summary of your education and work experience.

FIGURE 19.4 ■ Information for a Résumé

Essential

name	education (college, military, professional training)
address	job experience
telephone number	key words

Optional

goals or objectives	publications
language skills	patents
computer skills	scholarships
hobbies	honors
community activities	awards
church/synagogue activities	sports
political activities	interests
military status	test scores
security clearances	civil service ranking
professional organizations	travels
offices held	citizenship
volunteer work	references

Unnecessary

marital status	physical characteristics (height, weight)
birth date or age	health
race or nationality	home ownership
social security number	personality traits
religion	family background
clubs	fraternal organizations

The selection and sequence of the information depends on the conventions in your profession.

Name and Contact Information.   The heading of your résumé can begin with your name and contact information. It should not begin with the word "résumé," any more than a business letter would be headed with the phrase "business letter." The following suggestions will help you produce a professional-looking opening:

- **Name.** Use your legal name, not your nickname, even if that's what you prefer being called. Do not put a nickname in quotation marks, such as Jason "Chip" Mason. If your name is particularly difficult to pronounce, consider adding the phonetic spelling in parentheses, to make the person calling you to arrange a job interview more comfortable.

- **Snail Mail Address.** Use your permanent legal address. If you also have a temporary address (summer home, college apartment), include and clearly label both addresses, with ZIP codes. The only abbreviations should be the U.S. Postal Service two-letter capitalized abbreviation for each state.

- **Telephone Number.** Include your area code with your telephone number (and, if relevant, the country code). If you currently have a job and do not mind being called at work, you can include this number as well as your home number, but label them.

- **E-mail Address and URL.** If you regularly use e-mail, include your e-mail address. Do not include this address if you only check it occasionally. If you have a professional-looking Web site, include the URL, especially if the site includes samples of your professional work.

Education.   Whether you put your education or your job experience next depends on which will make a stronger impression on a prospective employer. Résumés should be organized in descending order, with the most important or impressive information coming first.

If you are entering the professional job market directly from college, you probably have stronger academic credentials than work experience, unless you have gained professional experience through a co-op or internship program or have found summer and part-time jobs related to your professional area. Entry-level college graduates usually list their education before their work experience on a résumé to emphasize their strength —current knowledge in the field.

An experienced professional has both academic credentials and job experience. Such people often place their job experience before their education, particularly if the experience relates directly to the desired position. However, people changing careers often place their education first, especially if their academic background relates more closely to the new position than their recent jobs do.

Employers are interested in four basic aspects of your college education: school, academic major, degree, and dates attended. You may provide additional information that reflects your level of achievement or breadth of knowledge by

Which would you probably place first in your résumé—the education section or the experience section?

indicating specialized courses, high grade-point averages, and academic honors. The order in which you present this information depends on what you want to emphasize, as shown below, but separate items are always listed in reverse chronological order, from most recent to earliest.

Emphasis 1 school (and location if it's not obvious)	**Education** University of Illinois, B.S. in Physics, 2002 Parks Junior College, A.S. in Aeronautics, 2000
Emphasis 2 degree (if applicable)	**Education** B.S.—University of Illinois, Physics, 2002 A.S.—Parks Junior College, Aeronautics, 2000
Emphasis 3 academic major	**Education** Physics, University of Illinois, B.S., 2002 Aeronautics, Parks Junior College, A.S., 2000
Emphasis 4 date of degree or dates of attendance	**Education** 2002, University of Illinois, B.S. in Physics 2000, Parks Junior College, A.S. in Aeronautics

You need not restrict information in the education section of your résumé to colleges. Include relevant military education and training provided by companies. Also, be sure to mention attendance at a community or junior college as well as specialized technical or vocational training. Education skills you have acquired informally—for example, electronics learned through a local community education program, computer languages you taught yourself—might be listed, if relevant. Generally, you needn't include high school education, unless it was specialized or highly prestigious, or unless you are entering the job market directly from high school. Some other elements of your education might be placed in your résumé:

- additional coursework in areas outside your specialty or major

- specialized courses in your major area

- course concentrations outside of or complementary to major area

- honors project or thesis

- grade-point average if above 3.0

- relevant military training/education

- relevant corporate training/education

How do you present yourself if you are in the working world and currently have or want a professional position but do not have a college degree? This situation is difficult if you work for a company that mandates a degree for recognition, raises, and promotions. Do not do what one person did: list school, academic major, dates, and then state, "Did not graduate." Instead, emphasize your job experience by placing it before the education section on your résumé. If you are pursuing a college degree while working, consider one of these versions of presenting your current college work:

Version 1   Merrimack College, 1999–present, Division of Continuing Education
                 78 credits of 120 required for B.S. in Accounting

Version 2   Accounting, Merrimack College, Division of Continuing Education
                 B.S. in Accounting anticipated next year
                 112 credits accumulated of 120 required for degree

Version 3   Merrimack College, Division of Continuing Education,
                 completed six semesters toward B.S. in Accounting

These versions express the nondegree status in a positive way, emphasizing ongoing education as well as indicating progress toward a degree. If you are not pursuing a college degree, focus instead on your on-the-job training and in-house seminar programs.

Experience.   Résumés can be separated into three types, according to how employment experience is presented:

Which résumé form— chronological, organizational, or functional—is most appropriate for you?

- **Chronological résumés** present information according to dates you have worked.

- **Organizational résumés** present information according to the type or name of the organizations for which you have worked.

- **Functional résumés** present information according to your job titles or job skills.

Regardless of the format, each listing is often accompanied by an explanation of the job, focusing on a person's primary responsibilities, and sometimes including major accomplishments.

Job experience is commonly organized chronologically. Many people choose this familiar form because it effectively shows continuous employment and steady expansion of responsibility. Even though chronological résumés are not particularly useful for entry-level people because they have little professional experience, they are the most common type. Chronological résumés are also inappropriate for people who have had breaks in their employment (pregnancy, illness, layoff) or who have held a series of jobs for short periods of time; the chronology merely stresses what some employers might consider undesirable qualities.

Like schools, jobs are always listed in reverse chronological order, with the most recent job first. Part of Mark Gordon's résumé, shown below, arranges his work experience chronologically.

■ **EXAMPLE**

2000–present   **BAYLOR RESEARCH CORPORATION,** Soren, VA
                      Staff Chemist

1999–2000	**CHEMCON, INC.,** Wheeler, VA
	Chemical Technician
1996–1999	**ADDEX CHEMICALS,** Leigh, VA
	Laboratory Technician

Organizational résumés stress the name or type of organization; they are useful for people who have worked for well-known and respected organizations. This form of presenting professional experience is also appropriate for people who have worked for short periods of time or have had unimpressive job titles. Before Mark Gordon was hired at Baylor Research Corporation, he presented his professional experience organizationally to emphasize the companies, while at the same time giving less attention to his technician status:

■ **EXAMPLE**

CHEMCON, INC., Wheeler, VA—Chemical Technician, 1999–2000

ADDEX CHEMICALS, Leigh, VA—Laboratory Technician, 1996–1999

An organizational résumé can be used to tremendous advantage by people who want to stress the variety of their professional experience. When Jan Peterson applied for a job in the training and development division of a company specializing in bioengineering, she separated her professional experience into categories to highlight the breadth of her background:

■ **EXAMPLE**

Teaching
Physiology Instructor, Trinity College, 2001–present

Biology Instructor, City Community College, 1999–2001

Biology Tutoring, Human Engineering Department,
  University of Bridgeton, 1996–1999 (part-time)

Medical Research
Project Assistant, 1997–1999
Human Engineering Laboratory
University of Bridgeton

Laboratory Assistant, 1996–1997 (part-time)
Human Genetics Engineering Laboratory
University of Bridgeton

Industry
Quality Control Inspector,
Medicus, Inc., 1995–1996 (part-time)

A functional résumé focuses on either job titles or skills. Organizing profes-sional experience by job title is particularly useful when the titles held closely match those being sought. If Mark Gordon applies for a new job as a chemist, he could develop a functional résumé because his background relates to the field in which he is applying:

■ **EXAMPLE**

Staff Chemist
   Baylor Research Corporation, Soren, VA, 2000–present

Chemical Technician
   Chemcon, Inc., Wheeler, VA, 1999–2000

Laboratory Technician
   Addex Chemicals, Leigh, VA, 1996–1999

Sometimes, however, a particular way of organizing a résumé can mask or even distort a person's experience. For example, without the organizational labels, Jan Peterson's professional experience seems scattered:

■ **EXAMPLE**

Physiology Instructor, Trinity College, 2001–present

Biology Instructor, City Community College, 1999–2001

Biology Tutoring, Human Engineering Department,
   University of Bridgeton, 1996–1999 (part-time)

Project Assistant, Human Engineering Laboratory,
   University of Bridgeton, 1997–1999

Laboratory Assistant, Human Genetics Engineering Laboratory,
   University of Bridgeton, 1996–1997 (part-time)

Quality Control Inspector, Medicus, Inc., 1995–1996 (part-time)

Another type of functional résumé organizes professional experience by categories of skills. This format requires careful analysis of your own background. Such a résumé is most appropriate for a person with a considerable amount of varied professional experience, often in widely differing fields. In his résumé, Carl Lawlor includes a job history that summarizes job title, employer, and dates, and then his professional experience. However, because of his distinctive work history, in which each position he held required two functions, he follows the job history with two functional categories—training and engineering:

■ **EXAMPLE**

Training
   ◆ Conducted on-site training in state-of-the-art electronics.
   ◆ Produced training tapes, focusing on industrial safety.
   ◆ Instituted a three-tier retraining program for electronics technicians.
   ◆ Created self-paced, interactive software as training supplement.

Engineering
- Developed and patented interface between X-1700 series mainframe and X-17 minicomputers.
- Designed circuitry for PC boards used in telecommunications projects.

Optional Elements

Your résumé may include other information that will influence the reader to invite you for a job interview. However, what's appropriate for you may not be appropriate for a friend or colleague. In fact, what's appropriate for you for one job may not be appropriate for another job. For example, if you're applying for a staff position with an industrial magazine, your photography hobby could be relevant; it would probably be irrelevant for a position as a quality control inspector.

You can decide whether to include any of the optional résumé elements listed in Figure 19.5 by determining whether the information creates a positive, professional image, advances your chances of being invited for an interview, or relates to the position for which you're applying. If the information does none of these things, omit it. These suggestions will help you make appropriate decisions about what information to include.

Which optional elements in Figure 19.5 would you include about yourself in your résumé?

Unnecessary Elements

Some elements are unnecessary in a résumé, either because résumé styles have changed or because privacy laws exempt people from having to reveal personal information that is not directly related to the job. (Look back at Figure 19.4.) On a résumé, you select the information to include, keeping in mind that gaining an interview is your goal. So, even though you seldom benefit from including certain kinds of information, add it if it will help persuade an employer to meet you in person.

When résumés are received, a worker in the personnel department usually sorts them into three piles: possible, questionable, rejected. Your goal should be to land in the "possible" pile or, at worst, in the "questionable" pile. So, when planning your résumé, consider whether to include information that might get your résumé tossed in the "rejected" pile.

Whether factors such as your age and height, your health and marital status, your religion and family background, your race and gender, your personality and social activities are "right" or "wrong" often depends on who reads the résumé. Remember that federal law prohibits employers from asking about personal information. Do not volunteer information that employers are prohibited from requesting. However, you should not omit information if the omission misrepresents your qualifications or background.

Design Elements

The visual impression made by a résumé is as important as the content. No matter how good the content of your résumé, if its design does not invite attention, your

FIGURE 19.5 ■ Optional Elements for a Résumé

Optional Elements	Reasons for Inclusion
Goal or objective	◆ Include a goal or objective as a way to relate your experience, education, and skills to a particular position.
	◆ Include a goal or objective as a way to suggest that you have thought about how your background suits the company's needs.
	Caution: Frequently, your cover letter is not duplicated and sent with your résumé when it is circulated in a company, so a stated goal or objective lets a reader know what position interests you.
Publications, presentations, and patents	◆ List if you have room on your résumé, especially if they demonstrate experience and skills related to the position for which you're applying.
Skills	◆ Identify skills outside your academic or career area.
	Hint: An English major wanting to be a technical writer could indicate knowledge of computer programming and industrial photography. An engineer applying to a multinational corporation might benefit from mentioning fluency in German and Spanish.
Church/synagogue, community, political, and volunteer activities	◆ Include if the experience relates to the position for which you're applying or to the organization as a whole.
	Example: Managing a political campaign, supervising a religious education program, chairing the finance committee, and coordinating a volunteer group all demonstrate experience that is relevant if you're applying for a managerial position, irrelevant if you're applying for a technical position.
Honors and awards, test scores, grade-point averages	◆ Include achievements if they relate to the position for which you're applying.
	Example: High scores on actuarial exams would be relevant for someone trained as a mathematician, accountant, financial analyst, or actuary.
Military status	◆ Note active military status; include previous military experience only if you have an honorable discharge.
	Hint. Military experience is particularly important to include if your training and experience relate to the position for which you're applying.
Nationality, security clearance, civil service ranking	◆ Indicate your citizenship or nationality if it might be relevant. Indicate whether you have a security clearance or civil service ranking if either is necessary to the position.
Professional organizations	◆ List memberships in relevant professional organizations and service on professional committees
Hobbies, sports, and travel	◆ Include these if they relate to the position for which you're applying.
	Example: If you are an oceanographer, your interests in scuba diving and underwater photography are pertinent.
References	◆ List if specifically requested; otherwise, state, "References available" or "References available upon request."

qualifications may be overlooked. Some people may interpret a sloppy or carelessly prepared résumé as a reflection of your attitude or work habits.

A critical design factor of a résumé is the length. An entry-level applicant should usually prepare a one-page résumé, whereas the résumés of experienced professionals can run to two or more pages. Executive résumés and academic vitae often run to many pages. In some cases, a person may enclose attachments listing credits, such as patents, presentations, or publications.

Design for Online Résumés.   Many companies today use résumé databases to keep track of potential employees. This means that your résumé may be scanned into a computer. When an employer wants to hire someone, a personnel officer scans the company's résumé database for key words relating to the open position (e.g., "BS Computer Science"). People whose résumés are identified in the search get calls. You would be wise to make your résumé scanner friendly:

- **Use key words.** Employers will search their résumé database for specific skills and abilities like "AutoCAD" or "Design Engineer." While you don't want your résumé to be just a list of key terms, you should try to include as many such key words as possible to increase the likelihood that yours will be selected by a search.

- **Use 10- to 12-point font in a common, simple typeface.** Scanners often have a difficult time reading ornate or small fonts, so you should select a standard, easily readable, and average-sized font.

- **Use a header on each page.** If you have more than one page, you should use a header with your name at the top of each page.

- **Avoid design features that might confuse a scanner.** These features include vertical and horizontal lines, shading, condensed printing, italics, graphics, and underlining. These features interfere with a scanner's ability to read your résumé and may result in your résumé being scanned incorrectly or even discarded.

- **Avoid colored or textured paper.** Anything except white paper interferes with a scanner's ability to read your résumé.

- **Avoid folding your résumé.** If your résumé is folded, especially over a line of type, the fold line may interfere with a scanner's ability to read your résumé.

Design Criteria.   Your reader is influenced by several visual factors. If you can answer affirmatively to each of the following questions, you probably have designed a visually appealing résumé:

- **Balance.** Are the sections arranged to avoid a top-heavy or lopsided appearance?

- **White space.** Does the amount of text approximately balance the amount of white space?

- **Typeface.** Is the typeface easy to read? Are there no more than two typefaces? Are there no more than three type styles?

- **Stock.** Is the paper a high-quality stock? Is the color appropriate: white, ivory, light tan, light gray?

- **Accuracy.** Is the typing or typesetting completely free of errors in spelling, punctuation, capitalization, and grammar?

- **Reproduction.** Is the copy clean and clear—easy to read with no smudges?

- **Visual coherence.** Does the résumé consistently use only two or three techniques for emphasis?

Sample Résumés

Figures 19.6, 19.7, and 19.8 present the résumés of three college seniors:

- One is about to graduate with a B.S. in Industrial Management.

- The second is a semester away from graduation with a B.S. in mechanical engineering with a minor in design.

- The third is coming up to the final semester for a B.S. in computer science.

Notice how the students use capitalization, indentation, and boldfacing to call attention to various parts of their résumés. The careful design of the three résumés makes them easy to read and creates a positive, professional image. Because all the students designed their résumés using sophisticated word-processing software, they can easily modify them for specialized positions and later update them when they have additional information to include.

Your Résumé and Your Development

A secondary purpose of a résumé is organizing your background so that you keep track of your expanding professional experience. At least once a year you should update your résumé to add new responsibilities and skills that increase your options and make you a more effective professional. Even if you are not looking for another job, updating your résumé helps you summarize your recent work when preparing for your annual review and gives you a chance to view your achievements.

If, during the year that you are reviewing, you have done absolutely nothing that can be added to your résumé, you should engage in careful personal inquiry. Are you happy with the status quo? Do you enjoy your current status and responsibilities? Have you gained or maintained personal and professional fulfillment from your job? If you answer affirmatively, consider yourself lucky—and keep doing your job. If you are not satisfied, then examine those areas of your professional responsibility that you would like to change. Maintaining your résumé can

FIGURE 19.6 ■ Résumé Emphasizing Chronology and Organizations

Jocelin Coady

2314 North 29th Street, Philadelphia, PA 19134, (215) 555-9186

EDUCATION

Carnegie Mellon University, Pittsburgh PA
B.S. Industrial Management, May 2001

Grade-Point Average: 3.25/4.0

Relevant Courses

Marketing	Statistics I, II
Publicity and Public Relations	Cost Accounting
Strategic Management	Optimization I, II
Organizational Behavior I, II	Finance
Business Communications	Econometrics

Computer Skills: Pascal, Lotus 1-2-3, Minitab, Displaywriter Four

EXPERIENCE

September 1997–
May 2001

Industrial Management Department, CMU, Pittsburgh PA
Office Assistant: Coordinated preregistration activities, advised students on procedural issues, edited notices and memos, and handled routine functions.

Summer 2000

Mobil Oil Corporation, Houston TX
Human Relations Associate: Designated and coordinated employee wellness program, which included hiring consultants, soliciting support of nonprofit organizations, managing publicity, and developing a budget for the event.

Summer 1999

Mobil Oil Corporation, New York NY
Human Relations Associate: Developed audio-visual guide for the corporate training center. Designed computerized directory of management topics. Worked with photography, graphics, and services departments.

September 1997–1999

Carnegie Mellon Action Project, Pittsburgh PA
Recruiting Assistant: Served as a liaison between prospective students and the Admissions Office. Prepared recruiting materials.

HONORS

National Society of Black Engineers, Achievement Award, 2000
Mobil Oil Scholarship Recipient, 1999–2000
Baptist Brotherhood of Ushers Scholarship Recipient, 1997

ORGANIZATIONS

Student Advisory Council, Co-Chair of Dean's Evaluation Committee
Philadelphia Regional Introduction of Minorities to Engineering (PRIME)
National Society of Black Engineers (NSBE), Outreach Committee
Spirit (Student Cultural Organization), Chair of Social Committee

ACTIVITIES

Tae Kwon Do, aerobics, and Young Adult Usher Board

References and professional portfolio available upon request

FIGURE 19.7 ■ Résumé Emphasizing Organizations and Positions

Kendra Thomas

Permanent Address	E-mail: kthomas@iastate.edu	*Campus Address*
176 Stevens Avenue	Web Site: http://www.public.iastate.edu/~kthomas	Johnson 143 Helser
Nashua, NH 03060		Ames, IA 50011
(603) 555-8140		(515) 555-3415

Objective

To secure a position as a mechanical design engineer that will enable me to use my interests and skills as a CAD designer

Education

Iowa State University, Ames, IA
Bachelor of Science in Mechanical Engineering, expected Fall 2002
Minor in Design
GPA: 3.92/4.00

Work Experience

Engineering Animation, Ames, IA, May 2001–present
Animator
 Work with several CAD systems in producing models of crime scenes for several court cases. Design, write, and user-test technical manuals for the presentation software for the crime scene models.

General Motors, Detroit, MI, September 2000–May 2001
Design Intern, Testing Department
 Worked as part of a design team that was responsible for producing three-dimensional simulations of power train failures—duties included constructing CAD models and developing animation routines. Wrote final report (collaboratively) and with the team presented results at several other General Motors facilities.

Iowa State University, Ames, IA, September 1999–present
Math and Physics Tutor
 Helped other students with concepts and coursework of Calculus I, Calculus II, Matrices, Physics I, and Physics II

Activities and Honors

George Washington Carver Scholarship
Tau Beta Pi Honor Society
Phi Kappa Phi Honor Society
Dean's List, Fall 1998–present
Member, American Society of Mechanical Engineers
Member, Society of Women Engineers

References

Available upon request

Gagan Prakash   3516 Lincoln Way #46, Ames, IA 50014 (515) 555-9978 gprakash@cs.iastate.edu

OBJECTIVE   To obtain a position as a software designer/developer in a field related to software engineering and informational technology.

EDUCATION   Iowa State University, Ames, Iowa
B.S. in Computer Science, May 2001
Cumulative GPA: 3.02/4.00

Computer Skills

Languages	C, C++, Visual Basic, Pascal, FORTRAN, Assembly 68000, HTML
Operating Systems	DOS, Windows, UNIX, Novell Netware
Software	Various applications and systems software
Hardware Skills	Assemble hardware based on the Intel 80x86 architecture

Selected Senior-level Course Work

Computer-Based Information Systems — Emphasis on software development, maintenance, documentation and quality control

Data Communication and Networks — The design and access mechanisms used in communication protocols and networks

Software Engineering — Development of reusable classes for OOP and formal specification of code

Project Work

Inventory Control Application (2000). Worked in a team of 6 to analyze, design, and implement an inventory application for a business using MS Access. Handled analysis of the manufacturing department and developed reporting portions of application.

Simple Message Passing Network (1999). Supervised the formal specification (SPECS C++) of a simple message passing network, and worked in a group of 5 to design and implement (C++) the project.

CAREER-RELATED EXPERIENCE

Developer of Inventory Control Package in Visual Basic for Bionics Engineering, India (2000). This application tracks raw materials purchased and used, finished goods produced and also stores a limited amount of accounting information.

Programmer and Hardware Technician for Bionics Engineering, India (1997–98). Developed software for numerical analysis of data and serial transmission of information from a PC to connected microprocessor based devices. Maintained the company's hardware and software.

Manager of Compu-Trend, India (1995–96). Supervised support and sales for software.

OTHER WORK EXPERIENCE

Library Aide for the Department of Computer Science, ISU (1999–98)
Maintained the faculty library and performed secretarial tasks.

HONORS AND ACTIVITIES

Recipient of ISU Academic Recognition Scholarship (1998–present)
Active trader in equities
Member of Iowa State University Computer Science Club

REFERENCES

Shashi K. Gadia, Associate Professor of Computer Science, ISU, Ames, IA
(515) 555-2253
Ghan S. Sharma, General Manager, Bionics Engineering Co., New Delhi, India
(011-91-11) 555-1186

be an effective vehicle for reinforcing job satisfaction or signaling the time for a change.

Preparing a Portfolio

In some fields (for example, architecture, computer graphics, journalism, graphic design, marketing, technical communication), a portfolio of your work is obligatory. In most other fields, a portfolio isn't expected, but it's a very nice plus that enables you to demonstrate your communication skills. In this section, you will read about what to include in a portfolio, how to decide whether to prepare a paper or electronic portfolio, and how to make the information usable.

Portfolio Content

Your portfolio can contain a variety of pieces, as suggested in the following representative list. Whatever you decide to include, it should be your best work—both individual and collaborative.

- memos and letters
- proposals
- reports
- flyers and brochures
- information sheets
- field or lab notes
- contracts
- business or management plan
- press releases
- marketing/promotional materials
- sales scripts
- marked-up and final versions of document to show editing skills
- documented computer code
- Web sites
- newsletters (ones you designed, edited, and/or wrote)
- newspaper/newsletter articles
- instructions and manuals
- online help
- training materials
- videotape of presentation
- radio, TV, video, or online scripts
- audio tape of radio broadcast
- PowerPoint slides
- conference or event planning
- "before" and "after" documents to show ability to revise documents
- tables, graphs, drawings, schematics, diagrams, maps, charts, and/or photos

What actually goes into a portfolio? The following examples, made by three entry-level employees, include a report and discipline-specific visuals, but they also include three other categories that demonstrate particular skills. Generally, four to six categories, with one or two examples in each category, are sufficient.

Biochemist	*Forester*	*Engineer*
▪ report	▪ report	▪ report
▪ visuals: graphs, microscopy	▪ visuals: tables, forest plots	▪ visuals: schematics, diagrams
▪ lab notes	▪ land management plan	▪ PowerPoint slides
▪ online safety training materials	▪ newsletter article	▪ instructions
▪ proposal	▪ videotape of presentation	▪ documented computer code

What would you select for your portfolio? What are the strengths of each piece?

If you want your portfolio to include proprietary documents (ones owned by your client or employer that are not available for public distribution, even though you designed, wrote, or edited them), you must respect confidentiality and obtain permission to use these documents. Kat Nagel, a freelance technical communicator and owner of MasterWork Consulting Services in Rochester, New York, explains the care she takes to respect confidentiality:

I make sure my contract includes a clause giving me at least one copy of the final document and permission to use it in my portfolio. Where confidentiality agreements prevent using the whole document, I am usually able to negotiate the right to use a specified portion of the document. For manuals and training materials, the cover and TOC and a sample chapter, suitably bowdlerized to remove sensitive material but with all company logos, etc. For shorter documents, a copy with sensitive text blurred out.[4]

Paper or Electronic?

Your choice of preparing a paper portfolio, a Web-based portfolio, or an electronic portfolio on a disk depends largely on your audience and purpose. Workplace professionals have differing opinions about how to present their portfolios. A recent discussion thread on TECHWR-L focused on portfolios. Marni Barilone, a senior technical writer at LHS Priority Call in Wilmington, Massachusetts, says that when a document she's written is externally available, she gives "the URL in my cover letter and/or résumé. If it's internal, I simply bring a laptop to my interview and let them poke around. One other option, send the site on a CD or floppy."[5]

In deciding whether to create a paper portfolio, a Web-based portfolio, or an electronic portfolio, consider the following list that summarizes some of the factors.

Paper portfolio in a three-ring binder
- appropriate if you have documents that are intended to be viewed on paper (for example, brochures, information sheets, booklets)
- appropriate if you expect most of your work to be paper based

- appropriate if you want to display and discuss your portfolio during a job fair or interview

- appropriate for people who like to touch and read paper versions of documents

- appropriate for potential employers who are unlikely to have easy access to equipment to review an electronic portfolio

- too expensive to leave entire portfolio with potential employers; need to prepare abbreviated version to leave with people

Electronic portfolio on a Web site

- appropriate if you have documents that are intended to be viewed online (for example, Web sites, online help, online newsletter)

- appropriate if you expect most of your work to be electronically based

- appropriate for potential employers who do most of their work electronically; very easy for employers to access if they have necessary technology

- appropriate way to display your Web skills without any fanfare

- very inexpensive (no paper, no disk)

- appropriate for potential employers who may want to save and/or transmit your portfolio; no paper to clutter or lose

- appropriate if you want materials easily distributed

Electronic portfolio on a disk

- an alternative if you do not have the Web space to put your portfolio online

- portable and inexpensive—that is, you can take disks to an interview or job fair and leave them with prospective employers

A Usable Portfolio

You need to make your portfolio—whether paper or electronic—usable. The care you take with the organization and design of the portfolio says as much to potential employers about your attention to audience needs and communication as the pieces you include. Making a portfolio usable involves three broad categories: labeling, navigating, and narrating.

Labeling.   Readers should have an easy time identifying each piece in your portfolio. Both the paper and the electronic versions should have a title page that includes your name, an indication that this is your professional communication portfolio, and the date. In addition, the three-ring binder for the paper version should be personalized by using a slip-in-spine label and cover sheet. Putting a copy of your résumé first reminds readers about your background.

Whether you have a paper or electronic portfolio, each individual piece should be labeled (tabbed labels or electronic links and headings). The labels provide identifying information as you give guided tours through your portfolio and aid readers who may look at the portfolio without your narrative comments.

Navigating.   Readers should have an easy time moving through your portfolio. In a paper version, this means having a table of contents, clear labels, and a logical organization. In an online version, this means having logical links to the main sections, clear descriptors for each, and clear navigational tools to help locate specific selections (including a *back* button and a button to return to the superordinate category, as well as the main menu).

What navigational aids have you included to help readers move through your portfolio?

Narrating.   A professional portfolio is much more than a slapped-together collection of work you've done. Instead, each selection should include enough information about the context, audience, and purpose of the document so that readers can appropriately interpret it. Your analyses should direct readers' attention to the features of each document that you most want them to see.

Tim Altom, vice president of Simply Written, Inc. (though his business card says "Head TechnoDude"), in Indianapolis, Indiana, advocates a portfolio that reads like a case study:

> The very best portfolio is a kind of case study. Present a facsimile of the original document. Then follow it with an analysis that has some basic categories: user profile, perceived need, layout decisions, your role in creation, tool used, problems encountered and solved, and credit to others. Keep the whole package to one or two pages for each project. Such a package shows several things. First, there's the physical appearance. Second, there are your superlative organization skills. Third, there's your knack for knowing what others want to know.[6]

When you are invited for an on-site interview, be prepared to discuss the pieces in your portfolio. Expect that the interviewer(s) may pick pieces and ask you about them—in detail. These pieces provide a focus for the conversation. Altom explains:

> We want to know what they did on the piece, how they did it, the tool they used, how that tool was set up, why they chose to use that layout, those phrasings, that graphic. How was the graphic done? Was it processed, resized, recolored? What problems did they have? Was it edited by someone else? If they had to do it

again, what changes would they make? How did they conduct interviews? What problems did they have with their SMEs [subject matter experts], and how were those solved? And on and on. . . . We want to know the process, not the outcome.[7]

You should create a template so that you discuss the same categories of information for each piece. The points in your template should display the most interesting features of the work in your portfolio and highlight your particular skills and experience. For example, if you're particularly skillful with a range of software, you might have a software category on your template. Similarly, if you have skill with usability testing or have participated in a variety of interesting and productive collaborations, you might include these as categories. Below you see four different templates of information, each of which works well.

What categories will be useful for informing potential employers about your strengths?

Version 1	Version 2	Version 3	Version 4
▪ purpose	▪ context	▪ context	▪ context
▪ audience	▪ audience	▪ audience	▪ purpose
▪ design	▪ purpose	▪ purpose	▪ audience
▪ collaboration	▪ design	▪ testing	▪ usability features
▪ software	▪ collaboration	▪ design/software	▪ software

Your analysis for each category—whether in a paper or an electronic portfolio—needs to be only a sentence or two. In a paper portfolio, the brief analyses are most useful if they're facing the first page of the document. In an electronic portfolio, the brief analyses can be static or pop-up callouts. In either case, the template should be consistent, and the information should be easy to read.

Bringing your portfolio to a job fair or an interview enables you to focus attention on what you've actually accomplished. In contrast to other job applicants who will only *talk about* what they've done, you can *show* what you've done.

Interviewing

Informational interviews are conducted when you are collecting information about a company but do not necessarily want a job with the company. Such interviews have several benefits:

- You can learn about a company: policies, practices, products.

- You establish new professional contacts.

- You practice interviewing techniques for a time when you really do want a job.

- You gain a sense of your value in the current job market.

If you want an informational interview, you first need to establish its specific purpose or goal. Then identify the person in the company best qualified to help you achieve the goal. By letter or telephone, arrange a convenient time to meet. The suggestions in Chapter 6 for interviewing will help you prepare.

Job interviews are different. You're not just collecting information; you're seeking employment. And whether you get the job you're applying for is usually decided in large part on the basis of the interview(s). You can prepare for an interview by doing some background investigation about the company and about the type of job you'll be doing.

Being nervous before an interview is normal; everyone gets nervous. You can allay some of your anxiety by practicing. Think of questions you'd like to ask, and practice saying them out loud. Anticipate questions you'll be asked, and practice possible responses. Consider how your skills and experience can specifically benefit the company, and plan how you'll convey that information to the interviewer.

You can also role-play an interview, with someone else acting as interviewer. If possible, videotape or at least tape-record the mock interview, then view it or listen to it to determine what you'd like to change. Much of the same advice for giving an oral presentation applies to interviewing: Make direct eye contact, speak clearly, listen carefully, wear comfortable, professional clothes, relax.

Personnel, a journal published by the American Management Association, has published an article that identifies questions an interviewer might ask or be asked when interviewing executive candidates. The article is prepared for the personnel interviewer, but the questions are equally useful for a person being interviewed for any professional position. You can skim through the lists of questions—both to get an idea of the kinds of questions you might have to answer and to identify questions you might want to ask. Typically, the questions fall into several broad categories:

Categories for Interviewers

- assessing your current or previous position
- assessing the organization with which you're interviewing
- predicting your own success in the organization
- making decisions
- handling personnel relationships
- motivating and evaluating personnel
- identifying your own interests
- defining your character
- assessing yourself

Categories for Applicants

- defining the position and related positions
- defining authority and expectations
- identifying personnel concerns
- determining areas of responsibility
- assessing my suitability
- evaluating performance
- asking about the position and the organization

In preparing for an interview, you can review the questions in Figures 19.9 and 19.10—both the ones that you might be asked and the ones you should ask. You can practice answering these questions and pose similar ones relevant to the situation. Practicing for an interview can mean the difference between a mediocre interview and an excellent one.

FIGURE 19.9 ■ Questions the Interviewer Should Ask[8]	
Assessing your current or previous position	◆ Which of your accomplishments at your current position or former positions are you proudest of?
	◆ What are your goals or schedule for accomplishment at your current position for the next year, for the next two or three years?
	◆ What would you have liked to accomplish in your current position that you have not accomplished, in whole or in part? What prevented you from accomplishing these things?
	◆ Why do you want to leave your current position?
Assessing this organization	◆ From what you know about this organization and the position available, what characteristics and accomplishments should we expect in the first six months from the individual we hire? During the first year? The first five years?
	◆ What do you think will be the toughest aspects of the job if you were to accept the position? What will be the most enjoyable aspects? The least enjoyable?
	◆ What problems do you think this organization faces in the next year? In the next two years? In the next five years? What do you think you can contribute to the identification and/or solution of those problems?
Predicting your success	◆ What do you think your greatest contribution to the job or to the organization will be? Where and how do you think you would be able to make your greatest contribution?
	◆ What would your personal goals in this job be for the next year? For the next five or ten years? For the rest of your working career?
	◆ From what you have been able to learn of the organization and the position, what short- and long-term problems do you think you will face, and how would you deal with them?
	◆ How long do you think the challenges of this job will excite and interest you? How would you deal with the problem many executives face after two or four years on the job when they have conquered most of the interesting problems or have set in motion a way to conquer them and their enthusiasm wanes? When will you be ready for your next job?
Making decisions	◆ Assume we faced a significant cut in expenditures—for example, 10 to 20 percent within a year or two. How would you go about planning and implementing such a cut in the areas of your responsibility?
	◆ Assume that we expected significant growth in your area of responsibility and ask you to give us a plan for growth. How would you do that?

FIGURE 19.9 ■ Continued

Making decisions (continued)	◆ Assume that the company was going to be merged with or bought by another company. What kinds of things would you like in the merger agreement and in the administrative operations plan covering your own area of responsibility and the company as a whole as you know it?
Handling personnel relationships	◆ If you are selected for this position, how would you deal with individuals in the company who were competitors for the job for which you are being interviewed, and who may feel that they are better qualified? (Assume that some of them may then be your subordinates.)
	◆ If you were conducting the selection process for this position, what would you have done differently, and why?
	◆ If you were promoted to the next higher position in the company, how would you select your successor, and what would you be looking for?
Motivating and evaluating personnel	◆ What criteria would you use in evaluating your subordinates' performance? How would you conduct an evaluation process?
	◆ What philosophy and techniques do you use in motivating subordinates and energizing them and, when necessary, disciplining them? Do you vary your approach for subordinates who are outstanding, good, satisfactory, mediocre? If so, how?
	◆ How would you deal with a subordinate (a) who does not appear to measure up to increasing demands of the job, (b) whose enthusiasm, motivation, and performance seem to be going down, (c) who seems to be under some sort of personal stress or tension?
	◆ What skills or attributes do you think the following should have: an outstanding subordinate, an outstanding peer, an outstanding supervisor of someone at your level? What skills or attributes do you possess that you think others would regard as being outstanding as compared with other individuals of your rank, experience, and accomplishment?
Identifying your interests	◆ What business, community, and public policy issues interest you, and why?
	◆ If a number of executive training sessions or continuing education sessions or conferences were to be scheduled, what types of sessions would you (a) care to attend and why? (b) feel competent to serve and interested in serving as a panelist, discussion leader, speaker, or teacher?
	◆ If you were able to meet with an outstanding management expert for (a) a one-to-one three-hour uninterrupted session and/or (b) an uninterrupted week or two, what kinds of things would you ask, and what would you hope to learn from the experience?

What five questions would you feel most comfortable answering? What five would you feel uncomfortable answering? Create a group or class matrix of these questions to determine if patterns exist about what makes people feel comfortable or uncomfortable. Discuss what causes the comfort or discomfort in responding to particular questions.

FIGURE 19.9 ■ *Continued*

Defining your character	◆ I assume that at some point you were in head-on competition with an individual in your current company for promotion or for status or project managership or something of that type. What would your competitor say about you in terms of your strengths and weaknesses?
	◆ What factors are: (a) most important to you personally in job satisfaction? (b) most important to your subordinates in job satisfaction?
	◆ How do you motivate yourself? How do you deal with stress, tension, boredom?
	◆ What do you expect from the social and public relations demands of this job?
Assessing yourself	◆ What criteria would you (a) use in measuring your own performance over the next year and the following years, (b) like your performance measured by, (c) use in measuring your superior's performance and your relationship to him or her?
	◆ How do you set priorities for your own time? For your subordinates' time?
	◆ From whom have you learned the most in your management career? What have you learned, and why is it valuable?
	◆ Why do you want this job? Why should we hire you?

FIGURE 19.10 ■ Questions the Applicant Might Ask[9]

Defining the position and related positions	◆ What specific responsibilities of the position do you regard as most important? What are the other responsibilities?
	◆ What are the major frustrations, as you see it, of my job? Of your (the supervisor's) job? Of your superior's job? Of my subordinates' job?
	◆ What are the major challenges/rewards/stimulations of my job? Of my supervisor's job? Of his or her superior's job? Of my subordinate's job?
Defining authority and expectations	◆ What are the company's goals, the supervisor's goals for his or her own area and for the area I might be in charge of? What are the long- and short-term goals of you, my prospective supervisor?
	◆ What short- and long-term problems and opportunities do you think exist for (a) the company, (b) the supervisor's area, (c) the supervisor's superior's area?
	◆ What long- and short-term problems and opportunities do you think my prospective area faces? What will I face in the first week, month, three months, six months, one year, two years?
	◆ How do you, the supervisor, like to operate in terms of assignments, delegation of responsibility and authority, general operating style? What are characteristics that you like in a subordinate, characteristics you don't like?

FIGURE 19.10 ■ Continued

Identifying *personnel concerns*	♦ What are the strengths and weaknesses of my prospective subordinates, as you see them?
	♦ What are the responsibilities of my peers, and what are their strengths and weaknesses?
	♦ With whom will I be interacting most frequently, and what are their responsibilities and the nature of our interaction? What are their strengths and weaknesses?
Determining areas *of responsibility*	♦ What are the limits of my authority and responsibility? What do I have to get permission for? Inform others about after the fact? Discuss prior to action?
	♦ What freedom do I have to act, and what budget is available to me for (a) changes in staffing, promotion, salary increases, (b) use of consultants, requesting or purchasing software and hardware systems, venture capital for new ideas and approaches, implementing planned growth, implementing planned cutbacks, (c) changes within my area in regard to policies, procedures, practices, performance expectations?
	♦ How frequently, and on what matters, do you, my prospective supervisor, interact with your superiors on a regular basis, and how are particular problems or crises handled?
	♦ How frequently, and in what manner, will I and my supervisor meet on a regular basis, and how will we deal with particular problems?
	♦ What contact on what issues will I have with my supervisor's boss, his or her superior, and others on a higher level?
Assessing my *suitability*	♦ What particular things about my background, experience, and style interest you? Make you think I'll be successful? Give you some amount of concern? What experience, training, attributes, operating style, accomplishments, and personality factors should the "ideal" candidate for this job have?
	♦ What professional, industrial, community, or public policy involvement do you feel it is necessary for me to have, and in what depth?
Evaluating *performance*	♦ What do you and/or my prospective supervisor hope I would accomplish in three months, six months, twelve months, five years, ten years?
	♦ What criteria will my supervisor use for my performance evaluation, and what is the time schedule for performance evaluations?
	♦ After six months, one year, two years, five years, how will you know you made the right decision in hiring the person for this position? If the position were offered, why should I accept it?
Asking about the *position and the* *organization*	♦ What opportunities are there for growth in my prospective area of responsibility and for advancement in the company? On what kind of timetable?
	♦ What social requirements does the job entail?

Chapter 19: Addressing Career Concerns

FIGURE 19.10 ■ *Continued*

Asking about the position and the organization (continued)	◆ How do you think the company and its top leadership are perceived in the industry and in the local business community, and why? What are its perceived strengths and weaknesses?
	◆ Why did my predecessor leave the position, what were her or his strengths, weaknesses, accomplishments, failures? (Or, if this is a newly created position, what factors led to the decision that this position should be created?)
	◆ Why did you come here? Why do you stay?

End-of-Chapter
Recommendations for Technical Communicators

1. Create a wide network of contacts when you're looking for a job.

2. Learn something about the companies you'd like to work for.

3. Prepare a sincere, informative letter of application.

   - Identify yourself in the opening.

   - Match your background to the job. Try to include some details that aren't in your résumé.

   - Indicate your availability.

4. Design a résumé that honestly highlights your strengths.

5. Decide which of the optional information you need or want to include.

6. Delete all unnecessary information (e.g., religion, private clubs, political affiliations, personality traits) unless you have a very good reason for including one of these elements.

7. Decide the order in which you want to present your education: school, academic major, degree, and dates.

8. Decide how you want to present your employment experience:

   - Chronological résumés present information according to dates you have worked.

   - Organizational résumés present information according to the type or name of the organizations for which you have worked.

   - Functional résumés present information according to job titles or job skills you have.

9. Design a visually appealing and readable résumé. Make sure the résumé can be scanned into a database without difficulty. Consider these elements:

- Balance
- White space
- Typeface
- Paper stock
- Accuracy
- Reproduction
- Visual variety

10. Prepare a print or electronic portfolio that highlights your strengths and is easy for readers to move through.

11. Prepare for both informational interviews and job interviews by practicing answers to questions you might be asked and by developing a list of questions for which you want answers.

Individual and Collaborative Assignments

1. **Locate a job ad.** Read ads for various positions in newspapers, technical publications, and on the Web (use one of the following search engines to begin your search):

   <http://www.excite.com/careers/>

   <http://www.lycos.com/careers/>

   <http://www.jobfind.com/>

   <http://directory.netscape.com/Business/Jobs/>

   <http://webcrawler.com/>

   <http://directory.hotbot.com/business/jobs/>

   <http://www.vjf.com/>)

   Select an ad or a job description for a position you would like to have.

2. **Analyze a résumé.**

   (a) Work with a classmate to create a generic rubric that you can use to identify features that characterize effective résumés. The rubric has been started below. Select the features you think are important; then fill in each cell in your own version.

Résumé Features	1 Excellent	2 Acceptable	3 Weak	4 Unacceptable
Accuracy				
Organization	Sequence of information is easy to follow and effectively labeled	Sequence of information is easy to follow	Sequence of information is difficult to follow	Sequence of information is confusing
Details	Includes all pertinent information about education and employment			
Format				
Etc.				

   (b) Locate a résumé posted on a Web site by using one of the search engines listed above.

   (c) Analyze the résumé according to your rubric.

3. **Conduct an interview.**
    (a) Work with a classmate to conduct mock job interviews for the positions each of you selected in Assignment 1.
    (b) After each interview, identify areas for improvement as well as strengths of both the interviewer and the interviewee.

4. **Prepare for an interview.**
    (a) Reread the questions that interviewers frequently ask during job interviews.
    (b) If possible, work in a small group with classmates who are in your discipline/field of study. Identify five questions that you would feel uncomfortable answering and five questions that you would feel comfortable answering.
    (c) Discuss why you feel this way.
    (d) Brainstorm five questions that you would like to ask an interviewer.

5. **Write a letter of application.**
    (a) Think about what would convince the employer to consider you for the position you selected in Assignment 1.
    (b) Write a letter of application for that job, following the guidelines in the chapter.
    (c) Work with a classmate who is willing to role-play the recipient of that letter and discuss your letter's content and organization.

6. **Identify decision-making factors.**
    (a) What would convince you to accept a position? Consider all the factors that will play a role in your decision. Some of these factors might include challenges of the specific job, opportunities for advancement, attitudes of co-workers, nature of supervision and evaluation, amount of travel, geographic location, size and type of organization, management philosophy, compensation (salary and benefits), local cost of living, available housing, lifestyle, and so on. Add as many more as you can.
    (b) Create a matrix that lists these factors in order of their importance to you and identifies the criteria for each factor that you'll use for accepting or rejecting a job offer.

7. **Write a résumé.**
    (a) Assess your strengths and weaknesses as they relate to the job you selected in Assignment 1.
    (b) Write a résumé for that position.
    (c) Explain to the classmate who read your letter of application why you chose a chronological, organizational, or functional form for your résumé.
    (d) Create an online version of your résumé.

8. **Design a résumé.** Use the following information to create two résumés: a print version and a scannable version.

Michael E. Williams

Current Address: 1929 Murray Avenue; Pittsburgh, PA 15216; 412-555-4752; mewilliams@cmu.edu

Permanent Address: 1404 North 21st Street; Boise, ID 83703; 208-555-3852

OBJECTIVE: A summer position in the field of materials engineering

EDUCATION
Carnegie Mellon University, Pittsburgh PA
Bachelor of Science degree expected in December 2001
Major: Metallurgical Engineering and Materials in Science
Overall GPA: 3.2 (4.0) GPA in major: 3.4 (4.0)

Selected Course Work: Senior Thesis; Plasticity & Fracture; Electron Optics; Technical Communication; Physical Metallurgy I & II; Process Metallurgy; Failure Analysis, Liability, & Redesign

EXPERIENCE
Chevron Corporation, Materials Division, Richmond CA
Co-op Materials Engineer, Nonmetallics group, September–December 1999
Compiled several years' worth of pipeline coatings testing into a final report; provided telephone consulting on nonmetallic materials; conducted several failure analyses with written reports of results.

Co-op Materials Engineer, Research group, January–May, 1999
Conducted large series of CTOD fracture mechanics tests and analyzed results; compiled a report characterizing drill-pipe properties and their relation to stress corrosion and cracking resistance; conducted several failure analyses with written reports of results

Co-op Materials Engineer, Metallurgy group, May–August 1998
Assisted with metallurgical failure analyses; gained first-hand experience with investigating techniques such as microscopy, metallography, and mechanical testing

Carnegie Mellon University, Pittsburgh PA
Research Assistant, Department of Metallurgical Engineering and Materials Science September–May, 1999–2001
Worked with several graduate students on their research involving fracture mechanics of ultra-high-strength steels

TECHNICAL SKILLS
Knowledge of SEM and TEM microscopy, metallography, photography, and the following computer software: Lotus 1-2-3, Wordperfect, Microsoft Word, Microsoft Excel, Statgraphics, Sigmascan

ACTIVITIES
Member of Society for Metallurgical Engineering
Member of American Society for Metals

Intertext

How Technology Is Changing
Privacy Issues in the Workplace[10]

When George Orwell penned his futuristic classic *1984* half a century ago, some readers were frightened by Orwell's depiction of late 20th century civilization. But the majority considered the novel a work of fiction, plain and simple.

And while the idea of a government spying on its citizens is nothing new, the technology of the last few years has made such intrusions much easier and more ubiquitous. Now, [more than] 15 years after Orwell's fictional opus took place, nowhere are Americans crying out more about Big Brother than the workplace.

"Spying is a lot easier and cheaper than it used to be," says Lewis Maltby, director of the American Civil Liberties Union's (ACLU) Workplace Rights Project in New York City. "It used to be if an employer wanted to eavesdrop on telephone conversations, they had to hire a private investigator to tap the phones. Now, you can eavesdrop on a business phone with the push of a button. There's really nothing to hold employers back anymore who are inclined to eavesdrop." According to studies by the ACLU, just 8 million Americans were subject to some form of workplace surveillance in 1991. That number ballooned to 30 million in 1999.

Yes, you are being watched

A recent poll by Louis Hams found more than 89 percent of Americans harbor concerns about invasions of privacy. What's more, surveys by the American Management Association reveal that 35 percent of companies monitor their employees by reviewing computer files or e-mail, videotaping them on the job, or listening to their phone calls.

As more employers have begun using these devices to keep tabs on their workforce, thousands of lawsuits have sprung up as workers claim their employers have invaded their privacy. The outcomes of these cases have been at best unpredictable, as virtually identical situations often elicit different verdicts based solely on the judge, jurisdiction, or argument presented by the legal counsel retained by the employer and employee.

"At this point, it's going to have to be on a case-by-case basis because we do not have an overriding federal law that deals with workplace privacy issues," says William Hubbartt, founder and president of Hubbartt & Associates, a St. Charles, Illinois-based human resource management consulting firm, and author of *The New Battle Over Workplace Privacy*. "Until that is defined on an overall basis, it's going to be that somebody feels offended, files a suit, and the judge makes a determination, applying appropriate state laws and answering the claims based upon the issues and facts presented and the law cited."

Indeed, most employees are surprised to learn that there is no overreaching federal law designed to protect their privacy while at work. A variety of state and local regulations do exist, but the legal perspective is still murky when it comes to this topic.

No legal precedence . . . yet

So what is an employer to do? Instances of workplace theft, discrimination, and violence have prompted the vast majority of companies to at least consider some forms of employee monitoring. But with the proliferation of lawsuits being filed, many are hesitant to put anything in place that might provoke claims of invasion of privacy.

"There's an employment law revolution going on in the country," says Michael Lotito, managing partner of the San Francisco office of Jackson Lewis, one of the nation's largest labor and employment law firms, and coauthor with Lynn Outwater of *Minding Your Business: Legal Issues And Practical Answers For Managing Workplace Privacy.* "You can't go to any company today of any size and not see a 'Let me tell you how to sue the company for free' bulletin board. And you are constantly treated in the press with stories of multimillion dollar damage awards by employees or former employees for these kinds of issues."

Before a company embarks on some policy or method of surveillance it's important that they consult with a lawyer. In addition, one of the keys to developing an effective, lawsuit-proof monitoring policy is to be clear upfront about the use and misuse of company property. This holds especially true in situations involving e-mail, telephones, and even lockers, where the employee is using company property and employers typically reserve the right to inspect and monitor as needed.

"Employers are trying to decrease the reasonable expectation of privacy that an individual can have in the workplace by promulgating policies and procedures that say things such as 'Keep in mind that the locker belongs to the company and we can take a look at it whenever we want to' or 'Keep in mind that the e-mail can only be utilized for company-related purposes and that we have the right to go into your e-mail,'" says Lotito. "If you can minimize an individual's reasonable expectation of privacy through policy development, communication, and reinforcement of that message from time to time, the company is in a much better position to say 'We didn't invade any reasonable zone of privacy.'"

The obvious, up-front approach

Another means of avoiding lawsuits is to avoid taking the hidden surveillance approach to employee monitoring. At Guess Inc., in Los Angeles, approximately 25 high-speed cameras have videotaped actions of the company's 1,000-plus employees for more than five years.

Located throughout the seven-building facility, the cameras are all located in plain view and don't play favorites, observing everyone from the CEO on down. According to Kevin Saucier, director of environmental health and safety, the cameras were originally put into place as a deterrent, but have since proven useful in numerous ways.

"The monitoring of the video cameras lets us know if someone is violating a safety regulation and needs to be made more aware of [his] safety environment," says Saucier. "If somebody is not using

733

the wire mesh gloves in the cutting area, for example, we can see that on the monitor, call the supervisor, and tell them of the problem."

The locations of the cameras are pointed out to Guess employees during new-hire orientation, and Saucier reports few, if any, complaints about their presence. In fact, he says, the majority of workers appreciate the system and the fact that those who fail to perform as expected will undoubtedly be caught.

"If somebody is going to jeopardize the health and safety of another person, you're going to want that person to be corrected," says Saucier. "The only ones that it bothers are people that are doing wrong. If you're doing everything right, why should you be bothered?"

Although the on-site camera system is completely out in the open, Guess does make use of hidden camera surveillance techniques in two necessary instances—to uncover workers' compensation fraud and to catch employees using drugs or alcohol on their lunch hour.

"If you are doing drugs outside the facility at lunchtime, we need to find that out," Saucier stresses. "People are operating high-speed cutters, working with heavy rolls of fabric, driving fork lifts, and operating heavy machinery. In those cases, you are not only jeopardizing your own health and safety, but that of everyone else as well."

Caught in the act
In addition, tapes of employees caught committing workers' compensation fraud are broadcast to their coworkers. According to Saucier, this technique only helps to strengthen Guess employees'

commitment to the company's camera system.

"You get a guy who's on light-duty work because he claims he has an injury, but you catch him in the afternoon moving an entire house," explains Saucier. "He's eating lunch next to the guy who's picking up his slack who suddenly sees him on TV moving furniture. It gets the other employees involved in the process as well."

Since the company began using cameras for monitoring its employees, Saucier estimates Guess has saved approximately $20 million in workers' compensation claims alone. In addition, he reports decreased workplace theft and an improved safety record, which has helped Guess set nine world records for workplace safety.

Although he concedes that most organizations have legitimate occasions to conduct workplace surveillance, Maltby feels the situation would better be handled if employers were to wait until a situation arises to monitor employee actions, rather than having surveillance devises permanently in place.

"If an employer runs a warehouse and there's a rash of TV sets disappearing from the loading dock, everyone understands you have to put a camera in place to get to the bottom of things," Maltby explains. "There's a far cry between conducting an investigation where you have reason to suspect wrongdoing and conducting an investigation of employees who haven't given any indication [that] they are doing anything wrong."

The security check is in the mail
At Guess, Saucier claims the company doesn't conduct any other kinds of work-

place surveillance, to the best of his knowledge. However, the proliferation of e-mail in today's workplaces has led 62 percent of companies to prepare written e-mail policies, according to a recent survey by Hubbartt & Associates. The personal use of e-mail has resulted in a growing concern over its misuse and the possibility of lawsuits resulting from sexually or racially charged messages. Hubbartt's survey reveals that 83 percent of those written policies prohibit sexual or other inappropriate e-mails, while 67 percent defined disciplinary procedures for those employees who disregard policy guidelines.

Granted, the majority of companies may be developing written policies, but without controls in place to actually monitor and screen the e-mails going in and out of a company, such policies are worthless, according to Richard Bliss, vice president of marketing for The Allegro Group in Dayton, Ohio. In order to help employers control the content of company e-mail, Allegro developed MailStop, a service that intercepts mail while still on the Internet.

Each client company sets their own rules, such as prohibiting mail containing sexually explicit terms or game files. As the mail passes through Allegro's filters, those that violate company rules are held up, and all involved parties are notified, including the owner of the domain name from which it was sent. Although employees typically complain about their e-mail being monitored, even by an outside service, Bliss explains that e-mail abuse is really no different than any other workplace infringement. "If you were to use the phone for an hour-long personal call or send your mom a 40-page fax,

your company might take offense to the fact that you are using corporate resources to conduct personal business," says Bliss.

A warning that works
Premium Financing Specialists in Kansas City, MO, recently put Allegro's Mail-Stop service in place, and the results have been phenomenal, according to network administrator Diana Fish. She soon discovered that a tremendous amount of personal e-mail was being sent out on company time using company resources. In fact, she found one situation where an employee was sending 50 to 75 personal messages every Friday afternoon. Since she began notifying employees of their e-mail abuse, Fish has seen outgoing mail reduced by 40 percent in a six-week time period.

"There were no threats or conditions put on it; it was just a simple advisory saying that our e-mail monitoring system has notified us that they may be sending e-mail of a nonbusiness content," says Fish. "It was amazing how quickly they stopped."

That's not to say all employees readily accepted the filtering of their mail. Fish was astounded when several workers asked how they were supposed to get mail from their friends or communicate with their parents. Her response was simple: Get your own Internet account at home.

Although opinions vary on whether or not a federal mandate would resolve the debate over workplace privacy, the ACLU has vowed to continue its efforts to convince Congress to update federal privacy laws. Maltby expresses frustration over the current Congress, which he says refuses to give privacy issues the time of day. However, that doesn't mean the topic is dead in the water, just placed on the back burner until a more receptive body of lawmakers are in session.

"There's no point of lobbying Congress now," says Maltby. "They're not interested in the subject, but someday they will be, and when they are, we'll be there."

Julie Cook is a business journalist, based in Rockford, IL, who specializes in human resources and marketing topics. She can be reached at JCookJourn@aol.com.

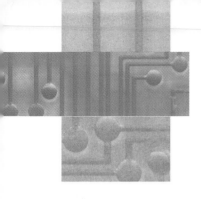

Usage Handbook

Words

1.1 Acronyms
1.2 Abstract Nouns Changed to Active Verbs
1.3 Substitutes for Inflated Words
1.4 Redundant Pairs, Modifiers, and Categories

Sentences

2.1 Sentence Structure
2.2 Sentence Fragments
2.3 Comma Splices
2.4 Run-On Sentences
2.5 Subject–Verb Agreement
2.6 Pronoun–Antecedent Agreement
2.7 Pronoun Reference
2.8 Dangling Modifiers
2.9 Misplaced Modifiers
2.10 Parallel Structure
2.11 Sentence Combining

Punctuation

3.1 Apostrophe
3.2 Brackets
3.3 Colon
3.4 Comma
3.5 Dash
3.6 Ellipsis
3.7 Exclamation Point
3.8 Hyphen
3.9 Italics
3.10 Parentheses
3.11 Period
3.12 Question Mark
3.13 Quotation Marks
3.14 Semicolon
3.15 Slash

Capitalization

4.1 Personal Names
4.2 Academic Degrees, Honors, and Awards
4.3 Groups of People
4.4 Place Names
4.5 Words Derived from Proper Nouns
4.6 Organizations
4.7 Historical and Cultural Terms
4.8 Calendar and Time Designations
4.9 Scientific Terms
4.10 Registered Trademarks
4.11 Titles of Works

Numbers—Figures or Words?

5.1 Ordinal vs. Cardinal
5.2 Beginnings of Sentences
5.3 Very Large Numbers
5.4 Physical Quantities
5.5 Percentages and Decimals
5.6 Age

Documenting Sources

6.1 Sources Cited
6.2 Source Notes
6.3 Formats for Documentation

Words

1.1 Acronyms

Acronyms are terms made by using the first letter of each word in a phrase. They are useful as a kind of shorthand that is recognized by people in the same field. However, indiscriminate use of undefined acronyms causes confusion because many acronyms are unfamiliar to those outside a particular specialty. Acronyms fall into several overlapping categories:

- Words that are so common that many people don't even realize they're acronyms are appropriate for use in any document although nonexperts may need to have the term explained. A simple definition of such acronyms won't help a person understand a concept such as *laser*.

  ### ■ EXAMPLES

  SCUBA   self-contained underwater breathing apparatus

  LASER   light amplification by stimulated emission of radiation

- Acronyms that most people recognize as words while still realizing that they're acronyms are also appropriate for any document. Often, people know what the term means but cannot identify the specific words from which the acronym is constructed.

  ### ■ EXAMPLES

  NASA   National Aeronautics and Space Administration

  BASIC   beginner's all-purpose symbolic instruction code

- Acronyms accepted in specific industries and recognized by most professionals in that field can be used in documents written for all levels of readers in a particular academic or industrial specialty. Outside these fields, however, such acronyms should be used sparingly.

  ### ■ EXAMPLES

  ANSI   American National Standards Institute

  PVC   polyvinylchloride

- Acronyms that would be familiar only to a specific organization and recognized by few others should be used with caution.

  ### ■ EXAMPLES

  VISSR   visible/infrared spin/scan radiometer

  HAC   Hughes Aircraft Company

Writers who use an acronym should first decide whether readers are likely to be familiar with the term. In any case, the first time the term is employed, the entire phrase should be spelled out, followed by the acronym in parentheses. The second time the term is used, the readers should recognize the acronym. If the second use follows within a few sentences, readers can look back to check the meaning. If the second use is several paragraphs or pages later, readers would probably benefit from repetition of the spelled-out phrase in parentheses. After that, the acronym alone will suffice. Acronyms are also appropriate entries for a glossary if a document needs one.

1.2 Abstract Nouns Changed to Active Verbs

Your writing will generally be clearer and more readable if you use direct, active verbs rather than their nominalizations (verbs made into nouns).

The biologist made a determination of the approximate age.   *nominalization*

The biologist determined the approximate age.   *direct verb*

Abstract Nouns	*Direct, Active Verbs*
allocation	allocate
assessment	assess
assignment	assign
avoidance	avoid
compliance	comply
comprehensibility	comprehend
conservation	conserve
conversion	convert
coordination	coordinate
decision	decide
deterioration	deteriorate
determination	determine
discussion	discuss
distribution	distribute
documentation	document
evaluation	evaluate
expiration	expire
explanation	explain
exposure	expose
formation	form
implementation	implement
information	inform
intention	intend
justification	justify
maintenance	maintain
promotion	promote

redemption	redeem
reliance	rely
specification	specify
transmission	transmit
utilization	use
verification	verify

1.3 Substitutes for Inflated Words

Your writing will generally be more appealing and readable if you avoid inflated, obscuring words.

	Inflated, Obscuring Words	*Simple, Direct Words*
Verbs	ascertain	discover, find out
	consolidate	combine
	construct, fabricate	make
	disseminate, transmit	send
	effectuate	carry out
	endeavor	try
	enhance	improve
	establish	show, create
	expedite	speed up
	formulate	design, create
	initiate, activate	begin, start
	interface	talk with, connect
	modify, redesign	change
	terminate	end, fire
	utilize	use
Nouns	capability	ability
	compensation, remuneration	pay
	compilation	list
	conceptualization	idea, plan
	conflagration	fire
	designation	name, label
	discrepancy	error
	implementation	start
	modification	change
	predisposition	tendency
	ramification	result, impact
Adjectives	advantageous	useful
	aggregate	total
	erroneous	wrong

expeditious	fast
explicit	plain
initial	first
numerous	many
optimum	best
subsequent	later
sufficient	enough

1.4 Redundant Pairs, Modifiers, and Categories

Redundant Pairs.   Some common terms contain two words, both of which mean the same thing. Eliminate one word or the other if you're tempted to use these phrases:

basic and fundamental	final and conclusive
thorough and complete	simple and elementary
each and every	issues and concerns
factual and accurate	null and void

Redundant Modifiers.   Phrases in which one of the terms implies the other are known as redundant modifiers. Choose one word or the other.

prioritize in order of importance	three different people
finally in conclusion	true facts
final outcome	consensus of opinion
most unique	new state-of-the-art
end result	future plans
circulate around	initial preparation
completely eliminated	mandatory requirement
actual experience	totally unified
optional choice	positive benefits
personal opinion	absolutely essential

Redundant Categories.   When one term in a phrase is in the general category to which the other term belongs, it's known as a redundant category. Typically, you can improve your writing by choosing the more specific term and eliminating the general category:

inspection procedure	promotion activity
seven in number	at this point in time
unstable nature	red in color
hot temperature	rectangular in shape
small size	rough in texture
manufacturing process	dull in appearance
reliability factor	excessive degree

Exercises: Abstract Nouns, Inflated Words, and Redundant Pairs

1. The manager announced changes in the plans for the documentation and distribution of our division's software.

2. The full and complete compilation of the total compensation packages will be available for examination tomorrow.

3. Deterioration of the end-product quality control process has led three different Q.C. supervisors to reach a consensus of opinion and make a recommendation about consideration of the possible conversion to an in-process system.

4. The endeavor to expedite the early and preliminary materials handling in the fabrication process should have certain benefits that completely eliminate the bottleneck in the process.

5. It is appropriate that we endeavor to thoroughly and completely ascertain the impact of the departmental allocation of the personnel resources in order to expedite the implementation of the analysis of the future budget plans. When the negative predispositions are completely eliminated, then the positive benefits of the conversion to a flex-time schedule can be identified. Once this is done, department managers can make the determination about which employees are absolutely essential for particular time blocks.

Sentences

2.1 Sentence Structure

Understanding sentence structure is valuable to writers because structure gives them the flexibility to express a single idea, coordinate equal ideas, and subordinate unequal ones. This flexibility comes from arranging independent and dependent (or subordinate) clauses in various combinations.

A clause is simply a group of words that expresses a relationship between subject and verb and sometimes a complement. An *independent clause* expresses an idea that makes sense by itself; a *dependent clause* must be complemented with an independent clause in order to make sense.[1]

Independent clause

subject   *verb*

A major decrease in the elk population could occur.

Dependent clause

subject   *verb*   *complement*

if winter conditions are especially severe.

The dependent clause must be connected to the independent clause.

■ EXAMPLES

If winter conditions are especially severe, a major decrease in the elk population could occur.

or

A major decrease in the elk population could occur if winter conditions are especially severe.

When the dependent clause introduces the main idea, a comma often separates it from the independent clause, as if to say, "Okay, the main idea is about to start." However, no comma is needed when the independent clause comes first and is followed by the dependent clause.

All sentences represent various combinations of independent and dependent clauses. A *simple sentence* contains one independent clause and no dependent clauses.

> *subject*   *verb*   *complement*
> Natural fires in national parks have benefits.   *Simple sentence*

Simple sentences are not necessarily short. Compound subjects, verbs, or complements and the addition of phrases can result in simple sentences that are quite long.

> *subject*   *verb*
> Without natural fires, the thick overstory of pines and other tall, mature trees grows,   *Simple sentence*
> increasingly shading out the aspen groves, preventing them from spreading.

> *subject*   *verb*   *complement*
> Natural fires encourage a diverse arboreal woodland suitable for a broad range of   *Simple sentence*
> wildlife and less susceptible to insect infestations than the current monoculture of lodgepole pine.

A *compound sentence* joins two independent clauses into a single sentence by using a *coordinate conjunction, correlative conjunction,* or *conjunctive adverb* between the two clauses. Coordinate conjunctions connect words, phrases, or clauses of equal (or parallel) grammatical rank:

and	but	or	for	nor	so	yet

Correlative conjunctions are simply pairs of coordinate conjunctions that connect independent clauses or other grammatically equivalent units:

not only . . . but also   either . . . or
neither . . . nor   though . . . yet
both . . . and

Common conjunctive adverbs also connect independent clauses in a compound sentence:

also	still then	hence
consequently	furthermore	instead
however	indeed	nevertheless
likewise	moreover	therefore
otherwise	thus	

Compound sentence with coordinate conjunction

The elk herd in Yellowstone was outgrowing its habitat, — *first independent clause*

coordinate conjunction

so park officials considered the traditional solutions of — *second independent clause* transplanting and hunting.

Compound sentence with correlative conjunction

correlative conjunction

The solution must not only maintain ecological balance without human intervention, but also it must respond to public concerns.

correlative conjunction

Compound sentence with conjunctive adverb

Most of the range deterioration was not due to overgrazing; instead, the damage was caused by human intervention.

conjunctive adverb

A comma before the coordinating conjunction properly separates two independent clauses in a compound sentence. Whenever a conjunctive adverb connects two independent clauses, it is preceded by a semicolon and often followed by a comma.

A *complex sentence* contains both a dependent and an independent clause. Adverbial dependent clauses are often introduced with one of the following subordinate conjunctions:

Time	after, before, until, when, whenever, while, since
Reason/Cause	as, because, whereas, since
Purpose	that, in order that, so that
Condition	if, unless, in case, provided that
Concession	although, though, even though
Result	so that
Place	where, wherever, everywhere
Manner	as, as if, as though

Complex sentence

subordinate conjunction

A good fire is better than trees dying out because nutrients are cycled back into the soil.

After severe fires killed some of the tall trees in the lower elevations where the elks live, the aspens below spread and flourished.

Complex sentence

A *compound-complex sentence* contains two independent clauses and one or more dependent clauses.

subordinate conjunction

Because managers have tools such as elevated boardwalks, campgrounds, and restricted areas, national park managers have the flexibility to limit human interference; therefore, terrain can recover from years of use.

conjunctive adverb

Compound-complex sentence

Understanding sentence structure allows writers to establish relationships among ideas by appropriate use of coordination and subordination. Clearly, important ideas belong in independent clauses whereas less important ideas should be expressed in dependent clauses or even in phrases.

2.2 Sentence Fragments

A sentence fragment is an incomplete sentence. Every sentence must have a subject and verb; a fragment is missing one of these essential parts. Often, a fragment is a phrase or subordinate clause that should be part of another sentence. Other times, a fragment represents only part of a thought the writer wants to express.

Pain relievers with extra ingredients such as caffeine.

missing verb

Offer no advantages over aspirin or acetaminophen.

missing subject

Though they are more expensive.

subordinate clause

These elements can be combined to create a sentence.

■ EXAMPLE

Though they are more expensive, pain relievers with extra ingredients such as caffeine offer no advantages over aspirin or acetaminophen.

Sometimes a writer creates fragments by mistakenly separating a subordinate clause from the independent clause.

Starting diesel engines is difficult. *Because high pressures are required inside the cylinders.*

fragment

Even though the fragment has a subject (high pressures) and a verb (are required), "because" is a subordinate conjunction. The subordinate clause "because high pressures are required inside the cylinders" should be connected to the sentence that precedes this fragment.

sentence   Starting diesel engines is difficult because high pressures are required inside the cylinders.

Other fragments are created when a writer begins but doesn't finish an idea.

fragment   Wild ducks harbor influenza viruses in their intestinal tracts, causing no illness in the ducks. *Spread influenza to many other species.*

"Spread influenza to many other species" is a fragment. It can be corrected when the writer completes the idea by adding a subject.

sentences   Because ducks migrate great distances, *they* spread influenza to many other species.

Ducks spread influenza to many other species during their migration.

Some fragments are created by carelessness. Others are caused by a writer's indecision. The following examples illustrate both situations.

fragments   Judging from recent radar scans. Venus appears to have mountain ranges similar to earth's Appalachians and Himalayas. Parallel mountains formed by horizontal movements of the crust.

This example has two fragments: "judging from recent radar scans" and "parallel mountains formed by horizontal movements of the crust." The first fragment is a phrase that should be part of the sentence. The second fragment can either be connected to the sentence or have a verb added to make it a sentence itself.

sentences   Judging from recent radar scans, Venus appears to have mountain ranges similar to earth's Appalachians and Himalayas, parallel mountains formed by horizontal movements of the crust.

Judging from recent radar scans, Venus appears to have mountain ranges similar to earth's Appalachians and Himalayas. Parallel mountains are formed by horizontal movements of the crust.

Exercises: Fragments

1. The access mechanism of the floppy disk drive contains two motors. One motor that rotates a floppy disk at 300 rotations per minute (rpm). Another motor is used to move the read-write head inward and outward on the tracks of the disk.

2. Modern strain gauges are manufactured by etching a very thin metal foil through a mask to obtain a grid pattern. The foil having been previously coated with a thin layer of epoxy to form the gauge backing.

3. Paperboard aseptic packaging has already revolutionized the beverage industry. Taking over a significant market share from metal cans and glass bottles. Developments in technology mean a rapid increase in production of more radical packaging. Plastic multilayer, high-barrier containers.

4. A vendor evaluation system should increase the number of good vendors and decrease the number of bad vendors. The effect being the acquisition of quality parts on time and at a reasonable price, lowering the overall product cost.

5. The iris diaphragm, a circular, variable-size door inside the camera that controls the amount of light that reaches the film in a given time.

2.3 Comma Splices

Comma splices are caused by connecting two sentences with a comma. The independent clauses in the next example are incorrectly connected by a comma.

Botulism requires immediate medical attention, the disease can be fatal.   *comma splice*

The sentences can be correctly separated by a period.

Botulism requires immediate medical attention. The disease can be fatal.   *revision*

However, if the clauses should be connected because the ideas are closely related and of equal importance, a writer can choose one of three ways to do it:

1. Two independent clauses can be connected by a coordinate conjunction (*and, but, or, nor, for, so, yet*) that is preceded by a comma. The coordinate conjunction expresses the relationship between the two clauses. The ideas in the independent clauses must be of equal importance.

   ### ■ EXAMPLES

   Botulism requires immediate medical attention, *for* the disease can be fatal.

   Synthetic substances such as Teflon have been used to reduce hoarseness, *but* they may be rejected by the body as foreign material.

2. Two independent clauses can be connected by a semicolon if the ideas in the clauses are closely related and of equal importance.

   ### ■ EXAMPLE

   Collagen, a natural protein, offers hope for people unable to speak or cough normally; it can fill out missing tissue in vocal cords.

3. A conjunctive adverb that connects two clauses is usually preceded by a semicolon and followed by a comma. The most common conjunctive adverbs include *accordingly, also, besides, hence, however, moreover, nevertheless, otherwise, therefore, thus, still.*

■ EXAMPLES

Botulism requires immediate medical attention; *otherwise,* the disease can be fatal.

Collagen may be useful for remolding delicate vocal cord areas; *however,* only preliminary research has been completed so far.

Exercises: Comma Splices

1. Some safety glasses have a sintered magnet molded into the temple portion of the frame, metal particles that float in the air in an industrial environment are attracted to the magnet, protecting the eyes from injury, a window exposes the magnet, both to attract the metal particles and to facilitate cleaning.

2. Financially, local companies are doing well. Spanner Associates is in excellent shape, sales for FY00 [fiscal year 2000] ended at $578 million with a net income of $37 million. Desktop Computer Corporation has done well until recently. Total sales for FY99 were $3.8 billion, net income was $417 million. FY00 was not as successful, sales were down 20 percent from the same period in FY99, FY01 should swing up.

3. Combustion toxicity of building materials and furnishings can be determined in laboratory tests, small quantities of materials are heated or burned in a miniature furnace, identifying the type and potency of toxic gases and materials, however, such tests do not consider ignition resistance, rate of flame spread, and extinguishability, therefore toxicity tests should not be the sole criteria for making fire safety decisions.

4. Many drugs can be absorbed through the skin, transcutaneous, or through-the-skin therapy, eliminates many problems associated with traditional treatments, transcutaneous application releases a constant amount of medication, reducing side effects, medication is distributed through a polymer pad that is bonded to a thin, flexible hypoallergenic foam and then to an adhesive bandage that is laminated with soft foil.

5. The solar pond project at Fort Benning, Georgia, covers 11 acres, 80 pond modules supply domestic hot water to 26 barrack buildings as well as the post laundry, each $15^{1}/_{2}$-by-200-foot pond has concrete walls, insulated sand bedding, and a water bag under an arched glazing cover of translucent glass-fiber reinforced panels, panels transmit 89 percent of the available solar energy, enabling the black plastic water bags, each filled with 4 inches of water, to reach 140° Fahrenheit to 160° Fahrenheit on

sunny afternoons, at peak temperature the heated water is pumped to the insulated 500,000-gallon storage tank for distribution during the night and next day, the system saves 11,300 barrels of oil each year.

2.4 Run-On Sentences

Run-on sentences (sometimes called fused sentences) result when two sentences are written as if they are a single sentence, without internal punctuation separating the clauses.[2]

> The diving reflex is the body's natural response to being immersed in water the heart rate slows dramatically and the blood supply to certain tissues and organs is restricted. *run-on*

A run-on sentence such as this usually results from haste in writing the draft. The writer is working so quickly that punctuation is momentarily ignored. A correction produces two separate sentences.

> The diving reflex is the body's natural response to being immersed in water. The heart rate slows dramatically, and the blood supply to certain tissues and organs is restricted. *revision*

Another common run-on error occurs in compound sentences—two independent clauses connected by a coordinate conjunction. Sometimes the writer forgets to insert the requisite comma preceding the coordinate conjunction.

> Weddell seals have a larger-than-normal blood supply and the blood itself is richer in red blood cells. *run-on*

The error is easy to correct by inserting a comma before the "and."

> Weddell seals have a larger-than-normal blood supply, and the blood itself is richer in red blood cells. *revision*

Writers do have to be careful not to indulge in "hypercorrection," inserting a comma every time they see an "and." Commas are necessary only when the "and" connects two independent clauses and when it connects three or more items in a series.

Another type of run-on sentence probably results from the writer's starting the sentence, getting distracted, and then finishing the sentence without rereading the first part.

> Weddell seals in Antarctica dive to extraordinary depths even beyond 1,500 feet they can hold their breath for an hour and fifteen minutes. *run-on*

In this sentence, the phrase "beyond 1,500 feet" can be part of the first sentence; however, it also fits as part of the second sentence. Which version presents accurate information?

revisions

Weddell seals in Antarctica dive to extraordinary depths, even beyond 1,500 feet. They can hold their breath for an hour and fifteen minutes.

Weddell seals in Antarctica dive to extraordinary depths. Even beyond 1,500 feet, they can hold their breath for an hour and fifteen minutes.

Exercise: Structure, Fragments, Comma Splices, and Run-Ons

A Pareto diagram is a special form of vertical bar graph or column graph data classifications are arranged in descending order from left to right. The only exception is a class referred to as "other." A composite of several very small categories. If it is used, "other" is always located on the far right of the diagram. Even when it is not the smallest of all the classes appearing on the diagram.

Pareto diagrams are useful in problem investigation, they show the priorities of a myriad of problems in a systematic manner. Particularly important when resources are limited. The analytical process has several steps. Selecting classifications, tabulating data, ordering data, and constructing the diagram. Employees who conduct this process often identify important relationships. Previously unnoticed.

Pareto diagrams are used in industrial settings in a variety of ways. They can analyze a problem from a new perspective, for example, rather than arranging manufacturing defects by frequency, the defects can be arranged by dollar losses. Which may change what is labeled as the most important defect. By arranging issues or problems in order of priority, Pareto diagrams differentiate major problems from minor ones and they also enhance communication because employees at all levels can see the same priorities. Another use for Pareto diagrams is to compare data changes during different time periods. Finally, Pareto diagrams provide a basis for the construction of a cumulative line. So that employees can determine the percentage of each prioritized item in relation to the overall problem.

2.5 Subject–Verb Agreement

The subject and verb of a sentence must agree in number—singular subject and singular verb or plural subject and plural verb.

error in subject–verb agreement

Because of inexperienced workers and old equipment, the *costs* to build the assemblies *is* increasing.

Even when a word or phrase comes between the subject and verb, they must agree. The plural subject "costs" requires a plural verb. Or, the singular verb "is" requires a singular subject.

Because of inexperienced workers and old equipment, the *costs* to build the assemblies *are* increasing.

subject–verb agreements

Because of inexperienced workers and old equipment, the *cost* to build the assemblies *is* increasing.

Errors in agreement also can result from using the wrong verb form with a compound subject. When two or more subjects are joined by *and*, they usually take a plural verb, even if one or more of the subjects is singular.

The Fahrenheit *scale* of temperature *and* the mercury *thermometer was* invented by Daniel Fahrenheit in 1714.

error in subject–verb agreement

The Fahrenheit *scale* of temperature *and* the mercury *thermometer were* invented by Daniel Fahrenheit in 1714.

subject–verb agreement

When the subject of the sentence is an indefinite pronoun, it usually takes a singular verb. Indefinite pronouns do not refer to any specific person or thing. (See a list of common indefinite pronouns on page 753 of the Handbook.)

Nearly 300 years later, *everyone* in this country *is affected* by Fahrenheit's invention.

subject–verb agreement

When an indefinite pronoun functions as an adjective preceding a compound subject, the sentence uses a singular verb.

Each observation and experiment toward developing a thermometer *was reported* in a paper Fahrenheit wrote in 1734.

subject–verb agreement

Some collective nouns can take either a singular or plural verb, depending on the meaning. When the collective noun refers to the group as a single entity, use a singular verb.

The research *team has reported* its experimental results in the next issue of *Science.*

subject–verb agreement

When the group's members are being considered as individuals, use a plural verb.

The research *team have reported* differing versions of their research.

subject–verb agreement

A common subject–verb agreement error results from making a linking verb agree with the complement rather than the subject of the sentence.

An important *part* of cattle breeding *is* clones developed from embryo splitting.

subject–verb agreements

Clones, developed from embryo splitting, *are* an important part of cattle breeding.

Exercises: Subject–Verb Agreement

1. Every engineering proposal, test plan, and test report written by the engineering staff are submitted to the engineering writer for copy editing.

2. The blade and rejection blade on a time-delayed fuse is soldered to the element assembly, a copper element soldered to a silver element.

3. The telecommunications system derive polled information from each store via EPOS (Electronic Point of Sale Registers), SATs (Store Administrative Terminals), and telephone lines.

4. Each time a customer buys something, the cash registers, which are small computers, remembers this information.

5. All government documentation are in the process of being classified or reclassified as confidential, secret, or top-secret.

6. The computer tape and the input that has been keypunched is given to the Internal Operations Department.

7. One benefit of running is that the number of red blood cells are increased, thus more oxygen can be carried per quart of blood.

8. The sinoauricular (SA) node is the key regulator of the electrochemical impulses that stimulates contractions of the heart muscles.

9. Two types of peptic ulcer is common: gastric ulcers in the stomach and duodenal ulcers in the intestine. Duodenal ulcers causes pain between the breastbone and navel, often relieved by food or milk. Gastric ulcers causes pain at a higher location, however, and is often brought on, rather than relieved, by eating. Diagnosis for both types of ulcers involve any combination of three basic procedures. The most common procedure are X-rays. Endoscopy uses a long fiberoptic instrument that light up the walls of the stomach and duodenum, take photographs, and even obtain samples for microscopic study. A third method, less frequently used, involves obtaining samples of gastric juices.

10. The result of the Sysgen procedure are program disks designed to load onto your computer. (Sysgen is a coined word, derived from System Generator.) Once the Sysgen is programmed into the terminal, a list of questions appear on the screen. The operator responds with the names of the source and destination drives. When all the system generation process are completed, the built-in commands and the operating system is on the new disk.

2.6 Pronoun–Antecedent Agreement

A pronoun substitutes for or replaces a noun; an antecedent is a noun or pronoun earlier in the sentence (or an immediately preceding sentence) to which a pronoun refers. A pronoun must agree with its antecedent in three ways:

- gender: feminine, masculine, neuter

- person: first, second, third

- number: singular, plural

Errors in pronoun–antecedent agreement cause awkward sentences that often confuse readers.

Many errors result from the misuse of indefinite pronouns, which are pronouns that do not refer to a specific person, idea, or thing. These are the most common indefinite pronouns:

all	both	many	no one
another	each	more	one
any	either	most	several
anybody	everybody	neither	some
anyone	everyone	nobody	somebody
anything	few	none	someone

With the exception of such obvious plurals as *all, few, many, more, most, several,* and *some,* indefinite pronouns are third-person singular. When such indefinite pronouns are antecedents to other pronouns, they generally require singular pronouns.

Everyone brought *their* bathing suit to the company picnic.   *error in agreement*

The error results because "everyone" is singular and "their" is plural. The correction can substitute "his" only if all the company employees are male, "her" only if all employees are female. To write, "Everyone brought his bathing suit to the picnic" would be inaccurate if both men and women employees brought bathing suits. However, to write, "Everyone brought his or her bathing suit to the company picnic" would be awkward. The most appropriate correction bypasses the stylistic problem of using *his/her* or *his or her* by making both the antecedent and pronoun plural.

All employees brought *their* bathing suits to the company picnic.   *agreement*

Collective nouns used as antecedents can take either a singular or plural pronoun, depending on the meaning. When the collective noun refers to the group acting together, the pronoun should be singular.

The *staff* discussed changes in organizational structure at *its* monthly meeting.   *agreement*

When the individual members of the group are acting independently, the pronoun should be plural.

The *staff* wrote *their* recommendations for changing the organizational structure.   *agreement*

2.7 Pronoun Reference

Pronouns can cause ambiguity and confusion for readers if the antecedents are not clear. Most problems result from inappropriate use of these pronouns:

you	this	they	these
it	that	which	there

Reserve *you* for situations in which you directly address the readers. Use *it, this, that, which,* or *there* only when you can identify a specific, concrete antecedent. These pronouns usually do not present a problem in speech, but they can make your writing unnecessarily wordy, vague, and sometimes confusing. You can easily rewrite common expressions that use pronouns ineffectively.

ineffective pronoun use

It is believed . . .

There are several competitors . . .

revisions

Our committee believes . . .

Several competitors include . . .

Clear writing requires that pronouns have stated rather than implied antecedents.

unclear

An air conditioner removes much of the humidity from the air. *It* either evaporates or runs off through a tube to the outside.

What is the antecedent of "it"? Air conditioner? Humidity? Air? "It" has no stated antecedent; rather, the antecedent is implied.

improved

An air conditioner removes much of the humidity from the air. As the humidity condenses, the resulting water either evaporates or runs off through a tube to the outside.

Sometimes the reference is so general that the pronoun has no antecedent. Often *this, that,* or *these* is used, referring broadly to several preceding ideas, thus confusing the readers.

unclear

Holding your work in your hand when using a screwdriver can be dangerous. Place your work on a flat surface or secure it in a vise or clamp. Do not put your body in front of a screwdriver blade tip. The blade can cause a bad cut if it slips. *This* is a good practice for any pointed tool.

improved

Holding your work in your hand when using a screwdriver can be dangerous. Place your work on a flat surface or secure it in a vise or clamp. Do not put your body in front of a screwdriver blade tip. The blade can cause a bad cut if it slips. *These safety rules* apply to any pointed tool.

Another pronoun reference problem occurs when the pronoun is so far away from the antecedent that the readers can't be sure of the reference without rereading the passage.

The *generalization* usually holds true that the lifespan of a mammal can be corre-lated to its size. The larger the mammal, the longer the lifespan. Most mammals take approximately the same number of breaths and have the same number of heart-beats. A shrew compresses its biological functions into one or two years whereas an elephant spreads its activities over 60 or so years. *It* does not apply to humans. *unclear*

The problem can be eliminated by substituting a noun phrase for the pronoun.

The *generalization* usually holds true that the lifespan of a mammal can be corre-lated to its size. The larger the mammal, the longer the lifespan. Most mammals take approximately the same number of breaths and have the same number of heart-beats. A shrew compresses its biological functions into one or two years whereas an elephant spreads its activities over 60 or so years. *The relationship between longevity and body size* does not apply to humans. *improved*

Pronoun references also cause a problem if too many pronouns create confu-sion or ambiguity.

Owls have round eyes that are so large *they* cannot turn in *their* sockets so *they* must rotate *their* entire head in order to follow a moving object. *unclear*

In order to follow a moving object, an owl must rotate its entire head because its eyes are too large to turn in their sockets. *improved*

An owl has round eyes that are so large they cannot turn in their sockets, so the owl must rotate its entire head in order to follow a moving object.

Exercises: Pronoun–Antecedent Agreement and Pronoun Reference

1. During a heart–lung transplant, it is standard procedure to sever the trachea, aorta, and right atrium of the heart in order to remove the organs.

2. The committee voted their approval of proposed research.

3. Pregnant women can exercise vigorously as long as her doctor approves.

4. When stressed to the near breaking point, all material emits their own characteristic sound waves.

5. Everyone in the department is ready to donate their time to establishing an apprentice program.

6. It is now claimed that milk may be one of the worst foods for peptic ulcers. The fat and protein in it stimulate the production of gastric acid; the calcium causes additional acid production. They can be treated with several types of medication. Traditionally, they were treated only with antacids, but then anticholinergics were developed to control gastric production. Most recently they are treated with new antihistamines called H2-receptor blockers.

7. The type of evening exercise people do may affect the time it takes them to fall asleep. Dynamic exercise such as jogging or cycling tends to lengthen the time it takes to fall asleep because of the generalized stress that results. Static exercise such as push-ups or isometrics tends to bring on sleep sooner, the result of a static muscle contraction that triggers fatigue in some people. It may help certain types of insomnia.

8. Trobriand Islanders are matrilineal, tracing their ancestors through their mother's side of the family. The women hold high status in the society and are actively involved in ceremonial and economic functions. Their opinions are respected. This may be because, traditionally, men are thought to play no biological role in conception.

9. The point angle of a twist drill is approximately conical; it is the angle between the lips measured in the plane parallel to the drill axis and the lips. It ranges from 60° to 150°. The point deviates from the conical shape due to the lip relief angle. This is necessary to permit the drill to advance into the work. For the drill to perform effectively, it is essential that it be accurately sharpened.

10. It has recently been discovered that the Wave 3000 units, beginning with s/n (serial numbers) 78-100213 through s/n 78-100713 were shipped containing a faulty 64K PROM chip. It was found that the error was in a program that has already been corrected. These 500 units should not have left the factory with this problem. It is clearly stated on page 27 of the *Wave Test Manual* the procedure to follow to verify that the memory is correct. It is absolutely essential that all procedures are followed to ensure that we are shipping a quality product. Effective immediately, if any technicians are found to be leaving out test procedures, it will result in dismissal.

2.8 Dangling Modifiers

A dangling modifier is a word or phrase that appears to modify the subject of the sentence, but doesn't. The modifier dangles because there is no word in the sentence that it can logically modify. A dangling modifier should be corrected because it gives the readers inaccurate information and may cause unintended humor. Correction is easy: Sometimes you can eliminate the phrase entirely, you can add or change the subject of the independent clause, or you can change the dangling phrase into a subordinate clause. Occasionally, rewriting the entire sentence produces the best result.

Let's examine some examples of sentences in which the writer had good intentions and a definite idea, but still confuses the readers.

When in production, the engineer is responsible for keeping the production lines running smoothly.

dangling modifier

Is the engineer being manufactured? Replicated? Assembled? The readers can figure out that the writer *means* the engineer works in the production department or is responsible for the production process—but that's not what the sentence says; it says the engineer is in production. Placing the questionable phrase immediately after the subject is a good test for some sentences. If the result is ridiculous or nonsensical, you know the sentence must be revised. The revision of the sample sentence is easy because "production" is repetitious; the dangling modifier is merely eliminated.

The engineer is responsible for keeping the production lines running smoothly.

revision

The next sentence has an unstated but understood *you* as the subject.

After 30 minutes at 250° Fahrenheit, raise the oven temperature to 300° Fahrenheit.

dangling modifier

Whoever is adjusting the oven temperature is going to be mighty warm! A person cannot possibly spend 30 minutes at 250° Fahrenheit without being cooked. The sentence can be corrected by making the dangling modifier into a subordinate clause by adding a subject.

After the oven has been at 250° Fahrenheit for 30 minutes, raise the temperature to 300° Fahrenheit.

revision

Sometimes a dangling modifier can be eliminated by turning the phrase into a subordinate clause with a logical subject.

After assembly, the index, middle, and ring fingers are inserted into the holes at the end of the control arm.

dangling modifier

Have you ever heard of a manufacturer offering ready-to-assemble fingers?

After you have assembled the control arm, insert your index, middle, and ring fingers into the holes.

revisions

After the control arm is assembled, insert your index, middle, and ring fingers into the holes at the end.

Often the confusion caused by a dangling modifier can be eliminated in more than one way.

dangling modifier	When investigating this problem, three major areas should be considered.

One way to correct this sentence is to add a logical subject.

revisions	When investigating this problem, consider three major areas.
	When investigating this problem, you should consider three major areas.

Another way to correct the sentence is to invert the phrase and the independent clause.

revision	Three major areas should be considered when investigating this problem.

A third way to correct this sentence is to rewrite it entirely.

revision	Three major areas should be investigated.

The next example illustrates the flexibility you have in revising dangling modifiers.

dangling modifier	With proper diet and exercise, the statistics on cardiovascular disease can be lowered.

The dangling modifier here makes "statistics" sound like they need proper diet and exercise. The phrase "With proper diet and exercise" actually modifies the omitted subject—people. Several revisions are possible.

revisions	With proper diet and exercise, people can lower their chances of having cardio-vascular disease.
	People who eat a balanced diet and exercise regularly reduce the risk of cardio-vascular disease.

Exercises: Dangling Modifiers

1. To compete in the CAD/CAM market, product quality must be ensured.

2. To develop the negatives, a combination of chemicals is poured into the tank.

3. Through the use of gear reduction, the speed is reduced to 600 revolutions per minute.

4. When determining the internal temperature of the autoclave, the figure indicated by the thermometer should be carefully observed because the steam pressure gauge alone may be misleading.

5. While changing the filter floss, the fish are not disturbed because the system is located on the back of the tank.

6. With a small amount of practice, a French curve makes an otherwise hopeless task easy to achieve.

7. To fully understand the air conditioning process, it is necessary to follow each step to see how the parts operate.

8. When taking a breath, the head rotates 90° to the side, keeping one ear in the water.

9. A planimeter is an instrument used for measuring the area of a regular or irregular plane figure by tracing the perimeter of the figure. By using a planimeter, a result is easily obtained that is not in error more than 1 percent, except for very small areas. When using the planimeter, the anchor point is set at some convenient position on the drawing outside the area to be measured. To determine the area, the tracing point is then run around the perimeter of the area to be measured.

10. Silversmiths can use a torch to produce designs on various metals. By controlling such factors as metallic alloy proportions, thickness of protective surfaces, amount of heat, and flame size and direction, the roughened surface texture is produced. With much experience, a textural surface with a definite pattern can be produced. For example, by angling the torch in one direction on the first row and in another on the second, a herringbone pattern is created. Controlling the amount of heat and the size and direction of the flame, the interior of the copper-silver alloy can be partially melted. By melting only the interior of the metal alloy, a wrinkled surface is produced.

2.9 Misplaced Modifiers

Like dangling modifiers, misplaced words and phrases cause confusion—and sometimes unintentional humor.

Adverbs are particularly easy to misplace because they can be correctly placed in several locations in a sentence; however, changing the location of the adverb changes the meaning of the sentence. The following words can be troublesome:

almost	exactly	just	nearly	scarcely
even	hardly	merely	only	simply

Notice how changing the location of "only" changes the meaning.

■ EXAMPLES

Only the technician adjusted the valve.

The *only* technician adjusted the valve.

The technician *only* adjusted the valve.

The technician adjusted the *only* valve.

A good guideline is to place phrases and subordinate clauses close to the words they are intended to modify. Incorrectly placed modifiers can change the meaning.

misplaced modifier   Endorphin is released during labor when a woman is having a baby *to dull her senses*.

Motherhood might, in some situations, temporarily dull the senses, but no woman begins with this as a goal. The revision places the phrase "to dull her senses" close to the word it modifies, endorphin.

revisions   Endorphin is released to dull a woman's senses during labor.

Endorphin, which dulls senses, is released during labor.

misplaced modifier   In the technical journal, she read an article about insect reproduction *that verified her own field study*.

The sentence is illogical if "that verified her own field study" modifies "insect reproduction"; instead, it should be placed next to "article," the word it modifies.

revision   In the technical journal, she read an article that verified her own field study about insect reproduction.

Exercises: Misplaced Modifiers

1. What are the differences between the following sentences?
   Just the manager approved the proposal this morning.
   The manager just approved the proposal this morning.
   The manager approved just the proposal this morning.
   The manager approved the proposal just this morning.

2. What are the differences between the following sentences?
   Our department has almost completed all of the investigation.
   Our department has completed almost all of the investigation.

3. What are the differences between the following sentences?
   Nearly everyone is ready for the quality control survey.
   Everyone is nearly ready for the quality control survey.

4. I ordered drills from the manufacturer with carbide tips.

5. The pilot sighted the missing fishing boat using a sonar scanner.

6. The personnel department recommended a candidate from a competitor who was already skilled in using CNC machines.

7. The buyer ordered a part from the distributor guaranteed for five years.

8. WANTED: Industrial site for precision manufacturing company with chemical drains and 220V.

9. The decision will only be made after all data are compiled.

10. The supervisor placed the damaged manual in the drawer of his desk with missing pages.

2.10 Parallel Structure

Parallel structure requires a writer to use equivalent grammatical structures for ideas or facts of equivalent importance.

This sentence identifies two results of accidents; both should be written in the same grammatical structure.

Accidents can be either personal injury producing or property damage.

error in parallel structure

The revision could be any of the following versions.

Accidents can either *produce personal injury* or *damage property*.

revisions

Accidents can result in either *personal injury* or *property damage*.

Accidents can either *injure people* or *damage property*.

In the next example, the parallel error is in the subject of the sentence.

Minimizing displacement of existing structures and avoidance of water bodies must be considered, or the cost of the roadway will increase.

error in parallel structure

Because the sentence has a compound subject, each part of the subject must have the same structure.

Minimizing displacement of existing structures and *avoiding water bodies* must be considered, or the cost of the roadway will increase.

revisions

Minimize displacement of existing structures and *avoid water bodies,* or the cost of the roadway will increase.

The last example shows that items in a list should be parallel. The following sign was posted in a shop to remind workers of safety guidelines.

ALWAYS OBSERVE SAFETY RULES:
a. Wearing of safety glasses
b. Proper tool for the job
c. Use only tools that are functioning properly
d. Maintain a clean and organized work area
e. Questions relating to procedures or the proper handling of tools should be presented to your group leader

error in parallel structure

The items in any list should adhere to the same grammatical form. Because the sign instructs workers to follow guidelines, the items can all be in imperative mood, as the revision illustrates.

revisions

ALWAYS OBSERVE SAFETY RULES:
a. Wear safety glasses.
b. Use proper tools for the job.
c. Use only tools that are functioning properly.
d. Maintain a clean and organized work area.
e. Ask your group leader questions about procedures or proper tool handling.

Exercises: Parallel Structure

1. The work-in-progress report is used by a wide variety of employees, ranging from dispatchers to those at managerial levels.

2. I judged the systems on price, effectiveness, special options, and how easily the alarm could be installed.

3. Documentation includes how to load your program into the computer, any error messages from the computer, and limitations on your program.

4. The amount of thermal mass for a house depends on the total area of south glazing, where the mass areas are placed, how much sunlight they will receive, and the types of materials used.

5. The amplitude corresponds to how loud a person is speaking, and the frequency is the pitch of the voice.

6. The first step is to measure the roll surface under ambient conditions. Second, place the test roll into a preheated 200° Fahrenheit oven for three hours. The last step is to remove the test roll from the oven and remeasure the roll surface.

7. The table of contents in a manual for assemblers lists these items:

---

   a. Air hookup and disconnect
   b. Proper holding of air-driven tools
   c. Changing tips safely on air-driven tools
   d. How to avoid stripping the hardware

---

8. This bulleted list is from a report:
   - STEEL—This material can corrode and is magnetic.

- STAINLESS STEEL—This material is noncorrosive and is nonmagnetic.
- PLASTIC—Nonmetallic and nonconductive

9. **a.** The insulation for a home can be chosen according to the area for installation. In areas of the country where it is cold or if heating or air conditioning is used, the R-value should be raised. Typically, contractors recommend that walls and crawl spaces have insulation rated between R-11 and R-13. Insulation for floors that are unfinished and finished floors should be between R-11 and R-19. Insulation for ceilings can range from R-13 to R-30.

   b. The type of insulation determines whether it's fire resistant. Fiberglass blankets and batts are naturally fire resistant. Loose insulation can be made from cellulose, vermiculite, and it is also of fiberglass. Vermiculite and fiberglass are naturally fire resistant; cellulose can smolder or it burns unless chemically treated. Plastic foam insulation is made of urea formaldehyde or polyurethane. Both types are combustible but are chemically treated for safety. Rigid board insulation can be made of polystyrene, polyurethane, or fiberglass. The polystyrene can be extruded or sometimes it is made of molded beads pressed together. Polystyrene and polyurethane, both combustible, are chemically treated for safety.

10. These definitions are listed in a reference manual glossary:
    - LOCK NUTS—prevent the nut from becoming loose after being properly torqued.
    - NUTS—are internally threaded fasteners designed to mate with bolts and screws. Nuts are two-sided. The flat side should be against the washer.
    - POP RIVETS—A rivet is a headed fastener with the shank end designed to be expanded or spread in order to join the work pieces. Rivets are used for inseparable assemblies. Rivets are made of aluminum or steel and come in different sizes. They are fastened with a rivet gun or hand tool.
    - RIVETS—Rivets that are solid, eyelet, or tubular should be fully seated. Stacking and rolling should be uniform.
    - SEMS—Are preassembled screws and washers in one unit. These units expedite assembly operations and ensure the presence of a washer in each assembly.
    - STANDOFFS AND SPACERS—Standoffs and spacers are used to separate work pieces. They may be plastic, metal, ceramic, or phenolic.
    - WASHER—A part, usually thin, having a centrally located hole or partial slot. The washer performs various functions when assembled between the bearing surface or a fastener and the part being assembled.

2.11 Sentence Combining

Sentence combining gives writers tools to connect and rearrange independent and dependent clauses so that sentences are direct and expressive, establishing relationships to make reading easier. (See Handbook Section 2.1 on sentence structure.) Judicious sentence combining usually clarifies the content and improves the style.

Sentence combining helps writers eliminate excessive use of short sentences. Although short, simple sentences are usually easier to understand than longer, structurally complex sentences, they can be overused, resulting in a primer writing style that often insults and annoys readers. A primer style contains unnecessary repetition and may, in fact, significantly lower comprehension because subordination is seldom employed; thus, relationships among the ideas in sentences are not clear.

As a reader, how do you react to this paragraph?

■ EXAMPLE

High acidity kills fish. Fish in the lakes of the Northeast and Canada are dying. Coal-burning plants produce sulfur dioxide. Some clouds retain this sulfur dioxide. Rain combines with sulfur dioxide. Weak sulfuric acid is formed from rain and sulfur dioxide. Coal-burning plants produce nitrogen oxides. Some clouds retain this nitrogen oxide. Rain combines with nitrogen oxide. The combination forms nitric acid. Coal smoke is produced in the Ohio Valley. Some snow and rain originate in the Ohio Valley. This rain and snow sometimes fall in the Northeast and in Canada. The rain and snow contain sulfuric acid and nitric acid. Canada blames the Ohio Valley for the high acidity levels in lakes.

Each idea is presented in a separate sentence, with no attempt made to establish relationships among the ideas. When you compare this choppy, primer version to the paragraph below (as it was originally published), you can see the importance of combining and subordinating ideas.

■ REVISION

High acidity levels are killing fish in the lakes of the Northeast and Canada. When rain combines with sulfur dioxide from a coal-burning plant it forms weak sulfuric acid, and when the cloud contains nitrogen oxides the product is nitric acid. Canada blames [the acidic] rain and snow originating in the smoky Ohio Valley for its problem.[3]

Because the relationships the writer intends are clearly expressed, the second version is easier to read than the first, which forces readers to make assumptions about these relationships that may be different from what the writer intended.

Writers use four strategies to combine sentences: adding, deleting, embedding, and transforming. Combining sentences by *addition* involves connecting sentence elements with punctuation (comma, semicolon) and either coordinate or subordinate conjunctions. In the following example, three separate sentences can be combined.

- The multiple layers of fossil-bearing deposits indicate that early humans first took shelter in the cave 460,000 years ago.

- The last of them did not abandon the site until 230,000 years ago.

- They were forced out by the filling of the cave with rubble and sediment.

In this case, combining requires no changes to the sentences themselves. The original article about "Peking Man" in *Scientific American* combined them by adding the coordinate conjunction "and" along with a comma and the subordinate conjunction "when."

■ EXAMPLE

The multiple layers of fossil-bearing deposits indicate that early men first took shelter in the cave 460,000 years ago, and the last of them did not abandon the site until 230,000 years ago, when they were forced out by the filling of the cave with rubble and sediment.[4]

When combining sentences, skillful writers often use *deletion* to eliminate redundant words or phrases. Pronouns are sometimes substituted for deleted elements. The remaining parts are combined into a series or a compound element:

■ The skull of the Peking man was much thicker.	(and)
■ ~~The skull of the Peking man was much~~ flatter.	(and)
■ ~~The skull of the Peking man~~ had protruding brows.	(and)
■ ~~The skull of the Peking man had~~ a marked angle at the rear.	

By deleting the repetitious "The skull of the Peking man," the writers have produced a clear sentence that is easier to read.

■ EXAMPLE

The skull of the Peking man was much thicker and flatter and had protruding brows and a marked angle at the rear.

A more sophisticated method of sentence combining involves *embedding*—placing elements of one sentence into another sentence. The following example of embedding takes the key concept in the first sentence and places it in apposition within the second sentence:

- One technique was called anvil percussion.

- In the technique a large flat stone (the anvil) was placed on the ground and forcefully struck with a piece of sandstone.

Usage Handbook

- ~~One technique was~~ called anvil percussion.
- In the technique ↙ a large flat stone (the anvil) was placed on the ground and forcefully struck with a piece of sandstone.

By deleting repetitious phrases and combining the two sentences into one, the writers have produced a smoother, more effective sentence.

■ EXAMPLE

In the technique called anvil percussion a large flat stone (the anvil) was placed on the ground and forcefully struck with a piece of sandstone.

The final combining strategy is called *transformation*, in which the form and order of words, phrases, and even clauses may be changed. In this example, combining makes one sentence subordinate to the other.

- The stone artifacts produced by the Peking man are primarily made of vein quartz, rock crystal, flint, and sandstone.
  (suggesting that)
- He did not rely exclusively on water-rounded pebbles for tools.

The second sentence is made subordinate to the first with the addition of "suggesting that."

■ EXAMPLE

The stone artifacts produced by the Peking man are primarily made of vein quartz, rock crystal, flint and sandstone, suggesting that he did not rely exclusively on water-rounded pebbles for tool material.

In combining sentences, emphasis is as important as grammatical correctness and accuracy of content. The most effective way to change the emphasis in a sentence is to change word order. The beginning of a sentence is the most prominent location; information presented first is assumed to be most important. The end of a sentence is the second best location for emphasizing information. Placing information in the middle of a sentence gives it the least emphasis.

The importance of location is demonstrated by revising the following sentence in several different ways to emphasize different ideas. The first example is a formal definition.

■ EXAMPLE

Hydrocephalus is a condition in which increased amounts of spinal fluid within the ventricles of the brain cause an enlargement of the head.

■ REVISIONS

Emphasis on "an enlargement of the head"

An enlargement of the head, resulting from increased amounts of spinal fluid within the ventricles of the brain, is a primary characteristic of hydrocephalus.

The ventricles of the brain collect increased amounts of spinal fluid, resulting in an enlargement of the head in the condition called hydrocephalus.

Emphasis on "ventricles of the brain"

Spinal fluid increases within the ventricles of the brain cause an enlargement of the head in victims of hydrocephalus.

Emphasis on "spinal fluid"

Awareness of audience is important for writers who are revising ideas and sentences through combining. The primer sentences in the next example all deal with the same subject, but they have no relationship established among them. They can be combined in different ways, depending on the needs of the readers.

- Plastic pails are used in industry.

- Plastic pails are often made of high-density polyethylene.

- Polyethylene pails cost 40 to 50 percent less than steel pails.

- The cost of polyethylene pails has risen.

- The cost of steel pails has risen faster than the cost of polyethylene pails.

One version is suitable for experts or technicians who want accurate information supported by specific facts:

■ EXAMPLE

Although the cost of plastic pails for industrial use has risen, the cost for comparable steel pails has risen faster. Now, pails made of high-density polyethylene cost 40 to 50 percent less than comparable steel pails.

Another version is more appropriate for readers who are interested in general information but who do not need specific details:

■ EXAMPLE

Plastic pails for industrial use, frequently made of polyethylene, cost less than comparable steel pails.

Cumulative Exercises

Exercise: Sentence Structure, Sentence Fragments, Comma Splices, Modifier Errors, Parallel Structure, and Sentence Combining

Using word-processing (wp) software, a document is accessible to the writer for unlimited revisions. Revision becomes easier because a writer does not have the physical burden of entirely rewriting a document. Instead, a writer incorporates necessary changes in the appropriate places. For example, sections of a document can be moved to any other place in the document, you can delete material and insert new material. Automatically adjusting the remaining content to fill in the lines and meet the margins. A writer can revise directly on the screen attached to the terminal or getting a paper printout and revising on paper appeals more to some writers. After completing the revisions, the final copy of the document is printed.

Exercise: Sentence Structure, Sentence Fragments, Comma Splices, Subject–Verb and Pronoun–Antecedent Agreement, Pronoun Reference, Modifier Errors, Parallel Structure, Sentence Combining

Excessive amounts of scrap and customer rejects has caused us to recommend three solutions to this. One, a new glue pot at a cost of $6,500. A more favorable solution is repairing the existing glue pot for $1,500 and then to purchase an International Glue Line Inspection System, the price for this system is $4,000. The new glue line system will decrease scrap and customer rejects by 75 percent. The system will detect breaks in the glue line and ejects defective cartons from the run. If the system detects more than five consecutive rejects, it automatically stops the machine. In the first year of use, the cost savings will exceed $10,000. More than covering the cost of rebuilding the glue pot and the new inspection system.

Exercise: Sentence Structure, Sentence Fragments, Modifier Errors, Parallel Structure, Sentence Combining

Machinists must follow blueprints and operating precision equipment including lathes and machines that do milling work. Working to very tight tolerances, some machined parts are accurate to 0.0001 inch. At regular stages in the machining of a part, the blueprint is checked. Dimensions of the part must match the dimensions specified on the blueprint. The application of the part determines the accuracy required by the blueprint. Even for medical and aerospace applications, some blueprints allow the part dimensions to vary slightly. Stating + (plus) or – (minus) the specified dimensions. Machinists must measure the part, determining that the dimensions are within the tolerances, and correct any errors. Because being undersized results in being scrapped, the machinists remove material from parts in extremely tiny amounts.

Exercise: Sentence Structure, Sentence Fragments, Comma Splices, Subject–Verb and Pronoun–Antecedent Agreement, Pronoun Errors, Modifier Errors, Parallel Structure, Sentence Combining

Although relatively high in initial cost ($50,000), a company using the pivoting arm industrial robot RX 784 will earn increased profit. Based on the salaries of the three workers it replaces, the payback period averages 16 months. By relying on hydraulic systems for movement, the manufacturer recommends the seals at the three main joints—hand, arm, and main rotary—be inspected and then only replace them if necessary every 400,000 hours.

The robot is more reliable than human workers and the noise and heat of the workplace does not affect it. Operates in hazardous and harsh environments. The RX 784 is made of tempered steel alloy that operate in radiation and up to temperatures of 2,000° Fahrenheit.

The RX 784 arm, which can extend from 500 mm to 1,000 mm and has an overall arc of 270°, is attached to a solid base. Although the base is stationary, it can be adapted to work from a moving track. It can be programmed in four hours to perform a variety of repetitive functions.

After the robot is installed, the highest expense is for electricity they require to operate. This cost, however, is 50 percent less than the cost of heat and cooling required to keep workers comfortable in the same work area.

Cumulative Exercise: Paragraphs, Fragments, Run-Ons, Agreement, Punctuation (Hyphens, Commas), Pronoun Reference, Verb Mood, Parallelism, Spelling

Radioactive (or nuclear) waste is the unusable byproduct, or obsolete, or discarded product, or nuclear actitities. There are several types of waste. High level waste (HLW) is the highly radioactive waste resulting from reprocessing spent fuel. (That is, fuel irradiated in a nuclear reactor). Currently in the United States, reprocessing involves removing the plutonium and uranium from spent fuel generated by the U.S. Department of Energy nuclear reactors. The plutonium and uranium is recycled for use in the Nation's defense programs, what remains after reprocessing is highly radioactive waste that must be remotely handled behind heavy protective shielding. It requires long term isolation (desposal in an underground repository) while it decays (stabilizes). The spent fuel resulting from the generation of electricity from U.S. commercial nuclear powerplants is currently not being reprosessed. Under provisions of Nuclear Waste Policy Act, it will be placed in an underground repository for long term isolation as will HLW. Both are shipped as a solid and is packaged in heavily shielded casks for storage and to be transported. Transuranic (TRU) waste contains synthetic elements heavier than uranium. Thus the name trans (or beyond) uranic. Although most TRU waste is no more radioactive than low level waste. It decays so slowly that it is radioactive for a long time, even though it does not require as much shielding, it requires the same sort of long term isolation as high level waste. In the United States, TRU waste is generated as a byproduct of the reprocesing of spent fuel from government reactors as part of the Nation's defense activities. Reprocessing removes usable plutonium and uranium. For use in defense programs as well as other isotopes useful in a variety of commercial applications. TRU waste is usually contaminated protective clothing, tools, glassware, and equipment. TRU waste is usually contaminated protective clothing, tools, glassware, and equipment. Low level waste (LLW) is radioactive material results from nuclear related research, medical, and industrial processes. The radiation level of these materials range from natural background levels to very radioactive. LLW are usually rags, papers, filters, tools, equipment, and discarded protective clothing contaminated with radio nuclides. These wastes are generated from research, operations, houssekeeping, and maintinence at medical reserch, commercial, industrial, or other nuclear facilities. Typically, LLW contains small amounts of radioactive material disperced in large volumes of other material. Generally poses little potential hazard. However, small volumes of very radioactive LLW material does require protective shielding during handling and transportation activities. All LLW is safely disposed at government inspected facilities. Uranium tailings are radioactive rock, and soil. The byproducts of uranium mining, and milling. Tailings contain small amounts of radium that decay, and emit a radioactive gas, radon. When radon gas is released into the atmosphere it disperses harmlessly but this gas might be harmful if a person was exposed to it in high concentrations for long periods of time.[5]

Punctuation

(*Note:* Conventions discussed in this section are based on the 14th edition of *The Chicago Manual of Style* and the 3rd edition of *Words into Type*.)

3.1 Apostrophe

3.1.1   Use an apostrophe to indicate possession. Add an apostrophe plus *s* to singular nouns and indefinite pronouns to form the possessive.

- **EXAMPLES**

Fire destroyed the company's data processing room.

The physician examined everyone's medical records.

Add an apostrophe plus *s* to plural nouns that do not end in *s*. Add only the apostrophe to plurals that end in *s:*

- **EXAMPLES**

women's locker room (locker room of the women)

schooners' crews (crews of more than one schooner)

3.1.2   Use an apostrophe to indicate omission of one or more letters or figures.

- **EXAMPLES**

doesn't = does not   '01 = 2001

3.1.3   Avoid a common misuse that confuses *it's* (it is) and *its* (possessive form of it), *you're* (you are) and *your* (possessive form of you). Do not use apostrophes with such possessive pronouns as *hers*, *theirs*, or *ours*.

3.2 Brackets

3.2.1   Use brackets to enclose comments or explanations inserted in a quotation.

■ EXAMPLES

"Production declined last month [May 2000]."

"The section manager [Thompson] identified the problem."

"Improper leveling [of the comparator] resulted in inaccurate data."

3.2.2   Use *sic* (meaning "so" or "thus") to indicate an error in the original document.

■ EXAMPLE

"The shipment was made on 5-33-00 [*sic*]."

3.3 Colon

3.3.1   Use a colon as a convention in salutations, citations, time, titles.

■ EXAMPLES

Dear Mr. Ellis:	5:30 a.m.
(January 2000): 342	*Synectics: The Development of Creative Capacity*

3.3.2   Use a colon to introduce a list or series when the words preceding the colon are a complete sentence.

■ EXAMPLE

The machinist regularly works with five metals: aluminum, beryllium, molybdenum, stainless steel, titanium.

Do *not* use a colon if the words preceding the list or series are not a complete sentence.

■ EXAMPLE

The machinist regularly works with aluminum, beryllium, molybdenum, stainless steel, and titanium.

3.4 Comma

3.4.1   Use a comma as a convention in dates, numbers, addresses, informal salutations, and titles or degrees. In dates listing month, day, and year, a comma goes before and after the year.

■ EXAMPLES

April 19, 1776, *or* 19 April 1776

317,554,203

1055 Thomas Jefferson, N.W.
Washington, DC 20007

Dear Kate,

Christopher D. Burnett, Ph.D.

3.4.2   Use a comma to separate two sentences connected with a coordinate conjunction—*and, but, or, for, so, yet.* Place the comma preceding the coordinate conjunction.

■ EXAMPLE

The printer was too slow, and most of the programs were never delivered.

3.4.3   Use commas to separate items in a series. Place a comma following each item in the series, except the final one.

■ EXAMPLES

Health, self-confidence, and self-esteem usually improve as a result of running.

To perform the test, an operator connects the coupler to the enclosure, evacuates the instrument, purges it with a reference gas, evacuates the system again, and then opens the coupler.

An automated coal-mining system would increase productivity, make mining safer, and protect the health of the mine workers.

Do *not* use commas to separate compound elements—two nouns, two verbs, or two modifiers.

■ EXAMPLES

The lenses and photodetectors are mounted on a plate.

Break-even costs vary widely with financing methods and tax structures.

The gas is noncorrosive and nontoxic.

3.4.4   Use a comma to separate introductory phrases and subordinate clauses from the main sentence.

■ EXAMPLE

Because solar-cell arrays can be built on roofs, they have low structural costs and can displace some costs of conventional roofs in new homes.

3.4.5 Use a comma to separate nonessential elements from the rest of the sentence.

- **EXAMPLES**

Before the IRAS (Infrared Astronomical Satellite), little could be learned about the formation of smaller stars, those like our sun, because of their faintness.

Scientists have isolated the worst-tasting substance ever discovered, a white powder so bitter it can be detected even when diluted to 1 part in 20 million.

3.5 Dash

Use a dash (made with an easy keystroke combination on your computer keyboard) to signal a break in thought. Do *not* separate the dash from the text with spaces.

- **EXAMPLE**

The interpreter of ancient clay tablets failed to recognize that one sign—a small circular impression—did not always have the numeric value of 10.

3.6 Ellipsis

Use ellipsis points (three spaced dots) to indicate that something has been omitted. If the omission comes at the end of a sentence, the first dot is the period, followed by the three dots of the ellipsis.

- **EXAMPLE**

Strokes in the temporal or parietal lobes of the left hemisphere of the neocortex characteristically result in the impairment of the ability to read, write, speak, and do arithmetic.

"Strokes . . . characteristically result in the impairment of the ability to read, write, speak, and do arithmetic."

3.7 Exclamation Point

Use an exclamation point at the end of a sentence to signal an extraordinarily startling idea or event. An exclamation point is seldom appropriate in technical documents.

3.8 Hyphen

3.8.1 Use a hyphen to signal the break of a word, showing that the word is carried over to the next line. Break words *only* at the end of a syllable.

3.8.2 Use a hyphen to create compound modifiers that precede a noun.

■ **EXAMPLES**

pollen-carrying hairs   word-length units

high-pressure valve   two-layer membrane

6-, 12-, and 16-foot fence   three-dimensional structure

3.8.3 Use a hyphen in most words that begin with *self-*.

■ **EXAMPLES**

self-examination   self-incrimination

self-regulatory   self-employed

3.8.4 Use a hyphen to avoid ambiguity.

■ **EXAMPLES**

coop: The chicken coop was freshly painted.

co-op: The food co-op has 200 members.

re-cover: After the storm, the plants were re-covered with cheesecloth.

recover: The plants would recover if protected from the sun.

3.8.5 Use hyphens in fractions and ratios that function as adjectives preceding a noun.

■ **EXAMPLES**

Committee rules require a two-thirds majority to pass resolutions.

The vote was carried by a three-to-one margin.

3.8.6 Use hyphens in compound numbers from twenty-one through ninety-nine.

■ **EXAMPLE**

Twenty-seven bus routes will be added on January 1.

3.9 Italics

3.9.1 Use italics to indicate titles of books, periodicals, newsletters, and newspapers.

■ EXAMPLES

Edgerton's work in stroboscopy and electronic flash photography is illustrated in *Moments of Vision*.

Aviation Week and Space Technology is an important trade publication.

3.9.2   Use italics to indicate material that deserves emphasis.

■ EXAMPLE

Each type of anesthesia available has specific risks. *General anesthesia* holds the greatest risk for the patient. . . .

In such a discussion, each type of anesthesia could be italicized as it is introduced. Emphasis through italics should be used cautiously or it loses its effectiveness.

3.9.3   Use italics to indicate legal citations. The *v.* (for versus) may be italic or roman, as long as it is consistent.

■ EXAMPLE

In *Technicomp* v. *Chemco,* industrial safety was established as the mutual responsibility of . . .

3.9.4   Use italics to indicate letters.

■ EXAMPLES

the letter *W*

mark it with an *X*

3.9.5   Use italics to indicate *algebraic variables*.

■ EXAMPLES

$a^2 + b^2 = c^2$

the *n*th power

3.9.6   Use italics to indicate textual references to visual points.

■ EXAMPLE

Plot a course from *A* to *Y* as shown on the navigational chart.

3.9.7   Use italics to indicate Latinate (usually scientific) names and terms.

■ EXAMPLES

Eel grass (*Zostera marina*) can take over a small pond if left unchecked.

Streptomyces griseus is a funguslike bacteria that produces streptomycin, a commonly used antibiotic.

3.9.8   Use italics to indicate names of vessels—spacecraft, ships, aircraft.

■ EXAMPLE

The *Voyager* space probe sent back data about the outer planets in our solar system.

3.10 Parentheses

3.10.1   Use parentheses to separate supplementary information within a single sentence or to enclose one or more sentences.

■ EXAMPLE

At short wavelengths (12 to 25 micrometers), the main contributor to infrared background is emission from zodiacal dust from the solar system.

3.10.2   Use parentheses to separate acronyms the first time they are introduced.

■ EXAMPLE

The Infrared Astronomical Satellite (IRAS) was launched in a joint undertaking by the Netherlands Agency for Aerospace Programs (NIVR), the U.S. National Aeronautics and Space Administration (NASA), and the U.K. Science and Engineering Research Council (SERC).

3.11 Period

3.11.1   Use a period to signal the end of a statement or command.

3.11.2   Use a period (without parentheses) to follow the numbers or letters enumerating items in a list.

3.11.3   Use a period as a decimal point.

3.11.4   Use a period following some abbreviations. Most scientific and technical abbreviations no longer require periods. However, use a period if the abbreviation spells another word: in. (inches), no. (number), and so on.

3.12 Question Mark

Use a question mark at the end of a question. See 3.13.3 for use with quotation marks.

3.13 Quotation Marks

3.13.1   Use quotation marks to indicate the titles of articles from periodicals and newspapers.

■ EXAMPLES

"Consumer Products Need Better Manuals" in *Technical Communication*

"Rolling-Contact Rheostat" in *NASA Tech Briefs*

3.13.2   Use quotation marks to enclose short direct quotations. Longer quotations (more than three lines) should be single spaced and indented from the regular margins, without quotation marks.

■ EXAMPLE

Gerontologist Lorraine Hiatt said, "Many of today's elders don't realize that the environment may be exaggerating and, in some cases, causing certain functional disabilities."

3.13.3   Place commas and periods inside quotation marks. Place colons and semicolons outside quotation marks. Place question marks, exclamation points, and dashes inside the quotation marks only if the punctuation is part of the quotation; otherwise, place them outside the quotation marks.

■ EXAMPLE

I asked, "Have you calibrated the scale yet?"

Did you hear him say "The scale is calibrated"?

3.14 Semicolon

3.14.1   Use a semicolon to separate two closely related sentences.

■ EXAMPLE

The world's earliest written records are inscriptions on clay tablets; they have been unearthed at the sites of two great ancient cities in Iran and Iraq.

3.14.2   Use a semicolon to separate two sentences connected by a conjunctive adverb. Precede the conjunctive adverb with a semicolon; follow it with a comma.

■ EXAMPLE

Penney's is a retail outlet; therefore, it is essential that the information from their stores be polled daily.

3.14.3   Use a semicolon to separate items in a series if individual items themselves contain commas.

■ EXAMPLE

The twist drill body contains the point, which is the cutting portion of the drill; the flutes, which convey the chips away from the cutting edges; and a number of other details.

3.14.4 Do *not* use a semicolon preceding a list; instead, use a colon.

■ EXAMPLE

wrong   The system has two parts; Filecreate and Crosstab.

right   The system has two parts: Filecreate and Crosstab.

3.15 Slash

Use a slash to separate elements in dates, to indicate a fraction, and in place of *per*.

■ EXAMPLES

6/6/47	(6 June 1947)
2/3	(two-thirds)
/order	(per order)

Capitalization

(*Note:* Conventions for capitalization are based on those suggested in the 14th edition of *The Chicago Manual of Style.*)

4.1 Personal Names

4.1.1   Capitalize names and initials of people.

■ EXAMPLE

Edward H. Burnett

4.1.2   Capitalize civil, military, religious, and professional titles that immediately precede a name as part of the name.

■ EXAMPLES

He said that General Jones had arrived.

The general has arrived.

4.2 Academic Degrees, Honors, and Awards

4.2.1 Capitalize the full name or abbreviation of an academic degree or honor.

■ **EXAMPLES**

The B.S. is awarded after four years of study.

Desmond Tutu won the Nobel Peace Prize in 1984.

Henry Kissinger, Nobelist and statesman, was born in Germany.

4.2.2 Do not capitalize general references to degrees or honors.

■ **EXAMPLES**

The bachelor's degree is awarded after four years of study.

The actor is returning to college to pursue a master of science degree.

4.3 Groups of People

Capitalize nationalities, as well as racial, linguistic, or religious groups of people.

■ **EXAMPLES**

German   Hispanic

Korean   Navajo

4.4 Place Names

4.4.1 Capitalize parts of the world or a country.

■ **EXAMPLES**

Arctic Circle   Pacific Northwest   the Middle East

Central America   Southeast Asia   Washington State

4.4.2 Capitalize countries, states, cities, and counties.

■ **EXAMPLES**

Southfield

New Marlborough

4.4.3 Capitalize specific topographic locations (rivers, lakes, islands, mountains), but lowercase general places.

■ EXAMPLES

Appalachian Trail	Penobscot Bay	Mekong River delta
Berkshire Hills	Matinicus Island	the mountains in Tennessee

4.4.4 Capitalize buildings, monuments, and public places.

■ EXAMPLES

Kenmore Square	Gateway Arch
Merchandise Mart	Bunker Hill Monument

4.5 Words Derived from Proper Nouns

Do not capitalize words derived from proper nouns. These should be lowercase.

■ EXAMPLES

curie	pasteurize
india ink	roman numerals
macadam surface	

4.6 Organizations

4.6.1 Capitalize governmental and judicial bodies.

■ EXAMPLES

Department of Health and Human Services

U.S. Supreme Court

4.6.2 Capitalize institutions and companies.

■ EXAMPLES

New Mexico State University

Digital Equipment Corporation, or DEC

4.6.3 Capitalize names of associations.

■ EXAMPLES

American Association for the Advancement of Science

Society of Technical Communication

4.7 Historical and Cultural Terms

4.7.1 Use lowercase for numerical designation of a period.

■ **EXAMPLES**

sixteenth century

nineteenth

4.7.2   Capitalize archaeological and cultural periods.

■ **EXAMPLES**

Renaissance   Stone Age

Industrial Revolution   Bronze Age

4.7.3   Capitalize acts, treaties, and government programs.

■ **EXAMPLE**

Declaration of Independence

4.7.4   Capitalize laws and legal citations.

■ **EXAMPLES**

Sherman Antitrust Act

Roe v. *Wade*

4.8 Calendar and Time Designations

4.8.1   Capitalize months and days of the week. Use lowercase for seasons.

■ **EXAMPLES**

June   spring

Monday   autumn

4.8.2   Capitalize holidays.

■ **EXAMPLES**

Christmas

Passover

4.9 Scientific Terms

(For more detailed assistance, refer to the *Council of Biology Editors Style Manual* and the U.S. Geologic Survey's *Suggestions for Authors.*)

4.9.1   Capitalize names of genus, family, order, class, and phylum, but not the species or subspecies.

■ **EXAMPLES**

Iris prismatica [genus and species]

Chordata [phylum]

4.9.2   Generally, use lowercase for common plant and animal names.

■ **EXAMPLES**

puffin   foxgloves

gerbil   hemlock

4.9.3   Capitalize geological terms.

■ **EXAMPLES**

Tertiary period

early Pliocene epoch

4.9.4   Capitalize astronomical terms.

■ **EXAMPLES**

North Star   Milky Way

Ursa Major   Halley's comet

4.9.5   Lowercase medical terms, except for proper names within the term.

■ **EXAMPLES**

Hodgkin's disease

measles

4.9.6   Lowercase generic drug names.

■ **EXAMPLE**

propoxyphene

4.9.7   Capitalize infectious organisms, but use lowercase for diseases based on such names.

■ **EXAMPLES**

Giardia lambia   *Trichinella spiralis*

giardiasis   trichinosis

4.9.8   Capitalize only proper names attached to laws and principles.

■ **EXAMPLES**

Boyle's law

first law of thermodynamics

4.9.9 Capitalize chemical symbols, but not the names.

■ **EXAMPLES**

sodium chloride   urea

NaCl CH_4ON_2

4.10 Registered Trademarks

Capitalize registered trademarks but not the generic derivative of the term.

■ **EXAMPLES**

| Levi's | Bufferin | Xerox | Vaseline |
| jeans | aspirin | photocopier | petroleum jelly |

4.11 Titles of Works

4.11.1 Capitalize first, last, and key words in titles of books, periodicals, pamphlets, newspapers, movies, television and radio programs, musical compositions, and works of art.

■ **EXAMPLES**

Technical Communication   PBS's *Nova*

American Journal of Nursing   *Amadeus*

Wall Street Journal   WGBH's "Morning Pro Musica"

4.11.2 Computer software is often in full capitals.

■ **EXAMPLES**

| APL | COBOL | Assembler |
| BASIC | FORTRAN | Pascal |

Numbers—Figures or Words?

(*Note:* These conventions for use of figures and words are based on those suggested for scientific and technical use in the 14th edition of *The Chicago*

Manual of Style. More specialized usage is presented in the United States Government Printing Office *Style Manual.*)

5.1 Ordinal vs. Cardinal

Generally, use words for numbers one through nine and figures for all other numbers, both cardinal and ordinal.

cardinal (count)

The office suite has seven rooms.

The manufacturing facility has 22,000 square feet.

ordinal (order)

The company was second in mass market sales.

She ranked 23rd out of the 300 applicants.

5.2 Beginnings of Sentences

Use words at the beginning of a sentence. If this is awkward, rewrite the sentence.

■ EXAMPLES

Two thousand three hundred and fifty seedlings were delivered.

The delivery of 2,350 seedlings arrived.

5.3 Very Large Numbers

Express very large numbers (over six digits) by a figure followed by *million, billion,* and so on.

■ EXAMPLE

Sales figures for last year reached $7 million.

5.4 Physical Quantities

5.4.1   Use figures for physical quantities—distances, lengths, areas, volumes, pressures, and so on.

■ EXAMPLES

17 inches	12 picas
1,700 square feet	220 volts
3.2 liters	5 cubic yards

5.4.2   Use figures with symbols or abbreviations.

90°	latitude 39°20′ N
55 MPH	32 psi
35mm film	4″ x 4″

5.5 Percentages and Decimals

5.5.1   Use figures for all percentages and decimal fractions. Use the symbol "%" in technical and scientific material.

■ **EXAMPLES**

A rejection rate of 7% is too high.

The manual had a readability level of 10.2 on the Fry scale.

5.5.2   Set decimal fractions less than one with an initial zero if the quantity expressed is capable of equaling or exceeding 1.00. If the quantity never equals 1.00, no zero is used.

■ **EXAMPLES**

ratio of 0.93

$p < .07$

5.6 Age

Use figures to indicate age.

■ **EXAMPLES**

age 39	women in their 70s
2-year-old	18 months old

Documenting Sources

Documentation can be separated into two major tasks: preparing a list of *sources cited* and preparing *source notes* (internal notes in the text, footnotes, or endnotes).

6.1 Sources Cited

Documents that are prepared with the help of other sources and include references to these sources should have a list of *Sources Cited* following the last page of document or appendix text. This list is also called *Bibliography* and occasionally *References, Sources, Works Cited,* or *Literature Cited.* Whatever the title, the list contains the sources the writer quotes directly, takes original ideas from, and refers to in the document. Sources that the writer examines while preparing the document but does not quote from or refer to are not included in the list of sources cited.

Several variations exist for ordering the entries in Sources Cited. Usually the entries are arranged alphabetically by the last name of the author. Less frequently, the entries may be arranged by order of citation in the document, by publication date, by primary and secondary sources, or by genre or subject of the source.

When you use a source, record all of the following information so that you don't have to locate the source again to find this information. The information usually appears in the following order:

1. *Author's name* List the author's name as it appears on the title page.

2. *Title of chapter or article* If you're only using a chapter from a book or an article from a periodical, give the chapter or article title.

3. *Title of the work* Give the full title of the book or periodical, including any subtitle.

4. *Name of the editor, translator* Identify any editor, compiler, or translator listed on the title page or at the beginning of an article.

5. *Edition used* Indicate whether a book is a second or succeeding edition, a revised edition, or an annual edition if such information is listed on the title page.

6. *Number of volume and issue* Identify the number of a work in a multi-volume work. Identify the issue number if there is one.

7. *Name of series* Cite the series and the Arabic numeral identifying the work's place in the series.

8. *Place of publication, name of publisher, and date of publication* Identify the city of publication; if more than one city is listed on the title page, identify only the first city. Then give the name of the publisher and the most recent date of the copyright.

9. *Page numbers* Identify the inclusive page numbers you use.

The Chicago Manual of Style presents formats used by professionals in a variety of technical fields. The models in sections 6.3.1 through 6.3.24 illustrate the *Chicago* formats for commonly used entries. If your instructor or company does not specify a format for your particular profession or discipline, use the one presented here.

6.2 Source Notes

6.2.1 Five situations require source notes:

- direct quotations, even excerpts

- quantifiable data (facts and statistics)

- information that is not common knowledge to your audience

- paraphrased presentation of original or unique ideas

- visual material, both content and design

6.2.2 Source notes can be presented in one of three ways:

- parenthetical notes within the text of a document (often called internal citations)

- footnotes, at the bottom of a page

- endnotes, at the conclusion of a document

Although there are three kinds of source notes, technical documents use parenthetical notes almost exclusively, so that's what is encouraged and illustrated in this Handbook. These parenthetical notes in the text of a document identify the author, date, and page number for the source of information. Readers can find the complete information in the sources cited list at the end of the document. In this style of documentation, a parenthetical reference immediately follows the quoted or paraphrased material:

- (Wallace 2000, 127–28) identifies the author, date, and pages

The models on the following pages illustrate the formats that *The Chicago Manual of Style* favors for parenthetical notes and the related full references that would appear in the sources cited list.

6.3 Formats for Documentation

(Citation formats for print documentation follow *The Chicago Manual of Style*.)

6.3.1   Book—One Author

Bibliography Entry   Batu, V. 1998. *Aquifer hydraulics: A comprehensive guide to hydrogeologic data analysis.* Wiley & Sons.

Internal Citation   (Batu 1998, 27–30)

6.3.2   Two Authors

Bibliography Entry   Schwartz, E., and L. Marino. 1999. *Digital Darwinism.* New York: Random House.

Internal Citation   (Schwartz and Marino 1999, 218)

6.3.3 Book—Multiple Authors

Bibliography Entry Locke, L. F., W. W. Spirduso, and S. J. Silverman. 1999. *Proposals that work: A guide for planning dissertations and grant proposals.* Thousand Oaks, Sage Publications.

Internal Citation (Locke, Spirduso, and Silverman 1999, 52)

6.3.4 Anthology

Bibliography Entry Sheth, A., and K. Wolfgang, eds. 1998. *Multimedia metadata management handbook: Integrating and applying digital data.* London: McGraw Hill.

Internal Citation (Sheth and Wolfgang 1998, 322)

6.3.5 Journal Article—One Author

Bibliography Entry McGee, L. 2000. Communication channels used by technical writers throughout the documentation process. *Technical Communication* 47 (February/March): 35–50.

Internal Citation (McGee 2000, 43)

6.3.6 Journal Article—Two Authors

Bibliography Entry Monnet, E., and F. Fauvel-Lafève. 2000. A new platelet receptor specific to Type III collagen. TYPE III COLLAGEN-BINDING PROTEIN. *Journal of Biological Chemistry* 275 (April): 10912–10917.

Internal Citation (Monnet and Fauvel-Lafève 2000, 10915)

6.3.7 Journal Article—Three Authors

Bibliography Entry Aguirre-Planter, E., G. R. Furnier, and L. E. Eguiarte. 2000. Low levels of genetic variation within and high levels of genetic differentiation among populations of species of Abies from southern Mexico and Guatemala. *American Journal of Botany* 87 (March): 362–71.

Internal Citation (Aguirre-Planter, Furnier, and Eguiarte 2000, 369)

6.3.8 Edition

Bibliography Entry   Lide, D. R., ed. 2000. *CRC handbook of chemistry and physics 1999-2000: A ready-reference book of chemical and physical data*, 80th ed. Boca Raton, FL: CRC Press.

Internal Citation   (Lide 2000, 64)

6.3.9 Volumes

Bibliography Entry   Mills, J., P. A. Volberding, and L. Corey, eds. 1996. *Antiviral chemotherapy 4: New directions for clinical application and research*. Vol. 394, *Advances in experimental medicine and biology*. New York: Plenum Press.

Internal Citation   (Mills, Volberding, and Corey 1996, 143–44)

6.3.10 Proceedings

Bibliography Entry   International Conference on Achieving Quality in Software. 1996. *Achieving quality in software: Proceedings of the third international conference on achieving quality in software*. London; New York: Chapman Hall, on behalf of the International Federation for Information Processing.

Internal Citation   (International Conference on Quality 1996, 143)

6.3.11 No Author

Bibliography Entry   Lasers in Cancer Treatment. 1999. CancerNet Cancer Facts at URL: http://cancernet.nci.nih.gov/genetics_prevention.html

Internal Citation   (CancerNet 1999)

6.3.12 Reviews

Bibliography Entry   Sullivan, B. Review of *The inmates are running the asylum*, A. Cooper, *Technical Communication* 47 (February/March 2000): 106–07.

Internal Citation   (Sullivan 2000, 106)

6.3.13 Newspaper

Bibliography Entry   Squires, S. 2000. Panel calls antioxidant megadoses ineffective. *The Washington Post.* April 10, 2000, A01.

Internal Citation   (Squires 2000, A01)

Citation formats for documenting electronic sources are relatively new. The
formats recommended here have been modified from those published by the
American Psychological Association (APA).

6.3.14 WWW (World Wide Web) Site

Bibliography Entry   Nuttall, Chris. (25 September 1999). It's only MP3 but I
like it. <http://news.bbc.co.uk/hi/english/sci/tech/
newsid_443000/443086.stm> (retrieved 9 April 2000).

Internal Citation   (Nuttall 1999)

6.3.15 WWW Journal

Bibliography Entry   Pinholster, Ginger. (September 1994). Rock 'n' Roll
Refrigerator. *Environmental Health Perspectives*
Volume 102, Number 9. <http://ehpnet1.niehs.nih.
gov/docs/1994/102-9/innovations.html> (retrieved
9 April 2000).

Internal Citation   (Pinholster 1994)

6.3.16 E-mail

Bibliography Entry   Nor, Terrek. (7 April 2000). Testing Plan Instructions.
Personal e-mail.

Internal Citation   (Nor 2000)

6.3.17 FTP Site

Bibliography Entry   Bradner, S. (March 1997). Key words for use in RFCs to
Indicate Requirement Levels. <ftp://ftp.iastate.edu/
pub/rfc/rfc2119.txt.Z> (retrieved 9 April 2000).

Internal Citation   (Bradner 1997)

6.3.18 List-serv

Bibliography Entry   Drapeau, T. *Integrating usability work in the design process.* ACM SIGCHI WWW Human Factors (Open Discussion). Tuesday, September 21, 1999, 1:23 PM

Internal Citation   (Drapeau 1999)

6.3.19 Posting from Mailing List

Bibliography Entry   Leighton, Luke Kenneth Casson. (8 April 2000). Re: TNG-1.9 smbd porblems[sic]. samba-ntdom Mailing List <http://us1.samba.org/listproc/index.html>.

Internal Citation   (Leighton 2000)

6.3.20 Mailing List from Archive

Bibliography Entry   One, Aleph. (3 April 2000). New Allaire Security Bulletin Posted. BUGTRAQ Mailing List <http://www.securityfocus.com>, archived at <http://www.securityfocus.com>.

Internal Citation   (One 2000)

6.3.21 Global Newsgroup

Bibliography Entry   Meron, Mati. (5 April 2000). Re: Antimatter vs. mass. <news:sci.physics.particle>.

Internal Citation   (Meron 2000)

6.3.22 Semi-Private Newsgroup

Bibliography Entry   Rosmanith, Herbert. (13 March 2000). reproducing machine crashes. <news://news.3dfx.com/3dfx.developer.linux>.

Internal Citation   (Rosmanith 2000)

6.3.23 Database

Bibliography Entry   Goverde, Angelique J., et al. (1 January 2000). Intra-uterine insemination or in-vitro fertilisation in idiopathic subfertility and male subfertility: a randomised trial and cost-effectiveness analysis. *The Lancet.* Lexis-Nexis database. (retrieved 7 April 2000).

Internal Citation   (Goverde et al. 2000)

6.3.24 CD-ROM

Bibliography Entry   Stimulants, Intoxicants and Hallucinogens. 1995. *The American Indian* (CD-ROM). Facts on File.

Internal Citation   (Stimulants 1995)

Rubrics

A *rubric* is an assessment tool that can be used in a variety of situations. The rubric on the next page is intended for the assessment of written communication. The criteria (content, context, purpose, audience, organization, visuals, and design) can be altered or amended to include the document features of different documents such as Web sites, reports, proposals, instructions, and so on. This rubric includes four assessment categories across the top: Exemplary, Proficient, Marginal, and Unacceptable. For a rubric to be useful, the cells under the appropriate category need to include narrative that explains why a particular criterion was given a particular assessment. Once you have mastered the use of rubrics for assessment, you can use them to assess your own documents, your peers' documents for peer review, or professionally developed documents for evaluation purposes.

Criteria	Exemplary	Proficient
Content	Content is complete and accurate. Information clearly and effectively supports a central purpose (thesis) and displays a thoughtful analysis of a sufficiently modest topic. Reader gains insights.	Content is largely complete and accurate. Information supports the purpose of the document and displays evidence of a basic analysis of a sufficiently modest topic. Reader gains some insights.
Context	The historical context as well as the social and political context of the document are clearly presented. The content is clearly situated. The occasion is well-defined.	The context of the document is clearly presented, but some details are omitted.
Purpose	The writer's purpose is clearly evident to the reader.	The writer's purpose is somewhat evident. The writer digresses from the intended purpose.
Audience	The document is clearly directed to a specific, well-defined audience or audiences. All features of the document are adapted to the audience(s).	The document seems directed to a specific audience but some features are not adapted to the audience.
Organization	The ideas are arranged logically to support the purpose. They are coherent so that the reader can follow the line of reasoning.	The ideas are arranged to support the purpose. They are usually coherent so that the reader can follow the line of reasoning.
Visuals	High-quality visuals clearly support the purpose of the document. The placement of visuals helps the reader to understand the content.	The visuals support the purpose of the document, and their placement is usually helpful to the reader's understanding of the content.
Design	Design elements help fulfill the purpose and appeal to the intended audience. The document is easily scanned, and information is easy for the reader to find. The document is usable.	Design elements usually help the reader understand the document. Most information can be easily accessed. The document is usable for most purposes and readers.

Marginal	Unacceptable	Notes
Content has some gaps and inaccuracies. Information sometimes supports the purpose of the document. Analysis is basic or general. Reader gains few insights.	Content is incomplete and/or inaccurate. Document does not successfully identify thesis. Analysis is vague. Reader is confused and may be misinformed.	
The context of the document may be acknowledged but minimally addressed or developed.	The context of the document is largely ignored.	
The writer's purpose is not consistently clear.	The writer's purpose is unclear and/or inconsistent.	
The document may be directed to an audience but is not adapted to that audience.	The document is not directed toward a specific audience.	
The ideas are not logically arranged. The reader has difficulty following any line of reasoning.	The writing lacks any semblance of organization. The reader cannot identify a line of reasoning.	
The visuals sometimes support the purpose. The placement of visual elements is sometimes distracting.	The visuals seem inappropriate and do not necessarily help the reader understand the content.	
Design elements are distracting. Information is difficult to access. The document is only marginally usable.	Design elements hinder the reader's understanding of and access to information. The document is largely unusable.	

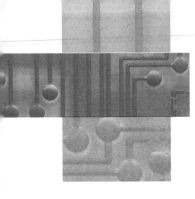

Endnotes and Credits

CHAPTER 1

Endnotes

1. Carol Barnum and Robert Fischer, "Engineering Technologists as Writers: Results of a Survey," *Technical Communication* 31 (Second Quarter 1984): 9–11.
2. Carol Berkenkotter and Thomas N. Huckin, *Genre knowledge in disciplinary communication: Cognition/culture/power* (Hillsdale, NJ: Lawrence Erlbaum, 1995) (see especially pages 1–25).
3. *New York Times Cyber Law Journal* 14 Jan 2000, <http://www.nytimes.com/library/tech/00/01/cyber/cyberlaw/14law.html>.
4. Cezar Ornatowski, "Between Efficiency and Politics: Rhetoric and Ethics in Technical Writing." *Technical Communication Quarterly* 1(1) (1992): 91–103.
5. Gary Tarcy, "Site Visit to Dalton Battery," Reprinted by permission of the author.
6. American Academy of Allergy and Immunology, *Allergy Relief Guide*. Reprinted by permission of the Academy.
7. Definition provided by ISTC, Institute for Scientific and Technical Communicators. See Web site at <http://www.istc.org.uk/index.htm>.
8. Ed Quigley, "Understanding and Avoiding the Leading Cause of Death Among Pilots," School of Communication and Information Systems, Robert Morris College, Pittsburgh, PA. Reprinted by permission of the author.
9. Deborah Grimstead, "Technical Writers are in Demand: Do you have the right stuff?" From *The Black Collegiate*, Feb. 1999, v. 29, i2, pp. 128–132. Reprinted with permission of the author.

CHAPTER 2

Endnotes

1. The following sources were used as background material for the discussion of creative problem solving: John F. Feldhusen and Donald J. Tressinger, *Creative Thinking and Problem-Solving in Gifted Education* (Dubuque, IA: Kendall/Hunt Publishing Company, 1977), Chapter 4; Linda Flower, *Problem-Solving Strategies for Writing*, 4th ed. (New York: Harcourt Brace, 1993); Marcia Greenman Lebeau, *A Teacher's Guide to Creative Problem-Solving* (ESEA, Title IVC Project Grant, 1981), Chapter V; William J. J. Gordon, *Synectics: The Development of Creative Capacity* (London: Collier-MacMillan, 1961).
2. <http://www.synecticsworld.com/whatis.htm>
3. Source: Nancy Downes, Mitsubishi Project PERT Chart (Carnegie Mellon University).
4. Source: Nancy Downes, Mitsubishi Project PERT Chart (Carnegie Mellon University).
5. Brenda Sims, "Linking Ethics and Language in the Technical Communication Classroom," *Technical Communication Quarterly*, 2.3 (1993).
6. Modified from "Stop the Presses," June 18, 1999, <http://www.mediainfo.com/ephome/news/newshtm/stop/st061899.htm>
7. Adapted from V. A. Johnson et al., "Grain Crops," in *Protein Resources and Technology: Status and Research Needs*, ed. Max Milner, Nevin S. Scrimshaw, and David I. C. Wang (Westport, CT: AVI Publishing Company, 1978), 244. Used with permission of AVI Publishing Company.
8. For an extended discussion of schema-driven, knowledge-driven, and constructive planning, see L. Flower, K. A. Schriver, L. Carey, C. Haas, and J. R. Hayes, "Planning in Writing: The Cognition of a Constructive Process" in *A Rhetoric of Doing* (pp. 181–243) ed. Cherry, Witte, and Nakadate (Carbondale, IL: Southern Illinois UP). For an equally useful discussion, see M. Scardamalia and C. Bereiter, "Knowledge Telling and Knowledge Transforming in Written Composition,"

in *Advances in Applied Psycholinguistics*, Volume 2: *Reading, Writing, and Language Learning*, ed. S. Rosenberg (New York: Cambridge University Press, 1987), 142–75.

9. Patricia Karathanos and Anthony Auriemmo, "Care and feeding of the organizational grapevine," *Industrial Management*, 41(2) (March–April 1999) pp. 26–31.

CHAPTER 3

Endnotes

1. Irwin S. Kirsch, Ann Jungeblut, Lynn Jenkins, and Andrew Kolstad, *Adult Literacy in America. Educational Testing Service and the National Center for Education Statistics* (Washington, D.C.: Government Printing Office, 1993).

2. Used with permission of James R. Carey, Lowell General Hospital, Lowell, Massachusetts.

3. Patricia Hynds and Wanda Martin, "Atrisco Well #5: A Case Study of Failure in Professional Communication," *IEEE Transactions on Professional Communication*, 38.3 (1995): 139–145.

4. Reprinted with permission of Iowa State University Extension.

5. Paul Levinson. *Soft Edge: A Natural History and Future of the Information Revolution.* (New York: Routledge, 1997), p. 146.

6. Used with permission of Kimberly Patterson, University of Massachusetts at Lowell, Lowell, Massachusetts.

7. © 1996, reprinted with special permission King Features Syndicate.

CHAPTER 4

Endnotes

1. Some of the discussion in this section is based on types of reading identified in two articles: William Diehl and Larry Mikulecky, "Making Written Information Fit Workers' Purposes," *IEEE Transactions on Professional Communication* 24 (1988) 5–9. Janice C. Redish, "Reading to Learn to Do," *The Technical Writing Teacher*, 15(3) (Fall 1988) 223–33.

2. © 1997–2000, Food Safety Project, Iowa State University Extension.

3. The discussion related to Figure 4.3 is based on a synthesis of information from several sources: (a) Janice A. Dole, Gerald G. Duffy, Laura R. Roehler, and P. David Pearson, "Moving from the Old to the New: Research on Reading Comprehension Instruction," *Review of Educational Research*, 61(2) (Summer 1991) 239–64. (b) Ann Hill Duin, "How People Read:

Implications for Writers," *The Technical Writing Teacher*, 15(3) (Fall 1988) 185–43. © Linda Flower, "Negotiating Academic Discourse," in Linda Flower, Victoria Stein, John Ackerman, Margaret J. Kantz, Kathleen McCormick, and Wayne C. Peck, *Reading to Write: Exploring a Cognitive and Social Process* (New York: Oxford University Press, 1990), 221–52. (d) Patricia Mulcahy, "Writing Reader-Based Instructions: Strategies to Build Coherence," *The Technical Writing Teacher*, 15(3) (Fall 1988) 234–43.(d) Wayne H. Slater, "Current Theory and Research on What Constitutes Readable Expository Text," *The Technical Writing Teacher*, 15(3) (Fall 1988) 45–206.

4. Christina Haas, *Writing Technology: Studies on the Materiality of Literacy* (Mahwah, NJ: Lawrence Erlbaum, 1996). (See especially Chapter 3: Reading Online.)

5. Karen McGrane Chauss, "Reader as User: Applying Interface Design Techniques to the Web." Rensselaer Polytechnic Institute. See abstract at <http://english.ttu.edu/kairos/1.2/features/chauss/bridge.html>.

6. Abstract to article written by researchers at University of California, San Diego, *Medicine and Science in Sports and Exercise*, Vol. 31, n. 6, pp. 864–869. Reprinted with permission.

7. J. J. Bromenshenk, et al., "Pollution Monitoring of Puget Sound with Honey Bees," *Science* 227 (February 8, 1985): 632–34. Copyright 1985 by the AAAS. Reprinted with permission.

8. *NASA Tech Briefs*, Vol. 24, No. 3, March, 2000.

9. Christopher D. Burnett, *How to Grow Shiitake Mushrooms Outdoors on Natural Logs* (Marquette, MI. Big Creek Farm, 1993). Reprinted with permission.

10. Chuck Megnin (Technical and Scientific Writing 42.225, University of Lowell). Reprinted with permission.

11. Adapted from Theodor Holm Nelson, "The Xanadu Ideal," <http://www.xanadu.com.au/xanadu/ideal.html/> (June 1996).

12. Stephen Katz, "The Ethic of Expediency: Classical Rhetoric, Technology, and the Holocaust" *College English* 43 (1992): 255–75.

13. Benjamin S. Bloom, ed., *Taxonomy of Educational Objectives* (New York: David McKay, 1956).

14. "Slowing the Course of Aortic Regurgitation," *Harvard Health Letter* (February 1995), 3–4. Illustration © 1995 Harriet Greenfield.

15. © 1996 Scientific American, Inc. All rights reserved. Reprinted with permission.

16. *Medicine and Science in Sports and Exercise*, 31(6) (1999), pp. 864–69.

17. © 1996 Scientific American, Inc. All rights reserved. Reprinted with permission.

18. "Sold on the Simplicity of Web Sites: Companies are getting back to basics with Web designs that enable users to find what they need," *PC Week*, June 7, 1999, v.16, i.23, p. 77. Copyright © 1999 Ziff-Davis Media, Inc. Reprinted with permission.

CHAPTER 5

Endnotes

1. Courtesy of Sharon Burton-Hardin.

2. For further information about the prevalence of collaboration in the workplace, check the following sources: P. Anderson, (1985). What survey research tells us about writing at work. In L. Odell & D. Goswami (eds.), *Writing in nonacademic settings* (pp. 3–83). New York: Guilford Press; L. S. Ede, & A. A. Lunsford (March 1986). *Collaboration in writing on the job: A research report.* Presentation at CCCC. (Also available from ERIC ED 268582.); L. Faigley, & T. P. Miller, (1982). What we learn from writing on the job. *College English, 44,* 557–69.

3. For additional information about workplace collaboration, refer to the following books and special issues of journals: A. Lunsford, & L. Ede, (1990). *Singular texts/plural authors: Perspectives on collaborative writing.* Carbondale: Southern Illinois UP; J. Forman (ed.). (1992). *New Visions of Collaborative Writing.* Portsmouth, NH: Boynton/Cook; M. M. Lay and W. Karis. (1991). *Collaborative Writing in Industry: Investigations in Theory and Practice.* Amityville, NY: Baywood; *Technical Communication,* November 1991 (Special issue of journal on collaborative writing). Guest editors Deborah S. Bosley and Meg Morgan; *Technical Communication Quarterly,* Winter 1993 (Special issue of journal on research about collaboration in technical communication). Guest editors Ann Hill Duin and Rebecca Burnett.

4. A. J. Meadows, *Communication in Science* (London: Butterworth, 1974), Chapter 7.

5. Courtesy of Allan Ackerson.

6. These questions were developed as part of the author's work for the Making Thinking Visible Project for the Study of Writing, Berkeley and Carnegie Mellon, funded by the Heinz Endowment of the Pittsburgh Foundation.

7. <http://www.usabilityfirst.com/groupware/intro.html>

8. Modified from information available at <http://www.usabilityfirst.com/groupware/intro.html>

9. Source: Brian Gillette, Richard Johnson, Emil Polashek, Jennifer Thornburg, and Christianna White. *The Art of Working Together: A Guide to Collaboration.* Ames, IA: Department of English, Iowa State University, p. 5.

10. Cohen, John and Gary Taubes. "The Culture of Credit." *Science* 268.5218 (1995): 1706–1712.

11. Cohen, John and Gary Taubes. "The Culture of Credit." *Science* 268.5218 (1995): 1706–1712.

12. Haskins, Mark, Jeanne Liedtka, and John Rosenblum. "Beyond Teams: Toward an Ethic of Collaboration." *Organizational Dyn*amics 26.4 (1998): 34–51.

13. For further information about conflict in collaboration, see Rebecca E. Burnett, "'Some People Weren't Able to Contribute Anything but Their Technical Knowledge': The Anatomy of a Dysfunctional Team." *Nonacademic Writing: Social Theory and Technology.* Ed. Ann Hill Duin and Craig Hansen. Hillsdale, NJ: Erlbaum, 1996. 123–156; Rebecca E. Burnett. "Productive and Unproductive Conflict in Collaboration." *Making Thinking Visible: Writing, Collaborative Planning, and Classroom Inquiry.* Ed. Linda Flower, David L. Wallace, Linda Norris, and Rebecca E. Burnett. Urbana, IL: NCTE, 1994. 239–244; Rebecca E. Burnett. "Conflict in Collaborative Decision-Making." *Professional Communication: The Social Perspective.* Ed. Nancy Roundy Blyler and Charlotte Thralls. Newbury Park, CA: Sage, 1993. 144–162; Rebecca E. Burnett. "Decision-Making During the Collaborative Planning of Coauthors." *Hearing Ourselves Think: Cognitive Research in the College Writing Classroom.* Ed. Ann Penrose and Barbara Sitko. NY: Oxford University Press, 1993. 125–146.

14. Dilbert reprinted by permission of United Features Syndicate, Inc.

15. See Deborah S. Bosley, "Whose Culture Is It, Anyway," *Technical Communication Quarterly* (Winter 1993).

16. © 1998 Massachusetts Institute of Technology Alumni Association.

CHAPTER 6

Endnotes

1. "EOA National Study Finds Nearly Half of American Workers Engaged in Unethical Hi-Tech Behavior Last Year." *EOA News* Spring (1998): 1, 4–5.

2. William Harvey, "On the Motion of the Heart and Circulation of the Blood." in *The Autobiography of Science*, ed. Forest Ray Moulton and Justus J. Schifferes, 2nd ed. (Garden City, NY: Doubleday, 1960), 106–107.

3. Barbara Peterson, Director of 3M Information Services. Telephone Interview.

4. Source: Office for Subject Cataloguing Policy, Collection Services. Library of Congress Subject Headings, 15th ed., vol. 1 A-C. Washington, DC: Cataloguing Distribution Service. Library of Congress.
5. <http://www.usabilityfirst.com/groupware/intro.html>
6. The definitions and explanations are modified from <http://www.netlingo.com>
7. "Internet Power Searching: Finding pearls in a zillion grains of sand," *Information Outlook*, April 1999, v.3, i.4, p. 285.

CHAPTER 7

Endnotes

1. Modified from Nick Jordon, "What's in a Zombie," Review of *The Serpent and the Rainbow*, by Wade Davis, *Psychology Today* (May 1984): 6.
2. A. B. Watkins, External and Internal Parasites—Causes, Symptoms, Treatment, and Control." *Dairy Goat Journal* 61 (August 1983): 14, 16. Reprinted with permission of the publisher.
3. <http://www.useit.com/alertbox/981018.html_useit.com>
4. Modified from Jeffrey M. Lenorovitz, "China Plans Upgraded Satellite Network," *Aviation Week & Space Technolgoy* 119 (21 November 1983): 71–75.
5. Dragga, Sam. "'Is This Ethical?': A Survey of Opinion on Principles and Practices of Document Design." *Technical Communication*, 43.1 (1996): 29-38; quotation from p. 30.
6. Dragga, p. 35.
7. Dragga, p. 35.
8. © 1990 IEEE. Reprinted, with permission, from Michaelson, Herbert B., "How an Author Can Avoid the Pitfalls of Practical Ethics," *IEEE Transactions on Professional Communications*, Vol. 33, n.2, (June, 1990), p. 58–61.

CHAPTER 8

Endnotes

1. Charles Kostelnick, "Visual Rhetoric: A Reader-Oriented Approach to Graphics and Design," *The Technical Writing Teacher* XVI, 1 (Winter 1989): 77–88.
2. <http://www.useit.com/alertbox/9703b.html>
3. Margaret F. Kinnaird, "Indonesia's Hornbill Haven," *Natural History* 105, 1. (January 1996): 40–44.
4. Daniel B. Felker et al., *Guidelines for Document Designers* (Washington, DC: American Institutes for Research, 1981), 85.
5. Thomas E. Pinelli et al., "Report Format Preferences of Technical Managers and Nonmanagers, *Technical Communication* 31 (Second Quarter 1984): 6–7.
6. Pinelli et al., "Report Format Preferences," 6–7.

7. TyAnna Herrinton, "Ethics and Graphic Design: A Rhetorical Analysis of the Document Design in the *Report of the Department of the Treasury on the Bureau of Alcohol, Tobacco, and Firearms Investigation of Vernon Wayne Howell also Known as David Koresh." IEEE Transactions on Professional Communication* 38, 3 (1995): 151–157.
8. <http://www.useit.com/alertbox/990124.html>
9. <http://www.useit.com/alertbox/990124.html>
10. Dell Computer Corporation, *Dell User's Guide* (for Dell® Midsize Pentium™ Systems) (March 1994): LX.
11. <http://info.med.yale.edu/caim/manual/pages/font_face.html>
12. For additional discussion of typography and color, check this source: Elizabeth Keyes. "Typography, Color, and Information Structure." *Technical Communication* 40 (Fourth Quarter, 1993): 638–654.
13. <http://info.med.yale.edu/caim/manual/pages/design_grids.html>
14. <http://www.istc.org.uk/design.htm> <http://www.useit.com/alertbox/>
15. Modified from Charles Kostelnick and David Roberts. *Designing Visual Language. Strategies for Professional Communicators* (Needham Heights, MA: Allyn & Bacon, 1998).
16. Copyright © 1999 by InfoWorld Publishing Corp., a subsidiary of IDG Communications, Inc. Reprinted from InfoWorld, 155 Bovet Road, San Mateo, CA 94401. Further reproduction is prohibited.

CHAPTER 9

Endnotes

1. For additional discussion, see Thomas R. Williams, "What's So Different about Visuals?" *Technical Communication* 40 (November 1993): 669–676.
2. James Gaines, "To Our Readers," *Time* (July 4, 1994).
3. Donna Kienzler, "Visual Ethics," *Journal of Business Communication*, 34, 2 (1997): 171–187.
4. *Nasa Tech Briefs*, Vol. 23, No. 1, January, 1999, p. 34.
5. Source: Illustration by Ellen Cohen in Allen L. Hammond, "Tales of an Elusive Ancestor," *Science*, v. 83, November 1983, p. 43.
6. Source: Roger W. Lewin, "Is the Orangutan a Living Fossil?" *Science*, v. 222, Dec. 16, 1983:1223. Copyright © 1983 by the AAAS. Reprinted with permission of the AAAS.
7. For additional discussion, see these two standard sources: Jan V. White, *Color for the Electric Age* (New York: Watson-Guptill Publications, 1990), and Elizabeth

Keyes, "Typography, Color, and Information Structure," *Technical Communication* 40 (November 1993): 638–654.

8. L. Dayton and Jack Davis, *The Photoshop 3 WOW! Book* (Berkeley, Calif.: Peachpit Press, 1996), p. 16.

9. Reproduced with permission.

10. Source: Dean Biechler, Chichaqua Bend Studios, Ames, IA.

11. Source: Dean Biechler, Chichaqua Bend Studios, Ames, IA.

12. Source: Leslie P. Gartner & James L. Hiatt, Color Atlas of Histology, Baltimore: Williams & Wilkins, (graphic 9.1, Lymphoid Tissues). Reprinted by permission.

13. John Deere.

14. AmTec, Bellevue, WA.

15. "Amazing Science of Space Photography." *USA Weekend* (October 24–26), 1997, 14.

16. Photo of nebula (Pillars of Creation in a Star Forming Region). Credit: Jeff Hester and Paul Scowen (Arizona State University) and NASA.

17. *Science*, Vol. 286, No. 5439, P. 30, Oct. 15, 1999.

18. New Hampshire DWI Prevention Council, *Know Your Limits* (Dover, NH). Reprinted with permission of the New Hampshire DWI Prevention Council.

19. "Meet the Bugs" table, *Nutrition Action Newsletter*, Oct. 1999, p. 9.

20. AFRL Technology Horizons, March, 2000.

21. Source: George M. Woodwell, "The Energy Cycle of the Biosphere," in *The Biosphere* (San Francisco: W. H. Freeman & Company, 1970, 72). Copyright © 1970 by Scientific American, Inc. All rights reserved. Reprinted with permission of Scientific American, Inc.

22. H. J. Heinz Company, Heinz Quarterly Report of Earnings and Activities, 1993 Second Quarter, p. 13. Used by permission.

23. S. Fred Singer, "Human Production of Energy as a Process in the Biosphere," in *The Biosphere* (San Francisco: W. H. Freeman and Company, 1970), 184. Copyright © 1970 by Scientific American, Inc. All rights reserved. Reprinted with permission of Scientific American, Inc.

24. "Consumer Alert: How to Choose Day Care for Your Child," *Masscitizen* (April 1985), p. 11. Reprinted with permission of the Massachusetts Public Interest Research Group.

25. Source: "Screws," *Sears Craftsman Master Shop Guide* (Hearst Corporation, 1969), sheet 3. Reprinted with permission.

26. Diagram of nesting in biological systems: *Taxonomic Diversity, from Status & Trends of the Nation's Biological Resources*, Vol. 1, U.S. Dept. of the Interior, p. 100.

27. Souce: *Des Moines Register* (January 19, 1993), p. 4A. Reprinted by permission of Tribune Media Services.

28. Photo of an insect (Short-Horn Grasshopper). Credit: Photographer: Tom Myers.

29. Photo of an insect (Wasp Moth). Credit: Photographer: Tom Myers.

30. Source: "Why Whales Leap," *Scientific American*, March 1985, p. 87. Copyright © 1985 by Scientific American, Inc. All rights reserved. Reprinted with permission of Scientific American, Inc.

31. MDO Exploits NASA's Discipline Breadth, *Insights: High Performance Computing and Communications*, NASA, Issue 10, August 1999, pg. 14. <www.hpcc.nasa.gov>

32. Source: *Environmental Restoration and Waste Management: An Introduction*, U.S. Department of Energy, DOE/EM-0104.

33. Source: Environmental Protection Agency, *Guides to Pollution Prevention: The Photoprocessing Industry* (October 1991).

34. *NASA Tech Briefs*, November, 1999, Vol. 23, No. 11, p. 54.

35. Source: Charles and Rae Eames, "Surface Tension," *Mathematics—IBM Exhibit Catalogue.*

36. *NASA Tech Briefs*, March, 2000, Vol. 24, No. 3.

37. Source: D. M. Canfield, *Elements of Farrier Science*, 2nd Ed. (Albert Lea, MN: Enderes Tool Co., 1968), p. 10. Reprinted with permission of Donald M. Canfield.

38. Source: *Easy Home Repair, Packet #2*, Pittsburgh, PA: International Masters Publishers, p. 2.

39. Source: Charles R. Hurburgh, Jr., "The Challenge of Marketing Soybeans by Protein and Oil Content," Presentation to the annual convention of the American Soybean Association, Des Moines, Iowa, 1989.

40. AmTec, Bellevue, WA.

41. "Mapping Web Sites" by Paul Kahn, Dynamic Diagrams Seminar on Web Site Planning Diagrams, Visualizing and Analyzing Existing Web Sites. Copyright © 2000 by Dynamic Diagrams, Inc.

42. Aerial Photograph Taken from Low-Flying Plane. Source: Iowa Department of Transportation.

43. Four views of California using computer technology, SAR image, interferogram, contour map, and perspective view, from *Operational Use of Civil Space-based Synthetic Aperture Radar (SAR)*, July, 1996, p. 10-8, NOAA.

44. Graph showing Per-capital Income Disparities from *New World Coming: American Security in the 21st*

Century, p. 33, U.S. Commission for National Security in the 21st Century.

45. Bar graph of a Dietary Fat Chart showing fat and fatty acid proportions from *Building for the Future: Nutrition Guidance for the Child Nutrition Programs*, 1992, p. 40, FMS-279, U.S. Department of Agriculture Food and Nutrition Service.

46. Source: Dr. D. E. Tyler, School of Veterinary Medicine, University of Georgia.

CHAPTER 10

Endnotes

1. *Encyclopedia Britannia*, copyright © 2000, Encyclopedia Britannia, Inc. With permission.

2. *American Pocket Medical Dictionary* (Philadelphia: Saunders, 1940), s.v. "focus."

3. George B. Thomas, Jr., *Calculus and Analytic Geometry*, 5th ed. (Reading, MA: Addison-Wesley, 1972), 479.

4. *Encyclopaedia Britannica*, 15th ed., s.v. "earthquake."

5. Polaroid Corporation, *The Square Shooter* (Cambridge, MA: Polaroid Corp., 1974), 3.

6. Alan Semat, *Fundamentals of Physics* (New York: Holt, Rinehart, & Winston, 1966), 96.

7. Bureau of Naval Personnel, *Principles of Naval Ordnance and Gunnery*, NAVPERS 10783-A (Washington, DC: US Navy, 1965), 4.

8. *Webster's New School and Office Dictionary*, s.v., "volt."

9. *Penguin Dictionary of Science*, s.v. "volt."

10. © 1999, *Peanuts* reprinted by permission of United Features Syndicate.

11. Joseph Snellar, "Mass Production of RRIM Parts Start up on Automotive Lines," *Modern Plastics* 59 (January 1982): 48.

12. Source: *Machinability Data Center, Machining Data Handbook*, (Cincinnati, OH: Metcut Research Associates), p. 3. Reprinted with permission.

13. Reproduced by permission. Copyright © 1995 by Netlingo, Inc. The Online Computer Dictionary. <www.netlingo.com>.

14. Reproduced by permission. Copyright © 1995 by Netlingo, Inc. The Online Computer Dictionary. <www.netlingo.com>.

15. Source: *Scott Foresman Advanced Dictionary*, s.v. "capillary attraction" and "capillary repulsion." Reprinted with permission of Scott Foresman.

16. Chris Drake, "Operational Definition of a Thermostatic Element" (Technical and Scientific Writing 42,225, University of Lowell).

17. *Webster's NewWorld Dictionary*, 2nd ed., s.v. "rivet."

18. Lee J. Foster, "Brief History of Carbon Black" (Technical and Scientific Writing 42.225, University of Lowell).

19. "Rayleigh-Taylor Instability and ICF," in "Diagnostics for Inertial Confinement Fission Research," *Energy and Technology Review* (July 1992). Livermore, CA: Lawrence Livermore National Laboratory.

20. Source: Dell® Midsize Pentium® *System User's Guide* (1994), Glossary -4 and -14.

21. Source: John A. Bittl and Patricia Thomas, "Opening the arteries: Beyond the balloon," *Harvard Health Letter* 21(3) (January 1996), 4–6. Copyright © 1996, President and Fellows of Harvard College. Reprinted by permission.

22. Alan Mandell, *The Language of Science* (Washington DC: National Science Teachers Association, 1974), 23.

23. *Chamber's Technical Dictionary*, s.v. "chemistry."

24. Reproduced by permission. Copyright © 1995 by Netlingo, Inc. The Online Computer Dictionary, www.netlingo.com

25. N. F. Hadley, "Lipid Water Barriers in Biological Systems," *Progress in Lipid Research* 28 (1989): 23.

26. NetLingo *http://www.netlingo.com/inframes.html*

27. From "Computerspeak Glossary," *Inc.* (May 1980): 102–103. Copyright © 1980 by Inc. Publishing Corporation, 38 Commercial Wharf, Boston, MA 02110. Reprinted with permission of *Inc.* magazine.

28. Source: Carolyn Stanhope, "The Fugue," *Technical Communication EN 4676*, Northern Essex Community College.

29. Source: Sue MacDonald, "Treating Stress," *Des Moines Register* (November 27, 1995), 3T. Reprinted with permission of the Des Moines Register. Copyright © 1995.

30. Rita Risser, "Sexual harassment training: truth and consequences, *Training & Development*, 53, 8 (August 1999), 21(3).

CHAPTER 11

Endnotes

1. Galileo Galilei, "The Sidereal Messenger," in *The Autobiography of Science*, ed. Forest Ray Moulton and Justus J. Schifferes, 2nd ed. (Garden City, NY: Doubleday, 1960), 75–76.

2. NASA—Jet Propulsion Laboratory, *Voyager Bulletin* Mission Status Report No. 36, 23 (February 1979), 3.

3. <http://www.spacescience.com/newhome/headlines/ast04oct99_1.htm>

4. Paul Dombroski, "Can Ethics Be Technologized? Lessons from Challenger, Philosophy, and Rhetoric," *Technical Communication Quarterly* 38.3 (1995): 146–150.

5. Robertson Parkman, "Management of the Newborn," in *Manual of Pediatric Therapeutics*, ed. John W. Graef, M.D. and Thomas E. Cone, Jr., M.D. (Boston: Little, Brown and Company, 1977), 99–100. Reprinted with permission of Little, Brown and Company.

6. Source: Dean Cocozziello (*Technical and Scientific Writing*, 42.225, University of Lowell).

7. Source: Thomas E. French and Charles J. Vierck, *Graphic Science and Design* (New York: McGraw-Hill, 1970), p. 79. Reprinted with permission of McGraw-Hill Book Company.

8. Source: *Air & Space*, June/July 1995, p. 35.

9. Source: Illustration by Harriet Greenfield, in Evan B. Dreyer, M.D., Ph.D., "Preserving Eyesight with Foresight," *Harvard Health Letter*, 19, 12 (October 1994), 4–6. Copyright © 1994, President and Fellows of Harvard College. Reprinted by permission.

10. Nancy Caswell Coward, "Cross-Cultural Communication: Is It Greek to You?" *Technical Communication*, 39 (May 1992): 264–266. Reprinted by permission.

11. Web page courtesy of The Boeing Company <http://www.boeing.com>

CHAPTER 12

Endnotes

1. Rude, Carolyn. "Managing Publications According to Legal and Ethical Standards." *Publications Management: Essays for Professional Communicators.* Ed. O. Jane Allen and Lynn H. Deming. Amityville, New York: 1994: 171–187.

2. Crowell, Todd. "After Tokaimura: Ratting on Japan's Nuclear Sloppiness." *Asia Now.* 13 October 1999. <http://cnn.com/ASIANOW/asiaweek/intelligence/9910/13/>.

3. Source: ATEX, Inc., *System Manager's Reference Manual* (Bedford, MA: ATEX, 1981), I-1-1–I-1-2. Reprinted with permission of ATEX.

4. Source: Frederick M. Oltsch, "Bog Development" (Becket, MA).

5. Source: James P. Shields, "Thermal Inkjet Review, or How Do Dots Get from the Pen to the Page?" from *Hewlett-Packard Journal* (August 1992), 67. © 1992 Hewlett-Packard Company. Reproduced with permission.

6. Source: "How Acid Rain is Formed," *Lowell Sun.*

7. Source: L. I. Slafer and V. L. Seidenstucker, "INTELSAT VT: Communications Subsystem Design,"

COMSAT Technical Review, 21 (Spring 1991): 61. Reproduced by permission of COMSAT Technical Review.

8. Source: Nilsa Cristina Zacarias, Iowa State University.

9. <http://www.spacescience.com/newhome/headlines/ast04oct99_1.htm>.

10. *NASA Tech Briefs*, December 1995, p. 58.

11. Susan E. Long and Catherine G. Leonard, "The Changing Face of Sexual Harassment," *HR Focus* (Oct 1999), p. S1.

CHAPTER 13

Endnotes

1. A useful and provocative discussion of document testing appears in K. A. Schriver, "Teaching Writers to Anticipate the Reader's Needs: Empirically Based Instruction" (Ph.D. dissertation, Carnegie Mellon University, 1987). The continuum described in this chapter—text-based, expert-based, and user-based testing—is derived from the classification presented in Schriver's work.

2. © 1998 IEEE. Reprinted with permission, from Karen A. Schriver, "Evaluating Text Quality: The Continuum from Text-Focused to Reader-Focused Methods," *IEEE Transactions on Professional Communications*, Vol. 32, (December 1998), p. 238–255.

3. For further information, see Kate Molitor, "How Participants' Expertise Influenced Expert Testing of a Technical User Manual," Unpublished M.A. thesis, Iowa State University, August 1995.

4. <http://www.plainlanguage.gov/cites/page1.htm>

5. Source: Tom Mansur, "Justification for the Purchase and Installation of Automatic Roll-Up Doors for the R&D Model Shop" (*Technical Writing* 42.225, University of Lowell).

6. <http://www.plainlanguage.gov/cites/memo.htm>

7. <http://members.home.net/garbl/writing/plaineng.htm>

8. <http://www.michbar.org/committees/penglish/def.html>

9. <http://www.plainlanguage.gov/>

10. <http://www.plainlanguage.gov/cites/page1.htm>

11. Case No. 96-36304. United States Court of Appeals for the Ninth Circuit. 1998 U.S. App. LEXIS 9846, May 18, 1998. For further information, including the court ruling, refer to <http://www.plainlanguage.gov/cites/page1.htm.>

12. <http://www.plainlanguage.gov/cites/page1.htm>

13. "Three-Fingered Robot Hand," *NASA Tech Briefs*, 8 (Fall 1983), 99.

14. Modified from John E. Bardach and Ernst R. Pariser, "Aquatic Proteins," *Protein Resources and Technology:*

Status and Research Needs, ed. Max Milner, Nevin S. Scrimshaw, and Daniel I. C. Wan (Westport, CT: AVI Publishing, 1978), 461.

15. Examples modified from Gary McMillan, "Finger-printing Moves into the Computer Age—Science of Fingerprinting," *Boston Globe* (January 30, 1984).

16. Mary Fran Buehler, "Defining Terms in Technical Editing: The Levels of Edit as a Model," *Technical Communication*, 28 (Fourth Quarter 1981), 13–15. Based on a system developed and used at Jet Propulsion Laboratory, Pasadena, CA.

17. Based on a study conducted by Gary F. Kohut and Kevin J. Gorman, "The Effectiveness of Leading Grammar/Style Software Packages in Analyzing Business Students' Writing," *Journal of Business and Technical Communication* 9 (July 1995), 341–361.

18. Allen, Lori and Dan Voss. "Ethics for Editors: An Analytical Decision-Making Process." *IEEE Transactions on Professional Communication*, 41, 1 (1998), 58–65.

19. Joe Montalbano, "Expansion Anchor Feasibility Report," Grand Gulf Nuclear Station, Port Gibson, MS. Used with permission.

20. New Hampshire State Fishing Laws, 1983, 6.

21. Scale from Rudolf Flesch, *The Art of Plain Talk* (New York: Harper & Brothers, 1946), 38. Sentences from David M. Worth, "DO 228–200 Offers Mission Versatility," *Aviation Week and Space Technology*, 119 (December 1983), 5.

22. Adapted from the *Boston Globe*, (July 5, 1983).

23. Joel R. Fried, "Polymer Technology—Part 7: Engineering Thermoplastics and Specialty Plastics," *Plastics Engineering*, 39 (May 1983): 39.

24. Philip J. Klass, "Software Augments Manual Readability," *Aviation Week & Space Technology*, 116 (January 11, 1982), 106.

25. Source: Edward Fry, "Fry's Readability Graph: Clarification, Validity, and Extension to Level 17," *Journal of Reading*, 21 (December 1977), 249.

CHAPTER 14

Endnotes

1. Netiquette guidelines, originally written by Peggy Pollock for this Web site, have been modified for this chapter. <http://www.public.iastate.edu/~rburnett/netiquette.html>.

2. The definitions and explanations are modified from <http://www.netlingo.com>.

3. Netiquette guidelines for newsgroups and lists, originally written by Peggy Pollock for this Web site, have been modified for this chapter. <http://www.public.iastate.edu/~rburnett/netiquette.html>.

4. The definitions and explanations are modified from <http://www.netlingo.com>.

5. Netiquette guidelines, originally written by Peggy Pollock for this Web site, have been modified for this chapter. <http://www.public.iastate.edu/~rburnett/netiquette.html>.

6. Copyright © 1999 Time, Inc. Reprinted by permission.

CHAPTER 15

Endnotes

1. MicroPro International Corporation, *WordStar Reference Manual* (San Rafael, CA: MicroPro, 1981), 2–2.

2. MicroPro International Corporation, *WordStar Reference Manual* E-13.

3. Source: A color 935/930, Fuji Xerox, No. TS-1543, 1995, pp. 286–87.

4. Source: Inframetrics, "Thermal Measurements of Building Envelope Components in the Field" (Bedford, MA). Reprinted with permission of Inframetrics, Inc.

5. Caher, John. "Technical Documentation and Legal Liability." *Journal of Technical Writing and Communication*, 25(1) (1995): 5–10; quoted material from p. 5.

6. Caher, p. 7.

7. Philip Rubens, "The Cartoon and Ethics: Their Role in Technical Information." *IEEE Transactions on Professional Communication*, 30(3) (1987): 196–201; quoted material from p. 197.

8. Caher, p. 10.

9. Pamela S. Helyar, "Products Liability: Meeting Legal Standards for Adequate Instructions," *Journal of Technical Writing and Communication*, 22 (1992): 125–47. The definition of products liability law and the list of requirements come from this article. Helyar's article is an excellent starting place for anyone interested in reading about products liability law. She not only discusses the legal requirements of adequate instructions, but she provides a number of interesting products liability cases that clearly indicate the importance of communicators being both legally and ethically responsible. See also ANSI Z535.5-1991, *Accident Prevention Tags*, which provides clear definitions of caution, warning, and danger.

10. Source: *User's Manual*, First Alert, Aurora, IL. Reprinted by permission.

11. Source: Dell ® *Diagnostics and Troubleshooting Guide* (1994).
12. Source: *Sears Craftsman (Model Number 917.380840) Owner's Manual*, Sears, Roebuck & Co., Hoffman Estates, IL 60179.
13. Source: *Getting Started with Your Macintosh.* Apple Computer, Inc.
14. Source: Reproduced by permission of Deere & Company. Copyright © 1990 Deere & Company. All rights reserved.
15. John A. Conrads, "'Illustruction': Increasing Safety and Reducing Liability Exposure," *IEEE Transactions on Professional Communication*, 30 (September 1987): 133–35.
16. Adapted from *Training & Development*, Copyright © 1999, American Society for Training & Development, www.astd.org. Reprinted with permission. All rights reserved.

CHAPTER 16

Endnotes

1. This differentiation of reports and proposals is discussed in more detail in a very useful book: Richard C. Freed, Shervin Freed, and Joe Romano. *Writing Winning Business Proposals: Your Guide to Landing the Client, Making the Sale, Persuading the Boss* (New York: McGraw-Hill, 1995).
2. Source: *Business Daily*, U.S. Department of Commerce A: April 1, 1993, Issue No. PSA-0815, p. 2; B: June 7, 1993, Issue No. PSA-0861, p. 4; D: June 8, 1993, Issue No. PSA-0862, p. 8.
3. The material on persuasive techniques is based on Roger Wilcox, "Persuading Your Reader or Listener," *Communication at Work* (Boston: Houghton Mifflin, 1977), 284–92.
4. Weiss, Edmond. "'Professional Communication' and the 'Odor of Mendacity': The Persistent Suspicion that Skillful Writing is Successful Lying." *IEEE Transactions on Professional Communication*, 38(3) (1995): 169–175; quotation from p. 169.
5. Weiss, p. 169.
6. Weiss, p. 169.
7. Weiss, p. 174.
8. Allen, Lori and Dan Voss. *Ethics in Technical Communication* (New York: Wiley, 1997).
9. Department of Health and Human Services, *NIH Peer Review of Research Grant Applications* (Washington, DC: Government Printing Office, 1983), 54; 148–49.

10. Source: Craig Wilder, "Proposed Merger: Mechanical Assembly with Final Assembly" (*Technical Writing* 42.225, University of Lowell).
11. Judith Harkham Semas, "Goof-proofing your RFPs," *Association Management*, Sept. 1999, v. 51, i. 9, pp. 41–46. Reprinted with permission.

CHAPTER 17

Endnotes

1. Grove, Laurel. "Speaking for the Environment." *IEEE Transactions on Professional Communication* 38.3 (1995): 165–68; quoted material from p. 165.
2. Grove, p. 165.
3. Grove, p. 166.
4. Grove, p. 166.
5. Grove, p. 168.
6. Source: George Buchanan, "FIP Packaging" (*Technical Writing* 42.225, University of Lowell).
7. General Henry M. Robert, *Robert's Rules of Order* (Glenview, IL: Scott Foresman, 1981), 389–391. Reprinted with permission of Robert's Rules Assn., John Robert Redgrave, Author's Agent.
8. Freda F. Stohrer and Thomas E. Pinelli, "Marketing Information: The Technical Report as a Product," *Technical Writing: Past, Present, and Future*, NASA Technical Memorandum 81966 (March 1981), 14.
9. Used with permission of Aaron Kurdle.
10. Maryann Z. Corbett, "Clearing the Air: Some Thoughts on Gender-Neutral Writing," *IEEE Transactions on Professional Communication*, 33 (March 1990): 2–6. Copyright © 1990 IEEE. Reprinted with permission.

CHAPTER 18

Endnotes

1. "Critical link between presentation skills, upward mobility." *Supervision* 52 (October 1991) p. 24.
2. Floyd Wickman, "Getting Them to 'Buy In' to Your Message," *Supervisory Management* (1992).
3. Modified from Jan V. White. *Color for the Electronic Age.* New York: Watson-Guptill Publications, 1990.
4. Laura Gurak, *Oral Presentations for Technical Communication.* Boston: Allyn and Bacon, 2000.
5. Brown, Stuart. "Rhetoric, Ethical Codes, and the Revival of *Ethos* in Publications Management." *Publications Management: Essays for Professional Communicators.* Ed. O. Jane Allen and Lynn Deming. Amityville, NY: Baywood, 1994: 189–200.

6. Adapted from Thomas Devine, *Listening Skills School-wide: Activities and Programs*, (Urbana, IL: National Council of Teachers of English, 1982).

7. J. Wesley Cochran, "Using Copyrighted Works for Meetings, Seminars, and Conferences," *Information Outlook*, July 1999, v.3, i.7, pp. 42–44. Reprinted with permission of Special Libraries Association.

CHAPTER 19

Endnotes

1. Salette Latas, TECHWR-L posting on March 15, 2000.

2. The example is from Maddocks, P. Merle, Sylvia Michelini, and Gover Porter. "Ethics Cases from Academe." *Management Accounting*, 76(4) (1994): 68.

3. Parrish, Debra. "Falsification of Credentials in the Research Setting: Scientific Misconduct?" *Journal of Law, Medicine and Ethics*, 24(3) (1996): 260-66.

4. Kat Nagel, TECHWR-L posting on March 15, 2000.

5. Marni Barilone, TECHWR-L posting on February 15, 2000.

6. Tim Altom, TECHWR-L posting on March 15, 2000.

7. Tim Altom, TECHWR-L posting on March 15, 2000.

8. Courtesy of Sigmund G. Ginsburg and the American Management Association, New York.

9. Figure 19.10 is modified from Sigmund G. Ginsburg, "Preparing for Executive Position Interviews: Questions the Interviewer Might Ask—or Be Asked," *Personnel*, 57 (July–August 1980): 32–36. © 1980 AMACOM, a division of American Management Association, New York: All rights reserved. Reprinted with permission of the author.

10. Julie Cook, "Big Brother Goes to Work," *Office Systems*, 99, Aug. 1999, v.16, i.8, pp. 43–46. Reprinted with permission.

USAGE HANDBOOK

Endnotes

1. Examples modified from Gary Blonston, "Where Nature Takes Its Course," *Science 83* (November 1983): 44–55.

2. Modified from Robert Cooke, "Understanding the Diving Reflex," *Boston Globe*, 30 May 1981, 45.

3. Joanne Omang, "A Primer for Debate Looming on Clean Air," *Boston Globe*, 19 August 1981.

4. Examples modified from Wu Rukang and Lin Shenlong, "Peking Man," *Scientific American* (June 1983): 86–94.

5. Modified from *Transporting Radioactive Material . . . Answers to Your Questions*. Department of Energy. August 1989. DOE/DP-0064.

CREDITS

Title page (iii) and Part 1 opener (p. 1) Leonardo da Vinci, Design for machinery. Art Resource, NY.

Part 2 opener (p. 161) Leonardo da Vinci, Design for machinery. Art Resource, NY.

Part 3 opener (p. 325) Leonardo da Vinci, Drawings of Parachute Experiments and Flying Machines. © Baldwin H. Ward & Kathryn C. Ward/CORBIS.

Part 4 opener (p. 485) Leonardo da Vinci, Studies on mechanical problems in nature related to fish and sustaining devices. Accademica, Venice, Italy. Scala/Art Resource, New York.

Part 5 opener (p. 657) Leonardo da Vinci, Manuscript page from treatise on optics. Codex Leicester. Collection of Bill Gates. Art Resource, NY.

Practicum graphic: Leonardo da Vinci, Design for machinery. Art Resource, NY.

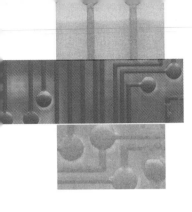

Index

Abstract indexes, 186
Abstracts, 106
  examples of, 107, 111
Academic degrees, UH43
Accuracy, of visuals, 551–552
Acronyms, UH2–UH3
Action, visuals to present, 303, 304
Active listening
  to collaborators, 139
  during presentations, 684
  strategies to promote, 685
Active voice
  inappropriate use of, 440–443
  in instructional texts, 547
  in process explanations, 407, 408
Administrative tasks, 445–446
Adverbs, conjunctive, UH7–UH8,
    UH12
Aerial photographs, 312–314
Affective conflict, 144
Agreement
  pronoun-antecedent, UH16–UH17
  subject-verb, UH14–UH15
Ambiguity, 241–242
Analogies, 336, 337, 338
Analysis questions, 113
Annotated bibliographies, 182
Antecedents, agreement between
    pronouns and, UH16–UH17
Antonyms, 336, 337
Apostrophe, UH34
Appearance, personal, 679–682
Appendixes, 346–347
Application questions, 113
Ascending/descending order, 218–220
Attitude
  of correspondence, 508–509
  of readers, 70–71
Audience analysis worksheet, 69
Audience(s). See also Reader
    analysis; Readers
  adapting visuals to, 279–280

analysis worksheet, 69
anticipating needs of, 4
constraints regarding, 19
of correspondence, 509
general, 665
identifying task of, 373–374,
    406–407, 536–537
for instructional texts, 531, 533
intended, 64
international, 533–536, 665
methods of engaging, 666–667
for oral presentations, 664–665
organizing for, 667–668
for reports, 608
for technical communication,
    6, 7
in technical description, 373–374,
    375
Audio recordings, 194
Authorities, data from, 43
Awards, capitalization of, UH43

Bar graphs, 297–299
Bias
  information design and, 257
  unfair, 240–241
Bibliographic essays, 182–183
Bibliography entries, UH51–792
Block charts, 305
Body, of reports, 625–627
Booklets, 16–17
Books in Print (BIP), 180–181
Boxed information, 262
Brackets, UH35
Brainstorming, 35
Bullets, 515
Business and industry guides, 182

Calculations, 170–171. See also
    Information Sources
Calendar designations, UH45
Call numbers, 183

Capitalization, UH42–UH47
Cardinal numbers, UH48
Careers. See Job search
Cartoons, 545
  Dilbert, 148
  Snoopy, 97, 331
Causal relationships, 44–46
Cause-and-effect analysis, 36
Cause-and-effect organization
  establishment of, 45–46
  example of, 225
  explanation of, 222
  in reports, 607, 627
  transitions in, 225
  types of, 222, 225
  use of, 224–225
Cautions
  example of, 548–549
  in instructional texts, 543–545
CD-ROM, writing for, 84–90
Chartjunk, 245, 254, 255. See also
    Information design
Charts, 304–306
Chat rooms, 493
Chat systems, 143
The Chicago Manual of Style, UH50,
    UH51
Children, as technical document
    readers, 66, 67, 84–90
Chronological order
  explanation of, 216–217
  instructions in, 541
  in reports, 607, 626
Chunks/chunking
  arrangement of related, 253–257
  color use and, 263
  decisions regarding, 248, 250
  example of, 249
  explanation of, 245
  headings to label, 252–253
  in instructional texts, 536, 537
  white space and, 250–252

Clauses
    dependent, UH6–UH7, UH28
    explanation of, UH6
    independent, UH6, UH8, UH11, UH28
    subordinate, UH9, UH10, UH24
Close reading, 170. *See also* Information Sources
Co-authoring, 136–137
Codes of conduct, 341
Collaboration
    conflicts and, 132, 144–151
    as constraint, 19
    in design process, 270–271
    ethical issues related to, 147
    global, 158–159
    groupware, 143
    guidelines for good, 131–132, 138–143
    interpersonal benefits of, 135
    reasons for, 131
    shared whiteboards, 143
    types of, 131
    ways to sabotage, 146
Collaborative writing systems, 143
Colleagues, 137
Collective nouns, UH15, UH17
Colons, UH35
Color
    to aid comprehension, 288–289
    appropriate use of, 283–290
    misuse of, 282–283
    to enable identification, 286–287
    to highlight components, 288
    to influence interpretation, 289–290
    in online documents, 283, 290–291, 295
    Pantone, 283
    production of, 283
    to show relationships, 294, 295
    to show structure, 287–288
    in visuals, 262–263, 273, 282–291, 303, 305–307, 310, 313 (*See also* Visuals)
    versus black and white, 285
    for Web use, 283–284, 290–291
Comma splices, UH11–UH12
Commas, UH11, UH13, UH35–UH37
Communication. *See also* Technical communication
    computer-mediated, 9
    contexts for constructing meaning and, 8–10
    cross-cultural, 392–395
    importance of effective, 3, 5–6
Communicators
    constraints faced by, 18–21
    employee requirements as, 13, 18
    noise from, 20–21
    processes of experienced writers, 49

Companies used as extended examples
    Big Creek Forestry, 349–353
    Boeing, 383–387
    CE Software, 470–474
    Engineering Associates, 228–233
    Iowa Public Television (IPTV), 84–90
    Lockheed Martin, 413–417
    Vidiom, 558–563
    Weisner Associates, 518–521
    Wellmark, 645–647
Comparison and/or contrast
    explanation of, 220–223
    in reports, 607, 627
Complaint letters
    domino effect of, 499–507
    example of, 496–499
    response to, 499
Completions, 178
Complex sentences, UH8
Components
    of instructions, 540–541
    separation of, 374
Composition fallacy, 45
Compound-complex sentences, UH9
Compound sentences, UH7
Comprehension, 288–289
Comprehensive questions, 113
Computer conversations, 140
Computer-mediated communication (CMC), 9
Computer software
    collaborative design, 270–271
    for editing, 445
    groupware, 142
    Multidisciplinary Design Optimization, 305
    project planning, 37
    word processing, 210–212
Computerized databases, 186–187
Computers, shared, 143
Concurrent testing, 430
Conflict
    affective, 144
    cultural differences and expectations and, 150–151
    procedural, 145–146
    substantive, 146–150
Conjunctive adverbs, UH7–UH8, UH12
Constraints facing communicators, 18–21
Constructive planning, 49, 50
Consultation, 137
Content
    accuracy of, 4
    of instructions, 540–547
    of technical communication, 6, 7
Content accuracy, 444
Context
    for constructing meaning, 8–10

    ethical issues and, 114
    identification of, 4
    noise from, 20
    physical and political, 68, 70
    of technical communication, 7, 8
Contour maps, 313
Contributing cause, 46
Conversation, 139–140
Coordinate conjunctions, UH7, UH8
Copyrighted materials, 690–692
Correlative conjunctions, UH7
Correspondence. *See also* E-Mail; Letters; Memos
    attitude and tone of, 508–509
    audience of, 509
    characteristics of, 487, 489–491
    domino effect of, 487, 493–506
    elements of composing, 487–488
    explanation of, 11
    format for, 488, 512–514
    guidelines for composing, 507–508
    mode of delivery of, 490–493
    organization of information in, 510–512
    questions to aid, 173
    visuals in, 488, 514–516
Credibility
    of information on Web, 190
    of personal observations, 169–170
    of persuaders, 578
Cultural issues. *See also* Context; International audiences
    color use and, 283
    conflict and, 150–151
    international business and, 392–395
Customer relations letters, 504–506
Customer services, 525–526
Cybergossip, 57–58

Dangers, presentation in instructional texts of, 543–545
Dangling modifiers, UH20–758
Dashes, UH37
Data
    inaccurate presentation of, 320–323
    omitted or incomplete, 43–44
    out-of-context, 44
    oversimplified or distorted, 44
    qualitative, 166
    quantitative, 166
    recording, 191–194
Data collection
    constraints in, 19–20
    distortion in, 319–320
Deadlines, 581
Decimals, UH49
Decision support systems (DSS), 143
Deductive reasoning
    explanation of, 224, 227, 622
    persuasive writing and, 580
    in reports, 622–623

Definitions
    construction of, 327, 334–335
    examples of, 16–17, 329
    expanded, 340–343
    formal, 335–336
    informal, 336–339
    multiple meanings, 330
    need for, 327, 330–334
    operational, 339–340
    placement of, 328, 343–347
    visuals as, 300–303
Demonstrations, 665
Density, in writing, 437–438
Dependent clauses, UH6–UH7, UH28
Description. *See* Technical description
Design. *See* Information design
Details
    in instructional texts, 542
    selecting concrete, 446
Dewey decimal system, 183
Diagrams, 306–307
Diction. *See also* Language; Words
    in instructional texts, 541–542
    for process explanations, 407
    of technical description, 374–378
Dictionaries, 182
Direct language
    in correspondence, 508–509
    editing for, 446–447
    use of, 446, 447
Directions. *See* Instructional texts
Distorted data, 44
Division fallacy, 45
Document cycling, 48
Document design. *See also*
        Information design
    accuracy and consistency of, 444
    ethical issues in, 226, 258
    revision of, 431, 434, 435
    for technical communication, 7, 8
Document planning
    collaborative, 38–39
    critical questions to ask during, 39
    ethical issues related to, 39–40
    explanation of, 37–38
Document testing. *See also*
        Evaluation; Rubrics
    categories of, 425
    expert-based, 429–430, 554
    explanation of, 427
    for instructional texts, 554–555
    observations about, 431
    procedures for, 425, 427–428
    text-based, 428–429, 554
    user-based, 430–431, 554
Documentation
    formats for, UH51–792
    list of sources cited and,
        UH49–UH50
    preparation of source notes and,
        UH50–UH51

Documents, noise from delivery of, 21
Drafts
    approaches to, 40–41
    electronic documents, 41–42
    of proposals, 582–583
Drawings
    function of, 307–308
    as source of information, 193
    versatility of, 308–310
Dual alternatives, 178

E-mail. *See also* Netiquette
    attitude and tone of, 508–509
    audience of, 509
    employer monitoring of, 732–735
    ethical issues concerning, 494
    explanation of, 143, 491
    format for, 512–514
    guidelines for composing,
        507–508
    guidelines for receiving, 492
    guidelines for sending, 491–492
    organization of information in,
        510–512
Editing
    for concrete words, 446
    for direct language, 446–447
    ethics and, 452
    examining decisions during, 451,
        453–468
    functions of, 47–48, 426, 443–446
    for noun strings, 449–451
    for positive phrasing, 447–448
    software for, 445
    for wordiness, 448–449
    in writing process, 47–48
Education, of readers, 71
Electronic documents, 41–42
Electronic mail. *See* E-mail
Electronic portfolios, 717–718
Electronic resources
    availability of, 186
    Web research and, 187–190
Ellipsis, UH37
Embedding, UH29
Emoticons, 492
Empirical investigations, 171–172.
        See also Information Sources
Employee monitoring, 732–735
Employee relations letters, 506
Encyclopedias, 182
End matter, 627–628
Environment
    ethical issues related to, 609
    noise from, 20
Equal Employment Opportunity
        Commission (EEOC), 422–424
Equipment lists, 541
Equipment operators, 65, 67
Ergo propter hoc fallacy, 46, 224
Essay questions, 178

Ethical issues
    collaborative situations and, 147
    context and, 114
    document design and, 226, 258
    editing and, 452
    e-mail and, 494
    environment and, 609
    instructional texts and, 545
    oral presentations and, 680
    pitfalls of practical, 237–244
    proposal writing and, 579
    reliance on precise facts and, 81
    resumes and, 701, 702
    technical description for, 370
    technical editing and, 452
    for technical professionals, 10
    technology use and, 167
    visuals and, 277, 319–323
    whistleblowers and, 401
    writing process and, 39–40
Etymology, 340–341
Evaluation. *See also* Document
        testing; Rubrics
    of presentations, 660, 684, 686
    of proposal drafts, 583
Evaluation questions, 114
Examples, 342–343
Exclamation point, UH37
Exclusionary language, 509
Executive summary, 632, 633
Expanded definitions
    explanation of, 340
    forms of, 340–343
    use of, 327
Expert-based testing
    explanation of, 429–430
    for instructional texts, 554
Experts, as readers, 65, 67
Exploded views, 309–310
Exploration, as stage in writing
        process, 31, 34–36
External views, 308–309

Face-to-face conversations, 140
Facts
    ethical issues and, 81
    reliance on precise, 81
    without drawing inferences, 43–44
Fallacies, avoiding. *See* Logic
Fax machines, 491
Feasibility report, 451, 453–468
Field journals, 191–192
Figurative language, 376–378
Films, 193
First-class mail, 491
First person, 443
5 Ws plus H, 45
Flesch-Kincaid Formula, 483. *See also*
        Readability formulas
Floating bar graphs, 299
Flowcharts, 306

Font. *See* Typefaces
Footing, 144
Formal definitions
    explanation of, 335–336
    use of, 327
Formal presentations, 662–663
Formal reports
    body of, 625–628
    explanation of, 605–606
    front matter in, 623–625
    function of, 603
    organization of, 604, 621–623
Format
    constraints regarding, 19
    for process explanations, 407–409
Forms
    effective design of, 622
    prepared, 621
Front matter, 623–625
Fry Graph, 483. *See also* Readability
    formulas
Fused sentences, UH13–UH14

Galileo Galilei, 367
Gantt charts
    example of, 38
    explanation of, 36–37
Gender-neutral writing, 650–655
General audiences, 665
General readers, 65, 67
Given-new analysis, 439–440
Global revision, 431–435
Glossary, 343
Government documents, 190–191
Grapevine. *See* Organizational
    grapevine
Graphic elements, 247. *See also* Visuals
Graphs
    bar, 297–299
    distortion of information with,
      320–323
    line, 294–295
    pictorial, 299–300
    pie, 296–297
    scatter, 296
Grids. *See also* Information design
    for designing Web pages, 264
    pages as, 245
    selection of appropriate, 253
Groups of people, UH43
Groupware
    common types of, 143
    use of, 142

Handbooks, reference, 182
Handouts, 676–677
Hasty generalizations, 44–45
Headings. *See also* Information design
    in correspondence, 513–514
    to label chunked information,
      252–253

Hierarchical organizations, 75
History, as form of expanded
    definition, 341–342
    Galileo Galilei, 367
    Leonardo da Vinci, xx–xxi, xxii,
      275
Honors, capitalization of, UH43
Hypertext documents, 82–83, 329
Hyphen, UH37–UH38

Illustration, 336, 337
Illustruction
    example of, 556
    explanation of, 555
Immediacy, 9
Imperative mood, 546
Incomplete data, 43–44
Incorporated information, 346
Indefinite pronouns, UH15, UH17
Independent clauses, UH6, UH8,
    UH11, UH28
Indexes
    abstract, 186
    newspaper, 185
    periodical, 185
    for research purposes, 183, 185
Indicative mood, 546
Inductive reasoning
    explanation of, 222, 225, 227, 622
    persuasive writing and, 580
    in reports, 622, 623
Inferences
    presenting facts without drawing,
      43–44
    strategies for drawing, 44, 105,
      110–113
Inflated words, UH4–UH5
Informal definitions
    examples of, 336, 338–339
    explanation of, 336
    types of, 337
    use of, 327
Informal presentations
    explanation of, 661–662
    use of, 663
Informal reports
    explanation of, 605–606
    function of, 603
    on meeting minutes, 616, 617
    organization of, 603–604, 610–611
    periodic activity, 611, 614
    progress-related, 614–616
    task-related, 611–613
    "to file," 620
    trip and conference, 616–620
Information
    color to aid in interpretation of,
      289–290 (*See also* Color)
    dissemination of, 510
    incorporated, 346
    outlining of, 207, 209–213

Information design
    arranging and relating chunks of
      verbal and visual information
      and, 245, 253–257
    chunking and labeling, 245,
      248–253
    cues, 107
    emphasizing information and, 247,
      257–263
    headings, to label chunked
      information, 252–253
    justification, chunking and,
      251–252
    leading, 252
    margins, to chunk information,
      250–251
    for Web, 246, 263–265
    white space, 250–252
Information notes, 343–346
Information organization
    ascending/descending, 218–220
    chronological, 216–217
    comparison/contrast, 220–223
    function of, 213–215
    parts/whole, 215–216
    spatial, 217–218
    use of, 224–226
Information services, 181–182
Information sources
    calculations as, 170–171
    close reading as, 170
    electronic, 186–190
    empirical investigations as,
      171–172
    government documents and
      agencies as, 190–191
    indexes as, 183–186
    internal records as, 172
    interviews as, 172–176
    letters of inquiry as, 174–177
    library resources as, 180
    online catalog as, 183
    overview of, 163–164, 166
    personal observations as, 168–170
    primary, 166–168
    recording data as, 191–194
    reference resources as, 182–183
    requirements for, 165
    research librarians and their
      references as, 180–182
    samples and specimens as, 171
    secondary, 166, 168
    surveys and polls as, 176, 178–179
Informational interviews, 720–721
Informative presentations, 665
Initial readers, 64
Instructional texts
    accessing information in, 528,
      538–539
    adapting task to audience of,
      536–537

audience analysis and, 527, 531–533
categories of, 527, 529
content elements in, 528, 540–547
defining, 529
ethical issues and, 545
explanation of, 11, 529
"illustrations" in, 555–556
international audiences and, 533–536, 553
online help, 347
organizing instructions and, 537–538
task analysis for, 527, 529–531
testing of, 554–555
training manuals, 567–569
visual and design elements in, 528, 547, 550–554
worksheet for, 532
Instructions. *See* Instructional texts
Intended audience, 64
Internal citations, UH51–792
Internal memos, 500–503
Internal records, 172. *See also* Information sources
International audiences
addressing, 392–395
example for, 409–411, 524–525
for instructional texts, 533–536, 553
oral presentations to, 664–665
International teams, 158–159
collaboration with, 150–151
International practices, 349–353
Internet. *See* World Wide Web
Internet relay chats (IRC), 493
Interpersonal benefits, 135
Interviews. *See also* Information sources
actions and attitudes for effective, 176
asking questions during, 173–175
developing questions for, 173–175
function of, 172–173
informational, 720–721
job, 720–726
thank you notes following, 175–176
Invention, as stage in writing process, 31, 34–36
Irrelevant functions, 45
Isotypes, 299, 300
Italic, 515
Italics, UH38–UH40

Jargon, 331–332
Job interviews, 720–726
Job search
application letters for, 693, 698–701
career knowledge and, 693, 695–698
interviews for, 694, 720–726

networking for, 695–696
online resources for, 697
portfolio preparation for, 694, 716–720
resume preparation for, 693, 701–716
Justification, chunking and, 251–252. *See also* Information design

Knowledge-driven planning, 49, 50
Knowledge questions, 113

Lab notes, 192
Labeling
decisions regarding, 248
example of, 249
headings for, 250, 252–253
in instructional texts, 536, 537
of visuals, 281–282
Language
direct, 446–447, 508–509
exclusionary, 376–378
figurative, 376–378
plain, 431, 435–443
Language conventions, 7, 8
Leading, 252. *See also* Information design
Leonardo da Vinci, xx–xxi, xxii, 275
Letters
attitude and tone of, 508–509
audience of, 509
complaint, 496–499
customer relations, 504–506
employee relations, 506
form, 621
format for, 512–514
guidelines for composing, 507–508
of inquiry, 174–177
job application, 693, 698–701
organization of information in, 510–512
response to complaint, 499
transmittal, 623, 629
Liability
product, 543–544, 548–549
related to copyright, 690–692
related to instructions, 543–544, 545
related to warning labels, 543–545
related to warnings, 548–549
Library of Congress Subject Headings, 181, 183
Library of Congress systems, 183
Library resources. *See also* Information sources
explanation of, 180
indexes as, 183–186
information services as, 180–182
online catalog as, 183
references as, 182–183
research librarians as, 180

Likert scales, 178
Line graphs, 294–295
explanation of, 294–295
Line length, 252
Listening. *See* Active listening
Lists, in correspondence, 515
Lists (Web), 189, 492–493
Literacy, limited, 72, 74–75
Local revision, 431, 435–443
Logic
using data from authorities, 43
drawing inferences, 44–45
establishing causal relationships, 45–47
presenting facts without drawing inferences, 43

Mail delivery, 491
Main points, 105, 110, 111
Manuals
designing learner-friendly training, 567–569
explanation of, 11
locating information in, 538–539
organizing instructions in, 537–538
process explanations in, 400
standard components of, 538
Maps
as source of information, 193
types of, 310–311
Web site, 311–312
Margins, to chunk information, 250–251. *See also* Information design
Marketing materials
explanation of, 11
process explanations in, 402, 404
technical descriptions in, 373
Materials lists, 541
Meaning, construction of, 3, 8–10
Memory, 667
Memos
attitude and tone of, 508–509
audience of, 509
form, 621
format for, 512–514
guidelines for composing, 507–508
internal, 500–503
organization of information in, 510–512
Metasearch engines, 202–203
Misplaced modifiers, UH23–UH24
Modifiers
dangling, UH20–UH22
misplaced, UH23–UH24
redundant, 449, UH5
Mood, 442–443. *See also* Verbs
Motivation, reader, 70–71
Movement, color to show, 288–289

Multidisciplinary Design Optimization (MDO), 305
Multimedia projects, 84–90
Multiple bar graphs, 299
Multiple-choice questions, 178
Multiple meanings, 330

Negative, 336, 337
Negative phrasing, 447–448
Netiquette
    chat, 493
    computer conversation, 140
    e-mail, 489–90
    explanation of, 491
    newsgroup and list, 490–491, 492
Networking, 695
Newsgroups
    explanation of, 189
    netiquette for, 492–493
Newspaper indexes, 185
Noise, 20–21
Nonhierarchical organizations, 75
Note cards
    recording information on, 192–193
    used during presentations, 668–669
Noun strings, 449–450
Nouns
    abstract, UH3–UH4
    collective, UH15, UH17
    words derived from proper, UH44
Number use, UH47–UH49
Numbered lists, 262
Numeric information, 292–294

Observation notes, 369–371
Omissions, 238–240
Omitted data, 43–44
Online catalogs, 183, 184
Online
    help, 347
    writing, 41
Open-ended questions, 178
Operational definitions
    explanation of, 339–340
    use of, 327
Oral presentations. See Presentations
Ordinal numbers, UH48
Organization. See also
        Ascending/descending order;
        Cause and effect organization;
        Chronological order;
        Comparison and/or contrast;
        Spatial order
    color to show, 287–288
    of information, 213–226, 668–669
    parts/whole organization, 215–216
    for process explanations, 407–409
    of proposals, 584–589
    of technical communication, 6, 7
    of technical description, 379–382

Organizational charts, 305–306
Organizational grapevine
    benefits of, 55–57
    in business, 54–55
    elements of, 55
    explanation of, 54
    implications for leaders and, 58–59
    potential pitfalls of, 57–58
    structure of, 55
Organizations (business), 75, UH44
Orientation and training materials.
        See also Training materials
    process explanations in, 400–402
Orphans, 245, 254, 256
Out-of-context data, 44
Outlines
    as body of document, 213
    function of, 193, 209
    questions to ask about, 212
    used during presentations, 668–670
    with word processing software, 210–212
Overnight mail, 491
Oversimplified data, 44

Pantone, 283
Parallel structure
    explanation of, UH25–UH26
    in instructional texts, 536, 544–545
Parentheses, UH40
Parts list, 541
Parts/whole organization, 215–216
Passive voice
    inappropriate use of, 440–443
    in process explanations, 407, 408
Percentages
    distortion of information with, 320
    use of, UH49
Periodical indexes, 185
Periods, UH40
Person, first, second, and third, 443, 547
Personal names, UH42
Personal observations. See also
        Information sources
    credibility of, 169–170
    explanation of, 168–169
Perspective view, 313
Persuasion
    credibility and, 578
    logic of message and, 578, 580
    in proposals, 571, 574, 577–580
    reader needs and, 577–578
Persuasive presentations, 665
PERT (Program Evaluation Review
        Technique) charts, 36, 37
Photographs
    aerial, 312–314
    color in, 313

function of, 312
    as source of information, 193–194
Pictorial graphs, 299–300, 321
Pie graphs, 296–297
Place names, UH43–UH44
Plagiarism, 242–243
Plain language
    active and passive voice and, 440–443
    characteristics of, 435, 436, 437–438
    density and, 437–438
    effects of, 436–437
    first, second, and third person and, 443
    function of, 435–436
    given-new analysis and, 439–440
    revising for, 431
Plain Language Action Network
        (PLAN), 436
Planning. See also Questions
    document, 37–40
    project, 36–37
    proposal, 581–582
    types of, 49
Polls. See Surveys
Portfolios
    content of, 716–717
    paper vs. electronic, 717–718
    usability of, 718–720
Positive phrasing, 447–448
Post hoc fallacy, 46–47, 224
Poster displays, 678–679
Presentation support systems, 143
Presentations
    active listening during, 684, 685
    appearance for, 679–682
    audience for, 664–665
    class, 663
    engaging audience during, 666–667
    ethics in, 680
    evaluation of, 660, 684, 686
    formal, 662–663
    handouts for, 676–677
    informal, 661–662
    noise constraints from delivery of, 21
    organization of, 659, 667–668
    poster displays for, 678–679
    puposes of, 665
    questions during, 681, 683–684
    transparencies for, 674–675
    types of, 659, 661–663
    using note cards or outlines during, 668–670
    visuals for, 671–676
    vocal characteristics for, 681
Previews, 109–110
Primary readers, 64, 608
Primary sources, 166–168

Primer sentences, UH28, UH30
Priority mail, 491
Privacy
    e-mails and, 494
    technology use and, 9–10, 732–736
Problem-solving strategies, 35–36
Procedural conflict, 145–146
Process, as reason for collaboration, 134
Process explanations
    audience for, 406
    characteristics of, 397
    defining, 399–400
    diction for, 407
    examination of, 398
    examination of sample, 409–412
    function of, 399–400
    in general-interest publications, 404–406
    identifying audience and purpose for, 406
    identifying steps involved in, 406–407
    in manuals, 400
    in marketing and promotional materials, 402, 404
    organization and format for, 407–409
    in orientation and training materials, 400–402
    planning for, 409
    preparation of, 397–398, 406
    use of, 397
    visuals to illustrate, 403, 407
Product, as reason for collaboration, 135
Product liability, 543–544, 548–549
Professional experience, 71
Professional nonexperts, 65, 67
Project planning, 36–40
Promotional material
    explanation of, 11
    process explanations in, 402, 404
    technical description for, 373
Pronouns
    agreement between antecedents and, UH16–UH17
    gender-neutral, 650–655
    indefinite, UH15, UH17
    reference problems with, UH18–UH19
Proofreading, 444–445
Proper nouns, UH44
Proposal preparation. See also Requests for proposals (RFP)
    drafting stage of, 582–583
    elements of, 571, 580–581
    evaluation stage of, 583
    managing stage of, 581
    planning stage of, 581–582
    revision stage of, 583–584

Proposals. See also Requests for proposals (RFP)
    elements of, 11, 573–574, 585
    ethical issues regarding, 579
    organization of, 572, 584–589
    sample, 589–594
    solicited, 574–575
    sources of RFPs and, 571, 575–577
    technical description for, 371–372
    types of, 571, 574–575, 585, 586
    unsolicited, 575
Public information
    process explanations in, 404–405
    technical description for, 373
Publication, indiscriminate, 243–244
Punctuation. See also specific forms of punctuation
Purpose
    explanation of, 4
    identifying, 63–64, 406
    of instructions, 540
    of presentations, 665
    for reading, 101–102
    of reports, 603, 606–608
    of technical communication, 6, 7

Qualitative data, 166
Quality control circles, 35–36
Quantitative data, 166
Quantities, UH48–UH49
Question marks, UH40
Questions
    for analyzing audience, 69
    for analyzing technical documents, 12
    for analyzing instructions, 546
    for collaborators, 141, 148
    during document planning, 39
    as element of collaboration, 140–141
    to identify purpose, 63
    interview, 173–175
    for job interviews, 722–726
    about logic of document, 47
    during oral presentations, 681–684
    for outlining, 212
    provocative, 148
    readers who generate, 105, 113–117
    survey, 178, 179
    for task analysis, 530
    about text difficulty, 73
    types of, 113–114
    about writing for the Web, 104
Quotation marks, UH41

Rank ordering, 178
Readability formulas
    explanation of, 72
    Flesch-Kincaid and Fry Graph, 482–483

function of, 479
    problems in using, 479–482
    restrained use of, 482
Reader analysis. See also Audience
    attitudes and motivations and, 70–71
    context and, 68
    education and, 71
    explanation of, 61, 67
    organizational role and, 75
    overview of, 67–68
    professional experience and, 71
    reading level and, 71–75
    worksheet for, 69
Reader-based documents
    creation of, 3
    elements of, 9
    explanation of, 209
Readers. See also Audience
    adjusting to, 61, 76–83
    analyzing, 67–68
    characteristics of, 66
    constructing meaning on Web sites, 82
    with differences in expertise, 76, 77
    external, 64, 65
    identifying, 61, 64–65
    roles of, 64, 78–80
    strategies used by, 105
    types of, 65–67
    of Web sites, 80–83
    writing for resistant, 70
Readers Guide to Periodical Literature, 185
Reading. See also Technical document reading
    close, 170
    drawing inferences, 110–113
    explanation of, 101
    individual differences, 119–123
    previews, 109–110
    purposes for, 101–102
    reading-writing relationships, 102–103
    reviews, 109–110
    strategies for effective, 103–105, 115–123
    visual cues for, 107
Reading level
    explanation of, 71–72
    factors that affect, 73
    limited literacy and, 72, 74–76
    readability formulas and, 72
Reasonable woman standard, 359–361
Reasoning
    deductive, 224, 227, 580, 622
    inductive, 222, 225, 227, 580, 622
Receptive readers, 70

Recommendation reports
    draft of, 634, 636, 639, 640, 642
    executive summary for, 632, 633
    final version of, 635, 637, 638, 639, 640, 643
    function of, 630–631
    table of contents for, 631
    title page for, 630
    transmittal letter accompanying, 629
Redundancy, 448–449
Redundant categories, 449, UH5
Redundant modifiers, 449, UH5
Redundant word pairs, UH5
Reference material, 370–371
Reference resources, 182–183
Reflection, as element of collaboration, 142–144
Registered trademarks, UH47
Relationships, visuals to show, 294–300
Reliability, 172
Reports
    audience for, 603, 607, 608, 622
    body of, 625–627
    end matter of, 627–628
    examination of sample, 629–643 (See also Recommendation reports)
    explanation of, 11
    formal, 603–606, 621–628 (See also Formal reports)
    format of, 604, 620–621, 628
    front matter of, 623–625
    informal, 603–606, 609–620 (See also Informal reports)
    of meeting minutes, 617, 618
    periodic activity, 611, 614
    progress, 614–615
    purpose and characteristics of, 603, 606–608
    task, 610–613
    technical description for, 371–372
    "to file," 620
    trip and conference, 616–620
Requests
    for information, 500
    making routine, 510–511
    responding to, 511
Requests for proposals (RFP)
    proposal preparation and, 581, 582, 583, 584
    solicited proposals in response to, 574–575
    sources of, 571, 575–577
    tips for, 597–601
    use of, 573
Resistant readers, 70
Resumes
    design elements of, 709, 711
    design for online, 711–712

educational background on, 704–706
elements of, 703–704
ethics issues related to, 701, 702
function of, 701–703
listing of experience on, 706–709
name and contact information on, 704
optional elements for, 709, 710
samples, 712–715
unnecessary elements for, 709
updating, 712, 716
Retrospective testing, 430, 431
Reviews, of technical documents, 109–110
Revision
    approaches to, 42–43
    examining decisions during, 451, 453–468
    factors involved in, 425
    global, 431–435
    local, 431, 435–443
    avoiding fallacies, 43–47
    for plain language, 435–443
    of proposals, 583–584
Route charts, 306
Rubrics. See also Document testing; Evaluation
    for print documents, 793–795
    for Web sites, 269
Run-on sentences, UH13–UH14

Sales materials, 11
Samples. See also Information sources
    as sources of information, 171
Sans serifs, 259
Scatter graphs, 296
Schema-driven planning, 49–50
Scientific method, 222
Scientific terms, UH45–UH47
Search engine information
    career guides on, 697
    characteristics of, 188–189
    further developments in, 204
    hints and tips of, 201–202
    information on changes in, 204–205
    list of popular, 189
    metasearch, 202–203
    power searching with, 198–201
    size of, 198–199
    specialty, 204
Search engine locations
    Alexa, 204
    AltaVista, 188, 189, 199–200
    Ask Jeeves, 189
    Corporate Information, 204
    Cyberspace Guide to Internet Research, 204–205
    DejaNews, 201–202, 204

Direct Search 203
Dogpile, 202
Excite, 188, 189, 200
Free Pint, 205
Google, 189
Hoover's Inc., 204
HotBot, 188, 189, 200, 205
Index, 188
InfoSeek, 188, 189
Integra, 204
Internet Sleuth, 202
Liszt, 204
Lycos, 188
MetaCrawler, 189
Northern Light, 189, 200–201, 205
On the Net, 205
Open Text, 205
Price's List of Lists, 203
ProFusion, 202–203
Pub-SCIENCE, 190
Savvy Search, 203
Search Engine Update, 205
VentureOne, 204
Vista Information Solutions, 204
WebCrawler, 188
XLS, 204
Yahoo, 188, 189
Second person, 443, 547
Secondary readers
    explanation of, 64–65
    of reports, 608
Secondary sources, 166, 168
Section headings, 515, 516
Semicolons, UH11, UH12, UH41–UH42
Sentence fragments, UH9–UH11
Sentences
    combining, UH28–UH31
    comma splices, UH11–UH13
    complex, UH8
    compound, UH7
    compound-complex, UH9
    numbers at beginning of, UH48
    run-on, UH13–UH14
    simple, UH7
    structure, UH6–UH9
Serifs, 259. See also Typefaces
Sexism, avoiding 650–656
Sexual harassment
    current standards and developments in, 421
    defending oneself against claims of supervisory, 422
    EEOC guidance and, 422–423
    investigating claims of, 423–424
    reasonable woman standard, 359
    Supreme Court decisions and, 421–422
Sexual harassment training program, 359–363

Shaded information, 262
Shared whiteboards, 143
Sidebars, 345–346
Simple bar graphs, 298
Simple sentences, UH7, UH8
Slash, UH42
Sliding bar graphs, 299
Society for Technical Communication
    (STC), 28, 133, 341
Software, *See also* Technology; World
    Wide Web
    for editing, 445
    robots, 523–524
Source notes, UH50–UH51
Sources
    EnergyFiles, 190–191
    government documents, 190–191
    Internet, 198–206
    NASA Space Science News Web
        Internet, 198–206
    primary, 166–168
    qualitative, 166
    quantitative, 166
    secondary 166, 168
    types of, 166
Sources Cited, UH49–UH50. *See also*
    Documentation
Spatial elements, 247
Spatial order
    explanation of, 217–218
    in reports, 607, 626
Specimens, 171
Speculation, 241–242
Spiders, 188
Spying, 732
Standards. *See* Codes of Conduct
Stipulation, 336, 337
Structure
    color use to show, 287–288
    document features and, 106
    identifying technical document's,
        105
    previews and reviews and, 109–110
    visual cues and, 107–109
Students, as readers, 65, 67
Subdivided bar graphs, 298
Subject
    agreement between verb and,
        UH14–UH15
    constraints regarding, 19
    as reason for collaboration, 134
Subordinate clauses, UH9, UH10,
    UH24
Substantive conflict, 146–150
Sufficient cause, 46
Surveys, *See also* Information
    sources
    design of, 176, 178
    questions for, 178, 179
Syllogism, 580
Symbols, 334

Synonyms, 336, 337
Syntectics, 36
Synthesis questions, 113

Table of contents, 623, 626, 631
Tables, organization of information
    in, 292–294
Task analysis
    for instructional texts, 527,
        529–531
    questions for, 34, 530
Team projects. *See also* Collaboration
    collaboration on, 137–138
    global, 158–159
Technical communication. *See also*
    Communication
    characteristics of, 6–8
    constraints facing, 18–21
    explanation of, 3
    importance of, 5–6
    standards for, 4
Technical communicators, 18, 27–30
Technical description
    background of, 367–368
    cross-cultural communication
        and, 392–395
    defining, 365, 368–369
    diction of, 374–378
    ethical issues regarding, 370
    identifying audience's task for,
        373–374
    for marketing and promotional
        pieces, 373
    for observation notes, 369–370
    organization of, 379–382
    planning for, 380
    preparing, 365–366
    for proposals and reports, 371–372
    for public information and
        education, 373
    for reference and training
        materials and manuals,
        370–371
    use of, 365, 369
    visuals for, 378–379
Technical document reading
    distinguishing main points while,
        110–113
    generating questions while,
        113–115
    identifying purposes while,
        101–102
    identifying structure while,
        105–110
    relationship between reading and
        writing and, 102–103
    strategies for, 99–100, 103–105,
        115–123
Technical documents
    context of, 8–10
    examples of, 14–17

    features of, 106
    guidelines and questions for
        analyzing, 12
    practical approaches for reading,
        118
    purposes of writing, 61, 63–64
    questions to ask regarding, 34
    standards for, 11, 13
    types of, 11
Technical editing, 452
Technical experts, 18
Technical professionals, 10
Technical reports, 14–15
Technical writers
    demand for, 28
    educational background for,
        29–30
    function of, 27–28
    salaries of, 28–29
Technicians, 65, 67
Technology. *See also* World Wide Web
    constraints in, 20
    effective use of, 142
    ethical issues related to, 167
    privacy and immediacy and, 9–10
Telephone calls, 490
Telephone conversations, 140
Terms. *See also* Words
    accurate, 375
    audience-appropriate, 375
    historical and cultural,
        UH44–UH45
    scientific, UH45–UH47
Testing. *See* Document testing
Text-based testing
    explanation of, 428–429
    for instructional texts, 554
Textual elements, 247
Textual references, 281
Third person, 443
Three-dimensional views, 308
Time constraints, 19
Time designations, UH45
Time management, 36–37
Title pages, 630
Titles, UH47
Tombstoning, 245, 254, 256. *See also*
    Information design
Tone, 508–509
Topic sentences, 214
Tracings, 193
Trademarks, UH47
Training materials
    designing learner-friendly,
        567–569
    process explanations in, 400–402
    technical description for, 370–371
Training sessions, 665
Transformation, UH30
Transitions, 214
Transmittal letters, 623, 629

Type. *See also* Typefaces
  size of, 259–261
  style of, 261
Typefaces
  characteristics of, 257–258
  effects of, 246, 257
  serif and sans serif, 259
  type size and, 259–261
  variations in, 259
  for Web pages, 258–259, 261
Typographic devices, 262–263

Underlining, 262, 515
URL (Uniform Resource Locator), 188
Usability
  of technical communication, 7, 8
  of portfolios, 718–720
  of Web sites, 265, 269
User-based testing
  explanation of, 430–431
  for instructional texts, 554
User-friendly
  explanation of, 531
  training manuals, 567–569
  Web sites, 128–130

Validity, 172
Variables, not correlated, 46
Verbs, *See also* Voice
  active, UH3–UH4
  agreement between subject and, UH14–UH15
  imperative mood of, 531
  linking, UH15
  mood, 442–443
Video communications systems, 143
Videotapes, 193
Visual cues, 107–109
Visual functions
  defining concepts, objects, and processes as, 300–303
  identifying facilities or locations as, 310–313
  illustrating appearance, structure, or function as, 306–310
  organizing numeric or verbal data as, 292–294
  overview of, 274, 291
  presenting action or process as, 303–306
  showing relationships as, 294–300
Visuals. *See also* Information design
  adapted to audiences, 279–280
  balance between verbals and, 551

benefits of, 273, 275–276
color use in, 262–263, 273, 282–291, 303, 305–307, 310, 313 (*See also* Color)
combined with text, 276–278
in correspondence, 514–516
cues, 107–108
distortion in use of, 319–323
ethical issues regarding, 277
in instructional texts, 547, 550–554
for international audiences, 534–536, 553
labeling, 281
methods of incorporating, 273, 276–282
noise constraints from delivery of, 21
placement of, 254–255, 289–282, 552, 553
during presentations, 671–676, 678–679
for process explanations, 407
referencing and placing, 280–282
size of, 673
for technical communication, 7
for technical description, 378–379
total, 553–554
and verbal combinations, 276–279
versus verbal presentation, 275–276
Voice. *See also* Verbs
  active, 407, 408, 440–443, 547
  in instructional texts, 547
  oral presentations and, 681
  in process explanations, 407, 408

Warning labels, 543–545
Warnings, 548–549
Web browsers, 188–189
Whistleblowers, 401
White space, 250–252. *See also* Information design
Widows, 245, 254, 256
Word processing software, 210–212
Wordiness, 448–449
Words. *See also* Definitions; Diction; Language
  accurate, 375
  audience-appropriate, 375
  editing for concrete, 446
  redundant, UH5
  substitutes for inflated, UH4–UH5
  used for numbers, UH47–UH49

Workflow systems, 143
World Wide Web
  color use on, 283, 285, 290–291
  constructing meaning, 82
  credibility and information on, 190
  customer services on, 525–526
  designing for, 246, 258–259, 261, 263–265
  domain names, 337–338
  dumping text on, 264–265
  EnergyFiles, 190–191
  evaluation of, 269
  government information on, 190
  important factors for reading sites on, 104
  Internet searches, 198–206
  job searches using, 696–698
  locating information on, 188–189
  NASA Space Science News Web site, 368
  online resumes and, 711–713
  organizing information for, 214–215
  overview of, 187–188
  power searching on, 198–205
  reader adjustments to sites on, 80–83
  resources for jobs on, 697
  robots, 523–524
  user-friendly design of sites on, 128–130
  Web-based portfolios and, 717–718
  Web site maps and, 311–312
  writing for, 41, 104
Writer-based documents, 209
Writing process
  drafting stage of, 31, 40–42
  editing stage of, 32, 47–48
  ethical issues related to, 39–40
  of experienced writers, 49
  individual variations in, 32, 48–50
  inventing and exploring stage of, 31, 34–36
  overview of, 33–34
  planning and organizing stage of, 31, 36–40
  revising stage of, 31–32, 42–47